Tourism Social Science Series
Volume 12

The Sociology of Tourism
European Origins and Developments

Tourism Social Science Series

Series Editor: **Jafar Jafari**

Department of Hospitality and Tourism, University of Wisconsin-Stout, Menomonie WI 54751, USA.
Tel (715) 232-2339; Fax (715) 232-3200; Email jafari@uwstout.edu

Associate Editor (this volume): **Dennison Nash**
University of Connecticut, Storrs, CT 06269, USA.

The books in this Tourism Social Science Series (TSSSeries) are intended to systematically and cumulatively contribute to the formation, embodiment, and advancement of knowledge in the field of tourism.

The TSSSeries' multidisciplinary framework and treatment of tourism includes application of theoretical, methodological, and substantive contributions from such fields as anthropology, business administration, ecology, economics, geography, history, hospitality, leisure, planning, political science, psychology, recreation, religion, sociology, transportation, etc., but it significantly favors state-of-the-art presentations, works featuring new directions, and especially the cross-fertilization of perspectives beyond each of these singular fields. While the development and production of this book series is fashioned after the successful model of *Annals of Tourism Research*, the TSSSeries further aspires to assure each theme a comprehensiveness possible only in book-length academic treatment. Each volume in the series is intended to deal with a particular aspect of this increasingly important subject, thus to play a definitive role in the enlarging and strengthening of the foundation of knowledge in the field of tourism, and consequently to expand its frontiers into the new research and scholarship horizons ahead.

Published

Tourism Social Science Series
Volume 12

The Sociology of Tourism
European Origins and Developments

GRAHAM M. S. DANN
Finnmark University College, Alta, Norway

GIULI LIEBMAN PARRINELLO
Università Roma Tre, Rome, Italy

United Kingdom • North America • Japan
India • Malaysia • China

Emerald Group Publishing Limited
Howard House, Wagon Lane, Bingley BD16 1WA, UK

First edition 2009

Copyright © 2009 Emerald Group Publishing Limited

British Library Cataloguing in Publication Data
A catalogue record for this book is available from the British Library

ISBN: 978-1-84663-988-3
ISSN: 1571-5043 (Series)

Awarded in recognition of
Emerald's production
department's adherence to
quality systems and processes
when preparing scholarly
journals for print

INVESTOR IN PEOPLE

For our colleagues in the research committee of international tourism (RC 50) of the International Sociological Association.

Contents

List of Contributors

Julio Aramberri	Department of Hospitality Management, Drexel University, PA, USA
Julian Bystrzanowski	College of Tourism and Hospitality Management in Warsaw, Poland
Graham M. S. Dann	Department of Tourism and Hospitality, Finnmark University College, Alta, Norway
Vasiliki Galani-Moutafi	Department of Social Anthropology and History, University of the Aegean, Greece
Jens Kr. Steen Jacobsen	Norwegian School of Hotel Management, University of Stavanger, Stavanger, Norway
Marie Françoise Lanfant	CNRS-URESTI, Paris, France
Jaap Lengkeek	Socio-Spatial Analysis Chair Group, University of Wageningen, Wageningen, The Netherlands
Giuli Liebman Parrinello	Department of Comparative Literature, Università Roma Tre, Rome, Italy
Krzysztof Przecławski	College of Tourism and Hospitality Management in Warsaw, Poland
Asterio Savelli	Department of Sociology, University of Bologna, Bologna, Italy
Hasso Spode	Institute of Sociology, Leibniz University, Germany

Paris Tsartas	Division of Postgraduate Studies in Tourism Planning, Management and Policy, University of the Aegean, Greece
Dorota Ujma	Division of Tourism, Leisure and Sport Management, University of Bedfordshire, UK
Boris Vukonić	Utilus Business School for Tourism and Hotel Management, Zagreb, Croatia

Editors' Biographies

Photograph by Brian Castledine

After obtaining his PhD in Sociology from the University of Surrey, **Graham Dann** lectured in that subject at the University of the West Indies in Barbados for 21 years. While in the Caribbean, he developed an interest in tourism, especially in its motivational components and in the semiotics of its promotion. From there, he was also invited to join the editorial board of *Annals of Tourism Research* and to be a founder member of the International Academy for the Study of Tourism. He additionally helped establish the research committee on international tourism of the International Socio-logical Association and served consecutively as president and vice-president. In 1996, he was appointed the first Professor of Tourism at the University of Luton (now University of Bedfordshire) and in 2003 received a DLitt from that institution. His association there is on an emeritus basis while his current professorial affiliation is with the Department of Tourism and Hospitality at Finnmark University College, Alta, Norway. Among his many publications, he is probably best known for his *Language of Tourism*.

Photograph by Sergio Parrinello

Giuli Liebman Parrinello was born in Trieste. She graduated with a degree in philosophy from that city's university, and at that time specialized in German language and literature and published extensively in that area. During the course of several stays in Germany, France, and United Kingdom, she began to combine linguistic and tourism studies. In 1983, she took up the position of associate professor at La Sapienza University in Rome, followed in 1993 by a similar appointment at *Università Roma Tre*. As an expert in the field, she was charged with teaching the sociology and psychology of tourism for the Masters program at the Rome-based *Scuola Internazionale di Scienze Turistiche* where she taught for a decade before taking up a position in the Masters program on the languages of tourism and intercultural communication at the *Università Roma Tre*. Having been president of the research committee on international tourism of the International Sociological Association, her tourism research interests and publications lie in anticipatory motivation; new perceptions of postindustrial tourism; mind, body, and the tourist experience; and the theoretical aspects of future technology. She has recently collaborated with Graham Dann in a research article on travelblogs. Not only do they share an additional interest in tourist motivation, but they are also both fascinated by the power of language.

Acknowledgement

Scholarly works are typically the result of an exchange of ideas. This observation is even more valid in the case of the present anthology where our principal editorial function was to catalyze and stimulate reflection among collaborators with different national, cultural, linguistic, and theoretical backgrounds. Thus our first substantial acknowledgement is to our 12 contributors representing European countries stretching from the Arctic Circle in the North to the Sea of Candia in the South, who overcoming numerous difficulties in three years of hard work, singly and collectively made this volume possible. Gratitude is also due to the anonymous referees who vetted the proposal, the Associate Editor—Dennison Nash, the Series Editor—Jafar Jafari, our mentor—Roberto Cipriani and the Publisher, for making a number of theoretical and practical suggestions for the improvement of the manuscript, but whose designated tasks often mean that they are not given separate mention in acknowledgements of this kind. However, in our case, they went well beyond the call of duty and such efforts are deeply appreciated. Thanks are similarly extended to those individuals and groups who wish to remain unidentified but who provided fundamental help and encouragement throughout this long period.

Chapter 1

Setting the Scene

Graham M. S. Dann
Finnmark University College, Alta, Norway

Giuli Liebman Parrinello
Università Roma Tre, Rome, Italy

INTRODUCTION

This is a book about tourism social theory. It includes contributions from a number of European regions tracing the origins of the sociology of tourism to Europe in the 1930s and the wide range of its early conceptualization. There is also a specific focus on the Continental roots of its four current mainstream theories and the continuing richness of its evolution in diverse cultures and many languages up to the present day.

A comparative study of tourism social theories and their initial appearance in various European countries prior to their subsequent Anglo-Saxon articulation is a new and challenging exercise. For an ambitious undertaking such as this it is necessary to go further than the simple accumulation of different perspectives, even if they display a fascinating patrimony expressed in a way beyond the habitual horizons of conventional wisdom. Instead, the sociology of tourism and its sociological object must somehow capture the multi-polarity of tourism as a "total social phenomenon" (Lanfant 1995; in this volume). To deal with tourism social theories means not only abstractly linking them with general sociology and its main paradigms, but also taking into consideration the socio-political,

The Sociology of Tourism: European Origins and Developments
Tourism Social Science Series, Volume 12, 1–63
ISSN: 1571-5043/doi:10.1108/S1571-5043(2009)0000012006

economic, geographic, cultural, and ideological contexts in which they arose, including the working conditions under which the sociologists of tourism lived, together with their institutions of affiliation. Our project thus requires the study of multiple, different strains and levels of analysis.

The inspiration for this volume derives from a concern about monolingualism in tourism theory, an unjustified dominance of English as the *lingua franca* of communication that stands in sharp contrast to the polyglot tradition in sociology, as pointed out on several occasions by a former, highly respected President of the International Sociological Association (ISA), Immanuel Wallerstein (1995, 1998) (see Touraine 1998). In fact, the research committee on international tourism (RC 50) within the umbrella and as a microcosm of the ISA, with its significant Anglo-Saxon, European, and cosmopolitan composition has acted as a kind of intellectual catalyst for our interest in this matter, particularly with the realization that several of the contributors to this book are members of that group (Liebman Parrinello 2008; RC 50 2008).

Moreover, there is the essential relationship between the sociology of tourism and other social scientific disciplines of tourism, whose multi-, possibly inter-, disciplinary treatment is well known. Although it can be argued (Dann 2000) that the sociological treatment of tourism has probably contributed more to the current stock of knowledge of tourism as a social phenomenon than any other discipline (Dann 2005b), among the most important disciplines a few, like anthropology, are closely allied to, and sometimes barely distinguishable from, sociology (Nash 2007; Sharpley 1994:28–29) in providing an understanding of tourism. For that reason the sociology of tourism, coupled occasionally with the anthropology of tourism, is heuristically the principal focus of the pages that follow.

To this end, socio-historical overviews have been invited from well-known scholars from a number of Continental countries. With the exception of some from far Eastern Europe, they range from France, Germany (Austria and Switzerland), Italy, Spain, Greece, the Low-Countries, and the region of Scandinavia to the former Yugoslavia and Poland.[1] By examining these individual contributions on a comparative basis, it is possible to explore them in their various social and ideological contexts, and thereby obtain a cumulative picture of their evolution.

Throughout this representative anthology (with typical brief excerpts from our carefully selected indigenous experts for different areas translated by them from their native languages into English for a mainly Anglophone readership), it is possible to discover the Continental origins of the sociology of tourism. In other words, we can grasp the application of a discipline *in fieri*, not only in its uncertainties and weaknesses, but also in the rich complexity of its development, strictly bound up with its historical and geographical-cultural aspects. Such an exercise also implies casting additional light on the global qualities of contemporary tourism theories. As Löfgren relatedly observes, "the lively and innovative research carried out in countries like France and Germany rarely travels across the English Channel or the Atlantic" (1999:284). In fact, and in spite of the dominant English literature, the sociology of tourism keeps on going in some European countries, without them abandoning their specific local linguistic ways of investigation. It is this development, as much as the origins of the field that will be traced in the pages that follow.

EUROPEAN ORIGINS AND DEVELOPMENTS

Before turning to a final section featuring the authors of these European contributions, readers are invited to pursue the four preliminary stages of this introduction:

- The Anglophone dominance of tourism studies today
- The sociology of tourism: some unsettled questions
- European origins of the sociology of tourism
- Major sociological theories of tourism and their European roots

After this introductory chapter, the nine-chapter anthology that follows constitutes the main body of this volume. There will then be a conclusion with tables summarizing the principal findings of this investigation in their original and evolutionary contexts.

The Anglophone Dominance of Tourism Studies Today

According to Norwood (2006), "only 30 percent of UK citizens have a level of 'conversational competence' in a second language…enough to order a beer, but not enough to buy a home" (in contrast to 99% of Luxemburgers, 91% of Dutch, and 88% of Danes). A similar state of affairs occurs in the United States (National Virtual Translation Center 2008) where only 9% of Americans can speak their native language plus another language fluently, as opposed to 53% of Europeans.

Catering to, and perhaps encouraging such linguistic limitation in an area where we would assume that a premium would be placed on the ability to communicate in another language, in 2003, it was estimated that there were in excess of 40 English language tourism journals producing more than 500 articles a year (Tribe 2003 in Botterill 2003:97). Just four years later, the quantum of such outlets had increased by over 25% (Jafari 2007:116), and in mid-2009 the incomplete total of journals with tourism and/or travel in their titles calculated by us from data supplied from the *Centre International de Recherches et d'Etudes Touristiques* (CIRET) (International Center for Tourism Studies and Research) and a listing prepared by Xiao (2009) was estimated to be 80 solely in English with a further 10 in English and another European language. By contrast, and from the same sources, the number of tourism journals located in Continental Europe and publishing in European languages other than English, such as *Revista de Estudios Turísticos* (Review of Tourist Studies), was as low as nine. Indeed, some Continental tourism journals, realizing that they are fighting a losing battle (e.g., the *Scandinavian Journal of Hospitality and Tourism*) have turned over the dissemination of their ideas to UK publishers. Here, all their original, culturally predicated thoughts appear in English even though the topics they treat and the literature reviewed are decidedly non-Anglophone in nature. Meanwhile, some other non-Anglophone tourism journals, such as *Acta Turistica* (Tourist Proceedings), find it necessary to publish in two side-by-side languages—in this instance Croatian and English—or produce separate issues in translation, for instance, the Polish *Nowe Problemy Turystyki* (New Problems of Tourism).

Yet, if we turn to the geographical spread of tourism research centers, it is possible to calculate from their most comprehensive listing (*Centre International de Recherches et d'Études Touristiques* 2008) that while English as a first language occurs in approximately 40% of the cases overall,[2] the published output emanating from such institutions is the complete reverse of such a minority linguistic situation.[3] This asymmetrical patterning should come as no surprise since the sociology of tourism, like its parent discipline has "a strong bias toward [academics from the] richer [Anglophone] countries" who have "much stronger financial support than scholars elsewhere, and have consequently found it easier to engage in research and produce scholarly writings"... "They thereupon receive a 'rent' in the form of a greater reputation and a wider acceptance of their views" (Wallerstein 1998:5).

Turning to this English-speaking world, and using the prime exemplar as a case study par excellence, an examination of past issues of what its founder editor and many peer reviews refer to as the leading academic tourism publication, *Annals of Tourism Research* (Jafari 2007:116), quickly reveals an almost exclusive concentration on English language material that carries over to the nationality of the contributors and their patterns of citation.

Swain et al. (1998), for example, after indexing 25 years of that journal's publication, confirm independent analyses conducted by Sheldon (1991), Kim (1998), and Turkulin and Hitrec (1998) that "the greatest number of *Annals'* individual authors reside in the United States, with Canada and all Europe second" (1998:1003), that the United States is the most indexed geographic location (1998:1003) and the most cited world region (1998:1003). An even more recent content analytical study of *Annals* conducted over a longer period by Xiao and Smith reinforces these trends by showing from the subject indices that the principal countries represented continue to be the United States, Canada, United Kingdom, Australia, and New Zealand, all Anglophone countries (2006:492). They, conclude, although without any supporting demonstration, that non-Anglophone authors tend to submit their work to regional journals such as *Anatolia* and *China Tourism Research*—seemingly oblivious of the irony that these journals themselves, in order to attract a clientele, feel obliged to publish most of their material in English (Sheldon 1991:477).

By way of illustration and taking a recent complete year of publication of *Annals* (2005), it can be seen that of the 51 articles appearing in those four issues, 37 are from authors whose first language is English, 7 from writers whose maternal tongue is European/non-English (6 Spanish and 1 Portuguese), and 7 from non-European countries whose primary language is non-European (Israel: 1, Japan: 1, South Korea: 2, Taiwan: 1, Turkey: 1). (In cases of multi-authorship, the nationality of the first or senior author is taken). However, of greater significance is the fact that practically all the publications quoted by these contributors are written in English. In the case of the dominant Anglophone group, of the 2,205 references they provide, fully 99.8% are to works in English, a figure which rises to a maximum 100% for the 13 UK authors, who display a total inability or unwillingness to cite material other than in their own language.

The situation is not much better for the non-Anglophone/non-European authors, whose citation of English works is some 96.9% of all quotations (the remaining 3.1% being allocated to non-European sources). Only when we come to the seven European authors does the situation change. Here 27.5% of cited works are written in European languages (mostly Spanish, thereby indicating a slight trend toward nationalism), but still the remaining three quarters of all citations are of Anglophone material. The overall message from this little exercise thus seems to be that, not only are there more English language tourism journals when compared to any other provenance, but their linguistic content is similarly biased. However, in order to substantiate this claim unequivocally it would be necessary to undertake a similar analysis of all journals of this kind and to generalize its conclusions.

A similar picture emerges from English-language tourism textbooks. Burns and Holden (1995), for instance, include only one Continental European publication out of total of 235 works in their list of references and in Brown (1998) as many as 169 of the 170 works cited are in the English language. Indeed, this is a skewed relationship that is probably replicated in every Anglophone tourism textbook and commentary that one cares to examine. However, what makes Brown's situation so ironic is that, within the very same covers, she notes "The continuing ignorance of each other's work among English-speaking researchers and those speaking other European languages remains a hindrance to a rounded appraisal of tourism" (1998:94–95).

While the same sort of pattern emerges in texts specifically dedicated to the sociology of tourism,[4] the scenario is somewhat different when we analyze edited works with contributors from a variety of national backgrounds. If there is an underlying trend, it is that within the pages of the same book, those from English-speaking countries tend to display far greater ethnocentrism than those from the non-Anglophone world.[5] This pattern is replicated in edited volumes with an even split between French and English-speaking authors all of whom write in English[6] and in edited works where contributors write in their own language.[7] A similar Anglophone hegemony is in evidence among the most prestigious group of tourism academics worldwide, the International Academy for the Study of Tourism (IAST) (2008) in terms of its composition and publications (Dann 2007a).[8]

In spite of the foregoing English-speaking domination of tourism studies, all is not lost. Fortunately, and apart from Brown's previously mentioned enlightened, though somewhat illogical attitude, a few additional examples can be found of an open-minded Anglophone minority whose comments can usefully serve as an inspiration for the current undertaking. Take Botterill, for instance. Although he admits (in English), in a bilingual tourism journal, that he forms part of "the sub-culture of the Anglo-centric tourism research community" (2003:99), he disassociates himself from it to the extent that his position of critical realism derives from Kantian transcendental idealism (2003:99), a German theoretical position. Additionally he acknowledges that his involvement with *Tourism Concern* is inspired by the Durkheimian notion of social inclusion (social solidarity) found in the French-language community (2003:99).

Relatedly one finds Franklin and Crang stating that there is a need "to challenge the predominantly Anglo-centric views of tourism presented in the current literature" (2001:19). Their message assumes greater significance with the realization that they are editors of a cutting edge journal in tourism theory (*Tourist Studies*) and that their remarks are contained in what is surely a declaration of editorial intent in that publication's first issue. Further poignancy is added to their proselytizing mission when they go on to claim that they will be "encouraging submissions from non-English speaking authors" (2001:19). Though it is still too early to discern whether their good intentions are borne out in reality, at least they would appear to be a step in the right direction.

Then there is the highly acclaimed Rojek who turns on his Anglophone colleagues for failing to understand the seminal concept of *flâneur* (stroller) that is used so frequently and uncritically today in tourism studies (1997:57–58). Had his compatriots been more familiar with the original (1927–1940) work of Benjamin on the *Arcades* project, instead of waiting for it to become available to them in translation (1999), they would, he argues, have been better able to appreciate the *flâneur* as emblematic of postmodern cosmopolitan tourism.

Inspired by such writers, who are quoted in a recent state-of-the-art paper, the situation may be summed up as follows:

> There is also an (unwitting) tendency for some scholars to over-quote persons from their own discipline, nationality and tongue. In the latter regard, tourism research seems to be dominated by monoglot Anglophones who are either unwilling or unable to learn another language, and hence are blissfully unaware of what is taking place elsewhere in the world (Dann 2005b:3).

Part of the foregoing analysis includes the identification of seven leading tourism researchers, only one of whom is from the non-Anglophone world. Most of the others are white, male, and from developed countries. Above all, though, they write in English, a strange situation, "given that tourism itself is supposed to be a global phenomenon *par excellence*" (Dann 2005b:3).

One of these distinguished scholars in Dann's listing is the Israeli sociologist, Erik Cohen, who is reckoned by many, unofficially at least, to be the number one in the field. Yet, according to Graburn and Leite in a perceptive review of this pioneer's life legacy (Cohen 2004), the "omission of works outside of the Anglophone tradition is also surprising for a polyglot such as Cohen, pointing up the question of Anglo-Saxon hegemony in the field and of academic linguistic Anglo-centrism more generally" (2006:270).

The previously mentioned odd one out in Dann's select group of tourism academic celebrities is Marie Françoise Lanfant (in this volume) who, it is interesting to note, has expressed her feelings on the intellectual isolation experienced by herself and her French colleagues. In a paper addressed to her compatriots, she laments the predominance of an Anglophone discourse in tourism studies, pointing out that work appearing in such influential journals as *Annals of Tourism Research* "ne correspond pas exactement à ce qui passe en France dans la même période" (does not correspond exactly with what took place in France during the same period) (Lanfant 1999:42) (translation of first editor; hereafter all translations into English are either carried out by the first or second editor or respective country authors, none of whom will be specifically acknowledged). Consequently, she has rightly insisted that, in making presentations to such gatherings as the research committee on international tourism of the ISA (of which she is a former president), she should be allowed, perhaps even encouraged, to deliver in French, particularly since over 10 years ago a former distinguished head of that organization has stated in unequivocal terms that "the use of multiple languages, while having some negative administrative effects, is intellectually essential to the scientific future of social science" (Wallerstein 1998:9). Even so, she, like many of her fellow nationals, has been obliged at the alternative risk of being intellectually sidelined, to publish a great deal of her output in English, and, since Wallerstein's remarks, the situation, if anything, has deteriorated.

Another person in a like predicament is the Norwegian sociologist of tourism, Jens Kristian Steen Jacobsen (also in this volume) whose most important theoretical insights have been published in English. Had they been left in Norwegian, the academic world of tourism would have been arguably none the wiser and a great deal intellectually poorer.

However, even if Continental specialists in the sociology of tourism are given the credit they deserve (and indeed this is one of the principal aims of this book), there are still some unresolved issues relating to the field itself, questions that must be tackled before we can proceed any further. To these matters we now turn.

Some Unsettled Questions

Around the middle of the 19th century, John Stuart Mill (1844) was dealing with political economy as a new science. Being confronted *inter alia* with the question of definition he suggested a chronological order which was different from the logico-didactic order, noting that the definition of a science had almost invariably not preceded but followed the creation of that science itself. In the more modest field of the sociology of tourism, and even though it has been established for quite some time, longer than many realize, we are today still faced with several unsettled questions. Macro-problems are at stake, such as the surrounding context and influence of European and national sociologies, the relationship between general sociology and the sociology of tourism, and particularly, strictly intertwined, the fundamental relationship free-time—leisure—tourism, the issue of definition, the multi-/interdisciplinarity of tourism studies, fundamental problems of language and translation and, last but not least, ideological discriminants. The (mostly diachronic) exploratory reviews undertaken by our different contributors and the resulting cross-cultural representation of diverse European areas offer many clues as to the richness and range of orientations on many basic issues, where signposted paths are often strayed from and, as a result, apparently attained certainties get lost. We could maintain that, in spite of progress in some of these areas, we are today not richer but poorer. Our research field has become restricted, and sometimes a veil of silence spreads over it, as if by way of tacit ideological acceptance. The introductory accent placed on unsettled questions should thus be seen as an ideological attitude to clarify before we begin to reconstruct in detail the European origins of the sociology of tourism.

European and National Sociologies. Is it legitimate to express ourselves in terms of a European sociology? By way of response to this rhetorical question, Nedelmann and Sztompka in their *Sociology in Europe in Search of Identity* propose and examine various European paths to sociology. In introducing their position, they declare:

> Sociology is a form of reflective self-awareness of societies, and as such it mirrors their concrete, particular experiences, their unique history, specific culture, local tradition. Nobody would doubt that European history, culture and heritage display some specificity. And, hence, it is a justifiable guess that sociology, reflecting European experience, will demonstrate some peculiarities as well (1993:2–3).

Sociology itself, because of its very nature as a science of society is ultimately tied to a national framework. European countries are no exception to this generalization. All have their traditions and sets of values which are historically defined, and trends which are not indifferent to sociology. These differences are more than just cultural; they imply power relationships and institutions, as well as networks of established behavior and of everyday functioning (Ferrarotti 1986:20). Since they constitute particular idiomatic visions of the world, they are best communicated in their own language (Touraine 1998:10; Wallerstein 1998:5).

Not only differences in sociological theories themselves are important, but also the determination of disciplinary fields and their encounters, where one can sometimes come across several names for the same discipline. Until quite recently, for example, Great Britain was reluctant even to accept the very term "sociology," and the discipline that in the United States was called "cultural anthropology" was defined in the United Kingdom as "social anthropology." Today these national contexts have of course to be understood within a twin process of unification and globalization. More-over, Anglo-Saxon sociology is no longer a relative Cinderella, but dominant all over the world. One more problem arises on account of the former Western-Eastern relationship. Stereotypes can be misleading. In retrospect, probably the so-called Iron Curtain was a less substantial divide than one might imagine in the field of sociology. Some particularly relevant Eastern sociologies were very much alive and well, especially the sociology of leisure (Dumazedier 1985; Lanfant 1972), as also the related field of the sociology of tourism. While some Eastern bloc countries like Poland and the former Yugoslavia (strictly speaking a nonaligned country) could be considered as contributions leading to chapters of this book, others unfortunately could not, even if they (like Hungary) would probably have been interesting in several aspects. Some relevant insights in the former East Germany (GDR) can be found in this volume (Spode), hinting at common research problems going through the Western-Eastern divide.

Another interesting European feature is that of the Mediterranean Association for the Sociology of Tourism. It is concerned with the common sociological interests of destination countries confronted with the evolution of traditional tourism, like Italy, Spain, Greece, and is attempting to extend a hand toward North-African countries. Born at the end of the 1980s, this association is very active and has already organized six conferences (Savelli in this volume).

General Sociology and the Sociology of Tourism.   It is still a contested relationship: the sociology of tourism depends on sociology in general, but not in the sense of a well-established subdiscipline. For the moment we can only realistically refer to the sociology of tourism with provisos that derive from its relationship with the sociology of leisure (see below). Were we to examine the evolution of sociology in general it would be evident that there is no single overarching theory of society that has been, is, or will be, universally accepted. Such theory that has emerged has been partial, dialectical, and perspective based. Proceeding under the same logic, we can expect a derived application to display a similar pattern. Thus, even though different sociological perspectives contributing to the sociology of tourism have been identified by Dann and Cohen (1991), the sociology of tourism, in spite of the efforts of its adherents, is still mostly a piece of the jigsaw, a fragment of the cumulative and kaleidoscopic understanding of tourism. In the case of France, Lanfant underlines the lack of systematization and causality, possibly the inadequacy toward the premises of a glorious and ambitious general sociology "La sociologie du tourisme s'est formée cahin caha de sorte qu'on peut se demander s'il existe en France une sociologie du tourisme répondant aux exigences d'une demarche sociologique et d'une théorie du social bien établie" (2005) (The sociology of tourism is so lamely put together that one can rightly ask if there exists in France a sociology of tourism that responds to the needs of sociological advancement and of a well-established social theory). Yet, in some Continental European countries, more so than in others, it is possible to trace the classical sociological pedigree of the (middle-range) theories that have appeared on the scene. In Germany, for example, much of the early theorizing was derived from the Formalist insights of mainstream sociologist, Georg Simmel, most of whose writings were published in the late 19th and first decade of the 20th century. Max Weber was another German sociological giant who acted as a paradigmatic mentor both for his compatriots (Knebel) and those in other countries with a similar language base (e.g., Aubert in Norway).

France has also displayed a healthy degree of the right variety of ethnocentrism in its approach to the adoption of classical sociologists for their application to tourism, even though none of these mainstream thinkers explicitly addressed the topic in his writings. In this vein, Marie-Françoise Lanfant (in this volume), for instance, has utilized the 1895 insights of Émile Durkheim on social facts (as outlined in his well-known *Règles de la Méthode Sociologique* (Rules of the Sociological Method) to support her 1995 notion of "tourism as an international social fact"—an external agent of constraint and consensus. Her ideas were eclectically reinforced by employing the insights of Mauss (1969, 1980) and Morin (1962), as well as those of Lacan (1975). Lanfant has additionally acknowledged the influence of the Swiss, Krapf (1953, 1964) on tourism as a form of consumption whose ideas were made available to her in translation by her longstanding colleague, René Baretje, and subsequently developed by another compatriot, Pierre Bourdieu. As Jacobsen and Lengkeek (also in this volume) respectively point out, a similar dependence on French thinkers is evident in the work of such outsiders as Löfgren (who relied on Barthes and Bourdieu) and Mordal (on Dumazedier) in Scandinavia, and Bouillin-Darteville (on Dumazedier) in Belgium. However, it was not until 1976 that the Anglophone MacCannell admitted his reliance on Durkheim (1912[1915, 1965]), in particular the area of social representation underlying the sight sacralization of markers, as spelt out in *Les Formes Élémentaires de la Vie Religieuse* (Elementary Forms of the Religious Life).

Polish sociology of tourism has a respected pedigree of its own with sociologists like Thomas and Znaniecki, who, even if they did not include tourism in their studies, through their theory of social disorganization and reorganization helped in explaining social encounters in tourism via a Symbolic Interactionist perspective (Przecławski, Bystrzanowski, and Ujma in this volume).

In examining the contributions from European countries other than Germany and France, it will emerge that they formed part of the *evolution* of the sociology of tourism rather than its *origin*. That is to say, many of them depended on France and Germany for their initial insights and frameworks that they subsequently developed and applied to their own idiosyncratic cultural situations. In the section devoted to the European origins of the sociology of tourism and in the conclusion it will be interesting to speculate as to whether the Northern Europeans would tend to follow more closely the German theorizing and those from the South the French way of thought. Similarly it should be worth exploring the extent to which later European countries interact theoretically with one another as a form of intra-dependency.

The Sociology of Tourism and the Sociology of Leisure. Without a longitudinal and enlarged view embracing the contested relationship between the approaches of leisure and tourism, it would not even have been possible to search for a common sociological basis for the contributions of this book. In fact the two focuses of interest that Lanfant presents in her long life's work are indicative of the whole range lying between these two fields. On the one hand, there is the sociology of leisure that she analyzed in her early research years (Lanfant 1972), the traces of which and developments from are still quite vibrant in some parts of Europe and elsewhere today (e.g., Lengkeek in this volume, in relation to the Netherlands). On the other hand, there is international tourism, object of her broad and long-sighted more recent theorizations (Lanfant 1995, 2005). Today, we could (erroneously) conclude that the problem has simply been solved by the domination of tourism over leisure. True, the current academic superiority of the sociology of tourism implies a corresponding crisis in the sociology of leisure, where there is even talk of the definitive demise of the latter (Franke and Hammerich 2001). Yet a sociologist of tourism like Erik Cohen singles out a trend, a fundamental merger of tourism and ordinary leisure as opposed to tourism and exploration (2004:318). Instead of a contrary active quest for the "totally Other" in the "center-out-there," a contrasting type of tourism implies passive recreation and diversion, excursionism, sightseeing, and the more sedentary roles associated with this kind of outbound tourism, along with the various species of a more modest domestic tourism closer to free-time occupations and to leisure.

It is difficult to disentangle the different concepts of time suggested by the sociology of leisure and the sociology of tourism. Yet, in the various formulations of tourism, fundamental, even if implicit, is always the conceptualization (or lack of conceptualization) of work-time and free-time (leisure) in its different species. Following the historical development of *temps libre* (free-time) and *loisir* (leisure), two theorizations, which were distinct at their origin, then brought nearer, inducing confusion, have in fact to be singled out. On this point, Lanfant's (2005) assessment is illuminating. She questions the relationship between tourism and leisure through a conceptual and linguistic analysis. Leisure derives from the Greek concept of *scholé*, subsequently translated into the Latin *otium*, with its well-known positive connotation which stands in contrast to its antonym *negotium*. As Lanfant underscores "L'idéologie du loisir a été un élément dynamique tour à tour positif ou négatif de l'évolution des sociétés précapitalistes et capitalistes" (2005) (The ideology of leisure has been a dynamic element, now negative, now positive, in the evolution of pre-capitalist and capitalist societies).

Relatively more recent is the dichotomy work-time/free-time associated with industrial societies. Here the sociology of work and the sociology of free-time are intrinsically bound together. It has been speculated whether it was because of the Marxist doctrine and/or the Protestant Ethic that the principal interest of sociology was directed at first mainly to the sociology of work, thereby consigning aspects of free-time to the territory of frivolity and superfluity (Lanfant 1995).

The phenomenon cannot be understood without remembering the traditional 19th century anxiety over the increasing free-time of workers and the consequent potential brutishness of their amusements, debauchery, drunkenness, and misguided occupations of every kind, not to speak of their possible attitudes of rebellion (Thiesse 1996:329). This bourgeois concern over the misuse of free-time and leisure by the proletariat and its resulting class-predicated, patronizing attitude were adopted by the International Labor Organization after World War I and directed more and more by governments, especially since the 1930s, through a policy of paid holidays.

Therefore, confusion arose between two concepts of leisure. The first derived from free-time was ideologically laden, originating as it did from Marx and Engels' manifesto (1959), with its emphasis on work, capital, and surplus value. Consequently there was a dichotomous antagonism between the leisured class (Veblen 1899[1970,1994]) and the servile working class, according to which free-time could be considered either as time outside work necessary for recharging one's batteries or time for the proletariat to overthrow the exploitation inherent in forced labor. Free-time was hence either recuperation from work (capitalist) or compensation for the alienation experienced in work (Marxist). It was the former (second concept of leisure) as a bourgeois target for the working class that gained the ascendancy with its accent on individual interest and motivation in the context of personal freedom in a humanist, Western, postindustrial society. There was thus a transition from the ideology of production and surplus value to one of consumption and surplus gratification—a quest for increasingly novel forms of pleasure.

As Lanfant demonstrates, France, too, was preoccupied in the 1950s in enlightened terms with leisure, as was evident in the pioneering work of Dumazedier and herself. She saw in the 1950s and in the 1960s a new humanism, possibly embracing Western and Eastern societies and a successful evolution from time freed from the productivity of labor to time becoming discretionary time for leisure. But the situation evolved and Lanfant's confrontation with Dumazedier predated the overall decline of the sociology of leisure. According to her (in this volume), in the 1970s, one could witness a progressive appropriation of the concepts of leisure and free-time by the disciplines of tourism.

Only later, in 1990, and then under the intellectual aegis of the ISA, did tourism become detached from leisure as a specific field of sociological inquiry with the establishment of its own dedicated research committee. Yet, if this position represented mainstream thinking in Europe, there were also territories like the very different Low Countries, embracing Catholic

Belgium and the Protestant Netherlands, where "for a long time, and in both countries, leisure studies constituted the common denominator for the approaches of leisure, recreation, sports, media and tourism" (Lengkeek in this volume). In Belgium, for example, Lengkeek also shows that the first area of concern was the domain of *leisure* and how it was (ideologically) perceived by bourgeois academics as a social problem (for the proletariat) before it constituted a sociological problem for all (requiring understanding and explanation). The Belgian Catholic milieu became more and more interested in tourism, initially as a form of charity, and subsequently organized in the institutionalized form of "social tourism." In the Dutch social and academic milieu the focus was on free-time, meaning first of all "outdoor recreation," and having its roots in the recreational pursuits of the Dutch Bicycle Union founded as early as 1883. In both countries, at the levels of research and teaching, proper tourism studies appeared very late and very slowly on the academic scene, and even when they did finally emerge, they were mostly coupled with recreation.

The Problem of Definition.   Some scholars of tourism still claim, and with a certain amount of justification, that there is a lack of a suitable definitional framework for their field. In Boyer's words, "Force est de reconnaitre qu'à la fin du XXième siècle aucune définition conceptuelle du tourisme n'est généralement admise" (It is necessary to acknowledge that at the end of the 20th century there was no generally accepted conceptual definition of tourism) (1999:14).

Yet, it is interesting to observe that a much more rigorous approach to definitions was adopted in earlier works of Continental European theorists. For example, and as pointed out several times by Durkheim (1897[1951, 1997] on suicide) himself, especially in *Les Règles de la Méthode Sociologique* (1895), much of the early work in establishing a discipline or an applied field is taken up with the act of classification, an exercise which in turn leads to definition.

However, it is especially in tracing the pages of this book devoted to the German speaking milieu that we realize just how important was the search for a *Begriffsbestimmung*, a conceptual definition, of tourism, which was at the same time an attempt to reach a sociological definition based on the German concept of *Fremdenverkehr* (literally "stranger traffic") (Bormann 1931; Glücksmann 1935) with its Simmelian influence and emphasis on social interaction. An essential focus on interaction was also apparent in the seminal definition of Hunziker and Krapf, heirs of the German tradition during and after World War II: "Tourism is the quintessence of relationships which result from travel and sojourn by outsiders, insofar as no principal residence is established by their stay and, as a rule, there is no associated professional activity" (1942:21). Although Spode claims that there is little sociology or psychology in this definition to be interpreted *ex negativo*, it is interesting to see that the word "quintessence" is distinctly reminiscent of Simmel's "form," especially when linked to relationships. Moreover, the notion of outsider (as opposed to insider) (Becker 1963) is also arguably more sociological in nature than the concept of guest when contrasted with host (Smith 1977a, 1977b). Therefore, it is not surprising that this definition became official not only for the "Swiss School," but also that the *Association Internationale d'Experts Scientifiques du Tourisme* (AIEST) (International Association of Scientific Experts in Tourism) adopted it in 1964. Furthermore, it is suggestive that, although the ambivalent organic notion is today largely abandoned and substituted by either the neutral United Nations World Tourism Organization (UNWTO) formula of "activities of people" or by an explicitly and exclusively economic "supply-side view" (Smith 1988), yet tourism academics needing a deeper definition often implicitly go back to Hunziker and Krapf. Such is the case of a textbook like that of McIntosh and Goeldner (1995), but also of a scholar like Tribe (1997), who adapts the formula to more contemporary circumstances.

The German term *Fremdenverkehr* was only little by little substituted by *Tourismus* (Tourism). With Enzensberger (1958) the definition was organic and ideology laden. It was also bound to the new term of *Tourismus*. For Enzensberger (1974) tourism as "a consciousness industry" (i.e., having mechanisms such as education and the mass media through which the human mind was reproduced as a social product perpetuating the existing order of man's domination over man), similarly stressed mobility and mass production. Thus, according to his definition tourism was "a set of political, social, technological, and intellectual symptoms with a common revolutionary impetus" (1996:124). There were, however, no further developments of this formulation, a matter to which we return in the next major section on "origins." Compared to later developments in the sociology and anthropology of tourism, it is interesting how pale the definitions of tourist are in the latter that link tourism with leisure, in the second case also adding a motivational component. Interestingly, the accent is necessarily on the individual tourist, not on the tourism phenomenon. For instance, Nash (1981:462) defines a tourist as "someone at leisure who also travels" and Smith as "a temporarily leisured person who voluntarily visits a place away from home for the purpose of experiencing a change" (1977a:1).

Nevertheless, the organic notion of tourism still seems to be central in the European heritage and continues to feature prominently in the writings of

Przecławski (see chapter on Poland in this volume). Although he concedes that definitions of tourism are not universally accepted, vary according to discipline, and that some do not distinguish clearly between the essence of the phenomenon and its effects, he nevertheless highlights many elements that should, in his opinion, feature in a definition of tourism, among which are the typical Polish accent on human values, the pedagogical attitude, and concern over the environment. Thus, even though Przecławski is influenced by a largely American inspired Symbolic Interactionism (according to which, if situations are defined as real they are real in their consequences), and by the Catholic thinker Teilhard de Chardin, it should not be forgotten that one of Symbolic Interactionism's principal exponents was a compatriot of his, a certain Florian Znaniecki.

Multi- and Interdisciplinarity. These issues are still open to discussion in contemporary English language debate. They are explicitly profiled in Tribe's (1997) seminal "indiscipline of tourism," while there are implicit hints at tourism theory, especially in contemporary German tourism studies.

As the previously mentioned Wallerstein puts it, "A discipline defines not only what to think about and how to think about it, but also what is outside its purview. To say that a given subject is a discipline is to say not only what it is but what it is not" (1999:1). This observation is even more valid for tourism. If we examine the terms of the question, multidisciplinarity and interdisciplinarity can be considered essential characteristics of tourism. Przecławski makes a distinction between them. According to him, interdisciplinary research is obviously more unified and integrated than a multidisciplinary inquiry (1993). Important examples of this kind of investigation were the so-called Vienna Center projects (Bystrzanowski 1989; Bystrzanowski and Beck 1989). The second one, in particular, singled out the social change induced by tourism, featured all the possible fundamental co-existing causes, and employed for many years dozens of international specialists from diverse disciplines. Therefore, it was not merely by chance that Polish scholars like Przecławski and Bystrzanowski (in this volume) were actively involved in the coordination of its activities.

Hunziker had tackled the idea of a tourism doctrine—strictly intertwined with a tourism definition—by proposing a revised structure of the tourism system and distinguishing between the "economic aspects of tourism" and "tourism as the object of noneconomic subjects." Among the noneconomic subjects, he included the "history of tourism," the "geography of tourism," the "sociology of tourism," and the "law of tourism" (Hunziker 1973:5).

It should be noted that sociology was not always the first social science discipline to explore this newly emerging field, a point made by many of the contributors to this book. As Savelli (in this volume) observes, in the case of Italy, already by the 1920s and 1930s, sociological analyses were preceded by studies based on political economy, business economics, and economic geography. According to Vukonić (in this volume), a parallel situation later occurred in the former Yugoslavia where the economics of tourism took center stage in the peculiar "self-managed" economy of a nonaligned country. Furthermore, as Aramberri (in this volume) shows, even in those countries with relatively easy access to foreign exchange, such as Spain recovering from a civil war, the economic aspects of tourism were paramount. In socialist Poland, however, the scenario seemed to be reversed, since as Przecławski, Bystrzanowski, and Ujma (in this volume) claim, a sociology of tourism had been in existence there for at least 50 years. Yet a glance at the European situation offered by this anthology illustrates a potential collaboration of different disciplines that has partly gone astray. The different countries analyzed in this volume also developed tentatively through alliances of varying emphases placed on diverse disciplines.

Although the coupling of the sociology and anthropology of tourism may sometimes be taken for granted (Dann 2005b), it should not be accepted uncritically. However, if nowadays this alliance of the sociology of tourism with cultural anthropology seems to be the only one possible, and it is a cooperation which has been productive over the last few decades, it may also threaten to become too obvious and reductive. Already in the early postwar years, anthropological interests in Scandinavian tourism were evident (Jacobsen in this volume). We should remember, too, the pioneering anthropological studies (field research, participant observation) undertaken by the *Studienkreis für Tourismus* (Study Circle for Tourism) in 1970s Germany (Spode in this volume) and the collaborative work illustrated by Tsartas and Galani-Moutafi (in this volume) in Greece.

One discipline in the study of tourism which is still missing today is (social) psychology, and the kind of amalgamation of disciplines (sociology-psychology of tourism) that used to be customary for many during the postwar years, especially in German-speaking countries (maybe also due to the double research interest in tourism-tourist), has been forgotten. However, and although the psychology of tourism seems to be a dying discipline ousted by the pragmatics of tourism marketing (Liebman Parrinello 1993), a reflection of the importance of the psychological approach can still be seen in some Scandinavian studies (Jacobsen in this volume) and partly in the Italian tradition of pairing disciplines (such as the sociology and psychology of tourism) at the institutional level (Savelli in this volume; Sessa 1974–1992).

In Italy especially, the geography of tourism has a long tradition. It developed here little by little from interests in rural sociology, which led to regional studies, the patrimony of food and wine, urban sociology, etc. (Savelli in this volume). Furthermore, in the Netherlands in geography a distinct approach is relevant, while in Germany geography has for many years been coupled with the sociology of tourism.

The educational aspects of tourism are also traditional in German-speaking countries especially when tourism became intensive mass tourism in the second postwar era. In this respect, an institution like the *Studienkreis für Tourismus* played a key role (Spode in this volume). Also relevant is the pedagogical concern in Belgium, especially at the University of Leuven, and in Poland as an intrinsic feature of the sociology of tourism. Moreover, there is a distinct impression that these educational interests are correspondingly expanding with the onslaught of an increasingly individualized tourism.

Among other main disciplines to be mentioned, and quoted by Hunziker, is the history of tourism, often associated with an "historical anthropology" (Spode 1995), where some scholars are very productive. Derived from the French "history of mentalities," Anglo-Saxon cultural anthropology, German philosophical anthropology, and debates on everyday history, historical anthropology is currently a transdisciplinary approach mainly prevalent in Germany and Austria (Spode 1999). After many years of oblivion, now a renewed interest can be declared, both on behalf of historians of tourism (Boyer 2007; Hachtmann 2007) and of historians in their own right (Baranowski 2001; Walton 2005). Indeed, without the basis of such a longitudinal cross-cultural perspective this book could not have been conceived.

There are also many, sometimes taken-for-granted disciplines in the field of tourism, like tourism medicine, for instance. While they used to belong to the research topics of early Scandinavian tourism (Jacobsen in this volume), they are still accepted in the current spectrum of tourism disciplines even though they are not linked anymore with the interests of the sociology of tourism. Nevertheless, at least there is a suggestion of tourism theory, an issue which still survives especially in the German world, one that could be considered either as the last gasp of a dying creature or the perennial need for a theoretical disciplinary framework. Under a different guise, especially over the last few decades, it is still an open discourse among some tourism scholars, even if the historical reference points are mostly ignored.

This discourse—which is intertwined with the disciplinary one—sometimes goes under the definition of the "field" of tourism studies, like in the discussion between Tribe (2000) and Leiper (2000), occasionally evoking the ghost of "tourismology" (controversially considered by some to be the unique meta-discipline which should deal with tourism and tourism theory). "Paradigm" is another term which cannot be found in the traditional European theoretical tradition. Yet, since its 1996 symposium in Jyväskylä (Finland) there has been an ongoing debate on paradigms in the research committee on international tourism (RC 50) of the ISA (Dann 1997a), as well as outside that institutional framework (Boyer 1999).

There are relatively few supporters of a "tourismology" as a specific science of tourism. A trace of this central European heritage can be found in the former Yugoslavia, where Jovičić was a supporter of this conceptualization with his discussed *Turizmologija* (1972) and there was even a chair of tourismology at the university of Belgrade for two decades (Vukonić in this volume). Yet, in spite of their Swiss matrix, Krippendorf and Müller are against a proper tourismology (tourist science) since they argue that tourism, like any other applied science should acknowledge the epistemological contributions of other fields of knowledge (Krippendorf 1997; Müller 2002).

Linguistic and Translation Problems.   If many of the ideas underpinning the sociology of tourism originated in Continental Europe, they remained buried there for several years in their own languages. Some of these works were never translated into English. A few, like Enzensberger's (1958) essay, for example, had to wait four decades before they were made available to the Anglophone world. Others, like the more fortunate Krippendorf (1987) only experienced a delay of three years before they appeared in English. Yet, in today's world of instant communication and dated knowledge, such procrastination is quite unacceptable.

Here there is a quasi inevitability to the whole process, the result perhaps of the domination of the field by publishers in the United States and United Kingdom, and, as a corollary, the emergence of a system of Anglophone gate-keepers (reviewers) to ensure the maintenance of linguistic standards and ultimately the control of scientific outcomes (Ammon 2008). Thus, in spite of Lanfant's (1972) expressed regret that her book on the *theories* of leisure, which, apart from Italian, Spanish, and Dutch versions, remained as it was written, in her native French, a more fundamental question arises as to whether it should have been translated into English for the benefit of her monoglot Anglophone colleagues as she had wished.

At this point we are reminded of the Italian expression *traduttore, traditore* which itself exemplifies the difficulties of translation since a literal English version would be "translator, traitor" which clearly lacks some of the idiomatic resonance of the original. Even so, the expression draws attention to the fact that insights articulated in one language cannot always easily be transferred into another. For example, *état, staat, estado* do not refer to the same reality as *state* and for that reason such terms are best left as they are (Touraine 1998:10). Furthermore, almost any classical work we might care to examine, if we compare the original with its rendition into English some of the meaning disappears on the way. In the words of a recent film title, "Lost in Translation" is the verdict and outcome.

Thus, it would seem to be that the optimal position would be to leave all works in the language in which they were written and encourage English speakers to learn foreign languages in order to become familiar with the literature in its entirety. After all, "from 1850 to 1945 the period of the creation of the modern social sciences," "it was apparently assumed that scholars could understand languages other than their own" (English, French, Italian, and German) (Wallerstein 1995:27), thereby encouraging Wallerstein to rhetorically ask, "is it so unthinkable that we can reachieve what was the expectation of our predecessors?" (1995:33). Carli and Ammon note that the shift was even more recent when they claim: "Until the end of the Seventies of the last century, a much higher degree of shared multilingualism was typical of academia...It was, in fact, only during the Eighties that a rapid and drastic change toward monolingualism took place, at first in the so-called *hard sciences*...and gradually also in the social sciences and humanities" (2008:1). What they also may have had in mind was the current state of affairs where non-Anglophones, having read European works in the original are obliged to cite them in English if they wish to communicate these ideas to their monoglot English-speaking colleagues—the *active* use of English (as opposed to the *passive* use whereby they are forced to use English if they wish to follow new developments in the field (Ammon 2008)). That matters are even worse than when these observations were made may be gauged from the fact that the University of Cambridge has recently removed its foreign language entry requirement and that several English secondary schools which once used to prepare students for higher education have also taken modern languages out of their curricula.

Thus, what we have today is a state of affairs where many younger Anglophone academics, lacking the necessary time, ability, and inclination, will never learn another language. For these cases, therefore, translation might be better than nothing at all. The same sort of reasoning would also apply to non-mainstream European languages such as Norwegian, for example. It would surely take the most dedicated of scholars to learn a language spoken by only four million people worldwide in order to capture the full meaning of a book or article in that language. Hence the reality of the situation is reluctantly accepted, in spite of Wallerstein's warning that "it is a serious handicap to scholars if they cannot read what other scholars write" and that "those with the biggest handicap are of course the native English writers, since they are the least likely to acquire the ability to read other languages" (1998:9). Thus, Anglophone colleagues are encouraged to become aware of works emanating from non-Anglophone countries. Indeed, without such a consciousness, they would still be under the mistaken impression that the sociology of tourism derived from the English-speaking world.

Paradigmatic is the change in fortune of Krapf's *La Consommation Touristique* (Touristic Consumption) (1953, 1964), which can be considered a paramount case of the spread of European tourism social studies. While at the beginning of the 1960s its importance had been recognized, in order to overcome the German language barrier, Krapf himself asked René Baretje to undertake the translation into French (1964). Krapf's early dramatic death (1963), along with the publication and circulation of this text through Baretje's person and offices of the *Centre des Hautes Études Touristiques* (Center for Advanced Tourist Studies) created a kind of European official version which had its diffusion in the last few decades and became a strong inspiration for Lanfant. Recently, at the turn of the millennium, the still current relevance of the book was confirmed by the need for a new translation, this time for a Spanish-speaking audience. This is now available on the internet at Biblioteca Virtual Eumednet (2004). Interestingly, the Anglophone scientific world is still excluded from this seminal work.

A particular linguistic problem is represented by the generally accepted definitional linking of the terms *Fremdenverkehr* and *Tourism*, a problem whose consequences as far as we know nobody has questioned in the field of the sociology of tourism (Liebman Parrinello, 2007; Spode 2007b). Even without accepting the Sapir-Whorf hypothesis of cultural relativism, according to which human languages determine thought and perception (Whorf 1986), it is clear that theoretical systematization developed over many decades within a specific linguistically anchored concept and was surprisingly accepted without objection all over Europe. Apparently, until World War II, Germany was still generally considered to be the main country for scientific language (Ammon 1998). A useful idea that provides an understanding of the complex cultural diversity, without subscribing to the radical consequences of Sapir-Whorf, is one offered by the German jurist, Carl Schmitt (1932 (1993)). His assumption of a "continental" versus an "oceanic" perspective, emerging from the field of geopolitics, but also applicable to the discipline of sociology, seems to correspond exactly to the semantic fields of both *Tourism* and *Fremdenverkehr*. Globalization apparently originates from/and privileges the "oceanic" perspective of those nations (like *Rule Britannia*) that used to/still claim mastery of the waves. Nevertheless we cannot ignore the central European formulation, which is much more than an isolated episode.

Ideological Discriminants. There is a classical French distinction of describing people as they are (Racine) or as they are supposed to be (Corneille). Ideological use of the latter is clearly addressed by several European theorists in their examination of tourism—one that is only partially reflected in later Anglophone discussions of reflexivity (Bruner 1995; Crick 1995). Marie-Françoise Lanfant, for example, readily acknowledges that, "the notion of ideology is an operational category that has given rise to many works [in the sociology of tourism], particularly in France and Germany" (2005). By ideology she intends "doctrines which rest on dubious or false theories which have a credibility that they do not merit" (2005), which means simply relating to or based on ideology (literally, the study of ideas). However, in the philosophy of knowledge as expounded by Weber and Mannheim, idea systems are the expression of certain vested interests. Following this reasoning, so-called scientific objectivity and value freedom would also be ideological.

Tourism also is obviously not a neutral field; indeed tourism social studies constitute a kind of litmus paper for ideological attitudes. In this regard, Lanfant was still concerned with leisure, which, as she put it, "place d'emblée le sociologue sur le sol piégé de l'idéologie" (that places the sociologist at the outset on a ground ensnared with ideology), and pointed to the "l'univers apparemment rose" (the apparently rosy universe) (1972:13) evoked by the word "leisure." This observation is even more valid for tourism.

The scientific systematization of tourism is not so quietly assessed in the four platforms of ideological attitudes suggested by Jafari (1987), to which a fifth of tourism development can be added, critically joined by a sixth represented by ethics (Macbeth 2005). In fact, these platforms—"advocacy," focusing on tourism's (mainly economic) benefits; "cautionary," critical of tourism's sociocultural costs; "adaptancy," seeking new strategies (such as alternative tourism) to overcome these negative effects; "knowledge-based," formulation of a scientific approach to understanding tourism—which may be interpreted as historical stages, can also be understood coterminously as ideological attitudes. For example, although the second platform of criticism originates from the 1960s and 1970s, it has never been completely forgotten.

Yet how many (not just Anglophone) academics discuss ideological attitudes or are even aware of a mainstream ideology in their own writings? A possible critical attitude can be detected not just in a direct and infrequently occurring anti-capitalistic position, but in more indirect forms as well. Such an attitude is also often linguistic, if only because language implicitly denounces through slogans and passwords, often wickedly lurking in the guise of democratic values, as has been shown, for instance, by those scholars who re-examine the assumption of touristic freedom (Dann 1997b) or who consider "the language of tourism" to be a language of social control (Dann 1996a). "Sustainable tourism" in turn represents more than a politically correct catch-phrase, since it can even be regarded as a fifth platform. Then, too, the universalistic ethics proclaimed by UNWTO with its much vaunted "new world order" can be ideologically laden (Lanfant 2004), as indeed can the related but unsubstantiated mantra that tourism leads to mutual understanding between peoples (Crick 1994).

Thus, it follows that the present volume cannot be anything but ideologically biased, even if our attitudes as editors are considered to be "objective." As collaborators, we are openly, honestly, and subjectively skewed, because of our formation and our experience in the field of tourism research. We are also value laden because we identify contributors whom we think are the most suitable in the interest of research in the field. These different contributors in turn probably try to be "objective," even though some seem to be more neutral than others. Indeed, ideology emerges everywhere in this book. For example, Lengkeek ably demonstrates how ideology is manifested along religious and political lines. As he indicates, the primary reason why tourism studies in the low-countries developed along different trajectories was that Belgium was principally Catholic and the Netherlands were mainly Protestant. Similarly, Scandinavian studies of the first postwar decades constitute more than mere social-democratic lip service since we can find, for example, ideological engagement in favor of human dignity against alcohol abuse, or a concern for minorities, as in the case of the Sámi (Jacobsen in this volume). Additionally the pedagogical attitude of the *Studienkreis für Tourismus*, due also to the presence of the churches (Spode in this volume), witnessed an ideological attitude that probably went hand in hand with the market economy.

Certainly it cannot be denied that our linguistic attention to "non-Anglophone" contributions may have brought with it more sensitivity for a certain set of cultural values. Nevertheless, these "unsettled questions" have to be read in the sense of an overall critical attitude, reminding us not only of the contradictions emerging through a diachronic and cross-cultural approach, but of the continuous need to re-open apparently closed discourses and to keep the doors open. Indeed, without exaggerating, there is no gainsaying that the foregoing unsettled questions imply a fundamental attitude of scientific doubt, an attitude which is always somehow "ideological"—"uncertainty" can be positively seen as an opportunity (Wallerstein 1999). By highlighting (though not necessarily resolving) them, the ground is now laid for an examination of the origins of the sociology of tourism.

European Origins of the Sociology of Tourism

The period before World War I can be viewed as the golden age of international tourism in which scholars recognized first and foremost its substantial economic contribution. Even so, it is not surprising that some works examining the economic aspects of tourism, like those of the Austrian Stradner (1905) and the Swiss Guyer-Freuler (1905) implied, even if sporadically, interests that extended beyond the limited domain of economics (Hömberg 1978; Spode in this volume).

With the possible exception of Bodio (1899), Mariotti is probably right in claiming to be the first to analyze tourism comprehensively in Italy, albeit from a quasi-exclusive economic perspective: the first edition of his *Lezioni di Economia Turistica* (Lessons of the Economics of Tourism) appeared in 1928 (Mariotti 1928). Apart from Italy, the countries most concerned with the theoretical treatment of tourism were Germany and Switzerland (Jacobsen 2003:10) to which Spode adds Austria and Greece (1998a). Most of the tourism academics from these countries were economists or applied economists, who were especially interested in hospitality, a field which had just attained the level of a degree in Italy at the University of Rome as a direct result of the pioneering work of Angelo Mariotti. Also worthy of note was the Tourism Studies Unit based in the Institute of Geography of the University of Kraków founded in 1936 (Przecławski, Bystrzanowski, and Ujma in this volume).

As far as sociology is concerned, in his review of tourism as a field of study within the social sciences, Cohen (1984) points out that the sociological treatment of tourism can be traced to Germany in the work of the sociologist von Wiese (1930), whose efforts were further advanced by Knebel (1960) (Dann and Cohen 1991). However, while Cohen is right in highlighting the importance of von Wiese and Knebel, it would be misleading to describe them as isolated forerunners, since there were many other individuals, institutions, and ideas surrounding them, from the 1920s till the end of the 1960s, that formed a cumulative part of the "Continental scene."

It is fascinating to follow this gradual emergence of sociological insights through contributions from different parts of Europe, involving theories, the prominent figures of scientists, institutions, important congresses, international events, and simple everyday realities in a variety of languages from the first post-World War I period onwards. Even if our focus is on consecutive stages of those European countries making significant contributions, which in turn lead the way for others to follow, all the diverse areas involved in this research are obviously—if not explicitly in the title—always taken into consideration. Yet in spite of this wide spatial and temporal coverage, there still seems to be a gap between the sociological evolution of tourism and its theories. That is to say, tourism social theory was not elaborated so simultaneously and so rapidly that it always managed to keep up with the complexity of the tourism phenomenon. Nevertheless, and in spite of this "cultural lag," its checkered development remains to be charted, and it is this tentative itinerary that is laid out through the identified stages of research that follow.

The European Laboratory.　While the overwhelming direction of tourism leading to so-called "mass tourism" in the post-World War II era does not require demonstration, the period between the two world wars is more contested. Indeed, the intervening decades, especially the 1930s, constituted a key phase in the development of tourism that is essential for an overall understanding. Up to that point, those writing grand histories did not care very much about tourism, to the extent that the development of the phenomenon, even during the Great Depression, was only indirectly acknowledged by general historical analysis. Of course there was frequent reference to mass unemployment and its huge and traumatic impact on the policy of industrialized countries (Hobsbawm 2004:116). Yet, according to Landes, the economies of Western Europe grew during these years, not just in absolute terms, but additionally in terms of per capita income, due to the effects of continuous technological change that stimulated investment and raised productivity (1969:419). Thus, technological progress was a fundamental issue (Mokyr 1996). As far as lifestyle was concerned, new demand by the middle and working classes for technical and luxury items could be described as a quest for "nonessential consumer goods" (Thomson 1960:49–50). Interestingly, this new consumer attitude which, when coupled with an increase in free-time, created an amalgam of elements that were exactly conducive to tourism.

In spite of this common aspiration, European countries and regions differed both in their traditional cultural practices and in their domestic and international tourism development, along with their diverse global ventures, so that the situation was far from homogeneous. Scandinavian countries, for instance, seemed for a time to be in the vanguard of outbound countries, while Spain began to stand out as an inbound destination with the consequences of tourism dividing supporters and opponents of the Franco regime. Then there was the former Yugoslavia—an international tourism destination with a vibrant domestic tourism. Meanwhile Belgium and the Netherlands, largely for historical reasons, went on their own idiosyncratic ways. Notwithstanding these diverse approaches to tourism, which were not simply a matter of domestic versus international tourism or of class attitudes, little by little, even if not straightforwardly, found their way in articulating the beginnings of a sociology of tourism.

Today the development of tourism from the 1930s is confirmed by different histories of tourism that concentrate mostly on countries like France and Germany (Boyer 2005, 2007; Hachtmann 2007), but which are nevertheless also open to a more cross-cultural approach (Baranowski 2001; Walton 2005). Between the world wars, surprisingly, the historical-political situation seemed to be less influential than the socioeconomic context. Even though different European countries experienced years of alternating totalitarianism and democracy, regardless of the prevailing power, the spread of tourism still took place.

Especially in the 1930s, Europe could even be considered as something of a laboratory, experimenting with various aspects of both tourism and its theory. Our journey follows the construction of this intellectual mosaic. The golden age of international tourism as the heritage of the traditional Grand Tour, albeit with more cosmopolitan and democratic features, corresponded to a unique world economy and to the globalization of trade. In the language of tourism studies, this stage was followed by the advent of the monolithic phenomenon of mass tourism. By contrast, reflection on the origins and the slow but indirect rise of the European sociology of tourism should be strictly bound to the complexity of the evolution of the European social situation.

If already in its golden age a more multifaceted approach to tourism could not be overlooked, it was between the world wars, especially in the 1930s, that its importance and binary expressions became more evident: international but also domestic tourism, world tours but also alpinism, day trips evolving to long stay tourism, models shifting down from the middle class to the emerging working class, imitating and aiming at the values of the privileged class (Boyer 1999).

Around 1925, many wage-earning workers of industrial countries had already gained the right to holidays with pay. By the late 1930s the situation had become even more widespread; legislation of paid holidays extended over all Europe largely as a result of enlightened government thinking. In 1936, for example, enactment of the Lagrange law made up for the French delay; interestingly, France, ruled by the Popular Front apparently applied the same holiday policies as National-Socialism with its *Kraft durch Freude* (Strength through Joy) (Spode in this volume). This common attitude was, of course, more easily understandable for European Fascism and National-Socialism. The promotion of domestic tourism by right wing regimes aimed at capturing consent through mass organizations like the Italian OND *Opera Nazionale Dopolavoro* (literally "after work"), which was taken as an example by National-Socialism and the Franco regime. *Kraft durch Freude* was concerned with an ambitious social program, implying holidays, sport, and the diffusion of the "Volkswagen." The organization became the biggest German tour operator, moving altogether with excursionism till the year 1939, 43 million Germans, including 700,000 cruiseship passengers (Spode 2003b).

Certainly, the German situation from 1919 to 1932 contained the seeds of future trends. If the bourgeois dream for every worker was to be lured by status enhancing cruises in the Mediterranean, one can also detect in the tourism of those years the heritage of proletarian social tourism, linked with excursionism and trekking (Keitz 1997:30). Thus, it is not surprising that the middle classes in particular took advantage of National-Socialism's efforts toward the democratization of tourism (Keitz 1997; Spode 2003b). There were also area differences, in the sense that the Latin world did not accept a model which was common in Central Europe and in the United States, interpreting holidays and weekend outings as nature-focused leisure activities (Boyer 2007).

So which sort of tourism and what kind of typology of it then became unavoidable questions for the laboratory profilers? Similarly if international tourism and the new mass tourism politicized domestic tourism in totalitarian countries, was there a need for a new consumer model? Questions relating to social class were also an issue. In Germany, for example, there was the confused aspiration of the proletariat to the holiday dream (Keitz 1997), while in 1936 France, although legislation was progressive, there was an overall lack of ideals concerning holidays (Boyer

2007). At that time there were also the ambivalent experiments of Swedish social-democracy (Löfgren 2001). Later, from 1945 to 1975, there was the establishment of mass tourism profiles along with the phenomenon actually deserving of the name (Boyer 2007). As Battilani, referring especially to the 1920s in the United States and to the postwar years in Europe, states: "L'epoca del turismo di massa coincide così con la creazione di una gamma sempre più ampia di servizi, visto che il turismo di élite non è scomparso ma è solo diventato relativamente meno importante" (The era of mass tourism thus coincided with an ever increasing range of services, given that elite tourism had not disappeared but had only become relatively less important) (Battilani 2001:13–14).

The 1920s and 1930s: Tourism Comes to Academia in Berlin. As far as European theorizing was concerned, Berlin could claim supremacy, especially in the person and activity of Robert Glücksmann, the founder of the *Forschungsinstitut für den Fremdenverkehr* (Institute of Tourism Research) in 1929, and with it, the establishment of a journal, *Archiv* (Archive) and the emergence of a scientific community, including high-profile individuals such as Bormann (1931) and von Wiese (1930) (Spode in this volume).

Even if Glücksmann might not nowadays be described as a trained sociologist, within his aspiration to provide a scientific definition of tourism, "die Summe der Beziehungen zwischen einem am Ort seines Aufenthaltes nur vorübergehend befindlichen Menschen und Menschen an diesem Ort" (The sum of the relationships between a person who finds himself only temporarily at the place of his sojourn and the people of that place) (1935:3), he emphasized that interpersonal relationships were more important than individual mobility. Thus, in the framework of what he called *Allgemeine Fremdenverkehrskunde* (General Teaching in Tourism) (Glücksmann 1935) in a book of the same title that had to be published in Switzerland on account of the forced closure of the Institute by the Nazis in that year, made a significant input to the sociology of tourism. In this book, notwithstanding those sections devoted to the economics and politics of tourism, there was an explicitly sociological chapter dealing with the effects of tourism. Here relationships and potential international approaches played a significant role. There was also an important attempt to explore the customarily neglected topic of motivation. In the framework of "relationships" attention was paid not only to tourists and locals, but also to places of origin and to tourist destinations. In some respects, his approach could be considered broadly "anthropological," since it focused on the encounters between hosts and guests, along with their conditions. Yet, the social effects of tourism were also taken into consideration, both on the destination and on the organization, thereby anticipating a later discourse on tourism's impacts.

Von Wiese's contribution to tourism cannot be considered separately from the Berlin Institute. It is probably no mere coincidence that von Wiese's offering appeared as the first article in the opening issue of Glückmann's *Archiv*. Von Wiese (1876–1969), an affirmed sociologist, and author of *Allgemeine Soziologie als Lehre von den Beziehungen und Beziehungsgebilden der Menschen* (General Sociology as a Theory of Human Relations and Relationships), in two volumes (von Wiese 1924), described his sociology as *Beziehungslehre* (Theory of Relations) which focused on social behavior. He believed that sociology dealt with conduct in society taking place in an environment which led individuals to maintain a "social distance" from each other. From this formulation (definition) there were various elements that could contextualize von Wiese's brief contribution on tourism, entitled *Fremdenverkehr als zwischenmenschliche Beziehungen* (1930) (Tourism as an Interpersonal Relation) as a special episodic case of interaction with strangerhood.

Inspired by Simmel's *Exkurs über den Fremden* (Excursus on the Stranger) (1908) and by that thinker's paradoxical mixture of proximity and distance, von Wiese made a distinction between three different types of stranger. If this taxonomy were accepted (Knebel 1960) it followed that there were also different corresponding types of inhabitants, along with a plurality of intentions and desires. Of major relevance are the contemporary considerations on the stranger and accompanying direct references to Simmel which are today quite frequent in tourism studies. However, only a handful of sociologists of tourism have adopted the complete tenets of Formalism whereby the essence or forms of behavior are treated as space- and time-transcendent. Maybe the overlooking of such rich insights has contributed to a current gap in theoretical understanding.

The 1940s and 1950s: The Swiss Connection.   After the short life of the Berlin Institute, further sociological developments were transferred to Switzerland (especially during World War II), with a continued emphasis on doctrine, systematization, and a general theory, efforts that would not have been possible without the pioneering work of Glücksmann.

Switzerland was conscious of its function of preservation of the tourism science during the war and wanted to be equipped and ready for the expected boom after the war. In 1941, two Institutes were founded, one in Sankt Gallen and the other in Bern. Walter Hunziker and Kurt Krapf became their respective directors (Spode in this volume). Later, Jost Krippendorf became the director of the Bern Institute for many years till his untimely death, and René Baretje, with a Swiss mother, and coming from the same Bern Institute, became the founder of the renowned *Centre des Hautes Études Touristiques* in Aix-en-Provence.

Hunziker and Krapf worked closely together. In a joint work written in 1941, tourism was considered a general cultural phenomenon that continued Glücksmann's ideas by introducing the notion of social relationships among individuals, since people were considered to be at the very center of tourism (see section on "unsettled questions" in this chapter). In 1942 they published a textbook, a genre that had been invented by Bormann (1931): the *Grundriss der Allgemeinen Fremdenverkehrslehre* (Outline of the General Teaching of Tourism). This book was also oriented toward practical needs and for decades it served as the "bible" in training and research all over Europe (Spode in this volume).

In 1943, and this time on his own, Hunziker published *System und Hauptprobleme einer wissenschaftlichen Fremdenverkehrslehre* (System and Main Problems of Scientific Research on Tourism) (Hunziker 1943), which could be generally regarded as more sociological in nature (Mariotti 1952). Relatedly, Spode is very definite on the subject: "The scientific 'Fremden-verkehrslehre' belongs now as an empirical cultural science to sociology; it is in no sense part of economics" (1998a:16). Hunziker's development, in the sense of a system and of a doctrine that were connected with the growing importance of sociology could only be verified in his later works. In the brief publication of 1973 *Le Système de la Doctrine Touristique*, edited in three languages, German, French, and English, with the latter's title of *The System of Tourism Doctrine*, Hunziker returned to this issue (1973). Tourism was defined as a cultural phenomenon. Referring to Weber and Sombart, and partially rejecting the system built up with Krapf 30 years earlier, Hunziker tackled the idea of a tourism doctrine, by proposing a revised structure of the system and distinguishing between the "economic aspects of tourism" and "tourism as the object of noneconomic subjects." Further-more, in his "structural scheme of a tourism doctrine," Hunziker outlined the sociology of tourism as comprising: "tourism as a sociological category," "objects and problems of tourism sociology," "special aspects" that embraced "tourism and the individual," "tourism as a mass movement" and "the inclusion of sociology in tourism doctrine and tourism training" (1973:1–2).

There are further echoes of the Swiss school which are obviously of current relevance. The International Association of Scientific Experts in

Tourism was chaired by Hunziker and Krapf in 1949. Some three years earlier the *Revue de Tourisme* (The Tourist Review) appeared. Traditionally a trilingual journal, even in its title, it still exists today as the oldest publication in the field, in spite of the irony that its articles are in English and the publisher is UK based. A continuation of the Swiss line of thought can also be found in the work of Claude Kaspar, who wrote profusely, especially during the mid-1970s, and tried to apply systems theory to tourism. The title of the later version of his work *Die Tourismuslehre im Grundriss* (1996) (Outline of the Teaching of Tourism) testified to the definitive transition from the concept of *Fremdenverkehr* into "Tourism," now fundamentally intended as its contemporary equivalent. True, his definition of tourism as a "sum of relationships and phenomena" went back to that of Hunziker and of the AIEST. However, Kaspar definitely abandoned the old framework of "quintessence" of the tourism phenomenon, possibly due to the need to extend the concept to neighboring disciplines and to the difficulty of reducing the complex "empirical reality" of tourism to an easily operationalized concept (Spode 1998b:917).

The 1950s.   On the way toward a sociology of tourism, Jacobsen (2003:10) points out a number of noteworthy attempts in the 1950s, such as those of Leugger (1956, 1958) (Spode in this volume). In fact, the 1950s also witnessed some more brief sporadic contributions, like those of the Dutch, Ramaker (1951), and of the Finnish, Waris (1951), quoted by the same Leugger (1956), which were indicative of a changing climate. It was Ramaker (1951) who hinted at broader economic and sociological problems such as those associated with demand and consumption. Moreover, and as regards the new field of the sociology of tourism, he argued that, if sociology were concerned with human groups, tourism should deal with the behavior of these groups as they related to tourism. In the meantime sociological developments like technology and social welfare were also briefly identified as factors of tourist development (Waris 1951). As an exception to the general use of the German language in central Europe and in Scandinavia at that time, it should be noted that Ramaker's contribution was written in French and Waris's in English. Both short essays were published in the *Revue de Tourisme*.

Leugger is a more or less forgotten name, whose work could be seen as a meeting point between the more conventional development in the framework of *Verkehr* (Traffic/Transport) and a broad range of interests appearing in those years in Europe, especially in Germany, since he took into consideration the attitude of the German *Studienkreis für Tourismus*, the new sociological ideas of Dahrendorf (a noted conflict theorist) and

Knebel himself (Leugger 1956, 1958, 1966), as well as works translated into German, like the contributions from the key French scholar, Joffré Dumazedier. Leugger's point of reference was, of course, that of the Swiss school, and still in the framework of *Fremdenverkehr*. Indeed, he stated that there was at the time neither a proper sociology of traffic/transport nor a sociology of tourism, since they only considered single aspects of *Fremdenverkehr*, and borrowed from industrial sociology and the sociology of leisure (1956). In the English summary of his article he stated that,

> Traffic/transport is, therefore, the scene in which a daily change of status and structure takes place [...] "Tourism" is characterized by a more extensive dissociation from its everyday-background i.e. the change of structure and function of the individual is much more pronounced in an extended weekend [...] than in the daily shuttle-service [...] (1966:158).

The French Milieu: From Loisir to Tourism. In the Italian edition of his *Sociologie Empirique du Loisir* (Empirical Sociology of Leisure), the French sociologist Dumazedier expressed in a very captivating way the sense of a scientific community:

> Qualsiasi ricerca sociologica, pena il pericolo di enunciare problemi già posti e di ricercare risultati già trovati, deve integrarsi non solo a livello dei singoli gruppi, ma anche in quella specie di officina reale e al tempo immaginaria costituita dagli specialisti più qualificati della materia, operanti in tutto il mondo e lontani tra loro migliaia di chilometri (1985:26).

> Any sociological research risking the danger of enunciating problems that have already been articulated or of researching findings that have already been discovered, must integrate itself not only at the level of individual groups, but also to that type of working relationship and to the imaginary time made up of more qualified specialists operating all over the world separated by thousands of kilometers.

It is in fact necessary to wait until France of the 1960s to discover the conditions and the symptoms of a new scientific community. One of the most important European contributions to the sociology of tourism cannot be fully appreciated without the background of the great French sociological tradition, the promising sociological structural studies of the 1960s, along with Dumazedier's sociology of leisure and the useful criticisms of Marie-Françoise Lanfant. Through her vivid description the images of the French scholars and milieu are evoked, and an up-to-date path of the sociology of tourism is traced (Lanfant in this volume). Here, by way of summary, and at the risk of occasional repetition, we can briefly identify the chronology of key events and persons associated with developments in the sociology of tourism in France from the 1950s to the 1990s—many of which are autobiographically supplied by Lanfant (2007).

In 1953 Joffré Dumazedier was asked to establish a team to study leisure at the prestigious *Centre National de Recherche Scientifique* (CNRS) (National Center for Scientific Research) and eight years later he invited Marie Françoise Lanfant to join him. Her postwar formation at the Sorbonne put her in direct contact with such influential thinkers as Roland Barthes, Jacques Lacan, Claude Lévi-Strauss, Jean Piaget, and Jean-Paul Sartre (and also prepared her for the ideas of other inspirational fellow countrymen like Baudrillard and Bourdieu), all of whom have provided interdisciplinary insights into tourism, even if they all did not tackle the topic directly. She was also exposed to the thinking of Lefebvre (1967) and Naville (1967), influential Marxists, which, though not converting her, nevertheless put her in good stead in her dealings with Dumazedier (of similar ideological persuasion) and enabled her to analyze critically the consequences of such an alienationist perspective on the sociology of leisure (Lanfant 1972). It also made it possible for her to engage in lively debate with members of the research committee on leisure of the ISA of which Dumazedier was president.

However, after such a radical break, Lanfant found it impossible to be part of Dumazedier's leisure team and as a result of this split she found herself applying for the position of *chargée* at CNRS and, with it, a project linking international tourism with leisure. It was this study which led to her articulation of tourism as an international social fact and a total social phenomenon (Lanfant 1980, 1990, 1995) based on the respective classical insights of Durkheim (1938) and Mauss (1980). Around this time also, there appeared a special issue of the journal, *Communications*, and with it, some extremely interesting, though surprisingly neglected reflections by the likes of Burgelin (1967) and Gritti (1967) on the notion of tourism as an agent of social control (Dann 1996a). A few years later, in 1975, she was appointed *chargée*, and with the responsibility came the opportunities for assembling her own research team, this time in the field of tourism, which in 1976 became known as the *Unité de Recherche en la Sociologie du Tourisme International* (URESTI) (Unit for Research on the Sociology of Tourism). Among members of her team engaged in a number of field studies examining the sociocultural impacts of tourism from an entirely new perspective were such younger scholars as Claude-Marie Bazin, Jacques de Weerdt, Michel Picard, and Danielle Rozenberg. This 10-year study eventually led to a significant debate on the topic held as a round table in Marly-le-Roi in 1986 to which a number of overseas researchers were also invited. The results of these important deliberations were published in the Polish journal, *Problems of Tourism* (Lanfant 1987a, 1987b, this volume).

With this coterminous expansion of interest now was the time to create parallel opportunities within the umbrella organization of the ISA. To this end and with the support of some international colleagues, dialog was initiated with the research committee on leisure at the ISA World Congress of 1986 in New Delhi. The result of these discussions was a sect-like split from the parent research committee (RC 13) and the subsequent formation of a separate thematic group on tourism. The following World Congress (1990 Madrid) produced a successful application for working group status, and the one after that (1994 Bielefeld) an equally rapid promotion to full research committee status (RC 50). Of course all this could not have come about with the unremitting efforts of Lanfant and, it must be said, the parallel growth in interest in the sociology of tourism demonstrated by an increasingly active Anglophone contingent which by now had been exposed to the English language theoretical formulations of their leading representatives, among whom were the likes of Crick, Dann, Graburn, Harrison, Jafari, MacCannell, and Selwyn. This French initiative was further cemented by subsequent World Congresses of the ISA held in Montréal (1998), Brisbane (2002), and Durban (2006).

However, and of at least equal significance was the holding of interim symposia with a thematic emphasis on tourism theory, among which were those of Nice (1992) "International Tourism between Tradition and Identity," Jyväskylä (1996) "Paradigms in Tourism Research," Mytilene (Lesvos) (2004) "Understanding Tourism: Theoretical Advances," Wageningen (2006) "Theoretical Innovations in Tourism Studies," and Jaipur (2008) "Ever the Twain Shall Meet: Relating International and Domestic Tourism". It was no mere coincidence and eminently appropriate that the first of these in-between events was organized by URESTI in collaboration with the Université de Nice. The resulting multi-lingual proceedings appeared two years later (Jardel 1994), the full significance of which was explained by the then Director of URESTI, Marie-Françoise Lanfant (1994). Apart from a number of overseas theoreticians of the caliber of Bruner, Graburn, and MacCannell, there was an excellent turnout of French-speaking scholars, including such names as Amirou, Boyer, Cazes, de Vidas, Jardel, Michaud, Micoud, Moulin, Picard, and Urbain. This highly successful French initiative not only demonstrated the depth of its own scholarship but also the fact that it was prepared to enter a fruitful dialog with academics from elsewhere, surely evidence if any were still required that the sociology of tourism had finally arrived and come to stay. Other edited books with a theoretical focus emanating from the same group were those of Lanfant, Allcock, and Bruner (1995) on *International Tourism: Identity and Change* and Dann (2002) on *Tourism as a Metaphor of the Social World*, while there was a special issue of *International Sociology* edited by Graburn and Barthel-Bouchier (2001) that was dedicated to "Relocating the Tourist."

Missing Link or Point of No Return: Krapf's Theory of Consumption.   As already anticipated in the subsection "some unsettled questions" Krapf's *La Consommation Touristique* (Touristic Consumption) (1953–1964) can be considered as an emblematic account and paradigm case of treating European tourism studies from a linguistic point of view. Here we intend to return briefly to this work because of its seminal theoretical approach to consumption.

Already by 1927 Morgenroth (in Knebel 1960:3) had defined tourists as leaving their usual domicile to sojourn in other places "lediglich als Verbraucher von Wirtschafts-und Kulturgütern" (uniquely as consumers of economic and cultural goods). The concept of consumption, which was only implicit in the classical definition of tourism (Hunziker and Krapf 1942) was subsequently taken up by Krapf as a key issue for an increasingly consumer-oriented tourism trend, singling out its importance in the framework of postwar tourism development. Interestingly, Galbraith's *Affluent Society* (1958) lies in between Krapf's 1953 dissertation and its 1964 French translation.

Here we are reminded once more of Krapf's theoretical depth in his previous works with Hunziker. In this book, the subtitle of which was "une contribution à la théorie de la consommation" (a contribution to the theory of consumption), Krapf, now in the role of international expert, also demonstrated an understanding of world economic development. As he put it in his foreword, the starting point was provided by sociology on the one hand and by a more economic-practical attitude on the other: "les touristes sont les 'consommateurs ultimes' des biens et des services fournis par l'industrie du tourisme" (tourists are the "ultimate consumers" of goods and services offered by the tourism industry) (Krapf 1964:1).

Tourism was singled out as important and ideal-typical case of consumption. It is not surprising that a sociological interest was linked to that of marketing, a field that was taking its first steps in Europe. (It was probably no mere coincidence that the Swiss Krippendorf published in 1970 the first European handbook of tourism marketing). Focusing on consumption, Krapf further asserted that the study of tourism could only be understood if consumption and the factors which determined it were always kept in mind. He went on,

> Ainsi compris, le tourisme est un exemple typique d'une satisfaction des besoins qui correspond à l'idée que l'on se fait du mode de vie approprié à son standing. Il ne recèle donc pas uniquement des considérations utilitaires, mais contient une grande part d'eléments extra-économiques, donc irrationnels (1964:30).

> Thus understood, tourism is a typical example of a satisfaction of needs which corresponds to the idea that one fashions a way of life appropriate to one's status. Therefore, it does not uniquely conceal utilitarian considerations, but comprises in large measure extra-economic, and hence irrational, elements.

Krapf's global framework not only involved economics, but also sociology and psychology. Moreover, the so-called "irrational" element that was considered the noneconomic aspect of tourism production was also this time placed under the protection of the guardian angel of Swiss psychoanalysis, C.G. Jung. Tourism was thus not only interpreted as an ideal-typical and paradigmatic case of consumption, with tourists being the ultimate consumers, but even as an example to increase our knowledge of the phenomenon of consumption itself at a more general level.

Lanfant (2005) sees this book as "prémonitoire" (a form of prophetic warning) and of perennial significance, all the while appreciating the realization that tourist consumption is treated as a borderline case of consumption in general. She considers the fact that Krapf is aware of the shortcomings of the Austrian school (marginalism) compared to the multifaceted aspects of the tourist consumer, and develops in her own way

Krapf's absolute consumption, tourism as the ultimate consumption. Lanfant's original interpretation consists of the integration of the apparently free consumption by tourists into their economic treatment as commodities in the framework of world trade. "En liant indissolublement consommation et tourisme, notre auteur aborde un des aspects les plus intrigants de notre civilisation" (In inextricably linking consumption and tourism, our author tackles one of the most intriguing features of our civilization) (Lanfant 2005). Moreover a certain heritage of the Swiss school can be found in her recent thoughts on marginal utility and leads from the "moindre jouissance" (least enjoyment), to the "plus-de-jouir" (surplus enjoyment), to Lacan's lust principle.

In conclusion, a fundamental more sociological and ideological issue has to be underscored. If the tourist is the consumer par excellence, if the implicit antinomy between social tourism and business tourism that can still be discerned *in vitro* in Hunziker and Krapf's formula is vanishing because even that contradiction is false, if only consumption itself matters, that means that by the beginning of the 1950s, the bets had already been taken. From consumption and from its theory we are led back to the concrete, empirical, ultimate consumer, the tourist as subject, with her/his apparently free, though "irrational" choice. This free choice is not as innocent as it appears, since it implies already a market politics not only with its front- backstage tricks, but with the nearly unavoidable front-stage of touristic freedom.

There is no direct heritage of Krapf's theory of consumption in the sociology of tourism. An obvious authority was the rediscovered Thorstein Veblen, whose work was taken by Riesman (1950) as a subtitle for his *Lonely Crowd*. Indeed, not even Knebel, in his leading work *Soziologische Strukturwandlungen im modernen Tourismus* (Sociological Structural Change in Modern Tourism) (1960), which led extensively to Riesman's building on Veblen's (1899[1970, 1994]) perspective of the leisure class as a conspicuous tourist experience, took into account Krapf's seminal results.

Return to Germany: The 1960s and 1970s.   In 1948, the right to holidays with pay was declared to be a fundamental human right. From 1950 to 1980, the general atmosphere was in favor of growth and progress, and tourism was included in this process. As in the German situation of the economic miracle, great expectations were realized and satisfied. All over Europe, the same sort of development took place, so that holiday travel was no longer regarded as a luxury, but, in sociological terms, became a "social norm" (Keitz 1997:285).

In spite of this common aspiration, European countries and regions differed not only in their traditional cultural practices, but also in their domestic and international tourism development and their diverse global ventures, so that the situation was far from homogenous. Scandinavian countries, for instance, seemed for a time to be in the vanguard of outbound countries, while Spain began to stand out as an inbound destination with the consequences of tourism dividing supporters and opponents of the regime. Then there was the former Yugoslavia which was both a destination of international tourism and a lively domestic tourism. Meanwhile Belgium and the Netherlands, largely for historical reasons, went on their own separate ways. Notwithstanding these manifestations of a diverse phenomenology of tourism, which was not simply a matter of domestic versus international tourism or of class attitudes, little by little, even if not straightforwardly, found its way in articulating the beginnings of a sociology of tourism.

The broad sociological discussion that developed in Europe, especially in the 1960s, which was concerned with mass consumption and with the new habits of the "affluent society," involved more indirectly than directly the sociology of tourism. While the vast front of the protest was to lead to the revolutionary movement of 1968, mass tourism was marching ahead on its triumphal path (Hachtmann 2007). The orientation of the Frankfurt School could only be against mass tourism, judging leisure and tourism critically as products of the consumer society. The clue was a new understanding of Hegel's concept of alienation derived from a re-reading of the scripts of the early Marx (Spode in this volume). Moreover, as Sessa assumes, the discourse of cultural alienation of Marcuse concerning the manipulatory techniques of the masses and the exploitation of leisure and its associated entertainments was sometimes still associated with the aristocratic romantic attitude of the good old times (1992:187–188).

Even though he still remained isolated and without followers, Enzensberger (1974) and his "consciousness industry" (see earlier) could not be imagined without the antecedent of Adorno's "culture industry." Knebel, too, while more academic and more familiar with the tourism literature than Enzensberger, was also original and without disciples. It is not a purely arbitrary exercise to link Enzensberger's and Knebel's names, and not just because they were both confronted with the realities of mass tourism generated by the economic miracle in Germany. Interestingly, in his acknowledgement of Enzensberger's ideas, which he was able to examine in 1958, immediately prior to the publication of his own work, Knebel stated that there were numerous parallels and similar points of view both in their socio-historical attitudes and in their analysis of the present (1960:176).

Knebel is given priority in this account, if only because he can be considered more closely identified with the German tradition, even if he displayed an openness already in the title of his principal work, *Soziologische Strukturwandlungen im modernen Tourismus*. Although Knebel was a sociologist acquainted with recent theoretical developments of that discipline in the United States, he felt the need to go back to the European theory of the 1930s. Terminologically, too, while adopting the more modern term "tourism," he still considered "tourism" and "tourist" as special cases of the superconcepts *Fremdenverkehr* and *Fremder* (Knebel 1960:1). Although rather stereotypical in the overall role he bestowed upon the tourist, Knebel's work could be regarded as the first serious attempt to investigate tourism from the point of view of sociology (Hömberg 1978). However, his offering was not well-received by sociologists. Not only did they object to its undeniable weaknesses (inadequate empirical framework, alleged journalistic language), but they also took issue with its basic approach, which, for them, represented merely an indirect sociological contribution via cultural criticism (Meyer-Cronemeyer 1960).

For his part, Knebel went back to such traditional sociological themes of European tourism as mobility, relationships with host people, the Veblenesque display of conspicuous consumption, and a longing for comfort and physical safety. Although in considering the tourist as an individual, Knebel was explicitly guided by Max Weber's ideal-typical method, he turned to David Riesman (now attracting quite a European following thanks partially to the efforts of Joffré Dumazedier), for his classification of the tourist. Here, the historical picture of tourism development was inspired by that American sociologist's distinction between the inner-directed and the other-directed individual, and the appropriateness of the latter for an understanding of contemporary tourism. Knebel also borrowed the concept of role from American social psychology (Sargent 1950), to the extent that the tourist's role was conceived as total. Knebel was read and studied extensively in his original language in Central Europe and in Scandinavian countries. In 1974, his work was translated into Spanish and was well received in Latin America and in Brazil (Barretto 2003).

Among the ideas he had in common with Enzensberger were the concepts of mobility and the mass production of tourism. If in Knebel there were many interesting suggestions, it was Enzensberger who could really be considered the forerunner of the emerging sociology of tourism. Yet, his original essay published with a short introduction appeared in English only in 1996 in the *New German Critique*. Indeed, it apparently enjoyed little success in Anglophone countries, and was certainly not included in the field of the English-speaking sociology of tourism. Enzensberger, a genial writer, even if not a sociologist in the strict sense of the term, made several important sociological contributions, for example in developing and transforming Adorno's critical attitude toward the culture industry, and in an examination of the "consciousness industry" that included both the mass media and other forms of communication, among which was tourism (Gemünden 1996). Furthermore, even if simulacra were not explicitly addressed by him, an anticipation of their postmodern treatment by the likes of Baudrillard and Eco could nevertheless be discerned. Already the title *A Theory of Tourism* was significant. Above all it expressed confidence in the potential of such a broad explanatory framework. As far as terminology was concerned, Enzensberger had no doubts and opted automatically for "tourism," especially international tourism (Liebman Parrinello 2006). According to Enzensberger's historical-genetical broad definition of tourism already quoted in the section on "some unsettled questions" (1996:124), the multidisciplinary nature of tourism was strengthened by its historical dimension which was both explicitly and implicitly underscored.

Interestingly, only two of the four themes of the sociology of tourism identified by Cohen (1984)—tourists and the tourism system—were evident in this relatively short work (only 19 pages in the English version), while the remainder—traditional relationships with locals and tourism's impacts—were overlooked. Enzensberger's mainly Eurocentric viewpoint allowed him to concentrate on and to deepen the social origin and development of the phenomenon, along with its social aspects and values, in a successful synthesis of tourism's structural, infrastructural, and superstructural layers. The Industrial Revolution and the pristine natural and historical attractions of European Romanticism were suggestively interwoven, and reminiscent of Hobsbawm's (1962) "dual revolution." An essential and crucial feature of his essay—basically interpreting tourism as a form of escape—was a kind of totalitarian mobilization, which was linked to the human condition of the "pursuit of happiness" and the "deceptive freedom" on which it was supposedly based (Liebman Parrinello 2006).

It has been noted that Enzensberger allowed stereotypes of the tourist to infuse his text, and, for that reason, his contribution was heavily criticized (Hömberg 1978; Pagenstecher 1999). Even so, it is not surprising to come across a comparison between MacCannell and Enzensberger, which can be seen as "a supplement, if not a corrective" to the semiological theses of the former and others (Gemünden 1996:114). In fact, while MacCannell considered the role of the tourist in postindustrial society, Enzensberger's accent was placed very firmly on the origins of tourism that were strictly connected with industrial society (Gemünden 1996). Furthermore, Enzensberger's essay can also be read in decidedly contemporary terms in the light of a globalization that is predicated on "standardization, packaging and serial production" which arguably go beyond industrial society considered as a homogenization (1996:128–129).

In his analysis, and as noted already, Spode (in this volume) pays due attention to an institution which was relatively unknown outside of Germany, but which was fundamental in tourism studies for three crucial decades, from 1961 to 1993—the *Studienkreis für Tourismus*—which carried out various innovative social and cultural studies, conducted an annual travel survey, and additionally published many books and booklets that seldom found their way to libraries. It was open to research and to the pedagogical aspects of tourism in encouraging mass education.

From the foregoing themes of this historical overview, it is quite clear that the elements of a sociology of tourism had their origins dating back to the 1930s in Continental Europe and continuing to develop thereafter. Forty or more years still had to pass before Anglophone writers made their equivalent theoretical mark on the academic scene, and even then they either felt obliged to acknowledge their reliance on the prior insights of their European colleagues or else were simply unaware of the seminal ideas of the latter. It is to this point of the story that we now turn.

Major Sociological Theories of Tourism and their European Roots

Although we have shown that a number of fundamental sociological insights in relation to tourism were evident in the 1930s, whenever the four major sociological theories of tourism are examined—those of authenticity, strangerhood, play, and constructivism (Dann 1996a)—in an act of collective amnesia, they are often treated without reference to their origins. Moreover, while these frameworks of understanding, explanation, and prediction are all predominantly associated with individuals who write mainly in English, an attempt will be made to demonstrate that the genesis of such thinking can be found in non-Anglophone Continental Europe. It should be noted, however, that whereas these theories are here treated separately, for analytical purposes there is often considerable conceptual overlap among them. It should also be noted that even today this 1996 paradigmatic model has endured to the point that it was accepted as the basis for ulterior theoretical discussion by the ISA research committee on international tourism in its 2008 symposium in Jaipur (RC 50 2008).

The Authenticity Perspective. The roots of the authenticity debate in the English-speaking world can be traced to Daniel Boorstin (1962, 1964). Writing in the 1960s, he nostalgically lamented that "the lost art of travel" had given way to a series of contrived experiences and pseudo events that constituted contemporary mass tourism. The tourist had thus become a cultural dope, lured by inauthentic places and attractions.

The principal academic reaction to Boorstin came from the same social stratum and language background in the figure of MacCannell (1973, 1976). While agreeing that much of present day life was inauthentic and that many individuals were deeply alienated, he took exception to the view that tourists were emblematic of such inauthenticity. Rather, he counter-argued, tourists sought out authentic experiences in other times and places, and that this search for meaning was a contemporary version of the premodern quest for the sacred. Thus, the tourist of today was a pilgrim of the secular world paying homage to various attractions that were symbolic of modernity and represented the differentiations of society. It was these manifestations of the real lives of others that the tourist tried to reach. However, the industry thwarted this quest by staging such realities as tourism attractions.

Soon MacCannell was joined by another California-based academic, Nelson Graburn. In a well-known essay entitled "Tourism: The Sacred Journey" (Graburn 1977, 1989), British born Graburn argued that tourism was a secular and universal equivalent of religion operating in nonordinary time. By leaving the domestic environment, passing through the *limen* of the sacred (in the center of the "Other") and re-entering the home situation anew, tourists were reflecting the stages of rites of passage analogous to the spiritual death and rebirth of baptism and pilgrimage.

Subsequently, Cohen (1979b) pointed out that it was inaccurate to assume that *all* tourists were either dopes or secular pilgrims. Most were simply out to have a good time. Only a few, and then of the noninstitutionalized variety, looked for meaning in their lives in the center-out-there (the world inhabited by the "Other"). Additional persons entering the intellectual fray included, for example, Pearce and Moscardo (1986), Selwyn (1996), and Wang (2000), the former providing an empirical base for the theory, the latter two employing more refined distinctions within it. The authenticity debate thus lasted for more than four decades among tourism scholars writing in English and, even if not stated in its original terms, could continue, possibly in some other guise, for several more years to come.

However, more germane to the present discussion is the provenance of these ideas and the extent to which their authors rely on European sociological thought. In this regard, MacCannell and Graburn, both of whom incidentally are quite *au fait* with the French language, also acknowledge the influence of Durkheim on their thinking. In particular, they rely on insights from *Les Formes Élémentaires de la Vie Religieuse* (1912[1915, 1965]) about the sacralization of society and its being treated like an object of worship in a similar fashion to a primitive totem and its collective representations. Indeed, MacCannell has several sections of his *magnum opus—The Tourist*—devoted to markers and the semiotics of attractions (the contemporary equivalent of collective representations), as also to the process of sight sacralization. The influence of (the younger) Marx is also acknowledged, especially his analysis of alienation, which, within a tourism framework, acts as an impetus toward the search for authenticity. Even the heavy reliance on fellow American, Erving Goffman, on back- and front-stage performances cannot take away from the Continental origins of some of his ideas, since in the latter's pioneering work, *The Presentation of Self in Everyday Life*, one finds him admitting, for example:

> To the degree that a performance highlights the common official values of the society in which it occurs, we may look upon it, in the manner of Durkheim …. as a ceremony—as an expressive rejuvenation and re-affirmation of the moral values of the community (1959:45).

Of course Goffman also relied on other European theoretical insights and these in turn could have thus indirectly influenced MacCannell.

The Continental European origin of MacCannell's and Graburn's Anglophone theorizing in the sociology/anthropology of tourism may also be traced to the German, Enzensberger (1958), who spoke of sightseeing as an obligatory ritual, an institutionalized duty and social constraint imposed upon the tourist. Thus, although neither of the two California-based academics cited the work of Enzensberger, and was possibly unaware of it at the time he wrote, there is no gainsaying that such an interpretation of tourism was evident in Europe a good 10 years before its first appearance in the United States.

Strangerhood.   Although it is tempting to interpret Cohen's initial reaction to the authenticity perspective in his 1979 "A Phenomenology of Tourist Experiences" as the antithesis to the respective positions of Boorstin and MacCannell that *all* tourists are either cultural nitwits or secular pilgrims, the appearance of an earlier typology from Cohen (1972) based on a continuum stretching from familiarity to strangerhood in fact predates MacCannell's works of 1973 and 1976. So for that matter did another Anglophone contribute to our understanding of strangerhood (Nash 1970).

Back in 1972, Cohen argued that people were interested in things, sights, and cultures that were different from their own precisely because they were different (1972:165). In other words, and now as tourists, they sought novelty and strangeness for their own sake—they were the very motives, and hence explanations, for tourism. Yet because some persons desired more strangeness than others, they preferred less institutionalization and more exposure to difference. They rejected the "environmental bubble" of familiarity, safety, and security of those who wanted home-from-home experiences and looked instead for meaning in the unfamiliarity of a foreign culture. It was thus possible to discern various types of tourist according to the amount of novelty and strangeness that they sought. At one end of the continuum was the organized mass tourist. At the other, was the drifter or wanderer. In between, were such other types as the individual mass tourist and explorer. Subsequently, in 1974, Cohen incorporated the ideas of novelty and change into his definition of a tourist.

Interestingly, in neither of his two early papers on tourism and strangerhood did Cohen (1972, 1974) explicitly acknowledge the influence of Simmel. That had to wait until a little-known monograph on expatriates appeared (Cohen 1977) (cf. Haug et al. 2007) with the full-blown typology some two years later (Cohen 1979b) in which a response to Boorstin and MacCannell was articulated with the addition of insights from Éliade in terms of "recreational," "diversionary," "experimental," "experiential," and "existential" tourists.

Yet it was Simmel's (1908) "Excursus on the Stranger" that was so replete with originality and insight. The idea that, by a process bordering on pure intuition, it was possible to abstract out the unique and recurring forms of human behavior that were associated with social types and institutions such as the blasé character, the metropolis, and secrecy, marked a definite watershed in social theory. The stranger was one of these types so emblematic of modernity, the product of an urban existence who, treated like an alienated number, looked for meaning in alternative times and places—a person who came today and stayed tomorrow—who responded to the *a priori* vocation in the society of the "Other." Had Simmel investigated the tourist in a like fashion, we would today have the essential attributes of such a figure that transcend the limits of space and time. Instead we have taxonomies which, by definition, are no more and no less than heuristic devices.

Yet, as has been seen, Simmel's insights were readily acknowledged by those Continental tourism scholars who provided the theoretical basis for the work of Bormann, Glücksmann, and von Wiese, and allowed the latter to elaborate the fundamental notion of strangerhood with its constituent elements. That taxonomy in turn was extended by Knebel to include corresponding host relations. All this theoretical development took place between 1930 and 1960, well before the English-speaking world was exposed to Cohen's (1979b) paper. As will be seen, Simmel additionally had a direct influence on the 1980s theoretical analyses of Jacobsen in Norway and Ostrowski in Poland. Here Jacobsen (in this volume) concedes that he was also influenced indirectly by Simmel via Knebel, as indeed were his colleagues, Aubert and Schmidt. In the former Yugoslavia, too (Vukonić in this volume), Vrignanin admits the indirect impact of Simmel's thinking via the German theorists Bormann and Glücksmann.

Play. The Anglophone play perspective as a hybrid may be said to derive from the first of Cohen's (1979b) tourists ("the recreational") who finds pleasure in familiarity. The other half of play can also be detected in Graburn's (1977) sacred tourist who experiences liminality in crossing the threshold that leads out of the ordinary and into the extraordinary. In this new found state of Turnerian *communitas* the ludic tourist can enjoy role reversal as a state of inversion—Gottlieb's (1982) king or queen for a day—just as Lett's (1983) liminoid charter yacht tourists do in the Caribbean. In terms of postmodern theory, however, it is left to Urry (1990) to provide the foundation in his "tourist gaze." Here the visual is given prominence (tourism becomes a performance), so much so that van den Berghe (1994) speaks of destination people making a spectacle of themselves. Whether the gaze is "romantic" (as in the case of nature, for example), or "collective" (as in such themed attractions as West Edmonton Mall), the accent is on the consumption of signs, a blending of high and low culture, immersion into anti-auratic pastiche.

Yet, whatever the appeal of this English-speaking variant of tourism theory, there is no denying its European origins. The play paradigm in general is, of course, based on the work of Huizinga (1949). More specifically, there is *Le Regard* (The Gaze), which is immediately traceable to Foucault, especially his *Birth of the Clinic* (1973). Then there is *flâneurie*, idle strolling amid signs of different cultures, like the post-shopper or people-watcher in a mall, that is derived from Benjamin's (1927–1934) *Arcades* project (1999). The consumption of signs or representations of reality (Crick 1989), or the spectacularization of the "Other" via a play of signs in order to transform cultures into consumable products (van den Abbele 1980), can be found in several postmodern French writers such as Baudrillard (1988), and even earlier in Veblen's (1899[1970, 1994]) work on conspicuous consumption as a means to status enhancement.

The iconization of signs, such as the Eiffel Tower, the *Guide Bleu* (Blue Guide), and photography, may be found in French semiology, particularly in the work of Roland Barthes (1984), just as the notion of "post-tourism" can be discovered in the writings of Bourdieu (1984) (on cultural capital, symbolic goods, and *habitus* as a system of social classification). As for travels in hyper-reality, among fakes and copies, where technology can provide more reality than nature, these are evident in the work of Umberto Eco (1986). Once all this Continental European infrastructure has been removed, there is very little original thought for Urry to transmit to his Anglophone readers. Again and again the pattern is the same: the real ideas have originated in the non-English speaking world. Anglophones have to wait several decades in a state of culpable ignorance before the acts of borrowing and translation take place.

Constructivist. The constructivist perspective in Anglophone tourism studies is as complex as it is multi-faceted. One important conflict variant derives from Said (1978) and his well-known work *Orientalism*, defined as "a mode of discourse," "a western style for dominating, restructuring and having authority over the Orient...for managing and producing the Orient." Such postcolonial discourse is about power and the unequal distribution of knowledge into texts. A textual dualism thus emerges in which Orientals are represented as "irrational, depraved, childlike, and different," while the Western author who creates them is self-portrayed as "rational, virtuous, mature, and normal." Orientalism is thus a discourse of misrepresentation, not describing what the world of the "Other" is, but what the writer and reader wish it to be, a language that "consciously contests" the insider's view of the world (Said 1978:2–3, 12, 40, 273; cf. Dann 1996a:24–25).

Hollinshead in his monumental (1993) PhD thesis entitled *The Truth about Texas: A Naturalistic Study of the Construction of Heritage* continues this line of thought. According to him, power in discourse relates to the ability of the speaker to turn addressees and referents into subjects through storylines—to control them antagonistically by privileging one version of the past over another. Tourism is thus a form of communication in which reality is represented by images, destinations assume a narrative style, and attractions constitute a form of speech. *The Truth about Texas* is one such battleground in which the tourism authorities select preferred narratives from the past. They present an interpretevist view of reality by editing history. Hollinshead is indebted to Foucault, especially in the premise that knowledge is power, the central motif of his entire thesis. Another variant of the constructivist perspective can be found in the work of Bruner. He argues for an "invention of culture position" in which culture emerges as a function of performance and its interpretation. As ethnographic examples drawn from the world of tourism, he takes Lincoln's New Salem (1994), three types of Maasai performances in Kenya (2001) and the slave fortresses in Ghana as differently perceived by locals and Afro-Americans in search of their roots (1996). In each instance, there are several types of performers defining and redefining their representational activities and equally many diverse interpretations of these various points of view.

However, what is interesting about Said's thesis is its overwhelming reliance on European sources, at least for much of the earlier material that gave birth to Orientalism. Said, as an academic, quotes a number of scholarly works to support his position by citing with approval such Continental heavyweights as Durkheim, Weber, and Foucault, and, with some reservation, Marx.

As for Bruner, when he discusses the origins of "constructivism" in a number of American writers (Berger and Luckmann 1966), he readily acknowledges that the roots of the perspective—what he calls "the invention of culture" or "the invention of tradition"—(Bruner 1994; see also Hobsbawm and Ranger 1984) are much older, going back to William Dilthey, John Dewey, and George Herbert Mead. Had he continued this exercise in provenance further, he would inevitably have been able to trace it to the Weberian debate on *Geisteswissenschaften* (literally: sciences of the spirit) and to the works of European symbolic interactionists such as Znaniecki. As it was, he at least admitted a reliance on Mikhail Bakhtin, Roland Barthes, the poststructuralists, and the performance theory of Bauman.

By way of summary of this last preliminary section, it can be seen that whichever variant of contemporary Anglophone theory on the sociology of tourism is employed, it can trace its roots to earlier theorizing in Europe. If authenticity is the mainstream paradigm, that framework can be seen to derive from the respective insights of two leading lights in the German and French schools of sociology: Marx and Durkheim. In the case of strangerhood, the influence is exclusively German, deriving as it does from Simmel before being picked up by compatriots in the figures of Bormann, Glücksmann, Knebel, and von Wiese, and later extended to the cross fertilization of ideas in the predominantly northern European climes of

Scandinavia, Poland, and the former Yugoslavia. As for play, that had mixed origins going back to the Netherlands, France, Germany, and Norway, while the prototypes of constructivism can be found in Germany, France, and Poland. When talking about the genesis of unit ideas in the sociology of tourism, the message is crystal clear. Whatever their subsequent Anglophone embellishment, their pedigree is distinctly European in nature.

This chapter reinforces the European roots of the sociology of tourism when contrasted with the Anglophone dominance of tourism studies today. Although it is shown that much of this hegemony is evident in the location of journals, books, and publishing houses of today, in a sense it is a self-fulfilling prophecy catering to the linguistic limitations of the English-speaking world, while at the same time ignoring the non-Anglo-Saxon foundation of the knowledge that is being communicated.

It is additionally revealed that there are still many unresolved issues that contribute to this scenario of intellectual amnesia by referring to the context of European national sociologies, the relationship of the sociology of tourism to its European-generated parent discipline, the European link with the sociology of leisure, as well as European-based questions of definition, multidisciplinarity, translation, and ideology. Thereafter, the origins and development of the sociology of tourism are traced to Europe of the 1920s and 1930s, particularly the pioneering work carried out in Germany and its later spread to Switzerland and parts of Scandinavia. It is also demonstrated that while France tended to take another direction in originally locating the sociology of tourism within the sociology of leisure, that position at least had the advantage of opening up its development to extra-European dialog within the structures of the ISA.

This necessarily lengthy outline of the European origins and development of the sociology of tourism now complete, it should serve as a prologue for an introduction to our contributors and the conclusion to this chapter.

CONCLUSION

From what has been stated already, it should be clear that much of the initial theorizing about tourism can be traced to Germany and, somewhat later, to the German-speaking countries of Austria and parts of Switzerland. For that reason, it constitutes the first and possibly the most important contribution to this volume. After that no particular salience should be attributed to the order of appearance of any given territory. That particular exercise can be left to individual readers after they have digested the specific contents of each offering.

German-Speaking Countries: Hasso Spode

The author of this chapter, Hasso Spode, is eminently equipped to chronicle the development of ideas in great detail. He is supernumerary professor of historical sociology at the Leibniz University in Hannover. As a leading figure in historical tourism research in his native Germany, he can combine this focus to embrace not only the sociology of tourism but also its roots in such European thinking as that of Weber and Marx and, more recently, Elias and Foucault.

In the late 1980s, Spode was appointed research fellow at the recently established Institute for Tourism in Berlin. In cooperation with that institute and with the *Studienkreis für Tourismus* in Starnberg, he co-founded and later headed the first German working group on tourism history which held numerous symposia under his leadership. Throughout the late 1980s and early 1990s, the number of German scholars interested in tourism history and theory remained manageably small. However, by 1997, when academic interest began to expand, Spode saw the need to establish a journal to disseminate their ideas. Thus, in collaboration with Christoph Hennig and others, *Voyage. Jahrbuch für Reise & Tourismusforschung* (Voyage: Studies on Travel & Tourism) was born, and later he became its editor-in-chief. It was this publication that became the forum for cultural and social studies in tourism.

The same year also saw the appearance of the *Tourismus Journal* (Tourism Journal), which was oriented toward classical tourism science, and on whose editorial board he was invited to serve. The following year, he became director of the *Historisches Archiv zum Tourismus* (Historical Archive on Tourism) at the Free University of Berlin. Spode is also a member of the board of the Czech journal *Cestování Vcera a Dnes* (Tourism Yesterday and Today) and of H-Travel. He has more than 150 scholarly books and articles to his name, a third of which deal specifically with tourism. Topics include working class tourism and "Strength through Joy" in the Third Reich, tourism in East German society, the grammar of the "Fordist" serial production of tourist experience in the Nazi seaside resort of Prora, tourism history as an object of research, the theory of leisure and tourism, the history of tourism science, the birth of modern beach life, the relation between air travel and mass tourism, the role of tourism in the making of Europe, German-Austrian tourism, and national identity, and

"The Post Tourist Gaze—Follies and Fallacies in Tourism Research" (2005). His latest book is the revised 2009 edition of *An Introduction to Tourism History* (2003b).

France: Marie-Françoise Lanfant

The one person whose name is synonymous with the development of the sociology of tourism for the last four decades in France is Marie-Françoise Lanfant. Recognized in a recent anthology (Nash 2007) as one of the pioneers in the field and invited to contribute her life history to that collection focusing on anthropological and sociological beginnings of the study of tourism, we are similarly privileged to have her represent her nation here, only on this occasion the accent is on non-Anglophone Continental Europe. Nevertheless, her self-authored personal history (Lanfant 2007) is useful in the present context as it is the product of a reflexivity which would otherwise be absent from a traditional *curriculum vitae*. According to her own account, Marie-Françoise Lanfant benefited enormously from her training at the Sorbonne, and exposure to the ideas of Barthes, Lacan, Lévi-Strauss, and Marx. Her broad education ensured that, in addition to sociology, she received a complementary grounding in philosophy and psychology, thereby gaining her a teaching license in all three disciplines from 1951 to 1957. At the end of this period, she turned her attention to research and became an assistant at the CNRS where she came under the influence of Joffré Dumazedier (1967) and the ideas of Henri Lefebvre (1967). In this intellectual environment, the accent was firmly on the sociology of leisure and indeed was partially responsible for her comprehensive treatment of the topic in *Les Théories du Loisir* (Theories of Leisure) (1972). Another influence on her book were her years of teaching at the *Centre d'Études Supérieures du Tourisme* (Center of Higher Studies in Tourism), also located at the Sorbonne, from 1964 to 1973, and exposure to the ideas of students from 28 different countries, many of them belonging to the developing world. Not only did she encourage them to openly debate about the effects of tourism as a total global phenomenon, but she herself felt obliged to think out her own position on tourism as an international social fact (concepts respectively derived from Mauss and Durkheim). Additionally she became interested in the Swiss theorist, Krapf (see earlier), and his notion of touristic consumption.

Throughout this formative period of twin focus on leisure and tourism, her academic attention was gradually moving in the direction of the latter. Her break with Dumazedier, who continued to concentrate on leisure, was thus inevitable, but happily it coincided with her appointment as *chargée de recherche* at CNRS in 1975 and, one year later, the establishment of the URESTI where she became Director from 1978 to 1985. With sponsorship available from several sources, she was able to conduct several international group projects until such financial support dried up. This funding also enabled her to host a round table in 1986 at Marly-le-Roi and to create an international network of tourism scholars. So the seed was sown for the subsequent emergence of the IAST some two years later under the inspiration and presidency of Jafar Jafari. The desire for internationalization was also manifested in her finding a niche for the sociology of tourism under the umbrella of the ISA. At the world congress of the ISA in New Delhi (1986), Lanfant, along with Graham Dann and Krzysztof Przecławski (both in this volume), initiated discussions that led to the amicable severance from the research committee on the sociology of leisure and the establishment of a thematic group on the sociology of tourism. In an unprecedented accelerated rate of promotion within the ISA the thematic group soon became a working group and then a full research committee (RC 50), and with it a series of seminars, conferences, and publications (RC 50 2008). (Later all three of these individuals were to serve as president of the research committee on international tourism, as indeed was the contributor on Belgium and the Netherlands, as well as the other co-editor of this book). Apart from her contributions to the macro-sociological treatment of tourism as an international social fact, Marie-Françoise Lanfant is also known for her tireless campaign to have languages other than English recognized for the dissemination of ideas in international forums. While her point is taken in the ISA (which has the additional official languages of French and Spanish), it is absent in many other organizations claiming to be international. Nevertheless, it constitutes the second reason why she is an ideal contributor to this volume.

Italy: Asterio Savelli

Our next contributor, Asterio Savelli, has been selected for the Italian section of this volume. From 1974 he has been institutionally affiliated to the Department of Sociology of Bologna University, where he has developed his studies on tourism. Most of his teaching has been devoted to the sociology of tourism, first at the *Centro Studi Turistici* (CST) (Center for Tourism Studies) in Assisi (1985–1993), and subsequently in the faculties of economics of the University of Perugia at Assisi (1992–1994) and the

University of Bologna at Rimini (1996–2001). From 1993 his activity has been located within the Faculty of Political Science at the University of Bologna at Forlì, where he is currently associate professor teaching the Sociology of Tourism and the Sociology of the Environment and Territory.

However, perhaps Savelli's greatest contribution to tourism knowledge has been the part that he has played as Secretary in launching, organizing, and sustaining the Mediterranean Association for the Sociology of Tourism. Meeting every four years the respective themes of its conferences have been "Tourism and Cultural Communication" (Bologna 1987), "Local Intermediate Groups and Structures for a Change of Image in the Tourist System" (Cervia 1991), "Tourism and the Environment" (Estoril 1995), "Local and Global in Tourism: Forms of Aggregation and Networks of Communication" (Ravenna 2001), "Mediterranean Tourism Beyond the Coastline: New Trends in Tourism and the Social Organisation of Space" (Thessaloniki 2005), and "Tourism as Development and Cohesion in the Mediterranean Region" (Granada 2008). Proceedings of the first three of these congresses were published in *Sociologia Urbana e Rurale* (Urban and Rural Sociology) 26 (Guidicini and Savelli 1988b), 38 (Guidicini and Savelli 1992), and 52/53 (Savelli 1997a). Other book length publications of Savelli include a wide range of topics focusing on meaning, motives, and structures of post-metropolitan tourism (Benini and Savelli 1986), tourism in a changing society (Guidicini and Savelli 1988a), sociology of tourism (Savelli 1989), community strategies in Mediterranean tourism (Guidicini and Savelli 1999), cities, tourism and global communication (Savelli 2004a), tourism, territory, and identity (Savelli 2004b), and touristic space and global society (Savelli 2008e). All were published by FrancoAngeli (Milan). Unfortunately each of these works was in Italian, thus depriving them of a wider readership. In that sense, Savelli illustrates, like many other contributors to the current volume, that unless European ideas are made available in English, they will simply be ignored by a prevailing Anglophone monopoly on tourism theory today.

Poland: Krzysztof Przecławski, Julian Bystrzanowski, and Dorota Ujma

As will soon be seen, the counterpart to the author of the chapter on Spain, Julio Aramberri, can be found in one of our Polish contributors, Julian Bystrzanowski. Not only did the two overlap at Drexel University from 1999 to 2005 when both held professorial positions in the Department of Hospitality Management, and in their linguistic proficiencies (Bystrzanowski is fluent in English, Russian, and French), but also in their early exposure to the workings of the tourism industry. After graduating with an MA in history at Warsaw University in 1963, Bystrzanowski spent the next seven years consecutively running a students' (1963–1967) and a teachers' (1967–1970) travel agency. Having gained this practical experience, he subsequently turned to teaching courses in tourism at the Academy of Physical Education and to research, emerging in 1973 with a PhD in tourism studies from the same institution. For the next 22 years (1973–1995) he assumed the positions of lecturer and Deputy Director at the Institute of Tourism in Warsaw. It was during this period that he conducted in two phases (1975–1977, 1982–1989) the international program of comparative studies *Tourism as a Factor of Change* on behalf of the Vienna-based European Coordination Center for Research and Documentation in the Social Sciences, and became editor of the seminal two-volume report (Bystrzanowski 1989; Bystrzanowski and Beck 1989) comprising a sociocultural study and several national case studies. Among his many publications on tourism in Poland are works devoted to the history of tourism (1964) and social tourism (1981), and, on the European front, economic and sociological problems of tourism (Bystrzanowski 1977), outbound tourism (1980a), and tourism information systems (1980b).

Another co-contributor to the Polish chapter is Krzysztof Przecławski, a close colleague of Julian Bystrzanowski. Their careers overlapped at the Institute of Tourism in Warsaw where Przecławski was Director from 1983 to 1991 and in their co-participation from 1983 to 1989 in the Vienna Center project. During his period of tenure at the Institute, Przecławski was additionally editor-in-chief of the quarterly *Problemy Turystyki* (and now of its current successor *New Problems of Tourism*) published simultaneously in English and Polish, and featuring articles from a number of well-known international authors and a special (1987) issue on the 1986 round table of Marly-le-Roi organized by Marie-Françoise Lanfant. Like Bystrzanowski (and many others in this volume), Przecławski is also something of a linguist, sometimes preferring to speak in French rather than English in presenting academic papers to international conferences.

Where the two compatriots differ is in their training and career paths. Initially Przecławski graduated in law from the University of Warsaw at the age of 22. In 1963 he completed his PhD in sociology and in 1970 was awarded a postdoctoral degree from the Institute of Philosophy and Sociology of the Polish Academy of Sciences (where he had worked from 1958 to 1972). After one year teaching sociology at the Jagiellonian University in Cracow he returned to his native Warsaw where he consecutively assumed positions at the Youth Research Institute (1973–1977) and the Institute of Re-socialization and Social Prevention of the University of Warsaw (1977 to the present), during which time he was appointed professor (1982). More recently, he was also granted a professorship in Warsaw's College of Tourism and Hospitality Management.

Like some other contributors to this volume, Przecławski was a founder member of IAST. He was instrumental in establishing the research committee on international tourism of the ISA and becoming its first president (cf. Marie-Françoise Lanfant). He was additionally founder and first president of the Polish Tourism Association. He has over 100 papers and 8 books to his name. Topics of the latter include works dedicated to tourism and education (1973), sociological problems of tourism (1979), humanistic foundations of tourism (1986), tourism and the contemporary world (1994), ethical foundations of tourism (1997), the sociology of tourism (1996, 2004), and the philosophy of tourism (2005).

The third contributor to the chapter on Poland is Dorota Ujma. After completing her Masters in Economics with a specialization in marketing in travel and tourism at the Kraków University of Economics in 1994, she taught there for another two years. Subsequently she enrolled for a doctoral program at the then University of Luton, UK where she was awarded a PhD in tourism in 2002 with a thesis entitled *Channel Relationships between Tour Operators and Travel Agents in Britain and Poland* (Ujma 2002). While at Luton she gained experience in teaching a number of tourism modules such as tourism marketing, public sector tourism and tourism practice, as well as the more theoretically oriented course in understanding tourism. Soon after the University of Luton, following a merger with De Montfort University, became the University of Bedfordshire, Dorota Ujma was promoted to Senior Lecturer and became field chair for two undergraduate degrees in travel and tourism and international tourism management. Her publications and conference presentations not only concentrated on disseminating her doctoral work to a wider audience, but in exploring the pedagogical aspects of tourism, in particular, student awareness, personal development, transferable skills, and online learning. She thus has an ongoing commitment to tourism education and its future directions. At the same time she maintains links with her country of birth, a significant initiative being her recently establishing an academic partnership between the United Kingdom and Poland. Her continuing interest in tourism theory facilitates such an endeavor and makes her a suitable co-contributor and complement to her compatriots.

The Former Yugoslavia: Boris Vukonić

Also from the former Eastern bloc is Boris Vukonić. Like Przecławski, Bystrzanowski, and Ujma, Vukonić was raised in a country with a centrally planned, supply-oriented economy, even if it did have greater autonomy in other areas. Where he differed from them was that he was trained as an economist whereas, and as noted previously, their backgrounds were in history, law, philosophy, and, above all, sociology. Born in the Croatian capital, Vukonić received his Bachelor (1962), Masters (1965), and PhD (1978), all in economics and each from the same University of Zagreb. Subsequently he was appointed Assistant Professor and, shortly afterwards, Full Professor, in that institution's Faculty of Economics where he also served as Dean and Vice-Dean. In 2004 he left his alma mater and became Dean of Utilus, a privately run Business School for Tourism and Hotel Management, also in Zagreb. His tourism related appointments have included Secretary of the Scientific Council for Tourism of the Croatian Academy of Science and Arts and President of the Croatian Society for Health Tourism. He has worked as a tourism expert for UNDP and UNWTO in Afghanistan, Bangladesh, Egypt, Guyana, India, Tanzania, and Zanzibar, and received an award from UNWTO for his "contribution to the global development, research, education and training in tourism." He is a member of the IAST and from 1972 to 2007 of the AIEST. He is also editor-in-chief of the bilingual *Nova Acta Turistica*.

Although the many publications (over 200 papers and 25 books and monographs) of this prolific writer tend to focus on economic issues (e.g., *Turizam i Razvoj* (Tourism and Development)) (1987), Tourist Agencies (1997b), and the first book on marketing tourism in Croatia (1981, 1983, 1989). He has also authored volumes on topics related to tourism that are more sociologically oriented. Some are in Croatian (e.g., *History of Croatian Tourism* (2005) and *Tourism and the Future* (1994). Others have appeared in Croatian and English; they include *Tourism and Religion* (1990, 1996) and *Tourism in the Whirlwind of War* (1997a; 2003).

Scandinavia: Jens Kristian Steen Jacobsen

Possibly the greatest linguist among our European contributors is Jens Kristian Steen Jacobsen who ably demonstrates the point by including Denmark, Sweden, Finland, and his native Norway in his chapter. However, his multilingual skills extend well beyond Scandinavia since he is also fluent in English and German, with a working knowledge of French, as is evident, for example, in his content analysis of foreign guidebooks on northern Norway (Jacobsen, Heimtun, and Dale Nordbakke 1998). Yet on many occasions he is obliged to publish in English or perish, thereby reinforcing the general theme of this book.

Jacobsen is the only one of our contributors who *currently* divides his time between academia and applied research since he is an associate professor of tourism at the University of Stavanger and a senior researcher at the Norwegian Centre for Transport Research in Oslo, with output from each institution appearing in equal measure. He is also the only contributor whose bachelor, advanced MPhil, and doctoral degrees are all in tourism, while he holds a master (*Candidatus Magisterii*) degree in general social science. (The English title of his *Magister Artium* (Master of Arts) thesis was *Modern Tourism: A Sociological Analysis of Central Aspects of Tourist Behaviour* (1983) while his dissertation for the *Doctor Rerum Politicarum* (Doctor of Political Matters) was *Exploring Tourism: Aspects of International European Holiday Travel* (2005)).

On the academic front Jacobsen is one of the leading sociologists of tourism in Norway and probably also in Scandinavia. Apart from being a frequent participant at the annual Nordic conferences on that region's tourism, he also regularly attends meetings of the research committee on international tourism of the ISA, and, when serving as vice-president-2, organized an interim symposium of the latter in Lesvos, Greece (2004). As a theoretician, Jacobsen has explored the insights of most contemporary sociologists in the field, especially the likes of John Urry. Coterminously, he also acknowledges the Continental European origins of their ideas. Among his many wide-ranging areas of eclectic research interest should be mentioned the topics of imagery, the making of attractions, perceptions of landscape, "smellscapes" (with Graham Dann), tourists' experience of place, anti-tourist attitudes, tourism in peripheral areas, the tourist role, travel dreams and myths, tourist motivation, sightseeing, and encounters with the "other." Apart from publishing in various international English language journals such as *Annals of Tourism Research, Tourism Geographies, Journal of Tourism and Cultural Change, Tourism Analysis, Landscape and Urban Planning*, and the *Scandinavian Journal of Hospitality and Tourism* (which, as noted previously, also feels the need to publish in English), he has contributed to such Scandinavian language journals as *Sosiologi i dag* (Sociology Today) and *Norveg* (Norwegian Journal of Ethnology). The remainder of his academic work appearing in Norwegian is to be found in six edited/co-edited books and over two dozen chapters in books. As for his applied research for the Institute of Transport

Economics, that can be found in 28 research reports, of which only two are in English.

Spain: Julio Aramberri

Unlike the author of the preceding chapter, the other contributor who *was* industry oriented, though *currently* only academically affiliated is Julio Aramberri. In a former role he was Director of the Tourist Office of Spain in the Netherlands (1985–1986), Miami (1991–1996), and *pro tempore* Los Angeles (1991), as well as press attaché to the Spanish Embassy in Chile (1987–1999). He was also Director General of *Turespaña* (1987–1990), the government corporation responsible for the worldwide promotion of tourism to Spain which included the activities of advertising, public relations, and marketing. He has additionally worked as a consultant for a number of tourism projects including EU programs in Poland and Vietnam.

Wearing his academic hat, he graduated with honors from Madrid University in 1964 and was awarded his doctorate from the same institution some three years later. From 1964 to 1984 he was Professor of Sociology at Madrid, taking time out from 1971 to 1974 to assume the position of graduate researcher at the London School of Economics. From 1999 to the present he has been Professor of Tourism at Drexel University, USA. However, he has taught at a number of other universities including those in the Balearics, Dongbei University of Finance and Economics, Dalian, PRC, Hanoi University in Vietnam, and with the ITHAS program that comprises four European universities.

As a founder member of the IAST, he was responsible for organizing the charter meeting in Santander, Spain and, as vice-president for organizing the scientific sessions of its recent 20th anniversary meeting in Mallorca, Julio Aramberri was additionally the first Continental European co-editor of its latest book, *Tourism Development: Issues for a Vulnerable Industry* (with Richard Butler), Channel View Publications (Aramberri and Butler 2005). He has also co-edited in 2004 (with Shalini Singh and Xie Yanjun) a special issue of *Tourism, Recreation Research* 29(2) (Aramberri, Singh and Yanjun 2004) and in 2005 edited a special issue of *Politica y Sociedad* 42(1) (Politics and Society) devoted to the sociology of tourism (Aramberri 2005). Like Jens Jacobsen, Julio Aramberri, while publishing mainly in English, is also something of a linguist. This ability is evident in the works that he reads and cites in several European languages.

Belgium and the Netherlands: Jaap Lengkeek

Our next contributor is Jaap Lengkeek. With over 100 publications to his name since 1995, over 60% are in his native Dutch while the remainder are in English. Whereas most of the latter can be found in conference proceedings, book chapters, and in such international journals as *International Sociology*, the former are mainly targeted at a domestic readership. Even so, some of these Dutch journals like *Vrijetijd en Samenleving* (Leisure and Society), *Recreatie en Toerisme* (Recreation and Tourism), and *Vrijetijd Studie* (Leisure Studies) (where he was either editor or editor-in-chief), also include occasional papers from overseas Anglophone scholars such as John Urry. What is also interesting to note is that most of these journals have leisure in their titles, reflecting perhaps the overall Netherlands' inclination to view tourism in these terms, both academically and historically.

A similar trajectory is evident in Jaap Lengkeek's personal history. Although his degrees from the University of Amsterdam are in cultural anthropology (BSc 1968), non-Western sociology (BSc 1969), and sociology (MSc 1973), and from the University of Wageningen his PhD (1994) is also in sociology, much of his career is applied or derived from these disciplines. For example, for most of the 1970s he researched and lectured in the area of physical planning and housing, while for the first half of the 1980s he worked for the Recreation Foundation in The Hague before becoming a coordinator for recreation studies at the Agricultural University of Wageningen. From that academic base he extended his teaching role through the various academic levels of lecturer, associate professor, and professor while maintaining his research interests in the coterminous position of senior researcher at the Mansholt Institute of the same university. Throughout this development, his fields of expertise were once more not simply limited to sociological theory, the sociology of leisure, and environmental sociology. They also extended to the philosophical aspects of leisure (e.g., Lengkeek 1996), the leisure of special populations (e.g., the disabled and elderly), voluntary associations, public policy, lifestyle and consumer patterns, landscape, and planning. Among other reasons it was this accent on leisure which led to the decision to relocate the World Leisure and Recreation Association's Centre of Excellence (WICE) from Leeuwarden to Wageningen. Likewise, and even when tourism became included in his purview, it tended to assume an applied dimension, as for instance in the areas of sustainable tourism and liveability, cultural heritage and tourism, community involvement in tourism development. Such a range of teaching and research is also reflected in the various PhD theses that he has supervised in topics such as "tourism-scapes"—an actor network perspective (van der Duim 2005), meaning and quality of place, tourism and representation of landscape, cross-cultural confrontations in tourism, new age tourism, and pro-poor tourism. (It is this last topic where local communities in the developing world are shown how they can benefit from the introduction of tourism that characterizes Lengkeek's practical and international approach to the subject). Relatedly, from 2002 until 2005, he was co-director of the "Landscape Centre" of Wageningen University and Research Centre. Under his management his former group Socio-spatial Analysis developed an academic Masters program in Leisure, Tourism and Environment, as well as a specialization of socio-spatial analysis in the Bachelor and Master program of Landscape Architecture and Spatial Planning both of Wageningen University.

That is not to say that Lengkeek is averse to theorizing in the sociology of tourism. He has, for example, provided a critique (Lengkeek with Elands 2006) of Cohen's (1979b) modes of tourist experience (especially the experience of out-there-ness), examined the discourse of authenticity in relation to heritage (Lengkeek 2006), and explored love as a metaphor of tourist longing (Lengkeek 2002). It is no doubt for his contribution to a sociological understanding of tourism, and as previously noted, that he is currently the president of the research committee on international tourism of the ISA. Although he has recently retired from his full-time position in Wageningen, it is perhaps typical that his valedictory address should have been entitled "From Homo Ludens to Homo Turisticus" summing up in a nutshell his life's work.

Greece: Paris Tsartas and Vasiliki Galani-Moutafi

Finally, attention turns to the second of our co-authored accounts, that provided by Paris Tsartas and Vasiliki Galani-Moutafi, to reflect respective theoretical developments in Greece. Tsartas's background, like that of some other contributors, is multidisciplinary and home-based. With a diploma in economics from the University of Piraeus, he was awarded an MA in regional development and a PhD in sociology from the Pantion University in Athens. His tourism research interests have tended to follow this three-pronged path with emphases on tourism employment, marketing, and management (economics), tourism development, special and alternative forms of tourism, sustainable tourism development (development), sociology of tourism, and tourism education (sociology). These research interests have, in turn, resulted in several corresponding projects (funded by such bodies as the EU, NCSR, GSRD, and GTO) in domestic tourism, city tourism, holiday homes in Greece, agro-tourism cooperatives, sustainable tourism in Athens, social impacts of tourism in Corfu and Lassithi, Balkan relations, xenophobia, and tourism as a factor of social change.

While many of these projects have subsequently been published in Greek (e.g., the social and economic impacts of tourism development in the Cyclades, women's agro-tourism cooperatives in Greece, the social impacts of tourism, multidisciplinary approaches toward tourism development, and the demand for domestic tourism), Anglophone readers have been exposed to only a few of these topics that have appeared in English in journals such as *Anatolia, Annals of Tourism Research, Journal of Sustainable Tourism, Sociologia Urbana e Rurale,* and *Tourism Today,* as well as in a number of edited collective volumes. Tsartas is currently Professor of Tourism Development and Director of Postgraduate Studies in Tourism Development, Management and Policy at the University of the Aegean. He maintains his international contacts through such organizations as the ISA and The World Leisure and Recreation Association.

Vasiliki Galani-Moutafi is a colleague of Paris Tsartas at the University of the Aegean where she is Academic Director of the Postgraduate Program on "Women and Gender: Anthropological and Historical Approaches." Member of the Department of Social Anthropology and History on the Lesvos campus, she underwent training in social-cultural anthropology at the City University of New York where she was awarded her BA, MA, and PhD degrees in that discipline. Her 1990 doctoral thesis was on "Tourism on Samos: Implications for Marriage, Dowry and Women's Status" which was subsequently published in *Ethnology* (1996 in Greek) and in two parts in the *Journal of Modern Greek Studies* (1993, 1994). Other topics of theoretical importance which she has explored in her publications include the construction of place identity (*Anatolia* 2004a), tourism research on Greece (*Annals of Tourism Research* 2004b), representing the self and the other (*Journeys* 2001), the self and the other: traveler, ethnographer, tourist (*Annals of Tourism Research* 2000), approaches to tourism: the contrived and authentic (*Synchrona Themata* (Current Issues) 1995 (in Greek)). She has additionally produced a book entitled *Tourism Research on Greece and Cyprus: An Anthropological Perspective* (in Greek) published by Propombos in Athens (2002), from which the present account is partially derived, plus some chapters in books dedicated to intercultural encounters in Aegean tourist destinations and issues of self-reflexivity.

Galani-Moutafi includes among her many tourism research interests the processes of socio-economic development affecting Greek island communities, cultural change and the renegotiation of local identities, the anthropology of tourism, travel and tourist discourse, tourist representations, the transformation of cultural products into tourist products, alternative forms of tourism, place identity, heritage management, and locally distinctive products, as well as the previously mentioned gender, consumerism, and identity. Like Paris Tsartas, she is a resource editor of *Annals of Tourism Research*. Additionally she serves on the editorial board of the recently launched *Tourismos: An International Multidisciplinary Journal of Tourism* based in the University of the Aegean, Greece.

From these brief introductions to our contributory authors, it should be evident that they are among the leading representatives for their respective countries and regions. It should also be clear that, had this self-contextualization been left to themselves, humility might well have prevented them from justifying their selection in deservedly glowing terms. That welcoming editorial task accomplished we are now ready to listen to what they have to say. The task of comparing their accounts in style and content is necessarily left to the reader.

NOTES

1. Their proportional distribution may be gauged from the number of tourism research centers in these regions/countries as derived from the related statistics available from the *Centre International de Recherches et d'Études Touristiques* (2008). With frequencies in parentheses they range from France (24), Germany (24) (Austria (14) and Switzerland (16)), Italy (21), Spain (25), the former Yugoslavia (3) (especially the modern nation states of Croatia (5) and Slovenia (4), Greece (5), the low countries (of Belgium (7) and the Netherlands (15)), the region of Scandinavia (comprising, Denmark (3), Finland (4), Norway (5), and Sweden (6)) to Poland (7). While their accounts do not pretend to be exhaustive of the pan-European effort (we could have included contributions from Portugal and Russia, e.g., even though they only constitute 7 out of a total of 221 tourism research centers in Continental Europe (CIRET 2008)), they are sufficiently representative of the main expertise on tourism in Europe today (accounting for some 86% of these centers).

2. Only 283 out of 708 worldwide have English as their mother tongue, and of the former 69 are located in the United Kingdom and 114 in the United States (the remaining 100 being shared between Australia 55, Canada 29, New Zealand 7, Ireland 5, Barbados 2, Bahamas 1, and Jamaica 1).

3. Indeed only 10% of the 50 most spoken languages worldwide is English <http://www.photius.com> (accessed 27 September 2008). Even though with 430.8 million internet usage out of 1,463.6 million users worldwide, Anglophones account for 29.4%, that still means that the remaining 70.6% of users do not have English as their mother tongue <http://www.internetworldstats.com> (accessed

29 August 2008). Even when one comes to blogging, 36% of English users are exceeded by the Japanese on 37% <http://globalvoicesoline.org> (accessed 1 September 2008). These statistics have recently become the object of separate commentary (Dann 2008).

4. Take Sharpley (1994) for example. Here there are 216 references of which 186 are to works written by Anglophones for Anglophones, while the remaining 30 are written by those who do not have English as their mother tongue but who nevertheless write in English for an English-speaking audience. Thus, although translation makes their offerings available to Anglophones, there are still no citations of original material in any Continental European languages.

5. See Singh's (2004) collection, for instance. Here there is only one non-English speaking contributor, Aramberri (2004), whose distribution of citations in his chapter written in English is 80.6% in English, 4.6% in English translation, 3.7% in French, 9.3% in German, and 1.8% in Italian. Since he is a Spanish national, it is interesting to see that he displays no ethnocentrism since there is a complete absence of references to works in his maternal tongue. For the remaining 13 Anglophone contributors, however, the percentages are 95.9% English, 3.2% in English translation, 0.0% French, 0.3% in German, 0.2% in Italian, 0.1% in Hindi, 0.1% in Dutch, and 0.1% in Spanish.

6. An example is the edited volume by Lanfant et al. (1995) where all chapters are in English and there is a more-or-less equal divide between seven French and six Anglophone authors, and where the variation in ethnocentrism and linguistic ability is highly significant ($\chi^2 = 181.29$ sign $p < 0.0001$). Here the French quote 39.2% of material in their own tongue, while the percentage for Anglophone authors rises to 98.3%.

7. This is the case in an edited volume by Jardel (1994) where the French contributors write in their own language, non-French Europeans write in English or Italian, and Anglophone authors write in English. When the focus is on English and non-English authors, variation in the quotation of Anglophone and non-Anglophone works is sufficiently striking as to be significant at $p < 0.0001$ with a χ^2 of 167.45. Here, English speakers cite their own material (84.3%) and French speakers do the same (though to a far lesser extent (59.2%)). In the middle are the non-French Europeans, who cite English material (44.7%) more frequently than do the French (23.6%). They also, however tend to demonstrate a far greater linguistic resource base, though with limited tendency to quote from it.

8. Although when the organization was first established in 1988, 61.4% of the 44 charter members had English as their principal language, a figure that has subsequently increased to 67.1% of the 73 current members, there are indications that Anglophone dominance is even more pronounced in other areas. When it comes to positions on the executive committee, for instance, 82.9% of a total of 35 elected officials from 1988 to 2008 have English as their mother tongue, a figure that rises to a full 100% for the influential positions of president and secretary. A parallel imbalance, though somewhat less exaggerated, can be seen in the academy's six publications. Here the English-speaking authors quote 87.2% of their works in English while for the non-English speaking authors the respective percentage is 65.3% ($\chi^2 = 146.05$).

Chapter 2

Tourism Research and Theory in German-Speaking Countries

Hasso Spode
Leibniz University, Germany

INTRODUCTION

Tourism "theory," or scholarly thinking about tourism,[1] originally emerged within the discipline of economics, and then mainly in Italy and the German-speaking Alpine countries. Comprising some 100 million persons, German speakers constitute an important element of the world's population that initially contributed and currently continues to make important contributions to tourism theory, but that fact in itself does not explain why tourism research began here. Rather, it was grounded in the fear of failing to capitalize on an emerging market. The rapid development of tourism in the Alpine areas around 1900 (the "rush to the Alps") took place in a very uneven way. The Western Alps (Switzerland) became the world's leading destination, whereas in the Eastern Alps, belonging to Austria and Bavaria, tourist traffic grew only moderately. During most of the 19th century, the Alps were regarded as virtually synonymous with the Swiss Federal Republic. Inbound tourism, principally from the United Kingdom and Germany, transformed this secluded, poor country into a prosperous one, a center of *high life* for the European upper classes. Although the German-Austrian Alpine Club successfully promoted climbing and hiking

The Sociology of Tourism: European Origins and Developments
Tourism Social Science Series, Volume 12, 65–93
Copyright © 2009 by Emerald Group Publishing Limited
ISSN: 1571-5043/doi:10.1108/S1571-5043(2009)0000012007

in the Eastern Alps, politicians and economists from these two countries looked with envy at the flourishing upscale tourism in their Western neighbor state.

In this connection, in 1894, a "congress for the enhancement of tourism" was held in the Austrian city of Graz. In all Alpine countries, a number of articles on tourism in relation to the national economy and statistics appeared, indicating a growing awareness of the role of tourism (Spode 1998a). "Our mountains," which used to be a barrier for trade and travel, are now "part of our national wealth," concluded the economist and journalist Josef Stradner from Graz (1890:257f). Generally, there was a widespread feeling of living in an age of travel, particularly in the German Empire which transformed itself from an agrarian country into a leading industrial nation. Indeed, among the middle and upper classes (some 10% of the population), the annual vacation had become quite commonplace. "Everybody travels," exclaimed the novelist Theodor Fontane (1894), who called the "regeneration" by vacation trips a necessity in the face of an ever faster pace of life in cities and offices. According to his rudimentary theory, tourism allowed for a time-out, a retreat from the alienated "modern" way of life.

In such a manner, "real life" shifted from everyday to the holiday: "Eleven months you have to live, the twelfth month you will live" (Fontane 1894:3f). Later, Georg Simmel, a founding father of sociology, made this growing mobility an object of theoretical reflection. In 1895, he published an essay on the "industrialized" consumption of nature in Switzerland in which he criticized the Alpinists for inflating their "egoistic" pursuits with moral claims (Simmel 1992). In 1908—on the occasion of his "habilitation" (state doctorate)—he introduced his innovative analysis of the *Fremde* (stranger) (Simmel 1923). In the network of the "spatial orders of the society" the stranger was both included and excluded, a situation that had its merits and disadvantages. Simmel did not speak of tourists in this connection but of tradesmen and minorities; for him, the *Fremde* represented one of the basic types of human relations. Of course one might conclude that this type also characterized the tourist, as later did von Wiese (1930) and Gleichmann (1969) (cf. Cohen 2003).

TOURISM RESEARCH AND THEORY

The initial spark that ignited tourism research occurred in 1902. The occasion was a lecture delivered in Munich by Adolf Brougier on the "impact of tourism for Bavaria." In this address, he defined tourism as leisure travel and identified many of its direct and indirect positive effects on the local economy, including an increase in beer consumption (Brougier 1902; Spode 2007a). Soon after, the Tourist Association for Munich and Upper Bavaria started to gather regular statistics and to promote this destination in order to benefit from the "gold stream" of international tourism which flowed from the "Rhine to the Swiss mountains."[2]

The Birth of the Fremdenverkehrswissenschaft

A milestone in the emergence of tourism research was the 1905 overview *Der Fremdenverkehr. Eine volkswirtschaftliche Studie* (Tourism: An Economic Study) by the previously mentioned Josef Stradner (here 1917). This first academic monograph on tourism stressed the fact that tourists were consumers; they spent money in a destination which had been earned somewhere else. In certain regions and countries, tourism had thus become a significant factor in the "balance of payments." Moreover, tourism helped to monetize—and so preserve—"nature" (such as forests). Like Brougier, Stradner consequently regarded tourism as essentially different from other forms of travel, and defined it in particular according to its voluntary and "luxury" character (a term signifying élitist access to tourist experiences).

From the time of Stradner onwards, the term *Fremdenverkehr* (literally, stranger's or nonresident's traffic)[3] had become firmly established in public culture, politics, and science. As in every new branch of research, the demarcation of the object was a crucial task. Roughly speaking, two opposing approaches were (and still are) applied. One tended toward a wide definition, leaving out motives and comprising nearly all varieties of travel. This could be traced back to the economist Hermann von Schullern zu Schrattenhofen (1911) who had defined *Fremdenverkehr* as the sum of all economic activities in connection with travel. The second approach took, however vaguely, specific motives of tourists into account and/or stressed their role as consumers and thus regarded tourism as a (novel) subset of all travel. This approach could be traced back to Brougier and Stradner and is particularly appropriate to social and cultural studies. The wide definitions, by contrast (Mundt 2001)—while suitable for economic and statistical questions about horizontal mobility in general—are, as Nettekoven rightly maintains, "completely useless for sociological orientated studies" since they cannot grasp the *differentia specifica* of tourism (1972:7).

With respect to tourism motives, again two basic explanations could be distinguished: sociological and biological. Like Fontane, the majority tended to perceive modern times as an era that ruined the "nerves" (of the brainworkers only) and thus created new needs for relaxation in order to regenerate the workforce.[4] The latter stated that there was a certain "drive" in humans that made them travel and that modern transport technologies and growing wealth provided the means to act out that nomadic instinct on a large scale. As in the case of the definitions of "tourism," by and large both positions are still evident today.[5] In the early debate on tourism, however, the question of basic motivations was of minor importance (so that Stradner could combine the two explanations), and the wide definitions prevailed.

The Berlin Institute

After World War I, Europeanization and globalization were replaced by a walling-off of nation states, and under the slogan "autarky" the balance of payments became a political dogma. First, cross-border traffic decreased dramatically and then, due to a series of economic crises and upheavals, domestic tourism in Central Europe also declined. In spite of this downturn, travel agencies, communities, and governments enhanced their efforts to stimulate tourism demand.

In this connection, several books, booklets, and dissertations appeared, dealing with the economic, statistical, geographical, political, and marketing aspects of tourism.[6] In 1927, for example, the *Handbook of Political Sciences* included an entry on the topic and thus ennobled it as worthwhile to scientists (Morgenroth 1927). At the same time, the widespread notion that tourism was a vital part of the economy and culture ushered in the first university courses. While in Italy the young economist and director of the national tourist board, Angelo Mariotti, from 1925 began to lecture on the economics of tourism at Rome University, in 1928–1929 the business economist Robert Glücksmann founded the *Forschungsinstitut für den Fremdenverkehr* (Research Institute for Tourism) in Berlin.[7] This institute, housed at the Commercial University, held seminars and, above all, started to carry out and organize systematic research (Glücksmann et al 1930; Grünthal 1962; Spode 1998a). To this end, a library and an historical archive were installed. Although mainly centered on economic issues, teaching and research were interdisciplinary. Stimulated by the progress made in Berlin and Rome, Arthur Bormann published a textbook on tourism defining *Fremdenverkehr* as the epitome of travel, provided the stay was not permanent (1931:10). Later, Glücksmann and his associates also authored a textbook or overview (1935) that included a similarly wide definition,[8] even though the research followed more Stradner's notion of tourism as leisure or pleasure travel. In addition to these economics oriented textbooks, Glücksmann's co-operator, Alfred Grünthal, published an outline of "tourism geography" (1934).

In order to establish the new discipline, Glücksmann launched a series and above all founded the *Archiv für den Fremdenverkehr* (Archive of Tourism). This journal, with a print run of 400 copies,[9] provided a breakthrough for tourism research. Although Glücksmann was more interested in practical questions, like hotel-management, he nevertheless knew that a new field of research needed an academic blessing. Hence it was no surprise that the lead article of the first issue was authored by the noted sociologist Leopold von Wiese (1930), a disciple of Simmel, who discussed *Fremdenverkehr* as an "interpersonal relation." Here, he distinguished three types of *Fremde*: the stranger as an agent of power (for instance, a conqueror), the stranger by chance, not interested in relations with locals, and the stranger as a "guest" (the tradesman or the "traveler for pleasure," i.e., the tourist). Today, von Wiese's article is sometimes counted among the pioneering works in tourism theory (Cohen 1984). But enumerating various types of "relations" that occurred in connection with travel was more a finger exercise of his formalistic "relationship theory" that he had erected on the base of Simmel's system. Not very inventive, too, was a subsequent essay by Franz Oppenheimer (1932) on the "sociology of tourism." Nonetheless, von Wiese's approach made clear that not only economists and geographers, but also sociologists can, and should lay claim to analyzing tourism.

The contributions of prominent scholars to the *Archiv* underscored the ambitious interdisciplinary objectives of the Berlin Institute and its journal. Even so, surrounding circumstances were inimical to the project. Due to cutbacks in the wake of the Global Economic Crisis, there was a constant shortage of money, and when, in 1933, the Nazis seized power, Glücksmann's position (he was a Jew[10]) became untenable. In 1935, the Institute was shut down and with it the last issue of the *Archiv* was published.

At that time, the "democratization of travel" (Glücksmann 1935:9) ranked high on the political agenda of many countries, especially Germany. More than any other previous government, the Nazis realized the economic and political value of tourism.[11] On the one hand, and in order to demonstrate the alleged integration of the working class into the "people's community," it built up organized mass tourism. To this end, the leisure organization *Kraft durch Freude* (KdF), (Strength through Joy) sold millions of cheap vacation trips—by far the world's biggest tour operator. On the other hand, the regime successfully fostered upmarket tourism as a source of national wealth as well as an instrument of foreign propaganda.

Likewise the regime produced an international leisure movement as an anti-structure to the League of Nations that was to disguise its long-term objective, namely war. Its propaganda sold the democratization of "bourgeois" joys, be they theater, sports, or travel, as an essential contribution to "inner and outer peace." In 1936, and running parallel to the Olympics, a bombastic "World Congress" on leisure and recreation was staged in Hamburg. Its honorary president, the doyen of the American sport officials praised the ideal of the "people's community" and delegates from 61 countries held political and scientific lectures (Internationales Zentral-Büro 1937). A similar congress in Rome followed suit; successfully the Fascist regimes globalized leisure politics and leisure research and made it their trademark.[12] By comparison, specialized research in tourism continued on a much smaller scale after the closedown of the Berlin Institute. Of this limited output, the most remarkable work was by the geographer Hans Poser (1939), whose landmark study on the Silesian mountains showed how tourism shaped this region according to its needs and aesthetic ideals.[13] In 1939/1941 two new research institutions were established. However, due to the war no major work—apart from a hefty tome on the cultural history of the public house—was carried out. Nonetheless, thanks to Glücksmann's activities, a small but significant scientific community had been formed around 1930, one that began to stimulate research in other countries such as Austria, Greece, Hungary, Switzerland, the United Kingdom, and even South Africa. A decade later the Berlin Institute and its journal were rightly praised as the "first and, at the same time, qualitative and quantitative unique step" toward a "scientific understanding of tourism" (Hunziker and Krapf 1942:27).

The Swiss Twins

By far the greatest scientific impact took place in Switzerland. Here a second (and institutionally successful) attempt was made to establish tourism research. Once more, the background was a crisis in tourism. During World War II inbound tourism virtually ceased, but Switzerland wanted to prepare this industry for the expected boom after the war. In 1941, two institutes were founded: the Seminar for Tourism in Sankt Gallen was to focus on teaching, while the other in Bern, whose name was identical with the former Berlin Institute, was to engage more in research (both institutes still exist). Their respective directors, Walter Hunziker and (since 1943) Kurt Krapf, worked closely together. In 1941 they authored a first outline on tourism research and tourism history. A year later, they published a sort of textbook,

Grundriss der Allgemeinen Fremdenverkehrslehre (Outline of the General Teaching of Tourism), a genre that had been invented by Bormann (1931). It was oriented toward practical needs, and for decades it served as the "bible" in training and research. While Stradner had implicitly concentrated on special tourism motives, Hunziker and Krapf only took *ex negativo* motives into account (Hunziker and Krapf 1942:21f). That is to say, they preferred the following wide nominal definition:[14]

> Fremdenverkehr ist somit der Inbegriff der Beziehungen und Erscheinungen, die sich aus dem Aufenthalt Ortsfremder ergeben, sofern durch den Aufenthalt keine Niederlassung zur Ausübung einer dauernden oder zeitweilig hauptsächlichen Erwerbstätigkeit begründet wird.
>
> Tourism is thus the epitome of the relations and phenomena arising from the sojourn of non-residents, provided that their stay does not lead to residence for the sake of a permanent or temporary main earning activity.

From this starting point onwards, the "functions" were listed which required or resulted in tourism. In order to visualize the "complexity" of the phenomenon, an accompanying figure was provided: In the center was located tourism as a *Verkehrsvorgang* (act of traffic), surrounded by the "factors" involved—public health, technology, culture, social policy, politics, and the economy—each of them linked with a line that stood for mutual influences. The authors commented, tourism equals a "crystal" that is visible only in the totality of its "glimmering" facets.[15] But despite the reference to social "relations" and the caption: "in the center is the human being," sociological and psychological aspects were of minor importance. The textbook summed up and arranged the field of knowledge in such a way that placed tourism research under the umbrella of economics.

However, in 1943, for reasons still unclear, Hunziker presented an alternative—more demanding and more prestigious concept—the *System einer Wissenschaftlichen Fremdenverkehrslehre* (System of Scientific Tourism Research). Here, tourism was defined as a cultural phenomenon by drawing on the Neo-Kantian notion of *Kulturerscheinung* and Weber's *Kulturbedeutung* (cultural meaning and/or relevance). In so doing, he intended "to create a completely new discipline" (Hunziker 1943:10ff; cf. Hömberg 1977; Spode 1998b).

Inspired by Max Weber, Werner Sombart, and early Functionalist thinking, tourism was conceived as entrenched in the "cultural system as a whole" (Hunziker 1943:32). Tourism research had to "orient itself" toward this totality and thus was no longer to be a branch of economics but of "sociology." While the economy formed a system in its own right that fulfilled "secondary" functions for other subsystems, such as religion or art, tourism was a "primary" function of such subsystems, and in addition fulfilled functions in or for the cultural system as a whole. Up to this point, Hunziker's observations were not perfectly thought out. It was not made clear whether tourism formed a system in "empirical reality" or (in the Weberian tradition) only in the mind of the researcher. In particular, the meaning of "function" remained vague;[16] depending on the perspective, the term could be interpreted both as an output and as an effect. Methodologically, a distinction between structure and event—rather misleadingly called "theory" and "history"—was proposed. Although this concept was hardly more than a thumbnail sketch, it was nevertheless a pioneering attempt to cope with the diversity and entanglements of tourist travel and experience. Hitherto no other work had provided such an inventive and far-reaching theoretical framework for an understanding of tourism than Hunziker's "System."

The Postwar Period

Even so, Hunziker's "new discipline" never came into being. With the birth of tourism science in the first half of the 20th century, its explanatory power was obviously used up. After the war, tourism science became a strictly applied discipline, based upon Hunziker and Krapf's *Fremdenverkehrslehre* (Teaching of Tourism) from 1942. Research had to meet the needs of clients, namely governments, communities, and the tourism industry. Such needs were not based in academic fields but in business.

The Established Tourism Science.   The established *Fremdenverkehrswissenschaft* (tourism science) was located mainly in Sankt Gallen, Bern, and at the University of Vienna, where, since 1951, Paul Bernecker (1962) had developed a close cooperation with Krapf and Hunziker. In addition to that "triumvirate," there were newly founded institutes in Munich and also, strangely enough, at the East German University of Dresden.[17] Following the example of Grünthal and Poser, geographers, too, began to study tourism. The scope of their questions and topics was similar, admittedly less economics oriented and partly more demanding with respect to theory. In particular, Walther Christaller (1955), an expert in regional planning,[18] contributed to tourism theory; he conceived tourism as a move from the "center" to the "periphery" and—long before Butler's theory—developed a model for the evolutionary lifecycle of resorts. For the development of "tourism geography" the Academy for Regional Planning in Hannover and later also the Geography Department at Trier University, where Christoph Becker since 1976 published a series,[19] became of great importance.

Central European economists and geographers initially dominated the *Association Internationale d'Experts Scientifiques du Tourisme* (AIEST) (International Association of Scientific Experts on Tourism) which had been founded in 1949 on the initiative of Hunziker and Krapf. Leading journals of that time included the *Jahrbuch für Fremdenverkehr* (Tourism Yearbook) from the Munich Institute and the trilingual *Tourist Review* edited by the AIEST containing articles in French, German, and English. Tourism researchers formed a small, and in later years increasingly international, scientific community engaged in solving limited problems—or "puzzles," to use a Kuhnian expression (1962)—in the fields of marketing and of regional, economic, and transport planning. Especially within the "triumvirate," historical and sociological questions were considered as distractions to this "puzzle solving." Hunziker's ambitious "System of Scientific Tourism Research" was discarded (last but not least by the author himself) and soon sank into oblivion. The result was the self-marginalization of that discipline. No longer did it contribute to a broader understanding of the phenomenon which it studied. Instead, reflection about tourism became the specialization and interest of other professionals.

In the beginning the *Jahrbuch* still contained some weighty contributions. With an article on the role of consumption, Minister Ludwig Erhardt, the "father of the economic miracle," wrote the lead article in the first issue of the journal, a strategy of gaining prestige that Glücksmann had previously applied. However, following the example of von Wiese, attempts to introduce sociological questions failed (Günther 1954, 1956). Sociology and social psychology, it was bluntly stated, "are not directly profitable and thus do not awake instant interest today" (cf. Geigant 1962; Hunziker 1954; Nyberg 1955).

Certainly, there were sporadic works which were theory-grounded, just to mention Krapf's habilitation (state doctorate) thesis from 1947 on "tourist consumption," Urs Keller (1973) who analyzed the tourist way of life as an "exceptional state of mind," and—influenced by the sociological debate—Hans Meinke (1968) who regarded tourism as an "escape" from an "industrial environment" based on high income. But these exceptions only proved the rule. Although closely related to the industry, German tourism research even failed to give birth to a national survey. This urgent "puzzle" thus had to be solved by other scientists.

In the wake of the postwar "economic miracle" in West Germany, tourism recovered quickly. By the mid-1950s, the prewar travel intensity was exceeded; by 1960 it reached some 30%, that is to say, tourism grew but the majority was still excluded.[20] Nonetheless, concern about the leisure time of the "masses" began to feature in the repertoire of social scientists. In this discourse, ideas from North America, but more especially from France, played an important role.[21] It is hence a bit arbitrary to split the discourse along language lines, even though there were certain idiomatic peculiarities. Be that as it may, in the postwar Central European discourse, it was mainly West Germany which set the tone.[22] Here, two main threads can be distinguished.

The Study Circle for Tourism.   On the one hand, within sociology and education an empirical "youth and leisure research" emerged. In this connection, and in 1961, the interdisciplinary *Studienkreis für Tourismus* (StfT) or Study Circle for Tourism, was founded by a handful of scholars from academia and experts from the industry and the church (Meyer and Meyer 2007; Schrand 2007). As the word *Tourismus* indicates, the Study Circle distanced itself from the narrow research on *Fremdenverkehr*. Mainspring and long-standing director was the psychologist Heinz Hahn. Although he published sparsely, he was nevertheless a brilliant organizer and mastermind, motivated by the ideal of European understanding and of the tourist emancipation of the lower classes. The StfT, sited in Starnberg near Munich, financed and carried out various social and cultural studies. The result was often a "gray literature" that rarely found its way into libraries. In this regard, there were several pioneering "observation studies" (ethnological field studies focusing on tourist behavior, such as beach life), even if they were rather descriptive in nature (Mayntz 1961). Methodologically, more sophisticated was the quantitative research, which from 1970 onwards ushered in the extensive yearly *Reiseanalyse* (Travel Survey) that instantly became the standard data source for the holiday behavior of West Germans.[23] In addition, the StfT initiated research in neighboring fields, such as social psychology and cultural history (Hahn and Schade 1969; Hartmann 1982; Spode 1987), and became a major contributor to the Yearbook for International Youth Encounter. Each year dozens of books and booklets were published or initiated by the StfT ranging from informative literature to extensive empirical studies (Kentler et al 1965; Studienkreis 1969) and valuable overviews (Wagner 1970).

The *Studienkreis* fostered mass education as well as research, thereby leaving behind the limited scope of the established tourism science. However, the nonprofit organization did not institutionally collaborate with universities. Instead, its main economic pillar was the Travel Survey financed by the industry, while a secondary source of income derived from its pedagogical publications on behalf of government agencies and foundations. Its proximity to politics and economics rendered the *Studienkreis* vulnerable and hampered the development of pure research. So did the diversity of its objectives. Consequently the StfT failed to establish an institutionalized academic field of cultural and social tourism science. No journal (according to Kuhn (1962), a precondition for a scientific community) was founded and there was virtually no cooperation with experts from abroad. Thus, its seminal work remained unknown outside Central Europe. Due to waning support from the industry and growing inner tensions, in 1993 the *Studienkreis* ceased operations.[24] The Travel Survey, however, was continued by a commercial institution (which, contrary to the practice of the StfT, strictly limited access to its data).

The Sociological-Historical Debate. On the other hand, exponents of *Kulturkritik* (cultural criticism) discussed the "problem" of leisure. In a nutshell, philosophers and sociologists, like Theodor W. Adorno (1969a, 1969b) and Jürgen Habermas (1973), criticized capitalism in general, and the "cultural industry" in particular, for "manipulating" people. For them, the freedom and individuality of leisure activities constituted an illusion, if not a dangerous fantasy preventing the "masses" from struggling for their rights. Here, the key concept was the Hegelian *Entfremdung* (alienation) which had been made popular by the "early" Marx[25] whose works had been rediscovered by the "New Left" (also called the "Frankfort School"). According to them, capitalism "alienated" persons from their "natural" needs, suppressed their "freedom," and dismembered the old, holistic *Lebenswelt* (lifeworld)—and, as the carrot to that stick, offered the surrogate joys of consumption and leisure time. Paradoxically enough, these "critical" Leftist analyses, especially those of Adorno, defended bourgeois high-brow culture against a growing tide of "shallow," commercialized mass culture, whereas the circle around Hahn assumed a principally positive stance toward mass tourism as a means of physical and psychological regeneration and of widening the horizon (even though Marxist positions were also published by the StfT). The controversy was thus about the "right" use of time[26]: another phase in the continual (from time to time expanding) moral and political struggle ongoing since the days of the campaign for "rational recreation" in 19th century England.[27]

With respect to tourism, the "critical" approach was further elaborated by the young author and philosopher Hans-Magnus Enzensberger (1958).[28] His "Theory of Tourism" was the first sophisticated attempt to explain tourist motives; at the same time it laid out the paradoxes of tourism in particular and of modernity in general. To this end, it drew on the concept of "alienation," but even more (as text analysis reveals) it was based upon the influential "Dialectic of Enlightenment" by Horkheimer and Adorno pointing out that rationality destroyed its own premises (an intellectual thread that could be traced back to Marx and Weber, if not to Rousseau). Enzensberger, in his ingenious historical master narrative linked the birth of tourism to the French Revolution and the subsequent period of romanticism, and concluded that tourism was an "escape from the self-made reality," namely from the restraints of bourgeois-capitalist society.[29] Although the Revolution had opened the window of "freedom," it was soon closed again, thereby leaving a scar in the hearts of the people. This desire became the motive for the rapid growth of tourism, while at the same time capitalism provided the means of cheap mass travel by "standardization, assembling, and serial production." Enzensberger held that such an escape would be in vain, since the tourist world would become as constrained and well organized as the ordinary world: tourists destroyed their goals the moment they attained them. Consequently, holiday trips resulted in a latent disappointment. Yet Enzensberger did not join in the widespread ridiculing of tourists. Instead he felt pity for tourists as victims of an inhuman society caught up in a futile search for "freedom and happiness"—since unconsciously "the tourist criticizes that from which he turns away."

The Austrian economist Arnold E. Pöschl, too, saw the roots of the "seasonal urban flight" in romanticism and regarded the tourist as a fugitive (1971). But while Enzensberger's tourist wanted to escape from a repressive society, Pöschl's tourist took flight from the unhealthy, crowded metropolises (1962)—a notion not in the Marxist tradition but resuming an anti-urbanism in vogue since the turn of the century, along with élitist concepts of the "masses" à la Ortega y Gasset. With less cultural critical verve, the Swiss sociologist Josef Leugger also analyzed tourism—just as Fontane had previously done—as a relief from the strain of everyday and working life, and called it "an indispensable element of social integration"

(Leugger 1959, 1966). Like Enzensberger, he maintained that the "economic principle" tended to pervert the tourist world. But more than Leugger or Pöschl, the layman Enzensberger, whose essay was reprinted several times, gained substantial influence in the scholarly debate about tourism, particularly from the Left—although, however, often in an oversimplified form. The sociologist Helmut Kentler, for example, defined tourism as a "counter-world" which allowed for an annual "departure from society" (Kentler et al 1965). This was not far from Leugger's Functionalism, but he drew the opposite conclusions when he rendered harsh political judgements; tourism provided a "surrogate satisfaction" for otherwise suppressed needs and thus became an instrument of power assuring the continuance of the repressive society.

Attention among experts attracted in particular the sociological dissertation by Hans-Joachim Knebel on the "Structural Changes in Tourism." He defined tourism as "travel that does not serve evident purposes" (1960:5) and the tourist role—in opposition to the daily and the weekend leisure time—as a "total role." Knebel outlined how tourism had developed from older forms of travel and then step by step had become a mass phenomenon. Drawing on David Riesman and Thorstein Veblen, he stated that it was an important field for *demonstrativer Erfahrungskonsum* (conspicuous consumption of experience) that had become part of the modern conformistic, "outer directed" lifestyle. Although Boorstin's famous critique of tourism and "pseudo-events" came up only after the dissertation, Knebel's highbrow view of mass culture was comparable to Boorstin's conservative mindset. For its historical and empirical shortcomings and the overestimation of social prestige as a main motive for vacation trips the study was harshly criticized (Nettekoven 1972). Still, this first sociological monograph on tourism was full of lucid ideas. Like Enzensberger's essay it was a courageous attempt to link tourist motives and behavior with historically changing "social characters" or mentalities, respectively.

The cultural criticism of tourism (be it of a Leftist or élitist nature) was attacked by liberal sociologists. René König, a leading light of "empirical social research," called it a "shallow pseudo-science" (foreword in Nettekoven 1972:xiv). In this connection, some scholars tried to grasp the functions and motivational structures of tourism in different ways. There was Peter Gleichmann (1969, 1973), for instance, who, drawing on Simmel, looked for *Agens* (the motive force) of tourism and found it in a parlous balance between farness and nearness: the universal "figuration of the stranger."

Simultaneously Erwin Scheuch drew on Simmel even though he regarded the "stranger" as a typical modern social type (Scheuch 1969, 1981).[30] In an extensive article for the *Handbook of Empirical Social Research*, he made good use of the empirical materials of the *Studienkreis*. Scheuch defined tourism formally as *Freizeitreise* (leisure travel); similar to Leugger and others (Mitscherlich 1965), he stated that the *leitmotiv* was to dissociate from the everyday environment. Yet, rebutting Enzensberger, he underlined that distance seeking did not mean negation of the ordinary; instead it helped testing the boundaries of the own character or role set, respectively. Thus, tourist behavior tended to act out the complete opposite of the respective everyday routine and varied accordingly. Rejecting the concept of alienation, Scheuch called the idea of an integral personality, which had been destroyed by the capitalist division of labor, a "lunacy." In certain contradiction to these arguments, however, he also remarked that the tourist world often corresponded to the *solidarité mécanique* (mechanical solidarity) as opposed to *solidarité organique* (the organic solidarity) of the ordinary world.[31] Scheuch disagreed with the assumption that the restraints in capitalism had grown at the expense of freedom of choice. Instead he believed that a gain in the latter had sharpened an awareness of the confining mesh of mutual obligations.

A contrary approach was suggested by the emigrant sociologist Norbert Elias. In his (up to the 1970s virtually ignored) benchmark study of 1939 (see also Elias 1982), he had analyzed the "civilizing process" as a growing network of "chains of interdependency" resulting in increasing self-control. Accordingly, in an essay he conceived leisure time as an enclave for "controlled de-controlling" (Elias 1972). Likewise, Paul Rieger, a co-founder of the *Studienkreis*, spoke of "islands in the industrial society" (Lutz 1992:243). This was not far from notions of the cultural critique even though neither was identified with the Frankfort School.

In summary, from the late 1950s to the early 1970s, there was a lively controversy on leisure time and tourism, often accompanied by innovative research designs. In this debate, the specialized *Fremdenverkehrswissenschaft* had fallen virtually silent. Instead, the interdisciplinary *Studienkreis* took over its role. In contrast to Hunziker and Krapf's wide but empty definition, the Study Circle as well as Enzensberger and most of the other theorists, regarded tourism—as Stradner once did, and as everyday conventional wisdom now does—as a modern, particular type of travel, driven by special motives. Thus, regardless of their directions, these approaches felt the need to argue historically in order to draw the line between pre-tourism and tourism.

From the 1970s to the 1990s

During the 1970s, however, the sociological-philosophical discourse petered out; in those times of upheaval the focus of the social sciences was on production rather than consumption, on "hard" rather than "soft" topics. While the English-speaking world set off to overcome its belatedness in tourism research and while new journals were founded and new approaches were discussed, the Central European debate stagnated and made itself comfortable behind its language barrier. The Neo-Marxist critique was confirmed by some (Armanski 1978, also 1997; Mäder 1982) who labeled tourism an "escape agent," others went further. As in many Western countries, there was a growing tide of anti-tourism which denounced tourists as exploiters and crusaders imposing their questionable values on the Third World (Beutel et al 1978).[32] A more balanced and well-informed overview of the past and present of tourism was provided by the sociologist Prahl and the geographer Steinecke (1979). Whereas they drew on Enzensberger and Kentler when they conceived tourism as a temporary flight from alienation, the dissertation by Hömberg (1977) took up Leugger's and Scheuch's ideas and tried to combine them with Luhmann's System Theory. This was a promising but misfired attempt—after all, the System Theory was still *in statu nascendi*. Also Claude Kaspar (1975) (and see in Haedrich et al 1998), the new director in Sankt Gallen, spoke of "systems" but did not make clear whether this framework referred to the established structural-functionalist theory of Talcott Parsons or the new communication theory by Niklas Luhmann. His often-reprinted textbook was a sort of update of the one by Hunziker and Krapf, and hence confirmed the insignificance of the *Fremdenverkehrswissenschaft* in the discourse on tourism. Yet, Bernecker et al (1984:29f), the first named then doyen of this discipline, made the daring claim that "the basic research is principally completed," and rejected all cultural approaches as an amateurish intrusion into the sphere of professional research. In the history of science such smugness had often turned out to be premature.

Tourism Critique.   Indeed, the Bern Institute had begun to assume quite a different tone. Under the direction of Jost Krippendorf, it became a bastion of "tourism critique." As a result, the *entente cordiale* between Sankt Gallen, Vienna, and Bern was substantially affected. Although Krippendorf derived many of his ideas from Enzensberger's escape theory, he nevertheless concentrated upon the effects of, rather than the reasons for that flight. According to him and his associates, the tourism industry was a "devourer of landscapes" (Krippendorf et al 1985). Unlike the older cultural critique, the starting point of "tourism critique" was not the traveler but the *Bereiste* (the "traveled"), or the threat to destination culture and the ecological environment. Activists of that movement—an offspring of the anti-tourism and part of the broader green movement—pleaded for a "soft," "alternative," or "different" tourism, in which the industry, but more so individual tourists, had to alter their behavior. Their basic text stemmed from Robert Jungk (once a futurologist and an ardent proponent of nuclear energy) who released a list of 17 commandments that should guide the "sympathetic" tourist: be tactful, quiet, eager to learn, inner-directed, and the like (Krippendorf et al 1985:60). Like its opponent, the established tourism science, "tourism critique" was only interested in practical issues. Although it claimed a "new understanding" (Krippendorf 1984), its theoretical contribution to that end was quite marginal.[33]

New Institutions and New Approaches.   These attacks shook up the small cadre of tourism researchers. Some began to cooperate with the Study Circle, while others sought to establish new institutions. Of great influence on the media was the commercial "British American Tobacco (BAT)-Leisure-Institute,"[34] founded in 1979 in Hamburg by the educationist Horst W. Opaschowski. Journalists called him the "tourism pope" but in the scientific community his reputation was not so infallible, in spite of his publishing a useful, often reprinted introduction to the structure and theory of tourism (Opaschowski 1989, 2002, 2006). More within the framework of the established tourism science fresh ground was broken in West Berlin when in 1984 geographers, economists, and historians founded the "Institute for Tourism" at the *Freie Universität*[35] as the first interdisciplinary university tourism institute after the war. In addition to its more conventional teaching and empirical research, it expanded its remit to the sphere of culture. Tying in with the *genius loci* of Robert Glücksmann, in the late 1980s it established the "Historical Archive on Tourism" (HAT) and, together with the Study Circle, launched a working group dedicated to "historical tourism research."[36]

The background to this initiative was a growing discontent with the a-historical, business-dominated tourism science (even within that scientific community). In cooperation with tourism researchers, the sociologist Dietrich Storbeck founded a project team in order to produce an inter-disciplinary synopsis that included historical, psychological, and sociological essays (1988a), even though its impact on the debate was limited. So, too, was von Böventer's Tourism Theory (1989) which—following the "rational choice" approach—analyzed the tourist as *homo oeconomicus* always eager to optimize his decisions. In 1993, however, the dissatisfaction led to the pioneering handbook on *Tourismuswissenschaft* (Tourism Science), edited by Heinz Hahn and H. Jürgen Kagelmann. Gathering entries from many different professions and viewpoints, it constituted a breakthrough in original thinking. The introductory articles outlined the historical development and then the theoretical approaches of the disciplines involved in tourism research, with a particular focus on sociological and psychological entries;[37] subsequent articles discussed key terms, like "authenticity" or "mental maps"; and finally, empirical topics and methods were presented (Hahn and Kagelmann 1993). The authors were unaware of Hunziker's "System of Scientific Tourism Research" but unconsciously they celebrated an anniversary because exactly 50 years later the *Handbook of Tourism Science* renewed Hunziker's claim that: "tourism research (is) a branch of the social sciences" (Hahn and Kagelmann 1993:ix). The compendium can be considered as the legacy of the *Studienkreis* which was closed down shortly after. Admittedly, not all entries were of the same excellent standard, but on the whole the compendium was a unique attempt toward an all-embracing perspective on tourism, still useful although unfortunately not updated in later years.

The reunification in 1990, which altered Germany in so many fields, had virtually no impact on the theoretical debate.[38] But since then the topic "tourism" ranked higher in the public consciousness than it did in the former West Germany. The number of private and public economics colleges and university institutes[39] that offered tourism studies increased massively and ended the "Alpine" hegemony (including the residual significance of their two journals). So too did related work in the social sciences correspondingly expand (Schimany 1999). Whether it was the decline of the old industries in Eastern Germany—comparable to the interwar period—or due to latent tendencies in the humanities becoming manifest, tourism certainly grew in stature.

Already in the 1970s, a couple of social historians had worked on tourism; in particular the Third Reich attracted their attention and gave rise to more general considerations on the role of tourism in different political and social systems.[40] Apart from this, Wolfgang Schivelbusch's dissertation (1977) on the 19th century "industrialization of time and space" was a landmark study in historical anthropology. By the 1980s, the folklore (also called European ethnology or cultural anthropology) and the history of art and of literature had discovered travel and tourism as an object of research (e.g., Wahrlich 1984).[41] The 1987 German folklore congress was on the "experience of strangeness" (Greverus et al 1988), followed by the formation of a tourism section and by several publications,[42] among them a programmatic outline by the Swiss Ueli Gyr (1988). Not too far removed from Knebel's ideas, it stated that tourist behavior was characterized by a break with the ordinary, by selective and standardized perception and by the ritualized consumption of symbols (and that it resulted *inter alia* in a gain of prestige).

Last but not least the historical-anthropological question was put as to how people view "nature," a thread that can traced back to Jacob Burckhardt's renaissance study from 1859. A bit ahead of his time was Ritter's philosophy of "landscape" from 1963 (here 1974:141–163) but then research gained momentum (Bodenstein 1972; Bopp et al 1981; Groh and Groh 1991/1996; Hartmann 1982; Pikulik 1979; Weber 1989); in particular there was Corbin's influence on the "delights of the coast" and Schivelbusch's notion of the "panoramic view"[43] (1977) which met with considerable response in and outside the scholarly debate. Long before John Urry coined the "tourist gaze," in-depth studies about long-term changes in the social construction of "nature" and "landscape" paved the way toward a better understanding of the origins and specifics of tourist perception (Spode 1995).

The Turn of the Millennium

The gradually growing interest among scholars from different fields had prepared the ground for the 1993 benchmark work by Hahn and Kagelmann and the atmosphere of departure that followed—a loose circle of two or three dozens scientists, divided in subgroups, set out to rethink tourism research. After the closing of the *Studienkreis* a number of denominational academies took over the twofold task of organizing interdisciplinary meetings and publishing numerous anthologies on the philosophy and theory of tourism; the newly founded publisher, Profil, also launched a series on tourism social science.[44] Finally, two new periodicals staked their claim for a broadened, theory-grounded research. Since they covered different fields, their relation was more of cooperation than concurrence. In 1997, an interdisciplinary group (Tobias Gohlis, Christoph Hennig, H. Jürgen Kagelmann, Dieter Kramer, and Hasso Spode) launched *Voyage. Jahrbuch für Reise & Tourismusforschung* (Voyage: Studies on Travel & Tourism). The yearbook or series, respectively, was to focus on sociological, historical, and cultural studies, including—in the sense of the Nietzschean "merry science"—philosophical essays and sometimes even poems (Spode 1997). Financed by the DuMont publishing house in Cologne, *Voyage* not only targeted the scientific community but also a broader audience. Moreover, in order to foster an international discourse it gathered essays by prominent foreign scholars, while others were appointed to the advisory board.[45] *Voyage* acted as a platform and catalyst for theoretical debate. So, too, although in a different way, did the second new periodical, *Tourismus Journal*, which was founded in 1997 as the brainchild of the sociologist Karlheinz Wöhler (1997) from Lüneburg University. Comparable to *Annals of Tourism Research* this quarterly intended more to reform tourism science from within than did *Voyage*. Unlike the latter it was peer reviewed and business economics played a prominent role; nevertheless most issues also contained stimulating articles of a theoretical or historical nature.

Previously Enzensberger had complained about the lack of "understanding" of tourism; now the established research was attacked for chiefly consisting of "short-winded polls, vacuous buzzwords and dubious future scenarios" (Spode 1997), and, in order to overcome the "reserve of tourism science towards theory" (Vester 1998a), new approaches were discussed. As in other countries (Dann 1997a), much debate was on the paradigmatic nature of a prospective *Tourismuswissenschaft* (e.g., Pompl 1994). While some orthodox tourism scientists rejected such a project as both uncalled-for and impossible, others pleaded for an "integrated discipline" (Wöhler 1997), a "trans-disciplinary tourism science" (Schrand 1998) or for a wide "platform" as an "interpretative frame" that could "organize" research (Spode 1998c; Wöhler 1998a; cf. Groß 2004; Reeh 2005:Chapter 3).

In this connection, the sociologist Heinz-Günter Vester (1997, 1999) analyzed some of the "classical" general grand theories with respect to their potential contribution to tourism theory; but none of it, he argued, was suitable to ground such a theory[46] and no synthesis was offered that could function as a "framework." This task was undertaken by a number of scholars who took up the threads of the earlier discussion and combined them with different grand theories. Here, the effects of tourism as well as its functional structures (staging, rites of passage, etc.) were discussed, but the most fascinating point remained the motive forces (or "push-factors"). Admittedly, a controversial exercise in face of the diversity of tourist practices (Scheuch 1969) ranging from "collective" to "romantic" types, from "autonomy" to "security," from "tension" to "relaxation" (Graf 2002; Pagenstecher 2003a)—at least, this task required a high level of abstraction. In this connection, the sociologist Ronald Lutz (1992) even tried to unite all reasonable explanations as conceptual approaches when he classified tourism as a "product of industrial society" that at the same time represented the universal phenomenon of an "upside-down world" and expressed a "specific human need." While omitting the latter point, the sociologist Hennig (see below) and the historian/sociologist Spode (2001) also developed anthropological perspectives on the interplay of universal and modern patterns.

Already by 1987 Spode had related tourism to the "simultaneity of the non-simultaneous" engendered by the "rationalizing" or "civilizing pro-cess." Drawing on Elias, Foucault, Koselleck, and others, this historical outline was elaborated into a complex theory (1995, 2009). As in the earlier debate, it conceived tourism as a novel type of travel that did not serve manifest purposes.[47] The tourist view and its performance, tourism, were based upon three intertwined developments that in the 18th century resulted in a synergetic process: technically upon an improvement of security and infrastructures, cognitively upon the "historification" of knowledge, space, and culture, and psychologically upon the deep ambivalence toward so-called "progress." This process allowed for a "backwards time-travel with return-ticket" (Spode 1995:112). Confirming Eric Leed's suggestions, this had both a cultural-cognitive and a biographic-psychological dimension. Tourists were in search of a "fountain of youth," of a world they had, supposedly or actually, lost (a Shangri-La of naturalness and hence of freedom, simplicity, authenticity, and coherence), be it in a lonesome Alpine hut or at an alcohol saturated beach party. Like Enzensberger, Spode regarded tourism as a clue to the modern *conditio humana* and linked its emergence to romanticism. Yet, here this term had, in opposition to the common usage since Goethe, a different, fundamental meaning: not a temporary successor of the enlightenment but its twin[48] and to this day part and parcel of our mentality. "Progress" (always perceived as "accelerated") produced both profits and losses; the one triggered belief in the "future," the other belief in "nature" and the "past." In other words modernization generated nostalgia[49] and thus, *inter alia*, tourism.

A different attempt to reveal the motivational and functional structures of tourism was made by Hennig (1997, 1998a, 1998b). While Spode sought the *specific* characteristics of tourism and to a certain degree agreed with Enzensberger's approach,[50] Hennig looked for the *universal* features that underlay tourist behavior and (comparable to Scheuch's analysis) strongly opposed the escape theory since it was grounded in a latent anti-tourism which labeled tourists fugitives, ignored the joys and fascination of travel, as well as its benefits for both the individual and society. Instead, Hennig highlighted the anthropological phenomenon of a temporary upside-down or time-out world, respectively. Applying a broad theoretical background ranging from Morin to Turner, he stressed the contrast between the ordinary and the extraordinary and the respective rites of passage as universal structures, whereby he was emphasizing the playful and fictional nature of tourist experiences and the distinctiveness of tourist roles, rules, and rituals, according to which tourism was "a functional equivalent to the pre-modern feast" (1998b:65). Of particular importance was the relation of "tourism and imagination." On this point, Hennig actually confirmed Enzensberger's ideas when he stated that the origins of tourism had been closely linked to the fictional spaces in arts and literature, and that tourists still tried to make dreams come true: they looked for "pictures" predetermined in the collective imagination (1998b:7, 2002). Thus, all pedagogical efforts to turn tourists into studious ethnologists would be inappropriate and futile. In his book "wanderlust" Hennig embedded this theory in a brilliant general view of the social, cultural, and economic aspects of modern tourism (1999).

While Hennig had given a more sketchy view on the tourism economy, Wöhler developed a complex economic theory along the "transaction cost" hypothesis and framed it within Luhmann's concept of the economic subsystem and Enzensberger's notion of the standardized travel business (1998b). Other theoretical reflections were more on present-day traits and recent developments in tourism than on basic structures. In this connection "lifestyle," "event," and "experience" were researched, often drawing on Gerhard Schulze's notion of the "Experience Society" (Berger 1999; Georg 1995; Kagelmann 2007). There was also some discussion of "cultural contact" (Thiem 1994), the tourist body (Wang 2003), and its nourishment (Lanfant 2002). But in particular the concepts of "space," "authenticity," and "postmodernity" were connected and vividly discussed. Modifying the classical definitions of tourism, Wöhler emphasized that tourism meant consumption of space and declared the abstract entity of "space" to be the central topic of a prospective tourism science (1997); and this space, he stated, was disappearing. In a series of articles, Wöhler analyzed the postmodern "tourism without space." In the 1970s, a "de-localization" had set in that had meanwhile reached a stage of an unlimited willingness and capability to make tourism spaces (Wöhler 1998c, 2003, 2005a; Wöhler and Saretzki 1996).[51] While in sociology the concept of postmodernity started to become passé, it was now fashionable in tourism research. Vester, for example, suggested that the "question of identity and authenticity" had emerged as a "sham-question," meaningless to post-tourists (1998b). Others, however, opposed such ideas. They objected that the philosophical destruction of reality,[52] and hence of authenticity, did not affect the psychological desire for genuineness (Häußler 1997; Hennig 1999: Chapter 9). In this vein, Regina Bormann—rejecting Marc Augé's term *non-lieux* (non-places) as a resurrection of alienation theory—argued that space was principally constructed, and moreover it was an inappropriate entity for sociological analysis which had to "explain the social by the social" in the Durkheimian sense (2000).

The discussion reached its peak in the late 1990s, in particular with a conference at the Loccum Protestant Academy in 1998,[53] where the leading tourism economist Walter Freyer exclaimed: "tourism is economically a giant but scientifically a dwarf"; it was also there that Hennig and Wöhler presented their tourism theories mentioned above, and where Spode analyzed mainstream research as *Kunstlehre*, as a device to produce instructions instead of posing questions. The discourse encompassed a wide range of disciplines, topics, and concepts, ranging from the notion of tourism as a modern form of universal structures or as a *longue durée* since the 18th century to the notion of an essentially new, postmodern tourism.[54] But once more the rebirth of the theoretical debate finally occurred separately from the tourism science establishment. Now calling itself likewise *Tourismuswissenschaft*, it looked for while as if it was about to transcend its economic-prone, if not anti-intellectual, narrowness. Particularly its geographical branch, traditionally more open to sociological and historical approaches, was affected by the pioneering spirit.[55] In 1996, and in certain contrast to the pedestrian AIEST, the "German Society for Tourism Science" (DGT) was founded. It was underlined that tourism was a "cross-section phenomenon" that called for interdisciplinary research, and in order to assure an appropriate level, membership was limited to holders of a doctorate; at least—as Glücksmann once did—the DGT felt the need to accumulate cultural, namely erudite capital.

However, the deep gap between pure and applied sciences proved to be all too deep. Step by step the DGT lowered the criteria for membership and the business economists took command. Under their supremacy it finally returned to the 1950s and became a platform for an ancillary science that tendered itself to the business world. Although the DGT backed the *Tourismus Journal*, social and cultural scientists increasingly raised the levels of discomfort, if not feelings of inferiority, among mainstream tourism researchers. "They use us as 'sparring partners,'" Freyer complained (2005).[56]

On one point, though, the new tourism research became reconciled to the old one. Now the "critical" Neo-Marxist attitude virtually vanished, and in its place a more descriptive or neutral attitude of their former "liberal" opponents set the tone, whenever, for example, problems of "sustainability" or "cultural contact" were discussed.

CONCLUSION

To everything there is a season. Placing the development of German language tourism research under review, a certain pattern emerges. There were three "hot" phases of theoretical innovation, each separated by two or three decades of "normal science" if not stagnation. These hot phases first comprised the 1930s and 1940s, when Glücksmann and his Swiss successors established the paradigm and the institutional backbone of tourism science; second they occurred in the 1960s, when the Study Circle boosted interdisciplinary research and the sociological debate on leisure and tourism flourished; and third they took place in the 1990s, when social scientists revolted against the "a-theoretical state" of established research and new journals provided an arena for equally novel ideas. If that pattern is correct, the next "hot" phase will be a long time coming.

As for today, with central "interpretative frames" of the 1990s continuing to structure debate, there has been a movement toward less spectacular work in research, and the vision of an "integrated discipline" that comprises new and orthodox science has vanished. Instead, and as an outcome of the recent "hot" phase, tourism social science, in addition to the economic and geographical branches, has been established as a third branch of tourism research. Among these scientists there is a wing that is oriented toward historically based theories and one that is oriented toward analyses of the present, each of them related to their respective mother-disciplines.[57] Although both work intimately together, the void left by the *Studienkreis* has still to be filled, especially against a background of backlashes: the *Tourismus Journal* ceasing publication in 2007, *Voyage* suffering from cutbacks,[58] and the Berlin Tourism Institute shutting down.[59] But although its institutional position remains weak, even more fragile than it was in the 1990s, socio-historical tourism research continues to flourish.

As it once was in 1960s, German tourism theory is (thanks, above all, to Hennig, Kagelmann, Vester, and Wöhler) involved in international developments again;[60] nowadays, moreover, its output in terms of conventions, books, and articles is considerably higher than it used to be. Thus, first it requires a dedicated analysis of its own to portray the current German discourse and second it is increasingly difficult to separate it from other "national" discourses. Of course there remain slight differences in theoretical mindsets. Roughly speaking, Central Europeans continue to look upon tourists as fugitives, whereas Anglo-Americans still tend to regard them as pilgrims. It also seems that among German-speaking scholars (as in many other Continental European countries), there is greater reluctance toward "free-floating" postmodern thinking than there is among their English-speaking colleagues. Both groups, however, make use of a shared vocabulary of general concepts like "construction," "gaze," "distinction," "liminality," etc., and as a further common denominator they usually[61] regard the tourism world as structurally distinct from the ordinary one.

In addition to general "classical" grand theories, those of Bourdieu, Elias, or Simmel, for instance, some non-translated works on tourism had and continue to have considerable impact on the Central European discourse,[62] especially Urry's ideas on the "tourist gaze." His application of *le regard* (derived from Foucault) became a sort of *de rigueur* fixed expression for scholars describing tourist behavior, and at times his work functioned as an advocacy for the notion of post-tourism. This popularity, however, may be seen as a setback compared to the general body of acquired knowledge.[63] Admittedly, it is extremely difficult to say what constitutes progress in such understanding (Spode 1999). One reason lies in the "inconceivable complexity" of the social world, to use the expression of Luhmann. Probably all ways imaginable of reducing that complexity have been principally explored by philosophers since the 18th century, or since the interwar period at the latest, when sociological and anthropological theorists sought to "fill the explanatory gaps of Marxism" (K.-S. Rehberg in Spode 1999:34). Another reason lies in the limited memory capacities of the sciences in tandem with the constant demand for "innovation" in the "business" of academia. However, while the natural sciences can abandon theories and other knowledge as "falsified," the social sciences lack the mechanisms for discarding theories once and for all; instead knowledge goes out of fashion and evaporates—and sometimes returns in a new guise. Yet, if the progress of knowledge is to be more than a cliché, we need to maintain a cumulative memory that in a disciplined manner builds on the past and present and points to the future. This essay should be seen as a small contribution to that goal.

NOTES

1. Although this essay is mainly about grand theories or "narratives" of the tourism social sciences, it also traces the development of applied tourism science; for the different meanings and usages of "theory" see Spode (1998c) and Vester (1998a). Here, due to limits of space, only a selection of the pertinent literature can be provided. For the same reason general "classical" grand theories, ranging from Durkheim to Giddens (on the corpus of sociological "classics" see Barlösius

2004), are not included in this review; neither are tourism studies from outside Central Europe, ranging from MacCannell to Urbain (see the respective essays in this book), except for selected overviews and for some articles published in German only. For other criteria concerning exclusion or inclusion see endnotes 6 and 37. I am deeply indebted to Graham Dann for reading the various drafts of this chapter.

2. See Spode (2007a:25). An offprint of Brougier's speech is held in the Historical Archive on Tourism (HAT) and in the Bavarian State Library, where there is also a small offprint by the Swiss Guyer-Freuler (1903) who likewise regarded tourist travel as a typical modern phenomenon.

3. The English word *tourist* entered the German language shortly after 1800; it solely referred to mobile tourists (hikers, excursionists, short-time visitors). The technical term *Fremdenverkehr* first appeared around 1850; in translated versions it also became common in Eastern and Northern Europe. In the late 20th century it was more or less replaced by *Tourismus*; cf. Liebman Parrinello (2007), Opaschowski (1989), Pagenstecher (2003a), and Spode (2007b). For the scientific definitions see also Arndt (1978), Bernecker (1952), Cohen (1974), Gleichmann (1969), Hömberg (1977), Mundt (2001), and Spode (1998a).

4. See Bausinger (1995), Schumacher (2002), and Spode (2009).

5. Today the hypothesis that tourism is "the realization of the wanderlust of the human being" (e.g., Gutzler in Tetsch 1978:81), although time and again rejected (e.g., Hennig 1997; Knebel 1960; Scheuch 1969; Spode 1995), has found new advocates in the wake of the rise of genetics as a shibboleth to explain human behavior.

6. Interwar publications on tourism science by German-speaking authors (Adler, Benscheidt, Dietel, Häußler, Jäger, Klafkowski, Krauß, Müller, Neff, Schmidt, Simon, Sputz, Warnecke, etc.) according to the HAT catalog and the *Archiv für den Fremdenverkehr* (Archive of Tourism); cf. also the sources given in Hunziker and Krapf (1942), Knebel (1960), Norval (1936), and Spode (1998a, 1998b). Here only the most important books are included in the references.

7. By 1914 he had already founded a college for "tourist and hotel business" that closed in 1921.

8. For an early discussion of definitions see *Archiv für den Fremdenverkehr* 1–5 (1930–1935), passim.

9. Today copies are held in Berlin (HAT), Leipzig (DNB), Frankfort (IHK), Cologne (UB), Kiel (ZBW), Basle (SWA), and Innsbruck (UB).

10. On Glücksmann's biography, see Moß (2000).

11. For references see Spode (2009) and note 40.

12. Due to war the next congress, planned for 1940 in Osaka, was cancelled. As a symptomatic case of academic amnesia, 24 years later in Japan a "First World Recreation Congress" was held.

13. Additionally, there were some dissertations, but mostly on juridical aspects (cf. Spode 1982).

14. It followed that of Gölden's excellent study (1939:8), and was adopted by the International Association of Scientific Experts in Tourism (AIEST) in 1954; it is—slightly modified—still the state-of-the-art. Also the statistics of the World Tourism Organization (UNWTO) lump together virtually all varieties of cross-border traffic under the term "tourism" (cf. note 3).

15. To this day graphics of that kind, though less poetically explained, are very popular with authors of tourism textbooks (for a critique cf. Spode (2003a) with a reprint of the "ur-crystal").

16. The works of Radcliffe-Brown and Malinowski on the one hand and Cassirer on the other were unknown to Hunziker, and Parson's grand theory was not yet written; based on apparently vague information, he created a Functionalism for his own purposes.

17. In the East there were later also institutes in Greifswald and Leipzig; in the West institutes in Heidelberg (already founded in 1941), Frankfort and later in Salzburg were of a short lifespan; cf. Drechsel (1988), Spode (1998a) on tourism geography cf. Becker et al (2007, part I), Steinecke in Hahn and Kagelmann (1993), Wolf and Jurczek (1986).

18. During the Nazi period Christaller was engaged in "relocation" planning in occupied Poland. After the war he converted to Communism and worked for the Polish government, and later as a Social Democrat he became a leading figure in the regional planning of West Germany.

19. The *Materialien zur Fremdenverkehrsgeographie* (Materials on Tourism Geography) from the Hannover Academy especially the anthology Akademie (1969) deserves mentioning.

20. Thanks to high subsidies in the GDR, travel intensity grew in a corresponding fashion (cf. Pagenstecher 2003a; Spode 1996, 2009).

21. To mention R. Barthes, D. Boorstin, S. de Grazia, J. Dumazedier, H. Lefebvre, and D. Riesman; in addition the inspiring essay by the Dutch historian J. Huizinga—first published in 1938 in German—on the role of playful action in human history became a best-seller (cf. note 1).

22. Although East German scholars contributed much to tourism history, few contributed to theory. However, an interesting definition was given by H. Uebel, Director of the Dresden Institute. He defined *Tourismus* as a subgroup of *Fremdenverkehr* characterized by recreation and voluntariness (cf. Nettekoven 1972:36f).

23. In contrast to the wide definitions of AIEST and UNWTO, the German *Reiseanalyse* (Travel Survey) only counted tourist travel (*Urlaubsreisen*).

24. The archive of the StfT had been split; its remains are now kept at the HAT in Berlin (*Reiseanalyse* etc.) and at the *Zentralarchiv für Empirische Sozialforschung* (Central Archive for Empirical Research) in Cologne (especially *Reiseanalyse*); some materials also found their way into the vaults of Dresden University.

25. Only in the course of the debate, by around 1970, the "late" Marx became the "bible" of Leftist thinking: in his *Kapital* he finally had broken with the concept of alienation.

26. … whereby a line of demarcation was drawn between the vulgar *Freizeit* (leisure time) and the noble *Muße*, a virtually untranslatable term that refers to the ancient ideal of *otium* (cf. Timm 1968 and Lanfant in this volume).

27. For a discussion of post-war leisure and tourism research see Andreae (1970), Bausinger (1981), Eichler (1979), Gemünden (1996), Giesecke (1968), Gleichmann (1969), Hammerich (1974), Hlavin-Schulze (1998), Hömberg (1977), Huck (1980), Nahrstedt (1972), Prahl (2002), Prahl and Steinecke (1981), Scheuch (1969), Schmitz-Scherzer (1973, 1975), Schumacher et al (1993),

Spode (1995, 2001), Storbeck (1988b), Tokarski and Schmitz-Scherzer (1985), and Vester (1988).

28. cf. Asmodi in Hahn and Kagelmann (1993), Liebman Parrinello (2006), Pagenstecher (1998a), Spode (1995).

29. Much of the historical material of the essay simply stemmed from an old encyclopedia. Nonetheless, as Pagenstecher and Liebman Parrinello rightly insist, it is all but outdated: For its brilliant style and far ranging insights Enzensberger's essay continues to merit the attention of scholars (in contrast to his later remarks on the connection between tourism and "our nomadic past"; cf. Hennig (1997:38).

30. In modified forms Scheuch published this article many times (e.g., in Scheuch and Meyersohn 1972).

31. ... in the sense of Durkheim; one might also speak of "community" (*Gemeinschaft*) versus "society" (*Gesellschaft*) in Tönnies's terms.

32. The anti-tourism combined "anti-imperialism" with the romantic notion of the "noble savage"; for an analysis of the latter see Flitner et al (1997).

33. In particular, it lacked an understanding of its own premises. "Tourism critique" was a new name for the old strategy of social distinction in tourism (cf. Hennig 1999 for additional references). It arose when travel intensity exceeded the 50%-barrier; entrenched in the needs and values of the educated strata it offered no solutions for the tourism of the "masses" (cf. Klemm and Menke 1988).

34. Recently renamed the "BAT-Stiftung für Zukunftsfragen."

35. In 1999 renamed the "Willy-Scharnow-Institut für Tourismus."

36. On this term see briefly the co-founders of the institute W. Eder and K. Klemm in *Touristik & Verkehr* No. 3, 1988:41f, and more detailed Spode in Hahn and Kagelmann (1993:27ff). Up to now the working group held nine symposia (Spode 1991, 1996).

37. Namely history and anthropology (H. Spode), sociology (H.-G. Vester), economics (H. Klopp), geography (A. Steinecke), folklore (D. Kramer), pedagogy (W. Günter, W. Nahrstedt), and psychology (H.-W. Opaschowski, H.J. Kagelmann, and others). At the same time, Kagelmann (1993) had edited an anthology on "tourism science" which gathered older essays, many of them translated. NB. Since Hahn and Kagelmann's compendium alone counts 111 entries, the single articles are not included in this review of the literature and the references.

38. The handful of East German tourism researchers—one of them, B. Benthien, in 1989 became the first and only tourism minister of the GDR—had been engaged in empirical work or, as in the case of Benthien, developed system-functionalist models as part of a "recreational geography," inspired by Soviet studies but rather similar to those in the West.

39. ... namely within the departments of economics, geography, pedagogy and applied cultural studies; see Klemm (1998) and also Becker and Job (2004).

40. Besides sketchy overviews (e.g., Fink 1970; Prahl and Steinecke 1979), the KdF tourism was analyzed especially in Bucholz' unpublished dissertation (1976) and in Spode's Magister Artium thesis (partly published 1982); for further early historical studies see the bibliographies by Hachtmann (2007) and Zimmers (1995).

41. See already Hinske and Müller (1979); an article by Kramer (1982) was only a digest from Prahl and Steinecke but there were four innovative exhibitions on tourism history; in the 1990s the number of such exhibitions increased massively (cf. Spode 2003b). In this context also research in pre-tourist travel was intensified (e.g., Brenner 1989; Griep and Jäger 1983) and an archive on early modern "travel culture" was founded.
42. Including Bausinger et al (1991), Cantauw (1995), Kramer and Lutz (1992).
43. A case already made by Sternberger (1938).
44. *Bensberger Protokolle* (e.g., Taxacher 1998), *Loccumer Protokolle* (e.g., Burmeister 1998), and *Tourismuswissenschaftliche Manuskripte* (e.g., Bachleitner et al 1998).
45. Links to *Voyage* via http://www.wikipedia.org. One such scholar was the French semiotician, Jean-Didier Urbain (1997). Another was Greenblatt (1997).
46. Wöhler (1998b:105) mockingly remarked that, a "theory of tourism" would be like having a "theory of the car"; nonetheless he pleaded for an "over-all model."
47. Only ex-post the 19th century the bourgeoisie invented good reasons to go on holiday, namely health, education, and international understanding. See also the philosopher P. Sloterdijk (2006) who stated that tourism had freed travel from purposes and so had to compensate its "needlessness by cultural signification."
48. After all, it was already Rousseau who made the term "romantic" popular.
49. See also the inspiring study by Fritzsche (2004) on the modern "melancholic" notion of history that allowed for "imaginative journeys backward in time"; unfortunately, like Enzensberger he had based its emergence upon the political event of the French Revolution (cf. Spode's review in *JSH* 38/2007:186ff).
50. He rejected Enzensberger's periodization and, more basically, his starting point: the concept of alienation was itself a romantic notion that stated timeless-universal "human needs," instead of deconstructing them as time-bound.
51. See also, for example, Borghardt (1997), Kagelmann et al 2004, Köck (2001), Shields (1998), and Wöhler (2005b).
52. ... which, by the way, was not an invention of post-modern thinkers but a "continuation of epistemological cleavages that already broke out in the 18th century" (Spode 1999:54).
53. See the report in *Frankfurter Rundschau* (Frankfurt Review) 2/21 (1998), reprinted in Burmeister (1998:239).
54. For the theoretical concepts and/or the research activities see Hennig (1997) as well as Hennig (1999) and Spode (2005); with an emphasis on sociology, see Bachleitner et al (2005), Schimany (1999), and Vester (1998a); on geography, see Hopfinger (2004, 2007), Job (2003), Jurczek (2007), and Reeh (2005); on economics, see Freyer (2005); and on history, see Kopper (2004), Pagenstecher (1998b), and Spode (2003a, 2003b).
55. For the body of knowledge of this subdiscipline see Becker et al (2007), Becker and Job (2004), and Steinecke (2006); for the more economically oriented branch see Freyer (2006), Haedrich et al (1998), and Seitz and Meyer (2005); among good general textbooks are Mundt (2001) and Müller (2002 (2005)).
56. This was not altogether wrong: for a critique of the underexposure of the economy in social and cultural studies, see Wöhler (1998b).
57. ... namely history and sociology, as well as psychology and folklore/anthropology, which itself is divided into an historical and a sociological wing.

58. So does the journal *Cestováni Vcera a Dnes* (Tourism Yesterday and Today) that gathers articles in Czech and German and also contributes to the Central European discourse.

59. A research center grouped around the Historical Archive on Tourism is said to continue, but the associated historical working group had virtually fallen silent and so had the tourism section of the German Sociological Society. Only the tourism section of the folklorists remains active.

60. ... sometimes all too involved: cutting off the theory building in Central Europe, the entry on "tourism sociology" in Hahn and Kagelmann (1993) almost exclusively refers to Anglophone literature. Its authors, conversely, all too often cannot cope with foreign languages, so that the international discourse looks more like a one-way-street; for overviews see Robinson and Phipp (2003) and *Annals of Tourism Research* 18 (1991).

61. For a different stance—the touristification of everyday life—see Gyr (1999), and Köstlin (1995). Already the post-war sociology of leisure was split over the question whether leisure time constituted a structure different from the ordinary world (cf. endnote 27).

62. To mention D. MacCannell as well as M. Augé, E. Cohen, A. Corbin, G. Dann, N. Graburn, J.-C. Kaufmann, E. Leed, O. Löfgren, D. Nash, T. Selwyn, R. Shields, and J.-D. Urbain—(cf. note 1).

63. Already the common English translation "gaze" indicates shortcomings in the understanding of Foucault's "archaeological" approach: applying a subconscious order of things, tourists (like all other people born into an "epistemological field") do not necessarily "gaze," they might as well simply look or view. In doing so, they might wield "power," as tourism critiques underscore, or they just reduce complexity, as sociologists of knowledge suggest. On these and other confusions of post-modern tourism theory see Spode (2005), with respect to the tourist view, cf. also Pagenstecher (2003b), Seyfarth (2007), and to tourist space Bormann (2000).

Chapter 3

Roots of the Sociology of Tourism in France

Marie Françoise Lanfant
CNRS-URESTI, Paris, France

Petit poisson deviendra grand
Pourvu que Dieu lui prête vie;
Mais le lâcher en attendant,
Je tiens pour moi que c'est folie.
(La Fontaine 1950).

A little fish will become a big fish,
As long as God lends him life.
But to let him go while waiting,
For me, that is foolishness.

INTRODUCTION

The formation of a sociology of tourism in France is full of idiosyncrasy and paradox. Because it is a reflexive account, its treatment here is conducted in the first person. Even though what follows has its own logical structure, it cannot be described as systematic, except perhaps in its chronological sequencing of the various links between the founding fathers of sociology, travel accounts, definitional and linguistic implications of the very word

The Sociology of Tourism: European Origins and Developments
Tourism Social Science Series, Volume 12, 95–129
Copyright © 2009 by Emerald Group Publishing Limited
All rights of reproduction in any form reserved
ISSN: 1571-5043/doi:10.1108/S1571-5043(2009)0000012008

tourism, the connection with the sociology of leisure, and finally the emergence of the sociology of tourism itself.

At first glance, we could consider France as a territory particularly suited to the emergence of a sociology of tourism. Over the centuries, it has become a great place for touristic attractions, one which, according to official statistics of the World Tourism Organization (WTO), assumes first place worldwide among countries that are destinations for foreign tourists. This progress did not just happen overnight. The further we go back in time, the more we discover that its territorial space has been ceaselessly crisscrossed by different types of traveler. Marc Boyer (1982) quotes the *Guide of the Ways of France*, "ancestor" of all guides, which dates from 1551. In the Middle Ages several beaconed routes for pilgrims led to the shrine of Santiago de Compostela. In the Gallo-Roman era, Gaul was traversed by armies of centurions, chain gangs of slaves, and by the citizens of the Empire going to and from Rome. There remain traces of routes crossing from Rome to Great Britain, of staging posts and numerous (other) vestiges. Its low cut coastline used to offer numerous possibilities of asylum for adventurers originating from Phoenicia, and further afield, sailing across rough seas. When Gaul was not yet "The Gaul," for centuries, man, whom the theory of evolution had elevated to the category of a superior species, lived on this earth and hollowed out his holiday home in caves where today amazing pictures are still being discovered, in as many niches which give the ethnographer of today an appetite for research.

Thus, France currently presents itself to tourists with its brand image, a repository of curiosities from the era of the Enlightenment, a reliquary, a library, a museum where precious items are assembled, thereby evoking the desire to visit them. Indeed, until quite recently, "To Sell France to Foreigners" was the slogan adopted by the *Maison de la France* (House of France), the official authority for France's tourist promotion abroad. The French State, and most of its governmental and nongovernmental institutions, has for a long time been active both in the promotion of tourism originating from inside its boundaries (domestic tourism) and from outside its borders (international tourism), through the export of its managerial techniques and the content of its political project encompassing tourism development. After all, the country has been involved in the WTO for many years, and, it should be noted, its former Secretary General, although bearing an Italian family name, was nevertheless of French nationality. However, above all, France is the place where a certain conceptualization of social life was molded in which tourism, associated with holidays, is integrated as a fundamental value. Indeed, the idea of paid vacations for everyone enacted by the *Front Populaire* (Popular Front) remains in the minds of French people as a right to leisure and tourism and as a part of the Declaration of Human Rights.

First, I will look at how sociological thought originated and developed in France and ask whether a sociology of tourism actually exists there. From this premise, and via some linkages, I will briefly try to show how sociological thought originated and developed. In order to be recognized as a field of studies legitimated by academia, tourism has to demonstrate its connections with Sociology (with a capital S), as it appears in the register of the Sciences of Man and Society. This naturally raises the problem of the relationship of the sociology of tourism with the *object of sociology*. That is something of an embarrassment because the object of sociology, which, regardless of the vast amount of work carried out under that label, still remains a matter of controversy. In spite of all the references to the social sciences, we still need to know what is meant by the term "social," and the status of the sociology of tourism as a separate field of research. More specifically, in the current contribution, which attempts to conceptualize different ways of dealing with social facts, the crucial epistemological issue to be tackled is "what is a sociological object?"—a question which has been continuously raised since the birth of the discipline. It should also be noted that in France, the process moved from the initial insights of its patriarch, Auguste Comte, who invented the word "sociology," which was soon adopted outside France, particularly in England, by Herbert Spencer.

However, since the work of its founding fathers, sociology has evolved a great deal. Their position of positivism soon surrendered to alternative perspectives. New social theories began to flourish under the influence of an advancing empirical sociology, the invention of survey techniques, the multiplication of research fields, sociolinguistic and cultural pluralism, and theoretical elaboration leading to a flourishing of topics via a thorough analysis of the epistemological bases of social research. Parallel evolutions emerged in the disciplines working more or less in tandem with the sociology of tourism, that is, history, geography, economics, ethnology, paleontology, etc. Yet, although sociology today engages in an identity quest for its points of reference, there is still talk of a crisis of sociology. Indeed, if we examine the content of bibliographies featuring in the catalogs of scientific research centers under the heading of "the sociology of tourism," we can surely say that it reflects such a crisis.

Under the caption "sociology of tourism," we find a mixed assortment of different topics bearing apparently little or no relationship with tourism in the usual sense of the word. They deal with religious practice, political independence, the consequences of globalization, the politics of heritage, crises of identity, the transformation of humankind, war, the situation of women, the family, conditions of recovery from mental illness, table manners and gastronomy, body techniques, sexual intercourse, etc. All major problems seem to appeal to this variant of sociology, as if this field of research and study can transcend the multiple branches of sociology, which become more and more autonomous as specialized research topics that go hand in hand with developments in general sociology. Thus, the epistemology of the so-called "sociology of tourism" refers back to a much more fundamental question, that of the "construction of the object of sociology." Here, there is a scientific discipline, *sociology*, whose bases are essentially in a state of flux and a subject/object, *tourism*, whose limits are borderless and whose meaning is manifold. The sociology of tourism is not a simple entity; it is more a question of method. In order to present its development, it is necessary to adopt the methodological criteria of historical research for the study of sources and the analysis of their content. This implies a reliance on the framework of general sociology and its history. The relevant questions are many. From what event can the birth of the sociology of tourism be dated? According to which criteria can its corpus be delimited? In what geographical place has it been applied? The most logical way forward would seem to depend on bibliographical data entered by research centers under the index items "tourism" and/or "sociology."

France is fortunate enough to possess an exceptional research center built up over the years by René Baretje. This *Centre des Hautes Études Touristiques* (Center of Higher Touristic Studies, CHET) (2008), located in Aix-en-Provence since the 1960s, contains thousands of titles. I have had the opportunity to glance through the documentation in relation to sociology. I was compelled to make drastic choices because of the variability of the discipline. After all, there is sociology and sociology. If we refer to the titles indexed in the thesaurus, the sociological or derived literature concerned with tourism is rich. But if we analyze the contents of this literature, they produce very meager results. There are plenty of descriptive studies without theoretical referents, texts expressing opinions devoid of critical reflection, definitions of tourism which are either products of the imagination or normalized by tourist practices or publishers' choice of catchy titles. Moreover, there are humorous texts, chronicles of events, literary essays, ideological speculations based on local notices, partial and parochial biases reflecting the ideas the author has in his mind, etc. Many studies derive from what Pierre Bourdieu, with a certain measure of contempt, calls a spontaneous sociology. Yet many of these kinds of publications would seem to have played a part in the beginning of the sociology of tourism and haphazardly contributed to its evolution.

In a more subtle way, the issue that took shape under the name of "sociology of tourism" derived to a great extent from the procedures stemming from the financial or political imperatives of tourism development. Such was the case of all those studies aiming at supporting tourist demand, and all those investigations dealing with the motivations, attitudes, and representations of tourists, which turned sociology in the direction of "social psychology," or more precisely tourism marketing. Additionally, the sociology of tourism has become handmaid to the operations of management over numerous regions of France and elsewhere, so that nowadays nearly all parts of the world give birth to all kinds of local monographs. Although many of these works sometimes provide a very rich and diversified picture, there is comparatively little consistency from which to draw major ideas. Moreover, the abundance of partial and parochial bias in these studies is reflected in the odor of sanctity surrounding the professors dominating their associated academic and scientific institutions. In the turmoil of the 1960s when multiple applications of sociological research were constituted as recognized subdisciplines, the sociology of leisure was one of the most dynamic and most criticized. Although this was not the case as regards the sociology of tourism, the word "tourism" nevertheless aroused the suspicion of the academic milieu. Its claim to scholarship could even be considered fraudulent. On one occasion, when I was Director of the Department of Human Sciences at the National Research Center (CNRS), a colleague (perhaps to discourage my aspirations) said that "tourism was not a sociological object." A researcher aspiring to a job at CNRS or at a university bearing a project dealing with tourism was accused of foolishness.

If this volume depends on the titles indexed under "sociology of tourism," there is always the risk of neglecting essential problems. In order to reconstruct its history, it is necessary to rely on the direct evidence of scholars who contributed toward the establishment of tourism as a research field for sociology and to analyze the obstacles they had to overcome. Since this history is not recorded in books, we need to construct it according to historical principles. That means adopting the methodology of sociohistory, or associating the historical method of research and of source verification with the sociological method that focuses on the memory of the actors making history.

In this context, my personality necessarily enters the scene. Since my admission to the CNRS in 1956, I had been intimately bound to the origins of a sociology of leisure, as a research assistant to Joffré Dumazedier.

Starting in 1972, I took the initiative of creating within the CNRS a team of specialized researchers. The aim was to create a research field in order to understand which crucial questions the spreading of tourism all over the world was posing for sociology. This team was officially recognized in 1976 by CNRS under the name of the *Unité de Recherche en Sociologie du Tourisme International* (URESTI) (Unit of Research in the Sociology of International Tourism).

SOCIOLOGY AND THE SOCIOLOGY OF TOURISM

This account does more than simply take stock of the various positions of the sociology of tourism in France. It also confronts an issue that has yet to be raised, which is the question of locating the sociological contributions to tourism that are contextualized within the heritage of the French School of Sociology. At the same time, it examines the epistemological bases of the different streams in which these contributions find their legitimation. It is, of course, a fundamental difficulty for a research field which is currently being established. The charting of this history is of major importance in order to grasp the wide problems raised for contemporary society by the expansion of international tourism. It is in fact a global process implying consequences in every field, be it economics, politics, or the ethics of social relationships. It also is of major importance in handling the question of the status of sociology/anthropology within the framework of social scientific disciplines interested in the study of tourism. This status has not been established in a unique or united paradigm embracing all its problems. It is crucial today that the sociology of tourism does not give up addressing the most serious issues accumulating in its research field, once the necessary opportunity for reflection and debate has been grasped. I am referring here to the French School of Sociology, but it is necessary to add immediately that this variant is not characterized by national features. First of all, it is permeated with the work of preceding philosophers, themselves shaped by a wider Graeco-Latin and Judeo-Christian tradition. It is sufficient to read the *Année Sociologique* (Sociological Year), Durkheim's review (originating in 1898 and still continuing today), to be convinced of this fact. Likewise, it is necessary to underscore that the sociology of tourism could not be authorized to bear a national brand.

Is tourism a sociological object? As far as I am concerned, it is first of all a research field where the most notable and pressing questions of contemporary societies arise, issues which relate to their economy and their development. It is in this problematic context that tourism is conceived as a metaphor of the social world, inasmuch as the individual is its actor and spokesperson (Dann 2002).

It has been argued that the major stages of the construction of sociology were grafted on to the huge social crisis which in the 19th and 20th centuries shook European societies to their political foundations. This statement is also valid for the creation of a sociology of tourism. The invention of tourism occurred simultaneously with the Industrial and French revolutions. Although both these revolutions manifested themselves under different registers, nevertheless both presented themselves to contemporary witnesses as moments of the disorder they raised on the public scene, and in the system of values as instances of irreversible rupture with the established *Ancien Régime* (Ancient Order). The French Revolution abolished the privileges of the aristocracy and the clergy; the Industrial Revolution overturned the traditional social order of relationships between town and country. For a more thorough analysis, one should realize that tourism, in its evolution since the 18th century, has been politically oriented toward these structural changes in Western societies. The evolution of world tourism brings new tests of our understanding of social disequilibrium. The origin of sociology and its subsequent evolution must be read through the lens of these periods of history where society was, and still is, in crisis. In the French case, we can distinguish several periods of precursors: the initial approach through the principles outlined by Auguste Comte, the laying of the foundations with Durkheim, and finally maturation until approximately 1960. Thereafter, sociology branches out into a variety of new perspectives.

Semantic Features

It should be noted that *tourism* and *sociology* emerged in different registers of the French language at the same moment—the first half of 19th century. Both expressions reflected movements of ideas and representations. In this history of the sociology of tourism, it is important for me to mention very briefly the origins of these words which struck the spirits of contemporaries with their novelty. Conventional wisdom has it that history attributes to modern tourism a place of birth (England), a date of birth (between the 18th and 19th centuries), and a certificate of baptism (the appearance of the name in a dictionary). In this light, works chronicling the history of tourism never fail to mention the Grand Tour, followed one century later by the enterprise of the clergyman Thomas Cook. However, in the present account, it is necessary to reject the simplicity of this narrative for generating a certain conception of history, a one-way conception, ignoring social relationships featuring in this historical period when the famous word "tourism" established itself, the focus of our attention.

The introduction of the word *touriste* into the dictionary of French language is usually ascribed to Stendhal, a writer enjoying a good reputation even while he was alive (see also Böröcz 1996, and Przecławski et al, this volume). Actually the word *touriste*, if not widespread, had already been in use for quite a while, a trace confirming this fact going back to 1811. Then, in 1837/1838, Stendhal published *Mémoires d'un Touriste* (Memories of a Tourist), aiming, according to his publisher who had commissioned the work, at describing his travels in France (his own country) in the same way as he had written about his peregrinations in Italy, especially in Rome and Florence (1973). Thereafter, Victor Hugo employed the word in 1842 in his work *Le Rhin* (The Rhine).

Stendhal's work can certainly be considered as sociological in nature even before the birth of sociology. Nevertheless, he is not original in his writings. In the 19th century, travel accounts were written by the majority of French literature authors, like Lamartine's (1835) *Voyage en Orient* (Voyage to the Orient), (de) Chateaubriand's (1811) *Itinéraire de Paris à Jerusalem* (Itinerary from Paris to Jerusalem), and (de) Nerval's (1848, 1850) two volume *Scènes de la Vie Orientale* (Scenes of Oriental Life). Then there was Victor Hugo (1842) who kept a travel diary along the Rhine at the French–German border, Georges Sand who described her excursions in the Creuse, and Flaubert (1966) who recounted his experiences in Egypt, to mention just a few of the most renowned. These accounts are sources that the ethnography of tourism should not neglect. From their travels, these authors report observations and analyses of the societies they visited which can be considered as precursors of the new science of society. Tocqueville studied democracy in America; Montesquieu examined political institutions in England; Jean-Jacques Rousseau, as the solitary walker and citizen of Geneva, proposed the social contract; and Lamartine through his travel to the Orient initiated a taste for exotism, of ethnological curiosity. Georges Sand, penetrating on donkeyback the mountain massifs of the Cevennes, raised an interest in remote and lonely places, whose legends and folklore became the object of French ethnology. Victor Hugo, whose 1842 work *Le Rhin*, because of its foresight, became a plea for the construction of Europe based on French–German consensus, while Chateaubriand was French ambassador after the restoration of the monarchy.

However, in Stendhal's case the key issue, the word *tourist*, lay elsewhere. Stendhal, having lived in England before, turned the tables on his detractors. "Here I am under a terrible curse of being labeled a tourist. A national hatred has taken hold of the stupid people of both countries" (1838). These reactions of chauvinist and anglophobe hostility highlight the fact that tourism is not a sociologically neutral object. This tourist is more than a walking individual, s(he) is a signifier characterized by the mark of a stranger. A tourist is the other, or rather the Other of the other; in the case of a Frenchman, it is an Englishman.

The word *touriste* was to remain for a long time with this meaning. In 1872, the dictionary *Littré* provided the following definition of the word *touriste* (Littré 1872):

> used for travelers scouring foreign countries solely because of curiosity and idleness, making a kind of round trip to those countries usually visited by their countrymen; used especially for English travelers in France, Switzerland, Italy.

In the beginning, tourism, taking its lead from "tourists" as individual subjects, defined the activity they practiced as tourists. At that time, nothing allowed people to foresee either the fortune which the word *tourism* would encounter, or the load of meanings which were to slip little by little under the signifier *tourism*. It would be up to sociology to discover the hidden meanings which had become welded together in the course of history.

The Origin of Sociology

The sociology of tourism had its origin in Europe during the last century, with a slight staggering of time in different countries. Nevertheless, while the word tourism was still infrequently employed in the French language, the theoretical and conceptual framework allowing the problematization and understanding of its social meaning had already been outlined by an emerging sociology. Authors who would open paths to sociological research and reflection belonged to a preceding generation and were themselves shaped in the tradition of sociological thought which was forged in stages. Rereading the founding texts, one realizes just how much the orientation of Auguste Comte and his disciple Durkheim, founder of the French School of Sociology, shaped the sociological thought that could later be applied to the field of tourism. These classical authors opened the way, even if we may have forgotten their initial contributions. They built up a framework of references, highlighted perspectives, oriented directions of research, proposed models of reasoning and of dissertation, forged concepts, and invented the theoretical bases on which progressively the perception of the whole of tourism was elaborated as a social phenomenon concerned with the production of the society in which we are living today. These works are like road signs which allow us to locate the sociology of tourism within the framework of general sociology. The works of those sociologists usually considered as pioneers of sociological development (Comte, Durkheim, and Mauss) left their mark on a certain attitude toward social phenomena, which still perpetuates itself in our way of confronting the sociological object. Because of this mark, we are led to conceive tourism not in the usual way as a sector of activity separated from ordinary life, but more broadly as a system of actions which are deeply intertwined with all acts of social life, generating structural changes at every level of expression of society considered as a whole.

Here, (De) Saint-Simon (1760–1825) has a special place worthy of mention. It was he who foresaw in the historical post-revolutionary context the soon to be science of social phenomena. According to Durkheim, it was De Saint-Simon (1966, 1997) who first conceived the aim of this new science, which was not called sociology, because that name was given later by Auguste Comte, but rather the science of man or science of societies, or social psychology. For Saint-Simon, sociology was the science of society in the act of society creating and producing itself. The work of Saint-Simon additionally represented a major point of reference that linked the sociology of tourism with the history of sociology. This was because, on the one hand, he introduced to research two major pioneers of sociology: Auguste Comte, who used to be his secretary and disciple before quarrelling with him, and Karl Marx, who, since his first student years, had encountered the ideas of Saint-Simon and who derived inspiration from him for his first writings on socialism and the social sciences. On the other hand, Saint-Simon is especially interesting because he conceived an analysis of society in terms of social class. Long before Thorstein Veblen (1899), Saint-Simon molded the sociological concept of a leisure class which was later to be studied by the author of *The Theory of the Leisure Class*, translated into French under the title of *Théorie de la Classe de Loisir*, which became a classic.

Moreover, it was Saint-Simon who first proposed a sociological theory of a life of ease, free from work or worry, predating Auguste Comte, Karl Marx, and Thorstein Veblen. The word *oisiveté* (ease) is one of those notions that are difficult to translate (see Spode this volume) and that can only be fully understood by locating them in their history. Etymologically, ease is derived from the Latin word *otium*. In the language of Ancient Rome, *otium* was the translation of the Greek *scholé* indicating the social condition of a free man toward the servitude of a man forced to work. *Otium* had a positive value when compared to *neg-otium*, where *neg* meant privation of *otium*, with a French equivalent of *negoce* (commerce). In Judeo-Christian culture, *otium* was of supernatural character, synonymous with a supreme condition of happiness, divine *otium* in Thomistic terms.

In the 18th century, characterized by progress in industry and trade and the ascent of capitalism, one can see in Western culture an inversion of values; ease derived from *otium* began to assume a negative meaning and, as a consequence, so did the word *loisir* (leisure) itself. In contrast, work started being claimed as having a positive value. It was in the framework of this movement of ideas that Saint-Simon proposed a sociological theory of the leisured class. Saint-Simon sided with the opinion of the theoreticians of industrial society. Industry was opposed to the military conquest of territories with wealth and power going to the victors. In the industrial economy, with the appearance of private capitalism, wealth was earned by industry as a result of productive work. This wealth engendered a new form of ownership, that is, the ownership of the means of production. The division of labor, made possible by the collaboration of producers, gave rise to new forms of social organization. For these theoreticians, progress was only possible due to new investment. A part of the revenue of work had to be taken away from the profligate expenditure enjoyed first of all by a privileged class, and invested in the means of production as a way toward the general development of society which would be of advantage to the whole of humankind. According to Saint-Simon, everything not industrial was parasitic, idle, thieving. The leisured class was the enemy of production and the progress of industrial society implied its elimination. No doubt, Saint-Simon had in mind the nobility of the *Ancien Régime* which, after the Revolution of 1789, perpetuated itself in the French society of the 19th century under the restoration of Bourbons, after the fall of Napoleon. This social class had to be eliminated, both because it was based on an injustice and because its way of life and its profligacy were opposed to the accumulation process, which, according to those theoreticians (and Saint-Simon himself), was the only source of wealth and productivity.

It was thus in the framework of economic growth that Saint-Simon criticized this life of ease, this idleness, which, according to him, implied more than a simple inactivity in the moral sense of the word. A life of ease meant being socially useless, economically harmful. It was a sociological category. It was always in pejorative terms that Saint-Simon defined people at ease. He spoke of property owners as a class still sillier and more contemptible than the feudal one, looking in their life for enjoyment achieved without work. The same conceptual scheme can be found as a critical base, albeit with different political attitudes, in Karl Marx, Thorstein Veblen, and Paul Lafargue (1965), who analyzed the same issue of ease as typical of the way of life of certain categories of the population. These authors insisted on the privileges of their time, the social criticism of idleness which had struck before the aristocracy of the *Ancien Régime* (Lanfant 1972:35).

Following the Saint-Simonians, several works analyzed industrial society and its evolution in capitalist and socialist contexts, including those of Karl Marx which have been thoroughly investigated by French sociologists according to this perspective. Such an analysis also lies at the basis of numerous works on the concept of free time, which is a fundamental concept in the sociology of tourism and of leisure, the evolution of which is treated below.

Birth of the French School of Sociology

Durkheim (1858–1917) is considered the true founder of the French School of Sociology, because following the principles outlined by Auguste Comte, what he built up was a strict methodology faithfully adhering to the scientific approach of test and demonstration encountered in the experimental sciences. First of all, he elaborated precisely the notion of a *social fact* (1895). A social fact could not be reduced to the sum of its individual parts. Neither could it be reduced to biological, economic, or other causal factors. It had a special determinism all of its own. Following the golden rule of the sociological method, the social as such had to be explained by the social. Social facts could not be explained except by means of other social facts. According to Durkheim, the sociological method appealed to the reasoning of modern logic, that is, on the detailed and systematic analysis of a series of propositions, variables, organized as a hypothetico-deductive model following the example of a system of axioms. The analysis proceeded through subsequent verifications reasoning progressively through deduction as well as through induction. Tools of verification were statistical tests that is based on a calculus of probability and every other procedure related to modern logic and to set theory (e.g., as correlations, multivariate analysis, combinatory analysis, network analysis). Durkheim offered an exemplary demonstration of his method in his classical work on suicide (1897), a "must have" in the repertoire of every elementary teacher of sociology.

By the tender age of 16, Durkheim had already chosen his academic career. First he studied at the *École Normale Supérieure* (Normal High School). There he became acquainted with the work of Auguste Comte. Subsequently, he was appointed professor at Bordeaux, where he wrote his most important works: *La Division du Travail Social* (1893) (The Division of Labor in Society), *Les Règles de la Méthode Sociologique* (1895) (Rules of Sociological Method), and *Le Suicide* (1897) (Suicide). A year after this last work, and with some colleagues, he initiated the review *L'Année Sociologique*, that was to become the reference point for the French School of Sociology, assuring him a worldwide reputation. Durkheim later invited his nephew, Marcel Mauss, to come to Bordeaux to assist him in his research. His last major work, and some would say his crowning glory, was *Les Formes Élémentaires de la Vie Religieuse* (1912) (Elementary Forms of the Religious Life).

Although Durkheim pursued his academic career with determination, he was not detached from the living realities of his time. In spite of his concern to preserve the objectivity of sociology, Durkheim, as a friend of Jean Jaurès from his time at the *École Normale Supérieure*, sided with the socialists. The Dreyfus affair revealing an anti-Semitic hatred smoldering in the French psyche led Durkheim (who was incidentally the son of a rabbi) to join a small group of intellectuals who founded the secular League of Human Rights. As for Auguste Comte, he considered that sociology was to be at the service of the education of citizens in order to reinforce their attitude to live in a democratic society.

After Durkheim

While some predicted that sociology would decline after the death of its leading light, Émile Durkheim, quite the reverse occurred. This new science, far from disappearing, gained in subtlety and depth, because the project continued under the direction and personality of his nephew, Marcel Mauss. Much later, at the opportune moment, and after the deep turmoil caused by the Nazi invasion of France, sociology was given a new lease of life, anchored in the spirit of the principles sown by Durkheim and Mauss. The latter, although remaining faithful to Durkheim's orientation, opened entirely new paths. If one wants to associate the sociology of tourism with the *École Française de Sociologie* (French School of Sociology), its premises can be found in the insights of Marcel Mauss. Mauss (1872–1950), accepted for a course in philosophy at Bordeaux, did not seek a career at that university. At the conclusion of his higher studies, he decided at first to continue his training in Paris, then in the Netherlands and at Oxford in order to complete his formation in ethnology and oriental studies. Later he was appointed lecturer at the department of religious studies at the *École Pratique des Hautes Études* (The Practical School of Higher Studies). Subsequently, he was affiliated with the *Institut d'Ethnologie* (Ethnological Institute) and the *Collège de France* (College of France), where he could devote himself completely to research and teaching without worrying too much about the duties and responsibilities linked with the position of a university professor. Like Durkheim, Mauss was very interested in ethnological data. He opened up sociology to fields of research located at the margins of academic institutions: sinology, indiology, and the sciences of religion. That is why disciplines other than sociology in the 1920s and 1930s derived from the heritage of the French School of Sociology, along with its spirit, a new dynamism. On the one hand, there was ethnology, to which Mauss devoted himself in association with the Institute of Ethnology of the University of Paris and the establishment of the *Musée de l'Homme* (Museum of Man) in 1936. On the other hand, there was history renewed by a kind of sociological graft (Marc Bloch and Lucien Febvre), synology (Granet), celtic studies (Hubert), linguistics (Meillet), and human geography (Demangeon).

When in 1936 some authors attracted by surrealism established themselves as a working group under the name of *Collège de Sociologie* (College of Sociology), they asked to be associated with Hubert and Mauss, especially since Mauss, more so than Durkheim, was politically engaged with the left. I mention these facts because they allow us to appreciate the status of the sociology of tourism which was to develop starting in the 1960s in France. More precisely, this was an interpretation of the sociology of tourism which was going to assert itself in its global dimension as a field of research lying at the intersection of a group of disciplines focusing jointly on some key issue, like the notion of "total social phenomenon," for instance. This idea, derived from Marcel Mauss and subsequently collectively adopted, was of extraordinary heuristic significance for researchers all over the world claiming their belonging to this field. Some French researchers thought that tourism referred to something social rather than the product of individual consciousness. For this reason, they straightaway located their empirical studies in a conceptual framework that sought to capture simultaneously tourism in both its global and local features, in order to clarify it as a phenomenon which could not be reduced to its mere representation in social discourse or to the subjective experiences of actors. From the post-Second World War (WWII) onwards, it was recognized that it was necessary to tackle a completely new phenomenon, one with no historical precedent. It is in this sense that sociology was challenged at this specific time, in that particular way, as a source of relevant knowledge. When in the 1970s another generation of researchers dedicated their theses to topics related to tourism, the principles applied by the disciples of Durkheim were somehow assimilated by these initiates, regardless of their prior formation, and these principles in turn became leverages for their investigations. It was as if their inquiries, starting from isolated cases, were revealing themselves as a practice leaving the same point of origin and emerging in disparate places.

The Premises of a Sociology of Tourism

After the WWII, sociology experienced in France a renewal of vitality. The day after the Nazis were defeated on French soil, a major turning point could be observed in the academic and scientific environment concerning the position of sociology. The teaching of sociology took a completely new turn with relevant professors entering the Sorbonne. One of these was Georges Gurvitch (1957, 1960, 1965), who held the chair of Morals and Sociology. His teaching was faithful to the tradition of Durkheim and Mauss, to which he further contributed by publishing their still little-known works. Primarily, however, his lectures were deeply embedded in personal experience, and equally marked by the tumultuous and dramatic events featuring in the first half of 20th century. Georges Gurvitch (1894–1965), of Russian origin, but Jewish by birth, originally participated in the October Revolution on the side of Trotsky. However, as a supporter of democratic socialism, he had to choose exile in 1920. He taught at the University of Prague for three years, established himself in France in 1925, presented a thesis in 1932, and was appointed to the University of Strasbourg in 1935. In 1941, due to threats to his person, he took refuge in England. After coming back to France in 1946 and before being appointed to the Sorbonne (1949), he created the first modern laboratory of sociology at the *Centre d'Études Sociologiques* (Center for Sociological Studies). He founded the *Cahiers Internationaux de Sociologie* (International Papers of Sociology), and, in collaboration with Henri Jeanne, the *Association Internationale des Sociologues de Langue Française* (International Association of Francophone Sociologists).

Another important figure in French sociology was Raymond Aron, who had studied at the *École Normale Supérieure* at Rue d'Ulm in the same group of students as Jean-Paul Sartre, and who had sought refuge from Vichy Regime in General De Gaulle's resistance movement in London. After the war, he became a professor at the Sorbonne and held the chair of Political Sociology. It was he who introduced the works of important Germans (Simmel, Tönnies, Weber, etc.) into French sociological thought (Aron 1935, 1967).

The first chair of Social Psychology was occupied by Jean Stoetzel, originally from of the east of France, who created the IFOP, *Institut Franç ais des Sondages d'Opinion* (French Institute for Opinion Research).

Merleau-Ponty was politically very active. Along with Jean-Paul Sartre, he participated in the *Revue des Temps Modernes* (Review of Modern Times). He was a disciple of Edmund Husserl. At the beginning of the 1950s, he held the chair of General Psychology at the Sorbonne, where he expounded his phenomenological theory and his new views on language, perception, body, and alterity. The teaching of anthropology was already dominated by the personality of Claude Lévi-Strauss linking himself to the work of Marcel Mauss, but renewing it through the method of structural anthropology.

To these figures some more observations can be noted. At that time, there was a growing interest in the Freudian discovery of the unconscious and its consequences for approaches to social phenomena. In this regard, there was the sociologist Castoriadis who attended the seminars of Lacan. There was also a return to philosophy which was evident in the close relationships existing between the *École Normale Supérieure* and the University of the Sorbonne. This proximity was fostered by the reduced space of the *Quartier Latin* (Latin Quarter) where the figure of Gaston Bachelard dominated, the well-known writer of the history of science. Additionally, after several somber years, there was a dazzling simultaneous opening to new fields of knowledge preparing the next generation, especially in the persons of Michel Foucault, Raymond Boudon, Pierre Bourdieu, and Jean Baudrillard, to mention just a few.

This was also a time of intense debates arising from the reading of Marx, to which all sociologists referred irrespective of their political leanings. Here, the likes of Raymond Aron, Georges Gurvitch, Pierre Naville, Henri Lefebvre, and Louis Althusser included in their well-documented works readings of Marx which were passionately commented on by students. Henri Lefebvre and Pierre Naville, in particular, proposed readings of Marx on the margin of official theses sanctioned by a Communist Party that was faithful to Soviet dogma. They both tried to understand the analysis of alienation, a key concept of critical sociology. During this period, too, there was a renewed reading of the major classics due to the publication of the complete works of Marcel Mauss which were double edited by Lévi-Strauss for ethnology and Georges Gurvitch for sociology. There was also the publication of Durkheim's correspondence and the renewal of the *Année Sociologique* by the Durkheimians of the *Centre d'Études Sociologiques* (Center for Sociological Studies). The formation received by students who were to become researchers in the 1970s or 1980s was quite different from the one received by researchers who, in 1946, founded this *Centre d'Études Sociologiques*. In 1958, a degree in sociology was created at the Sorbonne that involved crowning three years of studies in the following disciplines: sociology in the strict sense, ethnology, social psychology, general psychology, statistics, aesthetics, logic, and philosophy.

In 1946, the *Centre National de la Recherche Scientifique* (National Center for Scientific Research), created in 1939, resumed its activities and reconstituted itself with a *Département des Sciences Humaines* (Department of Human Sciences) embracing several disciplines: demography, geography, history, ethnology, sociology, etc. The latter, assembled in the *Centre d'Etudes Sociologiques*, was the cream of French sociology under the leadership of Georges Gurvitch. He was succeeded by Jean Stoezel and Georges Friedmann who held a weekly seminar at the *École Pratique des Hautes Etudes* (The Practical School of Higher Studies). A whole new generation of sociology researchers followed: Pierre Naville, Henri Lefebvre, the younger Roland Barthes, Alain Touraine, and Edgard Morin, who met there nearly every day, including, in 1953, a research team in the sociology of leisure headed by Joffré Dumazedier. The proximity of researchers working under one roof and specializing in diverse branches of sociology promoted in a unique and incomparable way an exchange of ideas, debates, and reciprocal criticism, in brief, a high quality of competitive ideas, which were soon to benefit ensuing research. By rereading those works published at that time, one can state that nearly all the researchers meeting at the *Centre d'Etudes Sociologiques* on the rue de Varenne were interested in the meaning of *loisir* (leisure) and *loisirs* (amusements). They then wrote some basic works to which we are still referring today. The reflections raised by the explosion of mass tourism were related to the different streams of sociological thought analyzing modernity. So tourism became a kind of sign of this modernity.

The first studies on tourism had as their theoretical backdrop the major works of synthesis examining the transition from an industrial to a postindustrial society, from a society based on production to a society based on consumption. These works represented avenues of transmission, passing on the intellectual baton of grasping the huge problems raised by the spreading of international tourism all over the world. They were published between 1950 and 1960.

The sociology of leisure profited especially in the conflict between the thought of Marx and of liberal thought. After the WWII, it established itself in industrialized countries. The concepts of free time and leisure were at the center of the analyses of theoreticians describing the respective advantages and disadvantages of the two powerful industrial, economic, and political systems dominating the world: socialist and capitalist. Leisure became an important symbol of the wealth and future of the contemporary masses, wherever they lived. These reflections reached a point where the two systems at the military and ideological levels were subject to internal crises stemming from their optimistic or pessimistic positions. Leisure thus represented a dualism: either for overcoming alienation and class antagonisms or fighting against scarcity and enjoying an alleged freedom for the self and others. Through these respective theses deriving from the advent of leisure and free time, one can sense the anxious concern of the authors, both capitalist and socialist, about the social finality of industrial production. These contradictory theses promoted controversy between the rival political regimes on the world scene.

In the beginning, the sociology of leisure developed in the context of a liberal economy. It grew as a reaction to a Marxist critique that predicted increasing contradictions at the core of the developing capitalist system. It moved from a rejection of a centralized, totalitarian socialist system that worked against individual freedom, yet remained inspired by socialist ideas. It was guided by the search for an alternative society through reformist ways inspired by democratic values. The result was that between the sociologists defining themselves as Marxists and those who could rather loosely be classified as liberal, there were no truly defined oppositions apart from those professing a radical Marxism and those opting for a well-established liberalism. In the 1960s, both approaches clashed, the first under the label of a sociology of free time (a concept inherited from Marx) and the second under the name of a sociology of leisure (a concept typical of humanistic thought). The latter focused on the social organization of time off work. This was said to be increasing due to the automatization of the means of production, with the underlying idea that free time could become the source of a new humanism, of a new culture (Lanfant 1972:65–67). The thesis prevailing among these sociologists was that leisure in its modern meaning was still a developing reality; although it had been born in the context of industrial society, it was a completely new reality which one could not contrast with the idleness of preceding centuries. Therefore, a new concept of free time was elaborated. In those societies that had passed through the first stages of industrialization, a change of meaning could be noticed. From time liberated by the productivity of work, free time became a period available for leisure. The modern concept of leisure thus developed by breaking off from its analysis of work. This rupture gradually came to signify a clear-cut separation between work and leisure. The latter became a reality *sui generis*, finding its justification and finality in itself. Hence, the well-anchored idea that this sphere of free time positioned itself in opposition to ordinary life. It was an idea which was clearly widespread among many authors proposing their theories of tourism.

We can date this seesaw moment to the middle of the past century in France. It was then that tourism became an object of study for the social sciences. These activities of free time were defined as "free from constraint," as opposed to work which was marked by the sign of necessity. This notion of "freedom from constraint" was to have a significant destiny; it allowed people to think of the sphere of free time as empty or hollow time, hence potentially open to the creation of new activities. It was a time for adventure, the pursuit of the imaginary, the search of another life, an elsewhere. In the same way, new conceptions of sociological determinism were emphasized. The sociology of leisure freed scholars from the sociology of work and the whole conceptual apparatus that went with it. It followed a concealment of the economic and technological aspects of the use of free time. In this explanation, subjective factors tended to prevail.

In this situation, Joffré Dumazedier was to play a decisive role, not only in France but at the international level. He constantly insisted on the correct articulation of his problematic, which emphasized the notion of *loisir* and not of *loisirs*. For him, this emphasis was essential, breaking with the idea that this sphere of sociology could become the repository of all the various studies concerned with the numerous activities emerging in time liberated from work. For him, leisure became a new concept, which carried thoroughly innovative values into every subsystem of social life: family, religion, work, individual and social persons, etc. (Dumazedier 1988). This conception was discussed and shared in France and (thanks to Dumazedier's international connections) also abroad, because Dumazedier as a founder president of the Committee on the Sociology of Leisure of the International Sociological Association (ISA) maintained numerous contacts with Eastern European countries, the United States, and Latin America. It was on this foundation that the sociology of tourism was built up in the 1950s and 1960s.

Dumazedier's views of the sociology of tourism gained ground as a result of his research program. In his first work published in 1962, *Vers une Civilisation du Loisir?* (Towards a Sociology of Leisure?) where he expounded his first investigations, one of the chapters bore the title "Leisure and Touristic Culture" (Dumazedier 1962:127–142). Here, it should be noted that essentially the phenomenon of holidays, defined as free time after work, was the object of his attention. Touristic culture was that revealed by the data collected through surveys of different categories of people. He stated this fundamental point that the majority of interviewed people were waiting for their annual holiday, for rest. According to him, these tourists were little itinerants; all they wanted was to take a siesta. Next to those focusing on this elementary need, there were many, especially among young people, who wanted to escape into "a concrete utopia" similar to that offered by the *Club Méditerranée*, which became in those years the "brand image" of holidays in the art of the French middle classes (Raymond 1960). Dumazedier was surely deceived by the results of his surveys, since for him, access to leisure should have engendered quite a different attitude toward existence.

Dumazedier's view of leisure was clearly libertarian. Leisure, for him, constituted a kind of rebellion against repressive culture with all its social constraints and worries, and he envisaged an opportunity of creating a new, less repressive society. Familiar, religious obligations were going to vanish, thereby providing space for individuals to respond to their free will. For him, leisure resulted from a free choice, and was characterized by the individual's search for a state of satisfaction that was an end in itself. The quest for well-being, pleasure, and happiness was one of the fundamental features of leisure in modern society. The fulfilment of leisure assumed the liberation from constraints imposed on the individual by the family, religion, and the state. Leisure was not lived any more in relationship to the virtues of work. The future was to prove him right.

This conceptualization of leisure proposed by Dumazedier, justified by the results of his surveys, was invariably repeated in the articles of those years concerned with the demand for holidays in the sociology of tourism of the 1960s and 1970s. Economics and geography followed the same trajectory. There are numerous examples where this definition was utilized. For instance, and as I observed at that time, tourism was considered to be a particular use of free time deriving from the logic of individual choice. Hence, desire for escape, orientation to pleasure, rejection of constraint, and search for individual fulfilment. However, in this way, there was an under evaluation of the impact of the tourist market on the consumption of free time and of the fact that it shared the same ground with a new meaning.

Dumazedier stimulated a global reflection on leisure, moving from the idea he had built of it as an aspiration of mankind to free itself from work seen as form of brutishness. Industrialization was able partially to free individuals from work in order to allow themselves to realize this ideal. There was in Dumazedier a genial intuition, which was no doubt inspired by his personal experience, his enthusiasm at the time of the Popular Front, his engagement in the resistance during the WWII, and his friendly relationships with stars of the theater, cinema, sport, and popular entertainment. As a partisan during the resistance, he prepared with his comrades a project for the constitution of a movement of popular education, which was to see the light of day after the liberation and the president of which he remained until 1969.

Soon after WWII, Dumazedier assumed charge of a group which found consensus among many sociologists of the time. Since its first operations, the *Comité de Recherche du Loisir* (The Research Committee on Leisure) of the ISA (RC13), founded in 1953, took upon itself the task of assembling an international catalog of the social sciences concerned with leisure. It was a way of bringing together sociologists who were working alone in a variety of social situations with the same aim. Dumazedier proposed a precise plan of research in the context of a dynamic sociology. The conditions and processes of the cultural change of social groups under the influence of leisure were the privileged object of this venture.

The third session of RC13 took place in December 1957 and received the support of three departments of UNESCO (youth, education, and social sciences). It included both French- and English-speaking sociologists, and it was coordinated by the team of CNRS directed by Dumazedier. Responding to the requests of the *Commissariat au Plan* (Department of Planning), Dumazedier widened CNRS by giving it a multidisciplinary structure. He brought into his program economists (André Piattier and Jean-François Bernard), a geographer (Françoise Cribier), an historian (Marc Boyer), a linguist (Georges Mounin), and a mathematician (Alain Degenne). All these scholars were researchers already engaged in the study of leisure. Before collaborating with Dumazedier, André Piattier had worked as an economist on numerous aspects of leisure, especially on tourism. From 1949 to 1955, he had chaired the research committee at the *Institut International d'Études Touristiques* (International Institute for Tourism Studies). He had published interviews and surveys concerned with tourism. He was one of the designers of a national sample survey carried out every year in France on the holiday departure tax by the *Institut National de Statistique* (National Statistical Institute). Additionally, he participated in a study of the extensive touristic settlement of the Languedoc-Roussillon coast. Eight reports were delivered to the ministries in 1962, 1963, and 1964. This type of study is rarely collated into an edited work that can be found in bookshops. It is thanks to René Baretje that all these documents were assembled in his scientific research center where they could be read on the premises.

From this time onwards, Dumazedier gave this research program a clear-cut, practical, and futuristic orientation. In this respect, France seemed to be ahead of what was being studied elsewhere under the heading of "sociology of leisure." An interdisciplinary methodology seemed to be gaining ground. The international context required new methodologies enabling comparisons among different countries. These methodological problems were constantly discussed and applied by the team of Dumazedier and propagated at the international level through RC13 of the ISA. As a sociologist, he unceasingly displayed an attachment toward empirical sociology, not so much to support the ideal of scientism, but rather to counteract right- and left-wing ideologies infiltrating social discourse in the postwar years. In this regard, he was faithful to the tradition of the French School of Sociology. In spite of his contacts with Marxist thought and his tolerance for the Communist Party, to which he belonged for a short period after the liberation, Dumazedier took his place among liberal thinkers criticizing and rejecting both the capitalism of free competition and every kind of totalitarian dictatorship. He located his research and his activities within the framework of a capitalist society, sensitive to technical, social, and cultural innovation, and oriented toward a model of pluralistic democracy.

At the end of the 1960s, and especially after the riots of 1968 and their turbulent effects on French society, the orientations of Dumazedier could be regarded as dangerously ambivalent. Although he saw in the students' revolt against the moral order a confirmation of his analysis, his call for the engagement of the state in the organization of *loisirs* and culture was judged severely by a whole class of left-wing intellectuals who considered the state to be the right arm of capitalism. The leisure proposed by Joffré Dumazedier as part of the vision of the democratization of society did not represent the ideal basis for a tourism policy, which in those years was already aligned with world capitalism. The team of Dumazedier did not survive him. Today the new breed of sociologists of tourism do not recognize what they owe him. His contributions to the field appear to have sunk into oblivion.

Other Precursors

In those years, Dumazedier was not the only person in France studying the phenomenon arising in those societies which had freed themselves from forced labor. Other research groups had also established themselves. Before the war, in 1940, a group of academics became dedicated to the works of Durkheim, Hubert, and Mauss on the elementary forms of religious life (Durkheim 1912) and the exchange of the gift (Mauss 1980), in order to discover the authentic nature of social ties from the data of archaic societies. This group, called the *Collège de Sociologie* (College of Sociology) (1937–1939), was founded on the margins of academia, at the crossroads of surrealism, ethnology, and phenomenology, by Georges Bataille, Jules Monnerot, Roger Caillois, and Michel Leiris. The ethnologist Alfred Métraux was also associated. The review *Acephale* (literally Headless) founded by Bataille and the painter Masson in 1936 was its principal outlet. After the "descent into hell" of the 1940–1945 war, Georges Bataille created the review *Critique* (Criticism) distancing himself from *Nouvelle Critique* (New Criticism), the review of the official Marxism of the French Communist Party. This group announced a new school of sociology, from which the sociology of tourism today draws some of its ideas, both on account of preexisting problems and of the ways of tackling these problems through their debates. That can be seen from some of the titles of their publications. For example, there was Roger Caillois's (1950) *L'Homme et le Sacré* (Man and the Sacred) and Georges Bataille's (1967) *The Cursed Part, Preceded by the Notion of Expense*. This last book, the result of over 30 years reflection under the influence of the ethnologist Alfred Métraux, saw Georges Bataille becoming acquainted with the theory of the potlatch (tribal feast) articulated by Marcel Mauss (1980) in his *Essai sur le Don* (Essay on the Gift), an archaic form of exchange, published in the *Année Sociologique* in 1925. This discovery pushed him more and more to take into account his reflection on contemporary economic reality, without dissociating it from the facts of anthropology deriving from the observation of traditional societies. Certainly, this aspect had been little exploited by French sociologists, with the exception perhaps of Jean Baudrillard, whose radical criticism of generalized economics or of the economist Marc Guillaume is well known in such works as *La Société de Consommation, ses Mythes, ses Structures* (The Society of Consumption, its Myths, its Structures) (1970); *Pour une Critique de le Politique du Signe* (For a Critique of the Politics of the Sign) (1972); *L'Échange Symbolique et la Mort* (Symbolic Exchange and Death) (1975).

At the beginning of his career, Jean Baudrillard was the assistant of Henri Lefebvre (1945), the author who had provided an extensive critique of everyday life. Lefebvre had a great influence in the 1960s. He had plenty of style, and showed off a freedom of dress which shocked some of his companions in the Communist Party to which he belonged for many years after the war, but which he loudly abandoned on account of the Kruschev report, and especially after the invasion of Hungary by Soviet troops. He was one of the theoreticians of Situationism, which promoted the student riots of 1968. Henri Lefebvre was an incisive man of learning with a ferocious pen to match. He could be counted among the finest readers of Marx (Lefebvre 1947, 1967). With a philosophical education, he had a sharp critical spirit. He was a dissident by vocation. It was he who contributed to the introduction in France works of the younger Marx which had been earlier published in France in a purged edition and were later proscribed by official Marxism. Jean Baudrillard, being at that time his assistant at the university, borrowed from Lefebvre his theses on ideology and the theory of need, and was himself highly versed in the work of Marx, and extended that critique to the consumer society. According to Lefebvre, the universe of leisure was an artificial universe. So-called modern man hoped to find in leisure what his work and his familiar or private life did not provide him. This way there was a tendency toward the constitution of a world of amusements of pure artificiality, approaching the ideal, and far removed from everyday life.

At that time, Roland Barthes (1957) published *Mythologies* (Mythologies) where his famous text on the Blue Guide can be found, followed shortly afterwards by a prediction where he foretold a method of discourse analysis inspired by structural linguistics approximating that applied by Lévi-Strauss in his analysis of myths. The chapter on the Blue Guide has become a classic in tourism research field. In this vein I have also worked on the application of discourse analysis to tourism.

From the emergence of tourism in 17th and 18th centuries until the period when I could locate the appearance of the sociology of tourism (around 1950), in these intervening years of the history of French society, marked by previously mentioned, consecutive social crises and by street riots seeking to overthrow the established social order based on authoritarian power (monarchical, imperial, or fascist), this new social phenomenon—tourism—unceasingly acted as a catalyst for the reflection of intellectuals. Thus, well before the first sociological works on tourism appeared, its development aroused an awareness of the phenomenon. Typical of this trend was the judgement of political scientist, André Siegfried, that tourism was one of the most important aspects of our civilization. This thought would be repeated time and again in subsequent publications on tourism.

Developments after WWII

It was only after WWII that under the heading "sociology of tourism" studies in France appeared that dealt with tourist practices, in spite of the fact that for more than 100 years one could witness in related geographical areas lasting changes in aspects of the occupation of spaces and of the rhythms of everyday life. These changes affected one another over the whole national territory. The social morphology of France transformed itself continually according to tourist supply and demand, depending on the evolution of both domestic and international tourism, what can be called in French sociological jargon the *mise en tourisme*, or the "touristification" of the territory.

After the war, the retreat of German troops and the liberation, holidaymakers rushed to the coastal areas. In just a few years the coast became saturated. The explosion of mass tourism engendered political measures aimed at mastering the migration of citizens' free time, while simultaneously making them profitable at the level of the global economy. It was a Frenchman, Jules Moch, who defended this position which resulted in making international tourism an item on the foreign trade balance of payments. Its importance in economic international exchange was going to grow so rapidly that by the turn of the second millennium, it would become an independent variable in the globalization process.

The tourist exploitation of developing countries, which was decided and planned since the beginning of the 1960s by the World Bank and other world bodies to aid development, were to change radically the data of the problem represented by the organization of free time and of holidays in the most affluent societies. The underlying thesis imposing itself was that, considered globally as an economic sector, tourism was a tool of development for the most disadvantaged regions. By this time no country could envisage the tourist phenomenon as starting only from national considerations. Tourism was a social fact unfolding itself on a worldwide scale. There is not necessarily a convergence between the stages of development of tourism and the stages of involvement of sociology in its study, no doubt because sociology was not so much interested in tourism as a phenomenon, as in its social dimensions. Since the end of 19th century, the representation of tourism in the minds of intellectuals and specialists in the human sciences was significantly modified. Tourism was not simply an individual activity of temporary relocation for the pleasure or consumption of some lucky idle people. The instrumentalization of this practice in the framework of transport, of the systematization of habitat, and of the organization of amusements brought the word *tourism* into the vocabulary of economics and later geography. This outcome led to important mutations in the definitions of tourism.

A fine example was provided by the *Académie Internationale du Tourisme* (International Academy of Tourism) (not the same as the International Academy for the Study of Tourism referred to in the introduction to this volume) created at Monaco in 1951, deriving from a sample survey of informed persons. Its mission was to collect words and terms typical of tourism, to establish their exact interpretations, and to publish them in different languages. Here, the word *tourism* assumed a conventional definition, which was subsequently taken up by dictionaries, as a "term applied to pleasure travel." Although this definition was derived from the 18th century, already other dimensions began to be added. It became a set of human activities that were designed to foster this kind of travel and, with the collaboration of industry, satisfying the needs of the tourist. It was in fact in the first half of the 20th century that the word *tourism* acquired a double meaning, referring to the individual tourist's activity as well as, on the social level, its meaning as an economic or commercial activity. This dualism was loaded with consequences for the study of tourism, in academia and elsewhere. This made the reconstitution of the origins of sociology of tourism very difficult, with the added problem that it began with the study of motivation in all its heterogeneity.

Different Facets of the Sociology of Tourism

It should be borne in mind that in this initial period, the sociology of tourism was constituted as a chapter in the sociology of leisure. The tourism phenomenon became identified with the holiday phenomenon. Indeed, the two words were sometimes confused, so that along these lines a regulated system of explanation following the rubrics of sociological analysis established itself, one which was going to lead to a false perception of the true reality of the tourism phenomenon.

The first so-called sociological field studies of tourism stemmed from the initiative of student-researchers choosing this approach for the topics of their dissertations. These students did not find support in the framework of the university. They attended the seminars of the team of the sociology of leisure, including such names as Françoise Cribier, Marc Boyer, Agnès Villadary, Henri Raymond, and Nicole Haumont.

At that time, mainstream sociologists drew from their travels works which could be attributed to a phase in the sociology of tourism. Edgard Morin, the most mobile, the most prolific, and the most verbose of them, published one book after another. He created the review *Arguments* (Arguments). His 1962 work *L'Esprit du Temps* (The Spirit of Time) opened masterfully with a reflection on the explosion of mass tourism, where could be found the renowned axiom that the value of vacations was the absence of values (see also Morin 1965). Additionally, he wrote his *Journal de Californie* (Diary of California), welcomed by the press as an admirable study of contemporary sociology (Morin 1970). Other authors of the period included Roland Barthes of Blue Guide fame (1957). There was also Henri Raymond (1960), who, delving into the very center of *Club Mediterranée*, described its inspiration as founded on good luck. Then there was Olivier Burgelin who in 1967 published in the review of CECMAS, *Centre d'Études de la Communication* (Center for Communication Studies) one of the first articles on the tourism phenomenon *Le Tourisme Jugé* (Tourism Assessed). In the same special issue of *Communications*, there was also a thought-provoking essay by Jacques Gritti (1967) on the social control exercised by travel guidebooks. Innovative texts such as these circulated and raised a new interest in this field of tourism.

Since an individually constituted research field in the sociology of tourism did not exist, studies on tourism were a by-product of works dealing principally with another domain. Tourism studies tended to adopt a research approach which had not yet adequately conceived the object being studied. At the same time, a quantity of isolated initiatives revealed themselves, which could not be put at the same level, but which all in all shaped the start of the sociology of tourism. At the end of the 1950s, courses such as sport, agriculture, and hotel management had already been introduced to universities and centers of vocational education. For example, at the University of Nice a *Centre de Motivation Touristique* (Center of Tourist Motivation) had been created by Professor Paul Gonnet, an historian, stimulating an interest among his colleagues at the university, like Jean-William Lapierre, Jean Poirier, Georges Condominas, and Georges Balandier, comprising a group of ethnologists specializing in studies of the Indian Ocean, South-East Asia, and West Africa. These professors would also later show an interest in my work, and would be of great support when people in my academic environment were showing not only a lack of confidence, but outright hostility against me.

The *Centre d'Etudes Supérieures du Tourisme* (Center for Higher Studies of Tourism) (CEST) linked with the Institute of Geography at the University of Paris Sorbonne, distinguished itself by creating at that time a multi-disciplinary educational program embracing geography, management, law, statistics, and the sociology of leisure which was entrusted to me. I have related elsewhere how my teaching at CEST was critical to my awareness of the tourism phenomenon and to my decision to create a research field in international tourism (Lanfant 2007).

At Aix-en-Provence, René Baretje started building a scientific research center at the margins of the University of Aix-Marseille in 1959. This *Centre des Hautes Études Touristiques* (Center for Higher Tourism Studies) began publishing some relevant works. As its Director, Baretje came from a center for tourism studies in Berne, where he assisted persons who had played a very important role in the promotion of European tourism research since the end of WWI. The first issue of *Les Cahiers du Tourisme* (Tourism Papers) of CHET was significantly the thesis by Kurt Krapf, translated into French and edited by him (Krapf 1964).

For the sociohistory of tourism, it is also necessary to deal objectively with the trajectory of very important personalities playing the role of pioneer and participating in the definition of a tourism policy where they place the accent on the social and cultural aspects of tourism. They have, as it is usually expressed, a sociological "sensibility." The Belgian, Arthur Haulot, for instance, drawing on his education in sociology, served in UNESCO where he proposed a charter for the protection of monuments and sites. Pierre Defert, and others affiliated with the *Association Internationale des Experts Scientifiques du Tourisme*, unceasingly strove for the participation of sociologists in that organization. M. Garai, the founder of the review *Espaces* (Spaces), gave it a definite sociological orientation. In the 1960s, when sociology was fashionable, other initiatives could be considered as moments of origin in a sociology of tourism, even though they maintained an often ambiguous connection with sociology.

A sociology of tourism took shape in relationship to the economic practices of the tourism industry. In the 1960s, in most French regions dedicated to tourism, whether coastal or mountainous, regional research teams were established. Tourism studies formed part of the perspective of the management of their territories along with policies of free time, the organization of weekends and yearly holidays. These works were mainly requested by the *Ministère de l'Equipement et de l'Aménagement du Territoire* (Ministry for the Manning and Management of Territory). The teams were often linked to a university, and this association occurred mostly within departments of geography. Such was the case at Paris Sorbonne with CEST. The same thing happened at Angers, in Rheims where Georges Cazes taught at the beginning of his career, and in Nice, with Yvette Barbaza. As far as the coast of Languedoc-Roussillon was concerned, at stake was the involvement of teams of sociologists with an analysis of the environment principally within the framework of a project of systematization. This project, starting from tourism activity led to a complete rearrangement of littoral space.

At the end of the 1960s, a change of direction could be noticed. The economic and political role of tourism was becoming more and more important in the politics of the civil authorities. This was evident in the change of orientation in the targets of the *Commissariat au Tourisme Franç ais* (Department of French Tourism), which demonstrated a thoroughly new awareness of tourism in the development of French society. In this regard, it showed a clear-cut turning point from former times when it declared that it was necessary to integrate tourism into the economic circuits and make it a constituent sector of the economy according to the industrial model. Hence, the requests for studies from the decision makers to which practically all the researchers who were to become renowned in this field responded. It was often the only way to obtain funds for research. In this sector, there were élites who were enlightened about tourism and those who were not. This imbalance in the knowledge of tourism's potential had negative consequences for the orientation of sociological research into the phenomenon. The situation was thoroughly examined by URESTI in the 1970s in a work published under the title *Sociologie du Tourisme: Positions et Perspectives dans la Recherche Internationale* (Sociology of Tourism: Positions and Perspectives in International Research), under my direction and with four researchers working in strict collaboration: Marie-Helène Mottin, Danielle Rozenberg, Michel Picard, and Jacques de Weerdt (Lanfant et al 1978).

Deviations of Sociology in the Study of Tourism

At the beginning of the 1960s, I began to explore the domain of tourism, examining all the publications indexed under the heading "sociology of tourism." Then, I concluded that most of the investigations, and perhaps the best of them, represented the output of isolated researchers who, although recognized because of the quality of their work, admitted that they had never studied tourism as a major subject. Their theses were often a second hand re-adaptation of disparate inquiries that had not been subject to sociological critique. Additionally, when opinions concerning certain forms of tourism development, and their ensuing social and cultural consequences, became more and more critical, sociology was suspected of raising problems which promoters did not like, so much so that it led to the following paradox. Although sociology was being more and more consulted on management issues, with a corresponding loss of its disciplinary focus, the result was often that of fundamental problems which it would normally be obliged to tackle, became buried in the process. Sociology, confronted with the objective of overseeing development, became prisoner of a problematic which was strange to it, that is, the economic problematic aligned to the market economy, in which tourism had become one of its most efficient leverages.

At this juncture, and in an *a priori* fashion, a place was defined for sociology, a subordinate position that reduced its status and rejected its questions, lowering it to the role of auxiliary in economic analysis (Lanfant et al 1978). Sociologists, as well as anthropologists, were asked to deal with the determinants of the demand for holidays and with the reduction of negative impacts on the social and cultural environment. In fact, the role of sociology was simply therapeutic in nature, active solely when social problems arose. From its analyses, a better knowledge of the holiday population was expected, in the framework of a democratization of amusements as well as an improved understanding of the cultural and social policies of tourism in the framework of policies of economic development in the chosen areas. In each case, the typical approach of the sociologist was inscribed in a logic which was alien to her, a logic of marketing tailored to prevailing circumstances.

On the other hand, institutional frameworks were not prepared to deal with the new situation that resulted from the development of tourism in the world. Students choosing for their final dissertations a topic dealing with an aspect of tourism were often discouraged from doing so by their professors. The latter frequently shared the prejudice of those intellectuals who regarded modern tourism as a destructive agent of classical culture. But above all, the location of a sociology of tourism within a university setting was still subservient to the artificial, administrative division of this field of knowledge into teaching and research. Thus, the study of society developed in France in two separate domains: ethnology and sociology. The result was a division of labor. The analysis of industrial societies oriented toward the future was deemed to be the prerogative of sociology, while the study of traditional societies seeking to preserve their past was reserved to ethnology. This separation constituted a real handicap to developing a global approach toward the tourism phenomenon. The ethnologists, confronted with the presence of tourists in the traditional societies which they had chosen for their fieldwork, considered tourists as intruders distorting the purity of the data that they had collected. Many students visiting these places as tourists, fascinated by the primitive character of these societies, proposed research topics on the social and cultural effects of tourism. They did not find in France the right sort of institutional framework at the university in order to support their research. Thus, URESTI had to take on the burden of these student researchers, at the risk of falling out with those professors who considered them as their game preserve.

Creation of a Research Field

It was because of the foregoing difficulties that I conceived a project to create a new area of research in the sociology of international tourism, a research field that was to be a place open to the collection of questions raised by the development and spread of tourism worldwide. Starting in 1972, and working at the margins of the team of the sociology of leisure and of cultural models, I set out on this path. The new research team received official acknowledgement in 1976 under the name of the *Unité de Recherche en Sociologie du Tourisme Internationale* (URESTI). The creation of this institution represented a decisive moment for the involvement of sociology in the study of the tourism phenomenon.

Although the period when this story began goes beyond the limits of this account, in order to place it in the perspective of the history of the sociology of tourism within the context of the *École Française de Sociologie*, it is useful to mention here the salient points of the problematic guiding the works of this team. Here, I provide only some elements of information. I have already written elsewhere about my personal journey and the stages of the creation of this research field in France until its broadening to become a permanent research committee of the ISA (Lanfant 2007).

From the very inception of this project, I adopted orientations which were clearly aligned to the international dimension of the tourism phenomenon. The basis of the project was to construct a methodology that permitted me to grasp the phenomenon in its globality beyond the diversity of representations spread by social discourse. From the outset, "a tourist fact" was treated as "an international fact" in the same manner that Durkheim (1938) and Mauss (1980) had indicated in their writings on the facts of civilization; the only difference being that in this case, the international dimension of tourism was tackled by following the principles of systemic analysis. According to these principles, it was no longer necessary to start from local or national contexts, but to define right away the sociological object as a phenomenon of interaction and interrelationship that transcended these limits. To locate myself in this perspective meant to sever connections with all the then dominant approaches treating the development of tourism as a consequence (nearly a consecration) of a demand for leisure emanating from postindustrial societies. Similarly, my position implied the need to overcome the differences between studies carried out separately in societies emitting foreign tourists (essentially Western societies) and societies called to receive them (essentially developing societies). It was truly a separation reinforced by the division of research departments according to disciplines, where the analysis of demand was more specifically allocated to sociology, the sociology of leisure in particular, while the analysis of the destination environment was still linked with anthropology/ethnology, with the resulting difficulty of treating the phenomenon in its totality.

In this same view, tourism was first of all tackled for its exchange value, with the specification that the concept of "exchange" was a fundamental concept common to both economics and anthropology. This concept allowed me to articulate in the same problematic the economic and the cultural dimensions of tourism, which were generally perceived as evolving toward antagonistic targets. According to this hypothesis, it was assumed that tourism movements, in propagating and amplifying themselves, would produce new types of exchange between differing human societies, cultures, or groups. Through these exchanges a process of civilization was at work, transforming contemporary societies in the idea they shaped of their identities and of their relationships with the Other.

Finally, the tourism phenomenon was studied as "a total social phenomenon" (Lanfant 1980, 1993, 1995). It was not a statement of principle qualifying the reality of the phenomenon. Rather, it was a methodological choice to start its study with a pluridimensional approach, paying attention to the eclectic and polymorphic aspects covered by the word *tourism*. Adopting this terminology, this research field drew on the anthropology of Marcel Mauss (1980), whose *Essai sur le Don* (Essay on the Gift) was one of the founding texts.

These working hypotheses helped frame the continuation of this research and in its enlargement into the international sphere. They permitted me a freedom from an explanation of the tourist fact moving from the Western ideal of leisure, as well as from a symmetric view of the term of exchange, and allowed me to quit the CNRS at the moment of my retirement in 1998, with the title of *Directeur Honoraire du CNRS* (Director Emeritus of

CNRS). The team of CNRS dissolved, but URESTI continued working, albeit in a fragmented way.

Today, the overall research field has consolidated and developed at an accelerated speed. This is suggested by the papers I have given from time to time, both in French and in translations provided by sympathetic colleagues. It is also testified by the countless presentations made to various universities and research centers, as well as to international conferences taking place periodically, particularly to the research committee on international tourism of the ISA (RC50) and the International Academy for the Study of Tourism. There has also been a steady development in a wide theoretical array of French tourism publications from the 1960s to the 1990s with, for example, works by Bruckner and Finkielkraut (1979) on anti-tourism, Cazes (1976) and Tresse (1990) on imagery, Dufour (1978) on myths, Picard (1992) on tourist culture, Thurot (1981) on the ideology of advertising, and Urbain (1993) on sociolinguistics.

At the Turn of the Millennium (1985–2000)

The sociology of tourism, originating from the sociology of leisure, neglected the theoretical background which was elaborated in the 1950s by the theoreticians of industrial society. Only the concept of leisure was maintained, and that was without any concern about how it had been shaped, by thoroughly ignoring its ideological and political dimensions and the implications at stake.

Nevertheless, and in spite of this limitation, there were some important initiatives undertaken in France prior to the millennium and they can be briefly mentioned here. The first took place at Marly-le-Roi and consisted in a round table that investigated in depth the theoretical basis of the sociocultural effects of tourism. Held under the initiative of URESTI, and under my direction, it witnessed the invitation of several international scholars to these discussions and, in that sense, continued the mission of Joffré Dumazedier of opening up French ideas to worldwide scrutiny and critique. Those interested in this seminal debate can consult the special edition of *Problems of Tourism* (Lanfant 1987a, 1987b) dedicated to this theme, especially as it contested the conventional wisdom on the topic and provided an alternative.

The second occurred in 1992 on the French Riviera town of Nice. Here, aforementioned colleagues at the University of Nice, especially those associated with the laboratory of ethnology, collaborated with me in extending an invitation to members of the by now vibrant working group on international tourism of the ISA. This was an interim conference devoted to the key topic of international tourism caught between identity and change which acted as a catalyst toward the rapid promotion of the group to its elevated status of a full research committee. The multilingual proceedings edited by Jean Pierre Jardel (1994) appeared two years later and now constitute an important resource book in the sociology of tourism, especially as it brought together for the first time contributions from leading Francophone and Anglophone scholars as well as a number of academics from continental Europe.

Then, in the year 2000, due to the initiative of Jean-Pierre Poulain, the *Centre d'Étude du Tourisme et des Industries de l'Accueil* (CETIA) (Center for the Study of Tourism and Welcoming Industries), organized a meeting at Foix in order to take stock of research in tourism, the proceedings of which were published the following year as a useful state-of-the-art text (Poulain and Teychenné 2001).

These are but three examples of international collaboration which are becoming a hallmark of the sociology of tourism and look like being the way that it will develop in the future. Even though there are academics on the international scene who from different parts of the world espouse diverse theoretical origins and developments in their field, without the significant input of the French School of Sociology and its application to leisure and, subsequently tourism, an important thesis in the ensuing dialectic would be missing. While this account has attempted to show how this thesis was formulated, it is up to others to demonstrate the various antitheses and syntheses which it evoked. Only with an appreciation of the heritage of the academic study of tourism in France and a variety of other countries, will it be possible to look forward to a fruitful and mutually beneficial future.

CONCLUSION

In this personal journey, I have attempted to show how the sociology of tourism emerged in France largely on account of its identification with the very foundations of its parent discipline in such pioneering figures as Saint-Simon, Comte, and Durkheim. Indeed, it was the *École Française* that laid the basis for key unit ideas that I identified in the sociology of tourism: tourism as a social fact and tourism as a total social phenomenon. I have also traced subsequent generations of French sociologists from modern to postmodern and the contributions they made to understanding society.

The litany of names stretching from Gurvitch and Aron to the likes of Naville, Lefebvre, Morin, Burgelin, Barthes, and Baudrillard is testimony to the rich sociological tradition of my country. In the midst of this evolution Joffré Dumazedier appeared and with him the crucial application of general sociology to the field of leisure. It was also at this juncture that the opportunity occurred for my own involvement in this domain and later to travel the path leading to the sociology of tourism. This was also the route that led to greater internationalization, from one European state to other European nations and beyond.

Acknowledgements—My thanks to Giuli Liebman Parrinello and Graham Dann for jointly preparing the translation of this account from the original French.

Chapter 4

Tourism in Italian Sociological Thought and Study

Asterio Savelli
University of Bologna, Bologna, Italy

INTRODUCTION

In Europe, the social sciences started to study tourism during the period spanning the first and second world wars. At first glance, the field seemed to be the prerogative of central European countries, with the manifestation of increasingly large and dynamic catchment areas for "active tourism." Investigations and observations there focused on topics such as the creation of demand, its social categorization and resulting consumer models with new, highly specialized forms of business for the organization of demand, and acting as go-betweens for the various functions and functionaries involved in the tourism industry.

However, Italy was a different case. It was a country whose tourism economy was largely receptive, or "passive," where hospitality services and their related businesses spread rapidly, affecting the economic, social, and territorial *status quo* of entire regions. Researchers here focused more on the modes of hospitality and the types of impact on the territory and the local community rather than on the genesis of tourism, its motivations, or what it meant for the society that generated it. Sociologists who began to analyze tourism in Italy directed their attention to the local economy, employment, businesses, relationships between groups of stakeholders, the use of

The Sociology of Tourism: European Origins and Developments
Tourism Social Science Series, Volume 12, 131–167
Copyright © 2009 by Emerald Group Publishing Limited
All rights of reproduction in any form reserved
ISSN: 1571-5043/doi:10.1108/S1571-5043(2009)0000012009

resources, urbanization, and changes in the environment and culture. Even when sociology did concentrate on demand and its motivations, it predominantly adopted the viewpoint of those (businessmen, the local community) who restructured their resources in order to cater for hospitality. This was apparently linked to the fact that the flow of tourists seemed to grow spontaneously, and managing it did not represent a problem, if one excluded organizational issues when tourists actually arrived on holiday. The Italian product was made up of local communities, families, and small businesses that "faced" the demand of a market whose presence and growth did not depend on any initiatives implemented by the product itself. It was more a case of adapting to demand rather than promoting it.

Economics and geography were classic disciplines in this area of the social sciences. Apart from a fleeting reference (in Cohen 1984) to the Italian, Bodio, writing the first brief scientific article on tourism in 1899, along with its link to foreign exchange, compatriots Angelo Mariotti (1974) and Umberto Toschi (1947, 1952, 1957) were considered the respective disciplinary leaders. Nevertheless, although scientific debate considered issues from many different angles, it did not always follow a clear path of development, often finding itself once again at the starting blocks, driven by an ongoing need to redefine a subject whose origins, motivations, and trends appeared very elusive. Hence the need for sociological and anthropological approaches to tourism which were capable of proposing and developing a systematic analysis of the collective factors that encouraged different stakeholders (tourists, visitors, organizers, and local communities) to come to their decisions and change their behavior.

There was no specific study of the sociology of tourism in Italy until the end of the 1960s and 1970s when initial approaches focused on rural sociology. Researchers such as Corrado Barberis, Claudio Stroppa, and Giampaolo Catelli first started to look into tourism as a result of its effects on the countryside and the social rural environment. These studies concentrated on the decisions taken by local communities and businessmen either to reject or participate in a phenomenon that was already challenging rural contexts because of the effects of mass tourism; whether they were prestigious or marginal, neither appeared equipped to cope with the new challenges from a cultural or organizational point of view. This posed the question of its potential extent and the necessary conditions for tourism to coexist or replace agriculture, ensuring the balance of employment in villages and preventing emigration (Barberis 1976). Tourism was seen as an opportunity to save the countryside by using the energies taken from the agricultural sector. Attention focused on sociological models of tourism development that depended on the local community's ability to control the scale of investment and to use the appropriate channels. In particular, analysis and comparison centered on models that related respectively to "local development" (the working class capitalism of local businessmen), "aristocratic colonization" (the programs developed by big business for vast areas), and "democratic colonization" (small-scale investment by individuals) (Barberis 1979).

Paolo Guidicini (1973) was the first Italian to discuss the social dimension of tourism in any detail. He claimed that the phenomenon of tourism's shifting focus between trends highlighted a restricting form of familiar "privacy" and tendencies, grouping individuals *en masse* in collective modes of travel and holidaying offered by the large tourism firms. He showed that there were none of the intermediate forms of social interaction, and that these would only be recovered or regenerated if individuals managed their leisure time and tourism independently within a framework of multiple groups and opportunities for association.

The idea of planning investment in the tourism sector led to the analysis of the behavior of consumers. With growth in per capita income and a decline in the amount of time spent at work, an increasing number of social groups now had the possibility of going on holiday. Tourism not only produced beneficial effects for specialist businesses (transport, accommodation providers, and restaurants), but also benefited a whole series of local businesses operating in a range of fields. Thus, the act of spending tended to prevail over the social act, overturning the scale of social values and lending more importance to leisure time activities than to work. This resulted in a hypothesis based on the increasingly cosmopolitan nature of individuals, of a tourism that was increasingly itinerant until the desire for something new had been satisfied. There was apparent variance between the tendency to create conventional images, prepared exclusively for tourists, and the concept of tourism as an opportunity for the development of an individual's personality and for social participation (Stroppa 1976).

Franco Martinelli considered the dynamics of tourism in parallel with the institutionalization and extension of annual holiday leave with the proliferation of means of transport, private cars in particular. From this perspective, a new reading could be given to the results of many of the investigations and studies of communities conducted in Italy with regard to leisure time, excursions, and travel (1976). Mass tourism was viewed as the consequence of a process of rationalization of employment, causing it to become a mere pragmatic fact. The lack of awareness of the condition of alienation at work also led to alienation in the private sphere, so that the domestic environment no longer fulfilled the role of giving vent to individual expressiveness, but had the task of reproducing the capacity to produce. The ensuing evasion also affected the private sphere and translated, from a territorial point of view, into escape from the city toward the "rabbit warrens" of leisure time, even though these presented the risk of reproducing the same negative elements of urban society. In the 1970s, the countryside was called the last frontier of leisure time, but was considered a "primitive area" by city dwellers, one that did not represent an alternative to urban values. As a result, the countryside was affected by a frenzy of building that was not linked to the local cultural substratum, but followed models copied from metropolitan culture. If each segment of a territory relinquished its inherent character and values, this inevitably led to the end of rural tourism and would only result in "areas unfit for human habitation" (Catelli 1976).

SOCIOLOGY AND TOURISM

Several higher education programs were launched during the early 1970s, mainly at private schools and colleges, aiming to address the needs of the new managers in the tourism industry. These programs grew and consolidated during the early 1980s, preparing the ground for the official advent of tourism studies at the university level.

Higher Education for Tourism Professionals and Initial Theorizing

The first examples at private colleges included the Free Faculty of Tourism Sciences based in Faicchio (Benevento) and Naples, the International School of Tourism Sciences (SIST) in Rome, Tuscia Free University in Viterbo, the Center for Higher Studies in Tourism and the Promotion of Tourism (CST) in Assisi, and "L. Bocconi" Commercial University, and the Free University of Foreign Languages and Communication (IULM) in Milan. The sociology of tourism made its first formal appearance in multi- or mono-disciplinary publications designed as teaching aids for the instruction of workers and managers in the private and public sectors. These publications expanded on the stimuli and thoughts arising out of general sociological theories and used specific national and international literature on the social dynamics of tourism (Costa 1985, 1989; Dalla Chiesa 1980; Fragola 1984–1985; Perrotta 1985; Savelli 1989; Sessa 1974–1992, 1979). These publications were followed by the advent of teaching manuals, used first at the "specialist schools" centered on tourism at various universities, then as part of the "sociology of tourism" courses formally incorporated into university studies in the early 1990s and now widespread throughout the Italian university system (Costa 2008; Martinengo and Savoja 1998; Nocifora 2001, 2008b; Savoja 2005).

Alberto Sessa published seven editions of his *Elementi di Sociologia e Psicologia del Turismo* (Elements of the Sociology and Psychology of Tourism) between 1974 and 1992. Here he considered and classified various social and psychological topics, such as motivation, the decision process, behavior patterns, types of advertising, forms of hospitality, and tourism's effects on local communities, with several references to the international sociological literature from France, Germany, and from English-speaking countries in particular (Sessa 1992). A later work on *Turismo e Società* (Tourism and Society) reflected a controversy felt at the international level: on the one hand, members of the International Association of Scientific Experts on Tourism (AIEST) maintained that research into tourism should be part of a theoretical framework focused on development; on the other hand, "anthropologized sociology"—backed by initial reports published by UNESCO and the World Bank on the social and cultural impacts of tourism—focused more on the degenerative aspects linked to the growth of tourism and emphasized the risks faced by local cultures for the preservation of their independence and their very survival. The social-anthropological approach was accused of a-historical immobility; the hope was for research that attempted to understand cultural dynamics in relation to economic change (Sessa 1979). This controversy was associated with the isolation of a number of authors who were grouped together for their shared "aprioristic ideological" approach (Adorno, Kentler, Lefebvre, and Marcuse). Sessa rejected their theoretical perspective while acknowledging that the increased potential of tourism had been misused in certain aspects (1979:55–57).

Ferdinando Dalla Chiesa provided a systematic benchmark for a truly sociological approach to tourism in 1980. He introduced the series of stakeholders and relationships that were involved in the sociology of tourism and paid particular attention to the social conditions when demand and the socioeconomic systems of supply came together, and offered his analysis of the changes induced by the development of tourism in the local society in terms of employment, demographic trends, and urbanization. He then considered the processes of "feedback," whereby the social effects produced at destinations affected and modified patterns of tourism demand. The development of the industry had led to an increasingly pronounced split between a person's private and public sphere. For a significant number of people, the private sphere had become the preferred or even exclusive environment for self-fulfillment. Tourism's new primary "compensatory" role was identified in the opportunities available for self-fulfillment (compensation for working hard and for what the city failed to provide), in addition to its traditional role as an alternative for recreation and rest and its symbolic function that in the mass dimension marked a shift from the emphasis on belonging to an elite or an egalitarian grouping (Dalla Chiesa 1980).

Dalla Chiesa applied the framework of the advanced industrial society, where tourism was given the task of representing the social system as a whole, over and above any division into social classes that was unequivocally promoted by the organization of production. Marcello Lelli took up the reference to a situation of Fordist production a few years later (1989). This was a situation where the repetitiveness and monotony of the tasks given to machines was reflected in societies using them, leading to the degrading of workers' activities both on the job and outside the factory. The factory also came to control leisure time activities, spending and tourism, reabsorbing them in its logic or giving them a merely temporary role, keeping them alive like remnants of the past. In this situation, Lelli said, "life is subordinate to the factory and the needs of people have to be turned into demand for the goods produced by the factory" (Lelli 1989:90). But he considered that this condition was destined to change rapidly when— and this was the case in the 1980s—radical changes occurred in the production process and in its relationship with other activities in social life. With the coming of new technologies, the value of the communication skills of stakeholders became fundamental and there was a "resurgence of personal creativity and a new centrality" (1989:92). In a society that had freed itself from mechanical work, culture became immediately productive and cultural consumption increased. Above all, there was the advent of manufacturing businesses founded on actual needs rather than stimulating needs based on current production. The distribution of given products led to the satisfaction of a broader sphere of needs and the promotion of increasingly higher standards of consumption. Social structure shifted from the portrayal of a classless society—overlapped and compensated for a rigid and complex contrast between social positions—evolution of a "no class" concept where people were placed into categories based on the worth of the job they did (1989:93).

Gerardo Ragone subsequently offered an important overview of the sociology of tourism. He focused on the relationship between tourism and social stratification, on the evolution affecting destinations over time, and the organization of tourism products. Ragone referred to Veblen's theory whereby spending was essentially a tool for the portrayal of social status: in the competition that arose between social classes, the displayed contents were defined by those who were more privileged, as they had more spending power. Most people harbored the aspiration to come within reach of the forms chosen by the elite as closely as possible, stimulating the latter to look for new alternatives to set themselves apart. At the root of the element of distinction, Ragone saw a relationship of subordination being formed between the host community and the tourist that still expresses the relationship between different social classes today. Being served became a major source of pleasure for tourists:

> I luoghi tipici, le cucine tradizionali, i cibi autentici non sono altro che ingredienti diversi di un'unica operazione tendente alla ricostruzione simbolica di una cultura subalterna e servile, idonea a richiamare alla memoria l'antico rapporto padrone-servitore (1998:678).

> Characteristic places, traditional and authentic food are simply different ingredients in a single operation attempting to offer a symbolic reconstruction of a subservient and servile culture, reminiscent of the old master-servant relationship.

Links with International Schools of Thought

In the mid-1980s, Rosalba Perrotta introduced Italian sociologists of tourism to the main theoretical concepts matured in the international context. The principal benchmark authors were David Riesman for his comparison between the different phases in history and the corresponding types of stakeholders (directed by tradition, inner directed, other directed); Dean MacCannell for his interpretation of the encounter between tourists and local populations and of the structure of tourism based on the representation of authenticity; and Erik Cohen for his categories of tourists based on the levels of organization of the tourist experience and on greater or lesser alienation compared to the "center" of the society to which they belonged. The different ways of considering tourism pointed out the complexity and vast potential of the phenomenon. In particular, the emergence of a new form of tourism for "study" was attracting growing attention, flanked by the more consolidated tourism for evasion that responded to the needs of an emerging postmodern culture (Perrotta 1985).

Nicolò Costa extended references to foreign authors in 1985 and again in 1989 in order to come to a more mature definition of tourism from a sociological point of view, to develop an analysis of the relationship of tourism with the local area, and to identify types of behavior and tourist experience. In addition to Cohen and MacCannell, authors such as Plog were now considered for his psychographical descriptions of the tourist, Philip Pearce for his study of the widespread image of the tourist, Snepenger for his segmentation of the market according to motivation for change and/ or new experiences, and Moore, the Turner's, Graburn, and Jafari for their interpretation of tourists as "pilgrims of modern life." The theoretical frameworks produced by international researchers were used to collect feedback and verify it in statistical surveys carried out in Italy by various institutes and research centers, such as the *Istituto Nazionale di Statistica, Roma* (ISTAT) (National Institute of Statistics, Rome), the *Centro Studi Investimenti Sociali*, Roma (CENSIS) (Center for Studies of Social Investment, Rome), the *Centro per gli Studi sui Sistemi Distributivi e il Turismo*, Milano (CESDIT) (Center for Studies of Distributive Systems and Tourism, Milan), the *Istituto per le Ricerche Statistiche e l'Analisi dell'Opinione Pubblica*, Milano-Roma (DOXA) (Institute for Statistical Research and the Analysis of Public Opinion, Milan-Rome), and *Trademark*, Rimini. They did not refer explicitly to the tourist categories established by the sociological literature except for the work by Dall'Ara (Trademark Italia 1985), where Plog's psychography was applied to the demand for tourism in Italy, as a tool to support the *marketing* conducted by hoteliers and travel agents. However, the data collected did provide significant information on the level of national demand based on different modes of travel. Furthermore, Costa paid particular attention in both volumes to the time-space cycle of tourism, providing conceptual tools and examples of surveys on the various stages when the experience occurred: the anticipatory dream, the journey toward the destination, behavior at the destination, the return journey, and the memory. He made a significant contribution that enhanced the awareness of the complexity of tourism phenomena, even those that seemed quite simple.

Asterio Savelli's *Sociologia del Turismo* (Sociology of Tourism) was also published in 1989. In addition to referring to the various interpretative approaches of the English-speaking authors mentioned above, he made ample reference both to Hans Joaquim Knebel and Marc Boyer for their method of historical comparison. This was fundamental for illustrating the links between tourist behavior and the structure of the society that generated it, as well as for the concrete connotations of behavior and their meaning in the various stages of development, to the complete affirmation of the "advanced industrial" society and the start of what some began to call "postindustrial" society. The crisis factors in mass tourism that came with an advanced industrial society were brought to light through the critical thought of Boorstin, Enzensberger, and Morin, while Burgelin, MacCannell, and Cohen referred to the paths for overcoming the limits of this experience (1989). Even the field studies conducted in Romagna's tourism area, whose format was based on the distinction between the "push" and "pull" factors proposed by Dann (1981), led to the affirmation that social pressure for the standardization of behavior was falling although still dominant, and a differentiation in motivations was emerging flanked by the need for new experiences, expressed in traveling alone without a set schedule, always visiting different places to meet people who had a different way of life. Savelli reported that there was a nascent need for identity and subjective protagonism, stemming from increasing social complexity and expressed through more selective behavior with regard to the opportunities available. For this reason, tourism information, with its territorial telematic networks, was viewed as a powerful pull factor regardless of its contents because it stimulated and simultaneously satisfied the selective approach of consumers with regard to tourist opportunities (1989).

A short but significant essay by Giuliano Piazzi offered some important theoretical references for understanding the dynamics that added value to the diversification of behavior. There he claimed that in the 1980s:

> Si esce dalla vacanza stereotipata e dall'ambiente turistico proposto unicamente come momento di eterodirezione ludica o come contrassegno di status sociale. Vacanze ed ambiente turistico vengono ora inventati e costruiti, scomposti e ricomposti, secondo trafile di significazione proprie ad una soggettività crescente, autodiretta e fine a se stessa (1988:23).

> Stereotypical holidays and destinations seen only as a moment of other-directed fun or as a mark of social status are coming to an end. Holidays and tourist destinations are now invented and constructed, broken down and built up according to procedures whose meaning is linked to a growing subjectivity that is inner-directed and an end in itself.

For Piazzi, this appeared to be the result of a change taking place in the form of social diversification: "the gradual emancipation and purity of *functional diversification* with regard to the residual forms of *stratified diversification*" (1988:23). He interpreted this change based on the theoretical contribution offered by Niklas Luhmann (1983); the new overabundance of options could be used as an increase in opportunities to enrich the types of difference (namely subjective identity), but in this case it was a difference without value, that did not produce hierarchies. Otherwise, it could be used to establish a difference between the experiences that continued to express variation in value, but in this case it became insecure, risky, and contingent (Piazzi 1988).

Tourism in Local Communities

Earlier it was seen how mass tourism represented the starting point for Italian sociological insights into the phenomenon, especially on account of the concern generated by its potential impact on vulnerable social structures, such as the countryside and small urban communities. Awareness of the ambivalent nature of tourism was a consistent theme in the sociological literature. It simultaneously provided "confirmation of identity through the mutual recognition of differences compared to a given object (the everyday environment for residents, the area of discovery and experimentation for tourists) and the denial of identity by suggesting different readings of a given object" (Palumbo 1992:361). This ambivalence was exacerbated by the commercial aspect of the exchange, whereby tourists paid for the authenticity they enjoyed and residents sold part of their identity, and by the implicit cultural dominance of tourists over residents. Within this framework, there was a growing interest in "identity tourism" the development of which apparently mitigated the privileges enjoyed by specialist destinations and benefited tourism products based on the inherent resources and values of individual territories, consequently posing the problem that there was no link between private businesses aiming to offer a traditional product and the public sector that was badly equipped for planning and promoting tourism products (Palumbo 1988).

   Emanuele Sgroi stated that the tourism industry transformed raw materials such as the environment, natural resources, the landscape, and the material and immaterial culture of a territory. As these local phenomena were "public assets," close interaction needed to be established with the local community. The business mentality had to engage in dialog with the local culture: "a businessman in the industry can do a bad job on his own; he can only do a good job by working together with the local community" (1988:139). Even if tourism assumed a global character by way of its mobility and its ability to take over space, it still remained a local phenomenon "because it is perceived as the entering—albeit briefly—of a place that is the sole and specific custodian of an *icon*." The tourist was "stimulated by the new culture of tourism to seek out, discover and perhaps invent 'his' (sic) own personal icon to proudly take back home from each place." Tourists pursued a wide variety of naturalist, artistic, ethno-anthropological, gastronomic stimuli and messages, and they were hence attracted by complex local realities. Therefore, tourism could not fill a "vacuum of development" on its own. Instead, it was "a perspective that can only move efficaciously if there are other dynamics of development going on at the same time" (2001:7, 9) to prevent the creation of single economy systems that were weak and carried the risk of a new dependence on external sources.

Widespread consideration of the process of globalization led many researchers to focus their analyses on the new found importance of information in tourist relations. According to Enzo Nocifora, an open and pluralistic society required people to handle different senses of belonging at the same time, building and interpreting specific paths of meaning. Distinct, individual choices led to homogeneous mass tourism being replaced with many different forms of tourism (2008a), all potentially present at the same time, while the marked volatility of demand thwarted attempts to find general explanatory principles in tourist behavior. Thus, the combination of tourism and information technology not only changed how tourism packages were sold; it also modified the ways in which they were designed and constructed. Consumers could compare various opportunities and choose their destination, resulting in global competition that was hitherto unknown (1997, 2008b). Everywhere was a potential destination and each place tended to stress its features in a sort of global competition between local areas, promoting its own image within complex tourism regions that were capable of offering inexhaustible options and experiences. Thus, tourism space expanded well beyond the specialized fields of historic towns, mountain resorts, and the seaside, involving the resources of minor localities and inland areas and designing new maritime tourism regions (Savelli 1997a, 2008a, 2008b, 2008d).

A particular point of interest for tourism stemmed from the desire to comprehend the dynamics taking place in the local community, within the framework of increasing mobility in a territory and growing exposure to global communication. Renzo Gubert and Gabriele Pollini (2002) researched this topic, focusing on the complex relationship between tourism and the local community. The fact that the variety of origins and the frequent change of people with whom tourism workers came into contact did not affect their attachment to the territory was explained by the weakness of the relationships that were created between workers and tourists, which were mainly utilitarian in scope. Although the decisions by tourists might be motivated by noninstrumental goals, they seemed to maintain contacts of a different nature compared to those of workers. Thus, "the diagnosis whereby contemporary modern society has lost its public traits and has only acquired corporate traits appears unduly stressed" (2002:307).

A projection of the feeling of belonging to a territory among workers could be seen in the relationship that each of them had with other employees in the same area and in the forms of cooperation that were established between the world of business and local communities, seen as a political and institutional system. It had been found that the weakness of such relationships had led to short-term strategic visions and short-term investments. In particular, Catalano, Fiorelli, and Marra (2008:105) noted that "the lack of planning and programming in the tourism sector has an immediate and negative impact on the landscape and on the health of the environment." A study in Calabria led by Ezio Marra (Catalano et al 2008), found clear heterogeneity in the levels of cooperation between public and private stakeholders in the various areas of the region. While it discovered meritorious examples of public-private cooperation, there almost always appeared to be a lack of cooperative strategies both among the same levels of local government (municipality to municipality) and between different levels (between provinces and regions). In certain cases, there seemed to be situations of veritable conflict. However, local mayors were expressing a new leaning toward projects open to collaboration between local municipalities. Studies dwelt on their portrayal of the status of tourism and on that expressed by workers in the private sector, measuring the gap between actual reality and perception, in order to comprehend the concrete prospects for the development of the areas in question (Catalano et al 2008:105–107). A similar study in Emilia-Romagna highlighted the tendency to extend the tourism area from the coastal strip to the hinterland and the Apennines (however uneven the spread), by developing relationships and alliances between local governments. Although it might have been true that even small localities could find their own space and a competitive edge in tourism's globalization process, it did appear that their success depended on being part of a wider "region," acknowledging variety as an asset while promoting their individuality within the broader tourism market (Manella 2008).

In Italy, the processes of territorial aggregation, bringing public institutions, and private business together to work on operational strategies for the definition and promotion of specific tourism products, were governed by law (n. 135/2001). This established Local Tourist Systems, considered "homogeneous or integrated contexts ... . with the integrated offer of cultural, environmental, and tourism attractions, including local farm products and local handicrafts, or by the widespread presence of individual or associated tourist businesses" (art. 5). As a result, a current of study containing sociological ideas and proposals had developed in recent years aiming to build a framework of professional skills and local interaction in order to support the establishment and operation of these systems. Here Paolo Corvo and Nicolò Costa were particularly active, studying the connection between the tourism system and the local community and defining some professional figures and "good practices" for planning and management of the new territorial and social aggregations in the industry (Corvo 2007; Costa 2005a, 2008).

The relationship between tourism and the local community immediately involved communications and the integration between different cultures and between global culture and local cultures. Tourism's potential role of go-between was addressed explicitly by several authors. They included Ulderico Bernardi who first highlighted the negative effects of ethnocentric closure, which had imposed "heavy existential costs on humanity and harm to nature affecting all people" (1997:55). Cultural anthropology offered a contribution that overcame the deterministic nature of positivism, whereby social progress came from nature, and of historical and dialectical materialism, whereby the future of humankind remained in the hands of the class struggle, by illustrating the inevitably local character of forms of knowledge. The acknowledgement that nothing justified discrimination between superior and inferior cultures facilitated mutual acceptance and exchange in an effective intercultural communication. Thus, Bernardi's contribution wound its way through cultures viewed as dynamic systems, considering tourism as a vehicle for the communication of local cultures. In particular, he noted how every society was being shown to be effectively multiethnic in the transition from the industrial age to the postindustrial age, yet cultural diversity was scarcely acknowledged as a value (1997:52–58, 212–220).

"Intercultural tourism" lay at the center of a study by Claudio Baraldi and Monica Teodorani. They considered "the set of communications that are based on a positive approach to the extraneousness of participants in a context that distinguishes between the roles of the tourist and the resident" (1998:9). It occurred in a destination society whose structural characteristics differed from those whence the tourists originated, and mediation developed between the two societies, enabling a link to be created between them.

However, this only took place when diversification according to functions occurred in the home society of the tourist compared to diversification by strata, and when the plurality of codes removed an image of the society itself, removing the value of contrast between those belonging there and strangers. The differences between individuals prevailed over social belonging. The protection of collective cultural resources was abandoned and every resource for intersubjective comparison was brought into play (1998:9–15).

Laura Gemini further stressed the relationship between tourism and subjectivity. She declared that "travel can be viewed as a meaningful experience….if it is part of the process of a person's individualization" (2006:270). The tourist experience came back to the notion of "vocational consumption," to individuals' need to represent themselves, to invest in their identity by expressing their vocation as tourists. Thus, everyone "considers his (sic) own journey as an opportunity for producing meaning from his specific perspective and with his creativity" (2006:271). With the resulting internal division and variety, tourism demand "produces behavior that promotes the complication of the product, the internal diversification of tourism, and the economic system" showing itself to be functional to society and its reproduction (2006:271). Recent changes in tourism and how it was conducted were viewed against the background of the shift from the "representational" imagination prevailing in modern times (from the 16th century to the mid-20th century) to the "performance" imagination, coming out of the changes in the relationship between leisure time and time spent at work in the post-Fordist economy. The first was based on a "set of images, symbols, and descriptions aiming to build an accurate and timely representation of reality" and led to the pursuit of "authentic things, places, peoples, and cultures" (2008:99). The second was based purely on an experience and was linked to "a constructive and subjective approach, where what counts is our own ability to take notice of ourselves, to understand what is genuine and meaningful for oneself" (2008:166).

The approach of cultural anthropology to tourism, whose development started with the study and reflection on specific issues, was largely systematized in a work by Alessandro Simonicca. After reviewing the traditions of Anglo-Saxon research and the French School, he referred to the patterns of analysis adopted by many scholars and researchers at the international level and focused largely on ethnographies of tourism in South-East Asia (1997). Important contributions of socio-anthropological investigations have also resulted from recent cooperative projects concerning the management of tourism, both within *UniAdrion* (a network of universities and research centers in the Adriatic-Ionian region established with the purpose of creating a permanent inter-association), and on the basis of a specific agreement between Bologna University and the Royal University of Phnom Penh, Cambodia (Callari Galli and Guerzoni 2004). Further evidence produced by a number of ethnographic experts on various tourism contexts in Africa, Asia, and Europe has been brought together in the dossier *Anthropological Gazes on Tourism* (VV. AA. 2001).

The Regional Dimension of Tourism

The analysis of the consequences of tourism on local communities and on social and structural equilibrium becomes particularly acute when the development of tourism takes place in regional contexts that have already experienced a severe contrast between traditional culture and industrialization. Here attention briefly focuses on Sardinia and Romagna.

Sardinia. An initial study with a socio-anthropological approach to the cultural cost of tourism and the disintegration of the Sardinian lifestyle was published in 1980. The author, Bachisio Bandinu (1980), focused on the most highly developed tourism area (the *Costa Smeralda*) (the Emerald Coast) resulting from the involvement of outsider entrepreneurs. Looked at semiotically, it was a universe of lies devised to destroy both the locals' *status quo* and the identity of tourists. Thus, sociology was led to question the effects induced by the development of tourism when changes occurred in their social context: was there an increase in development or degradation, in order or disorder? (Lelli 1983). Tourism was analyzed as an "ideological universe" aiming to involve both tourists and local residents through its ability to promote itself as an area where class conflicts were resolved and processes for collective identification were in place (Paolinelli 1983).

More recently, Sardinia again provided examples of the transformations concerning the relationship between tourism and the local population. In fact, the industry had become one of the most important factors of sociocultural transition, but no longer "from old to new, from country to factory" (Lelli 1989:98), but from industrial society to postindustrial society and leading to the "end of the hegemony of the iron culture" (Lelli 1989:98). The town of Olbia was a symbol of the new relationship between tourism and society in Sardinia; what was being offered here was "Sardinia as a resource: its landscape, its history, its people and its traditions in its true entirety; the real Sardinia, not the invented one." The Olbia case showed that "when Sardinia serves as the global resource ... the outcome is independent development" (Lelli 1989:100).

Toward the end of the 20th century, several towns, which had no aspiration of so doing a few years earlier, were starting to venture into the market in Sardinia. Such initiatives made a great effort to connect the coast and the mountains. Tourism involving the entire host community needed to be the focus of the cultural and social identity of the population. Antonio Fadda referred to "tourism of identity" where "the social lifestyle finds dignity in the formats that the inhabitants have assigned themselves over time" (2001:11). If the industry was to have economic and cultural potential for host communities, the local people had to be proactive and become managers of themselves, by discovering that tourism offered "an incentive for the exploitation of their daily life" (2001:13). The remains of the past were "a possible alternative to the standardization of thought and action" (2002:12), enabling the building of a future "that takes the human dimension and the sense of community into account" (2002:12).

According to Antonietta Mazzette, an increasingly vast and diverse public expressed demands that no longer went in a single direction: "those who choose their holiday destination for the sea and the beach also want to explore cities, monuments, and museums; they want to get to know a place and its traditions, adventure into the countryside and sample the local food" (2002:12). Moreover, supply and demand "begin to spread inland from the coast and the towns. An updated version of the local culture is being put on display" (2002:17) and added to the features of a beach holiday. The start of the globalization of tourism was fed by a multitude of local cultures that needed to take part in the large circuits of communications through efficient organization and networks and employing the support of professionals within a framework of clear and conscious political strategies (Mazzette 2002; Mazzette and Tidore 2008). This process was studied by Camillo Tidore and Marcella Solinas referring to Anglona, an area in the north of Sardinia where local administrators and businessmen had long been committed to the development of tourism based on local culture and environmental resources (2002:180–181).

Romagna. If the dynamics of tourism in Sardinia and the social contradictions and changes they brought to the surface, prompted a broad line of study and sociological research, a similar process took place in the area that is generally recognized as the very heart of mass tourism: the coast of Romagna. Vincenzo Buccino (1966) outlined the traits of the "pioneers" in the development of local tourism in an account written when the Italian "economic miracle" (the period between 1958 and 1963, when the economy was growing at its highest rate) was coming to a close and the first major phase of spontaneous development on Romagna's coast was at an end. Gualtiero Gori preferred an approach based on the experiences of the "pioneers" of the development of tourism in his analysis that explored the "internal dynamic tensions" typical of daily life in the suburbs and leading to the creation of the "tourism model" that Romagna was proud of for several decades. Personal narratives (autobiographical reports, accounts, in-depth conversations) were collected at Bellaria-Igea Marina between December 1980 and June 1981. They cast light on the conditions of life (from the food on the table to social life, where people spent their free time, and various forms of solidarity). They referred to forms of contact between residents and consumers that were used for developing a new "way of making a living," as tourism was considered. Finally, they expressed the forcing of relationships through which the family and the local community used to envelop visitors in a system of services, a system that was primarily a production of social relationships (Gori 1992:101–107).

Emilio Benini and Asterio Savelli examined the time frame of the dynamics affecting the Romagna model. Small hotels or *pensioni* (guest houses) were the main model for the expansion of tourism until the end of the 1950s, a period when the region enjoyed wide occupational mobility between the primary and tertiary sectors. This model had the advantage of the mutual support that businesses and the family offered one another (1986). The adoption of competitive pricing was allowed by two connected conditions: the running of businesses solely by family units and the practice of not keeping account of their labor costs (Battistelli 1993:229). The dimensions of business changed rapidly during the next phase: the model turned into a medium-sized hotel, involving investments beyond the possibilities of the families who worked in the local economy's traditional industry. The development of this category of hotels coincided with the period of maximum expansion of tourism in the early 1960s and matched the dominant characteristics of the movement itself, namely the large increase in demand from foreign tourists from central and northern Europe, partly controlled by international travel agencies (Benini and Savelli 1986:46–53). Hospitality services were cut and simplified. While the initial model of development could be mainly based on forms of solidarity within the family, the local community, and consumers, bureaucracy (local, regional) now intervened in the relationship between the industry professional and the outside world. Trade unions stood between businessmen and the workforce and travel agents became wedged between businesses and consumers

(Guidicini 1984:223). In the 1970s and 1980s, the strategies for coping with the changes in the market and the difficult times for businesses took two main directions. In the first place, a process started to modernize ventures aimed at higher levels of rationalization of facilities, services, and supplies. It was widely supported by new forms of association and cooperation and was mainly focused on strategies to maintain turnover and to safeguard the survival of businesses. The second strategy adopted at the time led to many entrepreneurs leaving the hospitality industry or turning their attention to property, demolishing the professional know-how and the social relationships that had been nurtured in the past, often in favor of short-term speculation (Benini and Savelli 1986:46-57). The priority given to property earnings was the most serious withdrawal on the part of industry businessmen, who tended to take refuge in the hidden economy rather than allocating resources in order to improve business management. Changes in accommodation facilities went with the specific development of entertainment services. In the past such function was not an institutionalized aspect of social life, but now it strengthened, becoming more autonomous, and attaining a longer activity period, just when foreign arrivals decreased and the length of tourist stay in Riviera was reduced (Battistelli 1993:69-72, 231).

Actually the 1980s registered a crisis in demand caused by the convergence of several negative factors. Decay in the quality of the environment was the main factor, the most blatant manifestation being the excessive amounts of nutrients caused by pollution of the sea. Added to this were factors linked to the economic climate of the day and the changing meanings in tourist behavior, originating in a society that had now reached the postindustrial stage. The 1990s also saw the emerging of two different paths to respond to the environmental and sociocultural challenges. One remained wholly within the tourism area along the coast and called for the replacement of the degraded environment via the production of artificial environments (swimming pools, water parks, theme parks, and leisure facilities). The other aimed to extend the range of local resources by involving the region's inland resources (traditions, events, festivals, fairs, pageants, wine, and gastronomy). At the turn of the 21st century, sociological research on the one hand undertook in-depth analyses of the reasons which motivated tourists who still came to the Adriatic coast, intending to understand their diversification and their reference to industrial and postindustrial cultural patterns (Savelli 2001). On the other hand, it sought to identify the main strategies adopted by businessmen in response to the different dynamics of the changing quantity and quality of the market, a range that shifted away from attempts to take refuge in the consolidated patterns of mass tourism and that was open to a local approach that promoted the specific features of a resort, regional resources, opportunities for mobility, and links offered by the sea (Savelli 2008a, 2008c).

Finally, Emilio Cocco and Everardo Minardi focused on the unity of the Adriatic region. Starting from the imaginative processes of territory, they stressed a maritime region in a way which was rare in sociology (2008:10–11). Unity and internal differentiation made them consider the Adriatic as a scaled-down representation of the Mediterranean Sea. The Adriatic basin was a border sea between different social and economic systems; now, it was becoming a mobility space and seemed to stimulate the production of trans-Adriatic institutional models (2008:19–23). The differentiation in tourist motivation and behavior opened new opportunities for territorial communities which were excluded or marginalized from the tourism market, and it favored a new multicentric regional dimension where even remote places were connected to an area which was recognizable (Iovanović 2008:217). That said, the project of an Adriatic euro-region will also have to rely on incentives from tourism, both through quality standards in order to integrate tourism packages of enterprises which operate on the Adriatic coasts, and through the development of mixed navigation societies and an integrated port system for people mobility (Cocco and Minardi 2008:251–252).

The Comeback of the City as a Destination

The first generation metropolis, the city of advanced industrial society, had a large infrastructure designed to cope with the pace of daily commuter mobility, which also enabled the extensive development of mobility outside the city, whose weekly or seasonal pace was dictated by holidays. Today, the postindustrial structure of the urban economy simultaneously enables and demands that the city itself be rediscovered as a destination. As documented by Guido Martinotti, new populations within the city are flanking and overlapping its residents and the commuters of the industrial age. A world of "city users" is being developed: they are involved in the city for various reasons, such as consumption, accessing services, and benefiting from the stimuli offered by the urban environment. In addition to its purely consumer-related, material, cultural, or aesthetic functions, more complex user modes are developing, representing the specificity of the postindustrial era. These come with "metropolitan businessmen," whereby work, social contact, cultural stimulation, scientific research, aesthetic creativity, and consumption seem inextricably linked, giving rise to the virtuous circles which increasingly feed a metropolis that has entered the so-called "second generation" (1993).

Thus, a "New Urban Renaissance" (as Giandomenico Amendola calls it), is currently underway, expressing a reaction to the attempts of standardization and "functionalization" made for over half a century by the modernity movement in the name of science and rationality. In Amendola's words:

> Se per il movimento moderno lo sforzo era stato di omogeneizzare, per il postmoderno è differenziare, se il criterio ieri era la razionalità, oggi è l'identità, se ieri era l'universalismo, oggi è il particolarismo, se ieri era la funzione, oggi è il piacere (1997:39).

> If efforts focused on standardization of the modern movement, the keyword is differentiation for the postmodern movement; if the criterion yesterday was rationality, today it is identity; if it was universalism yesterday, today it is individualism; if it was about functions yesterday, today it is about pleasure.

Although, "today, the city is becoming a major destination for contemporary tourism" (Amendola 1999:71), we should not consider this phenomenon simply a result of an increasing demand for tourism. The real reason for accelerated growth in the demand for city tourism "is the changing nature of the contemporary city itself" (1999:72) and its affirmation as a "consolidated and consolidating object of tourist demand" (1999:72). Today, the city is a place specifically "capable of promoting the feeling of being a tourist" (1999:73). It has this function within the framework of the new information economy where "more value is given to places, goods, or experiences that are able to produce the most consumable information" (1999:72). Thus, the "tourist town" product is no longer a mere container of tourism items but consists of a "city system," namely the city itself, a product with its own value that comes from being "a single field with multiple attractions to carry out in its complex and changing totality" (1999:78).

In Italy, the crisis and transformation of the city's image was particularly intense at the top of what was called the "industrial triangle," namely the cities of Milan, Turin, and Genoa. Milan was able to handle its switch to the new phase more gradually, relying on the image projected internationally by Futurism (the *avant-garde* art movement, founded in Italy in 1909 by F.T.

Marinetti; it was based on speed, the adulation of modernity, and technology), which lent it great dynamism. This image was already adopted in city-related "filmography" and is now being used by the fashion industry, by conference and business tourism, and by trade fairs: "Milan is a city that is full of attractions for tourists because it makes use of its collective cultural heritage" (Martinotti 2004:77). Whereas the transition from Fordist industrial production to postindustrial dynamism and tourism centrality in Milan was able to benefit from a continuity of images and support, the same cannot be said for Turin and Genoa, where the change of perspective of urban life is more recent and traumatic. According to research by Maria Cristina Martinengo and Luca Savoja, Turin's image currently appears to be in transition: while it is no longer strictly associated with the world of industry and motor vehicles, it has not yet been transformed by taking on other clear associations. The city's historical and cultural heritage is not easily recognizable to visit and enjoy. It still looks very authentic "precisely because it hides its features and the local character sought by the majority of tourists" (Martinengo and Savoja 2003:201; see also Martinengo et al 2001).

Even old port cities like Genoa (Gori 2004) are undergoing a restructuring of their economy and are driven to redefine a model of alternative development that replaces the now declining industrial model. The old docks are being redeveloped to become places of leisure activity, "aquariums, science museums, leisure facilities, restaurants, hotels, and *shopping centers* are all cropping up" (Guala 2004:130). However, the road for the regeneration of culture and tourism requires the development of analytical skills and the preparation of policies for the implementation of various intermediate objectives such as:

> The regrouping of skilled social groups and of legitimate social elites (social wealth), the recovery of "roots" and local identity, sustainable projects to identify common values and to promote the symbols of the community, coherent *city marketing* strategies to promote it as a cultural and tourist product (Guala 2004:130).

Chito Guala has studied the processes of transformation triggered by major events both at Genoa and Turin (Genoa 2004 "European Capital of Culture" and Turin 2006 "XXth Olympic Winter Games") and their effectiveness in the framework of policies to promote tourism in the city. The study of "mega-events" intends to feed hopes that "the critical skills of public decision makers are capable of planning truly unique events in contexts maintaining their appearance, their *genius loci*, without upsetting the urban fabric and the social and cultural balances created over the course of time and history" (2007:172).

Major events have also contributed to the revival of a city like Naples, which had experienced a long period of decline in tourism (1966–1993). The G7 summit and the UN Conference in 1994 led to the restyling of its organization, prompting an increased interest by tourism researchers in analyzing the new cycle. The slogan "Naples: City of Art and Culture" aims to point to "the regional capital's dual investment in its historical and artistic heritage and its identity" (Volpe 2004:161). For the first time, highly symbolic urban spaces are juxtaposed with the natural elements (of sea, sun, and Vesuvius) that were the focus of tourism in the past. But the author, Angelo Volpe, considers a series of factors of urban diseconomy that do not allow the pursuit of any form of mass tourism. He believes that the "updating for tourism" (2004:164), which started in 1993–1994, is uncertain and linked mainly to the growth of tourism connected with art and culture known throughout the country starting from the end of 1992, rather than specific local factors.

This review of the studies and thought relating to urban tourism in Italy cannot end without a reference to the recent contribution by Nicolò Leotta, who examines urban tourism using the method of visual sociology. He explores the specific interaction between visual culture and tourism involving various subjects, ranging from the representation of the territory to folklore, from history of art to architecture, from town planning to the history of photography. Following this approach, he focuses on three "itineraries" identified in the country: "Bel Paese" with the *Tour d'Italie*, "Dolce Roma" with the films shot during the 1950s and 1960s, and the "Po Valley Megalopolis" consisting of a constellation of cities stretching from Turin to Rimini. He compares the itineraries offered in the country before comparing them with the mother of all metropolises: New York City (2005:25–34).

Sustainability of Tourism Development

Several Italian authors have been particularly sensitive to the issue of the sustainability of tourism. Francesco Pardi notes how product policies are designed as a "planned moment of invasion followed by the destruction of an area and its art" (1992:128). He considers tourism as a sort of product of the die-hard industrial mentality, interpreting nature as an item to be exploited and leisure time as an opportunity for escapism. According to him, the tendency to cut the amount of time spent at work makes escape truly dangerous and counterproductive, inasmuch as it privileges the contemplation of the extraordinary over ordinary, everyday reality. Thus, he notes that either tourism should be rejected or else a new code is needed for the tourism system, independent of the economy and allowing everyone to "cross the boundaries between the different symbolic realms of society and the physical realms of the natural environment while maintaining a close relationship between the observer and the observed" (1992:129). Tourism should act as a:

> Proper social system that is different from any other, as it is an independent realm where most of our life finds a way to prolong our experiences according to a criterion of continuity and not according to a criterion of sequentiality, where everything is divided: time at work and leisure time, society and nature, daily life and absence (1992:129).

Osvaldo Pieroni and Tullio Romita complain that often new and immense artificial tourism spaces are designed and constructed regardless of the environmental resources available in any given physical space. Assuming that resources are neither infinite nor reproducible, expansionary-type logic leads to the self-destruction of tourism and considerable damage to humankind as a whole. The relentless deterioration of environmental resources make a lot of people aware of the indispensable nature of them for a better quality of life, and it contributes greatly to implementing changes in the way environmental resources are considered. Thus, where the economic benefits of the development of tourism prevailed in the past over the environmental damage it caused, today "public opinion is mainly beginning to be aware that it is time to reverse our priorities" (2003:13), and the concept of sustainable tourism is beginning to find specific applications. For some, it appears not only as a compromise solution, but also as a radical criticism of the development model based on endless growth, and as a "proposal for an alternative model centered on the quality of life, on friendliness, thrift and fairness" (2003:14).

Anna Rosa Montani considers the different types of the social impacts of tourism. First, there is the "image of the destination." Here the image created by marketing can represent the place in an unrealistic manner and local people may be tempted to offer tourists the imaginary reality for which they are looking. Then there are forms of "exploitation of vulnerable people," some of which are particularly objectionable, such as prostitution and sex tourism. The "skill for consideration," namely the ability to produce actual knowledge, may be affected, when the transitional and unequal nature of the relationship between tourists and local people once again proposes a typical colonial model, whereby locals are relegated to the margins of the activity taking place in their area and are forced into increasingly tight spaces. Finally, the imbalance in the "localization of costs and benefits" may result in feelings of frustration among locals due to their inability to benefit from the facilities and services reserved for tourists and generally for having to foot the bill while remaining almost completely excluded from the benefits of development (2005).

Luca Savoja also focuses on sustainability in his work on the "social construction of tourism." He says this should not be solely identified with the survival of natural ecosystems, the preservation of biodiversity, and the reproduction of resources. There is also the sustainability of the economy, requiring solutions to remedy the problems generated by the seasonal nature and monoculture of tourism, by the "return" of economic benefits to the countries of origin of tourists, by the processes of cultural contamination inherent in the tourism industry. There is also social sustainability, endangered by the disruption of the lifestyle and customs of local communities, by the increased cost of living, by the "falsification" of reality for the good of tourism. Lastly, there is also touristic sustainability, deriving from the need to meet the needs of visitors. The fact that the consumption of the latter cannot ignore the presence of other tourist-consumers implies that both a top and bottom limit to an area's capacity should be established. "Capacity needs" must be considered, meaning that tourism may be ecologically sustainable under the bottom threshold but may not be sustainable from an economic, social, and touristic point of view (2005).

Fulvio Beato places social equity at the center of the concept of sustainable tourism and refers explicitly to the ethical roots of the famous *Brundtland Report* of 1987. He considers sustainability to be an action to combat social exclusion, preventing the right to tourism to be exercised and above all illegitimate terms of employment being practiced at tourism resorts, especially seasonal resorts, such as failure to renew employment contracts, overtime not being paid, and insecure employment (2008).

The issues most often discussed by sociologists are illegal building and the destruction of cultural heritage. According to Enzo Nocifora, they are possible because local communities are identifying less with their territory, and this identification has been diminishing over time, "giving way to sham identification processes invented by the mass media" (2004:10). Hence, the working hypothesis used to tackle environmental degradation and to introduce innovation in development is based on the concepts of cultural tourism and environmental sustainability; nature and culture are no longer considered to represent opposite poles but are a continuum of situations and resources that, on closer examination, are the result of an historical construction that has taken a varying length of time (2004:7–47).

Osvaldo Pieroni (2008) discusses this issue, by conducting a detailed survey of legal, legalized, or illegal constructions that offend the landscape and are located within 300 m of the coast in Calabria. He highlights how unauthorized building erodes the potential of tourism linked to the attractions of the landscape and ends up creating a source of risk for the resident population itself. In particular, he denounces the ambivalent action taken by local governments, whose permissiveness, scant control, approval of changes in town planning, and the provision of urbanization result in the encouragement of unauthorized building. Also in Calabria, Tullio Romita investigates "invisible tourism," a unique phenomenon with many positive values for the economy and social life but also a cause of negative effects on the environment. This self-managed tourism is provided by private homes and "eludes any possibility of monitoring and evaluation" (1999:13). Given its dimensions, it outstrips the official tourist numbers for many areas in the region and thus it should not be overlooked. Instead, its best aspects should be enhanced and it should be brought within channels that guarantee its visibility, transparency, and governability with the aim of mitigating its negative effects on the territory (1999). Romita favors an investigation into social interaction based not on the relationship between tourists and host communities, but on the associations they establish on their own with the *stigturismo* (environment). He shows how the spaces where such relations develop come to form "spontaneous tourist contexts" that are much more widespread than literature on tourism might lead one to think. The main stakeholders are "Do-It-Yourself Tourists" whose ability to independently determine their own behavior enables them to stimulate the development of tourism spaces and influence their development and evolution. Other tourists and locals who start offering hospitality are falling in line with do-it-yourself tourists, carrying out the actions required of their role without necessarily interacting with one another (2008).

Meanwhile, over in Romagna, Asterio Savelli has conducted some studies that consider the new opportunities for the adoption of policies affecting local businesses intent on sustainable development, and the emerging tourism trend to make real time choices in a given context. More complex and multifaceted destinations are favored, where the options for action grow and change. In this case, the beach and the coast lose their privileged positions (along with the incentive for unauthorized building) within the framework of the new images of the tourism area. Such imagery is more and more linked to the concepts of network, itinerary, and a tourism "region" based more on the realm of communications than of buildings, at the service of the mobility of tourists rather than their immobility (2008c).

However, Carlo Ruzza argues that policies for competitive and sustainable tourism cannot disregard governance, namely a way of making public policies involving more flexibility, taking a cooperative viewpoint, including diverse stakeholders in society, and redefining interests through specific structures for participation and deliberation (2008). Enrico Ercole also takes up the concept of governance, indicating a new style of government focusing on the dynamics of processes and capable of bringing together a wide range of institutions and networks, especially with regard to strategies for the development of tourism in nature areas, rural locations, and medium size cities. These places are not tourism products themselves but could become so should their natural resources, landscapes, cultural, historical, or artistic resources be "made into a system" through a series of services targeting tourists. However, only part of these can be delivered by tourism businesses, since another part depends on the collective, local, economic, social, and political stakeholders, namely the local society's ability to support the initiatives of tourism businesses. This convergence of actions determines the transition from "resources" to "product," intended as a resource or set of resources made available not only in terms of logistics, but especially through the clarification of their "meaning" by a group of stakeholders (private sector, public sector, associations) operating in several areas (tourism, culture, infrastructures, etc.) (2008:172–174; see also Ercole and Gilli 2004).

In addition to environmental, economic, and social sustainability, there is also the problem of tourism sustainability: limiting the number of tourists to a given context in order to extend the duration of its appeal. Margherita Ciacci raises this issue in reference to the city of Florence and more generally to cultural destinations, where the value of tourism resources decreases when the number of those making use of it increases (1997:241). If the mass dimension is a positive outcome of the fact that traveling around the world is now easier and safer, the cultural experience also suffers the negative effects of crowding around "works that need space and silence to be properly observed, the depersonalization of travel, of haste and of the accumulation of must-sees" (2000:6). The creation of a "new" cultural tourism has to be fed by a "proactive desire to combine know-how, the processing and the coordination of information" and efforts to "close" the distance between those working in the industry, the local people and consumers and to enhance implicit "community" aspects, both in the management/promotion and usage of art sites (2000:99–110).

Gerardo Ragone suggests a precise reflection on the economic and social costs of the growth of tourism, distinguishing the "perverse effects" of demand from those originating in the supply. As regards demand, a drop in interest in the tourism product is related to its increasing standardization; competition coming from the urban areas closer to a tourist's home; and the "snob effect," whereby cutting prices enables new consumers to access a given market but causes others to abandon it. As regards supply, the largest limits to growth are posed by policies for the protection of the environment, cultural heritage, and the identity of host populations. The idea of these "fixed" or "programmed" numbers is to limit levels of tourist activity in certain contexts; indeed several cities and resorts in Italy are starting to implement them in their tourism policies (1992:85–90). The notion of placing limits on development stirs up much debate, which also embraces the evolution and decline of destinations and the revival of the "lifecycle" concept. Angelo Volpe provides a survey of the theories in this respect and of the debate that has developed in the national and international literature. He suggests concrete examples of its application and applies the lifecycle model in order to interpret the development of tourism in the city of Naples from the end of the Second World War until the end of the 20th century (Volpe 2004).

Over recent years, too, growing attention is emerging for tourism as an activity to favor sustainable development; in particular, such attention is increasing in areas with high environmental value. The point in the protected areas is to face the expectations of the local community, keeping the promise of social and economic development alongside the creation of natural parks. Starting from the cases of the 20 Italian National Parks, this topic has been studied by Rita Cannas and Micaela Solinas (2005). Their research introduces a systematic way of reading social relations in protected areas, providing a deep analysis of local dynamics. These authors stress current changes of meaning in the concepts of park and protection. Such changes make it necessary to include tourism in the strategies of environmentalists; at the same time, they influence a new consideration of the environment, which is no longer regarded as a picturesque scenario for package tours complete with hotels and transport facilities (2005:7–8). Protected areas have also made use of internationally developed tools in a variety of ways in order to promote the culture of quality (brands, certifications, Agenda 21, the European Charter of Sustainable Tourism). Several very interesting experiences have been accomplished in this way, demonstrating "the ability of parks to experiment with new forms of economic and social development based on the active involvement of local communities in decision-making processes relating to the development of the territory" (2005:19–20).

New Social Meanings for Tourism

"Who are tourists?" asks Gianfranco Morra. His answer is very different from the response provided years ago by Alberto Sessa, focusing on the continuity of needs and human behavior. According to Morra, "Tourists are an utterly new product of modern civilization ... .; they are inconceivable without the radical changes introduced by the process of modernization" (1988:17). This causes the transition from a sacred society, hostile toward anything new, to a secular society, "marked by its desire for discovery" (1988:18). Only a modernized society "could *have* tourism and consumption," in fact "in its very essence, it had *to be* a society for tourism and consumption" (1988:18). In other words, contemporary persons are "homeless," looking toward what is new, "ultimately reaching a goal only to look beyond it" (1988:19). But the pursuit of what is new is ambiguous. On the one hand, it is qualitatively different from everyday life (the "unprecedented, the genuine, the extraordinary, the wonderful"). On the other hand, it is based on instrumental rationality and cannot fail to pursue "comfort, organization, assurance, planning, efficient service" (1988:17–21).

Sociological study fervently resumes its analysis of the social significance of tourist behavior when the industrial phase gives way to the postindustrial stage, generally perceived through the production of services. For Giuli Liebman Parrinello, it represents a true leap in quality at both the macro- and micro-sociological levels. The class structure changes, embracing a new centrality of technicians, scientists, intellectuals and information managers, the emergence of a new category of *prosumers* (producer-consumers) and the new, central role of women. Leisure, culture, and scientific research are now the dominant economic sector. The former consumerism, pandering to the demands of social status, is replaced by the acquisition of a change in management skills. The synchronization of industrial society yields to de-synchronization, enabling "time to be chosen, individual and thus independent .... A new, psychic structure emerges out of this context, marked by dignity, self awareness, and a 'narcissistic personality' ..." (1987:216). The dismantling processes relating to space and time, taking place in contemporary society, lend "more weight and security to an individual's mental and physical intuition," giving rise to "mental maps" and "tourist images" used to express the dynamics of one's personality (1987:216–217). Ongoing territorial mobility is associated with the "continuous zigzagging between time spent at work and leisure time" (1987:204) until it eventually mimics a form of general mobilization.

Postmodern culture overlaps the postindustrial format of production and consumption. Claudio Minca focuses on this aspect and has identified "a sense of fragmentation of the present and of breaking away from the past, a lack of depth, a loss of stable references, the victory of the image, the euphoric and almost schizophrenic indifference of its protagonists" (1996:58) among its dominant features. It involves "the triumph of the ephemeral, the implosion of symbols, and the sublimate recycling of the past and of elsewhere ..." (1996:58). For tourism, in particular, "the recovery and commercialization of traditional heritage tends to radically simplify the social geography of the place-object" (1996:116). Furthermore, the non-places of tourism "recover their surroundings for use as their own (through the mass media), they suggest them on pretext, they take on their mark and confuse this with the mark of a distant past ... . The imploded space of non-places in tourism is the corresponding material of the victory of text over contents, the hinge of postmodern conception" (1996:188). "The visitor is the true protagonist; he (sic) is the one who provides the contents. The rest is choreography, story, text" (1996:189).

Mass holidays are submitted to an increasingly attentive and sophisticated analysis. They no longer appear to be "a goal or a social achievement of great significance" (Ferrarotti 1999:51) within the framework of a so-called "state of wellbeing." Instead, Franco Ferrarotti relates them to conditions of a widespread malaise in ordinary life, encouraging people to escape. He takes a historical viewpoint with a time frame consisting of centuries. He compares the travels of Bruce Chatwin with those of Rainer Maria Rilke and stresses the stark contrast between the end of the 20th century and the previous century. Once the harmony between artistic epiphany and scientific progress is shattered, once the ability to identify oneself historically in one's own era has been lost, an individual tends to travel for travel's sake, as if change itself offers a better condition (1999:116–117, 51–52). Further, "in the world where everybody travels, travel disappears, it vanishes," people do not need it to find themselves but to flee from themselves. Mass tourism runs idle: "it has no meaning and does not try to have any" (1999:102). The new modes of communication and travel create difficulties for subjective identity based on coherence. There is no more a single identity and it no longer needs to be strictly coherent: it has become "mobile, twisting, itinerant, rich, and unpredictable ... capable of developing, overlapping, and intersecting beyond any logical and formal *veto.*" A person is aware that multiple destinies are forming on the horizon, capable of "going beyond the very concept of *in-dividuum*, destroying and splitting the unsplittable at will" (1999:61). Without unity, without memory, a person can no longer "come back." S(he) will run idle, a victim of movement for movement's sake.

If there is to be salvation, it will not be the outcome of conscious programs or rational projects (...). Instead, what is needed is the humility of waiting, the gift of an unexpected favor. A journey must be started even if there is nothing certain, no confirmed bookings, with the full burden of anxiety and anguish that weighs on people today (...). Once again (...) the world will be saved, if it is to be saved, by the unexpected, mysterious support offered by a stranger (1999:148).

To find a way out of the crisis of a fragmented world, "where there are no longer any guarantees against the self-destruction of humanity," people have to accept the presence and the coexistence of different cultures, since:

> Nessuna cultura può considerarsi sovranamente autosufficiente. E nessuna gerarchia fra le varie culture come sistemi di significati appare oggi sostenibile (1999:158).
>
> No culture can consider itself utterly self sufficient and no hierarchy in the various cultures...can be said to be sustainable today.

The meanings of travel, how it is carried out, its interstitial nature, and the relationship between travel and tourism are all issues that have been investigated by several Italian authors, developing the questions and doubts above in recent years and illustrated in the work by Franco Ferrarotti. Myriam Ferrari finds tourism exercises the same fascination we feel when we approach the world of art, where "it is socially legitimate to avoid necessity by entering an aesthetic dimension of play and freedom." Becoming a tourist brings the potential of "supreme" experimentation of the world, an essential condition "in order to experience *a self* that is not subject to the criterion of usefulness and is open to knowledge and imagination for this very reason" (2004:143). Giovanni Gasparini uses freedom, research, separation-loss, and totality-pervasiveness, elements that are often complementary, in order to illustrate the most "interstitial" aspect of the experience of travel, referring to transit as a moment when a person is removed from the domain of a precise regulatory framework. The interstitial character of the experience tends to expand, going from a trip that ends with a return, or an arrival, to the person's whole life, acting as a metaphor of the postmodern condition (2000:30–37). Rossana Bonadei confirms that people now "live" mobility, "seeing themselves as people in transit who live according to the patterns and styles of travel." Thus life becomes "a floating series of greater or lesser organized interstices, in an exacerbated context of interconnection with a prevailing sense of simultaneousness." "*Casual* clothes, backpacks, sleeping bags, credit cards, mobile phones, and laptops are simply signs of belonging to a nomadic population, to a 'tribe' that is identified through the rituals of fashionable consumerism" (2004:143, 144, 146) even if it grants every member a certain degree of freedom, that can be used to move away from the dominant standard and express difference generated by the "micro context" of personal experience.

Hitches and setbacks play a significant role. Roberto Lavarini (2008) says it is important to be able to take advantage of them. Queues at motorway tolls, delays and strikes affecting trains and planes, time spent waiting at ports and airports, or unexpected events caused by bad weather or accidents, are all opportunities for discovery, communication, and aesthetic enjoyment that can give rise to amazement and stimulate the capacity of improvisation in a world where technology and professional organization tend to stifle any surprises along with their risks (2005:228–230). Setbacks slowing down the pace of travel and offering the potential to discover an area and the people who live there, tend to shift the focus from the destination and on getting there, to the journey needed to reach it, namely the period of transit and how this is accomplished. There is a new notion of "slow travel," traveling at a slow pace in order to discover places and people, be they close to home or on another continent (2008).

Marxiano Melotti, who focuses mainly on archaeological tourism, refers to its ability to involve a person in a "different" world, generated by various forms of discontinuity that act simultaneously: discontinuity of time, space, culture, and ontological status (such as a necropolis, tombs, and mummies). However, it is not necessary for the experience to be founded on the authenticity of a situation or of archaeological finds. It is the feeling of otherness that must be strong enough for any other element to become unimportant. Authenticity is no longer a major problem, indeed, the very concept of authenticity is changing profoundly in a relative system of tastes and values, itself in constant transformation (2007, 2008). On the contrary, the condition of otherness may belong to the very person who lives in the city, the suburbs and the malls. This is the case of *flâneurs* (see chapter one of this volume), a specific category of individuals investigated by Giampaolo

Nuvolati. The term comes from 19th century literature and, since its use by Benjamin, is back in vogue today "to describe certain modes of travel and exploration of places, of consciously relating to people and contexts" (2006:7). This person emblematically expresses the condition of humanity in late-modern society, with its processes such as "the individualization of the human experience, the composite expression of identification trajectories with the territory, the extension of the daily practice of *reflexivity*" (2006:8). He seems to prove the displacement of the person in a world of highly impersonal relations, but also the desire to create new relationships with the places visited, even in a temporary and insecure manner. "The *flâneur* is perhaps the last bastion of genuine nomadism, unencumbered by rules, the outcome of improvisation and driven by the desire to read the order of things at the same time" (2006:9).

According to Emilio Benini, such an experience should be considered a moment of legitimization of identity aiming more within than without a person. The increasing plurality of lifestyles and the resulting volatility for an individual profoundly alter the system of relationships into which a holiday fits. The desire to experiment a transient identity may try to find space in the potential offered by another reality, whose diversity comes from "unknown sources." Thus, "on the one hand, the growing subjectivity of behavior and choices brings uncertainty and a crisis of consolidated strategies, but on the other hand it offers the opportunity to recover the importance of the role of contexts and resources that were marginal before, if not actually ignored" (2008:30).

Sociology of Mediterranean Tourism

Throughout the 1970s and 1980s, some economic, political, and environmental events weakened the expectations of continuity in tourism development at the national and international levels. A crisis was particularly evident in the seaside holiday, the "heart" of mass tourism. After the "boom" of the 1950s and 1960s, changes in tourist behavior were related to an alteration in the social meaning of tourism: new motivations were emerging and they had to be interpreted through novel approaches. Here the role of sociology emerged. After some international debate, the similarity between Italian and Mediterranean problems was recognized and related to changes in economic production and to the everyday life of European societies. Since the passage from industrial to postindustrial society had to be considered, local phenomena needed to be connected to wider trends in the Mediterranean region. Consequently at the end of the 1980s, the

Mediterranean Association for the Sociology of Tourism was founded in order to study these changing trends. All the congresses of the association (six, from 1987 to 2008) constantly compared the development of cities and areas interested in tourism in the Mediterranean region, trying to connect them to wider trends of social life, the globalization of the economy, culture, and the tourism market.

The association was established in 1987 following the first Mediterranean Conference "Tourism and Cultural Communication. For an Active Role of Local Communities: New Services and New Professions" (held in Bologna in 1987). It was formally created with bylaws and the appointment of managing bodies during the general meeting convened on the occasion of the second Mediterranean Conference "Groups and Local Intermediate Structures: For a Change of Image in the Tourist System" (held in Cervia in 1991). From the papers and communications presented on these two occasions (Guidicini and Savelli 1988a, 1992) it was clear that, after many years in which the role of local communities in mass tourism had been essentially marginal, being merely a source of service personnel, this role was now changing. The vitality and the communication potential of these communities were beginning to be reappraised, being finally viewed as resources in their own right. The topics discussed at the two conferences examined the impact of tourism on the local communities of the Mediterranean area highlighting the values, meanings, and various opportunities then emerging in the trade. In the second conference, in particular, new forms of territorial organization and tourism activities capable of mediating between the local groups and operators, on the one hand, and the consumer and large-scale tour operators, on the other, were explored.

At the same time, an autonomous congress organized by the *La Sapienza* University in Rome, "Mediterranean Tourism as Resource and Risk" (held in Rome in 1993) noticed the continuous "fluctuation" between dialog and conflict among the various cultural roots which converged in the Mediterranean area, and tried to identify the necessary conditions of homogeneity giving rise to a communication field where people could use the same codes and establish positive cultural and social relations (Nocifora 1993:34–37). On that occasion, the conviction emerged that precisely because of its internal articulation, the Mediterranean area should avoid the ideology of escape tourism; instead it would offer a local dimension in which heritage and experience combined, producing "paths as social and cultural projects of the time and of the present" (Bonomi 1993:193). As a culture and folklore sea, the Mediterranean presented "a large range of possibilities for every user, regardless of his purchasing power, culture, age, or social project" (Amendola 1993:112).

The Third Mediterranean Conference "Tourism and the Environment" (held in Estoril in 1995) examined again the environment in which the local community lived, highlighting the different effects, whether negative or positive, arising from the impact of tourism. It was pointed out that the term "environment" was to be understood as referring not only to natural resources, but also to cultural heritage which contained the symbols expressing the memory and identity of the local community (Savelli 1997b). In 1999 the association published *Strategie di Comunità nel Turismo Mediterraneo* (Community Strategies in Mediterranean Tourism), which went over the previous conferences, collecting the more significant studies and linking them to some issues which were important for the association: local communities and tourism, tourism and the construction of social relations, the ambivalence of memory and cultural heritage, nature and rural space in new tourism relations, differentiation processes (Guidicini and Savelli 1999).

In the fourth Mediterranean Conference "Local and Global in Tourism: Forms of Aggregation and Communication Networks" (held in Ravenna in 2001), participants discussed the dynamics that existed in contemporary society which were leading to the creation of a global tourism market and which showed the differences between the areas at risk that could be reduced, obscured, or even cancelled completely through the diffusion of dominating models. Particular attention was given to the experiences in territorial and entrepreneurial aggregation that intended using the specific aspect of local supply in order to penetrate the large infrastructural networks on a global scale more efficiently (Savelli 2004a, 2004b).

In the fifth Congress "Mediterranean Tourism beyond the Coastline: New Trends in Tourism and the Social Organization of Space" (held in Thessalonica in 2005), some possible forms of alternative tourism were debated: farmhouse, environmental, sporting, cultural, and the like. The need for other solutions beyond the coastline was stressed: these remedies had to be connected with each other, in order to gain a new concept of holidays that united the resources of sea and hinterland (Iakovidou 2007; Savelli 2008b).

The sixth conference, "Tourism as Development and Cohesion in the Mediterranean Region" (held in Granada in 2008), stressed the importance of the social context in current international tourism. Globalization implied simultaneous challenges and opportunities; offering new products was seen as increasingly important in order to survive or access the tourism market. Several issues were debated. First, tourism products were considered, with particular attention to the relation between tourists and the local population, and to recent changes in the tourism labor market. Sustainability was also taken into consideration. The concept of "responsible tourism" was at the center of the debate: many case studies were presented, and all of them stressed the importance of the environment in local tourism development. Culture, too, frequently featured in the reflections of the conference; it was considered not only as paying attention to local heritage, but also as a process in which tourists influenced its perception and changes. With regard to the organization of tourism space, it emerged as a strategic point for several tourism regions; the importance of public-private cooperation was stressed, and also the need to involve all the local actors in the promotion of resources.

In summary, over the last two decades, the Mediterranean Association has become an important instrument for the circulation of scientific information, and it has stimulated research on the problems generated for local communities and social groups by tourism development. During this period, the sociology of tourism has been changing as it has begun to assume a greater Mediterranean perspective; such change is gradual but significant. Initially the sociology of tourism concentrated on the impact of mass tourism on the people who practiced it and the host communities of destinations. Then it adopted a more defensive attitude toward individuals and groups in the face of the de-structuring induced by international organizations, as it denounced the emerging contradictions and defended the peculiarities of local cultures. Subsequently, after years of entrepreneurial uncertainty and a weakening of collective behavior models, it turned toward the analysis of motivations and local aggregative forms which would promote the tourism economy. Today, the sociology of tourism is trying to capture the opportunities of globalization in order to underpin a broader range of activity of the local community and the entrepreneurial system. It encompasses new wide regional dimensions; the sea itself has gone beyond its frontier function bordering social and cultural systems, by assuming instead a connecting role tracing new images of territory. The network among the several resources of hinterland, coast, and sea gives back to the Mediterranean region its own propensity to attract, in a period which is characterized by a global but highly articulated tourism.

CONCLUSION

In this chapter, an attempt has been made to reconstruct a number of overlapping paths taken by the sociology of tourism in Italy over the last half century. The first drive to address tourism from a sociological perspective came from the processes of social change arising in the 1960s and 1970s. The privatization of leisure time and the standardization of behavior were the first topics to be examined. They were soon accompanied by changes in the social structure of the countryside, the role that tourism could play in these areas in order to curb migration, the risks associated with the various types of touristic colonization, and ultimately shifts in the values and leisure activities of local communities.

Stemming from this last issue was the focus of major interest in the early stages of the Italian sociology of tourism, namely the impact of tourism on local communities. Its extent was measured using such indicators as individual belonging, mobility, the relationship between tourism enterprises, the local community and the surrounding environment, the intensity of cross-cultural communication and the commodification of this exchange, tourism identity, the globalization of relationships, and the erosion of local culture. The significant differences noted in various areas of the country, both as regards the time frame of the development of tourism, the approach of business, and levels of participation among local people, gave rise to a particular focus on the regional dimension of issues and of policies for tourism, to the point where the main legislative and organizational needs related to the field were being covered by local governments themselves. Sardinia, Emilia-Romagna, and, more recently, Calabria, as typical instances of this regional trend, became the subject of in-depth research and analysis, aimed at recognizing and exploiting their respective specificities.

Subsequently attention was directed toward the comeback of the city. The post-Fordist metropolis and its emerging breed of consumers, the organization of major events, and marketing policies, gave rise to what was described as an "urban renaissance." The new dynamic nature of tourism, the differentiation of motives, goals, and behavior also led to novel ways of tackling problems of tourism's sustainability. The focus now centered on how tourism could be developed while preserving and enhancing resources, including protected areas, within a more dynamic interpretation of the concept of conservation and multilevel governance of the tourism sector.

Meanwhile, today new social meanings of tourism are appearing. Individuals in the postindustrial society, who are increasingly split over involvement in its various subsystems, try to rebuild their unity and past by recovering interstitial moments of freedom, play, improvisation, and awe. What matters now is no longer what they see, or the authenticity of a representation of the world they perceive as tourists, but their own performances, namely what they themselves experience as a way of enhancing their own subjectivities.

This contemporary attitude of tourists offers fresh opportunities for the recovery of local contexts and cultural resources that were previously ignored or marginalized as destinations. The Mediterranean Association for the Sociology of Tourism has examined these trends over the last two decades, leading to new comparative ways of imagining tourism, of projecting needs and desires on a spatial scale, of representing territory. The reevaluation of a destination through its specific features now occurs within a much wider context of a new image that allows experimentation on an intermediate scale with ideas emanating from the daily processes of globalization.

By sharing the concerns of the association with fellow Europeans the sociology of tourism in Italy has thus now reached the point of developing an attitude that is increasingly open to mobility and innovation in tourism. It does so from the perspective of building a more extensive range of choices for consumers, who tend to separate their experiences within a wider tourism region, be this linked to the sea or part of an international context, thus offering a reprieve for the specific history and culture of a place and its current capacity to build relationships.

Chapter 5

The Sociology of Tourism in Poland

Krzysztof Przecławski
College of Tourism and Hospitality Management in Warsaw, Poland

Julian Bystrzanowski
College of Tourism and Hospitality Management in Warsaw, Poland

Dorota Ujma
University of Bedfordshire, UK

INTRODUCTION

This account charts various stages in the growth of the sociology of tourism in Poland. Its origins can be traced back to the pioneers of sociology in general, whose published works date from the early 20th century. In their research, some of them ventured into allied areas, including history and literature, where they focused their discussions on travel and "wandering" and the resulting impacts on groups of people, their culture, and identity.

Initially the idea was to present these developments in chronological order. However, the journey to the sociology of tourism was rather repetitive and more of a "wander" itself, rather than traveling directly to a given destination. Many themes, often overlapping, were identified in the process and included definitions, linguistics, publications, reviews, and conferences in the area. Therefore, the first section introduces these pioneers whose thinking had an input in further theoretical developments. They are closely followed by those main researchers who planted the first seeds of a Polish

The Sociology of Tourism: European Origins and Developments
Tourism Social Science Series, Volume 12, 169–194
Copyright © 2009 by Emerald Group Publishing Limited
All rights of reproduction in any form reserved
ISSN: 1571-5043/doi:10.1108/S1571-5043(2009)0000012010

sociology of tourism. Their organizational efforts and political preparation for establishing the field is shown together with a brief summary of the "academic route" they followed comprising their principal publications. Subsequently there is a review of the literature featuring sociological topics relevant to tourism undertaken by leading contemporary authors. Analysis of definitions of and linguistic terms related to tourism are presented in order to illustrate a number of changes in the understanding of and attitudes toward it. Where and how the phenomenon was taught and established as an academic field is also indicated. Finally, there are reflections on associated publications in the new millennium, showing links between tourism and philosophy, ethics, anthropology, culture and technological developments, supporting the sharing of current ideas and the shaping of a likely future.

POLISH CONTRIBUTIONS

Well before the Second World War, Polish scholars were making a significant global contribution to the development of sociology in general. Thinkers of the caliber of Ludwik Krzywicki, Florian Znaniecki, and Bronisław Malinowski had become household names throughout worldwide academia. Stanisław Ossowski, Józef Chałasiński, Antonina Kłoskowska, and Piotr Sztompka followed in their footsteps and furthered themes developed by these pioneers. Their main achievements and publications are presented first, and then the impact of these on ulterior developments in the sociology of tourism is shown.

Sociology in General

Ludwik Krzywicki (1859–1941) was among the founding fathers of Polish sociology. He was considered one of the outstanding Marxist theoreticians. He developed the concept of "territorial societies which in historical development follow tribal ones" (Szacki 1981:551). His best known work, *Sociological Studies*, was first published in 1923 (Krzywicki 1950).

Florian Znaniecki (1882–1958) is also recognized as one of the leading lights of Polish sociology, especially in establishing it as a scientific discipline. He was first globally acknowledged as a consequence of the famous work he coauthored with W. I. Thomas entitled *The Polish Peasant in Europe and America* (Thomas and Znaniecki 1926). According to Szacki, "His sociological system is often considered as one of most comprehensive formulations of the so called 'theory of action', which *preceded* the theoretical renaissance of American sociology in the period of the Second World War" (1981:733; italics added). Znaniecki's theoretical system is often called "a culturalistic theory of values." Znaniecki is also known for his theory of the "humanistic coefficient." According to him, cultural phenomena as subjects of theoretical reflections are either experienced experimentally or as a result of conscious actions.

Bronisław Malinowski (1884–1942), held by some to be a father of Functionalism in the field of social anthropology, wrote in English and hence is better known among the international academic community. His major publications were *Argonauts of the Western Pacific* (1922), *Coral Gardens and their Magic* (1935), and *The Sexual Life of Savages in North-Western Melanesia* (Malinowski and Ellis 1929). These works present the results of thorough field research carried out on the Trobriand Islands. According to Szacki "The starting point of his theory was the biological organism equipped with a set of lasting needs" (1981:706), in Malinowski's words "human nature." He maintained that all components of society interlocked to form a well-balanced system, thereby integrating cultural theories with psychological science (1958).

Like Malinowski, Stanisław Ossowski (1897–1963) was "a representative of the humanistic orientation in sociology, who clearly noticed the basic differences between the biological and social sciences" (Sztompka 2002:28). Ossowski is referred to as the leading Polish sociologist and a "moral and intellectual authority during the second world war" (Sztompka 2002:28). The most significant books authored by Ossowski were *Więź społeczna i dziedzictwo krwi* (1939) (Social Ties and Blood Heritage), *Class Structure in the Social Consciousness* (originally published in 1957 and translated into English in 1963), *O osobliwościach nauk społecznych* (1962) (On the Peculiarities of the Social Sciences). His works were featured and analyzed by contemporary sociologists, including not only Sztompka, but also Mirosław Chałubiński (2006). The latter analysis has been published in English. As Chałubiński notes, there is only a very fragmentary familiarity with Ossowski's works internationally, which is

> ... in some respects the usual fate of outstanding scientists who did not publish much in foreign languages. They sometimes are appreciated only after many years when an acclaimed scholar reading a translation of their work notices the true novelty of the ideas and analyses contained within them (2006:304).

As mentioned in this review, Ossowski's book, *Więź społeczna i dziedzictwo krwi* (1939; translated in 1966), was published just before the beginning of the Second World War and devoted to the sociological analysis of racism and ethnic myths. It partially arose out of his concern about the progress of Fascism and other nationalist and authoritarian movements in Europe (Chałubiński 2006:285). Ossowski usually preferred to use the term "social sciences" rather than "sociology." He held views on many different theoretically significant problems of humanistic studies, such as "axiologism," that is, "a sociology engaged in values" (Chałubiński 2006:287–290). Although he possessed a clear awareness of sociology's axiological entanglement, he did not create a comprehensive system of sociology like, for example, Durkheim, Weber, or Znaniecki. He was not a founder of a new paradigm or school in sociology. Nevertheless, he put forth many innovative ideas, which later influenced the theoretical and research practices within various branches of sociology in Poland, as well as perceptions of the role of the sociologist and the function of the social sciences. Ossowski believed that sociology, in providing knowledge about different areas of social life, could increase human abilities, make people become aware of the various courses of action present in different situations, and help eradicate stereotypes and prejudices.

Chronologically Józef Chałasiński (1904–1979) is next on the list of established Polish sociologists. He had conducted a lengthy correspondence with his mentor Florian Znaniecki who lived in the United States. When, several years after the war, he was allowed to travel to America to meet Znaniecki, he learned on his arrival in New York City that his hero had died that very day. Chałasiński continued the traditions of the humanistic sociology of Znaniecki. He prepared a multivolume work *Młode pokolenie chłopów* (1938) (Young Generation of Peasants) the major study on youth in the rural areas of contemporary Poland. In his book *Społeczeństwo i wychowanie* (Society and Education) Chałasiński (1948) sought to establish the interrelations among the state political system, ideology, and models of education. He was editor-in-chief of two leading Polish sociological journals: *Przeglad Socjologiczny* (Sociological Review) (1948–1979), and *Kultura i Społeczeństwo* (Culture and Society) (1957–1966, 1970–1979).

Antonina Kłoskowska (1919–2001)—a student and eventually close collaborator of Józef Chałasiński—was primarily a sociologist of culture. She also succeeded Chałasiński as the editor-in-chief of *Kultura i Społeczeństwo*. Her most important writings were *From the History and Sociology of Culture* (1969) and *Sociology of Culture* (1981). It has been 25 years since the latter was published, yet it is the core element of any sociological studies in Poland and serves as a source of new ideas, inspirations, and links. Podemski's (2005) book (see below) often refers to Kłoskowska's monograph (1981), especially in the area of tourism. In the original work, Kłoskowska synthesized sociologists' investigations of culture and tried to define the boundaries of this subdiscipline, treating it as a bridge between the Polish tradition of sociological thought and humanistic sciences in the rest of the world. At the end of the 1990s, Kłoskowska intensely researched national identity and multiethnic relationships. The fruit of this labor resulted in the publication of *Kultury narodowe u korzeni* in 1996, with an English version *National Cultures at the Grass-root Level* in 2001, where she addressed the function of national identity in a modern society. She noted that, despite the trend toward globalization, the world continued to be riddled with national conflict. Based upon autobiographies by individuals belonging to various national minorities in Poland and other areas where ethnic borders were blurred, Kłoskowska examined the effects of ethnic differences on personal identity and the appropriation of national culture. In conclusion, Kłoskowska took the view that national cultures were either "open" or "closed" and stressed the importance of participating in more than one cultural medium (Księgarnia Życia Warszawy 2008).

Piotr Sztompka (born 1944), Professor of Sociology at the Jagiellonian University in Kraków and member of the Polish Academy of Sciences, was President of the International Sociological Association (ISA) from 2002 to 2006. His works have been published in 14 languages. They include *Socjologia: analiza społeczeństwa* (Sociology: Analysis of Society) (2002) and *Socjologia zmian społecznych* (Sociology of Social Change) originally published in English (1993) and translated into Polish in 2005, where he referred to the monographs created by the already listed Polish sociologists and developed their ideas further. He was awarded the highest Polish scientific prize—Award of the Foundation for Polish Science—the "Polish equivalent of the Nobel Prize" (Wydawnictwo Znak 2008).

The Sociology of Tourism

After the Second World War, the best traditions of Polish sociology were continued by the previously mentioned Józef Chałasiński, Stanisław Ossowski, Antonina Kłoskowska, and many others. As shown in the previous section and expanded below, their work touched upon tourism, along with its sociological impacts. In such a manner related themes became a topic for investigation for a new group of researchers and writers, including Jan Szczepański, Zygmunt Skórzyński, Andrzej Ziemilski, and

Krzysztof Przecławski, whose work gave rise to the sociology of tourism. Pioneers in the sociological research of tourism in the 1960s in Poland were Zygmunt Skórzyński and Andrzej Ziemilski. They were the first to introduce the field to Poland's academia and to conduct empirical research on it. In 1958, Ziemilski for the first time used the term "sociology of tourism" in his paper "Remarks on the Sociology of Tourism" (1958). In Ziemilski's words, tourism can be understood as a "social institution of individual and collective non-professional migrations meeting cognitive, hygienic (health), aesthetic, and other needs ..." (1958:488).

According to Podemski (2005:105–106), Ziemilski (in *Człowiek w krajobrazie*, 1976) (Man in Landscape), focused on the aspects of recreation, especially recreational space, relaxation around water, mountains, and tourism/recreational destinations, rather than travel. There were elements of his work which were referred to as the "sociology of scenery." Thinking of developing Snieznik (a peak in the Sudety mountains) for tourism, he distinguished three sociological views of scenery. First, a sociologist could identify "archetypes of scenery," such as the "sea," "mountains," and "forests" in literature, legends, and religion. Second, scenery might be viewed as

> ... zbiór przemieszanych elementów przyrody i dzieł czło-
> wieka, stanowiacy efekt działalności konkretnych historycz-
> nych ludzi, w ramach wyznaczonych przez technologię i
> organizację społeczna epoki (1976:75).

> ... a set of natural elements mixed with those created by
> human beings, as the result of a particular activity undertaken
> by an historically-known person, within the technological
> boundaries created by the social organization of an epoch.

Third, like artists or urban planners, sociologists could also be "vision-aries of scenery" as they imagined the future shape and infrastructure of a place, as individuals involved in the spatial planning process. When Ziemilski wrote *Człowiek w krajobrazie* (1976) he differentiated between dichotomous attitudes toward mountains (Podemski 2005:105–106). The typology he created was constructed around two measures in a matrix: agreement and disagreement versus autotelic properties and instrumental-ism. He also reconstructed a number of Polish mountain-based ideologies, including mountains for the economy of the country, mountains for improving body and soul, mountains for the disabled, mountains for sports, mountains for the élites, mountains for nature-lovers, and mountains for highlanders. He did not limit his typologies only to mountains; he also tried to establish various social spaces on beaches, as well as the social structure of skiers and skiing styles as fashion. In short, tourism could be a catalyst for and indicator of social change (Ziemilski 1973).

Skórzyński and Ziemilski edited *Wzory społeczne wakacji w Polsce* (1971) (Social Patterns of Leisure/Vacations in Poland). This research was followed by Saar et al (1972) *Weekendy mieszkańców Krakowa* (Weekends of Kraków Residents) and Przecławski's *Turystyka i wychowanie* (Tourism and Education) (1973), and *Socjologiczne problemy turystyki* (Sociological Problems of Tourism) (1979). Przecławski (2004:58) closed the circle by referring to Thomas and Znaniecki's (1926) work. Although they did not include tourism in their research, Przecławski stated that the theory of social disorganization and reorganization, which they created, was helpful in explaining social encounters in tourism (2004:58). He asked whether tourism was a factor that introduced disorganization to host societies, only to be followed by reorganization when tourists were accepted in those societies as a constant element of the system. This theme, in turn, was developed by Jan Szczepański. Szczepański (1913–2004)—from 1966 to 1970 President of the International Sociological Association and Head of the Institute of Philosophy and Sociology of the Polish Academy of Sciences—held a very special position among Polish sociologists after the war. In the 1970s as Chairman of the National Experts Committee he strove to establish a democratic educational system in Poland. He authored over 40 books, among which was his *Basic Notions of Sociology* (1972) and was considered the most significant follower of Florian Znaniecki in the field of systemic sociology. Szczepański always managed to combine his intellectual interests and scientific passion with an active involvement in current social problems of Poland.

Podemski draws attention to Szczepański's essay from 1980, which he calls "the most significant Polish sociological work about travel" (2005:107). Szczepański highlighted mass travel in the 20th century and referred to it as "the civilization of nomads." He asked about the motives and implications of this phenomenon and stated that its main cause derived from the monotony of everyday life, which awakened a need to escape, to run away and change it. One of the consequences of mass tourism noted by Szczepański, and elaborated by Podemski (2005), was the development of the techniques of invigilation. Podemski also observed:

> Współcześnie przestalismy być podróznikami, zostaliśmy sprowadzeni do roli lotniczych przesyłek. Dla wybitnego

polskiego socjologa najciekawszy jest metafizyczny wymiar podrózy (Podemski 2005:106).

> We are no longer travelers, we have become flying parcels. For the established Polish sociologist [Szczepański] the most interesting is the metaphysical dimension of travel.

Modern travel not only provided a grasp of other cultures, but also helped those involved to understand themselves better. The following excerpt illustrates this point:

> Podróz [...] natęza inność brutalnie i pokazuje ja ostro. Nagle znajdujesz siebie w zupełnej inności. Jakby przeleciało kilkadziesiat lat. Jesteś tu inny, obcy, nie czujesz się w pełni soba, jesteś wyrwany ze swoich zwykłych ram, musisz się przystosowywać tak, jak u siebie musiałbyś to czynić po wielu latach nieobecności. Wtedy mozesz sobie uświadomić, ze istota czasu i jego rzeczywistym upływem jest natęzenie inności między wcześniej i później. Wsiadam do samolotu i po kilku godzinach jestem w zupełnie innym świecie i sam jestem zupełnie inny. [...] Tu jestem obcy. Tu patrza na mnie oczy widzace mnie po raz pierwszy. Tu mnie ocenia na nowo i narzuca mi swoje kryteria postępowania. Tu muszę być napięty i gotowy na akceptacje tylu inności, które "u siebie" odrzuciłbym bez wahania. [...] Powrót nie jest odnalezieniem punktu, z którego wyjechałeś. Nie mozesz bowiem-chocbyś się bardzo starał (jak ten chłop, który w ogrodzie zoologicznym obejrzał zyrafę i powiedziawszy sobie "nie, takiego zwierzęcia nie ma", poszedł spokojnie do domu) powiedzieć sobie, ze to, co widziałeś i przeyłeś nie istnieje. Istnieje w tobie jako zastygły czas ucieleśniony w twojej inności' (Szczepański 1980:105–106, quoted in Podemski 2005:107).

> Travel [...] highlights otherness and exhibits it very clearly. Suddenly you find yourself surrounded by total strangeness, as if many years have passed you by. You are different here, a stranger. You are not totally yourself. You are taken away from your normal context. You have to become accustomed to the new situation, just as if you had lived away from home

for a long time. Then you may become aware that the notion of time and its actual flow are measured by strangeness compounded between before and after. I get into a plane and after a few hours I am in a completely different world, I am totally different ... I am an alien. Here I am observed by eyes which see me for the first time. Here I will be judged anew, and will have to respond to new behavioral expectations. Here I have to be ready to accept so many differences, which at home I would have rejected straight away and without hesitation... Coming back is not about finding the point from which you have left. You cannot, even if you try very hard (like the peasant who saw a giraffe in a zoo and, after saying to himself "no, an animal like that doesn't exist" peacefully went home), say to yourself that everything you have seen and lived through doesn't exist. It does exist in you as frozen time, acting as a reminder of your alienation.

Establishment and Growth

The growth of sociology within the field of tourism was advanced by a number of individuals working in the area and publishing the results of their endeavors. Authors introduced in this section include Wiesław Alejziak, Julian Bystrzanowski, Kazimierz Libera, Stanisław Lisiecki, Piotr Ostrowski, Krzysztof Podemski, and Krzysztof Przecławski. Some of these writers focused on the "organizational front," enabling tourism to play an active part in the Polish educational and political arena. Others mainly published the outcomes of their research, and by doing so developed existing ideas in the academic field. A few worked equally well in both dimensions: Bystrzanowski, Libera, and Przecławski, and constitute a good example of people who prepared the environment for the development of a sociology of tourism. As these two areas (organizational and academic) were intertwined and both to a varying degree contributed to the expansion of the sociology in tourism in Poland, the developments in both are now presented in parallel.

In 1969, Kazimierz Libera, (Founder of the *Centre International d'Études Supérieures du Tourisme* (CIEST)), introduced the sociology of tourism into the curriculum of the Center and entrusted Krzysztof Przecławski with the first lectures on the topic. In the introduction to one of his many texts Przecławski (1996:3) mentions that the invitation came in 1968. However the course did not start until the following year as initially the *Polska Akademia*

Nauk (Polish Academy of Sciences) refused to issue him with a passport, the justification being that anything as vague as the sociology of tourism did not exist. All the subsequent works by Przecławski and other Polish researchers have demonstrated not only that the field exists, but also that it covers a wide variety of mainstream sociological topics.

Przecławski in some of his books—such as *Tourism and Education* (1973), *Sociological Problems of Tourism* (1979), and *Tourism, Man and Society* (1984)—attempted to provide a sociological definition of tourism as well as an analysis of the social causes and effects of the phenomenon. Here Przecławski (1996:48) identified sociology as the study of social relationships, social groupings, social processes, and social identity. He argued that in tourism, social relationships revolved not only around tourists and hosts, but also tourists and local go-betweens, as well as among tourists themselves. Various collections of tourists and their typologies, as well as configurations of hosts could be distinguished in the category of social groups. "Touristification" was highlighted as the main process taking place, and both social identity and its strengthening were influenced by tourism as well.

In the 1980s, tourism research continued to grow slowly, but steadily. In 1981 Stanisław Lisiecki (in Przecławski 2004:60) defended his doctoral dissertation based on an investigation of tourist flows from West Germany to Poland. The same year, Krzysztof Podemski published his article, entitled "Sociological Research of Outbound Tourism." Referring to Antonina Kłoskowska's (1981) work, Podemski proposed that such tourism should be considered a "fifth dimension of culture." For him, it was a special form of participating in culture—and all the more special because of its unique characteristics, including compressed free time, contact with the best center of culture, several ways of disseminating and acquiring information, an idiosyncratic emotional aura, preparation for travel including assimilating new information and, finally, souvenirs playing a major part in making intangible elements on the journey more tangible and unforgettable (2005:108).

From the 1970s, Polish sociologists left their mark in the organizations and associations developing sociological research into tourism in Poland and abroad. The Vienna-based European Coordination Center for Research and Documentation in the Social Sciences (otherwise known as the Vienna Center) introduced the first major international study of tourism in Europe under the title "Sociological and Economic Problems of Tourism in Europe." A number of Polish academics were among the participants, and by 1975, the project was being overseen by Julian Bystrzanowski. In 1983,

Przecławski was appointed Director and Bystrzanowski Deputy Director of the Institute of Tourism in Warsaw. Under their auspices, the Institute became one of the major tourism research institutions in Europe. It coordinated a number of research and educational programs in various fields of tourism, with particular emphasis on their sociological dimensions. In 1985, the Institute initiated the publication of Polish and English versions of the journal *Problemy Turystyki* (Problems of Tourism), an international quarterly featuring Polish and international research in tourism.

Around that time, the short-lived Piotr Ostrowski also made a significant contribution in his often-quoted article "Understanding Tourism," published in *Problemy Turystyki*. There, Ostrowski (1988) expounded his theory of the "collective alien." He argued that "tourism introduces a more or less organized group of aliens (outsiders) into the social structure of a visited society." Each member of that group (a tourist) is only "... a wanderer who comes today and goes tomorrow" (Simmel 1969:257). Ostrowski continued, "I suggest that we call a collective alien any lasting concentration of tourists within visited societies" (1988:5). By making such a suggestion he reconnected with Thomas and Znaniecki's (1926) social theory of disorganization and reorganization. Bartoszewicz (1988), also in *Problemy Turystyki*, referred to tourism within exchange theory—as a flow of people, artifacts/things, money, information, and values. As a direct result of this flow hosts needed to accept "aliens" in their communities, people who were no longer "enemies," but "clients," consumers of services on offer, accepted in a reorganized society.

Another Vienna Center research program in the sociology of tourism was initiated at an important conference in Bratislava (Slovakia) in 1982. It was a cross-national comparative investigation of "Tourism in its Socio-cultural Context as a Factor of Change". Fieldwork had been carried out in seven European countries and in the United States. Members of the Polish team from the Institute of Tourism in Warsaw were among those responsible for the research design. The six-year inquiry was coordinated by Julian Bystrzanowski, while Krzysztof Przecławski was one of the international codirectors of the program. The resulting "Tourism as a Factor of Change" was edited and published one year later as a two-volume report by Bystrzanowski *Tourism as a Factor of Change: National Case Study* (1989) and Bystrzanowski and Beck *Tourism as a Factor of Change: A Sociocultural Study* (1989). It included a whole range of hitherto neglected methodological and theoretical issues in the cross-national analysis that had been undertaken in the implementation of the project. As such, it constituted a watershed, an opportunity for others to reflect on the difficulties of conducting comparative research that were soon to become a hallmark of tourism studies in general.

In 1988, Przecławski became one of founding members of the International Academy for the Study of Tourism. One year later, he organized its first scientific meeting in three Polish towns: Warsaw, Zakopane, and Kraków. In 1994, at the World Congress of the International Sociological Association held in Bielefeld (Germany), Przecławski was largely responsible for the establishment of a permanent Working Group, and subsequently a Research Committee dedicated to international tourism. In the 1980s and 1990s, Przecławski ran a regular course in the Sociology of Tourism at the University of Warsaw and the Jagiellonian University in Kraków. He also delivered a number of guest lectures in the United States, France, China, and Italy. Podemski (2005) notes that Przecławski was the only Polish sociologist who had devoted a number of books to tourism (e.g., 1973, 1979, 1984, 1996, 1997) and had been for many years the only Polish member on the editorial board of *Annals of Tourism Research*. In the 1990s, tourism research in Poland was principally concentrated within the Institute of Tourism. Among several important papers to emerge toward the end of that decade were Bartoszewicz's "Goals, Motives and Forms of Inbound Tourism in Poland" (1999).

In 1999, Wiesław Alejziak wrote *Tourism Facing the Challenges of the 21st Century* in which he analyzed the "dilemma of tourism development" (curse or blessing for destinations). He discussed contemporary trends in its globalization, and tried to integrate Polish investigations with the outcomes of international tourism research. With a question in mind as to what tourism would be like at the end of the 20th century (how it would be perceived and understood), he provided a comprehensive evaluation. Alejziak also examined various definitions of tourism and observed how difficult it was to find one that would satisfy everybody. In this assessment, he reinforced Przecławski's (1996) earlier argument that the expression meant something different for each person. He focused on qualitative tendencies and quantitative trends in the development of tourism and discussed factors that led to its growth by stimulating demand, increasing supply and planning, policies, and practices. In the final chapter Alejziak offered a prognosis on the future of the phenomenon, based on WTO and WTTC reports. Here he combined Polish research with worldwide approaches, including the futurologist Kahn's (1976) analysis of tourism development from 1929 to 2029.

In the new millennium tourism publications were no longer a rarity and showed a greater specialization based on a cumulative knowledge in tourism, sociology, literature, culture, social, and humanistic sciences. In 2005, for instance, Podemski published his *Sociology of Travel*, a compendium of theoretical approaches to travel in the social sciences based on Polish research conducted over the past 50 years. Although the main emphasis was on travel, rather than tourism, this text has been consulted and quoted throughout this chapter on a number of occasions due to a wide-ranging coverage of authors and thorough analysis of their works. Podemski (2005) compared Polish research with that conducted by non-Polish authors and noted the beginnings of sociological reflection on tourism in Germany and their connection with Polish thinking. In this regard, he referred to Georg Simmel (1969) and Alfred Schutz (1964) as the two leading authorities investigating the strangeness experienced by tourists in a new environment. He compared their and other ideas, concepts, and theories with Znaniecki's (1931) and, by reviewing them, formulated some 22 hypotheses relating to the phenomenon of travel. One of them spoke of a traveler as a "stranger," an "other," although not in a classical Simmelian (1969) understanding of the term as a permanent "outsider," nor as a Schutzian (1964) "newcomer," aspirant or candidate. Rather, Podemski (2005) placed the traveler in a special category, of a person being "estranged" only for a short period of time.

> What the traveler and a stranger have in common, is that both fall victim to the questioning of the obviousness of social reality. The traveler is more of Merton's (1977) "non-member" as long as he/she does not aspire in any way to become the member of a new society. Being the Mertonian non-member, the traveler sometimes becomes a "stranger" in the meaning assigned to this term by Znaniecki (1931). It is the case only, when a "conflict of meanings" takes place. Such a conflict arises, for example, when the traveler goes beyond the limits within which the natives are ready to tolerate him/her (Podemski 2005:360; from a summary translated into English by Podemski).

The year 2005 also witnessed the appearance of another book on the *Sociology of Tourism*, authored by Jerzy Suprewicz (2005), which presented a more mainstream approach to the phenomenon and focused solely on trends in Polish inbound and outbound tourism. Additionally, there were several works on pilgrimage and religious tourism. Studies of this nature had been carried out for years by Antoni Jackowski from the Jagiellonian University in Kraków (Jackowski 1991). In the two decades bordering each side of the 20th and 21st centuries, conference publications on this particular topic had been developing steadily, often influenced by the papacy of John Paul II. The Polish Pope's publications and comments on mountaineering, mountains, and tourism provoked a great deal of reflection among compatriot researchers and trekkers, which was subsequently presented during conferences and published. One of many examples was a conference organized in October 2005 by the Academy of Physical Education in Kraków in cooperation with the Center of Mountain Tourism PTTK (*Polskie Towarzystwo Turystyczno–Krajoznawcze*), the Polish Tourism and Sightseeing Association, and entitled "Rev. Karol Wojtyła: John Paul II, a Lover of Mountains and Nature" (Wójcik 2007).

Scope, Definition, and Reflections

In early Polish literature "travel" was treated with contempt, as a type of treason. Abramowska contrasted it with "szczególna zywotność niewędrowania w kulturze polskiej" (a particular liveliness of non-traveling in Polish culture). She quoted the definition of travel articulated in 1625 by Piotr Mieszkowski:

> Peregrynacja to nic innego, jak czasowe, zgodne z obyczajem poniechanie ojczyzny i domu rodzinnego. [...] Podrózujemy kierujac się nie tylko pewna korzyścia prywatna, ale pragnieniem dobra publicznego (1978:144).

> Travel is nothing else but temporary and customary abandonment of the home country and family home. We travel considering not only private gain, but also in the name of public duty.

In the Middle Ages the only justification for such "abandonment" was a pilgrimage. Only in the 17th and 18th centuries had learning from travel started to be acknowledged as a valid reason to do so. Podemski mentions Burkot, who listed travel as "zespół przedsięwzięć komunikacyjnych i społecznych" (Burkot 1988:6) (a set of enterprises of a social and communicative nature) comprising three types: with an aim, aimless, and enforced. He also suggested that the fashion in 16th century Poland to appreciate "one's own" meant that Poles began to be interested in discovering the rest of the world a bit later than other nations.

When was the term, *tourist*, first utilized in the Polish language? Although it had been employed worldwide since 1780 (Cybula 2007:16), Alejziak (1999:16) refers to Warszyńska and Jackowski (1978:21) where they note that *turystyka* was only introduced into Polish in 1847 by Xawery Łukaszewski. The general view expressed in the Polish literature was that the word should be attributed to Stendhal who used it in 1838 in his novel *Mémoires d'un Touriste* (see Cybula 2007, and Lanfant, this volume), and from there it spread to many languages. Interestingly, Cybula (2007) found out that, despite that general view, "tourist" was used in the Polish literature before 1847. She established that Milewski (2006:34) referred to a Polish author, A. E. Odyniec, who used the term on the 17 June 1830 in his letter to J. Korsak by stating:

> Z Anglikami znowu przeciwnie, (a nie mówię tutaj o wszystkich w ogólności, ale o egzemplarzach, które sam widziałem, stanowiacych jednakze większość ich zwyczajnych *turystów*) (Odyniec 1876:339, after Cybula 2007:16).

> With the English it is to the contrary (I'm not referring to all of them in general, but to the individuals I've noticed myself, who generally represented the majority of their normal *tourists*) (italics added).

She quotes Odyniec after Milewski (2006:34) and wonders if Odyniec was the first Polish author to use the term and considers it unlikely. He employed it to describe a group of English in such a way that the word seemed to have been commonly known in the 19th century in the Polish language.

In his *Socjologia podrózy* (2005), Podemski provides a revealing selection of quotes from the Polish literature, illustrating the changing approach to travel and later on, tourism. In his chapter on "Travel and Tourism in the Polish Humanistic Sciences" he refers to a number of interesting authors, starting with several historians investigating the literature. In this vein he cites Abramowska (1978:126; quoted in Podemski 2005:102) for whom travel or wandering was:

> ... pewien rodzaj doświadczenia społecznego o niezwykle istotnych konsekwencjach przenoszenia informacji i wartości

kulturowych, doświadczenia, które bywa rejestrowane w roznego typu periegezach, itinerariach i reportazach podrózniczych

... a form of a social experience with incredibly important consequences linked to the flow of information and cultural values; experience of this sort may be recorded in various types of itineraries and travelogs.

Podemski analyzes Abramowska's approach where travel was perceived along a spectrum of dichotomies: there was "a way" and "a point in space," "motion" and "stillness," which indicated being "closed in the house/home" or being "open to the world." Other dichotomies involved:

[...] cudze-swoje, obczyzna-ojczyzna, nieznane-znane, nowestare [...] zmiana-trwałość, ryzyko- bezpieczeństwo, przygoda-spokój, pogoń za zyskiem-poprzestawanie na tym, co się posiada (Abramowska 1978:127; quoted in Podemski 2005:102).

... yours-ours, foreign land-home country, unknown-known, new-old, change-stability, risk-safety, adventure-peace, searching for gold/income-being satisfied with what is owned.

These dichotomies were valued in a variety of ways, and each of them had a literary character assigned to them. If "home" was evaluated positively and the "world" negatively, travel was forced, a running away, where coming back home was the most important element. It was like Odysseus (Ulysses) returning home or Aeneas looking for a new abode, as the old one did not exist any more. When "home" was evaluated negatively, and the world positively, the character was a "traveler," a mariner (a nomad by choice) for whom wandering was the most valued activity. Accepting "home" and the "world" to the same extent characterized pilgrims, students, travelers, and tourists. Rejecting both was said to typify the Jews and their eternal "yearning for a promised land."

Przecławski (1979) pointed out that although there had been many attempts to define tourism, so far none of these definitions had been universally accepted. For that reason, some argued that it was not possible to establish a definition by total consensus. For example, in the most often-quoted definition in Polish tourism-related textbooks, which is now regarded as a classic one, W. Hunziker stated that:

> Le Tourisme—c'est l'ensemble des rapports et des phénomènes du voyage et du séjour de non-résidants en tant que ce séjour ne crée pas un établissement durable et ne découle pas non plus d'une activité lucrative (1951:9).

> Tourism is the sum of the relationships and phenomena of the travel and sojourn of non-residents inasmuch as this sojourn does not become permanent or a profitable activity.

This connection with Swiss scholarship (as noted in the introduction to this volume) is interesting since it provided a link with earlier European thinking. Subsequently L. Nettekoven expanded this definition.

> Mass tourism is the sum of social and economic phenomena stemming from a voluntary and temporary change of the place of residence taken up by strangers to satisfy their non-material needs while mainly making the use of installations meant for a large number of people (1972:34).

Tourism was typically defined by representatives of a number of social scientific disciplines, and their respective definitions reflected their various disciplinary perspectives. For example, it was perceived differently by economists, urban planners, and sociologists. Additionally, some definitions did not clearly distinguish the essence of tourism from its multiple effects: spatial, economic, cultural, social, and educational (Przecławski 2004:27–36).

Alejziak (1999) commented on the evolution of the definition of tourism in the Polish literature. He quoted Maczka (1974) to show that already, by the 1970s, and in Polish sources alone, one could find 33 different definitions of tourism, the two most frequently cited being Hunziker's (1951) and Przecławski's (1973). Alejziak noted the influence of the Swiss researcher on the Polish interpretation of tourism, as Hunziker's definition was the most popular in Polish tourism studies until a more indigenous perspective was proposed by Przecławski. Alejziak commented on Ostrowski's (1988) view that the difficulties in defining tourism indicated that tourism research might still be in its infancy, even though it was very much an interdisciplinary phenomenon. Although Alejziak recognized a number of typologies of tourism, he chose to focus on two of them by analyzing the functions and dysfunctions of tourism in relation to its roles listed by Przecławski (1996) and Gaworecki (1998). Przecławski (1996) defined tourism within psychological, social, economic, spatial, and cultural boundaries (Alejziak 1999:17). Gaworecki (1998) listed ten main functions of tourism as they related to: relaxation, improvement of health, education, personal fulfillment and development, politics, support of urban development, cultural education, economics, ethnicity, and raising ecological awareness. On the basis of these functions and their corresponding roles Alejziak demonstrated the positive and negative effects of tourism.

As early as 1973, Przecławski had suggested the following definition of tourism:

> Tourism in its broad sense is the sum of phenomena pertaining to spatial mobility, connected with a voluntary, temporary change of place, the rhythm of life and its environment, and involving a personal contact with the visited environment natural and/or cultural and/or social (1973:12).

According to him, tourism is, first of all, a form of interpersonal behavior related to human beings. Therefore, its essence must be mainly sought in the humanistic sciences. Tourism is a complex reality, which has various psychological, social, economic, spatial, and cultural dimensions. A specific feature of the phenomenon of tourism can be found in people's attitudes toward space, itself an element of the broader context of human spatial mobility. Additionally, however, tourism signifies a temporary change of place, thereby excluding migration (change of domicile) and/or employment. Tourism also represents a change in daily routine. Consequently, commuting and compulsory travel (such as military service) are not part of tourism.

Tourism is a psychological phenomenon because it is an individual who travels. Well before their journey, people experience certain needs to travel which later on become motivations for the journey. These persons establish a purpose for their trip which derives from a particular value connected with it. They usually create pre-trip images in their minds, on-trip images while traveling and, when the holiday is over, tend to compare experienced reality with their earlier expectations. Being on a trip becomes for them a source of intellectual and emotional experience. On reaching the destination and coming into contact with nature, culture, and people, they behave in specific ways. Tourism is a social phenomenon because, while traveling people assume the social role of a traveler: a tourist. They get involved in a number of social contacts with their fellow travelers, organizers of trips, guides, and local people. Such encounters may lead to the development of even deeper social ties. Moreover, in the choice of destination, means of transport and so on, tourists are socially influenced not only by such demographic factors as age and gender, but also by the social images and stereotypes associated with the trip.

Podemski (2005:104), in his review of the articles related to sociology of travel, refers to the cultural anthropologist, Wojciech Burszta (1996, 2001; quoted in Podemski 2005:104). For Burszta travel is mainly an educational activity. However, for travelers to understand a cultural gap/difference between themselves and the "other," they need to have a prior knowledge about their own culture, as well as the culture of the destination.

> Podróz—zauwazmy tedy—nie powoduje, iz dowiadujemy się w efekcie jej odbycia, ze świat jest zróznicowany; pojęcie podrózy zakłada wcześniejsza świadomość wielości kultur i ich zasadniczej niekiedy odmienności, podobnie jak pojęcie "człowieka pierwotnego" ma sens tylko wówczas, jeśli przyjmiemy wcześniej jako przesłankę pojęcie rozwoju i scharakteryzujemy "człowieka nowoczesnego". Antropolog, ale takze zwykły śmiertelnik z orbisowskiej wycieczki, w podrózowaniu znajduje wyłacznie potwierdzenie odmienności, o której wie wcześniej, moze on odkryć rozne formy jej przejawiania się, ale nie odkrywa odmienności jako takiej. Nie jest to tak naprawdę wyprawa w nieznane. Mozna nawet powiedzieć mocniej: świadomość zróznicowania nie jest analitycznym rezultatem podrózy; ale "konieczna forma przedistnienia" pojęcia podrózy, zarówno podrózy imaginacyjnej, literackiej, antropologicznej czy tez w sensie dosłownego "turystycznego szlaku"(Burszta 1996:61 quoted in Podemski 2005:104).

> Travel—let us note—is not the cause of our discovering while we are traveling that the world is varied; the concept of travel is based on the assumption that the awareness of many cultures and the differences between them already exist. Similarly naming a "pre-human" only makes sense if we know about development and we are able to describe "modern

man" (sic). Anthropologists, as well as common tourists, find in travel only a confirmation of existing differences, about which they had known before anyway; they may find various forms in which these differences will reveal themselves, but they are not discovered as such. It is not really a trip into an unknown. More fundamentally awareness of differences is not an analytical result of travel, but a "necessary pre-existing condition" to travel; and it may be an imaginary travel, literary travel, anthropological travel, or as a real "touristic path."

Przecławski argues that, although tourism is an economic and spatial phenomenon, in its broad sense tourism is a cultural phenomenon. Culture as a social achievement has been created by humans and is a consequence of their intentional actions. Tourism is also a form of human behavior. It is this realization that urges him to ask how the links between tourism and culture can be presented more clearly. By way of response, he indicates that there are five types of connections between tourism and culture, which bears some similarity to Podemski's (1981) tourism as a fifth element of culture, namely:

1. Tourism is a function of culture, or a manifestation of a given culture. If scholars try to understand why people behave in a specific way during a trip, the causes of such behavior must be sought not only in tourism, but also in certain phenomena typical of contemporary culture. In other words, it is impossible to understand modern tourism without being aware of what is going on in current culture.
2. Tourism is a permanent element of contemporary culture. That is to say, contemporary culture can only be fully understood and described if one takes into account the phenomenon of tourism and its role in present day culture.
3. Tourism is a transmission of culture. Certain values are communicated today not only by the mass media or by the agency of education but also, or perhaps to an ever greater degree, by tourism.
4. Tourism is an encounter of cultures, a "clash" of cultures. It provides for an exchange of values mainly between tourists, incomers and the residents of the regions visited by tourists. The greater the cultural gap between these milieux, the stronger the effects of the "clash."
5. Tourism can be also a factor of cultural change. It is thus no mere coincidence that the international program coordinated by the Vienna Center was called *Tourism as a Factor of Change: A Sociocultural Study*.

Relations between tourists and the inhabitants of visited areas are easier to explain in terms of Symbolic Interactionism (the perspective of Thomas and Znaniecki 1926). The essence of tourism is an encounter, a meeting with destination people, along with their past and present culture. Tourists seek to know these hosts and their artifacts. They try or at least are offered an opportunity to understand. They have the possibility of comprehending the symbols and signs presented by the persons they meet or through cultural artifacts. Tourism is thus more than an experience; it is an enrichment of the mind, a career (a typical theme of Symbolic Interactionism). Everything else, including the whole of the tourist industry and changes in visited societies, are only the effects of the first and basic element of symbolic interaction.

In recent years, Polish attention has turned toward the philosophy and ethics of tourism. Here, under the influence of the French thinker Teilhard de Chardin (1985; in Przecławski 1994:54–63), Przecławski's (1997) *Ethical Foundations of Tourism* and *Życie to podróz: wprowadzenie do filozofii turystyki* (Life is a Journey: Introduction to the Philosophy of Tourism) (2005) are both relevant. In these works he asks if there is an analogy between human life (during the entire course of life) and tourist wandering. If, indeed, such an analogy exists, tourism, like life itself, comprises four principal periods: childhood, adolescence, maturity, and old age. Time is not only objectively measured in seconds, hours, days, and years; but also "subjective time," which is measured by human experiences, their intensity, and human memory. Time can be measured according to the social division of individual periods: work, leisure, and holiday ("social time"). Finally, "cultural time" is how one manages social time.

Space where humans live is not homogeneous. There are four basic types of space: physical, psychological, social, and cultural. "Psychological space" comprises everything that people discover, experience, and memorize. For them, this space is fortunately limited in capacity. Social space refers to social groups and individuals in general, that persons encounter in their lifetime. Social and cultural space, thanks to mobile phones and the internet have greatly expanded in recent times.

Therefore, life is wandering through time and space. Sometimes this wandering is unplanned, especially in childhood. In later life (under normal conditions), wandering becomes more conscious and deliberate. In their journey through life, people determine their goals and select adequate means (material means, upbringing, and education) for achieving them. However, wandering must have a specific direction. As a result, being a human implies deliberation, to be able to sense qualities. It signifies the ability to decide freely, when faced with many situations and to choose the right path and means in order to reach a certain destination. These decisions are essentially conscious and free. A tourist also has a certain goal (apart from roaming without purpose, purely for pleasure, which ironically is an end in itself). There are many similarities among life, traveling, and tourism. In all cases, persons are *en route*. When they are on their way they are guided by specific signs. Their journey takes place in time and space. Both in life and travel one can distinguish a starting point and finishing point. Nevertheless, the journey is the most important. Life is also considered a path. All persons follow a certain route. They receive signs preventing them from getting lost. Tourists also take a certain path. Tourism is not only a physical activity but also a sort of symbolic communication. During roaming the skill to interpret signs becomes very important. Karol Wojtyła (John Paul II) used to say that in the mountains people need to tread in such a way that they do not miss the signs (quoted in Wójcik 2007:150). Life then requires constant cooperation. No one is an island. Tourism, especially some forms, requires strict cooperation. This cooperation is feasible, only if people abide by certain ethical principles. Ethics is essential to roaming. Only then will travelers reach their destination safely. Amid such happiness lie the goals of everyone.

Current Trends and Future Prospects

At the beginning of the 21st century (and coinciding with the anniversaries of a number of tourism departments across Poland) some leading indigenous scholars in various universities across the country tried to sum up and reflect upon what had been achieved so far in tourism studies. They noted the expansion of research in the field and tried to answer the question concerning its nature. From 2003 to 2004, Winiarski and Gołembski independently edited compendia of the study of tourism in Poland (Gotembski 2003; Winiarski 2004). One was published at the *Akademia Wychowania Fizycznego w Krakowie* (Kraków Academy of Physical Education), the other at the *Akademia Ekonomiczna w Poznaniu* (Poznań University of Economics). These two institutions were typical of tourism courses and research being conducted, with the first emphasizing leisure and sport, the second economic aspects of tourism. Both authors, working as academics in the fields related to tourism in the two universities encouraged a large number of leading Polish scholars to cover such areas as geography, economics, sociology, psychology, history, philosophy, and theology.

  Winiarski's compendium is in two parts. While the first focuses on the aforementioned disciplines, the second tackles managerial aspects of tourism research, including statistics, law, politics, marketing, finance, ecology, biometeorology, and medicine. In the preface to the first section, Winiarski (2003:7) notes that systematic tourism research had been established in Poland as early as the interwar period. In 1936, the initiative of Stanisław Leszczycki, Professor of the Kraków Jagiellonian University, had secured a place for a *Studium Turyzmu* (Tourism Studies Unit), based in the Institute of Geography. It was the first and only academic unit in Poland at the time, within which the teaching, research and publishing on tourism were quite extensive. These activities were halted in 1939 by the Second World War (Warszyńska 2003:18). Two expressions were distinguished at that time: *turystyka* (tourism as a pursuit including travel) and *turyzm* (defined below). That followed Leszczycki's (1937) suggestion voiced and published in 1937 (and quoted by Alejziak and Winiarski 2003) that all research related to tourism should be developed under the umbrella term *turyzm*, defined as "ogół zjawisk społeczno-kulturalnych, gospodarczych, przyrodniczych i organizacyjno-prawnych, zwiazanych z turystyka" (Alejziak and Winiarski 2003:160) (a set of phenomena of a socio-cultural, economic, nature-based, organization and legal dimensions, connected with tourism). Alejziak (2003) notes that the disadvantage of this approach was that too much emphasis was placed upon the geographical dimensions, not only in terms of the topics researched, but also the methods chosen.

Since the 1970s and 1980s, more emphasis has been placed on the economic aspects of tourism. Nowakowska (1982) refers to a "tourism economy," understood as "an organized part of economy where products, but mainly services are created to satisfy the needs brought on by the tourism mobility of societies." Rogoziński (1975) explains that tourism economics includes some of the elements of physical education, sport and exercise science, sociology, psychology, economic policy, planning, economic geography, and regional economy (both quoted in Nowakowska 2003:36).

Clearly, the sociology of tourism in Poland has come a long way. Indeed, there is growing evidence of a far greater cooperation among tourism academics than hitherto experienced. *Konfraternia Turystyczna* (Tourism Confraternity) for example, was created in September 2002, during a seminar organized by the *Wyzsza Szkoła Hotelarstwa Gastronomii i Turystyki w Warszawie* (WSHGiT) (University of Hospitality, Catering and Tourism in Warsaw). The seminar was entitled "The Place of Tourism Information in the Role and Responsibilities of Scientific Libraries: How to Disseminate Academic Information about Tourism." *Konfraternia Turystyczna* is now firmly established within a dedicated section of the libraries of the Polish Association of Librarians. It consists of academic libraries and research centers in higher education and other didactic institutions related to tourism. Its main task is to select, gather, and disseminate academic information relevant to the field.

The idea to further strengthen cooperation between units handling academic information derived from the *Gremium Ekspertów Turystyki* (Gathering of Tourism Experts) conference, which took place in 2003 in Poznań—to celebrate the 40th anniversary of the Tourism Department at the University of Economics in Poznań. One of the outcomes of this conference reads as follows:

> Istotnym wnioskiem jest poprawa informacji naukowej. Dlatego niezbędnym jest utworzenie (na podstawie istniejacych placówek) ośrodka informacji naukowej (o wydawnictwach, doktoratach, konferencjach, realizowanych tematach badawczych itp). Umozliwi to podejmowanie niezbędnych działań koordynacyjnych, pozwalajac zaoszczędzić czas i środki finansowe (Rozwadowski 2007).

> The academic (scientific) flow of information should be improved. It is essential to create (within existing institutions) a center of academic exchange of information (about publications, PhD topics, conferences, research topics under investigation). That enterprise should streamline co-ordination, which helps to save time and financial resources.

There are two practical components to this outcome. First, are various newsletters edited and published from September 2004 on the Webpage of *Wyzsza Szkoła Hotelarstwa Gastronomii i Turystyki w Warszawie* (WSHGiT 2008) (University of Hospitality, Catering and Tourism in Warsaw). Second, is a weekly communiqué produced in PDF format (also published from September 2004 and distributed via email to interested parties (academics and practitioners)). News and information are gathered in sections about conferences (advertising times and dates and providing feedback after the event), academic and industry-based events, publications, consultations, consultancies, and research (results of studies undertaken in a number of academic and industry-based institutions as well as public centers in Poland). Additional information covers issues of curriculum design and didactics in higher education).

Discussion includes topics for regulations and policies (organization and finance) regarding the research assessment exercise undertaken by the *Komitet Badań Naukowych* (Committee for the Funding of Academic Research): research assessment exercise by the *Ministerstwo Nauki i Szkolnictwa Wyzszego* (Ministry of Science and Higher Education, since 9 September 2005); ranking of academic journals by *Ministerstwo Nauki i Szkolnictwa Wyzszego* (Ministry of Science and Higher Education) and its comparison with the Philadelphia ranking; and creation of a digital tourism library. In other words, there exists a highly sophisticated Polish version of the electronic system of communication among English-speaking tourism academics, known as TRINET.

There are indications that many of Polish works in the sociology of tourism, if not reaching other audiences via translation, are becoming known in international fora. *Problems of Tourism*, for example, for many years a goldmine of works of Polish scholars, is now being given a fresh lease of life with the recent arrival of *New Problems of Tourism*. Then again, already in 2005 there has been a conference on "Turystyka w badaniach naukowych w Polsce i na świecie" (Tourism in Scientific Research in Poland and Worldwide) organized and held by the Academy of Physical Education, Kraków and the University of Information Technology and Management, Rzeszów (Alejziak and Winiarski 2005a, 2005b). This conference, marking the 30th anniversary of the Faculty of Tourism and Recreation in Kraków, was a state-of-the-art celebration based on the treatment of tourism in the human, natural, and economic sciences and involving a number of indigenous and overseas scholars. A few years ago such an event would have been virtually impossible due to lack of material. Today it indicates that the sociology of tourism is alive and well in Poland and that many of its ideas are being exchanged in settings as global as the phenomenon of tourism itself.

CONCLUSION

The review and discussion of this chapter suggests that as an applied field, the sociology of tourism in Poland has grown out of the parent discipline of general sociology, probably in a process similar to that experienced by other countries covered by this volume. Yet the nature of travel and tourism and the trends connected with the two were strongly influenced by the history of the country. As revealed in the literature, an initial appreciation of the home environment which was conducive to "a particular liveliness of non-traveling in Polish culture" (Abramowska 1978:143), became transformed into a great deal of "wandering" from the 18th century to the present day. Attitudes toward this "wandering" changed too. While originally many people left Poland forced by the twofold necessity of escaping death or finding food (as political or economic migrants), now when they travel they tend to return home more often. They "wander back" to the source, enriched by the experiences which they have undergone as "tourists" rather than as immigrants or asylum seekers. This is how the "wandering" itself and the identities of the "wanderers" have changed.

As suggested by Kłoskowska (1981), the development of the sociology of tourism is rooted in cultural identity and influenced by the historical developments of a nation. Thus, although some Polish commentaries on tourism, travel, and wandering may be lost in translation, it is still worth making the effort of peeling off the layers of idiom in order to discover their original meanings. Even so many Polish ideas and authors remain silent and undiscovered in the English literature. This account provides an opportunity to begin the process of shedding light on this body of knowledge. It thereby hopes to encourage international awareness of ideas that have for too long remained buried in national sources and which consequently have largely been missed by the wider tourism research community.

Chapter 6

Tourism Theory in the Former Yugoslavia

Boris Vukonić
Utilus Business School for Tourism and Hotel Management, Zagreb, Croatia

INTRODUCTION

In almost all countries, theoreticians of tourism usually spring up in periods when it is transformed from being a marginal activity to become a significant social phenomenon. Just like tourism itself in its historical evolution, its theory is characterized by different factors. Such theory is influenced by geopolitical, economic, cultural, sociological, and many other types of disciplinary environment. These are the settings which create a general interest in this field, as well as the particular interest of various experts in providing its theoretical explanations and critical analyses. The more developed tourism becomes, the greater the interest of its theoreticians, and this positive association is also evident in the former Yugoslavia.

The various areas and political entities in the former State, with their specific histories and cultural heritages, different languages and faiths, created a more or less homogeneous conglomerate upon the formation of a single State. However, this amalgam was not always able to function adequately, and tourism shared the same shaky fate. It emerged and developed with varying intensities and consequences in the individual parts of the former Yugoslav State. The first theoretical works appeared in the regions with the

The Sociology of Tourism: European Origins and Developments
Tourism Social Science Series, Volume 12, 195–219
Copyright © 2009 by Emerald Group Publishing Limited
ISSN: 1571-5043/doi:10.1108/S1571-5043(2009)0000012011

most robust resource base for the development of tourism, namely Croatia and Slovenia, and to a lesser extent Serbia. In these areas of the country, an awareness of the importance of the phenomenon was strong, as well as the need to provide complex answers to the issues of its development.

STAGES OF TOURISM DEVELOPMENT

It is difficult to trace the history of tourism theory in the former Yugoslavia without knowing the background of the general conditions in which it appeared and became one of the most significant economic options in large parts of the former State. This review begins with two hypotheses. The first assumes that the amount and quality of theoretical work corresponds to its individual phase of development. The second hypothesis assumes that the periods of its development can, with certain limitations, be generalized for the whole territory of the former State (Vukonić 2005). The rationale for this division into periods is that, in spite of the differences between the ex-Yugoslavia's geographic regions/republics, they shared the same fate at the precise time when tourism gained relevant economic significance, both globally and in the country. Thus, the last (sixth) part of this account refers to the time after the dissolution of the former State. Since the new States, the former Yugoslav republics, developed differently before the breakup, both economically and in the field of tourism, the first period after their gaining independence can be considered as the first development phase of their new history.

Initial Indications of Tourism

The development of tourism in those regions that would later become the State of Yugoslavia began much earlier than written evidence reveals. The 14th and 15th centuries marked the start of activities resembling tourism. As long ago as 1347, the Senate of Dubrovnik voted to open a hospice for foreigners in that city's Sponza Palace. The beginnings were also associated with pilgrimage, which, according to Fr Pietro Casole, in 1494, included Zadar and the islands of Korčula and Hvar. Until 1543, Dubrovnik subsidized inns which accommodated travelers, and in the same year lodgings were opened for Turks near the Rector's Palace. The first hospice in Hvar was mentioned in 1543 and again in 1561. An interesting written record from 1644 refers to the caravan-seraglio, a court, built for the vizier

Jusufpaša Matković. Guests were very much respected and enjoyed the best possible hospitality on the coast and in the interior, where at that time numerous inns and lodgings sprang up in larger settlements. The long rule of the Hapsburgs, the rule of Venice in one part of the country, and Byzantine rule in another, brought to these regions different languages, government institutions, and customs, including organized care for guests. The two major religions which dominated these regions, not only in the spiritual domain but also in general, social, and political life (Christianity and Islam), stressed that hospitality and the care of guests were among the most important values in human life (Vukonić 2005).

There are no reliable data that can answer the question why European nobles in the 17th century did not include the cultural wealth of this region in their travels, particularly the coastal towns, along with the buildings and architectural gems that they possessed. These settlements were not selected as destinations during their Grand Tours, although these same aristocrats visited almost every historical urban center in Italy, France, Germany, Bohemia, and some other European countries. Since there were no records about travels to the Balkans and the Adriatic coast, potential visitors could not acquire any written information on these locations. However, one possible word-of-mouth explanation as to why these aristocrats did not journey to this part of the world may have been that in the Eastern portion of what was later to become Yugoslavia, there were concerns over safety, and the roads were bad.

Nevertheless, that area formed a section of a very busy pilgrimage route from Venice to the Holy Land. *Viaggio in Dalmazia* (Voyage in Dalmatia) by Alberto Fortis (1774) was one of the first travel books of the time. The following year, Giovanni Valle from Kopar produced a drawing of the small Istrian town of Poreč showing people swimming in the sea. Another early account was an 1802 compendium of rare plants which promoted the natural richness of the Velebit mountain region. According to historical documents and early books, in the 17th and 18th centuries many writers, painters, poets, and others interested in the natural beauty of the country visited certain places and historic towns, mostly on the Adriatic coast, which were almost identical to those visited by tourists today. These odysseys brought forth more travel books, mainly by foreign authors, for example, the writings of H.J. Crantz on mineral springs and spas on the Croatian mainland. The nine-year rule of Napoleon over Dubrovnik and parts of Dalmatia was described in the literature as an exercise in decadence. As a result, Dubrovnik experienced economic collapse, and the number of visitors was significantly reduced.

Early Development

After the Vienna Congress of 1815, the return of Austrian rule to the Adriatic coast marked a new and relatively long period in the formation and functioning of a modern government administration, greater urbanization, and economic development. During this time, a large number of scientific and popular works on the impact of the sea, climate, and vegetation on the human body were published. These writings aroused interest and motivated foreign tourists to come, particularly to the northern part of the Adriatic coast, but also to spas on the mainland. They also showed that the then special interest tourism based on health and the healing properties of thermal springs (such as Vrnjačka Banja, Rimske Toplice, and Tuheljske Toplice) began to develop significantly. Yet, even though there were still no serious theoretical works during this era, tourism organizations/societies nevertheless began to be established. The first were set up on the islands of Krk and Hvar in 1866, and Vrnjačka Banka in 1868. They concentrated on promotional work and taught people in the local community how important it was to keep their streets clean, put flowers in their window boxes, and similar acts of domestic pride. Sometimes they organized funerals of important persons, but also festivals and other forms of entertainment. Obviously it was just the start, not yet of tourism but of some "forerunner" of future development. The government displayed an interest in tourism and influenced it through the passing laws of the Austrian Act on Health Services in 1889 and the Act on the Health Service legislated by the Croatian Parliament in 1906. These laws stipulated that certain places could be designated summer and winter resorts and demanded special bodies to serve as *zdravstvenbi turistički centri* (commissions in health resorts), bathing resorts, and spas. A large number of tourism societies were established after World War I, and, in 1922, regional associations were created in the most visited regions, with centers in Split, Sušak, Dubrovnik, and Ljubljana.

Between the Two Wars

The ex-Yugoslav State was founded after the end of World War I in 1918 as a kingdom consisting of three main territories: Croatia, Slovenia, and Serbia. From the beginning all three territories were very different—economically, nationally, and religiously. It was thus not surprising that the development of tourism suffered the same fate. At that time, individual travel to the newly formed country gradually acquired all the characteristics of tourism while numbers increased rapidly. However, all this activity was not sufficient to arouse the interest of experts, whether economists, geographers, or sociologists, for them to begin studying tourism as a universal phenomenon.

It is interesting to note that the first official definition of tourism dates back to this time. It was published in 1933 in an anonymous official document translated as *The Rules for Advancing Tourist Interest in the Settlements, Regions and Spas Important for Tourism in the Banovina of the Bannat of Sava*. Quoted by Vrinjanin, it stated that:

> Turizam u širem smislu je prvenstveno privredna radinost, kojoj je cilj da stvara povoljne uslove za putovanje i boravak posjetilaca u mjestima i krajevima, koji po svojim prirodnim osobinama, folklore, narodnoj istoriji, vjerskom kultu, kultur-nim objektima i zbirkama odnosno kulturnom značaju i privrednoj važnosti ili sportskim priredbama pružaju naročiti interes i privlačnost (1952:19).

> Tourism in a broader sense is primarily an economic industry whose aim is to create favorable conditions for the travel and sojourn of visitors in places and regions, which, on account of their natural characteristics, folklore, history, religion, archi-tecture, and artefacts, that is according to their cultural significance, economic importance or association with sport, are of particular interest or attractiveness.

The first written accounts of tourism in the ex-Yugoslav State coincided with the beginning of its strong development in Europe. There were many relevant works in Yugoslavia at that time, which was also a period characterized by a steep rise in visitor numbers, particularly international arrivals to the Adriatic Coast. Although there were some attempts to write about the phenomenon earlier, these articles, published in popular newspapers and magazines, were hardly scientific in nature.

Intensive Development of Tourism

Very soon after the end of World War II, two booklets appeared on tourism. The first, written by Vrinjanin (1952), had the simple title, *Turizam* (Tourism). In the same year, Apih published *Turizam u svetu i kod nas* (Tourism in the World and in this Country). A brief glance at the contents of the latter shows that the author was at least acquainted with the fundamental works of contemporary European tourism scholars, from Italy (Mariotti), to Germany (Bormann, Glücksmann), and Switzerland (Keller, Krapf, Hunziker). He attempted to convey their views to a still not a very interested local public. *Tourism in Theory and Practice* by Grgašević (1958) was the next volume to cover these issues. Here the author attempted to provide a very detailed description of terminologies, along with developments in international tourism in what was then the Yugoslav State. The third book on the topic was enti *Osnovi turizma* (Tourism Basics). It was a compilation of works by different experts in the field (Mazi, Esminger, Stojanovic, Bosnjak, Panic, Protic, Nikolic, and Popov 1967). Although only two of these writers survived the ensuing decades in which research took off, the number of authors shows that, at the start of the 1970s, the former Yugoslavia had a critical mass of tourism experts from which it was possible to recruit those who were ready to enter into theoretical debates.

There were two general approaches in explaining tourism: economic and social. It was then considered "travel for the purposes of entertainment, rest, health, enjoyment of nature, curiosity, seeing new regions and people, sport, etc." (Apih 1952:9–10), or "as a social movement for recreational and social needs" (Jovičić 1966:2). However, even at that time, some authors, like Mazi, opposed such a view and advocated tourism "as a specific form of consumption derived from the increase in income at a level which enables greater consumption than is necessary to provide for living in a permanent place of residence" (1965:12). It is not easy to explain what reasons led Vrinjanin to write a book on *Putničke agencije* (Tourist Agencies), as long ago as 1957, at a point when these organizations played only a marginal role in the development of Yugoslav tourism (Vrinjanin 1957). The text of the book was based on the experience of *Putnik*, the only State tourism agency in Yugoslavia at that time.

One of the first stimuli for investigating the phenomenon more thoroughly was the establishment of an investigation into the economics of tourism within the Faculty of Economics at the University of Zagreb in 1962. This study brought together all the existing experts in Yugoslavia, many of whom soon published their first works, which were subsequently used as the first university textbooks for students. In secondary-school programs tourism appeared much later, and with it, suitable textbooks. Among the first serious works were course materials and, a little later, a book by Janez Planina, *Ekonomika turizma* (Economics of Tourism) in 1964. This marked the beginning of a whole series of books of the same title which, with some breaks, appeared for more than 30 years, the authors of which were university lecturers from different Yugoslav universities (Zagreb, Belgrade, Ljubljana, Dubrovnik, and Novi Sad). This shows that from the very beginning an interest in tourism in the former Yugoslavia was very much focused on the economic benefits which were expected from its development. Here, the scientific interest of these authors concentrated on explaining the basic ideas and fundamental dilemmas found in the international literature that was then available. One of the frequently elaborated topics comprised the economic and noneconomic characteristics of those factors which made tourism a relevant social phenomenon. Since these factors appeared individually and fragmentarily in certain historical periods, and as an integral complex idea from around the middle of the 19th century, theoreticians in the former Yugoslavia worked a great deal on defining the stages in the development of tourism. Based on its political and economic analysis, Marković and Marković (1967, 1970) saw the two main development periods as tourism for the privileged classes and modern tourism. This classification corresponded with the political ideology of the time, and was based less on historical events and real practice.

The theoreticians of that period particularly dwelt on the fundamental methodological questions and definitions which more closely explained either tourism itself or the ideas and phenomena surrounding it—for example, the definition of a tourist, and the question whether employees on business trips should be considered as tourists. Taking as a starting point, the theories in Europe at that time, Janez Planina made the suggestion that business trips should not be included, since the expenditure structure of these travelers differed from that of tourists (1964:5). In the second edition *Osnove turizma* (Essentials of Tourism), S. and Z. Marković (1970:19) referred to the ideas of Paul Bernecker, one of the major authorities in European academia (see Spode in this volume), and concluded that it was very difficult to distinguish a tourist from a business traveler since the latter was often combined with private leisure and recreation. Mazi also accepted this view in *Ekonomika turizma* (The Economics of Tourism), since in business travels, "… expenditure is included which cannot be separated from other tourist expenditure" (1972:15). Unković, who embraced the ideas of American theoreticians in most of his works, clearly stated that "the very idea of 'tourist' should be understood as a matter of convention in given circumstances" (1968:14).

However, there were few original ideas or publications. The body of scientific works of that period was probably best described by Alfier who summarized them in the following way:

Premda historijsko i evolucionističko tumačenje geneze i razvoja turizma kao zasebne pojave ne može izdržati znanstvenu kritiku, ipak se ne može osporiti da i turizam ima svoju historiju. Ona je zasad još kratka, jer pojava turizma podudara se s počecima tehničko-industrijske revolucije, koja ujedno obilježava početak nove i do sada najkraće etape u razvoju društva. Pojava i razvoj turizma u tijesnoj su uzročnoj vezi sa svim dubokim i brzim promjenama ipopratnim pojavama što ih je tehnička revolucija izazvala i još izaziva u svim područjima života. Turizam je zapravo epifenomen svih tih pojava i promjena, a brzo omasovljenje turističkog prometa i brojne promjene turizma u uskoj su dijalektičkoj vezi sa svim pozitivnim i negativnim pojavama što prate nagli razvoj naše tehničke civilizacije (Alfier 1985:7).

Although historical and evolutionist explanations of the genesis and development of tourism have limited scientific foundation, we still cannot deny that it has its own history. However, it is a very short history as the development of tourism coincides with the beginning of the industrial revolution, marking the start of a new and so far the shortest historical period. The emergence and development of tourism are in close correlation with the deep and rapid changes that continue to take place as a result of technological revolution. Tourism is an epiphenomenon of these changes, and its rapid development and numerous transformations are closely dialectically associated with all the positive and negative features that accompany the rapid development of our technological civilization.

Probably, the real beginnings of serious research on the phenomenon occurred in the former Yugoslavia after the Markovićs published their textbook in 1967. This volume contained all the relevant views in Croatia at that time. Later these were used as a basis for developing a "Yugoslav tourism theory." It derived from the political doctrine known as *samoupravljanje* (self-management). This meant that the industry was not just important for the economic sector. It also indicated that developing domestic tourism in certain periods of the political life of former Yugoslavia became even more significant because state policy insisted that benefiting "working people" was a main policy goal of socialism in "providing" them with adequate possibilities for having a paid vacation and relaxation.

It needs to be said that such a theory emerged and developed during the era of socialism and a centrally planned state economy. Consequently, a number of assumptions from works published in the free market economies of European states had to be adjusted to the local situation. Almost all Yugoslav theoreticians used *Osnove turizma* as the basis for their own works, putting "finishing touches" to and "remodeling" the same theories.

Not much was written about the sociological features of tourism development in the former Yugoslavia. A possible reason for this omission was that the State authorities at the time showed a greater interest in the economic impact of tourism development (or foreign exchange inflow), since the industry was one of the major sources of external funds. It should not be forgotten that the then national currency, the dinar, was a soft currency, and that Yugoslavia could not use it for paying for much needed raw materials and other necessary commodities. In spite of this economic emphasis, among the first to examine the sociological aspects of tourism in the former Yugoslavia was Miro Mihovilović from the Department of Sociology, Zagreb University in the 1960s. He led several tourism projects with a sociological base. One of the focuses of his interest in the field was to research the profile of foreign guests who visited the former Yugoslavia, so that the industry could offer an adequate facility structure that would meet the needs of such a profile. Unfortunately, this valuable idea which underlay his empirical research did not bring tangible results in practice. Although the statistical part of the research was seemingly well designed, the results yielded "an average foreign visitor to Yugoslavia." This was a virtual tourist category since such a person did not exist beyond the level of ideal type.

The real flowering of scientific works on tourism took place in the former Yugoslavia during the 1980s, a period when it was growing strongly. The boom included not only analyses of its economics, which was the "most popular" topic among Yugoslav researchers, but also studies by authors of different scientific backgrounds that brought into the debate questions raised by their own fields (such as geography, sociology, and law). Even so, works of that kind were comparatively rare. Economic themes dominated the debate and for obvious reasons. The problems faced by the economy at that time were quite enormous. Therefore, it is not surprising that tourism received significant economic attention, given that it was the best way of getting hard currency into a country whose own currency was not convertible, and granted that the question of hard currency was a burning macroeconomic issue. For Western European researchers, this would have been a most unusual focus of attention because in their market economies such a problem simply did not exist. As many as eight books entitled

Ekonomika turizma (Tourism Economics) by an equal number of different authors provided evidence of the key debates and what was the perceived main vehicle of development. Other aspects were considered to be of marginal importance. Such a view was summarized by the Markovićs:

> Novije razdoblje turističkog razvitka pokazuje da su eko-
> nomske funkcije—bez obzira na bitnost neekonomskih motiva
> i funkcija—u suvremenim uvjetima ne samo postale neodvoj-
> ive od ostalih nego čine jedan od najupadljivijih, a praktično
> i najvažnijih i najsloženijih odražaja i djelovanja turizma
> (1967:44).

> The recent period of development of tourism shows that
> economic functions in modern circumstances—regardless of the
> importance of non-economic motives and functions—are not
> only almost inseparable from others, but are one of the most
> recognizable and most complex reflections of activities in tourism.

Mazi, Marković, Planina, Unković, and later Cicvarić and Kobašić are respected names among tourism experts in the former Yugoslav State; indeed their theories are still deemed to be as valid today as when they were first articulated. The issues of the economics of tourism were also dealt with separately by Kabiljo (1980) and Vukičević (1978, 1981). The areas these authors disagreed about were development policy and, in particular, the regional distribution of tourism. The huge political and financial rivalries between the various Yugoslav republics impacted on their disparate views on tourism, and these differences were the first intimations of what would later result in the dissolution of the Yugoslav State.

Geographers (e.g., Žabica 1967) viewed tourism through a different lens, and explained its significance in the former Yugoslavia in different ways, even placing its political implications before the economic ones. "Preventative health measures are of special social importance, with spontaneous recreation in the open air, as well as rehabilitation and medical treatment in the form of modern thallasso-, balneo-, and climato-therapy," were the words of the then often quoted professor of geography, Vladimir Blašković (1962:16). He added: .

> Kultura i kulturno-zabavna funkcija turizma imaju impresivni
> utjecaj na razvoj specifičvnih znanja o prirodnom fenomenu
> i specifičnih čimbenika, povijesnih objekata i spomenika,

kulturnih i povijesnih rijetkosti i vrijednosti, značajnih etnoloških i etnografskih karakteristika i vrijednosti, posebno nacionalnih karakteristika, iz kojih logički proizlaze načini na koje se manifestiraju političke funkcije turizma u formi snažnih patriotskih osjećaja i miroljubivih kozmopolitskih manira (1962:16).

Culture, and the cultural-entertainment function of tourism have an impressive influence on the development of a detailed knowledge of natural phenomena and specific features, historical objects and monuments, cultural and historic rarities and treasures, remarkable ethnological and ethnographic characteristics and wealth, national specific characteristics and social and economic achievements, from which logically follow political manifestations of the function of tourism in the form of noble expressions of patriotic feelings and peaceful cosmopolitan humaneness.

Among the Yugoslav geographers who studied tourism, Živadin Jovičić had primacy of place. In 1964, he first wrote *Turistička kretanja* (Tourism developments). This was followed in 1972 by a controversial article on methodology entitled "For the more rapid formation of tourismology as a separate scientific discipline" and in 1980 by *Osnovi turizmologije* (Essentials of Tourismology). According to Jovičić, the essence of this theory was that at a certain stage of its development it was necessary to refer to tourism as an independent science. While he insisted on the term "science," most other Yugoslav scholars and experts immediately opposed such an opinion. Based on his research, the University of Belgrade established tourismology studies, the title of which, as well as its methodology provoked much criticism and debate in ensuing decades. These studies ended with the collapse of Yugoslavia, but it is interesting that the same idea appeared in 2005 among a group of European experts, this time gathered in France. It had like content and similar supporting arguments as Jovičić's tourismology all those years before.

Academic Maturity

The real needs of the former Yugoslavia brought about the firm belief that tourism was crucial for the economy. This was the underlying premise of scientific thinking in Yugoslavia. In practice it meant that the majority of

studies by Yugoslav theoreticians concentrated on the economic characteristics and consequences of the phenomenon. Among several works
which discussed the topic, four stood out: Cicvarić's book *Turizam i
privredni razvoj Jugoslavije* (1984) (Tourism and Economic Development in
Yugoslavia), subsequently revised and published in 1990 under the title of
Ekonomika turizma (Tourism Economics); Pirjevec's *Ekonomski aspekti
jugoslavenskog turizma* (1988) (Economic Aspects of Yugoslav Tourism);
and Kobašić's *Turizam u Jugoslaviji* (1987) (Tourism in Yugoslavia). These
four works were primarily written as textbooks for university students. That
is why they not only contained explanations of many basic terms from the
economics of tourism, but also analyzed predominantly the economic
achievements in the former country. The same could be said the content of
Unković's *Ekonomika turizma* (1974) which was published in 14 editions
(during the time of the former Yugoslavia). It was then the basic textbook
utilized by students throughout the country. The reason for the preeminence
of Unković's book was not in its content but in the political circumstances in
which it appeared. Because Unković was a professor at the University of
Belgrade, his textbook was given preference over other ones of the same
kind. Thus, the fate of Unković's book mirrored the policy and State politics
of that time. It was obvious that many of his views drew on political ideas
of the State; consequently, it is difficult to determine today whether they
were always held by the author himself.

Pirjevec (1988) and Kobašić (1987) analyzed individual phases of
Yugoslav tourism, providing scientific arguments to support and explain
the characteristics of each. According to these two authors, the common
features of all the stages of its development were its seasonality, its territorial
concentration, and its orientation toward foreign markets. On the other
hand, Cicvarić (1984, 1990) advanced the thesis that Yugoslav tourism
would become an accelerator of economic development in the country and a
moderator of the instability which lasted for almost quarter of a century
in the former Yugoslavia. Cicvarić also supplied arguments against any
policy that would force the development of tourism as a monocultural
activity. He expounded similar views on the need to reduce seasonality.
Cicvarić's position was confirmed in later years in Yugoslavia, even after
the breakup of the country into those parts which objectively had, and still
have, the greatest potential for developing tourism: Croatia, Slovenia, and
Montenegro.

It is interesting to note that during the time that the former Yugoslavia
existed there were relatively few publications on hotel and catering, even
though theoretical works found these sectors to be a major contributor

toward the success of Yugoslav tourism. Yet these accounts were of a slightly lower quality than the parallel works on tourism.

Although sport and tourism were quite developed in the former Yugoslavia, and in some closely related destinations, the first professional publications did not appear until the end of the 1980s. Within the University of Zagreb, a Faculty for Physical Culture was established in 1973, later to become the Faculty of Kinesiology. Thus, the prerequisites for a scientific approach to sport were met, and the debate on the relation between sport and tourism became fruitful. Relac and Bartoluci, both lecturers in the Faculty, published *Turizam i sporstka rekreacija* (1987) (Tourism and Sport Recreation). Since the breakup of Yugoslavia, members of the Faculty have continued to publish. They have organized numerous conferences and workshops on the topics of sport and tourism and published the proceedings that include papers used as course material by the students of kinesiology.

In a country whose political ideology did not recognize religion, the Catholic Church nevertheless attempted to spread its own views on the relationship between that faith and tourism. The church did this at two symposia which resulted in two books. The first, *Turizam zbiližava narode* (1975) (Tourism Brings Peoples Closer), contained the papers from a Dubrovnik symposium. The second, *Obitelj i turizam* (1979) (The Family and Tourism), brought together the presentations from a Zadar symposium. Their opinions corresponded to those expressed by the Pope as the general view of the Catholic Church.

Tourism intermediaries (travel agencies and similar organizations) in the former Yugoslavia played an important role especially in relation to inbound tourism. Yugoslavia was a typical host country which shaped its development at the beginning of mass tourism and at the time of its expansion. That is why it had to cooperate with and seek help from travel agencies and later on from tour operators, particularly in international markets. Since domestic tourism was real mass tourism and was also oriented toward local travel agencies, and because the average disposable income of the majority of the population was not high, the role of intermediaries became important. It found its place in secondary-school books and university textbooks, and resulted in new research and the publishing of the first books on the activities of travel agencies. These included works by Gjivoje et al 1970, Knežević-Grubišić (1988), Pauko (1971), Popov (1979), and Rešetar (1981). Of these, a publication by Vukonić and Matović (1973) became the most widely used for all universities in the region for over 30 years. In these texts, the authors mainly described the practice of agencies in the world and in the former Yugoslavia at that time. Among the well-known works on intermediaries was that by Šmit (1977). Immediately before the breakup of Yugoslavia Šimić (1991) published a book on travel agencies and their role in the development of the industry.

By then tourism had come of age in Yugoslavia and that stage required the analysis of numerous factors in the development of its different forms and economic activities which ensured its success as a whole and for each of its components. It could best be seen in numerous theoretical works published from the middle of the 1980s to the end of the 20th century (i.e., until the breakup of Yugoslavia). Among these were works by Antunac (1985), Nejkov (1980), and Radišić (1981). A great number of authors published articles in different professional magazines and journals, including *Turizam* (Tourism), *Marketing, Ekonomski pregled* (Economic Review), *Turistični vestnik* (Tourism News), *Turizmologija* (Tourismology), *Lipov list ugostiteljstvo i turizam* (Catering and Tourism), *Acta turistica*, and others. Numerous authors published papers they had presented at domestic and foreign conferences organized by various universities, institutes, and tourism societies in Yugoslavia.

Most of the works on sociology of tourism were articles in journals and papers delivered at various conferences written by authors with very different profiles. It is interesting that other aspects of tourism began to be addressed at that time. Debates ensued when questions about the negative effects of its development were raised. But it was not only a Yugoslav peculiarity; such criticism was voiced throughout the world. This interestingly resulted in the first sociological debates about Yugoslav tourism. *Humanističke vrijednosti turizma* (Humanistic Values of Tourism 1977) was the title of the first major conference of its kind in Yugoslavia (held in Zadar in 1977). The Pedagogical Academy of Zadar published all the papers from that first scientific conference that dealt with the social impacts of tourism.

The reason for holding such a symposium was explained as follows:

> Temeljna i uporišna točka tom novom pristupu turističkom fenomenu krije se u onoj poznatoj i priznatoj činjenici da je turizam prije svega aktivnost pomoću koje čovjek ostvaruje i unapređuje ljudske osobine općenito, osobine čovječnosti, humanosti, bilo u međuljudskim odnosima, bilo u pogledima i spoznajama pojedinca, u njihovom odnosu prema svijetu i prema prirodi (Unković and Zečević 1977:15).

The cornerstone of this new approach to tourism phenomenon lies in the well-known and appreciated fact that it is the foremost activity through which people realize and foster human characteristics generally, humane qualities, either in their interrelations with other people, or in their individual views of and relations to the world and nature.

About 40 well-known experts in tourism at the time presented their papers at the symposium, among whom were Dragutin Alfier (Zagreb), Ivan Antunac (Zadar), Ratko Božović (Belgrade), Simo Elaković (Dubrovnik), Oliver Fio (Split), Vlatko Jadrešić (Zadar), Boris Jurić (Mostar), Nikica Kolumbić (Zagreb), Ljubica Radulović (Dubrovnik), Aleksandar Todorović (Beograd), and Momčilo Vukičević (Novi Sad). They offered fundamental sociological concepts applied to tourism, based on the works of a number of prominent European experts including Joffré Dumazedier, Arthur Haulot, and Jost Krippendorf.

There, Dragutin Alfier, one of the most prominent experts of the time, and professor at the Faculty of Economics, University of Zagreb, gave a keynote address (1977). The essence of his position was that, while the economic aspects of tourism had been given a great deal of prominence, their social effects had been correspondingly neglected. Indeed the negative consequences of its rapid growth, including the important role of people in tourism, had been studiously ignored. Ivan Antunac, the other protagonist of tourism theory, held a very similar position when he referred to the humanistic aspects of selective kinds of tourism.

A definite note of caution underlay Alfier's key message of this symposium, a warning that people should be given back the place they deserved in tourism. Persons should be in the forefront, not profit. Many authors believed that, in modern conditions of development, leisure time spent in tourist activities alienated individuals rather than humanized them. Humans had lost the ability to relax; instead they were buying a "product" that was being offered and sold on the market like any other mass product, oriented exclusively toward financial gain. They had been taught and were still being taught how to work, but not how to enjoy rest.

Ljudi koji ne posjeduju kulturu odmaranja ne umiju sami svrhovito, sadržajno i racionalno organizirati i provesti svoje slobodno vrijeme uopće, posebno ono koje je po trajanju pogodno za dokolicu izvan domicila. Takvi ljudi svoju vandomicilnu dokolicu provode ili u običnom ljenčarenju ili u pretjeranom uživanju, a to ih u jednom i drugom slučaju alijenira (1977:35).

People who do not foster the culture of taking rest are unable to organize and spend their free time purposefully and rationally while seeking meaningful activities. In particular, they do not have sufficient time for leisure pursuits outside the home. Such people spend time away from their place of abode either in lazy loafing or in indulging in excessive pleasures.

Alfier also spoke about the "incorrigible" sociological impact that "prodigal tourist consumption" exerted on local populations. Although he noted that local people prospered economically, they did so by going "straight from peasant to white tie and tails." Due to their inherited low cultural and spiritual standards they could not adequately accommodate such a change and so they morally deteriorated. Alfier further pointed out that consigning foreigners to luxury hotels, domestic visitors to holiday home ghettoes, and the owners of second homes to their isolated enclosures, summer cottages brought about social segregation; seasonal profits often deteriorated; and prices of all goods and services during the high season escalated chaotically. There were even opinions expressed that from the time when double flush toilets entered the homes of a local population, human beings were lost. However, a question was raised as to "whether development should be halted for the sake of purity of attitudes" (Gavranović 1977:225).

A large number of speakers stressed the negative effects that tourism had on nature and the environment, on urban heritage and its environs. It was pointed out that little had remained intact of the original built heritage on the islands, and not only on the islands, due to an unfortunate lack of cement, concrete, and prefabricated buildings which were strange and inappropriate for the environment. The local population, who lived in ultra comfortable houses and let rooms to visitors, threw litter, old refrigerators, and washing machines into the ruins of old valuable houses.

Poseban i još kritičniji problem predstavljaju hoteli i hotelsko-turistički kompleksi unutar starih urbanih prostora. Hotelske zgrade morale bi biti logičan nastavak tradicionalnog urbanizma, prilagođenog našim suvremenim potrebama i oblicima. One bi morale biti ono što su nekada bile crkve i palače—a to, na žalost, u većini slučajeva nisu. Prepotentno se nameću prvorazrednim urbanim cjelinama koji nije pridonio ni urbanom ni ljudskom prostoru, nego dapače predstavlja očiti primjer kapitulacije suvremenog urbanizma i suvremene arhitekture u odnosu na one tradicionalne (Kečkemet 1977:147).

Hotels and tourist facilities inside old urban centers constitute a special and more critical problem. Hotel buildings should be a logical extension of traditional town planning. They should be what churches and palaces once were, but in most cases, they are not. They overbearingly impose themselves on premier urban complexes and have not contributed to either urban or human space. On the contrary, they are a vivid example which shows that modern town planning and contemporary architecture have capitulated when compared with traditional ones.

It was further noted that tourism would gain in importance in realizing the concept of making leisure time more humane through decreasing the hours of work and increasing the income available for spending free time actively.

Prevaziđene su koncepcije da je sport povezan s turizmom amo prekosportskih manifestacija. Naprotiv, sport u turizmu je sastavni dio dnevnog života sve većeg broja turista. Napuštaju se postepeno koncepcije da je efikasan onaj turizam koji omogućuje podmirenje samo egzistencijalnih potreba. Aktivan odmor u turizmu danas je stvarnost. Dileme ipak postoje, a to je, što sve treba uključiti u aktivan odmor u turizmu (Marković, Relac, and Štuka 1977:253).

The idea that sport is linked to tourism solely through sport events has become outdated. Sport in tourism today is a part of everyday life of an ever larger number of tourists. Another concept which is gradually losing ground is that efficient tourism is the only one that meets existential needs. Spending a vacation actively is tourism reality now. However, dilemmas still exist of what should be included in active tourist vacations.

The contradictory nature of tourism was most clearly demonstrated by the fact that each of its positive functions on the social and economic plan was accompanied by a negative function.

> Jedna je od najvećih proturječnosti turizma zacijelo u tome što on istovremeno može igrati i igra ulogu resocijalizacije i desocijalizacije suvremenog čovjeka (Alfier 1977:21).

> Certainly one of the biggest contradictions of tourism is that it can, and does, simultaneously play a role of re-socialization and de-socialization of modern people.

In spite of its success, this gathering of social scientists did not immediately prompt more significant and systematic research into the sociological/psychological problems of tourism in the former Yugoslavia. However, authors who later did publish in the field included Čomić (1990), Elaković (1989), Geić (2002), Jadrešić (1993, 2001), Jokić (1994), Jurić (1975), Ravkin (1983), and Todorović (1982, 1984, 1990). Even so, the majority of their works were university textbooks, and most of them held few original positions, communicating, as they did, the views of foreign authors found in books published abroad. The works on tourism in Yugoslavia before 1991 (i.e., before the breakup of the country) reflected ideological standpoints of the time, socialist and partly communist.

Nevertheless, the social impact of tourism was the first of several specific fields of interest to be addressed by sociological perspectives. Yet ironically it was also one of the essential characteristics of tourism on which academic interest was rarely focused among experts in the former Yugoslavia. By that time its promotion had produced important results and brought about the first related works in the field, including those by Čulić (1965), Petrinjak and Sudar (1972), Rebevšek (1966), and Vukonić (1972). It is interesting to note that Čulić's book mentioned marketing for the first time in Yugoslavia. A year later, in 1973, Unković and Tourki published the results of their own research in Belgrade, which was an introduction to the later texts by Unković on implementing marketing in tourism.

Although this accelerated development required corresponding legislation, there were no theoretical works about it. The first works on the legal regulation of tourism appeared in the 1980s. The authors based their suggestions on foreign experience and unanimously advocated the need for legal regulations between partners in the market as an important prerequisite for the successful development of Yugoslav tourism. Among the first such books were those by Gorenc (1985) and Sušić (1985).

A more intensive interest in tourism in the United States in the second half of the 20th century resulted in new scientific concepts in tourism which were keenly followed in Yugoslavia. Some of these concepts, especially in marketing, were novel, not only in Yugoslavia but in Europe as well. It is strange that such an interest was shown in marketing in the socialist Yugoslavia, a country with no market in the classic sense of the term, in which a planned economy prevailed. It could be assumed that in such circumstances marketing would have little room for development in Yugoslavia. However, with the establishment of a Marketing Department at the Zagreb Faculty of Economics, University of Zagreb, this subject began to be studied as a scientific discipline in its own right and its use spread in business. Tourism was an example of why there was a need for marketing knowledge: one could not succeed in the international (capitalist) market without using the same methods and tools as the other participant competitors.

By the beginning of the 1980s, tourism in Yugoslavia had reached a high level of development owing to a corresponding growth elsewhere. Yugoslav firms had contacts with overseas partners and its destinations competed with foreign ones. Hence a huge interest arose in using marketing in tourism, both in practice and in theoretical studies (Kobašić 1975; Senečić 1988; Senečić and Kobašić 1989; Senečić and Vukonić 1993, 1997; Vukonić 1981). At about the same time when books on marketing tourism appeared in Zagreb, they were published in Slovenia too (Bunc 1974, 1986). Unković also published a relatively large chapter on the subject in his omnibus volume (1974). Although the authors aimed at a comprehensive analysis of the possible implementation of marketing in this industry, their works mainly concentrated on market research and promotion as the two most important factors, in their view, of tourism development. In the economic and political circumstances of the former Yugoslavia, unequal interest was shown in the components of the marketing mix, which is understandable. However, it was precisely due to marketing that the first discussions on the tourism product appeared in the Yugoslav professional literature. The above-mentioned authors, and some others, presented their papers at an international conference held in Zagreb in 1974, organized by the Faculty of Foreign Trade (*Turistički proizvod* 1974) (The Tourist Product). At this conference marketing theory applied to tourism met with approval and enthusiasm, while the theory of the tourism product, particularly the versions of older authors (Antunac, Marković, and others), faced numerous criticisms. The product they advocated looked for "theoretical weight" through this designation, but this technical term did not contain it, nor was it designed to be used in this context in either theory or practice. The idea of a "tourism product," as it was launched in the former Yugoslavia, aimed at eliminating the bad practice of using the expression "tourist offer" which excessively stressed the role of the hotel sector as the central economic activity in tourism minimizing other constituent elements. This was also an attempt to change the idea of tourism as a market of services into its conceptualization as a market of goods and services.

The Breakup of Yugoslavia

The breakup of Yugoslavia did not occur on one specific date. Every former Yugoslav Republic separated as a result of different processes at various times. Most of the dissolution took place in 1991, but in some territories, like Bosnia and Kosovo, it happened much later. After the breakup and following the war which ensued in Croatia, Slovenia, Bosnia Herzegovina, and Kosovo, tourism gradually returned to all parts of the former State, but most rapidly to Croatia. This was no surprise since by far the largest part (80%) of the former Yugoslavia's coast was in Croatia. That is why the return of tourists, primarily inbound, brought back an interest in tourism as a science. The organization of the new States placed a variety of priorities before their economies. As a result, tourism policy in each of the newly formed States sometimes went in different or even opposite directions than it did in the former Yugoslavia. Thus, the interest of tourism professionals and scientists in each of the States was predominantly directed toward the problems of their own environment. This "decentralization" required the writing of new books and textbooks in different disciplines of tourism, which was not an easy task. Former textbooks which used to cover the problems of Yugoslavia as a whole were no longer valid. In their stead writers, such as Unković and Zečević, prepared a new textbook entitled *Ekonomika turizma* (2004–2005) which had an edition every year or every second year with minor revisions or additions. Then there was Bakić (2002 (2005)) on management, Popesku (2002) on marketing, Spasić (2005) on tourism organizations, and Štetić (2003, 2004) on geography.

A wealth of publishing activity in the field of tourism continued in Croatia after its independence. This period was primarily characterized by the publication of new textbooks to help educate upcoming generations of professionals in the light of the recently formed State and its interests. The aim of many of these authors was to view tourism through its different features, while economic topics were mainly covered in professional journals and magazines. Although these writers comprised some well-known experts, several new names appeared as well. In this regard, Vukonić published another edition of *Turističke agencije* (1993) with a later edition in 2007. In 1994, Weber and Mikačić published a secondary-school textbook, while Jokić wrote her first book on tourism. In the same year, Šimić (1994) published a work in which he asked 100 questions and offered 100 practical answers based on his rich experience of working in tourism.

In 1996, a group of professors, headed by Mato Bartoluci, began an ambitious project of publishing literature from the field of sport and tourism. Over a period of 11 years a series of books was published which mainly dealt with the management and economics of sport and its relationship to tourism. Symposia were organized on various topics in the field and each resulted in a book containing the papers of the presenters. The first appeared in 1996 (Bartoluci 1996) and the last in 2007 (Bartoluci and Čavlek 2007).

In mid-1980s, immediately before the breakup of Yugoslavia, Vukonić published his research in *Turizam i razvoj* (1987) (Tourism and Development). By using an econometric model he sought to establish which of the most frequently mentioned factors in the foreign literature were more important than others in developing tourism in a given area. Political instability (wars, terrorism), along with religious beliefs and a country's indebtedness carried the most statistical weight. The author researched the first two phenomena in greater detail and published the results immediately after Croatia gained independence in 1987 and 1990, respectively. These were followed in 1994 with a book summarizing the author's views on the positive and negative circumstances in which tourism would develop in the years ahead.

During the same period, Jurić published two works on the sociology (1998a) and economics of tourism (1998b), primarily for the needs of the students of the University of Zadar. Following the tradition of analyzing the economic consequences of tourism, experts began to publish books with that content. Mihalić from the University of Ljubljana, for example, wrote on environmental economics in tourism (1995) and the activities of tourism agencies (1997). Meanwhile in Croatia, and as textbooks for the University of Zagreb, Čavlek was publishing on tour operators (1998), Pirjevec on the economic characteristics of tourism (1998), and Prebežec on airline companies (1998). Later, Jadrešić (2001) published his major work on the interdisciplinary theory and practice of tourism for students at the University of Split. Čavlek's volume received special attention since it was the first book in the world to cover this topic. It thoroughly and systematically analyzed the beginnings and activities of tour operators as representatives of the globalization process, companies with a new concept of mediation in tourism. Another Zagreb textbook by Pirjevec and Kesar (2002) outlined the principles of tourism.

Geographers were particularly active in producing books during that period (Bilen 1996; Bilen and Bučar 2001; Blažević and Pepeonik 1979). All these were "classical" standard textbooks, without including counter-arguments or introducing polemics of any sort. Their purpose was to replace editions from the time of the former Yugoslavia and to amend certain ideas in them that had been the result of political indoctrination. The approach had to be changed in accordance with the new market approach to the economy and with the interests of the new State of Croatia. An original and exceptional book with many sociological observations was written by Kušen (2002) which became a textbook for Croatian students of tourism. The volume emphasized the interrelatedness of several scientific disciplines (geography, spatial planning, culture, and the arts) and the author substituted the concept of the "natural tourist offer" with the more modern concept of "tourist attraction basis."

During this era which was rich in published works, readers were particularly attracted to the writings of Senečić, for example, *Istraživanje turističkog tržišta* (1997) (Research on the Tourist Market), as well as Mirić and Vlahović's *Zdravlje i turizam* (1998) (Health and Tourism). The titles of their books suggested topics of interest for tourism experts at the end of the 20th century. These volumes appeared during a time of a relative crisis in the territories of all the States which emerged from the former Yugoslavia. *Inter alia*, the aim of the books was to stimulate various activities and encourage further development of certain forms of tourism which would help revitalize arrivals, particularly in those parts of the former Yugoslavia where this was possible. Meanwhile, in Slovenia Mihalić wrote a textbook with Planina under the standard, and by now usual, title, *Ekonomika turizma* (2002).

At the beginning of the 21st century, the Institute of Tourism in Zagreb published two important books—the collected papers of two leading lights of Yugoslav and Croatian tourism—Alfier (2004) and Antunac (2001). Both of them were more than just testimonies to the doyens of scientific thinking in the erstwhile State, but offered historical reviews and discussed this development in the former Yugoslavia during its last 50 years.

A productive author, Dulčić from Split, published two significant works in 1991 and 2001. The first was a text which concisely explained the phenomenon of tourism, its history and modern principles which theoreticians used to explain the various reasons and ways in which contemporary tourism had been developing. Although Dulčić insisted on the term "tourist/tourism product," most other experts in Croatia at the time believed that he was wrong, because for them the term product as a notion could not be used on those occasions where there was no process of production—the case of tourism. This was not a routine volume which felt obliged to discuss standard concepts found in books on the economics of tourism. The second work provided a scientific foundation of a widespread practice in Croatia in which tourism development was seen and planned at the destination rather than at the resort level. It was within this basic framework that the author viewed the phenomenon, the criteria for making decisions in developing the industry, and discussed in detail its management. At the end Dulčić stressed that planning was the method in which a system could be efficiently managed. Another feature which made this book stimulating was the radical thinking of the author, and much of it differed from the mainstream thought of Croatian scholars in the field. The book was a radical departure from the thinking and activities of the international tourism market, which had also been advocated by some other theoreticians such as Mihalić in Slovenia; and Čavlek, Petrić, Pirjevec, Vukonić, and others in Croatia. In this context, the work of Geić, *Turizam i kulturno-civilizacijsko nasljede* (Tourism and Cultural and Civilizational Heritage) has proposed a modern concept of tourism and appropriate changes of approach to its development. Here, the author clearly stated that:

> Zbog nekritičkog prosuđivanja postignutih rezuktata I dostignuća minulih generacija, mikro i makroregionalni gospodarski i društveni razvitak na hrvatskim prostorima vrlo često se razvijao po konceptu drastčnih lomova, umjesto evolutivnih pocesa koji bi adekvatno vrednovali i valorizirali rezultate prethodnih generacija, promatrajući ih kao objektivno moguće dosage u odgovarajućem prostoru i vremenu (2002:9).

> Due to the uncritical evaluation of the accomplished results and achievements of past generations, the micro and macro-regional economic and social development on the Croatian territory has very often whirled through drastic break-ups, instead of evolving through evolutionary processes that would adequately value and evaluate the results of past generations, viewing them as objectively possible attainments in a given time and space.

Croatia had for years been preoccupied with establishing an adequate maritime policy, as well as with joining the EU, which was why the interest of many Croatian experts had focused on "European topics." Among these were Tihomir Luković (2002) from Split and Magaš (2003) from Opatija. The latter was different in the concept and understanding of how to manage a destination. It took into account new relations in the process of globalization and was a logical continuation of earlier books written by this author in 1995 and 1997 (Magaš 1995, 1997). Indeed these three works formed a specific trilogy. Books with a similar managerial theme were published by Cerović (2003), Marušić and Prebežac (2004), and Vrtiprah and Pavlić (2005).

The first accounts in the field about applying electronic communication to tourism have to be mentioned here. Two were published by the Faculty of Economics Zagreb University and edited by Željko Panian, a professor of this faculty: *Elektroničko trgovanje* (2000) (Electronic Business) and one edited by Antun Kliment, *Elektroničko poslovanje u turizmu* (2000) (E-Business in Tourism). During this millennial period, a fundamental lexicographic work also appeared, *Rječnik turizma* (2001) (Dictionary of Tourism), edited by Vukonić and Čavlek (2001), who collaborated with a group of authors, mostly from the Faculty of Economics in Zagreb. According to its preface, "The book provides, in a condensed form, the fundamental knowledge necessary to those employed in tourism, to entrepreneurs, managers and business people, as well as to journalists, students, and teachers." At the same time, this was a reference book for academic purposes and a reliable source of information for those employed in tourism or interested in it. The *Dictionary* had 2,300 entries and explained the most important concepts, abbreviations, institutions, and organizations from all sectors of the industry. In 2005, the Croatian Academy of Science and Arts, and Prometej, a publishing house from Zagreb, produced *Povijest Hrvatskog turizma* (The History of Croatian Tourism), edited by Boris Vukonić (2005). With this book Croatia gained an historical overview of the development of tourism, with numerous documents and photographs, from the 17th century till today. It was the first such book of its kind in the countries established after the breakup of the former Yugoslavia.

CONCLUSION

At a time when interest in tourism in Europe had become widespread, tourism incursions into areas of the former Yugoslavia were the result of the curiosity of a small number of people. Since the territory lagged behind in economic development and infrastructure, it is easy to understand why tourism, a significant phenomenon in the modern world, did not arouse as much fascination and awareness among Yugoslavs as it did in other European countries. As a consequence, the interest of different experts in the development of this new phenomenon was weak, and many were not eager to apply theoretical perspectives to it. That is why the first explanatory works on tourism in the former State appeared later than they did in more developed European countries. Theoretical positions reflected the political and economic developments of those times. Every geographical region of the former Yugoslavia experienced a different kind of tourism development, and consequently theoretical approaches varied in accordance with the geographical area from where these experts came.

Finally, it should be noted here that this review is based only on published books. Due to considerations of space, a huge amount of written material has been omitted, such as articles in domestic and international journals and magazines, papers presented at domestic and international conferences, and CD ROMs. Nevertheless, the impression should remain of a relatively large number of professional and scientific works in the field of tourism, particularly if one compares them with the size of the population which lived in the territory of the former State, and with a less than rapid social and political development of this region. For more than 50 years these people inhabited a single State. Yet they never had completely common interests or held views as to what those common interests should have been.

Chapter 7

Early Tourism Research in Scandinavia

Jens Kr. Steen Jacobsen
University of Stavanger, Stavanger, Norway

INTRODUCTION

Academic tourism research by Scandinavian sociologists and other social scientists commenced in the 1960s and expanded considerably from the 1990s. This chapter provides an overview of early tourism research in Scandinavia, primarily academic studies within sociology in a broad sense, though also to a lesser degree within such neighboring disciplines as anthropology, ethnology, and political science. While it does not claim to be exhaustive, it includes the most relevant Scandinavian contributions published in Danish, Norwegian, and Swedish, as well as some Nordic works appearing in English. The chronological account concentrates on the earliest works (those published before the mid-1980s). A range of writings is reviewed and the links to extra-regional research are briefly explored. Moreover, emphasis is placed on the offerings that anticipated Anglophone research contributions like those of MacCannell (1976) and Urry (1990). The last part of the chapter includes a short overview of Nordic academic tourism research propensities at the millennium and also the likely prospect of future studies within Scandinavian sociology is briefly discussed.

The Sociology of Tourism: European Origins and Developments
Tourism Social Science Series, Volume 12, 221–242
Copyright © 2009 by Emerald Group Publishing Limited
ISSN: 1571-5043/doi:10.1108/S1571-5043(2009)0000012012

Sociology in General

During the period under review, Scandinavian sociology could hardly be perceived as a unity even if several shared traits were exhibited. According to Allardt (1993), the various sociologies encountered in the Nordic countries had a common root, a belief in the discipline as an empirical science. However, Allardt also emphasizes that Danish postwar sociology had its origin in ethnology and social anthropology and had been mainly concrete and practical. At the same time, he regards Swedish sociology during the 1950s and the 1960s as predominantly manifest and methodical. Mjøset describes Norwegian sociology up to the 1970s as dominated by problem-oriented empiricism (1991:150–170). Moreover, Allardt finds this era in Norway to be typified by qualitative approaches (1993:127), even though it also encompassed quantitative elements. In an overview of Scandinavian sociology, Janson (2000:2450) maintains that until the late 1960s Scandinavian sociologists were characteristically engaged in empirical studies of social inequality, social mobility and the educational system, work conditions, problems of physical planning and social epidemiology, alcohol problems, and delinquency. In all the Nordic countries, there were early attempts to develop quantitative research (Allardt 1993:129) modeled on North American sociology. According to Allardt (1993:128), a Norwegian specialty in the 1960s was the unveiling of hidden role expectations, role strains, latent solidarities, and group ties. During the first postwar decades, Swedish sociologists were more critical and skeptical in tone, abhorring exaggerations and speculative statements. While Swedish sociology quickly reached a high level of sophistication in theory and methodology, it has been regarded as fairly pedestrian in its substantive descriptions of Swedish society in the postwar period up to the 1970s (Allardt 1993:129).

Typical of Scandinavia from the 1950s and onwards were also the many applied research institutions directed toward the establishment of knowledge-based platforms for industries and government bodies, mostly dedicated to concrete research on social problems. In Norway, the early development of applied research in the postwar epoch was inspired by North American sociology as also directly through a number of visiting Fulbright scholars (Janson 2000:2450). It was additionally assisted first-hand by the enterprising Paul Lazarsfeld (Lazarsfeld et al 1944; see Thue 1997:155–167).

Among the particular "Nordic" contributions to sociology particularly relevant to the context of tourism studies was research on the welfare state, well-being, and power, along with a concentration on gender and women's studies (Allardt 1993:132–134). Allardt has also argued that some of the sociologically most interesting Nordic cultural analyses up to the 1980s were produced by Swedish ethnologists focusing on how dominant cultural forms developed and how they related to the class structure in society (1993:135). Arctic ethnology and sociology as a Danish specialty contributed to the establishment of a professorship in cultural sociology in the early 1960s (Allardt 1993:121). From the end of this decade onwards, there was a weakening in Nordic sociology of a previously strong dependence upon North American sociology and also expanding theoretical pluralism, including a critique of positivism (Mjøset 1991). During the 1980s and the 1990s, one can observe increased fragmentation and loss of academic community (Allardt 1993:132), with a consequent difficulty in identifying national traits. In Norway in the 1990s, one still finds a commitment in sociology to empirically oriented research and the employment of middle-range theories (Birkelund 2006:60).

THE SOCIOLOGY OF TOURISM

Nordic tourism studies have often been conducted outside of universities and the tourism research endeavors of many sociologists in this region may be characterized as multidisciplinary, drawing on theories and methods from neighboring disciplines. As noted by Lanfant (1993), studies of international tourism have not been easily recognized by a number of reluctant sociologists as well as representatives of several other academic disciplines, and Scandinavia is hardly an exception to this observation. She writes that:

> Sociology is like an elderly lady concerned about her respectability and with preserving her own identity while dealing with other related disciplines ... Sociology cannot escape the rule to which the creation of any new field of research has to conform in order to be legitimized ... This academic position is destabilized when the study of tourism attaches itself to the phenomena of mobility (Lanfant 1993:71).

In contrast to such apparently widespread sociological reluctance toward tourism and other mobilities, Urry has proposed in the latter part of the 1990s to place journeys, flows, and connections, as also mobile theories and mobile methods, on top of the research agenda (2007:6).

There now follows a decade-by-decade account of the origins and development of the sociology of tourism in Scandinavia.

The 1950s and 1960s

In the middle of the 20th century, in Sweden and Norway, there were some proto-sociological or proto-social psychological writings on tourism, vacationing, and health, including mental health (Evang 1950; Huss 1951). More importantly, these works additionally speculated about various types of tourists and how they might react to the change of place that vacation travel necessarily entailed. Among these protagonists of the postwar period was the Norwegian Director General of Health, Karl Evang. It it was he who lectured on the social, cultural, and health aspects of vacationing a few years after a new law had enacted a vacation with pay allowance for a large proportion of the Norwegian workforce. Evang argued that persons, who constantly complained and were unwilling to shed their domestic woes, would be better off if they stayed at home during their annual leave. Evang maintained that such individuals:

> ... ville kunne få sin beste og mest givende ferie ... ved å oppholde seg i et miljø som de kjenner. Det vil være tilfelle for timide, engstelige, nevrotiske, kverulerende og andre typer, hvor det først og fremst gjelder også i ferietiden å skape et trygt, ufarlig og kjent miljø. Det finnes endel meget lett irriterbare typer som... det likefrem er risikabelt å slippe... ut i fremmed miljø... i alle samfunn finnes det en ikke helt liten gruppe avstikkende, skjøre individer, som bare kan få en god ferie under særlig gunstige vilkår. (1950:10).

> ... might have their best and rewarding holiday ... by staying in an environment they know. This would be the case for timid, fearful, neurotic, captious, and other types, for whom it is also important during holidays primarily to establish a confident, safe, and familiar environment. There are some easily aggravated types, who it is downright risky to let loose ... in an unfamiliar environment ... [I]n all societies there is more than a small number of incongruous, fragile individuals, who can only have a good holiday under particularly propitious conditions.

Here, Evang maintained that for some people, vacation environments similar to what later have been called "tourism bubbles" (Cohen 1972:166, based on Knebel 1960:137) might be beneficial. Evang also anticipated something akin to Cohen's distinction between a holidaymaker and a tourist. Relief from daily schedules and habits might generally be perceived as a sort of "holiday," contrary to "tourism." In this regard, Cohen argued that vacationers merely sought change, whether or not this brought anything new, in contrast to sightseer tourists, who primarily engaged in a quest for novelty (1974:544–545).

In Sweden, during the 1950s and 1960s, there were also some proto-sociological commentaries related to tourism issues other than health and well-being. In particular, tourism in Swedish Lapland, and its assumed influence on the Sámi population and their way of life, was discussed. Generally, the early writings on tourism in Sweden identified some of the problems that could arise from vacationing, such as various negative factors on those who traveled, including alcohol consumption. In 1962, the *Beredskapsnämnden för psykologiskt försvar* (The Preparedness Committee for Psychological Defence) in Sweden published a report entitled *Personlig påverkan och turism* (Personal Influence and Tourism) (Melén 1962). This seems to be the earliest known empirical study of tourism in Scandinavia that might be considered sociological, focusing on opinion leaders and vacation travel, and based on 450 interviews conducted in the autumn of 1960 in the city of Malmö. The main objectives of this research were to explore opinion-forming within Swedish holiday travel based on the two-step flow in mass communication (Lazarsfeld et al 1944) and to identify possible tourism opinion leaders (Melén 1962:6). One of the sub-goals was to explore the extent to which these opinion leaders might function as a tourism prognosis instrument, or serving as a tourism *avant-garde* (Melén 1962:8). Ola Melén here anticipated several subsequent studies on tourist decision making. For instance, he found that women were tourism opinion leaders to a greater extent than men, later verified in another context by Smith (1979). It is also interesting to observe that Melén's (1962) research forecast a Swedish interest in tours to Greece, as an alternative to their inclination toward France and Spain as particularly prevalent foreign destination countries at the time of the study.

One of the earliest genuinely theoretical contributions to tourism in Scandinavia was that of Vilhelm Aubert, Professor at the University of Oslo, and a central figure in postwar sociological research in Scandinavia. He had included a chapter on tourism in his book *Det Skjulte Samfunn* (The Hidden Society) (1969). This collection of essays originally appeared in English

(Aubert 1965), and the tourism entry was added to an enlarged version that was translated into Norwegian. In this volume, he demonstrated an ability to engage in social science debates through his analyses of such life world themes as sleep, love, and tourism. While Aubert developed a tourist typology in a rather impressionistic manner, his attempt also interestingly encompassed one of the consequences of the democratization of European vacation travel during this period (an anti-tourist attitude). His essay was partly related to role theory, but because the chapter did not include references, it is difficult to locate clear links to other social science works. However, Aubert had already studied the sailor—a transient figure (Aubert and Arner 1962) emblematic of early modernity. He argued that the tourist similarly belonged to the margins of the social structure, and here he was in agreement with Bachelard, who, strictly speaking, regarded structure and mobility as opposites (Bachelard 1943:2, 1988). Aubert also distanced himself from what in those days was a quite common functionalist approach to tourism and vacation travel. Even though he admitted that holidaymaking might have a "positive function," he argued that it had to be conceived as a reaction to work. Aubert comprehended tourism chiefly in terms of recreation and escape, which might be regarded as typical of the epoch when the essay was published: vacation travel was perceived as escape from the pressures and limitations of everyday life, what some people might regard as trivial and unsatisfactory in their quotidian existence (Aubert 1969:116).

In his attempts to develop a tourist typology, Aubert maintained that such a classification should be rooted in features related to the strains of the social structure from which tourists broke away. It should also be based on the social qualities that characterized the offerings that were tendered to tourists in the receiving societies where they arrived (1969:117). His types included the wilderness or outback tourist, the sun seeker, the emigrant tourist, the connoisseur traveler, the anti-tourist, and the itinerant sightseer (the participant in conducted tours). Here, Aubert's approach was Weberian. Aubert (1969:119–120) contended that what he was referring to were partly overlapping ideal types; pure types were rarely found. Aubert also linked tourism to consumption and believed that the tourist purchased a way of life for a limited period of time. He thus concurred with the German sociologist Hans-Joachim Knebel, who had argued that various touristic roles expressed certain consumption classes and styles. Touristic consumption thus became a criterion for stratification that constituted a not insignificant lure/appeal of the touristic role (1960:100). This contribution could also partly be seen as a follow-up to Veblen's (1899[1970, 1994]) "conspicuous consumption," that is, symbolic consumption to enhance social status (mostly based on nonfunctional aspects), rather than consuming goods and services primarily for their functional qualities. Functional aspects of holiday travel might include compulsory benefits and services like transport, overnight accommodation and food, while symbolic meanings encompassed more inherent and abstract ideas about travel consumption and its various forms (Brown 1992).

Some parts of Aubert's essay anticipated some of Graburn's (1977) and Turner and Turner's (1978:20) later ideas on tourism as a sacred journey. Aubert additionally laid out a discourse of anti-tourism; he regarded the anti-tourist as a type of vacationer who did not wish to be associated with other (fellow) tourists. This topic was elaborated a decade later by Bruckner and Finkielkraut (1979), Culler (1981), Fischer (1984), and afterwards, in a Scandinavian context, by Gustafson (2002) and Jacobsen (1983, 1984, 2000).

The 1970s

In 1971, the Swedish sociologist Gunnar Ekeroth published the research report *Turism och Alkohol* (Tourism and Alcohol) at the Department of Sociology, University of Uppsala. This was part of a wider project on drinking behavior, including Swedish imbibing in restaurants (Norén 1970, 1971). Here Ekeroth did not build on previous tourism research and referred to only a few studies of drinking behavior and attitudes toward alcohol consumption. His survey respondents were Swedes who had recently taken a vacation charter flight to a foreign destination, mainly to places in Mallorca. Some 14% of the interviewees stated that they had become more interested in spirits while 11% had become more attracted to wine as a result of their tour.

In his study, Ekeroth referred to group norms and maintained that Swedes abroad used alcohol for the purpose of "regulating interaction," in order to reduce tension. Swedish vacationers in foreign countries encountered different expectations to alcohol than those they were used to in their everyday life at home. Ekeroth further argued that norms relating to social control in daily life were inverted during the Swedish holidaymakers' stays in foreign countries; these travelers regarded the absence of everyday norms as normal during the trip (1971:52–53)—thereby anticipating Gottlieb's (1982) subsequent analysis of inversion. Ekeroth maintained that the expectations his subjects customarily held regarding their "fellow Swedes" were replaced by other, partly contradictory expectations, which were tied to the specific social settings which were at hand during their stay in a foreign resort (1971:8). In this report, Ekeroth also anticipated some of Cohen's arguments linking tourism with strangerhood (1972, 1974, 1979a, 1979b). Moreover,

Ekeroth's line of reasoning concurred with Turner's concept of "anti-structure" (1969, 1974) for describing liminality in ritual, later employed in tourism research by his compatriot Ulla Wagner (1977), since Ekeroth's survey found that most respondents' post-trip alcohol consumption returned to the same level as before their trip (1971:5–8). Ekeroth additionally discussed the use of alcoholic drinks during vacation trips in relation to risk, and maintained that beer or wine were considered the safest drinks to go with meals with regard to risks of infection abroad (1971:52). This part of the study also anticipated later Anglophone tourism research on safety and risk (Josiam et al 1998).

In 1972, the anthropologist Per Rekdal submitted his thesis for the *Magister Artium* (literally a Master of Arts degree, lying somewhere between a PhD and an advanced MPhil; see Sand 2008:255) at the University of Oslo. The topic was the development of modern sculpture production in Livingstone, Zambia. His study included how sculptors had modified their art to the presumed needs of foreign tourists, both symbolically (designs and ascribed meanings) and practically (sizes adapted to luggage limitations in air travel). Rekdal obtained the idea for his project when he accidentally came across some South-African souvenirs that allegedly were crafted by Zulus. Knowing that Zulus did not traditionally produce such sculptures and observing that the items had a catchy similarity with the witchdoctors' outfit as portrayed in Disney's comic strip Donald Duck, he wanted to explore what had really inspired the production of such souvenirs (Rekdal 1972:4), often called "curios" by visiting Europeans and "airport art" (Graburn 1967) by art critics. Several years later, some elements from this study were disseminated and further developed in two articles, also in Norwegian (Rekdal 1982, 1988).

Some of the main chapters in Rekdal's monograph were inspired by the work of Goffman (1959). Most of the thesis was actually a study of impression management in curio dealers' shops, and Rekdal's (1972) use of Goffman's notions of front stage and back stage to analyze tourism-related sculpture retailing predated some parts of MacCannell's argument in *The Tourist* (1976). In his thesis, Rekdal (1972) also foreshadowed some later Anglophone tourism discourses such as those of object-related authenticity and perceived authenticity (Bruner 1994; MacCannell 1973, 1976; Wang 1999, 2000).

Around 1970, traditional masks on offer in a "model village" did not appeal to tourists, because they were not perceived as African. Young white tourists also began to distance themselves from the traditional polished African sculptures, because, according to Rekdal, they regarded such objects as a response to vulgar tourist perceptions of African culture. Instead, some youthful visitors believed that roughly carved sculptures and masks were more genuinely African. As a result, several artisans in Zambia did not complete their tasks, because, as one of them concluded: "Rough work is art work." Here, Rekdal identified a paradox—that some tourists were highly satisfied with what they did not really want—as they shunned the authentic art that they were offered, and consequently chose only those items that Rekdal called fakes. Rekdal thus maintained that the perceptions of some young Westerners implied an exchange of one prejudice for another. A number of Zambian artisans also catered to tourists' wish for objects with magical meanings. These craftsmen thought that many white tourists were superstitious. Indeed, one of the sculptors observed, "For us Africans, this is only an object, while Europeans think they mean something. Then I just invent a story ... " (Rekdal 1988:151).

In the early 1970s, the Nordic Museum in Stockholm established a research program entitled *Turismen och den folkliga kulturen* (Tourism and Popular Culture), focusing on the vacation travel of "ordinary people." Among the affiliated researchers, ethnology students Berggren and Zetterström (1974) published a descriptive report on persons who stayed in self-catering cottages in "leisure villages." Their study found that guests were typically middle class families with children, and that they did not want any contact with fellow holidaymakers staying at the same site. Here, the authors identified a mindset akin to the anti-tourist attitude that had been earlier described by Aubert (1969). In other words, it was quite commonplace for considerable numbers of particularly educated upper middle class Norwegians and Swedes to avoid fellow tourists during their vacations (Löfgren 1979:57). Many years later, a similar feature was highlighted by Gunnar Alsmark, who maintained that a predilection for second homes far away from other people appeared to be a typically Scandinavian attitude, even if, to a large extent, it seemed to reflect what he termed a "bourgeois self-understanding" (1984:146). He further argued that the search for loneliness in Swedish vacation travel was something that characterized prosperous middle and upper class people (Alsmark 1984:146–147).

In 1977, the Swedish researcher Wagner published her pioneering article "Out of Time and Place: Mass Tourism and Charter Trips." Here, she employed Turner's (1969, 1974) analysis of pilgrimage to act as a theoretical framework for the sacred and liminal characteristics of coastal tourism that she encountered in the Gambia. Therefore, it comes as no surprise that her much cited article was included in Cohen's (1984) state-of-the-art paper, "The Sociology of Tourism: Approaches, Issues, and Findings," or that it appeared in the same year as Graburn's (1977) similar paradigm. Wagner later developed and disseminated some of these arguments in other contexts (1981, 1982, 1985).

In 1977, the Norwegian social science researcher Tord Høivik and the political science student Turid Heiberg at the International Peace Research Institute in Oslo published the paper "Tourism, Self-reliance and Structural Violence," which appeared three years later as a journal article (Høivik and Heiberg 1980). It was argued here that in industrialized societies, leisure was a compensatory sphere, and tourism and travel were ways of satisfying the needs of freedom (Høivik and Heiberg 1980:94). They also developed a vacation typology framework in relation to self-reliance. It was argued that while self-reliant tourists would generally live closer to the local population, and share more of the locals' daily life, at the same time the economic benefits tended to be less (Høivik and Heiberg 1980:80). Moreover, they discussed the emergence of various counter-cultures in the late 1960s and in the 1970s, and maintained that people who were able to realize an integrated lifestyle, "prefer(red) self-reliant tourism, avoiding the pre-planned itineraries and the artificial social groups set up by package tours" (Høivik and Heiberg 1980:95). This study anticipated later research on backpackers and similar international leisure travelers with a moderate interest in comfortable "tourism bubbles" (Cohen 1972:166; Knebel 1960:137). The self-reliant tourist described here might additionally be seen as an example of conspicuous consumption (Veblen 1899[1970, 1994]) in reverse, that is, tourists who also sought out destinations outside of tourism enclaves in developing countries might be analyzed as purchasers of a lifestyle for a limited period of time.

In 1978, yet another piece of tourism research was published by the International Peace Research Institute in Oslo (Mathisen 1978). This minor sociological study emphasized the social and cultural effects of tourism in Agadir, Morocco, which at this time had become something of a package destination. Basing herself on Forster's (1964) and Greenwood's (1972) stages of tourism development, Mathisen contended that Agadir was going through the third stage, institutionalization, when control and further development usually passed out of local hands (1978:24). Referring to Cohen (1971), she also discussed the phenomenon of the *drageur*, the equivalent to a beach boy or a gigolo—a young Moroccan male who profited from contacts with tourists. Mathisen was further told that some youth dropped out of school because they earned easy money from tourists. On the basis of interviews with various locals, Mathisen found that contact between tourists and locals was mainly regarded as superficial, the interviewees blaming the tourists for showing no real wish to communicate with them. However, the locals did not see their culture threatened by the appearance of tourists, even though the informants had noticed a certain degree of Westernization (Mathisen 1978:38–39).

In 1979, the sociologist Tove Mordal published an overview of the development of Norwegian vacation travel. Her study was partly influenced by French and North American leisure theory (de Grazia 1962; Dumazedier 1967, 1974; Kaplan 1975) and partly by the early theoretical insights of researchers such as Burkart and Medlik (1974), Cohen (1972), and Schmidhauser (1975). Moreover, Mordal's work included analyses of various social aspects that contributed to increased popular tourism. One of the most interesting reflections was her view of the Norwegian vacation law of 1947 which not only granted three weeks vacation for two thirds of the labor force but also introduced a vacation allowance or holiday pay, what Mordal (1979:47) termed "compulsory vacation savings." In a country such as Norway, holiday travel was increasingly considered like any other social right, even though the vacation allowance established by law was related to paid employment.

In a chapter entitled "Human in Nature," in the Swedish book *Den Kultiverade Människan* (The Cultivated Human), Orvar Löfgren (1979) included some telling observations on the origins of bourgeois urbanites' summer holidaymaking in the mountains, on the coast and in the countryside. Löfgren's writings on mountain tourism were influenced by Roland Barthes' well-known semiological essay on the *Guide Bleu* (Blue Guide) (1957) that was published in Danish in 1969. Although Löfgren's work concentrated on the origins of Swedish mountain tourism, it also contributed to an understanding of the cultivation of "wild" nature and "intact" landscapes in contemporary tourism. This chapter included aspects of landscape-oriented tourism that were dealt with in subsequent research publications.

The 1980s

In 1980, Vigdis Mathisen submitted her thesis for the *Magister Artium* degree in sociology at the University of Tromsø, a study of tourism in Agadir (Morocco) focusing on sociocultural aspects and interaction between tourists and locals. One of the central questions raised was whether tourism in this case could be regarded principally as an instrument of international understanding or as a contribution to cultural conflict. Participants in organized tours and individual travelers from various European countries were included in the structured qualitative interviews, and also tourist guides and destination people were interviewed. Both of the main research questions were answered negatively. Mathisen (1980) concluded that, overall, European tourism to Agadir contributed neither to international understanding nor to cultural conflict. She reached this conclusion as an outcome of the fact that most tourists stayed within their own "environmental bubble" thereby displaying a lack of interest in coming into contact with the local population. Moreover, Mathisen maintained that her interview data from Morocco disproved MacCannell's (1976) hypothesis that tourists searched for authenticity.

In the book, *Sommargäster och Bofasta* (Summerites and Locals), Anders Gustavsson (1981) reported from a study of cultural encounters and antagonisms related to summer holidaymaking on the Bohus littoral in south-western Sweden. Even if this was an ethnological study, the author acknowledged his links to sociological conflict theory in such works as those of Allardt (1971), Aubert (1974), Coser (1956), Swedner (1971), and Wiberg (1976). However, his study was also inspired by the previously mentioned Scandinavian tourism research conducted by the likes of Høivik and Heiberg (1980) and Wagner (1977). The book chiefly described the historical development of vacationing in fishing villages and spoke of related conflicts, for instance those connected with ownership of houses and a local interest in catering for mobile tourists, who did not own a second home in a village. Gustavsson additionally threw light on some contemporary protests against more massive development and the marginalization of coastal areas due to the merger of small municipalities in Sweden (1981:88–91). In this study, one finds the identification of more or less the same conflict dimensions as those later included in Robinson (1999).

Since 1968, the Central Bureau of Statistics of Norway (now Statistics Norway) has conducted holiday surveys, most of them published only as collections of tables with an introduction about data collection. However, in 1982, the sociologist Trygve Solheim published a study of Norwegian vacation travel in the 1970s. Based on time series data, he found that an increasing proportion of the population went on holiday tours. He also analyzed holiday patterns, and suggested four main types of motivating holiday factors: recreation, *opplevelse* (experience), social (family) gatherings, and status (Solheim 1982:9–10). Some 23% of the summer holidaymakers in 1978 reported that stays with relatives constituted the most important type of accommodation, a considerable proportion, though a decline from 30% in 1970. Another 5% stayed with friends or acquaintances, while 30% spent the nights in second homes that they either owned or borrowed (Solheim 1982:18). The surveys also showed that an overwhelming majority traveled either with the entire household or with some household members. Solheim thus demonstrated the importance of social interaction and upholding of social bonds as a central part of vacation travel, as large proportions of the population not only traveled together with household members but also spent time with relatives in second homes or they stayed with kin and, to some degree, with friends. Here, Solheim (1982) anticipated later Anglophone research contributions (Larsen et al 2007). Solheim additionally analyzed in great detail social differences in holidaymaking, in relation to customary demographic variables such as education, income, age, and place of residence.

In the Danish book, *Fotografi og familie* (Photography and the Family), Hansen (1982:161–171) included a chapter on vacation snapshots. This was principally a review of the relevant literature in many languages, such as the works of eminent authors like Pierre Bourdieu (1965) and Susan Sontag (1977), as well as early Swiss and German tourism researchers like Armanski (1978) and Fink (1970). Hansen's focus was on popular travel. He maintained that in the "classic" holiday photograph, the family achieved its true symbolic potential by depicting the destination as its private property, in the same way as it did when family members were photographed in front of their home (Hansen 1982:163–164). Hansen further described the importance of visual highlights in sightseeing and how sights influenced organized tourism trips, particularly through photo opportunities (1982:171).

In the 1980s, several Scandinavian tourism studies were related to planning, not only in Sweden, the bastion of social planning, but also to some degree in Norway. For instance, the sociologist Jan Vidar Haukeland and the social scientist Tore Eriksen published the report *Toleransenivå for reiseliv i lokalsamfunn* (Tolerance Level for Tourism in Local Communities) (1982). The idea behind this study was that rapid tourism development in small communities could possibly cause both positive and negative effects at a local level. This was one of the first comparative Scandinavian investigations of the socioeconomic impacts of tourism and also perceived ecological consequences were taken into consideration. Based on fieldwork in three communities in Denmark, Norway, and Sweden, it found that negative attitudes toward tourism were strongest among those engaged in traditional occupations, with corresponding value orientations. Moreover, negative attitudes were directly related to the level of tourism development. More liberal attitudes toward tourism were discovered among people working in the service sector. This research thus revealed strong conflicts inside communities that were previously dominated by farming and small-scale industries, being transformed as recipients of large numbers of tourists (Haukeland 1984). The work of Haukeland and Eriksen (1982) epitomized what Jafar Jafari (1990) later termed the "adaptancy platform." This way of thinking was typical of tourism scholars in the early 1980s and the center of attention was to be receptive to the interests of people of host communities while still providing novel products for visitors. Haukeland and Eriksen thus preceded the concept of sustainable development that was launched some years later, in the Brundtland Report (World Commission on Environment and Development 1987), comprising economic, social, and ecological components of tourism development.

In 1983, Jacobsen submitted his thesis *Moderne Turisme* (Modern Tourism) for the *Magister Artium* degree at the University of Oslo. This dissertation was influenced by the works of well-known general sociologists such as Goffman (1959, 1972) and Simmel (1968 [1908]), but also by German, Swiss, French, and Anglophone sociologists of tourism and a few other writers, such as Bruckner and Finkielkraut (1979), Cohen (1973, 1974, 1979a, 1979b), Keller (1973), Knebel (1960), MacCannell (1976), Opaschowski (1977), and Scheuch (1972, 1977). This study grounded a discussion of vacationing in leisure theory and the possible relations between the economy and the work sphere on the one hand, and leisure on the other, and the author further developed this topic many years later (Jacobsen 2002). Here, tourism was also regarded as consumption of and search for positional goods, that is, goods, services, and other social relationships that were scarce in some absolute or socially imposed sense, or were subject to congestion or crowding through more extensive use (Hirsch 1977:27). The perspectives employed on this theme were inspired not only by Hirsch (1977) but also by Douglas and Isherwood (1980) and their examination of the symbolic aspects of consumption. The central part of the thesis, however, was a discussion of the institutionalization of tourism, that is, the establishment of social order comprising standardized behavior patterns, predominantly in terms of role theory (Fennefoss 1982; Knebel 1960; Linton 1936). Some of these analyses of tourism and role-play were published in a separate article (Jacobsen 1984). The dissertation further attempted to develop a wider theoretical framework grounded in role theory, encompassing distinctive aspects of the tourist role, and central touristic activities (such as sightseeing and sunbathing) including forms of travel authentication (photography and the mailing of postcards) (Jacobsen 1983:183–185). Additionally, the thesis discussed the differentiation of vacation travel and tourism typologies such as those previously propounded by Aubert (1969) and Cohen (1974).

In the mid-1980s, the Nordic Summer University arranged a series of symposia on tourism and leisure travel, which could be considered as a breeding ground for academic research and the enhancement of multidisciplinary collaboration. Most of the participants were postgraduate students and young researchers, representing various disciplines such as history, the history of ideas, literary science, ethnology, anthropology, and sociology. A number of contributions from these seminars were published in two volumes: *Turisme og Reiseliv* (Tourism and Travel) (Schmidt and Jacobsen 1984) and *Friheten i det fjerne* (The Freedom Afar Off) (Jacobsen 1988). In the first of these two volumes, the Danish sociologist Øllgaard (1984) argued that there was a clear association between photography and tourism. He maintained that modern tourism was a condition under which a pleasure trip became pure gazing (1984:44). He thus anticipated some of the theoretical arguments later found in Urry's *The Tourist Gaze* (1990). As previously indicated, photography and visual travel experiences clearly constituted a key theme in some of the Scandinavian contributions of the early 1980s. Here the influence derived partly from Susan Sontag (1977) and a rediscovery of Pierre Bourdieu's work on photography (1965), but also partly from other Scandinavian works on imagery and photography. Moreover, there was an influence from Schivelbusch's exploration of the journey as panorama (1977).

Also in this first volume, the Danish historian of ideas Lars-Henrik Schmidt (1984) examined popular vacation travel within the context of consumption. Here he regarded holiday travel as establishing a detachment from everyday life, not as a lack of contact with reality but related to experience and revival (1984:71). He also dealt with the documentation of tourism through photography and postcards. Like several of his Nordic contemporaries, Schmidt was concerned with the question of social order and he linked the institutionalization of tourism as an industry to travel catalogs, guides, and travel handbooks (1984:70–71). In this respect, he was in agreement with Knebel (1960:26), who pointed out that the emergence of guidebooks made it possible to plan a trip. They promoted what Schmidt called "the reiterated journey." He further discussed tendencies toward the standardization of tourism and argued that under conditions of modernity, the sought-after journey among most people was the repeated journey. While adventurers and anti-tourists deliberately chose new journeys, mainly off the beaten track, people with less time and/or money would often want to imitate the excursions of those better off than themselves. Since travel experiences were personal, every trip was, strictly speaking, unique, and this also went for intended reiteration (Schmidt 1984:74). This meant that people did not necessarily experience the repetitions that characterized modern organized tourism. At least the frames of tourism were known and anticipated, Schmidt maintained (1984:74–75), an argument corresponding to Smith's notion of "the tourist bubble," envisaged partly as expectation (1977a:6). For most people, Schmidt emphasized, the tourist trip thus implied a departure from everyday life without going to the completely unknown.

Orvar Löfgren's article *Turism som kultur- och klassmöte* (Tourism as a Meeting of Culture and Class) (1984) dealt with the question of social class in vacation travel and with the standardization of package vacation tours to foreign countries. Like Jacobsen (1983) and Schmidt (1984), Löfgren was concerned with the institutionalization of tourism, a theme to which he returned many years later (1994). Löfgren maintained that, in the 1960s, a prototype of charter tours was developed from package holidays in destinations such as Mallorca and the Costa del Sol. Basing himself on similar experiences in Morocco, Löfgren argued that the tendencies toward the homogenization of such travel were related to vacationers' expectations. In other words, if an element in the winning tour formula was missing from a destination (such as local craftwork), the tour operator would invent it, referring to what North Americans have called commercial "fakelore" (Löfgren 1984:102). His conclusions here were similar to those of Rekdal (1972). Löfgren (1984:102) also analyzed tourists who looked for the authentic, and their being steadily ousted by what he called the expanding charter tour colonialism, inspired by the French writers Bruckner and Finkielkraut (1979).

The question of class distinction in contemporary tourism was discussed on the basis of a historical background. In Scandinavian academia in the 1980s, there was still an interest in social class, partly related to the relatively egalitarian tendencies in these societies that were far from classless but comprising political traditions that opposed social exclusion and poverty and emphasized the importance of minimum standards. Löfgren argued that holidays of the bourgeoisie were often characterized by a freedom *to*, while working class vacations were to a larger extent typified by a freedom *from*. Proletarian vacations, according to Löfgren, implied freedom from supervised and monotonous work, an understanding that seemed to be in line with the concept of alienation, which modern sociology derived from the writings of Karl Marx. Löfgren contended that working class holidays were thus mainly about rest and being left alone from bourgeois cultural policing. The upper middle class vacation, by contrast, concentrated on self-fulfillment, the realization of novelty, solitude, the cultivation of nature, and sensitivity (1984:122–123). In this pattern, he maintained, there was also an antagonism between cultivated asceticism and unrestrained hedonism, two fundamental orientations that, already in the 19th century, were class distinctive. Löfgren was partly inspired both by Bourdieu (1979) and British social history research (Bailey 1978; Cunningham 1980; Yeo and Yeo 1981). In this respect, Löfgren anticipated Wang's (1996) distinction between two main types of modernities in contemporary society: Eros-modernity and Logos-modernity, based on Lefebvre's (1991:392) *Logos–Eros Dialectic*. Löfgren concluded that, when cultivated academics looked disdainfully upon what they considered to be vulgar fellow holidaymakers, they should be aware of their heavy cultural heritage (1984:123–124).

Löfgren (1984) had highlighted the barbecue or the village feast as a *de rigueur* ingredient of the charter tour formula. The second tourism volume published by the Nordic Summer University included a follow-up on this theme: *Ett försök til grisfestens teori* (Towards a Theory of the Pork Feast) (Jokinen and Veijola 1988:101–117), an attempt to understand industry-organized, carnival-like, unrestrained tourist parties in coastal resorts in the Mediterranean and the Canary islands. The backdrop for this essay was, broadly speaking, that most package tours with charter flights from Northern Europe to these destinations were associated with uncultivated taste, something from which educated middle class people with anti-tourist attitudes should stay away. Considered typical of such uncouthness were the popular images of intemperate eating and drinking connected to the myth of the organized barbecue party, often called a "pork feast" by Scandinavians, because the traditional Mallorcan barbecue was based on suckling pig. Inspired by, among others, Bakhtin (1968), Elias (1982), Schivelbusch (1980), and Stallybrass and White (1986), the Finnish sociologists Jokinen and Veijola analyzed the barbecue party and its excesses, and compared this unbridled element of vacationing with carnival, when differences in social status were temporarily bracketed. They further referred to Bourdieu (1979, 1984) and argued that the disregard of social status in such collective vacation events implied that they appeared to be of little interest to middle class people, who strove to emphasize the differences between themselves and the lower class (Jokinen and Veijola 1988:113). Here, they anticipated Podilchak (1991), who argued that fun lasts only as long as inequality and power differentials are negated. However, and ironically, when these writings of Jokinen and Veijola were published, the pork feast was already on the wane in most types of package tours from the Nordic countries.

In this Nordic Summer University volume, one also finds some early sociological attempts to analyze gendering of certain parts of long-distance travel (Jokinen 1988; Veijola 1988). In her paper "What did Jane do to Tarzan: Hustruskap och resande" (What did Jane do to Tarzan: Wifehood and Travel), Veijola referred to Ehrenreich (1983) and her idea that the liberation from the "family centered" perception with its feelings of guilt was not only a merit of the women's movement but also the result of a male revolt that even predated women's liberation. Veijola contended that women's journeys had traditionally been related to taking care of kin relations. Wifehood had also confined travel and implied a limited access to the realm of freedom (Veijola 1988:62–63). This theme was further developed some years later in Anglophone tourism discourses (Swain 1995). Subsequently, Veijola and Jokinen (1994) published an article "The Body in Tourism," which was partly a follow-up to some of these themes. In this widely cited paper, they also commented on several non-Nordic tourism scholars. For instance, they opposed Krippendorf (1987:23), who had argued that many tourists wanted to get away from the monotonous, depressing, and stressful everyday life. From a feminist viewpoint, they maintained that there was nothing less routine than taking care of children (Veijola and Jokinen 1994:126). They also paid an imaginary visit to, among others, Urry and his tourist gaze, arguing that vacation travel was not only visual; rather it was the tourist body that broke with established routines and practices (Veijola and Jokinen 1994:133). In this article, they additionally referred to Glomnes (1990), a Norwegian sociolinguist who compared the space used in church to that of tourism.

CONCLUSION

It has been demonstrated that several early Scandinavian tourism studies predated theory building and findings in Anglophone research. One of the most striking examples is Rekdal's employment of Goffman's notions of front stage and back stage in his analysis of tourism-related sculpture retailing (1972), a contribution that predated some parts of MacCannell's argument in *The Tourist* (1976). Another interesting example shown here is Vilhelm Aubert's essay on tourism (1969) that anticipated some of Graburn's (1977) and Turner and Turner's (1978:20) later ideas on tourism as a sacred journey. Many Anglophone academics have obviously not been aware of or familiarized themselves with the Scandinavian studies and also a number of those presented in French and German, upon which some Nordic contributions rely. Early Scandinavian tourism research projects were less preoccupied with esoteric themes and exclusive tourism destinations than many of their Anglophone counterparts. Even so, postcolonial issues were tackled in a number of the inquiries presented here, such as the contributions of Høivik and Heiberg (1977, 1980), Mathisen (1978, 1980), Rekdal (1972), and Wagner (1977, 1981). Moreover, quite a few early Scandinavian studies were concerned with social problems that arose from or were related to increasing volumes of vacation travel, and they were thus in sync with some of the developments in the initial tourism research undertaken in the German-speaking parts of Europe.

A central issue in early Scandinavian tourism research was the question of social order, that is, the institutionalization of tourism and vacationing as an activity and industry. Tourism as an activity was dealt with primarily in relation to the notions of role and ritual, while analyses of industry contributions to social order focused on guidebooks, catalogs, and tour guides. In the early days of tourism research, the concept of role was frequently used (Cohen 1974; Knebel 1960; Jacobsen 1983, 1984; Pearce 1982, 1985). However, by the end of the 20th century, the concept of role had lost ground to a vocabulary of identity, both in sociology in general and within tourism research, presumably because identity connotes—more than most notions of role—a tempting and fashionable individuality (Fennefoss and Jacobsen 2002, 2004), with a subsequent research focus on the variety of tourist types (Fløtten and Solvang 1989; Haukeland 1993; Jacobsen 1993). We should also note that many of these early Scandinavian studies both avoided and critiqued the denigration of mass travel that was often found in early Anglophone tourism writings, particularly those of cultural critics (Boorstin 1962; Turner and Ash 1975), preferring instead to focus on aspects of popular vacationing such as the organized barbecue party. Thus, the importance of freedom was underlined in several Scandinavian tourism studies, including freedom from general social constraints in modern societies (Høivik and Heiberg 1980:94; Jacobsen 1985), supervised and monotonous work, and cultural policing (Löfgren 1984). The Swedish concern with alcohol consumption during vacations abroad (Ekeroth 1971) was an unparalleled case in early tourism research both in Scandinavia and elsewhere.

It has been shown that quite a few early Scandinavian studies considered vacation travel in relation to work and, to some degree, social class. Both in Sweden, a stronghold of social planning, and in other Nordic countries, welfare aspects and consequences of state regulations were reflected in social research on tourism, such as Mordal's (1979) focus on vacation legislation and compulsory vacation savings and Haukeland's (1990) and Kitterød's (1988) concern with non-travelers, those who are temporarily or permanently unable or unwilling to participate in holiday travel. Moreover, several early studies in Scandinavia understood tourism in terms of recreation and escape from the pressures and limitations of everyday life, which could be regarded as typical of the 1970s and first part of the 1980s, and they were thus in harmony with a widespread Nordic research concentration on peoples' well-being (Allardt 1993:133).

As has been seen (Jokinen 1988; Veijola 1988), the early Nordic sociological focus on gender and women studies (Allardt 1993:134) was also manifest in early tourism research in this region. Furthermore, Allardt (1993:135) accentuated Swedish ethnologists' research on dominant cultural forms and their relation to the class structure in society as sociologically noteworthy, and, as already shown here, these studies included tourism (Löfgren 1984, 1985). Some other general traits of Nordic sociology were additionally mirrored in tourism research during the period under review. For instance, the subtitle of the second tourism volume published by the Nordic Summer University was *Tourism Myths and Realities*, thereby constituting something of a legacy of what Allardt found to be a typical trait of Norwegian sociology (1993:127–128).

All the same, several of the early studies were not in line with the main trends of Nordic sociology during the epochs covered here. Moreover, a number of empirical studies conducted by Scandinavian sociologists and other social scientists in this era, (and also more recently), have predominantly comprised annotated collections of findings, thus not adding explicitly all that much to academic theory building, even if they apply scientific methods for data collection, regularly relate to previous research, and produce new insights relevant to ministries, local government, and segments of the tourism and hospitality industries. Often, such empirical investigations have provided data that might have been employed for academic publications while project funding has mostly not permitted such dissipation. Only very few such inquiries are referred to here, even if they might be considered demonstrative of a concrete and practical tradition found in Nordic sociology (Allardt 1993), particularly at the many applied research institutions in these countries but also at some colleges that pioneered tourism programs.

The 1990s and Beyond

The sociological and related research interest in popular travel has continued in Nordic countries from the 1990s onwards, even if the early focus on welfare and health aspects of vacation travel has declined. An interest in international tourism and independent travelers has prevailed since the mid-1990s (Cederholm 1999; Jacobsen 2004; Mehmetoglu et al 2001; Selänniemi 1999). Image research is another area that has been dealt with at the millennium, both by sociologists and other social scientists (Heimtun 1997;

Jacobsen and Dann 2003; Jensen and Korneliussen 2002; see also Dann 2004). An overall tendency in the Nordic countries is a continued interest in travel and identity, often in relation to gender issues (Birkeland 2005; Heimtun 2007) but also linked to specific destination people (e.g., the Sámi, see Olsen 2006; Tuulentie 2006; Viken 2006). Transnational identities associated with seasonal lifestyle and retirement migration have been scrutinized at the beginning of the 21st century (Gustafson 2002; Haug et al 2007), thus extending research on what Aubert named emigrant tourism (1969:130–133). Tourism related to second homes has additionally been studied (Bærenholdt et al 2004; Müller 2002, 2007; Tuulentie 2007). An earlier ocular-centric over-emphasis on the tourist gaze tended to disregard the fact that tourists also experience their temporary surroundings with senses other than sight, and several Nordic contributions from the 1990s onwards increasingly regarded tourism experiences as multi-sensory (Dann and Jacobsen 2003; Jacobsen 1997) and embodied (Heimtun 2007). But there has been a redoubled research interest as well in tourist experiences through the eyes, a key theme in a special issue of the Nordic academic journal *Sosiologi i dag* (Sociology Today) (Birkeland 1997; Viken 1997). During the 1990s, there has been a renewed Nordic focus on certain specific visual aspects of tourism including landscape perception research influenced by environmental psychology. At the beginning of the 21st century, one has also witnessed several contributions to the understanding of tourist experiences, not so much in sociology proper as in neighboring disciplines and in multidisciplinary approaches (Elsrud 2001, 2004; Gyimóthy and Mykletun 2004; Jacobsen 2001; Jansson 2007; Larsen 2007; Löfgren 2008; Nordbakke 2000; Olsen 2002; Selänniemi 2001, 2002; Selstad 2007; Sørensen 2003; Vittersø et al 2000). As unclear boundaries remain between "traditional" Nordic outdoor recreation and tourists' sightseeing-like experiences of landscapes, one can also find some outdoor recreation studies that contribute to the understanding of tourism (e.g., Vittersø et al 2004).

What is more, there is a parallel renaissance of sociologically inspired or related studies connected with environmental issues (Jacobsen 2007), tourism planning, and landscape management (Daugstad 2008). Environmental issues such as possible consequences of climate change have also been given more attention. Additionally, industry aspects and interests have become more prevalent in tourism investigations, mostly because of changes in funding sources for research. There has also been an increasing focus on the tourism sector as a workplace (Larsen and Folgerø 2008; Thrane 2007; Veijola and Jokinen 2008) and in the relation between tourism development and the local population (Tuulentie and Mettiäinen 2007). Some Scandinavian studies of transport and mobilities, too, have encompassed tourism-related issues (Bærenholdt and Granås 2008; Gustafson 2001).

In line with Allardt's (1993:135) observations on the overall development of Nordic sociology, Scandinavian sociologists as well as some other social scientists involved in tourism research during the 1990s appear to be less discipline-bound, resulting partly from requirements of funding sources. However, toward the end of the first decade of the new century, one can further witness a moderate interest in returning to academic studies with a stronger emphasis on disciplinary heritage. The "cultural turn" in the social sciences ushered in with the millennium can possibly strengthen sociological research interests in tourism in the Nordic countries. Mobilities as a sociological research approach has also been promoted in Scandinavia (Larsen and Jacobsen 2008) at the same time as Urry (2007) has argued that such a "mobility turn" is post-disciplinary.

However, since the field of tourism is less clearly demarcated than many larger thematic fields with longer traditions, such as the sociology of work and the sociology of the family, it may not receive future priority at several Nordic sociological university departments where there still exists a considerable reluctance to take up tourism as a "new" topic, partly based on a predominant and constricted perception of tourism as an industry rather than as a phenomenon covering an ample range of actors and activities. As a sociological subfield at universities, the prospects for Scandinavian tourism sociology seem uncertain. In Norway, some university departments of sociology still seem to act, as one has previously noted, "as an elderly lady concerned about her respectability and with preserving her own identity" (Lanfant 1993:71), while tourism appears to have become more accepted as a theme of research within Scandinavian anthropology and perhaps even more in human geography. But university fads might change, for instance, as a consequence of an increasing number of master students in tourism programs at several Nordic colleges and universities, for instance at Finnmark University College and at the University of Stavanger, and such expansion in turn could lead to innovation in sociologically related studies of tourism.

Acknowledgement—The author wishes to thank Graham Dann, Giuli Liebman Parrinello, Lars Mjøset, and Oddgeir Osland for helpful comments on earlier drafts of this chapter.

Chapter 8

The Sociology of Tourism in Spain: A Tale of Three Wise Men

Julio Aramberri
Drexel University, PA, USA

INTRODUCTION

This chapter reviews the work of three representative pioneers of Spanish tourism theory: a professional sociologist (Mario Gaviria), an accidental anthropologist (Francisco Jurdao), and a semiologist (José Luis Febas). They were all exotic flowers in an intellectual garden that prided itself in producing only white roses or red carnations. All of them worked beyond the pale of a scholarly milieu that displayed little or no interest in tourism, even though its growth was eliciting some of the most important economic and cultural changes that Spain had known in ages. It may be true that Minerva's owl only flies at dusk, but, in the case of tourism, its Spanish classmates waited until the sun set the next day. As for these three scholars, given the period in which their works were published, they would definitely have been highly regarded had they reached a livelier environment than Spanish academia. Alas, none of them wrote in English. Hence, the additional need to bring them to the attention of Anglophone scholars.

Attempts at building the intellectual equivalent of the Great Wall of China between different types of knowledge have often proved to be a case of "love's labor lost." Spanish research on tourism is no exception. Local interest in the matter revolved around a forceful issue: how to improve the

The Sociology of Tourism: European Origins and Developments
Tourism Social Science Series, Volume 12, 243–273
Copyright © 2009 by Emerald Group Publishing Limited
ISSN: 1571-5043/doi:10.1108/S1571-5043(2009)0000012013

performance of the Spanish economy. Indeed, arguments were mostly confined to economics because of the limits imposed on media debates by the dictatorship of General Franco. However, outside observers should not conclude that the discussion was all about numbers. A momentous political game was being played against the backdrop of determining who would lead Spain and in what manner in another of its often frustrated attempts to enter modernity. This chapter must not overlook this background. The limited production on the social and cultural dynamics of modern mass tourism mirrored basic political issues from a plurality of perspectives.

Under the right circumstances, tourism can make a sizeable contribution to economic growth. Spain is perhaps the protagonist in this correlation. Between 1960 and today, the country left behind its past as a less-developed nation and climbed to a top position in the world economy. One may make a good case that tourism played a substantial role in this process. Its development came unplanned, though not entirely by accident (Galiana and Barrado 2006). Spain had made a name for itself among many adventurous 19th century travelers. However, for all its wild glamour, the country had been unable to attract large numbers of vacationers before the 1960s. The aristocratic and moneyed élites of imperial Russia or of the Austro-Hungarian dual monarchy preferred the Venice Lido or Istria for their summer holidays. Once the First World War had wiped them out, the interwar European leisured classes plus the beautiful but damned Americans of the period contributed to the success of the French *Côte d'Azur* and, in a lower key, to that of the Italian Riviera.

Spain's later tourism success was based on other social groups with very different demands. After the Second World War, paid vacations became part of the Western European social compact that has since been known as the Welfare State. With free time on their hands and increasing disposable income in their pockets, millions of Europeans were ready to leave home every year. An available fleet of discarded war aircraft made it possible for Northern Europeans to travel to lands where the sun always shone and the atmosphere was warm and energizing (Čavlek 2005). Moreover, in some of these places, prices were so low that it was cheaper to spend a vacation there than at home. All this gave the country a remarkable opportunity to progress.

In the mid-1950s, after two centuries of decadence, Spanish élites were eager to catch up with the wave of economic growth that was engulfing Western Europe. Until then, all previous attempts to modernize its economy had failed (Velarde 2001). Throughout the 19th century, the country had seen its former vast empire melt away and the mainland had been unable to avoid internal political turmoil and an economic all-time low. Spain had a traditional social structure and, in a nutshell, it was the spitting image of what has been called oligarchic capitalism (Baumol et al 2007). General Franco's dictatorship (1939–1975) did not falter in its determination to sustain the oligarchic structure lock, stock, and barrel (Anderson 1970). The initial period of the regime, until 1959, catered to the interests of traditional elites securing their privileged control of the paltry national market and stifling at the same time any demand for an open economy and democracy. This period of so-called autarchy came to a dead end in the second half of the 1950s (Salmon 1991). In the bureaucratic prose of the International Bank for Reconstruction and Development mission (IBRD), now The World Bank, that visited the country in 1961 at the behest of the government, Spain's economy faced serious structural problems (IBRD 1963).

In the past, and under similar circumstances, Spanish bells usually tolled a temporary end of authoritarian solutions. However, even though that country's élites had traditionally favored uncompromising nationalism, they could now see that integration in the international economy offered a better chance to preserve their future hegemony. Most Western European nations were registering rapid growth, and Spanish élites saw this as the mother of all opportunities to share in the international bonanza. In 1959, witnessing national foreign reserves close to bankruptcy, they implemented a stabilization plan that became extremely successful (Estefanía 1998; Rodríguez 2007). Between 1959 and 1973 "[a]mong the member states of the OECD [Organization for Economic Co-operation and Development], only Japan enjoyed faster and more sustained growth" (Harrison 1985:144).

The new policy amply relied on the performance of the foreign sector of the Spanish economy. Traditionally, the country had been plagued by balance-of-payments deficits that prevented transfers of technology (Tamames 1968). Now the old vicious circle of deficits/low technology/ underdevelopment had finally been broken, not because of overnight improvements in the productivity of agriculture or of manufacturing, but because the country now could turn to new sources of foreign exchange that would subsequently finance an export-led takeoff fuelled by trade and services. However, the Spanish case had its peculiarities in the way that foreign reserves expanded. In total, all types of foreign investments increased 26 times between 1959 and 1973 (Harrison 1985). Foreign investment in real estate was impressive, outgrowing foreign direct investment (FDI) and increasing sevenfold between 1965 and 1974 (Vidal Villa 1981). A significant, though not easily quantifiable, fraction of it financed hotel and residential projects linked to tourism.

Two unconventional exports, in particular, solidified Spanish foreign reserves. One was migrant labor. During the 1960s between one and two million people left Spain in search of work in Western Europe (Temprano 1981). The amount of their remittances is not easy to calculate. One source (Fontana and Nadal 1976) reckons that between 1962 and 1971, they covered a yearly average of 7.9% in the balance-of-payments deficit. The other largely positive item in foreign exchange was tourism receipts, which takes us to the beginning of this chapter and to the focus of our quest. Between 1951 and 1960, both the number of international visitors and the income derived from their trips had trebled, and, according to the IBRD, this was just the beginning. Spain's numerous cultural attractions, its beach products and its price levels, augured well for laying an ambitious wager on tourism. If the strategy proved successful, foreign money would flow and could later jump-start the rest of the economy. The tourism policies of the government followed closely the IBRD template (Fraga 1964), and the outcome came to fruition exactly as planned.

The Spanish economic "miracle" thus owed much of its luster to the development of international and domestic tourism and both have remained crucial items ever since. At the time, this new dependency created a number of tensions both among the pro-dictatorship elites mainly between the Falangist old guard and the newly fangled *desarrollistas* (developers) linked to *Opus Dei* (literally Work of God), a conservative Catholic institute that favored what today would be called neoconservatism, as also among the opponents of the dictatorship (e.g., the Spanish Communist Party). However, once adopted, the decision to follow a so-called European strategy soon created an economic bonanza that did not provide much credibility to its challengers. A majority of Spaniards would accept willy-nilly the social covenant offered by the dictatorship, one that would make Spain truly different.

AWOL in Academia

While all this happened in real life, did Spanish academics pay any attention to the development of tourism? The answer, as previously mentioned, was a resounding, though qualified "no." In short, one can say that tourism research grew, and even flourished, in the realms of econometrics (variable construction and measurement, forecasting, impact evaluation, competitiveness) and hotel management (Bote and Esteban 1996). However, at the same time, and with few exceptions, Spanish academics were unable to grasp the social and cultural aspects of these new events. It may have been because of the frivolous image that the subject projected; or because sociologists and anthropologists could not grapple with its intricacies; or because Spanish intellectuals could not envisage that its study might contribute any theoretical innovation; or because of the reception of French deconstructionism with its dislike for allegedly manipulative new social practices such as fashion, sports, advertising, or tourism (Bourdieu 1984); or because of widespread censorship, to name just a few causes. The outcome, however, was obvious: tourism did not register as an academic subject. Even a recent collection of essays on the economic history of Spanish regions in the 19th and 20th centuries (Germán 2001) has practically nothing to say on the significance of tourism in Catalonia or Valencia, in spite of the high number of tourists these two regions host every season. The same applies to the case of the Balearic Islands, where it is impossible to overlook its magnitude, and there is a resistance to decisively acknowledge the economic and social dynamics unleashed by mass tourism (Manera 2001).

At any rate, since the 1970s, economic research on tourism was clearly favored by the few academics ready to follow their modest calling. Economics seemed to provide a less controversial ground for a discussion of tourism development. Nevertheless, most published research was carried on outside academia, and it found a home in the pages of *Revista de Estudios Turísticos* (RET) (Review of Tourist Studies). The journal was and still is produced by the *Instituto de Estudios Turísticos* (Institute of Tourist Studies). Though the institution changed its name from time to time, it has always been a branch of the Spanish National Tourism Administration. The first RET issue appeared in 1963. Since then and until 2006, the journal published 166 issues and 809 articles (*Centro de Documentación Turística de España* (CDTE) (2007)) (Spanish Center for Tourist Data). It is no exaggeration to say that most Spanish tourism research became public, thanks to RET. Its contributors were overwhelmingly Spanish. Indeed, the journal did not show much interest in following developments beyond the Spanish borders. Among the few foreign contributions, one can find some earlier European authors such as W. Hunziker and K. Krapf, but not much else. Indeed, the new Anglophone tourism research that started with the work of Erik Cohen, Jafar Jafari, Dean MacCannell, Valene Smith, and their colleagues remained far from its pages.

It was perhaps safer to keep the social sciences at arm's length in order to avoid analyses that might cause trouble for the powers that be. Even when Spain started its transition to democracy after General Franco's death in 1975, and until today, RET has preferred the alleged seriousness of math-based economics to the vagaries of political science, sociology, and anthropology. When one further examines its economics articles, the journal also made a clear decision to support noncontroversial topics. Econometrics, along with the industry's problem solving and best practices, constitute the bulk of its papers in preference to such supposedly divisive matters as development, the international division of labor, or globalization. In fact, most economic articles deal with forecasting and measurement, marketing, and structural aspects of the industry.

These observations are not meant to detract from the valuable work accomplished by econometric experts such as Angel Alcaide, Manuel Figuerola, Venancio Bote, Agueda Esteban, or Ezequiel Uriel. With different emphases, they fought a hard battle to show that the contribution of tourism to the Spanish economy was more than a mere trifle. However, RET, especially after the end of the dictatorship, although it could have cast a wider net, in practice opted to travel along a less-risky path. While it played a valuable role, its bureaucratic ownership and its limitations of choice prevented it from becoming one of the main international journals in the field of tourism. Spanish researchers paid the price for such myopic caution, as they remained practically unknown beyond the country's borders. This setback, however, was neither their last nor their largest hurdle.

TOURISM RESEARCH: THE THREE WISE MEN

After the 1970s, tourism research was overwhelmingly written and published in English and, unfortunately, not many Spanish professionals were at ease in that language. In this way, low academic status, concentration on economics, and limited skills in the use of English all conspired until quite recently to keep Spanish tourism research within the national boundaries. In some cases it was quite unfair. Some authors, especially Mario Gaviria, Francisco Jurdao Arrones, and José Luis Febas, blazed a number of trails in the sociology or the semiotics of tourism that deserved greater recognition, since they were both original and innovative.

Mario Gaviria: The Social Fabric of Mass Tourism

In 1975, Mario Gaviria and his team published the first overall treatment of tourism in Spain, complemented by another work containing the results of the survey (methodology and tables) on which the first one was based

(Gaviria et al 1975). Both studies were the outcome of a research project financed by the Spanish *Fundación Juan March* (John March Foundation) between 1972 and 1974. Gaviria, born in 1938, occupied and still holds a very special place among Spanish sociologists. First, this was because most of his work was carried out in teams that included a large number of collaborators in different capacities; for instance, 69 names are listed among the contributors to his tourism project. Among them, as the top consultant, appeared Henri Lefebvre with whom Gaviria studied in Paris during the 1960s and whose work influenced him deeply (Wikipedia 2007). One of the perpetual issues Gaviria grappled with in various studies was the production of space and the unequal access of different social groups to it. A second telling feature was that for most of his career, Gaviria was not a professor and toiled on the periphery of Spanish academia, never too eager to welcome critical thinkers in its midst.

His tourism project was intended to obtain a better understanding of the dynamics of the massive and growing presence of international tourists on the Spanish coasts and islands since the 1960s. As Gaviria and his team stressed, at the time, the only attempts to grasp its dimensions were the statistical data provided by the Spanish Ministry of Information and Tourism that mostly tracked flows of international arrivals. These data, it was argued, were both limited in scope (they did not include Spanish residents) and collected with the utilitarian goal of adapting tourism policies to the new demand. For the authors of the report, this approach was badly flawed, ignored the importance of tourism as a spatial fact, and overlooked its effects on the inhabitants of the new leisure towns. For their part, Gaviria and his colleagues favored a broader approach that would provide "a diagnostic on the problematic of the high use of spaces by tourists from the viewpoint of the users of those spaces" both international and domestic (Gaviria et al 1975:5) (here and henceforward all translations provided by the author).

To reach this goal, they conducted a survey of international and domestic tourists using questionnaires circulated in 16 towns (beach resorts on the Spanish coasts, the Balearic Islands, and the Canaries) in the first two weeks of August 1973 when tourist demand was at a peak. The sample was selected according to the main nationalities present in each of the towns. The questionnaires were accompanied by an unspecified number of in-depth interviews with hotel managers, travel agents, guides, and hotel workers. Additionally, a chapter on the dynamics of excursions employed the mostly anthropological method of participant observation. Though the study purported to achieve a holistic treatment of tourism, in fact the final analysis revolved mainly around foreign beach tourists and the foreign tour-operated business that catered to their needs. At any rate, even in this more limited scope the work represented a clear departure from the way tourism was regarded at the time by academics and the media.

For Gaviria, and his team, modern mass tourism was not an exclusive Spanish phenomenon. It also said much about the new affluent European societies that emerged after 1945. The peoples of Northern Europe were facing deteriorating home environments, cold climates, and increasingly expensive habitats. They coveted new zones where land was still cheap and beaches and sunshine were abundant. Thus, began an increasing redistribution of the settlement patterns of European populations. The Spanish Mediterranean coasts and Spain's islands became a magnet for the inhabitants of the new industrial societies ready to transfer out of their cities for a vacation in the sun. The exodus, whether of independent travelers or of tourists packaged by tour operators and real estate agents, started a new type of colonialism based on the exploitation of new quality destinations. In addition to the numbers of transient tourists, many Europeans were relocating to Spain permanently.

> De seguir así las tendencias podemos pensar que para el año 1980 haya permanentemente viviendo cinco millones de extranjeros en los mejores lugares del país, a la vez que varios millones de españoles están trabajando en los puestos que los extranjeros no quieren en sus lugares de origen. Esta misma situación se plantea, por ejemplo, con los puertorriqueños, que forman el subproletariado de Nueva York, y los norteamericanos que van de vacaciones a Puerto Rico (Gaviria 1975:14).

> If this trend keeps growing, one can expect that in 1980 there will be over five million foreigners living permanently in the best areas of the country while millions of Spaniards will take the jobs those foreigners shun in their countries of origin. Something similar happened to the Puerto Ricans. They became New York's sub-proletariat while US residents vacationed in their island.

In Gaviria's view, assessing the new trend would require a two-pronged approach dealing with both the temporary inflows of foreign tourists and the real estate developments that catered to those segments willing to find a new home in Spain. As available Spanish statistics did not help much to understand the facts, the best method to this end would be a behavioral study of European mass tourism to Spain coupled with an assessment of the strategies of tour operators and real estate companies. Starting with the European masses, after Second World War they created an increasing demand for leisure that reflected both the desire to leave drabness behind and to maximize the rising living standards of millions of Northern Europeans. There were also other, more immediate causes. The end of the war created a big market for second-hand turboprop aircraft that could be easily bought or leased by a number of European tour operators looking for bargains. This opening coincided with the emergence of small family and mid-sized hotels on the Spanish Mediterranean coasts looking for clients and offering decidedly competitive prices when contrasted with those of their French or Italian counterparts. A big window of opportunity thus appeared, in Gaviria's words, to combine all those factors under the logic of the market, and to take advantage of the new international division of labor. Some areas in the Mediterranean, with Spain at their head, took the lead in providing much sought quality leisure space and beach amenities to millions of Europeans. When existing hotels could not cope with increased demand, new ones were quickly built. Construction unleashed an upward economic cycle that, in turn, bred new resorts and new hotels to accommodate new clients.

Most Spanish hoteliers, however, owned family or mid-size properties and lacked the resources to finance larger resorts on their own. For their part, Spanish banks were wary of entering a market that they did not know well. They thus agreed that financing the boom would be the job of European tour operators. Since they needed beds for their clients and had some ready cash, the operators would fund the construction of new hotels advancing up to 50% of their cost. In exchange, they would sign preferential agreements with hoteliers to provide accommodation at stable prices for four to ten years. The deal was very attractive for the operators, as it helped them to plan their offer over the midterm. Additionally, if for unspecified reasons an operator was unable to fill the rooms it had booked, the hotelier would not request compensation for the missed business. The result was a burst of overbooking as hoteliers tried to cover themselves against the odds by selling more beds than they really had. However, both sides learned to cooperate in finding solutions whenever the problem appeared.

If they wanted to be profitable, the new hotels had to conform to a number of conditions that, in the end, jeopardized their quality and their facilities. The tour operators' strategy determined that hotels should be built close to the beach and the center of holiday resorts, as well as in the vicinity of shopping areas and nightspots. They should have sea views and be near, though not too close, to other hotels and resorts, thus forming leisure clusters. Together with favorable locations, hotels should have facilities such as gardens, tennis courts, and eventually golf links; above all they could not do without a swimming pool, ideally with warm water in winter. Economies of scale favored large hotels (500 + rooms) with low per-room investment and good common facilities. Small rooms pushed clients to common areas thus creating a captive demand. Clients would spend much of their time running up a drink account at hotel bars; shopping at the hotel's commercial gallery; or using in-house services such as hairdressing, spas, beauty salons, foreign exchange, gambling, and other extras. These hotels, different from both the traditional family and luxury properties, became par for mass vacations. Tour operators used to call them "convenience hotels," but they should have been better known as leisure factories that met the requirements of industrial tourism.

Why did the tour operators not take over the hotel management themselves? Specialization was one of the reasons. Their business was to steer tourist flows, not to run hotels. Another ground, no less important, was the regulatory framework. In the early 1970s Spain erected many hurdles for foreign tour operators. For instance, operators were barred from incorporating their own Spanish subsidiaries to sign contracts with hotels. This created a need for local legal intermediaries to run those operations. These intermediaries (often owned by the tour operators through a middleperson) gave local hoteliers some peace of mind as they could obtain compensation in case the tour operator went bankrupt at home or did not fulfill its obligations. Additionally, for the tour operator, local representatives provided excellent information on the local market, and intelligence on the economic health of hoteliers, the local and national business atmosphere, and other aspects that gave them an edge when negotiating prices and rates of occupancy. In the end, tour operators, thanks to their control of foreign demand, could determine the prices charged by hoteliers. The deal seemingly offered advantages to both parties, but was in fact an unequal exchange.

In a nutshell, on the hotelier's side, the new tourism industry developed following the needs of the tour operators and was often financed by them; their financial leverage gave tour operators almost complete control of the industry; and in order to increase their benefits, Spanish hotels would cut corners by imposing low salaries on their workforce and, at the same time, by reducing the quality of their services to tourists.

On the tour operators' side the outlook was rosier: Not entering directly into the hotel business while having key access to their own market allowed them to fund and control a higher number of hotels and beds; funding was quickly recovered as increasing vacation demand allowed for quick pay offs in the new properties; and excursions and other complementary activities allowed them to increase their profitability with relatively low investments.

One should not overlook the importance of the latter. Usually they included a number of entertainment activities such as donkey or camel riding, barbecue meals, visits to nearby localities of interest, wine tasting, nightclub hopping, and participation in local *capeas* (bullfighting shows). Quite often excursions had add-ons that were great opportunities to cash in on the tourists' additional discretionary income: dancing, all you can drink *sangria*, abundant low quality wine, and photo opportunities to capture pleasurable memories. People on shorter stays or winter vacations, as well as adults unaccompanied by children, were top spenders in excursions and related items. Selling the product was usually done on the same day the tourists landed, while they still retained most of the money budgeted for the trip. Just after arrival, tour operator representatives (reps) would call a meeting to explain their offers at the same time as welcome free drinks were served. These reps had a high interest in selling excursions for they produced a vital boost to their otherwise low salaries. Tour operators would typically outsource excursions to local agencies that often pooled clients from different hotels. Their role as providers of excursions was compensated by a third of the price, with the rest usually shared between the tour operator and the guides. Tour operators would additionally reap between 50% and 60% of the remaining benefits if the local agency that managed the excursion did in fact belong to them. Gaviria estimated that for a donkey-riding excursion, benefits were four times greater than expenses. In this way, by controlling the flows of incoming tourists, funding the construction of factory hotels, and keeping excursions under their command, tour operators were able to make huge profits while keeping investments low. Additionally, their control of foreign demand (that extended even to the vacation resorts, thanks to their network of guides) allowed them to impose low pricing policies on local hoteliers, to obtain sizeable benefits from the excursion business, and not to pay taxes to the Spanish government as the bulk of their business would take place in their countries of origin.

The report also included a review of the role of brochures in the strategy of tour operators. Researchers examined some 200 brochures with a total of 20,000 pages and 100,000 photos. They all had a similar format: glossy magazine-like publications with an average of 100 pages. Most of them portrayed holiday resorts controlled by the tour operator, while the rest offered information on how to buy the vacation, specified services to be delivered, and pushed the client to make her buying decision through this particular tour operator. Catalogs were an important investment on the part of tour operators and their cost served them well to keep low the prices that they paid to hoteliers. They had an additional political dimension. Tour operators used the power they got from their advertising efforts to threaten local governments and the industry with channeling demand to other destinations in case they would not get their desired goals in pricing and regulatory bonanzas.

Brochures followed the unique selling proposal (USP) logic. Their main goal being to close deals, they insisted on the commercial rather than providing real information about the destination, as though life and reality stopped beyond the hotel premises they advertised. Reps and excursions were the only conduits through which tourists would have a peek into the "real" world of the destination. Together with the USP logic they elided the nature of destinations.

> Puede hablarse asimismo del absoluto desprecio que los folletos muestran por los países turísticos. Adopción de unos aires a menudo imperialistas que se traducen en actitudes despectivas tanto hacia la persona que trabaja para los turistas; [...] como hacia las manifestaciones culturales del país; [...] y aun a los animales que de alguna forma representan el turismo en cada zona—un visible desafecto hacia el camello o el burro. Todo ello, conjugado con el enorme desinterés por el paisaje, muestra la verdadera imagen de un tipo de vacaciones, de un tipo de turismo nacido a partir de la década de los 60 y que permite a las clases media y baja de los países industriales gozar del sol y del buen clima mediterráneo (Gaviria 1975:87).

> One should also speak of the total contempt of brochures vis-à-vis host countries. [Brochures] often put on imperialist airs and spiteful attitudes towards the working people that cater to tourists; [...] to the country's cultural manifestations; [...] to the very animals (camels, donkeys) that epitomize tourism in the area. All this, together with the absolute lack of interest towards the natural environment, shows the real essence of the

vacations and types of tourism that appeared in the 1960s to allow the middle and lower classes of industrialized countries to enjoy the sun and the good Mediterranean climate.

At the same time, the USP was packed within the ideology of vacations as needs, and oriented to the lowest common consumer.

En resumen, podemos afirmar sin temor a equivocarnos que el folleto es una torpe elaboración publicitaria que paradójicamente alcanza su pretendida efectividad, lo que demuestra los condicionamientos a los que está sometido el ciudadano de los países industriales más desarrollados (Gaviria 1975:84).

In summary, [one] can state without fear of being mistaken that brochures are clumsy advertising tools of low quality, which show just how conditioned the citizens of the most developed industrial countries can be.

A close analysis of brochures showed that their agendas went beyond advertising.

Los folletos tenderán a introducir al "hombre acrítico" dentro del circuito del consumo turístico, prometiéndole la accesión a mundos míticos presentados de forma que su fruición resulte posible, [...] que imposibilita toda reflexión y, desde luego, toda crítica (Gaviria 1975:79).

Brochures tend to include an a-critical subject in the circle of tourist consumption, offering access to mythical worlds presented in such a way that their alluring enjoyment [...] will short-circuit thought, especially critical thought.

Brochures conveyed an ideology of unbridled consumption. On the one hand, they denied consumers real capacity to choose in the same act of offering them a choice—the products offered by the brochure were so similar to one another that consumers could not really decide what to choose. On the other hand, access to mythical leisure worlds offered an illusion of enhanced status through sophistication, vignettes of aristocratic existence, and a life of pleasure in contrast with everyday domestic chores, thus dodging any hint of difficulty or unpleasantness for the consumer—showing easy and comfortable travel, no hassles, fair prices, and protection from the dangers derived of too much exoticism. Reality was contrived through captions and intelligent use of photography to produce an ideology of naturalism. Vacationers could expect encounters with naïve locals in a happy natural environment that negated the increasing separation from nature that was so characteristic of modern life. Scantily clad bodies and natural environments created the illusion of attractive and pristine landscapes and hid the low quality of urban agglomerations and of hotel buildings. The message was clear: push and insist on everything that promises happy holidays and buy this particular seller's offer. Gaviria's conclusions were clearly in anticipatory line with the later analysis by Dann of the people of British brochures (Dann 1996c).

The sustainability of the whole operation would be impossible without another pillar: the Spanish workforce. The tourism miracle relied on the existence of surplus labor or *braceros* (day laborers). They were abundant and low in skills, that is to say, well adapted to the poor wages and job instability of the hotel sector. About 65% of the hospitality workforce came from distant areas far removed from destinations. Many made their way there through friends or relatives with employment in the tourism area that encouraged them to meet up or even found them a job before they left their villages. Once the season was over, they would typically return to their points of origin to look for menial employment over the winter months. Seasonality in tourism went hand in hand with seasonality in work. Given the hard conditions of the industry, most migrants were youngsters. Two-thirds of hotel employees worked only temporarily and had low protection *vis-à-vis* their employers. Trade unions (at the time the report was written, there were no trade unions other than the official, mandatory ones) did not even request the enforcement of existing labor laws. Workers who demanded their rights were easily blacklisted or fired. Much was made of the low skills of the workforce, Gaviria stressed, but the truth was that it went hand in glove with the structural arrangements of the hotel sector. Therefore, a vicious circle ensued in which seasonality and temporariness favored low wage levels while hard working conditions made the acquisition of higher skills very difficult. Out of a sample of 157 hotel workers, only 6 had completed junior high school and only 1 had a high-school diploma; 150 had learned their jobs onsite. One-third had neither social security nor health coverage. For the majority (128 workers) their workday lasted eight hours or more (10–11-hour workdays were the lot of many) and less than half had one free day per week. Only one in three workers had a permanent job and these were mainly directors and mid-level managers.

For Gaviria, better knowledge of the real tourism market would have opened the way to greater control by the Spanish. The government did not have a clear picture, while tour operators did, which gave them the higher ground to optimize their benefits. At the same time, Spanish ignorance of the real situation in the market was a lose/lose position, both on the commercial side and on the political one.

> Estas compañías tienen conexiones muy altas con la banca internacional, los productores de aviones, compañías especializadas en seguros y transportes y, lógicamente, con los gobiernos respectivos. Esto es lo que hace que lo que empezó siendo vacaciones para los europeos se haya convertido en un objetivo político-social de los gobiernos europeos: facilitar vacaciones baratas para las clases populares a costa de los trabajadores de los países del Mediterráneo (Gaviria 1975:74).

> These companies are intimately connected with international banks, aircraft builders, insurance and transportation companies, and clearly with their governments. In this way what started as providing vacations for the Europeans has become a socio-political objective of European governments—providing cheap holidays for the popular classes at the expense of Mediterranean workers.

Such policies bolstered the interests of conservative and social democratic governments, as well as the trade unions, in the main European countries, not those of Spain.

This new colonialism did not stop at seaside hotels. Along with the increasing migration of tourists, a new industry was growing. The report called it the "neocolonialist production of quality space" that was creating a vast movement of *apartamentos* (condominium) building and *urbanizaciones* (urbanizations, or urban sprawl) on the coastline. By the time the report was written, the race was in full swing, though Gaviria suggested that it would even increase over the next few years. Just in Málaga province (where the Costa del Sol was located) the researchers counted 226 new suburban developments.

> [...] ya que las urbanizaciones están, en general, situadas en
> las zonas más bellas de las costas y las redes excesivas de
> carreteras necesarias para dar acceso a todas las parcelas
> destruyen el paisaje aún más que la concentración de torres y
> bloques en ciertos puntos dados (Gaviria 1975:288).

> ... the urbanizations are located as a rule in the most beautiful
> of coastal spots while the excessive road networks needed to
> access all plots ruin landscapes even more than the accumula-
> tion of towers and condo blocks.

They were responsible, for instance, for the destruction of the Corralejo
sand dunes in Fuerteventura (Canary Islands). For Gaviria, residential
tourism had an even deadlier potential than sun and sea vacations.

The conclusion of this evaluation of the then bourgeoning Spanish
market mixed the denunciation of the new imperialism with nationalistic
proposals. The Spanish case epitomized the new wave of colonialism: the
production of quality leisure space. The Spanish industry and its workforce
had become subservient to the interests of foreign tour operators and real
estate developers. However, it was not too late to change the flow of the tide.
Spain had become a first-class power in mass tourism. Therefore, it had an
opportunity to build its own counterstrategy taking advantage of its
idiosyncratic strengths: excellent weather, fine sandy beaches with clear
waters, quality food and wine, hospitality know-how and technology, night
life, and happy people. The opportunity was there for the country to grab, as
those strengths could not be easily destroyed. Although tour operators
might threaten to send their tourist flows to other areas in the
Mediterranean, even if they so wanted, it would not be easy to substitute
what Spain had already developed.

> En resumen, hay muchas razones para pensar que es posible
> hacer pagar por la utilización de España, acabar con la
> imagen de España como paraíso fiscal, paraíso de inversores,
> y plantear una política turística de país moderno que ha salido
> de la situación de país neocolonial y subdesarrollado (Gaviria
> 1975:356).

> In summary, there are many reasons to think that we can
> make others pay for the use of Spain, that it is possible to get

rid of the image of an investor's fiscal paradise and that we can formulate a tourism policy worthy of a modern country that has outgrown its neocolonial and underdeveloped past.

Gaviria did not deny the economic importance of tourism for Spain and he did not propose doing away with the present market-oriented framework. In this way, he was a reformer who claimed a larger slice of the tourism cake for Spanish interests.

Twenty years later, Gaviria (1996) briefly revisited his former subject. This time his assessment was more general and more sober. Even though since 1973–1974 mass tourism had not ceased to grow (reaching some 45 million tourists in 1995), and even though the growth of residential tourism had followed an even quicker development than he had anticipated, his views had now changed. From 1975 to 1995, he said, Spain had become the seventh economic world power, and he had no doubt that tourism development had greatly contributed to this outcome. Now the situation he had so critically analyzed in the mid-1970s seemed different. Somehow the Spanish Model had worked. Even in 1996, the main details of how this happened still escaped one's attention, he said. But, be it as it may, turning a backward country into a great destination required a lot of business acumen and sophistication on the part of Spaniards. Spain had learned how to adapt itself to the demands of millions of visitors, both national and foreign, like no other country in the Mediterranean. Sun and sea tourism was no longer as suspect to him in 1996 as in 1975.

> Las playas españolas son la materialización sobre el espacio del ocio del goce merecido de los obreros del Estados del Bienestar Europeo. Parece grandilocuente, pero es una realidad sencilla. [...] Se ha hecho tan bien en material turística en los últimos 35 años, y se sigue haciendo tan bien, que se diría que el turismo marcha por sí mismo, viene sólo, atraído por la calidad de vida, de paisaje y de clima de España, por la amabilidad de nuestras gentes y la seguridad del ambiente y, sobre todo, por la relación calidad-precio de las playas (Gaviria 1996:336–337).

> Spanish beaches materialize in a leisure space the enjoyment deserved by the workers of the European Welfare State. This may sound like grand-standing, but is at heart a simple truth.

> [...] On the tourism side, Spain has been so successful over the
> last 35 years that one might say that our tourism just grows on
> cruise control attracted by Spain's quality of life, landscapes
> and weather, by our friendly people, by general safety and,
> above all, by the value for money to be found in our beaches.

Rather than standing still, Spain had further room to develop in other
products beyond the beaches. City trips, heritage, and cultural tourism
would be the new magnets for growing numbers of European youngsters.
An attentive listener would say that she had heard the same discourse
somewhere in the past. Mind you, it was in the articles and speeches of the
desarrollistas of yore.

Gaviria, regretfully, did not explain how and why he had changed his
position of 20 years earlier. Foreign tour operators still had an important
presence in Spain and, at the same time, urban sprawl accommodating
foreign residents remained a fixture of the landscape, while the nationalistic
policies he advocated in his younger years had been completely discarded.
Javier Gómez-Navarro, a socialist minister of Trade and Tourism at the
time Gaviria was writing this later work (1996), could still stir up the specter
of a Spanish tour operator responsive to national interests, but nobody took
him seriously—least of all his fellow socialist ministers. In fact, the U-turn
Gaviria now appreciated had been reached by letting the markets follow
their course. The big difference between 1973 and 1996 was that, after a long
period of economic growth, Spaniards could now participate in mass
tourism and other leisure amenities as much as other Europeans. They built
their affluence later than other Europeans, but they now had full access to it.
The former anticolonial approach that made tour operators, foreign
tourists, and their governments responsible for the vagaries of Spanish
underdevelopment seemed less defensible at a later date. It is a pity that
Gaviria refrained from explaining whether his change of mind was just a
case of mellowing with age or, rather, one of better understanding the
benefits of integration in the international market (or globalization).

Jurdao Arrones: From Uncertain Anthropology to Flimsy Populism

Francisco Jurdao Arrones shared with Gaviria a distance from academia,
but not much else. Though he was pronounced an anthropologist, he had no
degree in this field and his fieldwork in Mijas seems to have been due to an
accident. He started as a civil servant in the local government and there he
became deeply impressed by the remarkable changes the locality and its

people were experiencing as a result of mass tourism. His work, though, is better known than Gaviria's within Anglophone academia, thanks to the positive reception given to it by the Spanish-speaking Dennison Nash (1996; see also Nash 1989; Pattie 1992; Pearce 1992).

His first work (Jurdao Arrones 1979; here quoted in its 2nd edition of 1990) opened with a hypothesis close to Gaviria's and with a similar complaint. Spain was losing its sovereignty as a result of an uncontrolled transfer of property to foreign hands. The trend started under General Franco, but the progression deepened during the new democratic era that began in 1978. In fact, the massive land sale did not stop at the coasts but spilled all over the country. This was nothing less than a new imperialist episode of which the peasants had to bear the brunt. Their rural culture made them defenseless before the foreign developers who frequently acted in cahoots with local power brokers. Fraud and graft unleashed tourism developments that would decimate agriculture and turn peasants into construction workers. Jurdao followed the process and its alleged dynamics at the micro-level of one Andalusian town. Mijas was a small inland city in the area that had become known as the Costa del Sol in Málaga (southeastern Spain). Together with Majorca, the Costa del Sol was the cradle of foreign mass tourism in the 1960s. Before that, Mijas was a sleepy backwater in a predominantly agricultural area. Like most of Andalusia, since the mid-19th century it was torn by landlord–peasant conflicts similar to those described by Brenan (1990). After the Civil War and under General Franco's dictatorship, the town seemed poised to reproduce inequality and poverty as it had done for generations. Then, the masses of tourists arrived, and with them Jurdao's research on the impacts of tourism.

Historically, Mijeño society had the usual preindustrial features. Land was the center of economic activity and social stratification and power revolved around its ownership. It was composed of four main social groups: big, often absentee landowners living in Madrid or in the regional capital, Málaga, and their *caciques* (local retainers); mid-sized and small landowners; *aparceros* (sharecroppers), *braceros* (day laborers), wood cutters, and craftsmen; and professionals (doctors, chemists, school teachers, civil servants, etc.) with social prestige, though not particularly rich. The power of the big landowners not only flowed from their extensive holdings, it included few existing industries and commercial enterprises, so that their economic and political clout was buttressed by limited economic development. In the years before the advent of mass tourism, sharecroppers and day laborers represented 95% of the town's working population. The majority could not make enough from their work to feed their families.

However, the situation started to change at the end of the 1950s. The surrounding areas of Torremolinos, Marbella, and Fuengirola became new leisure towns given over to tourism. New hotels and condominium blocks required a growing workforce, thus offering new jobs in the construction sector to local peasants and to those of close-by areas such as Mijas. While official statistics and political sound bites extolled the importance of foreign tourism, the undertow went in another direction: the country being sold bit by bit to the highest bidder. For Jurdao, it was not so much the hotel business which should take the blame for this. Even though its growth was far from insignificant, the real driving force in the new period was the expansion of residential tourism. Jurdao showed scant respect for the new industry. The new leisure towns, he stated, became:

> Lugares donde pronto se dan cita golfos, bribones, especuladores, traficantes de drogas, hampones, prostitutas, que en un santiamén, convertirán el mundo de los negocios en simple especulación y la especulación del suelo será el motor del cambio económico (Jurdao 1990:125).

> ... [P]laces that will soon attract misfits, tramps, bums, drug dealers, thugs, prostitutes; soon business will turn into speculation; and speculation will become the engine of economic development.

The old traditional order started to fade away quickly. Towns and villages that had developed more or less harmoniously for centuries, each proud of its culture and identity, were being replaced by suburbs alien to the old world. According to Jurdao, 85% of the new *urbanizaciones* were foreign owned, and old local communities were on the wane.

Changes did not spare the local labor market either. Before the Civil War (1936–1939), Mijas residents did not look for jobs beyond the town's limits. Since the 1960s, mass tourism and the construction boom changed the landscape. Mijas became a Petri dish where one could observe the momentous changes that were shaking the traditional fabric of Spanish society. From 1900 to 1940, the agricultural workforce declined from 68% to 55%. Over the next 30 years, it would be quickly reduced to about a quarter of the labor force. In Mijas, day laborers were the first to initiate the exodus because they could find better wages in construction. Later they were followed by people who had previously resisted leaving their land.

Many sharecroppers and small landowners sold their village homes and farms to buy apartments in the new development areas. This helped further property concentration in the hands of old big landowners and of foreign interests. In many cases, says Jurdao, the peasants sold their holdings for a pittance thinking that they were doing excellent business. Their lack of accurate information about the real estate market made them easy prey to local *caciques* (retainers) who quite often worked hand in hand with foreign interests.

Damages to traditional society did not stop at the economic sphere.

> Mediante la división del trabajo, que ha introducido en la zona en pocos años el turismo, se ha roto la familia campesina. Los hijos han obtenido salarios independientes y el orden jerárquico del padre en la familia ha desaparecido. El campesino mediano o pequeño [...] [s]e siente cercado y abandonado en su soledad, ante un Nuevo mundo, que se planea desde fuera (Jurdao 1990:199).

> Because of the division of labor introduced in just a few years by tourism development, the peasant family had been broken. Children are now able to secure independent incomes and the hierarchical role of the father within the family has vanished. Small and median peasants [...] feel isolated and abandoned in their solitude before a new world planned in places far away from their society.

It was the victory of capitalism over traditional communities.

Mijas was now a schizophrenic society: on the one hand the autochthonous Spanish population of laborers and peasants; and on the other the planned communities with their villas and bungalows inhabited by foreigners, who usually enjoyed a higher standard of living than the locals. Those were two separate worlds with very few common interests. While locals had to do in a simple way, foreigners required their home comforts. A number of products had to be imported for their consumption, thus depleting their contribution to the local economy or, in more modern jargon, increasing leakages.

The second edition of the work, published 11 years later (1990), insisted that the process had deepened. In 1990, according to Jurdao, 80% of the population was foreign and 56% of the land now belonged to them.

A new theme appeared that Jurdao would pursue in a work written at around the same time (Jurdao and Sánchez 1990). Not only was the foreign population growing significantly, it was also mostly composed of elderly (over 47% older than 60). If the tide did not turn, Spain would soon become a huge geriatric ward, a new Florida. This process developed with the complicity of the Spanish government. From Madrid, the Spanish administration looked down its nose at the tourism towns of the Mediterranean seaboard as so many other colonies. It allowed foreign colonization to deepen without caring to protect the native communities, to prevent the disappearance of Spanish villages, or to hold back the sale of land to foreigners at bargain basement prices. In his view, this was a shortsighted policy that might become suicidal for Spanish entrepreneurs. If the sale of resources was allowed to proceed unabated, they would lose control over the national economy.

Among Anglo-Saxon academics, Nash has insisted that Jurdao's is a genuine denunciation of tourism and its imperialist dynamics (1996). However, if one looks at his argument a bit closer, any similarity with Gaviria's informed stand is but lexical. Essentially, the prime mover in Jurdao's argument was not an evaluation of national interests at a time of growing international integration, rather it was nostalgia for the passing of rural society and the old communitarian order. For all the acknowledged flaws he said it had, Jurdao still idealized it (1992). According to him, it was indeed unfair, but more palatable when compared with the countless problems visited upon the locals by the inflow of foreigners. Jurdao, however, refrained from attempting to understand or explain the process. In his view the Spanish actors, especially day laborers and poor peasants, made the wrong choice. They exchanged the ways of their traditional communities for the deceptive comforts of the new towns. Asking why did not interest him, though he might have found the reason just by reading what he wrote himself. Many workers in old Mijas were unable to cater for most of their families' needs. Hunger, early death, and squalor were their everyday lot. Leaving their land in droves they acted out of the conviction that the old order definitely was the worse possible of two evils. Even with their low skills, construction and the tourism industry offered better living opportunities than tilling the fields in endless days of misery. It was a voluntary choice. Nobody forced the *Mijeños* to sell their land or, in the case of the landless majority, to abandon it, except the desire to have a better life in places where good schools and adequate health care would be provided. The vaunted old communitarian order seemed to them less fair than the new one; accordingly they voted with their feet. Jurdao, however, for all his professed love for the local people seemed unable to understand their decision and showed his personal preference for the old order. At heart, he could not handle modern society. For him, agriculture—nature, not industry or the services—was the only real creative force. The rest, especially trade and tourism, thrived in contrived needs that wound up unleashing all types of social evils as in his tirade against the new leisure towns quoted above.

Even more difficult to condone was his open chauvinism. Every foreigner was a swindler and each *urbanización* an enclave. Jurdao was not alone in rejecting the consequences of a united Europe, among them the right for Europeans to settle where their fancy would take them. His, however, was but the option of a small minority rejected by most Spaniards. The country embraced Europe keenly, among other things because for years it enjoyed being a net recipient of European largesse. It is difficult to build a rational argument against this choice. Additionally, if he took seriously his idea that tourism, both transient and residential, was just imperialism, Jurdao should have denounced as well the high number of second residences Spaniards had bought on the coast. After all, they were also foreigners in the old agrarian communities. He kept silent on this issue, though. Does imperialism just depend on the passport one bears?

In brief, Jurdao's position was that of classical populism that made José Antonio Primo de Rivera, the founder of the Spanish Fascist movement known as Falange, and Federico García Lorca, the bard of Andalusian identity, strange bedfellows singing from the same hymn sheet. He shared with them the illusion of rural society's moral superiority over modernity; he accepted their mistrust of everything foreign; he also seemed to partake in their views on the redeeming virtues of youth. Why otherwise should Spain have feared becoming a magnet for retirees? Once costs and benefits were balanced, there were plenty of the latter in catering to an elderly population. For Jurdao, though, such ruminations were but fare for accountants, not arguments about identity. A good point if one thinks it is possible to define identity in an undisputed way.

In spite of using similar words, Gaviria and Jurdao were divided by a wide ideological chasm: the abyss between the will to know and populist nostalgia.

José Luis Febas: A Limited Wink to Semiotics

At the end of the 1970s, José Luis Febas published in RET a long essay *Semiología del Lenguaje Turístico* (1978) (Semiotics of Tourist Communication). Once again, Febas came from the outskirts of academia. He received his PhD from the Paris Catholic Institute in 1976 with a thesis on theological semiotics. After that, he became interested in the application of communication theory to tourism. Together with his main published contribution just noted, he also coauthored with Aurelio Orensanz a number of unbound papers on various aspects of tourist communication, notably the role of posters and brochures (Febas and Orensanz nd, 1980, 1982). After this bout of creativity, Febas disappeared off the radar and did not follow up on his initial interest in tourism. His work remains very little known and is mostly unquoted by the new generations of Spanish tourism researchers.

Febas' contribution, however, was highly original in the Spanish cultural environment of his time. He was among the first to import the techniques of what was then called French structuralism, especially as formulated by Lévi-Strauss. Significantly, even though he quoted in his piece the best-known names in the field (from Saussure to Jakobson to Barthes) one would in vain look for Foucault. Perhaps because of this omission, his writings lacked an open critique of tourism as the realm of the inauthentic and consumerism that played such a key role in the later work of Anglophones such as MacCannell (1976, 1992). With a quick formula one could say that Febas was postmodernism minus deconstructionism. For Febas, the key to Lévi-Strauss' theoretical revolution was his notion that all social facts could be interpreted within a general theory of communication. Accordingly, one could find the appropriate grammar to locate the role of tourism within the system of signs. Tourism became embodied in a number of messages susceptible to interpretation, and this applied to all its expressions whether marketing, promotion, or advertising. In his case, Febas selected 256 brochures published by the Spanish Ministry of Information and Tourism between 1963 and 1978 as the object of his analysis. Among the reasons for his choice, the author explained that they were a homogeneous body that included both textual and iconic techniques; that they were massively diffused and could be appropriated privately; that they were freely distributed and thus unfettered by economic or commercial constraints; and that they were easy to collect in their entirety.

How could one analyze the selected brochures? Were they a disparate ensemble deprived of inner logic? If not, what were their common elements? Was there a hierarchy of meaning? The best way to probe all those questions was offered by what Febas called the triangulation technique. According to it, the whole problematic of tourism communication could be organized around a number of triangular structures as detailed in Figure 1.

The four isotopic triangles thus obtained developed a more basic communicational scheme that went from the communicator or Ego to the

GRÁFICO I
LA TRIANGULACIÓN TEMÁTICA

Figure 1 The Tourism Communication System. *Source*: Adapted from Febas and Orensanz (1980).

interlocutor or You at the other end of the chain through a message that was included in a wider referential space or Id. Following this sequence each one of the isotopic triangles had a special function. Triangle A referred to the Id, the geographical environment of the given attraction or product. Triangle B was the space of the Ego, the emissary of the information. It included the human and cultural infrastructure. The You triangle (C) referred to the act of consumption proposed to the receiver. Finally, the specific services that the consumer could expect to obtain were included in Triangle D, where the Ego, the You, and the Id converged. By combining these different aspects of all four triangles, it was possible to reach the complete repertoire of the themes all the class *brochure* had in common. In alphabetical order the

themes comprised: accommodation, communication, consumption (cultural), consumption (individual), consumption (environmental), culture,
facilities, folklore, geography, landscape, main features of the attraction and
of its residents, and weather. Not all of them had equal weight; they recurred
in a different quantitative order that allowed one to reckon their respective
ranking (Figure 2).

More than half of the brochure messages (53%) referred to Triangle B
that Febas called the autochthonous contribution.

> En la comunicación turística, el "EL" referencial sobre el que
> versa el mensaje coincide con el "YO" del emisor. No se trata
> tanto de exponer las excelencias de un producto destinado al
> consumo, como sucede con la propaganda publicitaria, cuanto
> de que el productor se manifieste por sí mismo (Febas
> 1978:34).

> In tourism communication the referential Id—the substance of
> the message—coincides with the Ego of the communicator.
> Rather than bragging about the excellence of a product meant
> to be consumed, as happens in advertising, its goal is to let the
> communicator introduce itself.

Consequently, Triangle D (services) with 7% of the messages became the
least mentioned, while the other two (A with 19% and C with 21%) had
a similar weight. In a nutshell, tourism communication mainly revolved
around the referential aspects of the object conveyed.

Brochures' Contents

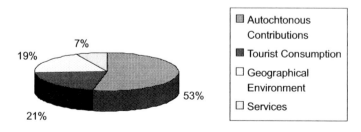

Figure 2 Analyses of Brochure Contents. *Source*: Febas and Orensanz
(1980).

Did the iconic portion of the brochures have a similar organization? In the 256 brochures subject to analysis, icons occupied 70% of the printed space. The distribution was not uniform as there were differences in the relative weight of the textual and the iconic in each brochure. Their proportion, however, did not change much—only between two-thirds and three quarters of the available space. If there was a significant feature in the whole group it was due to the moment when they were created. Older brochures reserved a smaller extension to icons than did new ones. Was this variation significant enough to maintain that both fulfilled their role in exactly the same way?

Indeed, there was a certain redundancy between the texts and the graphics that accompanied them. It was required by the importance of the referential over the other aspects of the brochures. But these two languages had specific nuances, styles, and functionality.

> El texto sitúa, comenta y define la imagen. La imagen ilustra objetiva y colabora tácticamente en la transmisión del texto. En buena camaradería ambos remedian lagunas mutuas y nivelan posibles desequilibrios temáticos o funcionales (Febas 1978:118).

> The text sets, comments, and defines the image. Images illustrate, make objective, and collaborate in expressing and transmitting the text. As good comrades, both palliate their mutual gaps and level their eventual imbalances, whether thematic or functional.

With this in mind, the conclusions seemed to flow freely from the analysis. In Febas' opinion, the best way to understand this relation between the basic elements of the brochures was to retrace their mythology in the Barthesian sense. The 256 brochures studied, says the author, had a notable degree of homogeneity, covered the totality of the country, had their own "house-style," and defined a space, both geographical and referential, that made them different from those of other countries.

Such a positive view of Spanish brochures notwithstanding, one should qualify their eventual communicational success in a triple dimension. Above all, information somehow still appears too fragmented and limited. Physical geography is often completely divorced from social, human, or cultural aspects, and descriptions of monuments omit the real life of people that surround them. Provincial capitals tend to be described with a richness of detail that is lacking when portraying nearby localities. Important aspects of social life such as health care, the economy, or local lifestyles seldom make an appearance in the literature. In contrast with the brochures of tour operators, practical dimensions of travel remain unexplained.

Self-reference is the second problematic element of Spanish brochures. Most text and icons refer to the communicating Ego either extolling its culture and folklore or giving positive self-evaluations of its character. On the other hand, the message recipient is often left unattended. Only 11% of texts and 20% of the iconic material engage the You. Finally, Spanish brochures prioritize the arts over all other aspects. The image of the country is that of a museum where art reigns supreme. Art somehow represents the unchanging features of a Spanish identity beyond time. It is the symbolism of eternal Spain represented by Castile where chauvinistic factors go hand in hand with the celebration of austerity, old age, and tradition.

> Esta es la imagen por la que optan los folletos españoles, con todo el cortejo de blasones, venerables monumentos [...], apologías del románico y del gótico, relegamiento de los aspectos que manifiestan la real industrialización y urbanización del país, etc., en contraste con la política aperturista y europeizante a la que está vinculado el milagro turístico español desde los 60 y a la imagen frívola, exótica y folklorizante que los operadores turísticos logran imponer, durante la misma época, en todo el mundo (Febas 1978:120).

> Such is the image favored by Spanish brochures, with all their paraphernalia of coats of arms, old monuments [...], celebration of the Romanesque and Gothic period, disregard for everything related to the industrialization and urbanization of the country. This contrasts both with the pro-European economic policies of openness that lie at the base of the Spanish tourist miracle since the 60s and with the frivolous, exotic and folklorizing images tour operators imposed during that time the world over.

However, the contrived vision of reality that flows from such a treatment of its subject is not specific to Spanish brochures. In fact, all brochures, whether Spanish or from any other nationality, respond to a mythical role with three main features. They are interpellative, that is, they seek acceptance over argument; they mix objective data with subjective gesturing though always trying to lean on referential reality; and they try to impress, that is, look for immediate attention stressing the iconic elements or suggestive connotations over texts. Their final goal is to push the reader to go from semiotics to ideology, making her live the myth by accepting it in fact and in consumption. In this way, brochures thrive in a depoliticized language that turns history into nature. In the Spanish case, this especially shows in their domineering and scholarly tone, in their lack of contemporariness, and in their simplistic cultural views. The very fine arts that are so much vaunted push human dimensions out of the picture. Monuments, above all religious monuments, overpower real people. If brochures want to keep their role as motivators, and symbols of tourism communication, they urgently need to reshape their language (Febas and Orensanz 1980:124). Febas comes to similar conclusions in the case of Spanish promotional posters (Febas and Orensanz nd).

As already noted, Febas' contribution was highly original for Spain in the 1980s. It opened a line of research that remained undeveloped by the strange disappearance of this author from the tourism environment. Perhaps, it followed too closely the semiotic grammar learned from French writers. It was, however, one of the first contributions to an evaluation of the official self-production of a national image by Spanish governments. A follow-up on his methods and a critical evaluation of later productions along the same line is a task that, to the best of one's knowledge, remains largely unexplored among Spanish researchers.

A few years later, Dann conducted similar analyses of tourism brochures (1996b) and of what he called "the language of tourism" in general (1996a). Although in the latter publication he devoted pages 36–40 to Febas, their conclusions differed considerably. For Dann, at that time, the language of tourism, irrespective of the media through which it was conveyed, or the expectations of its audience, exerted wide-ranging social control over its recipients. In fact, all tourism language, even that in seemingly innocent tourism notices (Dann 2003), played an identical role—ensuring control on behalf of those who shaped tastes while making handsome profits in the process. However, as has been pointed out by Harrison (1997), Dann's insistence in seeing the language of tourism as a one-way road made his argument self-fulfilling and, at the same time, dissonant with the real behavior of tourists.

From this point of view, Febas' approach seems more nuanced. He shares with Dann, and in fact with the entire deconstructionist current, the notion that tourism communication is a mythological pursuit that rates assent over dialog, and creates *syntagmata* that convey bias in the guise of information, but he clearly sees that this drive is far from all-powerful. Audiences know how to read the tourism lingo and they react to control in many different ways. Febas, for instance, was well aware that no matter how much the depoliticized jargon of Spanish brochures of the 1960s and the 1970s praised the Eternal Spain that the dictatorship wanted to restore, the Spanish Tourism Model required a different image. Official brochures could extol churches and museums till kingdom come; still over 80% of international tourists were looking for something completely different: leisure, sun and sea, night life, and all of that at reasonable prices. In this way, Febas understood the differences not just between bureaucratic and industrial brochures, but also the reason why the language of the latter was by far more successful than the illusions entertained by the former. His approach offered a lesson in subtlety that should not be forgotten.

However, interestingly, and particularly with the advent of the Internet and travelblogs, Dann (2005a) has modified his original (1996a) position to one of increasing trialog between the tourism industry, tourists, and destination peoples as the phenomenon of tourism becomes less monological and correspondingly more democratic (Dann and Liebman Parrinello 2007). One wonders whether his initial analysis and subsequent revision would have come to pass were it not for the original contribution of Febas, an example of the inspiration of Anglophone tourism academics deriving from insights of their European predecessors.

CONCLUSION

This quick tour around the origins of Spanish sociological and anthropological research on tourism allows one to draw a number of conclusions. The first should be that, in spite of initial appearances, one should acknowledge the existence of an interesting Spanish current of tourism research beyond the most traveled road, that of economic analysis. The relative obscurity that plagued its members is mostly due to two factors: their detachment from Spanish academia and their lack of publications in English. Both contributed to make the three best representatives of a social-sciences approach to tourism relatively ignored in their own country. For their part, all of them surrendered their initial interest on tourism in their later professional lives. The second refers to RET. In spite of its relatively early birth among tourism journals, both during Franco's dictatorship and until today, RET has preferred the comforts provided by hard economic analysis over other more controversial issues raised by soft social sciences such as sociology, anthropology, or semiotics. In so doing, the journal squandered its chance to become an influential vehicle for tourism research and discussion in the Spanish-speaking world. The recent appearance of *Annals of Tourism Research en Español* as well as new journals on the subject both in Spain and in Latin America will make it even more difficult for RET to become an important medium.

Of the three authors discussed in this chapter, Mario Gaviria seems to be the one that provides the most comprehensive analysis of the role of tourism in the Spanish Model to economic growth. The analyses supplied by Gaviria and his team of colleagues deal with a great number of key issues on both the sustainability of this model as well as its shortcomings. Many of his conclusions were indeed deeply influenced by the novelty of the phenomenon and the absence of accurate theoretical hypotheses to grapple with it that plagued people with leftist positions at the time. Gaviria's later reassessment of the key role played by tourism in the transformation of Spain into a modern society clearly shows that there was more than one way to skin this cat. If Gaviria, for all his serious efforts to the contrary, was initially unable to find a better one than the woolly premises of neo- or postcolonialism, it is no accident that Jurdao would buy into one shade of it—populist nostalgia for the bygone good old days of communitarian values. Foreign tourism, together with its real estate ramifications, was one of the main suspects in their demise. Thus, unable to understand the real causes of the latter, Jurdao could only smudge tourism, not reason it away. Finally, Febas made an interesting contribution to the semiotics of Spain's image building. Armed with the dubious weapon of deconstructionism, he had enough skills to avoid many of its pitfalls. Above all, he understood that tourism speaks in many languages and that to explain it fully, one should understand their differences.

The footsteps of this group of innovators have been nearly erased by the sands of time, and, even though they are cited by a few English-speaking tourism academics with the necessary foreign language skills, they are barely quoted today by younger Spanish researchers. Hopefully, the contributions of these three pioneering wise men will be one day valued for what they are really worth by both Anglophones and Hispanophones.

Chapter 9

Tourism Studies in Belgium and the Netherlands

Jaap Lengkeek
University of Wageningen, Wageningen, The Netherlands

INTRODUCTION

The Roman writer Plinius once described the Low Countries as damp,
unpleasant, and definitely not a place to be. Two thousand years later they
have somehow become "must see" destinations. Ghent, Bruges, Brussels,
Amsterdam, and Volendam, the tulip fields, the dykes and windmills have all
been transformed into icons of tourism. However, although tourism
developed significantly in the last century, scientific interest in the subject
has only been a recent corollary. It took almost 75 years in this part of the
world to find a foothold in academia. This intellectual lag seems all the more
puzzling because tourism is a considerable agent of change that has now
surpassed the importance of agriculture, which had been the pillar of the
economy in the Low Countries ever since Plinius first commented on their
sorry plight.

   In this chapter, it will be shown how tourism, once a part of leisure
studies, remained conceptually hidden until the last two decades when it
became a substantive scientific field in its own right. The account only covers
the Netherlands and Belgium. Luxemburg is omitted since no relevant
information could be found to illustrate its evolutionary process within the
overall designation of the "Low Countries." The historic overview is to some

The Sociology of Tourism: European Origins and Developments
Tourism Social Science Series, Volume 12, 275–297
Copyright © 2009 by Emerald Group Publishing Limited
ISSN: 1571-5043/doi:10.1108/S1571-5043(2009)0000012014

extent further imbalanced. Having been involved in tourism studies in the Netherlands, the author is more familiar with the Dutch situation. In any case, developments in Belgium were not as clear as in the Netherlands, partly because of dividing linguistic, cultural, and political walls between Flanders and Wallonia and a corresponding inconsistency of material on tourism studies in the latter.[1] In this essay, many key players will be introduced to English-speaking readers. However, explicitly mentioning some individuals always entails the danger of unintentionally overlooking others.

TOURISM IN THE PROCESSES OF SOCIAL CHANGE

In order to understand the sociological approaches and perspectives of tourism studies in Belgium and the Netherlands, it is necessary to go back a century and understand how the developments of travel and holidaymaking were addressed by the politics, policy, and knowledge production that accompanied them.

Early 20th Century

Whereas hardly any information is available on the travel of the bourgeoisie in Belgium, more is known of the Dutch situation (Kikkert 1985). The year 1883 saw the founding of the *Algemene Nederlandse Wielrijders Bond* (ANWB), the "General Dutch Bicycle Union." Initially an élitist club for cycle enthusiasts, within a few years, it became a general travel organization producing maps, guides, and insurance. It also furthered the interests of nature travelers and motorists. Nature tourism subsequently became the goal of other specialized organizations and leisure clubs.[2] Another significant organization was the *Verbonden Zeilvereenigingen van Nederland en Belgie* (United Sailing Clubs of the Netherlands [highly élitist] and Belgium), constituted in 1890 and including four Belgian water-sports clubs, aimed at the organization of controlled sailing competitions, and facilitating water tourism in general (Jorissen et al 1990:47).[3] The objectives of both organizations reflected an overall conceptual mixture of leisure, sports, recreation, and tourism which lasted for at least eight decades, making it difficult to identify "genuine" tourism policies, let alone studies, for a long time. In these early years, tourism was a "catch all" term comprising daytrips, travel in general, and holidaymaking.

There were significant differences between the two countries in religious orientations, rates of urbanization, and population growth. Although after the 16th century "Reformation" the Netherlands were mainly Protestant, at least in the underpinning of the nation state's ideologies, in the 19th century the Catholic Church successfully regained part of its social and political power. Liberal movements came up and even took over control of the parliament around the mid-century, and finally socialists started to organize themselves into a political party. When, between 1917 and 1919, the right to vote for men and women became legalized, each of the social divisions around religious convictions and political views (Protestants, Catholics, Liberals, and Socialists) started to secure power and influence based on their own social back-up: schools, leisure activities, commercial connections, and social services. This separation became evident in almost every realm of society and is generally referred to as *verzuiling* (pillarization). This separation of sociopolitical entities meant that there had to be cooperation in politics and decision making in general. The attitude toward negotiations still resonates in the present day, also typically Dutch, concept of the "polder model." The polder stands for the large-scale project and the polder model for negotiating all the different interests in such a way that the project finally ends successfully. After the Second World War, pillarization faded away, the polder model remained, and national policies began to focus on spatial planning (with integrating interests), much more than on a particular educational design for leisure, recreation, and tourism.

Both Belgium and the Netherlands have changed from agricultural to industrialized societies. In Belgium, the Catholic Church dominated the sacred and secular domains, influencing education and scientific work to a high degree. Each country had to deal with the rapid growth of the urban working class during the course of the 19th century. This increase led to a preoccupation with the question "how to *civilize*" the working class masses. This *beschavingsoffensief* (civilization attack), as it was called, took place in the Netherlands from the perspective of pillarization. In Catholic Belgium, the *moralité de la classe ouvrière* (morality of the working class) was an unambiguous religious-political issue that stimulated early geographical studies conducted by the Royal Academy of Belgium on leisure activities and the misuse of free time. One of the early people interested in role of holidaymaking was Vliebergh (1872–1925), a professor of law in Leuven (Louvain) and active as vice-president of the Farmers Union. He was one of the first in Belgium to teach on that subject in the *Leuvense Vakantieleergangen* (Louvain Holiday Courses) of 1907 (Persyn 1909) The movement of Catholic Action against Secularization and Modernization, which aimed to educate the uncontrolled lower classes, expanded its activities from 1930 to 1950. Its position toward free time and vacation was paternalistic and moralistic. In 1937, the *Semaine Sociale Universitaire* (University Social Week) dedicated its sessions to the topic of leisure and social classes as an academic subject.

In 1936, public policy ensured that laborers were granted a yearly holiday. A little earlier, Jacquemyns (1932–1934) applied sociological empirical methods for researching working class people and their leisure patterns. The "mandatory" yearly holiday resulted in the concept of "social tourism," a policy with different projects and initiatives to "teach the workers how to spend their holidays" (Geilen 2008:3). The concrete provision arising from this policy was the establishment of holiday centers along the Belgian coast which offered workers the opportunity to take a vacation at an acceptable price. The labor unions fought for paid holidays (Descan 1994). Social tourism remained the dominant factor in politics in Belgium until the present time, with its heyday between 1960 and 1970 (Smits and Claeys 2008). In 1963, Arthur Haulot, from 1946 until 1978 Commissioner-General of Tourism in Belgium, founded the *Bureau International du Tourisme Social* (BITS) (The International Office of Social Tourism), with its headquarters in Brussels. This agency currently embraces 35 countries. Its definition of social tourism has been adopted by Belgian policymakers, comprising the right of access to tourism for all; a tool for social integration; based on sustainable infrastructure; with a beneficial effect on employment, and a contribution to worldwide development. However, this last goal was well beyond the vision of the prewar period. According to Geilen:

> Het "Bureau International du Tourisme Social" is opgericht in 1963 met het doel het Sociaal Toerisme op een internationaal vlak te ontwikkelen en te ondersteunen, sociaal toeristische activiteiten te coördineren en informatie uitwisselen over het sociaal toerisme te promoten. Het BITS speelt ook een belangrijke rol in het theoretische kader over het Sociaal Toerisme (2008:8).

> The "Bureau International du Tourisme Social" was established in 1963 with the aim to develop and to support Social Tourism on an international level, to coordinate social tourist activities and to promote exchange of information on Social Tourism. BITS also plays an important role in the theoretical framework of Social Tourism.

In the Netherlands, there was some parallel with the Belgian preoccupation with the lower classes. The strongest impetus did not come from the churches alone, but from the much diversified political field as well, consisting of religious-political parties, liberals, and socialists. From 1900, free time was an important issue in Dutch politics. Prior to that period, politics aimed at utilizing long working hours in order to subdue the working classes, hoping to prevent alcohol abuse, prostitution, moral decay, disintegration of family life, and the rise of revolutionary activities. Only a few "enlightened" entrepreneurs created leisure facilities for their workers (social recreation) as part of their civilizing efforts. But in general, free time was seen as a "social problem" (Beckers 1983b:515). In 1910, a "right to vacation" was accepted for selected groups of workers and formed part of labor contracts. In 1945, it became incorporated into public law.

A Dutch Laborers' Travel Society dates back to 1928. From 1923 onwards and within the context of pillarization, several Catholic and Protestant travel societies came into being, as well as the Dutch Youth Hostel Organization and the Labor Union Holiday Resort in 1927 and 1929, respectively. At that time, the authorities were worried about the leisure and holiday patterns of the working class. The Labor Inspection Organization produced a report on workers' leisure patterns in 1923. Two "early" social geographers, Blonk and Kruijt (1933), raised the issue of leisure time as a sociological problem in 1933, and their work was complemented with Blonk, Kruijt, and Hofstee's empirical research on leisure patterns in 1936 (Blonk et al 1936 in Beckers and Mommaas (1991)). Yet, it must be noted that sociology as a discipline in the Netherlands was only in its infancy, since it still lacked a firm institutional academic basis. Blonk et al (quoted in Beckers and Mommaas 1991:36–37) formulated the problem in their 1936 report as follows:

> Een groot deel van deze bruto-vrije-tijd is men genoodzaakt te besteden aan tijdsvullingen, die onmisbaar zijn voor het behoud van de physieke kracht, nl. slaap en rust, physieke verzorging [wassen en baden, kleden, gebruiken van maaltijden. Het geheel van deze vier rubrieken is feitelijk een gedwongen tijdsbesteding en moet dus van de bruto-"vrije"-tijd worden afgetrokken. Wat overblijft is de netto-vrije-tijd, besteed op één der manieren, vermeld in de 17 rubrieken van tabel C.

> A large part of the gross free time is needed for maintenance of physical strength, such as sleep and rest, and physical care

(washing, bathing, dressing, eating). The totality of these four (physical strength, domestic work, care and assistance with "specific female duties") is in fact expending forced time and has to be subtracted from gross free time. What remains is net free time, spent on any of the ways, mentioned in the 17 categories of Table C.

The table comprised the following: simple family interaction; family interaction with play; spending time with the children; hobbies; listening to the radio; reading at home or in a library; courses, meetings, museums, excursions; visiting the theater/cinema, going to concerts; attendance at balls and dancing; visits to a bar (for social interaction or play); attendance at sporting events and matches; sauntering in the streets and in markets; outings, biking, hiking, sports outside the club context; visits to relatives, friends, and neighbors without play; as the latter with play; club life; and attending church or carrying out other religious duties.

Interestingly, the highest score was on reading, followed by the tradition of spending much time visiting relatives and friends *without play*. Yet tourism still did not feature as a separate item. Leisure in general was the predominant focus for empirical studies. An intriguing contribution came from Andries Sternheim (1939), who was a Dutch participant in the so-called Frankfurt School. He discussed the policies of totalitarian states, such as Germany and Italy, to directly intervene in leisure activities of the common people. According to him, these states had deprived civil society of freedom of movement and the choice over how to spend free time. Leisure as a diffuse concept was debated within the context of popular education, the position of workers and the education of youth. Tourism, as far as it was regarded as a leisure activity, was largely synonymous with "domestic tourism." Whereas tourism during the change from the 19th to 20th century fell under the dominant heading of leisure practiced by the elite, during the phase of emancipation of the lower classes and religious factions the emphasis shifted almost entirely to leisure as described in Blonk et al's Table C. For the lower and middle classes travel was not a widespread option.

In the Netherlands, the Second World War meant a breaking with the preexisting situation of academic interest in leisure and recreation. During the German occupation, the Nazi regime installed a Department of Popular Information and Arts. Its fascist ideology implied abandonment of class controversies and, in their stead, the use of leisure activities and tourism organizations for creating the "right" egalitarian and nationalist "spirit." The Germans, ever fond of centralized control, established a National

Planning Service, which continued to exist after the war and played a crucial role in the postwar reconstruction of the Netherlands and the development of leisure areas.

The Democratic Discourse of 1945–1980

Where the history of tourism policy and studies initially shared a more or less comparable past, in the postwar period the Netherlands and Belgium developed in different directions. In the latter a preoccupation with "social tourism" continued as an effort to bring greater opportunities for holidaymaking to larger groups of workers, as well as the elderly and disabled. The related emphasis on educating the common people also persisted. The Labor Unions had started to open vacation homes for their own members. Although the initial Catholic morality of segregation of the sexes still played a role in the supply of these properties, a kind pillarization now appeared in Belgium, where socialists and liberals started to offer their own vacation facilities. An example of this was the establishment of a kind of savings bank where people could deposit a percentage of their wages in order to provide for their annual holidays.

An important idea in this accommodated policy was that working class people were to be guided in their leisure behavior. For this reason professionals were trained as "monitors," and "agology" and "animation" started to flourish as scientific and practical fields with respect to tourism and recreation. Agology was a paraphrase of pedagogy and a variation on "agogy" which was a little more common concept, not reserved solely for the socialization of children, but for anyone, adults included. In fact it aimed to "mould" human action according to certain ideals or normative models. In this respect it was about control over leisure and free time, which could be either disruptive or inefficient as a tool of growing up and living well. Animation was also an approach to guide people in spending their leisure time, for example during their holidays. Where agology was the science of knowing what people and society needed in this respect, animation was the practical application of it. Animation was not a concept reserved to Belgium. Also in the Netherlands in the late 1970s the Dutch Center for Recreation Work was established to organize (mostly volunteer) work on campsites to entertain children and organize play for adults.

The domination of the educational, social, and emancipatory ideals in Belgium inspired Frans van Mechelen, a professor of sociology at Leuven University, to investigate the politics of leisure with applied research, paying particular attention to culture, sports, tourism, and democratization.

In 1964, he published the results of his "Sociological Research among the Active Dutch-speaking Population of Belgium," under the title of *Leisure Activities in Flanders*. In the introduction he wrote:

> In onze westerse kultuur is het volstrekt ondenkbaar dat in deze vrije tijd geen aktiviteiten zouden worden ontwikkeld. Naast rust en ontspanning groeien diverse vormen van vrijetijdsbesteding in een sfeer van hobby, vervolmaking, sport en kultuur (1964:5).

> In our Western culture it is absolutely unthinkable that in free time no activities should be developed. Next to rest and relaxation several forms of leisure grow such as hobbies, personal growth, sports, and culture.

He also emphasized the crucial role of "popular education" as part of leisure (1964:27–32). He articulated the dilemma of free time as follows:

> Het hoeft dan ook geen verwondering te wekken date r soms enige aarzeling bestaat om de vrijetijdsbesteding te integreren al seen volwaardig element in het social bestaan. Als uitdrukking van deze onvoldoende integratie moet de noodzaak worden aangezien van rationele rechtvaardiging van de vrijetijdsbesteding. Hoe vaak worden immers rust en vakantie niet een beetje vergoelijkt door een redenering als: 'Nadien zal ik beter kunnen werken en presteren'. Als waarde op zichzelf schijnt men de vrijetijdsbesteding nog maar nauwelijks te durven waarderen (Mechelen 1964:32).

> It is not surprising that there is some hesitation concerning the integration of leisure as a full element into our social existence. As an expression of this insufficient integration many express the justification of leisure as rational. How often do people explain away rest and holiday with reasoning: afterwards I will better work and achieve. As a value in itself not many seem to appreciate it.

He closed his discussion with recommendations to pay more attention to servants, laborers, and farmers, and further concluded that there was a need to do research on regular returning forms of leisure such as free weekends and holidays.

Urbain Claeys, who would later play a leading role in tourism policy and research in Belgium, was one of his research assistants at the time. Mechelen inspired several other young scientists who followed his interest in sports and animation, such as Livin Bollaert, who became professor in Brussels at the Free University and established leisure studies there within the Institute for Physical Education in 1970. The emphasis was on sports and leisure "agology." In 1971, Frans van Mechelen became Minister of Culture, which included responsibility for sports and youth policy. He stood at the very foundation of the Flemish Advice Council for Tourism. Later Mechelen returned as professor in Leuven and head of a study group for the advancement of culture. Claeys became the head of the Sociological Research Institute. At its peak, the institute employed some 20 research assistants. Between 1963 and 1990, the *West-Vlaams Economisch Studiebureau* (West-Flemish Economic Study Institute) carried out many surveys of tourism, particularly in the Belgian coastal areas (Vanhove 1973).

In the early 1980s, a state-of the-art appraisal of "social tourism" was the subject of a longitudinal research project by Hertogen and Naeyaert (1981). The occupancy of holiday homes was declining and the core of Flemish tourism policy was at stake. The social tourism concept was about to fail and become a problem again. Hertogen and Naeyaert undertook another object of study: nonparticipation. The idea and image of holiday resorts began to outlive their original social ideal. Later this turned for the better when the notion of social tourism changed into "tourism for all." According to most recent information (Geilen 2008; Smits and Claeys 2008), the heritage of social tourism has come to life again. The guests of the holiday resort reflect much more the typical average of the Belgian population. The vacation houses register full occupancy during the holidays. What was originally intended for the lower classes has become an acceptable provision for many people who want to spend an "economic" holiday. This opportunity is a growth market since Belgium as a whole has a low holiday participation rate (69% in 2004) compared to the Netherlands (81%, according to Geilen 2008:4). As Corijn later complained, academic research remained pragmatic, without paradigmatic discussions (1998:89, 93). There was hardly any critical, conceptual, or theoretical research, let alone a consistent scientific tradition. Positivist empiricism prevailed, linked to solving social problems. Social pedagogy or agology was not critical. Research lacked institutionalization and attention to the postmodern consumption of culture was entirely absent.

In the Netherlands, and directly after the war, there was a short lived revitalization of the pedagogical ideal, with a strong emphasis on educating the younger generation and offering holiday opportunities for less advantaged children (Beckers 1983a). In 1946, the sociologist Oldendorff undertook research into the conditions of leisure education, and some 14 years later co-authored a study of the reduction in working hours (Kuin and Oldendorff 1960). In 1947, The Central Organization for Youth and Holiday Making (with educational objectives) changed its name to The Camping Council. It began to imitate the British "Butlin's camps," which were still educational in purpose, albeit with a strong measure of social control. Soon a radical change in policy took place. Outdoor recreation became in 1965 a major policy domain of the new Ministry of Culture, Recreation, and Social Affairs.

As a consequence of the establishment of a Central Planning Service during the war, the orientation in national policy for leisure, recreation, and tourism soon shifted from education to spatial planning. Rapid urbanization, the restoration of the housing supply, and agricultural restructuring—all for taking care of the needs of the population—led to the creation of a large-scale infrastructure for day tourism or, in the terms of that time, "outdoor recreation." Recreation became the dominant title for policies related to sports, daytrips, and "overnight recreation" (this typical Dutch formulation—*verblijfsrecreatie*—is difficult to translate into English, but it is nonetheless "tourism"). The implication of bringing domestic tourism under one common policy category that it shared with outdoor recreation had the advantage that this policy was considered as clear, one-dimensional, and socially important. The underlying idea was that the state assumed responsibility for all citizens, providing what was needed on the basis of collective taxes. The emerging welfare state took this realm of civilian life as one of its core objectives. Free time was no longer a problem, but a collective concern for "self-development." This concept became an important policy objective in the 1970s, when the welfare state started to expand at a high rate.

During this period, mass recreation and tourism became important. From the early 1950s the ANWB argued strongly for "tourism for all" and for camping as an undertaking for the public and private sector. The Ministry of Economic Affairs supported these efforts with a Directorate of Tourism (1954) and subsidies for tourism infrastructure. At the same time, the Ministry of Education, Arts, and Sciences assumed a policy interest in leisure (education). A background ideology was strongly inspired by Karl Mannheim's idea of "planning for freedom" (Mannheim 1940). This concept supported the importance of active state intervention in social affairs in order to guarantee freedom of choice for the individual. This middle course between liberalism and socialism constituted the basis for a strong centralist recreation policy from 1950 until 1980 in the Netherlands. The then responsible Ministry of Education, Arts, and Sciences commissioned in 1954 the *Centraal Bureau voor de Statistiek* (National Office for Statistics) to conduct an empirical overview of free time activities and of holidaymaking (CBS 1954).

Before academic interest started to follow the foregoing political and social developments, private organizations began to enter into their discussions. The ANWB which survived the German occupation of the Second World War started to present itself more and more as a power alongside governmental institutions. In 1958, private organizations from different realms of leisure established the *Stichting Recreatie* (Recreation Foundation). This body positioned itself as a critical but constructive commentator on all the policies of the ministries which had any say on leisure opportunities in the Netherlands. The ANWB and the Recreation Foundation held conferences and think-tanks on every subject of leisure, recreation, and tourism (Stichting Recreatie 1983). Both groups produced their own journals, offering a platform for the exchange of knowledge between practitioners and academics.

In 1966, a new institute for the study of tourism, was founded—*Nederlands Wetenschappelijk Instituut voor Recreatie en Toerisme* (NWIT) (Dutch Scientific Institute for Recreation and Tourism)—which, since 1987, became known as the Dutch High School for Traffic and Tourism, NHTV,[4] a school with "neutral foundations," not related to any religious or political pillar in Dutch society (Koster 1985:486). This institute offered a program for vocational education. It was not a university, but a domain-specific specimen of the so-called Higher Economic and Administrative Education. Its curriculum acquired a subsidy from the Ministry of Education and Sciences. The research department was subsidized by the Ministry of Economic Affairs. In 1970, this research group became an independent institute—*Nederlands Research Instituut voor Toerisme en Recreatie* (NRIT) (The Dutch Institute of Tourism and Recreation Research). The institutional background of the different ministries of culture and welfare on the one hand, and economics on the other, illustrates a rising conceptual distinction between recreation (welfare, collective goods) and tourism (commercial, private enterprises). This point will be returned to later on.

In order to support a growing public interest in recreation as part of leisure and modern society, as a public and democratic "right," sociologists had started a substantial "program" of empirical research (Beijer 1967; Berting et al 1959; Heinemeyer 1959; Hessels 1973; Jolles 1957; Kerstens 1972). Hessels' work on *Vakantie en Vakantiebesteding sinds de Eeuwwisseling* (Holiday and Holiday-Making from the Beginning of the Century) was the most comprehensive study on tourism in the 1970s. In the meantime, after a period of dominance of geography as a descriptive discipline, paying attention to the diffuse phenomenon of free time and holidaymaking, many sociologists freeing themselves from empirical studies of the changes of postwar society, became theorists of social modernization. In 1967, sociology developed its own faculties with chair holders who gave a boost to the discipline. This development also resulted in more fundamental investigations of (the determinants of) leisure behavior (Blok-van der Voort 1977; Groffen 1967, 1970; Wippler 1968). The Ministry of Culture, Recreation and Social Work established a committee to attain greater theoretical depth in studies of free time (Have 1977), unfortunately with little effect. In 1977, Kamphorst and Withagen undertook a comprehensive "state-of-the-art" inventory of scientific publications (about 500 in all) on leisure over a period between 1935 and 1970. They concluded that most studies were scientifically superficial, with too much emphasis on spatial planning. In their later works (e.g., Withagen 1984), they proposed an alternative explanatory perspective of "socialization" and family lifestyles.

In 1976, the first structure was created for cooperation between scientific institutes engaged in the sociology of free time (including sports, media, recreation, tourism)—*Interuniversitair Werkverband Vrijetijd* (the Interuniversity Working Association on Free Time)—an association of 14 Dutch and Flemish institutes (Kamphorst 1982:5). Its aims were to promote academic discussions among scholars in the field, thus providing a structure for documentation and accommodation of exchange among institutes involved in the sociology of leisure. In 1982, this resulted in a journal *Vrijetijd en Samenleving* (Leisure and Society), with the Recreation Foundation assuming editorial responsibility for it, and featuring not only Dutch but also well-known English-speaking scholars (e.g., Urry 1991). This new scientific publication found a position next to the more professional periodicals: *Recreation* (Recreation Foundation) and *Recreatievoorzieningen, ANWB* (Recreation Provisions). Further, in 1982, the NWIT and the Polytechnic of Tilburg (later the Catholic University of Tilburg) jointly established a *Centrum voor Vrijetijdskunde* (Center of Leisure Studies). Its aim was to develop a scientific (predominantly sociological) course on leisure, to create a thesis track for leisure studies within the disciplinary programs of sociology and economics, and to engage in fundamental research into the broad phenomenon of leisure (Bijsterveldt 1983).

Toward Conceptual Specification and Institutionalization

Up to this point in the Netherlands, an interest in free time covered a widespread domain of sports, home-based leisure pursuits, day trips, and holidaymaking. All these activities were strongly connected to spatial policies in a country with limited land and disappearing spatial qualities due to population growth, urbanization, and agricultural reconstruction.

In Belgium, the emphasis on social tourism, sports, leisure education, and animation continued. In 1988, Claeys became head of the new *Vlaams Commissariaat voor Toerisme* (Flemish Commissariat for Tourism). Some 10 years later, it was transformed into *Toerisme Vlaanderen* (Tourism Flanders), an independent agency with the aims of supporting tourism, touristic recreation, leisure activities related to tourism, and to further professionalization of the sector. In addition to Tourism Flanders, and also in 1998, the Belgian government instituted the Flemish Council for Tourism. In a retrospective article on the geography of leisure, recreation, and tourism, Dietvorst and Jansen-Verbeke (1986:247) concluded that in the early 1980s there was hardly any scientific consensus on the very subject and definition of leisure. Recreation equalled leisure and tourism was regarded as a subset of recreation. In the early 20th century, tourism was the most common denominator, gradually changing into free time and leisure, with recreation as the most appealing concept because of its relationship to policies, at least in the Netherlands. Hekker (1983) suggested using only the word "recreation," considering tourism as an economic and commoditized variation of it. When tourism prevailed as a concept, scientific studies hardly existed. As sociology matured, it was the notion of leisure that gave direction to an integrated approach of its different manifestations, including tourism. Now conceptual discussions came to a zenith. The orientation became much more other-directed, as for example in the work of the Anglophone Jack Kelly (1987, 1990).

In the same period, discussions were shared with (particularly) British leisure scientists, such as Brian Bramwell, Mike Featherstone (1987), Ian Henry, Guy Jackson, and Alan Tomlinson (1981, 1986). The relationship originated from joint activities with the British Leisure Studies Association and the Center for Cultural Studies. Much theoretical inspiration came from the work of sociologists such as Anthony Giddens and later Scott Lash and John Urry. The discussions were embedded in meetings of the Interuniversity

Working Union on Free Time and publications in the previously mentioned scientific journal *Vrijetijd en Samenleving*—with Krijn van Bijsterveldt as the key player—in which Flemish researchers played a significant role, such as Livin Bollaert, Urbain Claeys, Marc Elchardus, Myriam Jansen Verbeke, Danny Naeyaert, Ronald Renson, Michelline Scheys, Sybille Van Hoof, and Bart Van Reusel. The Belgian center of gravity consisted of the universities of Brussels, Ghent, and Leuven. Urbain Claeys participated actively as the professor from Leuven in a post-academic course on leisure, an inter-academic joint venture of Leuven, Delft, Brussels, Wageningen, and Utrecht. In the Netherlands, the main centers were the Catholic University of Tilburg (Mommaas, Van der Poel), with an emphasis on leisure and work/time and involved in the Center for Leisure Studies (with Van Bijsterveldt), Utrecht University, related to leisure, family, and socialization (Kamphorst, Spruijt, and Withagen), the Agricultural University Wageningen (Beckers, Lengkeek, Van der Voet) with a main concern for outdoor recreation, and the Geographical and Planning Institute of Nijmegen University, with a particular interest in urban environments (Dietvorst, Jansen Verbeke).

Wageningen had its traditional link with land restructuring and land use for recreation. The Wageningen geographer/sociologist, Willem Hofstee, played an important role in social and demographic studies related to the radical changes which the Dutch landscapes were experiencing. Together with his colleague, Bijhouwer, of land use management, he acted as a catalyst for more systematic attention to countryside recreation in Wageningen. In 1976, he appointed Theo Beckers to the position of "recreation sociologist." Beckers started to play a key role in the growing scientific field of leisure, recreation, and tourism. His PhD thesis in 1983 elaborated on Mannheim's concept of planning for freedom. Its approach to recreation was "actor-centric," placing the emphasis of leisure phenomena on social individuals giving meaning to their own actions. A source of inspiration for him was the book *Leisure and Recreation Places* of Cheek et al (1976). These authors approached human beings not so much as facts and figures, but as intentionally acting persons who gave changing meanings to time-space related situations (Beckers and Mommaas 1991:227). Beckers found similar inspiration in Symbolic Interactionism and Phenomenology, for example as used by his Wageningen colleague Pennartz (1979). As Beckers (1979) put it:

> Bij de actorcentrische benadering staat niet de structuur van de samenleving central maar de mens, die zijn sociale situatie interpreteert en vanuit die interpretatie aktie onderneemt.

Voor de studie van de rekreatie zijn de volgende kenmerken van belang:

(a) Rekreatie is meer dan een konkrete handeling. Het is een beleving of ervaring van plezier, ontspanning, genoegen, in vrijheid gekozen, zonder extern doel. In deze visie is geen enkele aktiviteit rekreatief voor iedereen en kan anderzijds elke aktiviteit een rekreatieve betekenis hebben.

(b) Er wordt meer aandacht besteed aan het dynamische en integrale karakter van het rekreatiegedrag en aan de samenhang met andere levenssferen als arbeid en wonen. Het segmentalisme van de systeembenadering heeft plaats gemaakt voor het holisme.

(c) Onderzoek en planning richten onder andere hun aandacht op de vraag hoe sociale groepen bepaalde ruimten als rekreatie definiëren. Er wordt minder gedacht aan totale milieu's. Het rekreatiebeleid wordt duidelijker een welzijnsbeleid.

(d) Dat aan kwaliteit meer waarde wordt gehecht dan aan kwantiteit blijkt ook uit de wijze van onderzoek: observaties, case-studies, experimenten' (1979:2–2, 2–3).

The actor-centric approach does not focus on the structure of society but on the human individual who interprets his situation and takes action from this interpretation. For the study of recreation the following characteristics prevail:

(a) Recreation is more than a concrete action. It is the perception of the experience of pleasure, relaxation, feeling good, chosen in freedom, without an external goal. In this perspective no action is recreational for everybody and, on the other hand, each action can have a recreational meaning.

(b) More attention is paid to the dynamic and integrated character of recreational behavior and to the connection with other life spheres such as work and living. Segmentation from the systems approach makes way for holism.

(c) Research and planning aim at the question of how social groupings define certain spaces as recreational. Less attention is given to total environments. Recreation policy becomes more a policy for wellbeing.

(d) More emphasis on quality than on quantity appears from the research approach: observations, case-studies, experiments.

Due to his inspiration, in 1985, an Interdisciplinary Recreation Working Group in Wageningen initiated an integrated course on recreation in which an ecologist, economist, sociologist, psychologist, a planner, and landscape architects participated. The group, with Jaap Lengkeek as scientific coordinator, started with a specialization in recreation which was embedded in several disciplinary programs and a research program called "Recreation in a Changing Society." In Nijmegen, in the Department of Geography and Planning, Adri Dietvorst and Myriam Jansen Verbeke worked on tourism from a geographical perspective. Their objective was mainly urban tourism. Jansen Verbeke, a Belgian, studied geography in Leuven. She submitted a PhD thesis (1988) on leisure, recreation, and tourism in inner cities. In 1990 she published a study on tourism in the inner city of Bruges, Belgium (Jansen-Verbeke 1990). The focus there was not so much on the tourist as on the tourism system, its spatial locus, and the management of the tourism product.

From his adopted home in the northern Netherlands, Gregory Ashworth, a British geographer coming from the University of Portsmouth, worked from 1977 at the Geographical Institute of Groningen University. He published on marketing in the tourism industry, tourism and the local economy in India, and impacts of tourism development on disadvantaged regions. However, his main focus became tourism in historic cities (Ashworth 1984; Ashworth and de Haan 1986; Ashworth and Tunbridge 1990), and most recently he has directed his attention to dark tourism and sites of atrocity. In 1994, he accepted a position as Professor of Heritage Management and Urban Tourism in the Department of Planning at the Rijksuniversiteit Groningen (Ashworth 1994).

Between Dutch anthropologists and tourism scholars, no cordial relationship developed until a few years ago. An expression of this rare ecumenism was the article written by the anthropologist Jan Abbink, "Anthropologists are no Tourists" (1995). According to him, tourists spoiled the exotic world. Anthropologists (at least the Dutch variety) left it intact. No other interest in tourism came from the anthropology departments in the Netherlands, with one notable exception. Jeremy Boissevain, who held a chair in anthropology in Amsterdam, showed active interest, publishing and supervising students' theses on the subject (1986,

1996). The explanation of his position seems to have stemmed from his personal situation. Part of his time he lived in Malta, where he observed the growing impact of mass tourism. In 1992, he organized a workshop in Prague for the European Association of Social Anthropologists on "European Reactions to the Tourist Gaze." The contributions to the workshop resulted in a well-received book *Coping with Tourists*, which appeared in 1996 under his editorship.

Where other academic institutes developed their expertise on leisure, recreation, and tourism, the group in Utrecht lost most of their relationship with the subject when Kamphorst left the university in 1990. In Tilburg, the Center for Leisure Studies developed into an active academic department with its first full study program in Leisure Sciences. In 1988, Beckers moved from Wageningen to Tilburg, where he became the first professor in this new realm of social studies. In 1997, he managed to create another chair in Tilburg (Leisure Sciences), in particular the sociocultural and socioeconomic aspects of leisure. The position was taken up by Wim Knulst, a sociologist who worked for many years at the National Social and Cultural Planning Institute. To complete the professorial team, the Belgian sociologist Paul de Knop received an endowed professorship in "didactics and policy aspects of physical education and sports in the Netherlands." He combined this function with his position as professor at the Free University of Brussels, in sports policy and management, where he explicitly linked sports to tourism. Initially the whole team of professors and staff covered a broad area, including tourism, with such researchers as Heidi Dahles (anthropology of leisure) (1990) and Greg Richards (cultural tourism) (1996). Later this special area of attention disappeared, when these people left Tilburg. Mommaas who, years later, succeeded Beckers as professor, shifted the emphasis to urban culture and the (predominantly) leisure and experience economy (Pine and Gilmore 1999).

When Beckers left Wageningen, that university installed a part-time professorship in recreation studies, taken up by Dietvorst in 1989. The working group on recreation became gradually transformed into a small department of its own, establishing a stronger foothold in the Agricultural University. Inspired by the publications of such Anglophones as Graham Dann, Nelson Graburn, and Dean MacCannell, as well as the Israeli scholar Erik Cohen (who wrote mostly in English), academics who founded separate theoretical approaches to tourism from sociological and anthropological perspectives, Lengkeek started a course on the sociological aspects of tourism, within the specialization of recreation studies in Wageningen. René van der Duim, who was lecturer at the NHTV was appointed in

Wageningen, in order to further develop the field of international sustainable tourism. He was also one of the first to apply Actor Network Theory to tourism (2005). Meanwhile, Dietvorst expanded the field of recreation with a more general geographical approach to landscape transformations. The title of his professorship changed into Sociospatial Analysis, with special reference to recreation and tourism.

The Belgian and Dutch worlds of tourism studies came together in 1990, in a joint Master's Degree in Leisure and Tourism, supported by an international association, the *Homo Ludens* Network. The initiators were Adri Dietvorst from Wageningen and Willy Faché, professor at the Center for Leisure Agology in Ghent. The international master program was sponsored by the EU Erasmus program and included, apart from Ghent and Wageningen, several participating European institutes.[5] In order to explore the possibilities of this Master's, Faché had approached 21 European universities in nine countries. The program offered three tracks: leisure and tourism policy, leisure and tourism management, and animation and education in leisure and tourism. The curriculum was innovative in the sense that is had an international subject, with an international comparative approach, interdisciplinary, and methodologically advanced with problem-directed projects and teamwork. The idea was to transform the cooperation between the originally 28 participating universities to four leading institutes. Although the interest from institutes was overwhelming, the program ceased in 1994, because the Erasmus office decided to limit the subsidies to student mobility only (for a comprehensive overview, see Faché 2000).

Another cross border initiative was the establishment of the Erasmus Leisure Studies Group in 1991. The main promoter of this was the Department of Leisure Studies of Tilburg. Initially, this network consisted of 12 European institutes, among which were Leisure Studies at Brussels University, Wageningen Agricultural University, and the Polytechnic of Higher Education *Christelijke Hogeschool Noord-Nederland* (CHN) (Christian High School of the North Netherlands) in Leeuwarden, Netherlands. The latter offered a new graduate program Leisure Studies since 1988, with a course on Recreation and Tourism. The Erasmus Leisure Studies Group annually organized between 1991 (in Brussels) and 1995 a so-called international Winter University for European students. The main emphasis was on leisure studies, with only marginal attention being paid to tourism. In 1993, the tendency to give greater recognition to tourism studies resulted in a joint PhD program of Tilburg (Beckers), Wageningen (Dietvorst), Rotterdam (Jansen Verbeke), and Eindhoven (Timmermans, Urban Planning Group of the Eindhoven University of Technology). The program FUTRO stood for fundamental research into tourism and recreation. Many years later a group of students graduated with PhD theses within this wide realm of tourism and recreation.

In 1994, Myriam Jansen Verbeke was appointed endowed professor in Rotterdam, a chair in tourism management sponsored by large tourist agencies and the Dutch national airline, KLM. The emphasis in her work remained on urban contexts, but expanded to include tourism and cultural heritage. When the temporary chair expired, it was reinstituted and taken over by Frank Go, a specialist in tourism marketing. Jansen Verbeke returned to Belgium and the Catholic University of Leuven, remaining very active in international networks of tourism, particularly with respect to management and heritage. In Wallonia, interest in tourism developed far more sporadically than in Flanders. At the University of Liège, the Laboratory of Anthropology of Communication promoted cooperation with Asian countries on exchange in the area of heritage tourism. Here Tomke Lask was the main researcher in tourism.

In 1990, Teus Kamphorst left the University of Utrecht and started to dedicate himself to the development of an international educational program on leisure. As a board member of World Leisure and Recreation Association (WLRA), he embedded this initiative within that organization, designing a network of WLRA scientists of high quality to teach in the new program. The curriculum was based in the previously mentioned *Christelijke Hogeschool Noord-Nederland*, and received the status of MA program. The courses started in 1992 with 25 students coming from 23 countries and featured a number of well-known experts in leisure and tourism who visited in teams of two for a week at a time. However, a problem was that international students preferred to receive a diploma that was not just accredited by the CHN, but by the Dutch Government, one of the reasons to look for a home at one of the academic universities. In 1996, an agreement was signed between WLRA, later called "World Leisure" and Wageningen University to jointly operate World Leisure's International Center of Excellence (WICE) and to run an international Master of Science Program called "Leisure and Environments." Wageningen could grant a Master of Science degree.

Specialized Curricula

In 2002, important transformations took place in the Dutch national structure and legislation for higher education. One major change was the adoption of the Anglo-Saxon Bachelor/Master system. An agreement was made to bring together the WICE program and the Wageningen specialization in recreation and tourism in a single Master program: Leisure, Tourism, and the Environment. The integration implied a stronger emphasis on tourism and sociospatial conditions, while the very broad approach in the original WICE program became more focused, removing general leisure issues such as media and sports. In 2002, Jaap Lengkeek was appointed to the Wageningen chair in Sociospatial Analysis and became responsible for the teaching section of the curriculum. The model of inviting international visiting professors was continued, but the expertise was much more focused on tourism. The role of the Wageningen staff determined the structure and content of the courses.

The Wageningen curriculum currently extends over two years. The first year offers courses in fundamental concepts and approaches, experiences in leisure and tourism, the role of tourism in globalization, and sustainable tourism development. The program additionally provides a course in advanced methods and techniques. The second year consists of an internship and a large thesis project. Directly linked to the educational program, a research program exists with a threefold emphasis on the relationships between tourism, nature development and poverty reduction, tourism and heritage, and tourism and governance. Paradigmatically, there is no strict favoring of any given sociological perspective, but most of the teaching and research revolves around critical theory, phenomenology, and actor-network approaches. Closely connected are historical geography, rural sociology, and environmental psychology, which are not specifically limited to tourism. The courses are all in English, students come from all over the world and the visiting faculty represent a corps of outstanding international scientists.

For some years, the more scientific approaches of tourism in Belgium were to be found in the so-called post-academic "Specialized Complementary Studies" in Antwerp. However, their work was superseded by an initiative undertaken in 2000 by The Flemish Council of Tourism chaired by Myriam Jansen Verbeke. It recommended that the universities and institutes of professional higher education be brought together in a new curriculum "Master in Tourism." The Council started its advice with the words:

> Volgens de internationale normen heeft Vlaanderen een achterstand op het niveau van een coherent en interdisciplinair academische onderwijsaanbod. Het onderwerp "Toerisme" komt alleen in de bestaande universitaire onderwijsprogramma's versnipperd aan bod en is in Vlaanderen onbestaand als hoofdstroom, als specialisatie of als "herkenbaar" universitair diploma (Vlaamse Raad 2000:3).

> According to international standards Flanders is lagging behind on the level of coherence and the supply of interdisciplinary academic education. The subject of tourism receives only an outside chance in existing university programs in a fragmented way, and as a mainstream, specialization or diploma it is non-existent.

This initiative of the Flemish Council of Tourism required an enormous effort in unifying nine different institutes (three universities and six polytechnics) under one umbrella.[6,7] Cooperation between academic and higher education institutes was exceptional, because, according to government regulations, the standard of cooperative curricula had to be academic. The one-year program started in 2004 with provisional official accreditation. In 2007, it received its definitive accredited status. The program covered the structure of the industry, the significance of tourism, its international context and developments, and the multidisciplinary nature of tourism studies. According to Belgian legal regulation, but despite its international orientation, the language used in the curriculum was Dutch.

Another recent development is the multiplication in the Netherlands of professional institutes of higher education with programs in leisure and tourism. Apart from NHTV in Breda (formerly the NWIT, now presenting itself as a professional university) and the CHN in Leeuwarden, many more have appeared in the last decade. Some of them, the NHTV in particular, have outspoken ambitions to strengthen their international orientation and to develop into an academic university. The NHTV offers an applied bachelor in tourism, a management bachelor, and an international bachelor. At the master level, the institute offers MAs in International Destination Management, in Imagineering, and in European Tourism Management, which are offered in five European universities/polytechnics and accredited in the United Kingdom.[8] In 2008, Wageningen University and the NHTV agreed to develop a first academic BSc Tourism Sciences, and aim to start it in 2009.

CONCLUSION

This overview of tourism knowledge development in Belgium and the Netherlands has covered almost a century. It is only in the last two decades that tourism as an academic field appeared from under the covers of leisure and recreation studies. In both countries tourism knowledge was tightly connected to policy and practice. The Belgian authorities displayed a somewhat patronizing attitude toward tourism, from a socialist and Catholic moral standpoint, as expressed in the so-called social tourism, which still can be recognized today. The knowledge needed was practical and applied, and, as far as theory was concerned, with an emphasis on pedagogy, sports, and leisure. Recently a more integrated approach toward tourism has been adopted, linking different kinds of tourism, such as coastal, rural, urban, and heritage tourism, as well as tourism geography and management.

In the Netherlands, more so than in Belgium, tourism was predominantly a concern of the tourism industry, comprising a few large companies, but mainly small entrepreneurs. No Ministry or Minister of Tourism existed. State policy toward tourism coming from the Ministry of Economic Affairs was in fact neo-liberal, supporting and stimulating where necessary, but leaving tourism development to the private sector. The industry never appeared to be in need or in favor of fundamental knowledge. A strong state intervention from the ministries of welfare and of spatial planning for many years was concerned with outdoor recreation, sports, and media. This no doubt explains why tourism as a commercial and spatial phenomenon was hidden behind recreation in academic and higher educational institutes.

For a long time, and in both countries, leisure studies constituted the common denominator for the approaches of leisure, recreation, sports, media, and tourism. In Belgium and in the Netherlands, tourism is a young academic field. Interestingly, it expands from industry-related approaches to multi- or interdisciplinary scientific analysis and assessment as a major agent of change (Theuns 1984). Because of its many facets, it is impossible to credit this phenomenon only to sociology, although its manifold relevance draws it out of the realm of economics (cf. Vanhove 2005) and management into the wider realm of the social sciences. In this respect, the developments reflect the observations made by Tribe, who portrayed tourism studies as an "in-discipline" (1997, 2005), without a disciplinary body of knowledge of its own. Tourism knowledge derives its concepts, theories, and paradigms from different disciplines, benefiting from the contributions of researchers from varying backgrounds, including many sociologists.

Another recent development is the international orientation in tourism studies in both countries. In Wageningen, this seems only natural. When Wageningen University was still an agricultural university, its expertise on food production and international development spread all over the world. Students came from everywhere. The Master in Leisure, Tourism, and Environment follows this open tradition. With a strong emphasis on interpretative/critical theories and a crosscultural approach (Ateljevic et al 2007;

Lengkeek and Swain-Byrne 2006), prospects look bright for the development of the interpretative sociology of tourism in the years ahead. The Master in Tourism in Belgium, with a curriculum in Dutch, has a somewhat longer way to go, but is building up its integrated and international expertise rapidly.

NOTES

1. The author would like to thank Urbain Claeys, Rik de Keyser, Myriam Jansen Verbeke, Diane Nijs, and Dominique Vanneste for introducing him to and correcting him on the history of Belgian tourism studies.
2. The ANWB still exists as the largest voluntary and semipublic tourist organization of the Netherlands, with more than 3 million members.
3. The Belgian connection ended in 1920, after the First World War, and the organization changed its name to the Koninklijk Nederlands Watersport Verbond (Royal Dutch Water Sports Union).
4. In 1987 the NWIT merged with Academy of Traffic, Tilburg. The name changed into NHTV (Dutch Polytechnic of Tourism and Traffic).
5. Differing over the years and including among others: Department of Leisure Management Cheltenham, Deutsche Sporthochschule Köln, Manchester Polytechnic, Scuola Superiore del Commercio, del Turismo e dei Servizi, Milano, Sheffield University, Università di Roma La Sapienza, Universitat Autónoma de Barcelona, Universität Hamburg, Université Aix-Marseille II, Université François Rabelais Tours, Université Joseph Fourier Grenoble, Université Paris V, Université René Descartes Sorbonne, University of Modena, University of Surrey, and University of Wales at Cardiff.
6. The professional schools for higher education (Hogescholen) are indicated here as polytechnics.
7. Involved are: Catholic Polytechnic Bruges-Ostende, Catholic Polytechnic Mechelen, Catholic University Leuven, Erasmus Polytechnic Brussels, Free University Brussels, Plantijn Polytechnic Antwerp, Polytechnic West Flanders, University Ghent, and XIOS Polytechnic Limburg.
8. Bournemouth University, UK; Fachhochschule Heilbronn, Germany; Högskolan Dalarnay, Falun/Borlänge, Sweden; Universidad Rey Juan Carlos, Madrid, Spain; and Université de Savoie, Chambéry, France.

Chapter 10

The Sociology and Anthropology of Tourism in Greece

Paris Tsartas
University of the Aegean, Greece

Vasiliki Galani-Moutafi
University of the Aegean, Greece

INTRODUCTION

Though Greece plays host to millions of tourists, until recently the indigenous academic community has not treated tourism as a major research field within the social sciences. Several reasons explain this delay in orientation. Initially, the disciplines of sociology and anthropology lacked a presence in universities and research centers. This situation gradually started to change in the 1970s, and especially the 1980s, with the establishment of university departments in these disciplines at the Panteion University and the University of the Aegean. However, research in these disciplines concentrated in other areas of investigation, such as the exploration of social change, the characteristics and composition of social structure, political sociology, the sociology of education, social mobility, etc. This trend was reflected in the publications of the Εθνικό Κέντρο Κοινωνικών Ερευνών (EKKE) (The National Center for Social Research) (NCSR) founded in the 1950s. Generally, there was much skepticism on the part of Greek social scientists as to whether tourism constituted a "social phenomenon" worthy of research. Nevertheless, a

The Sociology of Tourism: European Origins and Developments
Tourism Social Science Series, Volume 12, 299–322
Copyright © 2009 by Emerald Group Publishing Limited
ISSN: 1571-5043/doi:10.1108/S1571-5043(2009)0000012015

number of constructive criticisms were expressed by "traditional" social scientists with backgrounds in agricultural sociology and educational or political sociology, who understood that tourism was a complex phenomenon requiring approaches based on multidisciplinary perspectives. Since the 1980s, there was an increasing interest on the part of state agencies and researchers in changes resulting from the growth of tourism on social and economic structures, as well as on the cultural life and value system of local communities. Parallel to this development, the emergence in other European countries of specialized studies and scientific publications dealing with tourism in sociology and anthropology was another critical factor orienting Greek academia positively.

The first publications on tourism by social scientists appeared in the early 1970s and, as the two relevant disciplines became established in the academic environment, production became more systematic. However, this trend was a result primarily of other causes such as the rapid development of mass tourism in the country's "traditional" coastal areas and island destinations, thereby stimulating an interest in tourism as a factor contributing to important modifications in social structure, family practices, and the organization of everyday life. A recognition of these new conditions led Kousis, Moutafi, and Tsartas in the context of conducting research for their doctoral theses, to analyze tourism-related socioeconomic changes in host communities.

Over the years, the course followed by the anthropology of tourism in Greece initially converged with but later diverged from the sociology of tourism. Although tourism, as a subject, appeared in the curricula of three university departments and attracted the interest of a few scholars, it was nevertheless regarded as a "peripheral" subject. Instead of being approached as a specialized field, it was studied as a phenomenon the analysis of which could be subsumed within, and enhance or modify the investigation of subjects such as socioeconomic transformation, gender, identity, tradition, sociality, and culture. Most of the early studies emanated from doctoral dissertations, followed by publications in English and/or Greek, while practically no works were produced as part of programs carried out at research centers. Whereas earlier anthropological investigations of tourism tended to bridge the gap and minimize the distance that separated the discipline from sociology—through methodological and analytical perspectives—increasingly this effort was abandoned. Nowadays, anthropologists whose research in Greece focuses on issues related to tourism tend to find more common ground with scholars from fields such as cultural and economic geography, architecture, and cultural and media studies. What accounts for this shift are epistemological changes in the discipline at large marked by post-structuralism as well as the paradigms of feminism, postcolonialism, and cultural criticism. In addition, the heavy reliance of ethnographic practice on qualitative methods, which provide a deep understanding of realities at the micro-level (including the construction of subjectivities), coupled with the absence of an applied orientation, account for the divergence in the approaches of the two disciplines.

Ethnographic research in Greece spans approximately half a century and has occupied three successive generations of anthropologists, both foreign and indigenous. The study of gender, kinship, and domestic realities in rural communities has dominated the production of anthropological knowledge before and after the discipline's institutional recognition and establishment within the national academic structure. Furthermore, the adoption of an historical orientation has enabled anthropologists to build a constructive dialog with historians in analyzing processes of social and economic transformation. In view of this orientation, representations of the past as well as social memory and "tradition" have been key issues examined in the context of processes related to the negotiation of identity. Since the decade of the 1990s, there has been a growing interest in the production and negotiation of cultural and social "otherness" within Greek society and ethnography. It is particularly in the context of this interest that the anthropology of tourism has developed.

This fascination with alterity has been stimulated by the drastic, macro-level changes and challenges accompanying large waves of immigrants and refugees settling temporarily or permanently in the country; the escalating interpenetration of national and local borders; political developments in the Balkans rekindling nationalist (ideological) claims; as well as the intensification of institutional developments associated with European unification in the post-Maastricht era, which testifies to the restructuring of the world system in the direction of growing globalization. In view of these developments, issues related to identity, cultural otherness, Europeanization, globalization, and consumption, as well as new methodological challenges, which can be met by the approach of multi-sited ethnography, draw increasing attention to and bring tourism into the realm of anthropological questioning.

In preparing this account, anthropology was included because related research in the country has contributed to tourism theory from the point of view of analytical issues—such as gender, identity, entrepreneurship, tourism representations, and tradition—that are at the forefront of debates both within the discipline and tourism studies. The following overview of investigations falling within the sociology and anthropology of tourism in Greece seeks to conform to the parameters set by this volume. The framework for this chapter is constructed by two considerations. First, works of Greek and non-Greek sociologists and anthropologists are presented as well as inquiries of scholars from related social science disciplines that facilitate (empirically and theoretically) a dialog with the two disciplines. Second, references are made to research, which is published in Greek or in other languages in scientific journals, conference proceedings, or refereed collective volumes. Additional reference is made to published and unpublished doctoral dissertation theses.

SOCIOECONOMIC CHANGES, TOURISM, AND RESEARCH

Empirical research on the sociology and anthropology of tourism in Greece closely followed European and international studies dealing with its social and economic effects. Overall, what characterized this research was the frequent use of destination case studies; many of these places (such as islands and seaside areas) had been locations for fieldwork in earlier and more recent investigations. Indeed, tourism hotspots constituted "ideal" field sites since rapid changes and cultural developments allowed a comparative and holistic approach for the period from 1970 to the present.

Among some early works, those of Kalfiotis (1976) and Lekkas (1925 [1996]) are worth commenting upon; others tend to be descriptive and have little scientific value. Lekkas was the first director of the Office for Foreigners and Fairs, established in 1914 in order to attract foreigners to visit the country, and his work basically contained a series of ideas and proposals concerning the organization and necessary regulations of the tourism phenomenon. He argued that tourism policy could be organically integrated into the country's overall economic and social development since it combined all the relevance and intervening processes of both the public and private sectors. He also proposed the establishment of an Administrative Council of the Office for Foreigners and Fairs, as a regulatory organ that would have included *ex officio* all the state agencies representing the ministries, which had co-jurisdiction for solving the problems of tourism. From a different perspective, Kalfiotis argued that once tourism was conceptualized as a social and economic phenomenon, it should have been recognized that tourist needs and tourism products were constantly changing. Following his proposals, these needs and products constituting the driving force and the means of tourism have been evolving throughout the years. Both tourism demand and supply have adjusted to meet the requirements of the society they serve.

The earliest scientific research on tourism was conducted by Lambiri-Dimaki (1972) and Stott (1973) on the island of Mykonos. Both investigations relied on specific types of samples in order to trace the economic and social influences of tourism. Conducting questionnaire-based research principally with heads of households, the former gathered data concerning their way of life, attitudes, and social values. Her research documented for the period 1961–1971 a transition from the social positions of farmer and laborer to that of small entrepreneur, as well as a rise in the economic and occupational hierarchy for most social groups. These changes for Lambiri-Dimaki indicated that Mykonos' social structure had started to undergo a process of "urbanization." As for the role of tourism in shaping the younger generation's value system, the responses of the students attending the three-grade gymnasium of Mykonos, whom she interviewed, revealed an interest in higher education, social mobility, and urban living.

Stott (1973) focused her analysis on the changes affecting women's position and family strategies in the "urbanized" economic and social structure of Mykonos. Concurrently, she compared the post-tourism reality with what she reconstructed as the "traditional" pre-tourism structures and approached the subject of socioeconomic transformation through the structural-functional perspective (Stott 1973, 1979, 1985). She stated that in the post-tourism society and economy of Mykonos the nuclear family had lost many of its "traditional" crucial functions: providing a dowry, supervising the behavior of single women, making instrumental marriage arrangements, and maximizing the chances of young women in contracting good marriages. Since these young women could earn income and contribute to their own dowries, the family's role in contracting marriage agreements had declined. Furthermore, with tourism development, accessibility to the means of status mobility had increased and a social ranking system had emerged characterized by fluidity and relativity. However, Stott argued that these social changes could be attributed as much to developments in broader Greek society as to contacts with foreigners through tourism.

From 1979 to 1986 Stavrou carried out another study on behalf of the Ελληνικό Οργανισμό Τουρισμού (EOT) (Greek National Tourism Organization) on the social awareness of tourism in different clusters of Greek islands: Mykonos-Naxos (1979), Kalymnos-Leros (1980), and Paros-Santorini-Kithira (1986). Despite its descriptive nature and limited scientific quality, this study provided the first in-depth social and economic analysis of the influences of tourism on destination areas. The basic conclusion drawn was similar to that of other European and international inquiries, indicating that local residents' views tended to be ambiguous: positive as far as economic benefits were concerned and negative or skeptical regarding tourism's social effects.

In the mid-1980s, following international scientific and research orientations, the first investigations were carried out within the sociology of tourism. Initially, Tsartas (1989) in his doctoral thesis, based on field research on the islands of Ios and Serifos in 1982, focused on their stages of tourism development and traced their influences on various social changes. The establishment of a "tourism scientific team" under his direction led, in 1987, to the launching of an extensive research project, supported by governmental and European research funds, concerning the social aspects of tourism development for the 1988–2000 period. Under the aegis of EKKE [NCSR] 2 (Tsartas et al 1995), it was the first interdisciplinary study dealing with the social influences of tourism in the prefectures of Corfu and Lasithi, Crete— areas which had reached different stages of tourism development. Besides the overall aggregate social study, more focused ancillary research concentrated on the effects of tourism in domains such as public health, specific social groups (teenagers and women), and the environment (new-building architecture and land use planning). A few years later, the same domains were explored to assess trends toward mass tourism and its influences, as well as local residents' skepticism concerning this path of tourism development.

The subject of tourism-related economic transformation and family change was also examined by Kousis (1985, 1989) from a diachronic perspective. She argued that the development of mass tourism in the rural community of Drethia (Crete) stimulated a process of proletarianization, which began in the 1960s. In the initial stage of development, changes in land ownership resulted in the loss of a significant part of the subsistence base for many local families, who turned to wage employment. During the period of full-scale tourism, the greatest portion of profits went to outside investors who owned the largest and most expensive hotels. In the early 1980s, the community's occupational structure was characterized by an increase in the labor supply of wage earners who lacked control over the means of production. Regarding social change, Kousis noted that endogamy patterns became modified, but the influence of family control, the importance of marital arrangements, and the dowry did not lose the significance which they had enjoyed prior to tourism.

A more dynamic perspective that revealed conflict-ridden processes was adopted by Kenna (1993) who examined tourism development in the context of transformations affecting both the island of Anafi and its repatriated urban migrants. Her research revealed that, over a period of two decades, seasonally or permanently returning migrants made use of their urban experiences and investment capital, and took advantage of their local kinship networks and island contacts to assume the ownership and management of the majority of Anafi's tourism-related enterprises. Furthermore, these repatriated migrants, because of their active role in local politics, often found themselves in conflict over development plans with long-term residents and other urban-based migrants.

Since the task of attributing changes to tourism required an historical approach that could highlight complex processes linking local communities with extra-local entities and forces, a reconstruction of a community's pre-tourism economic, social, and cultural structure was required. Thus, Zarkia (1996) reconstructed Skyros' pre-tourism social structure and argued that tourism had contributed (along with rural depopulation, urbanization, and the dissolution of the landowning families) to the transformation of the island's social strata. The poorest stratum benefited initially from tourism because it owned fields bordering the coastline (considered previously as the least productive land). With the development of tourism, the value of these fields multiplied many times and their owners managed to improve their position economically and socially.

The social influences of tourism constituted the subject of a study conducted by Haralambopoulos and Pizam (1996) who deployed empirical research on the island of Samos to investigate how local residents assessed changes in social and production structures. Another inquiry, in the prefecture of Rethymno, based on research carried out by Papadaki-Tzedaki (1999) for her doctoral dissertation, examined the wider influences of tourism on productive processes, particularly changes brought about by tourism development in the employment market. In his doctoral thesis (2000b) and in a paper with Vaughan (2003), Andriotis also investigated the influence of mass tourism development on Crete (Andriotis 2000a, 2001), but from the perspective of different sample groups and members of the tourism industry. Moreover, he emphasized the need for analyzing the role of local stakeholders and their relationship to tour operators. Further, Pappas (2006) studied the wider social, economic, and land use changes resulting from the development of mass tourism in the city of Rhodes over a 50-year period. In particular, Pappas traced the intervention of local interest groups in the design of policy and its implementation.

Social and Structural Change

Several researchers examined the issue of social mobility in the context of economic changes associated with tourism. Bidgianis (1979), after surveying the changes emanating from the construction of the Porto-Caras complex in Chalkidiki, sketched the profile of a new, vigorous, "bourgeois" peasant who had access to three income sources: as an employee in tourism (apart from engaging in agricultural activities or in the construction industry); as a wage earner in the room-to-let business or an owner of rental accommodation; or as a trade-oriented businessman. The issue of mobility particularly preoccupied sociologists, as Zagkotsi's doctoral dissertation thesis (2007) testified. Via empirical surveys, this work examined the question of social, geographical, and professional mobility in two communities in Chalkidiki, focusing on the crucial role of tourism as a medium of wider changes in social and productive structures. In the "urbanized" environment of these communities, Zagkotsi located various patterns of horizontal and vertical social and professional mobility.

An EKKE [NCSR] survey conducted on Corfu (Aghios Mathaios) in 1988 and authored by Tsartas (1991) documented the social and economic mobility patterns in the agricultural sector and shed light on new social and productive arrangements springing from the local farmers' multi-activity. Of two additional surveys carried out by the EKKE [NCSR], one (Tsartas et al 1995) aimed toward a comparative investigation of two prefectures with varied levels of tourism development in order to discern differences and similarities in changes occurring in local residents' attitudes and perceptions, the position of women in the new social structure, the reactions and practices of the youth, patterns of social mobility, and the like. In the other survey, which was part of an international research program (Manologlou et al 1999), the areas chosen on account of their different levels of growth were Nea Moudania and the community of Dionysos in Chalkidiki (as experimental sites) and Lavrio, an industrial region (as a control area). The study investigated attitudes concerning the protection of the environment, cultural heritage, and the family, as well as the cultural perceptions and patterns of sociability affected by tourism. Professional and social mobility, in conjunction with the prevalence of multi-activity among the rural population of Chalkidiki was also examined by Iakovidou (1991). The latter documented differences in the gender distribution of different types of employment within the tourism industry, particularly in the hotel industry where segregation between male and female employment was a common practice.

The comparative study undertaken on behalf of the *Κέντρο Κοινωνικής Μορφολογίας και Κοινωνικής Πολιτικής* (ΚΕΚΜΟΚΟΠ) (Center of Social Morphology and Social Policy) by Kassimati et al (1995) explored the characteristics of women's tourism employment in three areas of Greece, each with a distinct type of development: Athens, Arachova, and Delphi, as well as Rhodes. Documenting the low position of women in all branches of tourism, the study highlighted the following factors which accounted for such status: women's occasional and erratic employment; the tourism policy's drawbacks in the areas of education and women's employment; the parallel presence of a formal and an informal employment market, each structured on the basis of inequalities at the expense of women; the family inhibiting women's choices regarding education and professional career; and the social biases and stereotypes surrounding gender roles, which were reflected in the entrepreneurs' hiring practices and choices concerning personnel advancement. Thanopoulou (2003) also focused on female employees, concentrating on issues of wages, labor problems, occupational mobility, and the special characteristics of their employment "positions," especially in the hotel business.

Changes in the family associated with the growth of tourism was a theme on which Kousis focused, drawing from her research in the rural community of Drethia, Crete (1985, 1989) referred to earlier. More specifically, she examined family strategies in relation to tourism, changes in the role of women, professional mobility patterns, the processes of urbanization and modernization, and attitudes toward and perceptions of tourism, especially as they related to repercussions on social life. On the other hand, Galani-Moutafi's research on Samos (1993, 1994, 1996), apart from treating within a wider frame and through a historical perspective the social and cultural processes of transformation associated with tourism, documented women's strategies and perceptions of their tourism-related employment—the ways they practically and conceptually incorporated such work both into their daily family lives and their project of self-construction. Despite the dominance of family enterprises within the tourism industry, the central issue of the "family and tourism enterprise" had only been approached tangentially. For this reason, Nazou's doctoral dissertation (2003) set a precedent for future research on the subject, especially since it drew from extensive ethnographic research on Mykonos. She explored the views and practices of families with a tourism business (in the hotel sector) in order to investigate the gendered nature of entrepreneurial identity. More specifically, Nazou analytically approached women's work experiences in association with domesticity, as well as male qualities or characteristics of entrepreneurial identity. Her interpretive approach also led her to examine self-perception of younger members of families in relation to the mixed pattern of family/enterprise.

Gender Relations, Ideology, Sexuality, and Consumption

With a shift toward a post-structuralist paradigm, the recognition of the structure-action dialectic, which acknowledged individuals as actors, and the constructivist approach to identity, issues related to the cultural construction of gender, gender relations, and ideologies of sexuality emerged in several anthropological works. One such approach was pursued by Galani-Moutafi (1993, 1994) in her analysis of the transition from agriculture to tourism in the village of Kokkari on Samos. Tracing shifts in property and labor in terms of their implications for gender and kinship, she documented a change of emphasis from the patrilateral to the matrilateral kinship organization. She found that this was associated with a decline in the system of agricultural land ownership in the village prior to the advent of tourism and men's involvement in economic pursuits for which male kinship did not function as an organizational principle for the achievement of cooperation in work tasks.

Prior to its decline, the agricultural system in Kokkari had given prominence to men as the principal actors in kinship practices and had strengthened the agnatic type in a structural sense. In the post-tourism period, women's tourism-related economic activities and their dowry-mediated relationship to property, in conjunction with marriage patterns and postmarital residence, set the terms for the following changes: the dominant presence of women in domestic life and kinship, the prevalence to a large extent of matrifocality, the projection of the importance of relations among women in structuring kinship and, particularly, the strengthening of the mother-daughter bond. The study demonstrated that women's activities at the intra- and inter-household level, centered on the mother-daughter axis, and played a crucial role in the organization of kinship. However, the changes taking place in the economic and domestic life of women in Kokkari had not been accompanied by equivalent ideological transformations. The division of labor in the household and the cultural ideas, which helped define female identity, had not altered.

Outside the realm of the household, gender ideology and activities were examined in Zinovieff's analysis (1991) of the *kamaki* (the Greek male practice of "hunting" female tourists), which shed light on the issue of class divisions as well as on certain male beliefs concerning gender and prestige. She argued that men (typically of low social standing) established "alliances" among themselves and gained prestige or symbolic capital in the process of using female tourists as their objects. In addition, these men expressed their antagonism toward a "superior" Europe; by "deceiving" female tourists, they took vengeance, symbolically, as members both of an underprivileged social and economic class and a subordinate European country. Zinovieff also maintained that action in the field of tourism allowed men to find marriage partners among tourists; the issue arising in these cases was not only the contradictory representations of foreign women as "victims" of male aggression but also as mothers.

Moore (1995), too, treated gender ideologies in his analysis of changes in drinking behavior resulting from tourism. He argued that foreign and domestic tourism in Arachova had contributed to a change in the normative patterns of alcohol consumption in the context of constraints imposed by local gender ideologies. According to Moore, the 1960–1980 period was marked by alterations in male drinking patterns, which were a consequence of inbound tourism. With the appearance of bars and the introduction of beer for the satisfaction of foreign demand, beer also became a significant addition to the locals' drinking repertoire. In the case of women, however, it was after 1980 that social restrictions on their drinking were loosened, as a result of the development of domestic tourism.

From a different perspective, consumption and sexuality entered the analysis of how spaces and places constructed gender and were constituted by it through a dialectical gender/place relationship. The question raised by Kantsa (2002) concerned the role that women consumers of tourism played in the construction of gendered scapes. She assessed the spatial transformations of Skala Eressos, on Lesvos, since the beginnings of its lesbian tourism community, and argued that Eressos was a place where sexualities were lived—a location that enabled a lesbian gaze, which was not feasible in other destinations. Kantsa also noted that, whereas in the 1980s, tension and hostility prevailed between gay women and local residents, in recent years, strains had decreased significantly because of changes both in attitude and economic parameters; in addition, the boundaries between lesbians and locals were no longer strictly defined.

Interactions with the "Other"

Tourist representations and identities, tourist-local encounters, the ambiguities of tourist activities, and the production and dissemination of knowledge in the context of tourism were issues that had not drawn the attention of sociologists, but which had been treated in a few anthropological studies. In the literature, there was a "biased" or a one-sided emphasis on the effects of tourism on local communities, and a limited preoccupation (in terms of both empirical research and analysis) with intercultural, inter-subjective encounters, as well as with the experiences of the tourist or the traveling self. The earliest available study of this kind, carried out on Mykonos by Lambiri-Dimaki (1972), revealed a process whereby an initial phase (1950–1955) of criticizing tourism led to the development of a positive attitude. What accounted for this change were the local community's modernization and the economic benefits accruing from tourism, especially in comparison with threats to "moral values." Another piece of research, conducted by Stavrou on behalf of the EOT (1979–1986), highlighted a more positive attitude adopted by businessmen toward tourists compared to that of locals, as well as a dichotomous attitude: positive toward economic benefits and negative or ambivalent when it came to social influences.

The relationship between tourists and locals in regions with different levels of tourism development was examined by Tsartas in his doctoral thesis (1989). He identified differences in attitude according to the level of tourism development and attitude changes which depended on whether the locals' assessment related to economic or social benefits. In areas with a more advanced level of tourism development, residents tended to express greater skepticism concerning its social effects. Interestingly, along with the formation of national stereotypes, different preferences were revealed concerning the origin of tourists: Greeks were preferred over foreigners in areas where tourism was not as intensely developed. Although foreign tourists were viewed as a more profitable economic source, in the long run, tourist nationality ceased to be an issue of concern.

On the other hand, Haralambopoulos and Pizam (1996) concluded that residents on Samos expressed a favorable attitude toward tourists which was associated with the positive effects of anticipated tourism development. Moreover, based on the expressed views of locals, these authors discovered tourism's contribution toward improving the position of women both in the home and in the community. However, they also acknowledged a tendency of residents to attribute a series of negative developments (drug addiction, vandalism, brawls, sexual harassment, and incidents of crime) to inbound tourists. Adding to the debate, and along the same line of reasoning, Tsartas (1998) and Tsartas and Thanopoulou (1995) assessed the role of tourism and tourists' presence as a crucial factor influencing young people's process of socialization on Ios and Serifos. In addition, they highlighted those factors accounting for the characteristics of the contact and communication between tourists and locals at different phases of tourism development: 1960–1980 and from 1981 to the mid-1990s. More recent studies (Andriotis 2000b, 2006; Pappas 2006; Tsartas 2003; Zagkotsi 2007) found that locals' views and attitudes toward tourists had not changed; a few recorded differences were related to foreigners being responsible for or contributing toward the negative or positive effects of tourism development.

Some of the analytical issues posited at the beginning of this section were basically dealt with by researchers who used qualitative methods; such techniques allowed for an understanding of the phenomenon of tourism from the perspective of the research subjects' experiences and actions, as well as the meanings they attributed to them. The following investigations did not rely on statistically based samples but instead used methods dictated by (or appropriate for) an ethnographic approach. Galani-Moutafi's work (2000) drew examples from the area of ethnographic practice, tourism discourse, and travel narratives in order to shed light on the dual process of self-discovery and self-representation, which resulted from gazing into the elsewhere and the "Other." Analyzing the narratives of several travelers who visited Greece in the 18th and 19th centuries, she unraveled the construction of the "familiar-foreign" relationship, along with images of the self and Other which the traveler held. Turning to the tourism literature, she examined representations of modern Greece as well as the construction through signs of the tourist gaze. To bring her argument full circle, she also searched for common characteristics and differences in the experiences of the ethnographer and the tourist. In another investigation, Galani-Moutafi (2001) sought to apply her theoretical problematic to a case study of American college students visiting Lesvos as part of their study abroad program. She analyzed the reactions to their experiences and the images they used to construct the island and themselves while visiting it. A key issue her inquiry centered on was how the students confronted the cultural Other along the lines of maleness and femaleness, as well as through the notion of privacy. Her research showed that the students' attempts toward self-representation focused mainly on their discovery and confirmation of the positive qualities of self-independence and self-reliance. However, because of their tourist-like stance, their encounters with otherness occurred largely on their own terms, in an *aestheticized* space, and could not allow for self-transforming experiences; their self-reflexivity operated against the image of the tourist with whom they shared the consumption of signs.

Taking into account the increasing cultural heterogeneity of Greece, Lazaridies and Wickens (1999) compared the employment experiences of Albanian migrant workers, who entered the country illegally and found themselves in the periphery of the labor market, to those of tourists who chose to "go native" and turned to seasonal employment in the host country in order to finance their alternative lifestyle. They argued that even though both groups were found in low-paid occupations, the Western tourist-workers were treated more favorably by their Greek hosts, when contrasted with the Albanians, who were not just trapped in conditions of inferiority, immobility, and ultra-exploitation, but also treated as scapegoats in various political arenas. The point raised by these researchers hinged upon the issue of classification and definition of multiple Others and their differential treatment by the host country, suggesting it was a problem of ideology, identity, and politics.

Deltsou (2005), in a more in-depth analysis of identity (national and/or European) in view of the presence of Others, showed that depending on context, the particular choice of a specific identity might exhibit ambiguity, flexibility, or rigidity of boundaries. From her ethnographic research in a coastal tourism village in northern Greece, she ascertained practices aiming primarily at exclusion related to neighboring villages, owners of summer homes, tourists, and Russian-Pontic economic immigrants who resided permanently in the village. What accounted for the convergence and/or divergence between Greek and European identity and the different (in each case) perceptions of the self were the experiences of tourism and of immigration from the former Soviet Union. Deltsou concluded that while locals negotiated their ambiguous position and identity with regard to "Europe" (Western European tourists), at the same time they constructed their European and Greek identity in relation to Russian-Pontic immigrants ("Easterners") as rigid and non-permeable.

The issue of identity was treated from a different perspective by Nazou (2005), who examined various forms of intercultural exchange between tourists and the local Mykoniate community in the context of the provision of services. Nazou focused on the performance of identity on the part of female entrepreneurs as well as their practices, insofar as they related to material, symbolic, and emotional exchanges (gift giving, hospitality treats, and personal communications) with tourist customers. Their practices in the hotel sector could be characterized as a type of cultural mediation based on multiple exchanges and engagements with cultural others. Additionally, the skills women mobilized as entrepreneurs, in their attempt to deal with cultural difference, contributed toward the construction of a distinct entrepreneurial and domestic identity.

The works on tourists in Greece by Jacobsen (2000; in this volume) and Selänniemi (1994a, 1994b, 1997) are significant because they suggest the category "tourist" cannot be treated conceptually as a unitary one, but rather must be redefined by taking into account the meanings and experiences of the research subjects. In this regard, the Norwegian Jacobsen

(2000) examined the theme of tourist self-perception and practices in a comparative study of vacationers traveling in an organized or semi-organized fashion in selected destinations in Greece, Spain, and Turkey. He found a significant number of "anti-tourists" (defined as having a negative attitude toward the role of tourists) in offbeat Greek destinations, such as Chios. These "anti-tourists" considered the smaller Greek islands as the most appropriate destinations which they claimed they wished to experience, but in fact what they really wanted was a holiday on the beach. Nevertheless, for a significant number of vacationers with anti-tourist attitudes, the local flavor was experienced as more distinctive in certain Greek destinations (the smaller islands of Sporades) than in most of the destinations in Majorca, where an international style tended to prevail.

In his ethnographic research of Finnish tourists visiting Athens, Selänniemi (1994a) used his compatriots' motives and behavioral patterns as criteria to distinguish three types of tourists: "holidaymakers" (for whom a visit to the Acropolis was simply an obligatory part of their itinerary); "cultural tourists" (who recognized the symbolic values of the Acropolis, even though the latter was not their main reason for traveling to Athens); and "pilgrim-tourists" (whose devotional visit was more like a ritual performed in honor of the symbolic values of the Acropolis). Selänniemi described the type of tourism practiced by holidaymakers as "image-oriented" tourism, while he referred to the other two types as "site-oriented' tourism. Also, drawing from additional fieldwork among Finnish tourists visiting Rhodes, Selänniemi (1994b, 1997) noted that the average Finnish tourist on that island (compared to his/her counterpart visiting Athens) was younger, had a lower level of education, lived outside the metropolitan area of Finland, considered the climate to be the most important factor for his/her holiday experiences, and did not show an interest in cultural history. These tourists had a gaze (what he called a "traveling eye") that wandered over the landscape without fixing on details. In the Finnish type of mass tourism on Rhodes, people traveled more to a different state of being (enjoying the sun, sea, and sand) than to a different place.

Local Sustainable Development Issues

The importance of the environment as a basic resource for local tourism development was an issue that appeared frequently in sociological studies (Thanopoulou and Tsartas 1991; Tsartas 1998). Examining changes—at the economic, social, and policy levels—brought about by mass tourism on the island of Karpathos, Epitropoulos (1992) noted that the incentives for its development came from the then socialist government and its policy concerning the provision of grants, long-term, low-interest loans, and various tax benefits to investors. However, because such incentives were offered before the establishment of the necessary infrastructure, this development tended to be accompanied by various shortcomings in the area of environmental maintenance. Also, at the economic level, the abandonment of agriculture and fishing, coupled with higher consumer prices, exemplified the islanders' increased dependence on outside markets. In the case of another island—Zakynthos—Apostolopoulos and Sonmez (1999) documented the endogenous nature of its tourism development. Here they drew attention to tourism's rapid growth there during the 1980s and 1990s, as well as the more recent trend associated with the island's growing dependence on British tour operators and its transformation into a mass tourism destination. The study then assessed the ways three Zakynthian constituencies (residents, entrepreneurs, and local government) perceived tourism. It showed differences in local people's reactions to its development were attributed to: the latter's endogenous nature, the inhabitant constituency, the tourists' nationality, and the level of carrying capacity (high tourist concentration). The protection of the environment and the conservation of natural and sociocultural resources constituted an additional serious concern.

In another work Kousis (2000, 2001) focused on the social dimension of environmental problems ensuing from tourism and approached the issue of social sustainability through the case of an environmental protest. She examined the environmental impact of tourism on Crete (particularly in the intense tourist zone of the prefecture of Iraklion) for the period 1983–1993, and analyzed the local environment-related claims whose target was tourism. Kousis' study revealed that the environmental protests of these islanders reflected the problems of tourism's productivity on Crete. The latter stemmed from the over-exploitation of natural resources and the corresponding environmental pressures linked with both tourism's uneven geographical distribution and the unregulated construction of accommodation. Her study also suggested that economic dependence tended to hinder environmental mobilization; from the point of view of actors, economic sustainability was more important than environmental sustainability.

Aside from specific case studies, Thanopoulou and Tsartas (1991) formulated the hypothesis that in urban areas tourism development implied a partial and integrated change, while in rural areas it brought about a subversive modification in social structure. In urban areas, the tourism-environment relationship was explored through a focus on the fate of monuments and historic sites, as well as changes affecting the inner functions of the city and their impacts on specific professional and social groups. In rural areas, the implications of tourism development were located in conflicts over the use of land, problems of environmental and aesthetic pollution, and the formation of a new social ecosystem geared to the needs of mass tourism. In another critical review of various dimensions of Greek tourism, Apostolopoulos and Sonmez (2001) attributed the prolonged stagnation of the country's tourism industry to uneven supply and demand; the slow and uncoordinated emergence of new tourism forms; "irrational" political intervention in the market; a lack of strategic marketing policy; and fragmented and often bizarre public policies. In their assessment, tourism's lack of articulation with other productive sectors had prevented it from "revitalizing" the Greek periphery and reducing regional inequalities.

The issue of sustainability was approached from a different perspective by Galani-Moutafi (2004a) in her analysis of a case study that used the cultural economy approach in order to link the promotion of a regionally distinct product—Chios' *mastiha* (aromatic resin)—to endogenous development. The investigative techniques, she used included interviews, textual analysis of promotional material, and an analysis of events linked to product campaigns. Echoing Lash and Urry's assertion that "the economy is increasingly culturally inflected [while] culture is more and more economically inflected" (1994:64), Galani-Moutafi highlighted the various meanings attributed to *mastiha*. These were mainly derived through production and marketing practices, as well as the constructed images that linked it to place, thereby informing the island's representations of identity, including tourist identity. She also explained that "branding" and the creation of distinctiveness in marketing reflected the power of local agencies to shape current symbolic and economic realities. *Mastiha*-related endeavors were part of a larger scheme of endogenous development that included equity, in the sense of increased income-earning opportunities which countered economic vulnerability and forces of migration. Tourism, therefore, was not so much an end in itself but was integrated into what might be referred to as sustainable commercial marketing aiming at developing and promoting the circulation of *mastiha* and its products, thereby strengthening the island's image as a destination endowed with a distinct natural monopoly. The analytical orientation adopted in this work was guided by the premise that advertising practices constituting a cultural industry in their own right could easily serve as a separate context of economic and cultural production (Miller 1997) and also facilitate the promotional needs of tourism.

Alternatives to Mass Tourism

Special Interest Tourism (SIT) constituted a field of particular interest largely for sociological studies in Greece. Two main reasons accounted for this: first, the assessment that these forms of alternative tourism enhanced the possibilities for a viable growth and development, in contrast to mass organized tourism; and, second, their analysis allowed for a reexamination of issues and themes prevalent in both the anthropology and sociology of tourism (changes in local social and productive structures, women's entrepreneurship, family business strategies, and forms of cooperative action). Furthermore, interest in this area of research prompted the collaboration of scholars from different disciplines. Most related studies were published in the 1990s and what characterized them was an over-concentration on agro-tourism. More specifically, what drew the attention of researchers were women's agro-cooperatives.

During the 1990s, several works (almost all sociological) focused on the subject of agro-tourism, in general, and related cooperatives in particular. They examined the legislative framework of such cooperatives in Greece and the European Community's policy for its promotion; outlined the criteria for the entrance of candidate areas into a program of development; discussed its interconnection with "soft" types of tourism development; and assessed it from the perspective of the integrated economic development of rural areas. These studies also accounted for factors (national policy and agencies) which had affected the development and viability of agro-tourism ventures (Apostolopoulos et al 2001; Karagiannis 2004; Manologlou 1993; Papageorgiou 1998; Papakonstantinidis, 2002; Tsartas and Thanopoulou 1993). Regarding proposals made for treating organizational or other problems associated with women's agro-cooperatives, Iakovidou (1992) discussed expansion of their activities into relatively new services and products; the differentiation of the services offered by these cooperatives from those provided by other types of tourism; the creation of a central agency which would deal with organizational, bureaucratic, and investment-related problems; and the continuous education of the female members in areas related to cooperative organization, self-management, and service provision. Even so, because these studies dealt mainly with institutional and organizational problems linked to the establishment and functioning of the cooperatives, they did not contribute much to tourism theory, but instead added to tourism practical knowledge. They treated agro-tourism as a type of practice which could strengthen gender equality and promote local economic growth, but not as one that might allow hosts and guests to share experiences, nor as an entrepreneurial endeavor enabling women to play a key role in the (re)construction of cultural identity and tradition.

The earliest published work in Greek on women's agro-cooperatives was that of Papagaroufali (1986, 1994). She examined the agro-industrial cooperative of Anogeia (Crete), whose members engaged in the production/sale of traditional textiles. Her investigation also focused on three cooperatives in Petra (Lesvos), Ambelakia (Thessaly), and Pyrgi (Chios), which rented rooms to tourists. The study, based on qualitative methods, revealed that income accruing to females constituted a short-term solution to the problem of unemployment or underemployment. More importantly, these cooperatives tended to support the existing stereotypes identifying women with the home, since the products/services offered by them adjusted both to the ideology which restricted them to the role of housewife and to demands for the woman farmer's labor. A majority tended to abstain from the cooperatives' operational or collective type activities and restricted their plans to the extension of those areas of operation linked to the house (room rental or preparation of various edible goods). They preferred the mixed rather than "women exclusive" composition of cooperatives, in order that male members who were "by nature" "smarter" and "more capable" could run the external operations, leaving for their female counterparts the internal operations (carrying for customers, etc.). The attitudes of these women, according to Papagaroufali, reflected their tendency to perceive themselves as "home workers." Weighing the positive and negative effects of women's involvement in the cooperative of Petra, Castelberg-Koulma (1991) referred to the cooperative experience benefiting female guests, who felt safe from sexual harassment and gained an understanding of the local culture from the perspectives of their hosts. However, she expressed concern as to how effectively a centrally conceived plan could be implemented in a traditional rural economy and how successfully the cooperatives could work alongside a capitalist system in a culture that harbored women's oppression.

Tsartas and Thanopoulou's study (1995) confirmed but also differed from the conclusions drawn by Papagaroufali. Their empirically based analysis of five women's agro-tourism cooperatives led them to conclude that the lack of coordination and technical know-how at the initial stage of their development, coupled with the failure to set specific goals when starting out (1985–1989), had negative consequences on the cooperatives' development. On the other hand, the positive effects included the opening up of additional sources of income for the female members and the assumption on their part of professional responsibilities. Giagou and Apostolopoulos (1996), who surveyed the women's agro-cooperative of Petra a decade after

Papagaroufali, added to the debate by noting it had neither succeeded in promoting the active participation of its members, nor had it developed a team spirit among them; also, the cooperative was regarded as one more tourism enterprise, in the sense that its particular importance was no longer distinct from the point of view of both its members and its customers. Concerning agro-tourism's role in preserving the environment through agricultural activities, Anthopoulou (2000), who had also studied the women's agro-cooperative of Petra, argued that such a role diminished as tourism became socially and economically more enticing when contrasted with farming.

An overall assessment with which most scholars agreed was that the spread of agro-tourism in touristically developed zones of Greece did not serve the primary objective of promoting agricultural resources and contributing toward the socioeconomic revival of declining rural areas (Anthopoulou et al 1998). On the other hand, as a factor of economic development, agro-tourism was extolled in certain cases where the blending of agriculture with tourism had provided a new and profitable income earning productive activity. One such case was discussed by Theodoropoulou (2005) for the prefecture of Trikala. Her survey-based research showed that it was primarily the younger and more educated farmers who turned to agro-tourism, which also played a significant role in preventing further depopulation of rural areas, since it enabled earning a family income comparable to that of urban incomes. The other case concerned the area of Lake Plastira, where agro-tourism was integrated into a wider developmental scheme which facilitated its interconnection with the remaining productive activities and resources in the area (Anthopoulou et al 1998).

The limited presence of alternative forms of tourism in Greece beyond agro-tourism is reflected in the dearth of relevant works. However, one theoretically oriented study by Deltsou (2000) examined the ecotourism programs of Nympheo (in the prefecture of Florina) and of Prespes and, for comparative purposes, referred to the community of Nikiti in Chalkidiki. Deltsou argued that the ecotourism perspective tended to idealize not just traditional production methods but also an entire rural past, which was presented as homogenized and a-historical: a type of balance with nature. One way to achieve this balance between nature and culture was through the establishment of protected natural areas, which—along with their resi-dents—represented the past and a state of isolation. Thus, ecotourism contributed toward the shaping of a particular perception concerning both the past and the peoples' present. In another study, Deltsou (2007) maintained that the attraction of agro- and ecotourism places stemmed not so much from the antithesis between rurality and urbanity, but from the construction of rurality as a commodity. She examined various electronic sites, a ministry, and tourism enterprises, as actors involved in this construction process, as well as social relations defined with reference to the contexts of time and place. Her analysis showed all network sites oriented the attention of the tourist-consumer to concepts such as "nature," "environment," and "tradition," which contributed to defining localness in aesthetic, historical, and cultural terms. Tourism enterprises, by emphasizing the "authenticity" of the buildings they used, projected a conceptualization of the past as unchanged historicity. In addition, in all the cases examined, the nostalgic agro- and ecotourism destination was imbued with meanings derived from a discourse about food. Deltsou concluded that the meaning-making process concerning the relevant representations did not just depend on the use of texts, but on the internet itself as a symbol of modernity.

Sociological works focusing on agro-and/or ecotourism used an applied and nonanalytical approach in order to deal mainly with issues of development. Thus, Maroudas and Tsartas (1997) commented on the role that alternative forms of tourism could play for the smaller islands of the Aegean as a means for attaining viable tourism growth. Similarly, Maroudas and Kyriakaki (2001) focused on the role of ecotourism from the perspective of local growth by considering the case of several small islands in the northern Dodecanese. An article by Tsartas et al (2001) comprised an attempt to link alternative forms of domestic tourism (spa, mountaineering, ski, ecotourism, and congress) to the prospect of development. The authors used the findings of a research project in order to highlight the qualitative characteristics of domestic tourism in Greece, reveal the dominant tendencies of domestic tourists, and assess the importance of this business for the national economy. They concluded that since 1980, the above alternative forms of tourism had played an important role in the overall development of the country's domestic tourism.

CONCLUSION

In Greece, works examining analytical issues and theoretical approaches in the fields of the anthropology and sociology of tourism are low in number, because of the relatively few scholars who systematically probe into the phenomenon of tourism. Nevertheless, as this chapter has shown, research has been increasing over the last few years, partly because of the addition of doctoral dissertation theses whose contribution—empirically and theoretically—is especially significant. These new studies focus mainly on two themes: the role of motives behind tourism endeavors and tourism-related development processes, along with the changes they bring to various areas.

The first works investigating tourism in light of analytical approaches within the anthropology and sociology of tourism are those of Chtouris (1995), Galani-Moutafi (1995), and Tsartas (1995). Their contributions appear in a special volume (55) dedicated to *Τουρισμός: Κοινωνικές Ταυτότητες και Χώρος* (Tourism: Social Identities and Space) of the social science periodical *Σύγχρονα Θέματα* (*Synchrona Themata*) (Current Issues). Galani-Moutafi discusses anthropological arguments concerning the issue of authenticity in tourism; Tsartas presents sociological approaches to tourism; while Chtouris comments on the characteristics of modern tourists. In the case of the first two authors, the dialog established between sociological and anthropological perspectives at the time is apparent. Chtouris, on the other hand, bases his work on the phenomenological approach and treats the tourism-culture relationship from the point of view of experience.

Tsartas (1997), in a three volume collective study by Lambiri-Dimaki (1997), presenting the contributions of Greek sociologists for the period 1959–2000, examines the challenges that arise in the process of theory building in a sociology of tourism. It brings together a body of research emerging from several doctoral dissertations which treat the subject of tourism (Andriotis 2000b; Gkrimpa 2006; Kousis 2000; Moutafi 1990; Pappas 2006; Stavrinoudis 2005; Tsartas 1989). These scholars, in papers published from their theses, link their empirical studies with theoretical approaches in the anthropology and sociology of tourism. Recently, the University of the Aegean has become a forum for the investigation of tourism from the perspective of different disciplines, while continuing the "tradition" of combining theoretical approaches (mainly sociological) with empirical research.

A second group of studies takes the form of handbooks, which seek to meet the teaching and research needs arising within those university departments and *Ανώτατα Τεχνολογικά Εκπαιδευτικά Ιδρύματα* (ATEI) (Higher Technological Educational Institutes), whose curriculum and/or research orientation includes tourism. Among these, Lytras' handbook published under the title *Κοινωνιολογία του Τουρισμού* (The Sociology of Tourism) addresses tourism as a research topic within sociology (1998). Tsartas follows with *Τουρίστες, Ταξίδια, Τόποι: Κοινωνιολογικές Προσεγγίσεις στον Τουρισμό* 1996 (Tourists, Travels, Places: Sociological

Approaches in Tourism), where he integrates the approaches of different schools of sociology and social sciences with those of the sociology of tourism as "an autonomous scientific field." Recently, another work in Greek, by Moira-Mylonopoulou et al (2003), under the title *Κοινωνιολογία και Ψυχολογία του Τουρισμού* (The Sociology and Psychology of Tourism), addresses the wider approaches of sociology and psychology, as well as those of tourism as a scientific field; it is primarily intended to be used by students studying at Τεχνολογικά Επαγγελματικά λύκεια (ΤΕΕ) (Technological Occupational High Schools).

Of particular significance is the contribution of Galani-Moutafi's (2002) monograph (written both in English and Greek), *Έρευνες για τον Τουρισμό στην Ελλάδα και την Κύπρο: Μια Ανθρωπολογική Προσέγγιση* (The Analysis of Tourism in Greece and Cyprus: An Anthropological Approach). Though the presentation of the anthropological perspective carries a special weight in this work, the author covers in detail works of the last three decades from disciplines such as economics, sociology, geography, urban planning, business management, and political science. For researchers, the book is an extensive introductory base for relevant methodological, theoretical, and practical issues.

A critical assessment of the body of literature presented can conclude with a few remarks on the lack of communication and exchanges by scholars representing the disciplines of anthropology and sociology. The analytical approaches, methodologies, and research practices of these disciplines, as they have developed in Greece, are far apart from each other. Researchers in social anthropology, following the steps of a long-established Anglo-American tradition, tend to be theoretical rather than applied-oriented, place a great emphasis on "thick" ethnographic description, adopt a bottom-up perspective, avoid generalizations, and rely mostly on the research subjects' own conceptualizations or "categories." The sociological tradition in Greece, on the other hand, especially since it carries traces of a strong Marxist and/or political economy orientation, tends to place a more European theoretical emphasis on structure rather than action, explains phenomena rather than processes, understands complex realities through representative samples, and, generally, makes proposals for the solution of social and economic problems. Furthermore, what marks most Greek sociological studies of tourism is a failure to "exploit" certain broader, intra-disciplinary theoretical debates and paradigms from the Anglophone world, such as those of Urry, Lash, and Harvey, or those relating to globalization, commodity flows, national ideology and localism, the politics of culture, and the role of bureaucracy. Nevertheless, and despite these drawbacks and weaknesses, scholars of both disciplines have made important contributions not only through their innovative research, but also in establishing tourism as a "legitimate" subject or field of scientific investigation. The collaboration of a sociologist and an anthropologist in writing this chapter has the advantage of capturing a broad spectrum of research which is both applied and theoretical. It also reveals the diverging courses the two disciplines have followed in Greece.

Chapter 11

Origins and Developments: The Overall Picture

Giuli Liebman Parrinello
Università Roma Tre, Rome, Italy

Graham M. S. Dann
Finnmark University College, Alta, Norway

INTRODUCTION

English-speaking academics with an interest (but no formal training) in tourism did not share many of their ideas with their Anglophone colleagues until the 1970s. In that decade, Cohen published his first relevant tourism articles (1972, 1974), though not in specialized sociological reviews devoted to the field. In 1973, the first issue of *Annals of Tourism Research* was published, and in 1976 *The Tourist* by Dean MacCannell, which was to mark an epoch, saw the light of day. One year later, the first edition of Smith's (1977a) *Hosts and Guests* made its appearance. From the point of view of tourism studies, in those early years, the so called "critical platform" prevailed, to be followed shortly after by the "adaptancy" and "scientific" platforms (Jafari 1987). The most informed European tourism scholars were aware of these new contributions, which were duly recognized and absorbed little by little in Germany, Scandinavia, some other European countries and, last but not least, in France. But interestingly, and for the main part,

The Sociology of Tourism: European Origins and Developments
Tourism Social Science Series, Volume 12, 323–342
Copyright © 2009 by Emerald Group Publishing Limited
All rights of reproduction in any form reserved
ISSN: 1571-5043/doi:10.1108/S1571-5043(2009)0000012016

Continental European research continued in its own idiosyncratic way. By way of summary, it is worth recalling what happened country by country.

German-Speaking Countries

Symptomatic of a "globalized" trend in Europe was the volume *Tourismuspsychologie und Tourismussoziologie* (Tourism Psychology and Tourism Sociology) (Hahn and Kagelmann 1993). As already mentioned in the introductory section on "some unsettled questions" (Chapter 1), this comprehensive handbook lined up and blended the most recent insights of Anglo-Saxon and German research. Disciplines consonant with sociology (in tandem with psychology) were considered, such as economics, geography, (cultural) anthropology, and pedagogy, with contributors like Spode, Steinecke, and Vester. Theoretical concepts of the new Anglo-Saxon literature, "authenticity" and "play," for example, were placed alongside those derived from the German tradition, "mobility" and "psychogeography," for instance. Particularly, noteworthy was the contribution of Kagelmann (1993) who introduced in the form of an anthology, with authors such as Gottlieb and Cohen, recent Anglo-Saxon and German research in the three principal social science disciplines of tourism (sociology, psychology, and anthropology), under the title of *Tourismuswissenschaft* (Tourism Science). Throughout this exercise, marketing was not neglected; nor were different methodological issues of the social sciences (Spode this volume). At the same time, it is not surprising that leisure continued to play an important role in Germany, as for instance at the British American Tobacco (BAT) Leisure Institute in Hamburg. Here Opaschowski, mainly interested in the pedagogical aspects of leisure, extended the field to tourism with a "systematic introduction" (2002). All in all, German research proceeded on its own course, less fascinated by the issue of post-modernity, and more interested in both the scientific fundamentals of tourism and in mainstream theoretical research. Names like Hennig, Spode, Vester, and Wöhler featured in this intellectual journey (Spode this volume).

Yet, in spite of this progress, the presence of German scholars in RC 50 of the International Sociological Association, and other tourism congresses and conferences continues to be very limited. This strange state of affairs should give cause for thought. Since most German academics can read, write, and speak English, it cannot be simply be a linguistic problem that deters their participation. It is precisely on account of this shortcoming that Spode's contribution to this volume is so relevant.

France

As already seen, France was even more captivated by the question of leisure, so much so that under the inspiration of Joffré Dumazedier and Marie-Françoise Lanfant the very origins of the sociology of tourism could be located in that domain. Once sociology began to direct its attention toward international tourism, it too looked to mainstream sociology for its theoretical foundations. Thus, even though a sociological giant of the caliber of Durkheim never studied tourism, since its mass variant was well before his time, one of his important unit ideas, the concept of a "social fact," was put to good use by his compatriots in understanding this new global reality. Indeed the reliance of the field of the sociology of tourism on its parent discipline of general sociology was, as it should have been, a prime exemplar of locating sociological insights in the French School of Sociology. From there, it was just one step to contextualize advances in the sociology of tourism from the insights of second (Mauss) and third (Barthes, Baudrillard, Bourdieu, Foucault, and Lyotard) generations of French sociologists. Without their respective contributions to the notion of "a total social phenomenon," the sphere of semiotics, social control, postmodern theory, and the sociology of consumption, corresponding progress in the sociology of tourism over the decades from such names as Burgelin, Boyer, Cazes, Dufour, Gritti, Jardel, Picard, Rozenberg, Thurot, Tresse, and Urbain would have been severely limited, if not virtually impossible.

Italy

Italy, as a popular inbound destination, tended to develop a traditional framework for its initial sociological understanding of tourism, one that was nevertheless open to the forces of globalization. From some main issues like the countryside, and also perhaps because of the importance of cultural tourism, research was led back to urban aspects and to the city. Moreover, its location in the Mediterranean led naturally to the foundation of the *Associazione Mediterranea di Sociologia del Turismo* (Mediterranean Association of the Sociology of Tourism). Today, a continuous and steady topic is a focus on the tourist subject, including its psycho-sociological and geographical characteristics (Savelli this volume). Not to be forgotten is the pioneering work of Alberto Sessa, not only in bridging the disciplinary gap between the psychology and sociology of tourism, but also for his founding the *Scuola Internazionale di Scienze Turistiche* (SIST) (International School of Tourist Sciences), active from 1974 to 2004. This school, a then WTO training center, was an example of internationalization at both the theoretical and practical levels. In addition to its library, it was also responsible for the *Rassegna di Studi Turistici* (Review of Tourist Studies).

Turning to the next generation, among the liveliest Italian sociologists of tourism, the name of Costa (2005b) has to be mentioned, as the author who introduced MacCannell's *Il Turista* (The Tourist) (2005) to his compatriots. There are also today a growing number of Italian tourism academics who have recently started displaying an interest in the sociolinguistic dimensions of tourism. Here come to mind, for example, works by Palusci and Francesconi (2006), De Stasio and Palusci (2007), and Calvi (2005). In order to establish dialog with the principal Anglo-Saxon treatment of this theme (Dann 1996a), they recently hosted a conference on the topic and invited that coauthor of this chapter to deliver a keynote address on intervening changes in the language of tourism (Dann 2007b). There are some indications that these latest initiatives, along with a steady supply of publications in this specialized domain, may bode well for the future. If they spread outward to other areas of Europe, the ensuing exchange of ideas also has potential for the years ahead.

Poland

In Poland, since the 1990s, a cultural humanistic emphasis traditionally belonging to the high level social sciences, but also extending to the philosophy and ethics of tourism, seems to counterbalance the advance of economics (Przecławski et al this volume). In spite of the former constraints of the Iron Curtain, Przecławski has exerted a continual, unflagging presence on the international scene. As a result, there are now younger scholars, among them Podemski (2005), especially interested in tourism (Przecławski et al this volume). After Poland's entry to the EU and facing the problem of globalization, noteworthy also is the academic development of sectors like hospitality and catering and the collaboration between the state and industry, particularly with the realization of increasing amounts of information exchange over the internet. International contacts, conferences, university studies, and the appearance of an old review in a different skin— *New Problems of Tourism*—complete the picture.

The Former Yugoslavia

After the splitting of the former Yugoslavia, different national states arduously managed their former heritage. Here an emphasis on economics, along with the production of numerous textbooks, and a focus on different destinations were more evident than a tradition of the sociology of tourism. Nevertheless, special attention is given by Vukonić (this volume) to tourism studies in Croatia which are of special sociological and academic relevance (names like Alfier, for instance), along with several publications, a broad range of topics linking tourism with health and sport, a renowned journal issued both in Croatian and in English, and a growing tradition of holding international conferences in destinations such as Split and Dubrovnik. Altogether, there has been a considerable amount of scientific output, especially when compared to the relatively small population of the former Yugoslavia and the current Croatia (even though less is known about Serbia and tourism studies emanating from the former Yugoslav capital). Still, with such recent interest as that displayed in the specialist area of the critical turn in tourism studies, an interest shared with Dutch colleagues, largely due to the inspiration of Wageningen based Atlejevic and her associates (see Lengkeek this volume), theorizing of this nature is already becoming an avenue of worthwhile investigation that has managed to capture the imagination of several English-speaking scholars.

Scandinavia

In spite of their diverse sociological traditions, Scandinavian countries illustrate successful and balanced research in the sociology of tourism that is oriented both toward various areas of Continental Europe and to a consideration of anticipated Anglo-Saxon ideas. The works of the Swedish Löfgren and of the Norwegian Jacobsen can be considered typical of this twofold orientation. Names like Bakhtin, Barthes, Bourdieu, Dumazedier, Elias, and Schivelbusch rarely feature in the most recent Anglo-Saxon literature; yet they appear quite normally in Scandinavian works. Thus, it is not surprising to encounter some pioneering lectures concerning such tourism topics as liminality, gender issues, Eros-modernity, and Logos-modernity in various Nordic conferences and publications (Löfgren 1984; Jacobsen this volume). Social awareness is typical of the whole Scandinavian region, as a heritage of the welfare state. Although sociological research in popular travel has continued from the 1980s onwards, since the 1990s in Norway the focus seems to be on international tourism and independent travel. While new aspects deriving from these interests include emigrant tourism, outdoor recreation, and experience of landscapes, there has also been a renaissance of tourism planning studies (Jacobsen this volume). Although Jacobsen's main interest is in his native Norway, he also takes other Scandinavian countries into consideration. For example, Veijola and

Jokinen (1994) from Finland direct their attention to gender and the body, as well as summer rites; there is a Danish interest in travel photography; and there are fieldwork issues relating to three Scandinavian communities. In spite of this broad range of high-level tourism research and of specialized journals publishing mainly in English, there is no adequate acknowledgement of this effort by the rest of academia. The main reason for this lack of awareness and enthusiasm may be because the sociology of tourism is considered only as a subfield in Nordic universities. Nevertheless, there is hope for a change in attitude corresponding with the inclination toward multidisciplinary tourism research (Jacobsen this volume).

Spain

In Spain one does not have the impression of a vibrant sociology of tourism, in spite of the three relevant names of Febas, Gaviria, and Jurdao Arrones discussed by Aramberri (this volume), and notwithstanding the appearance of *Annals of Tourism Research en Español* in 1999. Far from the central European literature, this small group of sociologists and anthropologists of tourism tends to be more oriented toward anthropology and semiology, following French models and on account of frequent contacts with that country (e.g., Gaviria's links with Lefebvre). Interestingly Jurdao Arrones is known in the Anglophone academic world because he was "discovered" by Nelson Graburn, Dennison Nash, and Douglas Pearce. (Pi-Sunyer, of Catalan origin, is also familiar to English-speaking scholars due to his inclusion in Valene Smith's (1977b) pioneering work in the anthropology of tourism and his studies of Catalan communities opened up to the onslaught of mass tourism.) Noteworthy, too, is the realization that all the three authors highlighted by Aramberri (this volume) were working with only minimal links to Spanish academia, which in any case, and apart from a overwhelming concern with the economics of tourism, did not and does not seem particularly interested in the sociology of tourism. Indeed there appear to be no dedicated institutions or a specific scientific community covering the fields of the sociology or the anthropology of tourism comprehensively. Filling the gap, in this volume, but also elsewhere through his many publications, is Aramberri himself, who through his critical approach to conventional wisdom has livened up discussion in such otherwise mundane areas as tourism statistics and the sociocultural impacts of tourism.

Belgium and the Netherlands

After many years of different attitudes and politics, the Belgians and Dutch came together in 1990 for a joint Master's program sponsored by the

European Union, a common initiative embracing leisure and tourism, and for other common enterprises, like an Erasmus Leisure Studies group. After 2000, the Dutch Wageningen WICE international program was explicitly concerned with Leisure Tourism and the Environment, with a focus on tourism and socio-spatial conditions. Also in Flemish-speaking Belgium traditional leisure themes were implemented through efforts at the university level (Lengkeek this volume), and there has additionally been a resurgence of interest in social tourism that has finally captured the attention of the Anglophone world, as evidenced, for example in the work of Minnaert et al (2006) and the conference convened by Maitland et al (2008).

Greece

In Greece an interest in tourism studies is only relatively recent. Even if academia is not correspondingly structured, numerous PhDs, handbooks, journals, state agencies, and local communities testify to growing research in the field. Contrary to the experience of most other European countries, in Greece the anthropology of tourism prevails over the sociology of tourism. Thus, although our specialist contributors describe a rather backward attitude of the Greek sociology of tourism, by contrast a rich palette of theory and research develops in the anthropological treatment of tourism (Tsartas and Galani-Moutafi this volume). These Hellenic anthropologists have common interests with other disciplines like geography, architecture, and cultural and media studies. Ethnographic practice, qualitative methods, paradigms of feminism, post-colonialism, cultural criticism, identity, gender, entrepreneurship, tourist representations and traditions, represent the features of their investigations. Also evident is a particular constructive dialog with historians, one that opens ethnographic research to the presence of historical reconstruction, which adds greater depth to such research than the mere compilation of case studies.

TRENDS IN ORIGINS AND DEVELOPMENTS

Having looked at the general picture country by country, at this juncture it is worthwhile summarizing the specific origins and developments of the sociology of tourism in more detail by highlighting trends that emerge from its protagonists and their theories in different time periods. Here readers are invited to go to the two tables in the Appendix which serve as an empirical basis for the respective commentaries which follow.

The Protagonists

Bearing in mind that it has been decided that here authors cited separately should feature only once (from the time of their earliest contribution) and that Spain, though included in Appendix Table 1, is not analyzed due to its low cell counts, while the Anglophone world is excluded because it represents the point of contrast, a number of quantitative observations can be made (Appendix Table 1) which permit cross territory comparisons. Where authors have a nationality that differs from the country in which they are cited, that entry is made according to place of work. Thus, Selänniemi, for instance, is referred to under Greece because of much of the research he conducted there. For that reason he appears in that territory's sources rather than in Scandinavia under his Finnish place of origin. Moreover, where authors are cited in collaboration with others, they may appear under the nationality of their cowriters and in an earlier or later time period from their separate entries (e.g., Jacobsen and Dann (2003) under Scandinavia, and Dann and Jacobsen (2003) under Anglophones).

From Appendix Table 1, it can be seen first, that once the Anglophone and Spanish authors are temporarily removed, of the 540 cited among the 8 remaining countries/regions, a calculated overall mean of 67.5 is exceeded by German-speaking territories (142), the former Yugoslavia (93), and Italy (87), but rests below average for Scandinavia (61), Belgium and the Netherlands (52), Greece (52), Poland (34), and France (19). However, this distribution may say less about the impact of such writers than the reasons held by a given contributor for identifying and including them. In other words, the number of authorities selected may be a function of their perceived importance by a particular commentator rather than their objective salience. Yet, given the *de facto* subjectivity of the social sciences, this finding should be regarded as prone to occupational hazard rather than an excuse for not engaging in the exercise.

Second, and as to be expected, there is an even cumulative spread of authors from the pre-1930s (15) to the 1930s (9), and 1940s (6). In the 1950s and 1960s, these totals respectively increase to 17 and 47, before rising again to sums well in excess of these figures that range as follows for the next four decades: 1970s (81), 1980s (93), 1990s (114), and 2000s (158). This strong pattern of growth should bode well for the development of the field. It does mean, however, that the current, post-millennium momentum has to be maintained and surpassed if prospects for the future are to remain healthy.

Third, with authors identified in each period for the German-speaking countries, and with a similar characteristic being displayed for Belgium and the Netherlands, the former is the region which most clearly demonstrates both origins and development of the field, especially since 28.2% of its writers are to be found up to and including the 1960s. With an overall mean of 17.4%, percentages for other areas in descending order are France (42.1), Belgium and the Netherlands (23.1%), Poland (17.7%), the former Yugoslavia (16.1%), Scandinavia (9.8%), Italy (6.9%), and Greece (1.9%). The comparative statistic for Anglophone countries is 6.7%. This demonstrates a time lag particularly with respect to the first four countries; especially since English-speaking tourism scholarship has no entries prior to the 1960s. That of course reconfirms the principal thesis of this book, namely that there is a dependency of the Anglophone world on Continental Europe as far as theorizing in the sociology of tourism is concerned. As a result of the foregoing analysis, however, it needs to be reemphasized by way of distinction that this dependency is far from even and is not evident across the board. In fact, if Germany, France, Belgium and the Netherlands, and Poland (those above the mean) are contrasted with the former Yugoslavia, Scandinavia, Italy, and Greece (those below average), the differences yield a χ^2 of 27.43 which, with one degree of freedom, is significant at $p < 0.0001$. Furthermore, if the Anglophone countries are added to the analysis χ^2 increases to 33.13, thereby reinforcing the distinction between the former (old) and latter (new) even more.

The Theories

So far, and with the exception of Spain, the analysis has simply focused on the single, diachronic contributions made from each territory. However, in order to decipher the comparative trends according to their principal topic of concern, time period, and country/region, thereby treating the data as cumulative and cross-cultural, it is first necessary to categorize the material by themes (where clearly the number of themes is less than the number of previously identified authors (Appendix Table 1) when two or more authors tackle a given topic). The classification that results from this form of content analysis, with frequencies in parentheses (Appendix Table 2), is as follows:

1. Sociology of tourism, general theories, definitions, and terminology ($n = 39$).
2. Tourism as a form of consumption and/or social prestige ($n = 22$).
3. Tourism as escape from alienation; issues of freedom, and strangerhood ($n = 19$).

4. Tourism as interpersonal relations, communication, and imagery ($n = 26$).
5. Self-reliance, meaning, identity, socialization, liminality, and pilgrimage ($n = 22$).
6. "Tourist bubbles," mass tourism, and anti-tourists ($n = 16$).
7. Space and place: nature, coast, countryside, and city ($n = 20$).
8. Sociocultural effects, communities, jobs, policy, sustainability, and conflict ($n = 43$).
9. Tourism and gender; tourism and the family ($n = 17$).
10. Tourist motives and decision-making ($n = 15$).
11. Leisure, free time, recreation, sport, and holidays of workers ($n = 19$).

These classifications are found to be mutually exclusive with no residual category. However, where given authors employ more than one theoretical category, (unlike Appendix Table 1) they are entered separately on each occasion, even when more than one time period is involved. Otherwise, they are only entered once under the earliest time period when they make an initial appearance. Where two or more writers are involved, in accordance with academic convention, seniority is attributed to the first, and, as a consequence, there is only one entry under that individual's name. In this analysis, the frequencies indicate the relative popularity of the different themes. According to this count, sociocultural effects (category 8) are dealt with the most often, and to these can be added the specific cases of gender and family issues (category 9). However, that picture could be somewhat misleading since tourism theory in general (category 1) is the second most frequent item and, when that is added to the four specific examples of such theory (2–5), then theory, both general and specific, accounts for 128 of the cases, almost half of the 258 total. This should be borne in mind when the separate instances of such theorizing are analyzed.

Category 1: Theory in General, Sociology of Tourism, Definitions, and Terminology.   The temporal distribution of this category shows a gradual increase over all time periods except the 1940s, 1950s, and 2000s (pre-1930s: one; 1930s: two; 1940s: one; 1950s: one; 1960s: three; 1970s: five; 1980s: eight; 1990s: ten; 2000s: eight). However, when country as a variable is taken into account, the greatest contributions come from the former Yugoslavia (ten), Poland (eight), and Belgium and the Netherlands (six), a pattern that is replicated in the temporal sequencing through all stages. By contrast, while Italy, France, and Greece are under-represented, what appearance they do make tends to be mainly limited to later periods. Another distinction that emerges is a greater concern with definition (Poland and the former Yugoslavia)—both previous Communist states—when compared with establishing a sociology/anthropology of tourism (Greece). Interestingly, the German-speaking countries do not play much of a part in the *general* theorizing about tourism, with only Hunziker and Krapf establishing a definition in the 1940s, and with later contributions not occurring until the 1980s and 1990s. The fact that Hunziker and Krapf's handbook was well received in central Europe also adds to the popularity of definitions in that part of the world.

Category 2: Tourism Specifically as a Form of Consumption and/or Social Prestige. This category also shows a gradual progression through all time periods up to and including the 1980s, before dipping in the 1990s, and increasing once more after the millennium. There are, however, a number of significant differences between this and the previous category. In the present case, the initial contributions are made in the pre-1930s by two eminent sociologists (Veblen and Simmel) respectively representing Scandinavia and Germany (once it is acknowledged that, while Veblen spent most of his life in the United States, his father was of Norwegian extraction). Thereafter, until the 1980s, contributions are made solely from German-speaking countries, the former Yugoslavia, and Scandinavia. Beginning in the 1980s, and continuing into the 1990s and the new millennium, there is a huge Italian interest in this theme, accounting for all but one of the instances (from Greece), and representing fully 50% of all cases. Much of this enthusiasm may be derived from a parallel fascination with the postmodern condition and a renaissance in the city as a new tourism destination. By way of significant omission, there is no French or Polish presence in relation to this category, even though the former contains such illustrious names as Baudrillard, Bourdieu, De Saint-Simon, and Lyotard when discussing sociology in general.

Category 3: Tourism as Escape from Alienation; Issues of Freedom; and Strangerhood. Once more Simmel features as a mainstream contributor from the turn of the 20th century, this time attracting more of his German-speaking colleagues and such pioneering names as Enzensberger, Krapf, Leugger, and von Wiese, up to and including the 1950s. The German influence not only monopolizes this period but also extends into the 1960s, 1970s, and 1980s in the respective persons of Gleichmann, Kentler et al, and Krippendorf, before disappearing in the 1990s and 2000s. There is also an important Scandinavian presence from the 1960s (Aubert), 1970s (Ekeroth;

Høivik and Herberg), 1980s (Löfgren), and 2000s (Haug et al). Contributions from other countries are more sporadic: France in the 1960s with an interest in freedom and social control in tourism (Burgelin; Gritti); Poland in the 1980s (Ostrowski) and 2000s (Podemski); and Italy in the 1980s (Lelli). Here the significant omission is the former Yugoslavia, particularly since an absence of freedom is often associated with central state control.

Category 4: Tourism as Interpersonal Relations, Communication, and Imagery. This is another category that shows a gradual increase. With three entries each in the 1970s and 1980s, there is a rise to seven in the 1990s and five in the 2000s. Early theorizing on this theme originates in the pre-1930s German-speaking countries (Glücksmann), before the famous definition of Hunziker and Krapf and a contribution from the French Bachelard in the 1940s. In the 1950s, the German-speaking Hunziker is joined by Barthes from France and Apih from the former Yugoslavia, while in the 1960s Knebel is joined by Mihovilović, also from the former Yugoslavia. The Slavonic influence continues in the 1970s with the well-known Zadar conference in which Alfier is a key player, but on this occasion there are established links with Dumazedier and Krippendorf. Not surprisingly the 1970s sees other French scholars contributing to this theme in the persons of Cazes and Dufour. The French influence continues into the 1980s with Thurot, at which point he is joined by two Scandinavians (Øllgaard and Hansen). Apart from the Francophone Picard, Tresse, and Urbain, the 1990s are equally dominated by possibly less internationally known Italian contributors (Baraldi and Teodorani; Bernardi; Gori) whose influence carries over to the 2000s in the person of Montani. The millennium also sees the reappearance of contributors from the former Yugoslavia (Kliment; Panian) and two more Scandinavian entries. What marks out the initial Scandinavian contributions is an emphasis on photography (visual sociology), and in one of the later contributions there is a focus on photographs as a method for eliciting tourist verbal imagery.

Category 5: Self-Reliance, Meaning, Identity, Socialization, Liminality, and Pilgrimage. In spite of the fact that most of the seminal ideas for this category can be found in Veblen at the end of the 19th century, this theme does not emerge in the sociology of tourism until the 1970s, where it is tackled by three Scandinavian single or joint authors (Eckeroth; Høivik and Herberg; Wagner) two Poles (Abramowska; Przecławski), and one German-speaker (Keller)—all of whom are from Northern Europe. Thereafter and with only one exception (the Norwegian Heimtun in the 2000s), this topic becomes the total preserve of Southern Europeans: one Italian in the 1980s; four Italians and three Greeks in the 1990s; and five Italians and one Greek in the 21st century. Just why this is such a tardy topic in tourism theory may perhaps be attributed to the equally late theme of individualism in postmodern society along with the emergence of reflexivity and constructivism.

Category 6: "Tourist Bubbles," Mass Tourism, and Anti-Tourists. Although the idea of "tourist bubble" originated from Knebel in the 1960s, fully 50% of those contributing to the extended theme are from Scandinavia where they are represented in the 1950s, 1960s, 1970s, 1980s, and 2000s. A popular period for this topic is the 1970s where one Italian and two French authors join four Scandinavian scholars, while Greeks do not tackle the theme until the 1990s and 2000s.

Category 7: Space and Place: Nature, Coast, Countryside, and City. While this category originates with the German-speaking Simmel in the pre-1930s period, it reemerges with Barberis and Catelli, two Italians, in the 1960s. Thereafter, in the 1970s, it is tackled by one Greek, one Pole, one Belgian, and one Scandinavian, the latter, Löfgren, under the influence of the Francophone, Roland Barthes. Two more Dutch speakers focus specifically on the city in the 1980s, especially the historic city, and they are joined by the German-speaking Gyr with links back to Knebel and Veblen. However, the 1990s are dominated by Italian (two) and Greek (one) authors, as are the 2000s (four and three, respectively). The Italians initially focus on the countryside but later turn their attention to the renaissance of the city, while the Greeks tend to concentrate on such issues as agro-tourism and the link between rurality and the nostalgic past.

Category 8: Sociocultural Effects, Communities, Jobs, Policy, Sustainability, and Conflict. Although this is the largest of the categories in terms of frequency of contributors, it is also relatively recent. Apart from category 7 (space and place), sociocultural effects belong to the only category where there are numerically more authors ($n = 18$) in the 2000s than in any other period. Category 8, unlike category 7, has a theoretical start with the Italian Catelli in the 1960s and another compatriot, Martinelli, in the 1970s, when the latter is joined by one Scandinavian and three Greeks, one of whom (Bidgianis) focuses on peasant employment in the tourism industry. In the 1980s, with contributions from all countries, such subthemes as development are tackled by Greeks, former Yugoslav, and Scandinavian authors (the latter focusing on sustainable development), while sociocultural costs are treated by Italians, Poles, and the important French round-table of Marly-le-Roi. Cultural studies constitute the framework for Dutch scholars, while (class) conflict is taken up by Italians and Scandinavians. The 1990s appear to be dominated by Greeks (six) exploring such issues as local community and employment, although one Pole and one Italian can be found who respectively analyze the positive effects of tourism and invisible tourism. In the 2000s, apart from three Scandinavians dealing with the environment and the Sámi people, the remainder of the category is treated by 12 Italians investigating social equity, employee belonging, conflict between private and public sectors, social relations in a post-tourism community, local communities and globalization, unauthorized building, governance, and sustainability, while three Greeks tackle ecotourism, professional mobility, and environmental protests. Yet even though this is the largest category, some may argue that it is the least theoretical in nature, at least in so far as the sociology of tourism is concerned.

Category 9: Tourism and Gender; Tourism and the Family.   This is another relatively late category. Although it commences in the 1970s with a former Yugoslav church conference and the Greek author, Stott, before moving to the 1980s with two Scandinavian, one Italian, and one Greek entry. However, it is the period of the 1990s which dominates this theme with six Greek contributors, leaving the remaining three slots to representatives from the former Yugoslavia, Italy, and Poland (with a continuation of Scandinavian interest generated by the Finns, Veijola, and Jokinen). The popularity of gender issues in the 1990s is mirrored in the Anglophone world, even though the focus is less on family matters than it is in Greece. Finally, the 2000s are entirely represented by Greek contributions in spite of the fact that there are only three of them in total. Overall most of the contributors to gender and family studies are female. There is also no German or French treatment of this theme among the contributions identified in the country chapters.

Category 10: Tourist Motives and Decision-Making.   Whereas motivation in tourism studies can be traced back to the likes of the great German classicists of Weber, Simmel, and Schutz, authors who subsequently take up the theme are spread across most of the contributing territories. Initial interest is shown by two Scandinavians in the 1950s and 1960s as well as two Italians in the 1960s and 1970s. There are two more Italians in the 1980s as well as a Scandinavian and a German. However, one of these Italians, Savelli, acknowledges reliance on the German Enzensberger and Knebel, and the French Boyer, Burgelin, and Morin. The 1990s see representatives from Scandinavia, Poland, the former Yugoslavia, and Greece, although the latter is an instance of a Finnish researcher, Selänniemi, working in that country. In the 2000s there is a decline of interest in the topic with only two contributions, one from Italy and one from the Netherlands.

Category 11: Leisure, Free Time, Recreation, Sport, and Holidays of Workers. In the current exercise with an overall focus on the sociology of tourism, it is inevitable that leisure becomes the center of attention where tourism is regarded as a subset of that life domain. Such is certainly the case in the pioneering work of Dumazedier and Lanfant in the 1950s (with respective publications appearing in the 1960s and 1970s), as also the necessary split from the research committee on leisure within the International Sociological Association and the sect-like creation of a separate research committee dedicated to international tourism. However, within this category of leisure it emerges that the Dutch speakers are making two contributions in the pre-1930s era as well as three more in the 1930s. Those from the low-countries also exclusively dominate the 1960s with four more contributions, before tailing off in the 1970s, 1980s, and 1990s, with one, two, and one contributions, respectively. Nevertheless they account for 13 out of the 19 authors identified, the remaining places being taken up by three theoreticians from the former Yugoslavia, one each in the 1970s, 1980s, and 2000s (all focusing on sport), two previously identified from France in the 1960s and 1970s, and one from Scandinavia in the 1970s. It is worth repeating that this Scandinavian preoccupation with free time is also linked with an ideological concern on how workers utilize it for the good of society.

Taking all 11 categories together, with their identifying numbers in parentheses, they fall into four main groupings:

- Those categories with a lengthy tradition, predating Anglophone contributions of the 1970s by at least 40 years and continuing steadily from that time comprise: (1) general theory (pre-1930s); (2) consumption and social prestige (pre-1930s); (3) strangerhood, alienation, escape, and freedom (pre-1930s); (4) interpersonal relations, communication, and imagery (pre-1930s); (11) leisure, free time, recreation, sport, holidays of workers.
- Those categories which commence slightly later (though still 20–30 years ahead of Anglophone contributions), and continue thereafter: (6) "tourist

bubbles," mass tourism, anti-tourism, social tourism; (10) motives, and decision-making.

- Those categories with relatively early beginnings (pre-1930s), but not developing continuously until much later (1960s and 1970s): (5) self-reliance, tourist experiences, meaning, identity, socialization, liminality; (7) space, place, nature, coast, country, city.
- Those categories that begin and develop late (from the 1970s onwards): (8) social effects, local communities, employment, policy, conflict, sustainability; (9) gender and family.

Thus, all but the last group predates Anglophone theory (some 76.7% of the total). Interestingly, it is the constituent categories 8 and 9, which are the most descriptive and consequently the least theoretically oriented. There additionally appears to be an association, insofar as their early stages are concerned, between the first three groups and Northern European origins/ preliminary development. This pattern is also evident from cross-country citation of sources. For example, Jacobsen (this volume) writing in the 1980s, acknowledges the ideas of Knebel and Simmel, while Hunziker, writing in the 1950s, indicates dependency on von Wiese from the 1930s and the latter in turn derives many of his insights from Simmel (in the first decade of the 20th century). However, there are exceptions to this generalization, as Savelli (a Southern European), for instance, writing in the 1980s, indicates his reliance on Enzensberger and Knebel (both from the North). Even so, the general trend is for Northern Europeans to cite fellow Europeans from North of the Alps, thereby setting up an interesting hypothesis of ethnocentrism for a future study, but which limitations of space prohibit ulterior investigation here.

FINAL THOUGHTS

Putting together this volume has not been an easy task. In fact, throughout the lengthy three-year period taken to assemble what some may still regard as an over ambitious work we have of necessity had to enter numerous exchanges of dialog with our anonymous referees, our editors, our external mentor, our publisher, our contributors and, last but not least, ourselves. Hardly a day has gone by without at least two or three e-mails passing back and forth between us, and individual chapters have undergone several revisions, some as many as ten times, in order to bring them up to date with past, present, and future developments in each of the selected territories. Yet interestingly, and germane to the topic of this book, while none of our authors has English as a mother tongue, each can communicate in that language to a level that could well be envied by native speakers.

We have now turned full circle. Some concluding ideas have already been outlined in the preceding sections, which focus on further developments and future trends from a more comparative perspective. Rather than repeat these observations, the following final thoughts return instead to the very first pages of the introduction, thereby paying attention, however brief, to those more general methodological considerations that are strictly intertwined with a broad sociolinguistic issue. Even so, such an exercise may be regarded as non-mainstream, even eclectic, because of the ideology contained therein as well as the pluralistic content of the material. Throughout this book, tourism has repeatedly been confirmed as a multifaceted sociological phenomenon that takes into account different cultural interpretations and their correspondingly diverse linguistic articulations. In this framework, the contours of the sociology of tourism stand out, not so much along undisputed lines, but rather as constituting a heuristic device of a vibrant, but possibly still unsettled field. There are no definitive answers to our project. Indeed, some questions, according to the canons of scientific inquiry, remain just that—questions. They represent not only the traditional outcome of Socratic doubt, but also of a more permanent uncertainty in the sense of "an incredible opportunity to imagine, to create, to search" (Wallerstein 1999:23). Thus, if any readers prefer a managerial style, with ready-made set solutions and universally accepted cutting edge definitions, they will probably be disappointed in this book, even though it does possess its own strict internal logic and encompasses many areas of consensus. Its basic perspective is evolutionary, that is to say, attentive to historical origins, present developments, and future prospects. These outlooks must also be contextualized today amid the uncertainties of a global economic crisis, which is probably going to compel us all to rethink the customary parameters of tourism by redefining it as a "post-post-industrial" phenomenon. It is into this volatile framework that the blurred boundaries of other allied tourism social science disciplines can also be envisaged, presenting not only traditional scientific rigor but also innovative post-disciplinary trends.

The linguistic aspect (especially in its sociolinguistic variant) has to be considered as a key issue of this volume, revealing itself in many ways as a paradox with inter-tangled implications. It means first of all acceptance of certain aspects of Anglo-Saxon dominance as a language of science with its own set of consequences, implying the passive and active use of English by scholars (Ammon 2008), both in the so called "hard sciences" and in the social sciences. In any case, it would be reductionist to speak simply of the menace of monolingualism in the face of national differences in tourism. This notion of a universal *lingua franca* also implies a threat to unique thought, affecting not only the act of self-expression in scientific contributions, but also in adopting legitimate mainstream theories. On the other hand, and this is intrinsic to the paradox, the discourse of this volume could not be conceived other than in English, in order to reach beyond an Anglophone audience to those non-English speaking students (and other interested persons) for whom English represents the language of science in Europe and elsewhere. It is at this point that the anthropological implications of the book are at stake (Nash 1996). Here, anthropology can be understood in the sense of the cultural relativism of the discovery of unknown European frontiers from an Anglo-Saxon point of view. It can also signify not just a *modus operandi* for English-speaking readers, but also a key to the open doors of a diverse literary-scientific world (Nash 1993). An important issue is that the anthropological dimension cannot be enhanced unless it also brings a vertical diachronic dimension of historical depth implicit in most of the contributions. That said, the sociology and anthropology of tourism should not be considered, as one might at first sight initially suppose, simply as sister disciplines, but also in the wider sense of the above anthropological implications. (For an understanding of current differences and similarities between anthropology and sociology see Nash (2007:13–15).)

At this final juncture we would like to focus on the role of the cultural intermediation of the editors and of all the contributors through their writing and via their attempts to make understandable to colleagues and to a wider audience of scholars interested in tourism the vibrant context of their respective countries via passages in their original languages and in their translations. We are now led back to the issue of multi-, inter-, post-disciplinarity raised in the section on unsettled questions. This concern will never go away; indeed, it will probably require a complete rethink, due to the new parameters dictated by the expected lengthy global financial crisis of today, especially in sociology's relationship with economics and its subtle domination under the guise of marketing and management. By contrast, and almost swimming against the tide, Lanfant's contribution in particular reminds us of the incredible value of literary texts as sociological documents. Obviously the rapidly evolving new frontiers of communication require continuous attention. Moreover, in the case of the sociology of leisure that might seem to be superseded by the sociology of tourism, there is both a prospect of a possible returning to less mobility and a more holistic framework, where both fields can be seen again as intimately interconnected. It must be further emphasized that the sociology of tourism will also have to confront the increasingly solid background of neuroscience (the problem raised at the ISA Congress of Montréal in 1998 and at the interim symposium of RC 50 in Mytilene in 2004).

As anticipated at the beginning of the introductory chapter, the task of this volume was not to focus on the external façade of an abstract history of ideas, but rather to explore the internal context of an emerging, underlying social reality. In so doing, the multiple evocation of a tormented European history stands out amidst corresponding sought after panaceas: the shadow of the Nazi regime leading to the expectations of the postwar years, a new generation of social actors seeking identity in an economic and political community, mass tourism as a fundamental social phenomenon and human right, as well as the affluent society and the illusions of consumption of Continental Europe. A particularly vivid picture is provided by Germany of the 1930s and France of the 1960s and 1970s. Scandinavian countries also display an active profile. Not only are scientific institutions singled out; there are additionally several significant meetings and conferences, as well as some important scholars with their own spheres of influence.

It is here that some sort of response has to be made to two possible objections. The first relates to ethnocentrism, especially Euro-centrism in an increasingly global context. While the charge of the former can be refuted by referring to the multicultural premises of the present volume, the issue of the latter, which is more pressing, has to be rebutted in a twofold manner: the absence of the United Kingdom and an exclusive concentration on European countries. As far as the absence of this country is concerned, we pay heed to the points raised in the French contribution to this volume (especially as the champion of the British cause is paradoxically a French sociologist of tourism). In fact, there is overall talk about the contested construction of Europe, a region that is not so clear-cut either over the centuries or in contemporary political reality. Of course the United Kingdom was the forerunner and then a fundamental protagonist of the tourism movement and of its culture, still leaving its mark through many English names (of hotels, tourism structures, etc.) on the Continent. However, especially in relatively recent years, after WWI and particularly WWII, there was no corresponding dominance of tourism studies probably due to the increasing prevalence of English and monolingualism. It was against this backdrop that Europe in its turn was divided for a certain period according to two different concepts, *Tourism* and *Fremdenverkehr*, with a completely different cultural background which we tried to illustrate in Chapter 1. In fact, and in order to avoid misunderstandings of this nature, we as editors were tempted in the beginning to use the subtitle *Continental Origins and Developments*, and, were it not for its reductionist connotations, we might well have employed it. In this regard, it has to be remembered that for many people in the United Kingdom itself, Europe means the Continent (suggesting that Europe is synonymous with Continental Europe, a foreign super-state with its own currency, something with which it only partially identifies). The second implication of the objection against Euro-centrism can be transformed into a positive message. It is true that this book is confined to Europe, but the foundation of its message can also be adapted to other geographical areas and situations; it thus represents a new point of view and something of a challenge.

Last but not least, a fundamental question remains: that of the scientific community of the sociology of tourism and its relationship to this volume. It has been underscored from the outset that this book was borne out of the research committee on international tourism (RC 50) of the International Sociological Association. Furthermore, the epistemological need for this volume can be traced to a solid common background and to a steady communication among the members of RC 50, to which many contributors belong in their role of collaborators, while they and others additionally share similar disciplinary interests in applying their sociological knowledge to the same vibrant field. Hence the question: "Does a European tourism social scientific community exist?" should be answered in the sense that RC 50 as a scientific community is wider than its European membership (or, as Durkheim would say, greater than the sum of its parts), since it additionally comprises Anglophone scholars from the United States, the United Kingdom, Canada, Australia, and New Zealand, as well as some from non-European, non-English speaking countries. Apart from a dearth of membership from Africa, South America, Japan, and China, it is really only Germany and France that are relatively under-represented in RC 50 and they ironically were at the forefront in the origins of the sociology of tourism. If these are the contours of a scientific community, from this point of view the present book represents much more than an anthology or a random collection of loose papers. The English language as a contested vehicle of communication has to be accepted and understood with all the provisos of the still existing scientific vitality of European tongues.

References

Abbink, J.
  1995 Antropologen Zijn Geen Toeristen (Anthropologists Are No Tourists). Facta, Sociaal wetenschappelijk Magazine (Facta, Social Sciences Journal) 3(4):2–5.
Abramowska, J.
  1978 Peregrynacja (Travel). *In* Przestrzeń i literatura (Space and Literature), M. Głowiński and A. Okopień-Sławińska, eds., pp. 125–158. Wrocław: Ossolineum.
Adorno, T.
  1969a Freizeit (Leisure). *In* Stichworte. Kritische Modelle (Catchwords. Critical Models, vol. 2) pp. 57–67. Frankfurt: Suhrkamp Akademie für Raumforschung und Landesplanung, ed.
  1969b Wissenschaftliche Aspekte des Fremdenverkehrs. Forschungsberichte des Ausschusses Raum und Fremdenverkehr (Scientific Aspects of Tourism: Research Reports from the Committee on Space and Tourism). Hannover: Jänecke.
Alejziak, W.
  1999 Turystyka w obliczu wyzwań XXI wieku (Tourism Facing the Challenges of the 21st Century). Kraków: Albis.
  2003 Perspectywy i kierunki rozwoju badań naukowych nad turystyka (Perspectives and Directions for the Development of Scientific Research in Tourism). Paper Presented to the Conference "Gremium Ekspertów Turystyki" ("Gathering of Tourism Experts"), Poznań, 24–26 September.
Alejziak, W., and R. Winiarski
  2003 Perspektywy rozwoju nauk o turystyce (Perspectives in the Development of Tourism Studies). *In* Nauki o turystyce. Część I (Studies of Tourism, Part One), R. Winiarski, ed. (2nd ed.). Studia i Monografie (Studies and Monographs) vol. 7, pp. 157–166. Kraków: Akademia Wychowania Fizycznego im. Bronisława Czecha w Krakowie.
Alejziak, W. and R. Winiarski, eds.
  2005a Tourism in Scientific Research. Kraków-Rzeszów: Academy of Physical Education, University of Information Technology and Manage ment.
  2005b Turystyka w badaniach naukowych (Tourism in Scientific Research). Kraków-Rzeszów: Akademia Wychowania Fizycznego im. Bronisława Czecha w Krakowie, Wyzsza Szkoła Informatyki i Zarzadzania w Rzeszowie.

Alfier, D.

1977 Uloga turizma u socijalizacijii desocijalizaciji suvremenog čovjeka (The Role of Tourism in the Socialization and De-Socialization of Modern Man). Proceedings of the Symposium "Humanističke vrijednosti turizma" ("Humanistic Values of Tourism"), pp. 19–48. Zadar: Pedagoška akademija.

1985 Pokušaj dijalektičkog objašnjenja pojave turizma (The Tourism Phenomenon Explained—Attempts at a Dialectic). Teorija i Praksa Turizma (Theory and Practice of Tourism) 1/2:3–7.

2004 Turizam—izbor radova (Tourism—Collected Papers). Zagreb: Institut za turizam.

Allardt, E.

1971 Konflikt-och Konsensusteoretiker (Conflict and Consensus Theorists). *In* Sociologiska Teorier: Studier i Sociologins Historia (Sociological Theories: Studies in the History of Sociology), J. Asplund, ed., pp. 184–209. Stockholm: Almqvist and Wiksell.

1993 Scandinavian Sociology and its European Roots and Elements. *In* Sociology in Europe: In Search of Identity, B. Nedelmann and P. Sztompka, eds., pp. 119–140. Berlin: de Gruyter.

Alsmark, G.

1984 Landet Lagom: Några Aspekter på Svensk Kultur (The Suitable Country: Some Aspects of Swedish Culture). *In* Är Lagom Bäst?: Om Kulturmöten i Sverige (Is Just Right Also Best? About Cultural Meetings of Sweden), pp. 133–153. Norrköping: Statens invandrarverk.

Amendola, G.

1993 Lo Stile Mediterraneo ovvero le Architetture Improbabili della Scena Turistica (The Mediterranean Style, that is, the Improbable Architectures of the Tourist Stage). *In* Il Turismo Mediterraneo come Risorsa e come Rischio: Strategie di Comunicazione (Mediterranean Tourism as a Resource and Risk: Communication Strategies), E. Nocifora, ed. Roma: Seam.

1997 La Città Postmoderna (The Post-Modern City). Roma: Laterza.

1999 Il Turismo Urbano e le Politiche per il Cittadino (Urban Tourism and Citizen Policies). *In* Turismo: Una Tappa per la Ricerca (Tourism: A Research Step), M. Colantoni, ed. Bologna: Pàtron.

Ammon, U.

1998 Ist Deutsch noch internationale Wissenschaftssprache? (Is German still the International Language of Science?). Berlin: de Gruyter.

2008 Global Scientific Communication: Open Questions and Policy Suggestions. *In* Introduction to Special Issue on Linguistic Inequality in Scientific Communication Today. Association Internationale de Linguistique Appliquée (AILA) (International Association of Applied Linguistics) Review 20, A. Carli and U. Ammon, eds., pp. 123–133.

Anderson, C.

1970 The Political Economy of Modern Spain: Policy-Making in an Authoritarian System. Madison: University of Wisconsin Press.

Andreae, C.
1970 Ökonomik der Freizeit (Economy of Leisure). Reinbek: Rowohlt.
Andriotis, K.
2000a Scale of Hospitality Firms and Local Economic Development—Evidence from Crete. Tourism Management 23(4):333–341.
2000b Local Community Perceptions of Tourism as a Development Tool: The Island of Crete. Unpublished PhD thesis, International Centre for Tourism and Hospitality Research, Bournemouth University, UK.
2001 Tourism Planning and Development in Crete: Recent Tourism Policies and their Efficacy. Journal of Sustainable Tourism 9(4):289–316.
2006 Hosts, Guests and Politics: Coastal Resorts, Morphological Change. Annals of Tourism Research 33(4):1079–1098.
Andriotis, K., and R. Vaughan
2003 Urban Residents' Attitudes towards Tourism Development: The Case of Crete. Journal of Travel Research 42:172–185.
Anthopoulou, T.
2000 Agro-Tourism and the Rural Environment: Constraints and Opportunities in the Mediterranean Less-Favoured Areas. *In* Tourism and the Environment: Regional, Economic, Cultural and Policy Issues (Revised), H. Briassoulis and J. van der Straaten, eds., pp. 357–373. Dordrecht: Kluwer Academic Publishers.
1998 Χωρικές και Αναπτυξιακές Διαστάσεις του Αγροτουρισμούστην Ελλάδα, Ετσήγηση στο 5° Πανελλήνιο Συνέδριο Αγροτικής Οικονομίας (Spatial and Development Dimensions of Rural Tourism in Greece). 5th National Conference of Agricultural Economy: Reconstruction of Rural Space, Athens.
Antunac, I.
1985 Turizam i ekonomska teorija (Tourism and Economic Theory). Zagreb: Institut za istraživanja u turizmu.
2001 Turizam—teorijsko-znanstvene rasprave (Tourism—Theoretical and Scientific Papers). Zagreb: Institut za turizam.
Apih, M.
1952 Turizam u svetu i kod nas (Tourism in the World and in this Country). Beograd: Biblioteka Zavoda za unapređenje turizma i ugostiteljstva FNRJ.
Apostolopoulos, Y., and S. Sonmez
1999 From Farmers and Shepherds to Shopkeepers and Hoteliers: Constituency-Differentiated Experiences of Endogenous Tourism in the Greek Island of Zakynthos. International Journal of Tourism Research 1:413–427.
2001 Greek Tourism on the Brink: Restructuring or Stagnation and Decline? *In* Mediterranean Tourism: Facets of Socioeconomic Development and Cultural Change, Y. Apostolopoulos, P. Loukissas, and L. Leontidou, eds., pp. 72–88. London: Routledge.

Apostolopoulos, Y., P. Loukissas, and L. Leontidou, eds.
  2001 Mediterranean Tourism: Facets of Socioeconomic Development and Cultural Change. London: Routledge.
Aramberri, J.
  2004 Will Travel Vanish? Looking beyond the Horizon. *In* New Horizons in Tourism: Strange Experiences and Stranger Practices, T. Singh, ed., pp. 195–212. Wallingford, CT: CAB International.
  2005 Sociologia del Turismo (Sociology of Tourism). Politica y Sociedad (Politics and Society) 42(1):1–13.
Aramberri, J. and R. Butler, eds.
  2005 Tourism Development: Issues for a Vulnerable Industry. Clevedon: Channel View Publications.
Aramberri, J., S. Singh, and X. Yanjun
  2004 Domestic Tourism in Asia. Tourism Recreation Research 29(2):101–116.
Armanski, G.
  1978 Die kostbarsten Tage des Jahres (The Most Precious Days of the Year). Berlin: Rotbuch.
  1997 Manna und Moneten. Zur Dynamik des modernen Tourismus (Manna and Dough: The Dynamics of Modern Tourism). Prokla 27:487–508.
Arndt, H.
  1978 Definitionen des Begriffs Fremdenverkehr im Wandel der Zeit (Definitions of the Term Fremdenverkehr in the Course of Time). Jahrbuch für Fremdenverkehr (Tourism Yearbook) 26:160–174.
Aron, R.
  1935(1981) La Sociologie Allemande Contemporaine (Contemporary German Sociology). Paris: Alcan; PUF.
  1967 Les Étapes de la Pensée Sociologique (Stages of Sociological Thought). Paris: Gallimard.
Ashworth, G.
  1984 Recreation and Tourism. London: Bell and Hyman.
  1994 De Pijl der Tijds in het Ruimtelijke Doel. Erfgoedplanning voor een Actueel Gebruik van het Verleden (The Arrow of Time in the Spatial Target: Heritage Planning for Present Use of the Past). Groningen: Geopers.
Ashworth, G., and T. de Haan
  1986 Uses and Users of the Tourist-Historic City: An Evolutionary Model in Norwich. Groningen: Rijksuniversiteit.
Ashworth, G., and J. Tunbridge
  1990 The Tourist-Historic City. London: Belhaven.
Ateljevic, I. A. Pritchard, and N. Morgan, eds.
  2007 The Critical Turn in Tourism Studies. Oxford: Elsevier.
Aubert, V.
  1965 The Hidden Society. New Brunswick, NJ: Transaction Books.

1969 Det Skjulte Samfunn (The Hidden Society). Oslo: Pax.

1974 Socialt Samspel (Social Interaction). Stockholm: Almqvist and Wiksell.

Aubert, V., and O. Arner

1962 The Ship as a Social System. Oslo: Institute of Sociology, University of Oslo.

Bachelard, G.

1943 L'Air et les Songes: Essai sur L'Imagination du Mouvement. Paris: Librairie José Corti.

1988 Air and Dreams: An Essay on the Imagination of Movement. Dallas, TX: Institute of Publications, Dallas Institute of Humanities and Culture.

Bachleitner, R., H. Kagelmann, and A. Keul

2005 Lexikon zur Tourismussoziologie (Tourism Sociology: An Encyclopedia). München: Profil.

Bachleitner, R., H. Kagelmann, and A. Keul, eds.

1998 Der durchschaute Tourist. Arbeiten zur Tourismusforschung (The X-Rayed Tourist: Studies in Tourism Research). München: Profil.

Bailey, P.

1978 Leisure and Class in Victorian England: Rational Recreation and the Contest for Control. London: Routledge and Kegan Paul, pp. 1830–1885.

Bakhtin, M.

1968 Rabelais and his World. Cambridge, MA: MIT Press.

Bakić, O.

2002 (2005) Menadžment turističke destinacije (Management of a Tourist Destination). Beograd: EFCID.

Bandinu, B.

1980 Costa Smeralda. Come Nasce una Favola Turistica (Emerald Coast: How a Tourist Dream was Born). Milano: Rizzoli.

Baraldi, C., and M. Teodorani

1998 Avventure Interculturali. Il Turismo Alternativo nell'Era della Globalizzazione. Il Caso Avventure nel Mondo (Intercultural Adventures. Alternative Tourism in the Age of Globalization. The Case of World Adventures). Bologna: Calderini.

Baranowski, S.

2001 Strength through Joy: Tourism and National Integration in the Third Reich. *In* Being Elsewhere, Consumer Culture and Identity in Modern Europe and North America, S. Baranowski and E. Furlough, eds., pp. 213–236. Ann Arbor, MI: University of Michigan Press.

Barberis, C.

1976 Proposta di Lavoro per una Sociologia del Turismo (Work Suggestion for a Sociology of Tourism). *In* Sviluppo del Territorio e Ruolo del Turismo (Territorial Development and the Role of Tourism), C. Stroppa, ed., pp. 11–20. Bologna: Clue.

1979 Per una Sociologia del Turismo (For a Sociology of Tourism). Milano: FrancoAngeli.

Barlösius, E.
   2004 Klassiker im Goldrahmen. Ein Beitrag zur Soziologie der Klassiker (Classics in the Gilt Frame: A Contribution to the Sociology of Sociological Classics). Leviathan 32:514–542.
Barretto, M.
   2003 O Imprescindivel Aporte das Ciências Sociais para o Planejamento e a Comprensão do Turismo (The Imprescindible Contribution of the Social Sciences for the Planning and Understanding of Tourism). Horizontes Antropologicos (Anthropological Horizons) 9(20):15–29.
Barthes, R.
   1957 Mythologies (Mythologies). Paris: Éditions du Seuil.
   1984 Mythologies. London: Paladin.
Bartoluci, M. ed.
   1996 Menadžment i poduzetništvo (Management and Entrepreneurship). Zagreb: Fakultet za fizičku kulturu.
Bartoluci, M. and N. Čavlek, eds.
   2007 Turizam i sport (Tourism and Sport). Zagreb: Školska knjiga.
Bartoszewicz, W.
   1988 The Dynamic Analysis of Tourism. Problems of Tourism XI(3):21–31.
   1999 Goals, Motives and Forms of Incoming Tourism in Poland in 1998. Warszawa: Institute of Tourism.
Bataille, G.
   1967 La Part Maudite Précédé de la Notion de Dépense (The Cursed Part, Preceded by the Notion of Expense). Paris: Minuit.
Battilani, P.
   2001 Vacanze di Pochi, Vacanze di Tutti (Holidays for the Few, Holidays for All). Bologna: Il Mulino.
Battistelli, F.
   1993 Il Modello Rimini tra Crisi e Mutamento (The Rimini Model between Crisis and Change). *In* Il Turismo Mediterraneo come Risorsa e come Rischio: Strategie di Comunicazione (Mediterranean Tourism as a Resource and Risk: Communication Strategies), E. Nocifora, ed., pp. 227–236. Roma: Seam.
Baudrillard, J.
   1970 (1974) La Société de Consommation, ses Mythes, ses Structures (The Society of Consumption, its Myths, its Structures). Paris: Gallimard.
   1972 Pour une Critique de la Politique du Signe (For a Critique of the Politics of the Sign). Paris: Gallimard.
Baudrillard, J.
   1975 L'Échange Symbolique et la Mort (Symbolic Exchange and Death). Paris: Gallimard.
   1988 Selected Writings. Cambridge: Polity Press.
Baumol, W., R. Litan, and C. Schramm
   2007 Good Capitalism, Bad Capitalism and the Economics of Growth and Prosperity. New Haven, CT: Yale University Press.

Bausinger, H.
1981 Arbeit und Freizeit (Work and Leisure). *In* Funkkolleg Geschichte (Radio Seminar on History), W. Conze, et al, vol. 1, pp. 114–135. Frankfurt: Fischer.
1995 Bürgerliches Massenreisen um die Jahrhundertwende (Bourgeois Mass Travel at the Turn of the Century). *In* Soll und Haben. Alltag und Lebensformen bürgerlicher Kultur (Debit and Credit. Everyday Life and Forms of Life of Bourgeois Culture), U. Gyr, ed., pp. 131–147. Zürich: Offizin.
Bausinger, H., K. Beyrer, and G. Korff, eds.
1991 Reisekultur. Von der Pilgerfahrt zum modernen Tourismus (Travel Culture: From Pilgrimage to Modern Tourism). München: Beck.
Beato, F.
2008 Il Turismo Sostenibile. Note sull'Approccio Multidimensionale (Sustainable Tourism. Notes on a Multidimensional Approach). *In* Tracce di Turismo Sostenibile (Traces of Sustainable Tourism), F. Beato, et al, pp. 17–29. Rende: Centro Editoriale e Librario dell'Università della Calabria.
Becker, C., H. Hopfinger, and A. Steinecke, eds.
2007 Geographie der Freizeit und des Tourismus. Bilanz und Ausblick (Geography of Leisure and Tourism. Result and Outlook). (3rd ed). München: Oldenbourg.
Becker, C. and H. Job, eds.
2004 Nationalatlas Bundesrepublik Deutschland (National Atlas of the Federal Republic of Germany). vol. 10: Freizeit und Tourismus (Leisure and Tourism), (2rd ed). München: Elsevier
Becker, H.
1963 Outsiders: Studies in the Sociology of Deviance. New York: Free Press.
Beckers, T.
1979 Achtergrond en Verklaring van de Rekreatieve Groei (Background and Explanation of Recreational Growth). *In* Grenzen van de Recreatieve Groei (Limits of Recreational Growth). Capita Selecta (Selected Chapters) 1978–1979, pp. 2/1–2/15. Wageningen: Landbouwhogeschool.
1983a Planning voor Vrijheid (Planning for Freedom). Wageningen: Landbouw Hogeschool.
1983b Tussen Hoop en Vrees (Between Hope and Fear). Vrijetijd en Samenleving (Leisure and Society) 1(5):509–528.
Beckers, T., and H. Mommaas
1991 Het Vraagstuk van den Vrijen Tijd. 60 Jaar Onderzoek naar Vrijetijd (The Question of Free Time: 60 Years of Research into Leisure). Leiden/Antwerpen: Stenfert Kroese.
Beijer, H.
1967 Volksjeugd en Cultuur. Enige Beschouwingen op Grond van Waarnemingen te Maastricht (Lowerclass Youth and Culture: Some Thoughts Based on Observations in Maastricht). s.l.: Dux.

Benini, E.
2008 Superare l'Evidenza, Rompere l'Omologazione dello Sguardo (Going beyond the Evidence, Breaking the Homogenization of the Gaze). *In* Spazio Turistico e Società Globale (Tourist Space and Global Society), A. Savelli, ed., pp. 24–32. Milano: FrancoAngeli.

Benini, E., and A. Savelli
1986 Il Senso del Far Vacanza: Motivazioni e Strutture nel Turismo Postmetropolitano (The Meaning of Holidaymaking: Motivations and Structures in Postmetropolitan Tourism). Milano: FrancoAngeli.

Benjamin, W.
1999 (1927–1934) The Arcades Project. Cambridge, MA: Harvard University Press.

Berger, P., and T. Luckmann
1966 The Social Construction of Reality. New York: Doubleday.

Berger, W.
1999 Die Technologisierung des Erlebens (Technologization of Experience). Voyage 3:33–47.

Berggren, M., and M. Zetterström
1974 Att Bo i Stugby: Intervjuer med Gäster i Fyrklöverns Stugby och Siljansnäs Fritidsby (Staying in a Leisure Village: Interviews with Guests in Fyrklöverns Stugby and Siljansnäs Fritidsby). Stockholm: Institutet för Folklivsforskning/Nordiska Museet.

Bernardi, U.
1997 Del Viaggiare. Turismi, Culture, Cucine, Musei Open Air (About Travel. Tourisms, Cultures, Cuisines, Open Air Museums). Milano: FrancoAngeli.

Bernecker, P.
1952 Die Wandlungen des Fremdenverkehrsbegriffes (Metamorphoses of the Term Fremdenverkehr). Jahrbuch für Fremdenverkehr (Tourism Yearbook) 1:31–38.
1962 Grundzüge der Fremdenverkehrslehre und Fremdenverkehrspolitik (Main Features of the Teaching of Tourism and of Tourism Politics). Wien: Österreichischer Gewerbeverlag.

Bernecker, P., C. Kaspar, and J. Mazanec
1984 Zur Entwicklung der Fremdenverkehrsforschung und -lehre der letzten Jahrzehnte (The Development of Tourism Research and Tourism Teaching during the Last Decades). Wien: Service.

Berting, J., W. Heinemeijer, and H. Philipsen
1959 Status en Vrije Tijd (Status and Free Time). Sociologische Gids (Sociological Guide) 6(2):122–136.

Beutel, M., et al
1978 Tourismus: Ein kritisches Bilderbuch (Tourism: A Critical Storybook). Bensheim: Päd-Extra.

Biblioteca Virtual Eumednet
2004 Biblioteca Virtual Eumednet (html://eumed.net/cursecon/libreria/).
Bidgianis, K.
1979 Οι επιπτώσεις της οικοδομικής επέμβασης της εταιρείας Καρράς στη Νότια Σιθωνία (The Effects of the Carras Company Intervention in South Sithonia). Οικονομία και Κοινωνία (Economy and Society) 7:25–35.
Bijsterveldt, Q.
1983 De Ontwikkeling van de Vrije Tijd in Nederland (The Development of Leisure in the Netherlands). Vrijetijd en Samenleving (Leisure and Society) 1(2):159–187.
Bilen, M.
1996 Osnove turističke geografije (Essentials of Tourism Geography). Zagreb: Mikrorad and ekonomski fakultet.
Bilen, M., and K. Bučar
2001 Osnove turističke geografije (Essentials of Tourism Geography). Zagreb: Školska knjiga.
Birkeland, I.
1997 Visuell Erfaring som Situert Kunnskap (Visual Practice as Situated Knowledge). Sosiologi i dag (Sociology Today) 27(1):73–89.
2005 Making Place, Making Self: Travel, Subjectivity and Sexual Difference. Aldershot: Ashgate.
Birkelund, G.
2006 The Genesis of Norwegian Sociology: A Story of Failures and Success. Sosiologisk Årbok (Yearbook of Sociology) 3/4:41–67.
Blašković, V.
1962 Geografske karakteristike turizma u Jugoslaviji (Geographical Characteristics of Tourism in Yugoslavia). Ljubljana: Zbornik VI kongresa geografa FNRJ.
Blažević, I., and Z. Pepeonik
1979 Turistička geografija (Tourism Geography). Zagreb: Školska knjiga.
Blok-van der Voort, E.
1977 Vakantie Nader Bekeken: Een Roltheoretische Exploratie (Holiday Considered: A Role Theory Exploration). Leiden: Rijksuniversiteit.
Blonk, A., and J. Kruijt
1933 Oproep tot medewerking aan een onderzoek naar de besteding van der vrije tijd (Call for Cooperation in Research on Leisure Spending). Socialistiche Gids (Socialist Guide) 18:659–660.
Blonk, A., J. Kruit, and E. Hofstee
1936 De Besteding van de Vrije Tijd door de Nederlandse Arbeiders (Leisure Spending of Dutch Workers). Amsterdam: Nutsuitgeverij.
Bodenstein, E.
1972 Der Wandel touristischer Landschaftsbewertung seit Beginn des 18. Jahrhunderts am Beispiel des Harzes (Changes in the Tourist Valuation of

Landscape from the Beginning of the 18th Century. The Example of the Harz). *In* Landschaftsbewertung für die Erholung (Landscape Evaluation for Recreational Purposes), Akademie für Raumforschung und Landesplanung, ed., pp. 21–32. Hannover: Jänecke.

Bodio, L.
1899 Sul Movimento dei Forestieri in Italia e sul Denaro che vi Spendono (On the Movement of Foreigners in Italy and the Money that they Spend). Giornale degli Economisti (Economists' Journal) 15:54–61.

Boissevain, J.
1986 Tourism as Anti-Structure. Paper Presented at the Anthropology Seminar of the University of Utrecht, Netherlands.

Boissevain, J. ed.
1996 Coping with Tourists: European Reactions to Mass Tourism. New Directions in Anthropology, vol. 1, Oxford: Berghahn Books.

Bonadei, R.
2004 I Sensi del Viaggio (Meanings of Travel). Milano: FrancoAngeli.

Bonomi, E.
1993 Le Identità Molteplici, i Disagi e le Virtù (Multiple Identities, Troubles, and Virtues). *In* Il Turismo Mediterraneo come Risorsa e come Rischio: Strategie di Comunicazione (Mediterranean Tourism as a Resource and Risk: Communication Strategies), E. Nocifora, ed., pp. 189–194. Roma: Seam.

Boorstin, D.
1962 The Image; or, What Happened to the American Dream. New York: Atheneum.
1964 (1987) The Image: A Guide to Pseudo Events in America (25th anniversary ed.). New York: Atheneum.

Bopp, P., et al
1981 Mit dem Auge des Touristen. Zur Geschichte des Reisebildes (With the Eye of the Tourist: On the History of Travel Images). Tübingen: University of Tübingen.

Borghardt, J.
1997 Die Entgrenzung des touristischen Blicks (The Limitlessness of the Tourist Gaze). Tourismus Journal 1:405–418.

Bormann, A.
1931 Die Lehre vom Fremdenverkehr (The Teaching of Tourism). Berlin: Verkehrswissenschaftliche Lehrmittelgesellschaft.

Bormann, R.
2000 Von Nicht-Orten, Hyperräumen und Zitadellen der Konsumkultur: Eine sozialtheoretische Reise durch postfordistische Landschaften (On Non-Places, Hyperspaces and Cathedrals of Consumption Culture: A Social Theoretical Journey through Postfordist Landscapes). Tourismus Journal 4:214–233.

Böröcz, J.
1996 Leisure Migration: A Sociological Study of Tourism. Oxford: Elsevier.

Bote, V., and A. Esteban
1996 Introducción to Special Issue: La Investigación Turística Española en Economía y Geografía (The Investigation of Spanish Tourism in Economics and Geography). Estudios Turísticos 129:5–9.

Botterill, D.
2003 An Autobiographic Narrative on Tourism Research Epistemologies. Loisir et Société (Leisure and Society) 26(1):97–110.

Bourdieu, P.
1965 Un Art Moyen: Essai sur les Usages Sociaux de la Photographie (A Middle-Brow Art: Essay on the Social Uses of Photography). Paris: Éditions de Minuit.
1979 La Distinction: Critique Sociale du Jugement. Paris: Éditions de Minuit.
1984 Distinction: A Social Critique of the Judgment of Taste. Routledge and Kegan Paul, London; Cambridge: Cambridge University Press.

Böventer, E. von
1989 Ökonomische Theorie des Tourismus (Economic Theory of Tourism). Frankfurt: Campus.

Boyer, M.
1982 Le Tourisme (Tourism). Paris: Éditions du Seuil.
1999 Le Tourisme, une Épistémologie Spécifique (Tourism, a Specific Epistemology). Les Cahiers du Groupement de Recherche Tourisme: Lieux et Réseaux (Papers of the Tourism Research Group: Places and Networks) 2:7–20.
2005 Histoire Générale du Tourisme. Du XVIe au XXIe Siècle (General History of Tourism: From the 16th to the 21st Centuries). Paris: L'Harmattan.
2007 Le Tourisme de Masse (Mass Tourism). Paris: L'Harmattan.

Brenan, G.
1990 The Spanish Labyrinth: An Account of the Social and Political Background of the Spanish Civil War. Cambridge: Canto.

Brenner, J. ed.
1989 Der Reisebericht. Die Entwicklung einer Gattung in der deutschen Literatur (The Travelogue: The Development of a Literary Genre in Germany). Frankfurt: Suhrkamp.

Brougier, A.
1902 Die Bedeutung des Fremdenverkehrs für Bayern (The Impact of Tourism for Bavaria). München: Oldenbourg (offprint).

Brown, F.
1998 Tourism Reassessed: Blight or Blessing? Oxford: Butterworth-Heinemann.

Brown, G.
1992 Tourism and Symbolic Consumption. *In* Choice and Demand in Tourism, P. Johnson and B. Thomas, eds., pp. 57–71. London: Mansell.

Bruckner, P., and A. Finkielkraut
1979 Au Coin de la Rue, l'Aventure (Street Corner Adventure). Paris: Editions du Seuil.

Bruner, E.
1994 Abraham Lincoln as Authentic Reproduction: A Critique of Postmodernism. American Anthropologist 96(2):397–415.
1995 The Ethnographer/Tourist in Indonesia. *In* International Tourism: Identity and Change, M.-F. Lanfant, J. Allcock, and E. Bruner, eds., pp. 224–241. London: Sage.
1996 Tourism in Ghana: The Representation of Slavery and the Return of the Black Diaspora. American Anthropologist 98(2):290–304.
2001 The Maasai and the Lion King: Authenticity, Nationalism and Globalization in African Tourism. American Ethnologist 28:881–908.
Buccino, V.
1966 La Strada Difficile (The Hard Way). Ravenna: Longo.
Bucholz, W.
1976 Die nationalsozialistische Gemeinschaft "Kraft durch Freude". Freizeitgestaltung und Arbeiterschaft im Dritten Reich (The National-Socialist Community "Strength through Joy": Leisure Activities and the Working Class in the Third Reich). München: Diss.
Bunc, M.
1974 Tržna ekonomika in marketing turizma (Market Economy and Tourism Marketing). Ljubljana: Državna založba Slovenije.
1986 Integralni marketing u turizmu (Integral Marketing in Tourism). Ljubljana: Delo.
Burgelin, O.
1967 Le Tourisme Jugé (Tourism Assessed). Communications 10:65–96.
Burkart, A., and S. Medlik
1974 Tourism: Past, Present, and Future. London: Heinemann.
Burkot, S.
1988 Polskie podrózopisarstwo romantyczne (Polish Travel Writing in the Period of Romanticism). Warszawa: Wydawnictwo PWN.
Burmeister, H.-P. ed.
1998 Auf dem Weg zu einer Theorie des Tourismus (Towards a Theory of Tourism). Loccum: s.n.
Burns, P., and A. Holden
1995 Tourism: A New Perspective. Hemel Hempstead: Prentice-Hall.
Burszta, W.
1996 Czytanie kultury. Pięć szkiców (Reading of Culture. Five Essays). Poznań: Instytut Etnologii i Antropologii Kulturowej Uniwersytetu im. Adama Mickiewicza w Poznaniu.
2001 Asteriks w Disneylandzie. Zapiski antropologiczne (Asterix in Disneyland. Anthropological Notes). Poznań: Wydawnictwo Poznańskie.
Bystrzanowski, J.
1964 History of Tourism in Poland. Warszawa: Mountain Guides Association.
1977 Notas sobre la Participación de España en el Estudio Comparativo Multinacional sobre los Problemas Económicos y Sociológicos del Turismo en

Europa (Notes on the Participation of Spain in the Multinational Comparative Study of the Economic and Sociological Problems of Tourism in Europe). Estudios Turísticos (Tourist Studies) 55/56.

1980a Structure of International Outgoing Tourism in Selected European Countries. Warszawa: Institute of Tourism.

1980b Information System for the Tourism Pool of Eastern European Countries. Warszawa: Institute of Tourism.

1981 Development of Social Tourism in Poland. Warszawa: Institute of Tourism.

Bystrzanowski, J. ed.

1989 Tourism as a Factor of Change: National Case Study. Vienna: International Social Science Council, European Coordination Center for Research and Documentation in the Social Sciences.

Bystrzanowski, J. and G. Beck, eds.

1989 Tourism as a Factor of Change: A Sociocultural Study. Vienna: International Social Science Council, European Coordination Center for Research and Documentation in the Social Sciences.

Bærenholdt, J. and B. Granås, eds.

2008 Mobility and Place: Enacting Northern European Peripheries. Aldershot: Ashgate.

Bærenholdt, J., M. Haldrup, J. Larsen, and J. Urry

2004 Performing Tourist Places. Aldershot: Ashgate.

Caillois, R.

1950 L'Homme et le Sacré (Man and the Sacred). Paris: Gallimard.

Callari Galli, M., and G. Guerzoni

2004 Tornando a Casa. Flussi Turistici nei Mondi Contemporanei e Analisi Antropologica. Turismo Culturale e Cooperazione Universitaria (Coming Back Home. Tourist Flows in the Contemporary Worlds and Anthropological Analysis. Cultural Tourism and University Cooperation). *In* Turismo, Territorio, Identità (Tourism, Territory, Identity), A. Savelli, ed. Milano: FrancoAngeli.

Calvi, M.

2005 Il Linguaggio Spagnolo del Turismo (The Spanish Language of Tourism). Viareggio, Lucca: Mauro Baroni Editore.

Cannas, R., and M. Solinas

2005 Primo Rapporto sul Turismo nei Parchi Nazionali Italiani (First Report on Tourism in the Italian National Parks). Roma: CTS.

Cantauw, C. ed.

1995 Arbeit, Freizeit, Reisen. Die feinen Unterschiede im Alltag (Work, Leisure, Travel: Social Distinctions in Everyday Life). Münster: Waxmann.

Carli, A., and U. Ammon

2008 Introduction to Special Issue on "Linguistic Inequality in Scientific Communication Today". AILA (Association Internationale de Linguistique Appliquée) (International Association of Applied Linguistics) Review 20:1–3.

Castelberg-Koulma, M.
1991 Greek Women and Tourism: Women's Cooperatives as an Alternative Form of Organization. *In* Working Women: International Perspectives on Labor and Gender Ideology, N. Redclift and T.h. Sinclair, eds., pp. 197–212. London: Routledge.

Catalano, G., S. Fiorelli, and E. Marra
2008 Il Turismo Difficile. Reti Territoriali e Collaborazione Pubblico-Privato nel Caso Calabria (Difficult Tourism. Territorial Networks, Public-Private Cooperation in Calabria). *In* Spazio Turistico e Società Globale (Tourist Space and Global Society), A. Savelli, ed., pp. 105–127. Milano: FrancoAngeli.

Catelli, G.
1976 Turismo Agricolo e Società Industriale (Farm Tourism and Industrial Society). *In* Sviluppo del Territorio e Ruolo del Turismo (Territorial Development and the Role of Tourism), C. Stroppa, ed., pp. 183–194. Bologna: Clue.

Cazes, G.
1976 Le Tiers-Monde vu par les Publicités Touristiques. Une Image Mystifiante (The Third World Seen by Tourism Advertising. A Mystifying Image). Cahiers du Tourisme (Tourism Papers), série C, no. 33.

Cederholm, E.A.
1999 Det Extraordinäras Lockelse: Luffarturistens Bilder och Upplevelser (The Attraction of the Extraordinary: Images and Experiences among Backpacker Tourists). Lund: Arkiv Publishers.

Centraal Bureau voor de Statistiek (Central Office of Statistics) (CBS)
1954 Vakantiebesteding van de Nederlandse Bevolking (Holiday Making of the Dutch Population). Zeist: de Haan.

Centre des Hautes Etudes Touristiques (Center for Higher Touristic Studies) (CHET)
2008 (http://www.ciret-tourism.com, accessed 30 June).

Centre International de Recherches et d'Études Touristiques (CIRET) (International Center for Tourism Studies and Research)
2008 (http://www.ciret-tourism.com, accessed 30 June).
2009 Message to TRINET (accessed 24 July).

Centro de Documentación Turística de España (CDTE) (Spanish Center for Tourist Data)
2007 Índice General de la Revista de Estudios Turísticos (General Index of the Review of Tourist Studies) (RET). Madrid: Instituto de Estudios Turísticos.

Cerović, Z.
2003 Hotelski menadžment (Hotel Management). Opatija: Fakultet za turistički i hotelski menadžment.

Chałasiński, J.
1938 Młode pokolenie chłopów. Procesy i zagadnienia kształtowania się warstwy chłopskiej w Polsce (Young Generation of Peasants. Processes and Issues in the Creation of a Peasant Class in Poland), vol. I–IV [reprint], Warszawa: Spółdzielnia Wydawnicza "Pomoc Oświatowa".

1948 Społeczeństwo i wychowanie. Socjologiczne zagadnienia szkolnictwa i wychowania w społeczeństwie współczesnym (Society and Education: Sociological Aspects of Education and Upbringing in Contemporary Society). Warszawa: Nasza Ksiegarnia.

Chałubiński, M.
2006 The Sociological Ideas of Stanisław Ossowski. His Life, Fundamental Ideas and Sociology in Polish and World Science. Journal of Classical Sociology 6(3):283–309. Accessed from http://jcs.sagepub.com/cgi/reprint/6/3/283.pdf (18 February 2008).

Cheek, N., D. Field, and R. Burdge
1976 Leisure and Recreation Places. Ann Arbor, MI: Ann Arbor Science.

Christaller, W.
1955 Beiträge zu einer Geographie des Fremdenverkehrs (Contributions to a Geography of Tourism). Erdkunde 9:1–19.

Chtouris, S.
1995 Πολιτισμός και Τουρισμός: Ο Τουρισμός ως Δίκτυο Παραγωγής Βιωμάτων (Culture and Tourism: Tourism as a Network for the Production of Experiences). Σύγχρονα Θέματα (Current Issues) 55:48–56.

Ciacci, M.
1997 Fra Universalismo e Particolarismo: Il Turismo nelle Città d'Arte (Between Universalism and Particularism: Tourism in Cities of Art). Sociologia Urbana e Rurale (Urban and Rural Sociology) 52/53:235–242.

Ciacci, M. ed.
2000 Viaggio e Viaggiatori nell'Età del Turismo. Per una Riqualificazione dell'Offerta Turistica nelle Città d'Arte (Travel and Travelers in the Age of Tourism. For a Requalification of the Tourist Offer in Cities of Art). Firenze: Leo S. Olschki.

Cicvarić, A.
1984 Turizam i privredni razvoj Jugoslavije (Tourism and Economic Development in Yugoslavia). Zagreb: Tiskara "Zagreb".
1990 Ekonomika turizma (Economics of Tourism). Zagreb: Tiskara "Zagreb".

Cocco, E. and E. Minardi, eds.
2008 Immaginare l'Adriatico. Contributi alla Riscoperta Sociale di uno Spazio di Frontiera (Imagining the Adriatic: Contributions to the Social Rediscovery of a Frontier Space). Milano: FrancoAngeli.

Cohen, E.
1971 Arab Boys and Tourist Girls in a Mixed Jewish-Arab Community. International Journal of Comparative Sociology 12:217–233.
1972 Toward a Sociology of International Tourism. Social Research 39: 164–182.
1973 Nomads from Affluence: Notes on the Phenomenon of Drifter Tourism. International Journal of Comparative Sociology 14:89–103.
1974 Who is a Tourist? A Conceptual Clarification. Sociological Review 22(4):527–555.

1977 Expatriate Communities. Current Sociology 24:5–129.

1979a Rethinking the Sociology of Tourism. Annals of Tourism Research 6: 18–35.

1979b A Phenomenology of Tourist Experiences. Sociology 13:179–201.

1984 The Sociology of Tourism: Approaches, Issues, and Findings. Annual Review of Sociology 10:373–392.

2003 Stranger. *In* Encyclopedia of Tourism, J. Jafari, ed., pp. 559–560. London: Routledge.

2004 Contemporary Tourism: Diversity and Change: Collected Articles. Oxford: Elsevier.

Corijn, E.

1998 De Onmogelijke Geboorte van een Wetenschap (The Impossible Birth of a Science). Brussels: VUB Press.

Corvo, P.

2007 Turisti e Felici? Il Turismo tra Benessere e Fragilità (Happy Tourists? Tourism between Wellbeing and Frailty). Milano: Vita e Pensiero.

Coser, L.

1956 The Functions of Social Conflict. New York: Free Press.

Costa, N.

1985 Le Vacanze Estive. Geografia e Sociologia del Comportamento Turistico (The Summer Holidays. The Geography and Sociology of Tourist Behavior). Milano: Cooperativa Libraria Iulm.

1989 Sociologia del Turismo. Interazioni e Identità nel Tempo Libero (Sociology of Tourism. Interactions and Identity in Leisure). Milano: Cooperativa Libraria Iulm.

2005a I Professionisti dello Sviluppo Turistico Locale (The Professionals of Local Tourist Development). Milano: Hoepli.

2005b Introduction to D. MacCannell's Il Turista. Una Nuova Teoria della Classe Agiata (The Tourist. A New Theory of the Affluent Class). Torino: UTET-De Agostini.

2008 La Città Ospitale. Come Avviare un Sistema Turistico Locale di Successo (The Hospitable City. How to Start a Successful Local Tourist System). Milano: Bruno Mondadori.

Crick, M.

1989 Representations of International Tourism in the Social Sciences: Sun, Sex, Sights, Savings and Servility. Annual Review of Anthropology 18:307–344.

1994 Resplendent Sites, Discordant Voices. Sri Lankans and International Tourism. Chur: Harwood Academic.

1995 The Anthropologist as Tourist: An Identity in Question. *In* International Tourism: Identity and Change, M.-F. Lanfant, J. Allcock, and E. Bruner, eds., pp. 205–223. London: Sage.

Culler, J.

1981 Semiotics of Tourism. American Journal of Semiotics 1(1/2):127–140.

Cunningham, H.
1980 Leisure in the Industrial Revolution: c. 1780-c. 1880. London: Croom Helm.
Cybula, I.
2007 Pierwsze uzycie terminu "turysta" (First Usage of the Term "Tourist"). Rynek Podróży 11, Listopad 2007, 16 (accessed from Konfraternia Turystyczna, November 2007).
Čavlek, N.
1998 Turoperatori i svjetski turizam (Tour Operators and World Tourism). Zagreb: Golden Marketing.
2005 The Impact of Tour Operators in Tourism Development: A Sequence of Events. *In* Tourism Development: Issues for a Vulnerable Industry, J. Aramberri and R. Butler, eds., pp. 174–192. Clevedon: Channel View.
Čomić, Đ.
1990 Psihologija turizma (Psychology of Tourism). Beograd: Turistička štampa.
Čulić, D.
1965 Turistička propaganda (Tourism Advertising). Zagreb: Panorama.
Dahles, H.
1990 Mannen in her groen: de wereld van jacht in Nederland (Men in Green: The World of Hunting in the Netherlands). Nijmegen: SUN.
Dalla Chiesa, F.
1980 Sociologia del Turismo (Sociology of Tourism) (Typed). Corso di Perfezionamento per Funzionari e Impiegati dell'Ente Nazionale Italiano del Turismo (Course of Improvement for Functionaries and Employees of the National Tourist Board of Italy). Milano: Università Commerciale "L. Bocconi".
Dann, G.
1981 Tourist Motivation: An Appraisal. Annals of Tourism Research 8:187–219.
1996a The Language of Tourism: A Sociolinguistic Perspective. Wallingford, CT: CAB International.
1996b Tourists' Images of a Destination: An Alternative Analysis. Journal of Travel and Tourism Marketing 5(1–2):20–27.
1996c The People of Tourist Brochures. *In* The Tourist Image: Myth and Myth Making in Tourism, T. Selwyn, ed., pp. 61–81. Chichester: Wiley.
1997a Paradigms in Tourism Research. Annals of Tourism Research 24: 472–474.
1997b Tourist Behaviour as Controlled Freedom. *In* Tourism Research: Building a Better Industry, R. Bushell, ed., pp. 244–254. Canberra: Bureau of Tourism Research.
2000 Theoretical Advances in the Sociological Treatment of Tourism. *In* The International Handbook of Sociology, S. Quah and A. Sales, eds., pp. 367–384. London: Sage.
2003 Noticing Notices: Tourism to Order. Annals of Tourism Research 30: 465–484.

2004 Tourism Imagery Research in Norway: Classification, Evaluation and Projection. Scandinavian Journal of Hospitality and Tourism 4:191–207.

2005a Remodelling the Language of Tourism: From Monologue to Dialogue and Trialogue. Paper Presented to the International Academy for the Study of Tourism, Beijing, July.

2005b The Theoretical State-of-the-Art in the Sociology and Anthropology of Tourism. Tourism Analysis 10:1–13.

2007a How International is the International Academy for the Study of Tourism? Paper Presented to a Seminar of the International Academy for the Study of Tourism, Lykia World, Olüdeniz, Turkey, 15–19 May (Forthcoming in Tourism Analysis 14(1), 2009).

2007b Revisiting the Language of Tourism: What Tourists and Tourees are Saying. *In* The Languages of Tourism. Turismo e Mediazione, C. de Stasio and O. Palusci, eds., pp. 15–32. Milano: Edizioni Unicopli.

2008 The Topsy-Turvy Distinction between Centre and Periphery. Address to a Symposium in Honor of Arvid Viken, Finnmark University College, Alta, Norway, 17 October.

Dann, G. ed.
2002 The Tourist as a Metaphor of the Social World. Wallingford, CT: CAB International.

Dann, G., and E. Cohen
1991 Sociology and Tourism. Annals of Tourism Research 18:155–169.

Dann, G., and J. Jacobsen
2003 Tourism Smellscapes. Tourism Geographies 5:3–25.

Dann, G., and G. Liebman Parrinello
2007 Od putopisa do "putobloga": Redefiniranje identiteta turista (From Travelog to Travelblog: (Re)-negotiating Tourist Identity). Acta Turistica 19:7–29.

Daugstad, K.
2008 Negotiating Landscape in Rural Tourism. Annals of Tourism Research 35:402–426.

De Chateaubriand, F.-R.
1811 (1963) Itinéraire de Paris à Jerusalem (Itinerary from Paris to Jerusalem). Paris: Production de Paris.

De Grazia, S.
1962 Of Time, Work, and Leisure. New York: Twentieth Century Fund.

Deltsou, E.
2000 Η Οικοτουριστική Ανάπτυξη και ο Προσδιορισμός της Φύσης και της Παράδοσης: Παραδείγματα από τη Βόρεια Ελλάδα (Ecotourism Development and the Definition of Nature and Tradition: Examples from Northern Greece). *In* Ο Ορεινός Όγκος της Βαλκανικής: Συγκρότηση και Μετασχηματισμοί (The Mountainous Region of the Balkans: Its Constitution and Transformation), V. Nitsiakos and Ch. Kasimis, eds., pp. 231–248. Municipality of Konitsa, Konitsa: Plethron.

2005 Negotiating European and National Identity Boundaries in a Village in Northern Greece. *In* Crossing European Boundaries: Beyond Conventional Categories, H. Kopnina, Ch. Moutsou, and J. Staccul, eds., pp. 197–209. Oxford: Berghahn Books.

2007 Time, Place and Nostalgia in Representations of Alternative Tourism. *In* Economy and Society Confronting the New Challenges of the Global Agro-Food System. Electronic Publication of the Papers Presented in the 9th Conference of the Society of Rural Economy (ET. ΑΓΡ.Ο). The Rural Landscape of the Greek Countryside: Changes of Production Systems and the Representations Associated with the Landscape.

De Nerval, G.
1848 Scènes de la Vie Orientale, Tome I, Les Femmes du Caire (Scenes of Oriental Life, vol. I, The Women of Cairo). Paris: Sartorius.

1850 Scènes de la Vie Orientale, Tome II, Les Femmes du Liban (Scenes of Oriental Life, vol. II, The Women of Lebanon). Paris: Souverain.

De Saint-Simon, C.-H.
1966 Œuvres (Works). Paris: Anthropos.

1997 Histoire de la Sociologie (History of Sociology). Paris: Armand Colin.

Descan, J.-P.
1994 De Jaarlijkse Vakantie in België: Het Ontstaan en de Evaluatie tot op Heden (Annual Holidays in Belgium: Origin and Evaluation up to the Present). Brussel: Rijksdienst voor Jaarlijkse Vakantie.

De Stasio, C. and O. Palusci, eds.
2007 The Languages of Tourism. Turismo e Mediazione (Tourism and Mediation). Milano: Edizioni Unicopli.

Dietvorst, A., and M. Jansen-Verbeke
1986 Een geografische visie op de interrelatie Vrijetijd, Recreatie en Toerisme (A Geographical Perspective on the Interrelationship between Leisure, Recreation, and Tourism). Vrijetijd en Samenleving (Leisure and Society) 5(3):241–256.

Douglas, M., and B. Isherwood
1980 The World of Goods: Towards an Anthropology of Consumption. Harmondsworth: Penguin.

Drechsel, W.
1988 Zur Neugestaltung der Tourismusausbildung an der Hochschule für Verkehrswesen "Friedrich List" Dresden (The Reform of Tourism Education at the "Friedrich List" College for Transportation in Dresden). Mitteilungen aus der kulturwissenschaftlichen Forschung (Communications from Cultural Science Research) 24:174–184.

Dufour, R.
1978. Des Mythes du Loisir/Tourisme Weekend: Aliénation ou Libération? (Myths of Leisure/Tourism Weekends: Alienation or Freedom?) Cahiers du Tourisme (Tourism Papers), série C, no. 47.

Dulčić, A.
  1991 Turizam—načela razvoja i praksa (Tourism—Principles of Development and Practice). Zagreb: Institut za turizam.
  2001 Upravljanje razvojem turizma (Management of the Development of Tourism). Zagreb: Author and MATE.
Dumazedier, J.
  1962 Vers une Civilisation du Loisir? (Towards a Civilization of Leisure?). Paris: Éditions du Seuil.
  1967 Toward a Society of Leisure. New York: Free Press.
  1974 Sociology of Leisure. Amsterdam: Elsevier.
  1985 Sociologia del Tempo Libero (Sociologie Empirique du Loisir) (Sociology of Free-Time). Milano: FrancoAngeli.
  1988 La Révolution Culturelle du Temps Libre (The Cultural Revolution of Free Time). Paris: Méridien Klinckssieck.
Durkheim, E.
  1893 (1964) La Division du Travail Social (The Division of Labor in Society). New York: Free Press.
  1895 (1938) Les Règles de la Méthode Sociologique (Rules of the Sociological Method). New York: Free Press; Chicago, IL: University of Chicago Press.
  1897 (1997) Le Suicide (Suicide). New York: Free Press.
  1897 (1951) Suicide. *In* G. Simpson, ed. Glencoe: Free Press.
  1912 (1915) Les Formes Élémentaires de la Vie Religieuse (Elementary Forms of the Religious Life). London: Allen and Unwin.
  1912 (1965) Elementary Forms of the Religious Life. New York: Free Press.
Eco, U.
  1986 Travels in Hyperreality: Essays. San Diego, CA: Harcourt, Brace, Jovanovich.
Ehrenreich, B.
  1983 The Hearts of Men: American Dreams and the Flight from Commitment. Garden City, NY: Anchor Press.
Eichler, G.
  1979 Spiel und Arbeit. Zur Theorie der Freizeit (Play and Work: On the Theory of Leisure). Stuttgart: Frommann-Holzboog.
Ekeroth, G.
  1971 Turism och Alkohol (Tourism and Alcohol), Special Series: Alcohol Research. Uppsala: Department of Sociology, University of Uppsala.
Elaković, S.
  1989 Sociologija slobodnog vremena i turizma (Sociology of Leisure Time and Tourism). Beograd: Savremena administracija.
Elias, N.
  1939 The Civilizing Process: The History of Manners. New York: Urizen.
  1972 Leisure in the Sparetime Spectrum. *In* Soziologie des Sports (Sociology of Sport), R. Albonico and K. Pfister-Binz, eds., pp. 27–34. Basel: Birkhäuser.

1982 The Civilizing Process: State, Formation and Civilization. Oxford: Blackwell.

Elsrud, T.
2001 Risk Creation in Traveling: Backpacker Adventure Narration. Annals of Tourism Research 28:597–617.
2004 Taking Time and Making Journeys: Narratives on Self and the Other among Backpackers. PhD dissertation, Department of Sociology, University of Lund, Sweden.

Enzensberger, H.
1958 Vergebliche Brandung der Ferne. Eine Theorie des Tourismus (The Futile Lure of the Blue Yonder: A Theory of Tourism). Merkur 12:701–720.
1974 The Consciousness Industry: On Literature, Politics and the Media. New York: Seabury Press.
1996 A Theory of Tourism. New German Critique 68:117–135.

Epitropoulos, M.-F.
1992 The Socioeconomic Effects and Political Economy of Mass Tourism in Karpathos, Greece. Annual Meeting of the American Sociological Association (ASA), Chicago, IL, August 1999.

Ercole, E.
2008 Governance, Capitale Sociale e Pianificazione Strategica del Turismo nelle Aree Rurali e nelle Città di Medie Dimensioni (Governance, Social Capital and Strategic Planning of Tourism in Rural Areas and Middle-Size Towns). In Spazio Turistico e Società Globale (Tourist Space and Global Society), A. Savelli, ed., pp. 172–182. Milano: FrancoAngeli.

Ercole, E., and M. Gilli
2004 Il Turismo come Fattore di Sviluppo Locale nelle Aree Rurali: Studio del Caso Astigiano (Tourism as a Local Development Factor in Rural Areas: A Case Study of the Asti Region). In Turismo, Territorio, Identità. Ricerche ed Esperienze nell'Area Mediterranea (Tourism, Territory and Identity. Studies and Experiences in the Mediterranean Area), A. Savelli, ed., pp. 79–108. Milano: FrancoAngeli.

Estefanía, J.
1998 La Larga Marcha (The Long March). El País, May 3.

Evang, K.
1950 Ferien som Helsemessig, Sosial og Kulturell Faktor i Samfunnslivet (The Vacation as a Health-Related, Social, and Cultural Factor in Social Life). Address to Nordic Conference on Vacationing, Dombås, Norway.

Faché, W.
2000 Internationalisering, Conceptualisering en Operationalisering van Internationalisering van Universitair Onderwijs (Internationalization, Conceptualization and Operationalization of Academic Education). In Liber Amicorum Karel de Clerck (Book of Friends of Karel de Clerck), F. Simon, ed., pp. 267–309. Ghent: CSHP.

Fadda, A.
  2002 Isole allo Specchio. Sardegna e Corsica tra Identità, Tradizione e Innovazione (Isles in the Mirror. Sardinia and Corsica Amid Identity, Tradition, and Innovation). Roma: Carocci.
Fadda, A. ed.
  2001 Sardegna: Un Mare di Turismo. Identità, Culture e Rappresentazioni (Sardinia: A Sea of Tourism. Identities, Cultures, and Representations). Roma: Carocci.
Featherstone, M.
  1987 Lifestyle and Consumer Culture. Theory, Culture and Society 4(1):55–70.
Febas, J.
  1978 Semiología del Lenguaje Turístico (Investigación sobre los Folletos Españoles de Turismo) (Semiology of The Language of Tourism (Analysis of Spanish Tourist Brochures)). Revista de Estudios Turísticos (Review of Tourist Studies) 57–58:17–203.
Febas, J., and A. Orensanz
  n.d. Los Carteles Turísticos Españoles (Contribución al Estudio Semiótico del Cartel de Turismo). (Spanish Tourist Posters (Contribution to the Semiotic Study of the Tourist Poster)). Madrid: Instituto Español de Turismo (Photocopied).
  1980 El Folleto Nacional de Turismo como Autoformulación de la Imagen Turística (The National Tourist Brochure as the Self-Representation of the Touristic Image). Madrid: Instituto Español de Turismo (Photocopied).
  1982 Promoción Turística e Imagen (Touristic Promotion and Imagery). Madrid: Instituto Español de Turismo.
Fennefoss, A.
  1982 Roller: Et Historisk Perspektiv (Roles: An Historical Perspective). Working Paper 175. Oslo: Institute of Sociology, University of Oslo.
Fennefoss, A., and J. Jacobsen
  2002 Forståelse av Turisme og Turister (Understanding Tourism and Tourists). *In* Turisme: Turister og Samfunn (Tourism: Tourists and Society), J. Jacobsen and K. Eide, eds., pp. 25–55. Oslo: Gyldendal Akademisk.
  2004 Has "The Tourist Role" Disappeared? Vocabulary Changes in Sociology and their Implications for the Understanding of Tourists. Paper Presented to the Interim Symposium of the Research Committee on International Tourism (RC 50) of the International Sociological Association (ISA), University of the Aegean, Mytiline, Greece, 14–16 May.
Ferrari, M.
  2004 Come si Diventa Turisti. Teorie e Indagine Empirica sui Comportamenti Turistici (How to Become Tourists. Theories and Empirical Research on Tourist Behavior). Cagliari: Cuec.
Ferrarotti, F.
  1986 Manuale di Sociologia (Handbook of Sociology). Bari: Laterza.

1999 Partire, Tornare. Viaggiatori e Pellegrini alla Fine del Millennio (To Leave, to Come Back. Travelers and Pilgrims at the End of the Millennium). Roma: Donzelli.

Fink, C.

1970 Der Massentourismus: Soziologische und wirtschaftliche Aspekte unter besonderer Berücksichtigung schweizerischer Verhältnisse (Mass Tourism: Sociological and Economic Aspects with Particular Reference to Swiss Conditions). Bern: Paul Haupt.

Fischer, H.

1984 Warum Samoa? Touristen und Tourismus in der Südsee (Why Samoa? Tourists and Tourism in the South Sea). Berlin: Reimer.

Flaubert, G.

1966 Lettres d'Egypte (Letters from Egypt). Paris: Nizet.

Flitner, M., P. Langlo, and K. Liebsch

1997 Kultur kaputt. Variationen einer Denkfigur der Tourismuskritik (Broken Culture: Variations on a Pattern of Tourism Critique). Voyage 1:86–98.

Fløtten, T., I. Solvang

1989 Klasse, Livsstil og Reising: En Studie av Norske Pakketurister (Class, Lifestyle and Travel: A Study of Norwegian Package Vacationers). Cand. Sociol. dissertation, Institute of Sociology, University of Oslo, Norway, Oslo.

Fontana, J., and J. Nadal

1976 Spain: 1914-70. *In* The Fontana Economic History of Europe, C. Cipolla, ed. London: Fontana.

Fontane, T.

1894 Von vor und nach der Reise. Plaudereien und kleine Geschichten (Before and After the Voyage. Small Talk and Little Stories). Berlin: s.n.

Forster, J.

1964 The Sociological Consequences of Tourism. International Journal of Comparative Sociology 5:217–227.

Fortis, A.

1774 Viaggio in Dalmatia (Dalmatian Journey). Publisher unknown.

Foucault, M.

1973 Birth of the Clinic. London: Tavistock.

Fraga, I.M.

1964 El Turismo en España: Balance y Perspectivas (Tourism in Spain: Balance and Perspectives). Revista de Estudios Turísticos (Review of Tourist Studies) 1:5–50.

Fragola, U.

1984–1985 Teoria Generale del Turismo (A General Theory of Tourism). Napoli: Libera Facoltà di Scienze Turistiche.

Franke, B., and K. Hammerich

2001 Vom Ende der Freizeitsoziologie: Einige vorläufige Festlegungen (The End of Leisure Sociology: Some Provisional Statements). Tourismus Journal 5:352–363.

Franklin, A., and M. Crang
  2001 The Trouble with Tourism and Travel Theory. Tourist Studies 1(1):5–22.
Freyer, W.
  2005 Ganzheitliche Tourismuswissenschaft oder disziplinierte Tourismusökono-
  mie? (Holistic Tourism Science or Separated Tourism Economics?). *In* Zukunft,
  Freizeit, Wissenschaft. Festschrift für H. Opaschowski (Future, Leisure,
  Science: Record in Honor of H. Opaschowski), R. Popp, ed., pp. 58–82.
  Münster: Lit.
  2006 Tourismus. Einführung in die Fremdenverkehrsökonomie (Tourism:
  Introduction to the Tourism Economy) (8th ed). München: Oldenbourg.
Fritzsche, P.
  2004 Stranded in the Present: Modern Time and the Melancholy of History.
  Cambridge, MA: Harvard University Press.
Galani-Moutafi, V.
  1993 Part One. From Agriculture to Tourism: Property, Labour, Gender and
  Kinship in a Greek Island Village. Journal of Modern Greek Studies 11:241–
  270.
  1994 Part Two. From Agriculture to Tourism: Property, Labour, Gender and
  Kinship in a Greek Island Village. Journal of Modern Greek Studies 12:113–131.
  1995 Προσεγγίσεις του τουρισμού: Το επινοημένο και το "αυθεντικό"
  (Approaches to Tourism: The Contrived and the "Authentic"). Σύγχρονα
  Θέματα (Current Issues) 55:28–39.
  1996 Dowry and Socio-Economic Transformation in Samos during the 19th
  Century (in Greek). Ethnology 4:31–66.
  2000 The Self and the Other: Traveler, Ethnographer, Tourist. Annals of Tourism
  Research 27(1):203–224.
  2001 Representing the Self and the Other: American College Students in Mytilene,
  Greece. Journeys. The International Journal of Travel and Travel Writing
  2(1):88–113.
  2002 Έρευνες για τον Τουρισμό στην Ελλάδα και την Κύπρο: Μια Ανθ
  ρωπλογική Προσέγγιση (Tourism Research in Greece and Cyprus: An
  Anthropological Approach). Athens: Propombos.
  2004a A Regionally Distinctive Product and the Construction of Place Identity:
  The Case of Chios *Mastiha.* Anatolia 15(1):19–38.
  2004b Tourism Research on Greece: A Critical Overview. Annals of Tourism
  Research 31:157–179.
Galbraith, K.
  1958 The Affluent Society. New York: Houghton Mifflin.
Galiana, M.L., and T.D. Barrado
  2006 Los Centros de Interés Turístico Nacional y el Despegue del Turismo de
  Masas en España (Centers of National Tourist Interest and the Take-off of
  Mass Tourism in Spain). Investigaciones Geográficas (Geographical Studies)
  39:73–93.

Gasparini, G.
2000 Per una Sociologia del Viaggio (For a Sociology of Travel). *In* Il Viaggio (Travel), G. Gasparini, ed., pp. 3–48. Roma: Edizioni Lavoro.

Gaviria, M.
1975 España a Go-Go. Turismo Charter y Neocolonialismo del Espacio (Go-Go Spain: Charter Tourism and the Neocolonization of Space). Madrid: Turner.
1996 La Séptima Potencia: España en el Mundo (The Seventh Power: Spain in the World). Barcelona: Ediciones B.

Gaviria, M., J. Iribas Sánchez, F. Sabbah, and J. Sanz Arranz
1975 El Turismo de Playa en España. Chequeo a 16 Ciudades Nuevas del Ocio (Beach Tourism in Spain: A Review of 16 New Leisure Towns). Madrid: Turner.

Gavranović, A.
1977 Turizam i sredstva javnog informiranja (Tourism and the Media). *In* Zbornik: Humanističke vrijednosti turizma (Proceedings: Humanistic Values of Tourism), pp. 225–230. Zadar: Pedagoška akademija.

Gaworecki, W.
1998 Turystyka (Tourism) (2nd ed). Warszawa: PWE.

Geić, S.
2002 Turizam i kulturno-civilizacijsko nasljeđe (Tourism and Cultural Civilization Heritage). Split: Sveučilište u Splitu.

Geigant, F.
1962 Der Urlaubs- und Ferienverkehr als Objekt wissenschaftlicher Forschung (Tourist Traffic as an Object of Scientific Research). Jahrbuch für Fremdenverkehr (Tourism Yearbook) 10:39–50.

Geilen, B.
2008 Sociaal Toerisme (Social Tourism). Master in Toerisme Paper. Leuven: KU.

Gemini, L.
2006 L'Immaginario Turistico e le Forme Performative del Consumo Vocazionale (Tourist Imagery and the Performative Forms of Vocational Consumption). *In* Cum Sumo. Prospettive di Analisi del Consumo nella Società Globale (Cum Sumo. Outlook of Consumption Analysis in the Global Society), E. Di Nallo and R. Paltrinieri, eds., pp. 256–273. Milano: FrancoAngeli.
2008 In Viaggio. Immaginario, Comunicazione e Pratiche del Turismo Contemporaneo (Traveling. Imagery, Communication, and Contemporary Tourist Practice). Milano: FrancoAngeli.

Gemünden, G.
1996 Introduction to Enzensberger's "A Theory of Tourism". New German Critique 68:113–115. (also online).

Georg, W.
1995 Lebensstile in der Freizeitforschung. Ein theoretischer Bezugsrahmen (Lifestyles in Leisure Research: A Theoretical Frame of Reference). *In* Arbeit,

Freizeit, Reisen. Die feinen Unterschiede in Alltag (Work, Leisure, Travel: Social Distinctions in Everyday Life), C. Cantauw, ed., pp. 13–20. Münster: Waxmann.

Germán, L. ed.
2001 Historia Económica Regional de España en los Siglos XIX y XX (Regional Economic History of Spain in the 19th and 20th Centuries). Barcelona: Crítica.

Giagou, D., and Y. Apostolopoulos
1996 Rural Women and the Development of the Agro-Touristic Cooperatives in Greece: The Case of Petra, Lesvos. Journal of Rural Cooperation 24(2):143–155.

Giesecke, H. ed.
1968 Freizeit- und Konsumerziehung (Pedagogy of Leisure and Consumption). Göttingen: s.n.

Gjivoje, D., V. Gjivoje, and M. Rešetar
1970 Turističke agencije (Tourist Agencies), (text book). Dubrovnik: Viša turistička škola.

Gkrimpa, E.
2006 Προϋποθέσεις και Προοπτικές Ανάπτυξης του Επαγγελματικού Τουρισμού στην Ελλάδα (Conditions and Development Perspectives of Business Tourism in Greece). Unpublished doctoral dissertation, Department of Business Administration, University of the Aegean, Chios, Greece.

Gleichmann, P.
1969 Zur Soziologie des Fremdenverkehrs (On the Sociology of Tourism). *In* Wissenschaftliche Aspekte des Fremdenverkehrs. Forschungsberichte des Ausschusses Raum und Fremdenverkehr (Scientific Aspects of Tourism: Research Reports from the Committee on Space and Tourism), Akademie für Raumforschung und Landesplanung, ed., pp. 55–78. Hannover: Jänecke.
1973 Gastlichkeit als soziales Verhältnis. Ein Baustein zu einer Theorie des Tourismus (Hospitality as a Social Relation: An Element of a Theory of Tourism). Mitteilungen des Instituts für Fremdenverkehrsforschung der Hochschule für Welthandel (Communication of the Institute for Tourism Research of the College for International Trade) 8:27–36.

Glomnes, E.
1990 Church Space and the Television Service. Paper Presented to the Summer Session of the Nordic Summer University, Viborg, Denmark.

Glücksmann, R.
1935 Allgemeine Fremdenverkehrskunde (General Teaching in Tourism). Bern: Stämpfli.

Glücksmann, R., et al
1930 Der Fremdenverkehr in Theorie und Praxis (Tourism in Theory and Practice). A Course of Lectures in Co-Operation with the Federation of Tourist Offices. Berlin: s.n.

Goffman, E.
1959 The Presentation of Self in Everyday Life. New York: Anchor Books.

1972 Relations in Public: Microstudies of the Public Order. Harmondsworth: Penguin.

Gölden, H.
1939 Strukturwandlungen des schweizerischen Fremdenverkehrs, 1890–1935 (Structural Changes in Swiss Tourism). Zürich: Diss.

Gołembski, G. ed.
2003 Kierunki rozwoju badań naukowych w turystyce (Directions in the Development of Tourism Research). Warszawa: Akademia Ekonomiczna w Poznaniu, Wydawnictwo Naukowe PWN.

Gorenc, V.
1985 Poslovno pravo u turizmu (Business Law in Tourism). Zagreb: Školska knjiga.

Gori, G.
1992 Quando il Mare Brucia (When the Sea Burns). Imola: La Mandragora.
2004 Trasformazione Urbana, Cultura, Turismo: Genova 2004 (Urban Transformation, Culture, Tourism: Genoa 2004). *In* Città, Turismo e Comunicazione Globale (City, Tourism and Global Communication), A. Savelli, ed., pp. 129–145. Milano: FrancoAngeli.

Gottlieb, A.
1982 Americans' Vacations. Annals of Tourism Research 9:165–187.

Graburn, N.
1967 The Eskimos and Airport Art. Trans-Action 4:28–33.
1977 Tourism: The Sacred Journey. *In* Hosts and Guests: The Anthropology of Tourism, V. Smith, ed., pp. 17–31. Philadelphia, PA: University of Pennsylvania Press.
1989 Tourism the Sacred Journey. *In* Hosts and Guests: The Anthropology of Tourism, V. Smith, ed. (pp. 21–36. 2nd ed). Philadelphia, PA: University of Pennsylvania Press.

Graburn, N., and N. Leite
2006 Review of Erik Cohen's "Contemporary Tourism: Diversity and Change". Annals of Tourism Research 33:269–271.

Graburn, N., and D. Barthel-Bouchier
2001 Relocating the Tourist. International Sociology 16:147–158.

Graf, B.
2002 Reisen und seelische Gesundheit (Traveling and Mental Health). Berlin: Diss.

Greenblatt, S.
1997 Warum reisen? (Why Do We Travel?). Voyage 1:13–17.

Greenwood, D.
1972 Tourism as an Agent of Change: A Spanish Basque Case. Ethnology 11: 80–91.

Greverus, I.-M., et al ed.
1988 Kulturkontakt—Kulturkonflikt. Zur Erfahrung des Fremden (Cultural Contact—Cultural Conflict: The Experience of Strangers and of Strangeness), vol. 2, Frankfurt: s.n.

Grgašević, J.
  1958 Turizam u teoriji i praksi (Tourism in Theory and Practice). Beograd: Privredni pregled.
Griep, W. and H. Jäger, eds.
  1983 Reisen und soziale Realität am Ende des 18. Jahrhunderts (Traveling and Social Reality in the Late 18th Century). Heidelberg: Winter.
Gritti, J.
  1967 Les Contenus Culturels du Guide Bleu: Monuments et Sites "à Voir" (Cultural Contents of the Blue Guide: "Must-See" Monuments and Sites). Communications 10:51–64.
Groffen, W.
  1967 Keuzeprocessen in de Vrije Tijd: Een Empirisch Onderzoek onder de Nederlandse Beroepsbevolking (Choice Making Processes in Free Time: Empirical Research among the Dutch Professional Population) vol. 1. Groningen: Rijksuniversiteit.
  1970 Keuzeprocessen in de Vrije Tijd: Een Empirisch Onderzoek onder de Nederlandse Beroepsbevolking (Choice Making Processes in Free Time: Empirical Research among the Dutch Professional Population) vol. 2. Groningen: Rijksuniversiteit.
Groh, D., and R. Groh
  1991/1996 Zur Kulturgeschichte der Natur (Cultural History of Nature). vol. 2, Frankfurt: Suhrkamp.
Groß, S.
  2004 Die Entstehung einer Tourismuswissenschaft im deutschsprachigen Raum (The Emergence of a Tourism Science in German Speaking Countries). Tourismus Journal 8:243–263.
Grünthal, A.
  1934 Probleme der Fremdenverkehrsgeographie (Challenges of Tourism Geography). Berlin: Diss.
  1962 Die Tätigkeit des Forschungsintituts für den Fremdenverkehr in Berlin, 1929-1933 (The Activities of the Research Institute for Tourism in Berlin, 1929-1933). Jahrbuch für Fremdenverkehr (Tourism Yearbook) 10:3–16.
Guala, C.
  2004 Trasformazione Urbana, Cultura, Turismo: Genova 2004 (Urban Transformation, Culture, Tourism). In Città, Turismo e Comunicazione Globale (City, Tourism and Global Communication), A. Savelli, ed., pp. 129–145. Milano: FrancoAngeli.
  2007 Mega Eventi. Modelli e Storie di Rigenerazione Urbana (Mega Events. Models and Experiences of Urban Regeneration). Roma: Carocci.
Gubert, R., and G. Pollini
  2002 Turismo, Fluidità Relazionale e Appartenenza Territoriale. Il Caso degli Imprenditori Turistici in Alcune Aree del Nordest Italiano (Tourism,

Relational Fluidity, and Territorial Belonging. The Case of Tourist Entrepreneurs in some Italian North-Eastern Areas). Milano: FrancoAngeli.

Guidicini, P.
1973 Il Sociale nel Turismo (The Social Dimension in Tourism). *In* Regione Veneto, un Turismo Nuovo per una Società Nuova (The Veneto Region, a New Tourism for a New Society), pp. 13–19. Bassano: Grafiche Bassotti.
1984 Dinamica Sociale e Domanda Turistica (Social Dynamic and Tourist Demand). Politica del Turismo (Politics of Tourism) 2:217–224.

Guidicini, P. and A. Savelli, eds.
1988a Il Turismo in una Società che Cambia (Tourism in a Changing Society). Milano: FrancoAngeli.
1988b Il Mediterraneo come Sistema Turistico Complesso (The Mediterranean as a Complex Tourist Area). Sociologia Urbana e Rurale (Urban and Rural Sociology) vol. 26, special issue.
1992 Gruppi e Strutture Intermedie Locali, per una Reimmaginazione del Sistema Turistico (Local Intermediate Groups and Structures, for a Change of Imagination in the Tourist System). Sociologia Urbana e Rurale (Urban and Rural Sociology) vol. 38, special issue.
1999 Strategie di Comunità nel Turismo Mediterraneo (Community Strategies in Mediterranean Tourism). Milano: FrancoAngeli.

Günther, A.
1954 Fremdenverkehr, soziologisch gesehen (A Sociological View on Tourism). Jahrbuch für Fremdenverkehr (Tourism Yearbook) 2:1–16.
1956 Soziologische Kategorien im Fremdenverkehr (Sociological Categories in Tourism). Jahrbuch für Fremdenverkehr (Tourism Yearbook) 4:24–45.

Gurvitch, G.
1957 La Vocation Actuelle de la Sociologie (The Real Vocation of Sociology). Paris: PUF.
1960 Traité de Sociologie (Treatise of Sociology). Paris: PUF.
1965 Déterminismes Sociaux et Liberté Humaine (Social Determinisms and Human Freedom). Paris: PUF.

Gustafson, P.
2001 Roots and Routes: Exploring the Relationship between Place Attachment and Mobility. Environment and Behavior 33:667–686.
2002 Tourism and Seasonal Retirement Migration. Annals of Tourism Research 29:899–918.

Gustavsson, A.
1981 Sommargäster och Bofasta: Kulturmöte och Motsättningar vid Bohuskusten (Summerites and Locals: Cultural Meeting and Antagonisms on the Bohus Coast). Lund: Liber.

Guyer-Freuler, E.
1903 Fremdenverkehr und Hotelwesen (Tourism and Hospitality). Bern: Verlag Enzyklopädie (offprint).

1905 Fremdenverkehr und Hotelwesen (Tourism and Hospitality). *In* Handwörterbuch der Schweizerischen Volkswirtschaft, Sozialpolitik und Verwaltung (Handbook of Swiss Economics, Social Policy and Administration), N. Reichesberg, ed., vol. 2, pp. 77–85. Bern: Verlag Enzyklopädie.

Gyimóthy, S., and R. Mykletun
2004 Play in Adventure Tourism: The Case of Arctic Trekking. Annals of Tourism Research 31:855–878.

Gyr, U.
1988 Touristenkultur und Reisealltag (Tourist Culture and the Tourist Routine). Zeitschrift für Volkskunde (Journal of Ethnology) 84:224–239.

1999 Entgrenzung durch Mundialisierung? Dynamisierungsprozesse im massentouristischen Konsumsystem (Limitlessness by Globalization? Dynamic Processes in the System of Mass Tourism Consumption). *In* Grenzenlose Gesellschaft—Grenzenloser Tourismus? (Boundless Society—Boundless Tourism?), R. Bachleitner and P. Schimany, eds., pp. 55–66. München: Profil.

Habermas, J.
1973 Arbeit, Freizeit, Konsum (Work, Leisure, Consumption). Gießen: s.n.

Hachtmann, R.
2007 Tourismusgeschichte (Tourism History). Göttingen: Vandenhoek und Ruprecht.

Haedrich, G., C. Kaspar, K. Klemm, and E. Kreilkamp, eds.
1998 Tourismus-Management (Tourism Management), (3rd ed). Berlin: de Gruyter.

Hahn, H. and H. Kagelmann, eds.
1993 Tourismuspsychologie und Tourismussoziologie. Ein Handbuch zur Tourismuswissenschaft (Tourism Psychology and Tourism Sociology: A Handbook of Tourism Science). München: Quintessenz.

Hahn, H., and B. Schade
1969 Psychologie und Fremdenverkehr (Psychology and Tourism). *In* Wissenschaftliche Aspekte des Fremdenverkehrs. Forschungsberichte des Ausschusses Raum und Fremdenverehr (Scientific Aspects of Tourism: Research Reports from the Committee on Space and Tourism), Akademie für Raumforschung und Landesplanung, ed., pp. 35–53. Hannover: Jänecke.

Hammerich, K.
1974 Skizzen zur Genese der Freizeit als eines sozialen Problems (Delineation of the Genesis of Leisure as a Social Problem). Kölner Zeitschrift für Soziologie und Sozialpsychologie (Cologne Journal of Sociology and Social Psychology) 26:267–284.

Hansen, A.W.
1982 Fotografi og Familie: En Historisk og Sociologisk Undersøgelse af Private Familiefotografier (Photography and Family: An Historical and Sociological Examination of Private Family Photographs). Odense: Bidrag.

Haralambopoulos, N., and A. Pizam
    1996 Perceived Impacts of Tourism: The Case of Samos. Annals of Tourism Research 23(3):503–526.
Harrison, D.
    1997 Barbados or Luton? Which Way to Paradise? Tourism Management 18:393–398.
Harrison, J.
    1985 The Spanish Economy in the Twentieth Century. New York: St. Martin's Press.
Hartmann, K.
    1982 Zur Psychologie des Landschaftserlebens im Tourismus (Psychology of the Experience of Landscape in Tourism). Starnberg: StfT.
Haug, B., G. Dann, and M. Mehmetoglu
    2007 Little Norway in Spain. From Tourism to Migration. Annals of Tourism Research 34:202–222.
Haukeland, J.
    1984 Sociocultural Impacts of Tourism in Scandinavia. Tourism Management 5(3):207–214.
    1990 Non-Travelers: The Flip Side of Motivation. Annals of Tourism Research 17:172–184.
    1993 Den Norske Feriedrømmen (The Norwegian Holiday Dream). Research Report 164. Oslo: Institute of Transport Economics.
Haukeland, J., and T. Eriksen
    1982 Toleransenivå for Reiseliv i Lokalsamfunn (Tolerance Level for Tourism in Local Communities). Oslo: Institute of Transport Economics.
Häußler, O.
    1997 Reisen in der Hyperrealität. Baudrillard und das Problem der Authentizität (Journeys into Hyper-Reality: Baudrillard and the Problem of Authenticity). Voyage 1:99–109.
Have, T.
    1977 Beleid en Vrije Tijd: Een Speurtocht naar Normatieve Uitgangspunten (Policy and Free Time: An Exploration into Normative Starting Points). The Hague: Staatsuitgeverij ('s Gravenhage).
Heimtun, B.
    1997 Norges Image blant Tyske Turister (Norway's Image among German Tourists). Research Report 356. Oslo: Institute of Transport Economics.
    2007 Mobile Identities of Gender and Tourism: The Value of Social Capital. PhD thesis, University of West of England, Bristol, UK.
Heinemeyer, W.F. ed.
    1959 Jeugd en Vrije Tijd in Amsterdam (Youth and Free Time in Amsterdam). Amsterdam: Bureau voor Jeugdzorg.
Hekker, A.
    1983 Recreatie en Toerisme, Begrip en Beleid (Recreation and Tourism, Concept and Policy). Recreatie en Toerism (Recreation and Tourism) 12(2):12–15.

Hennig, C.
   1997 Jenseits des Alltags. Theorien des Tourismus (Beyond Everyday Life: Theories of Tourism). Voyage 1:35–53.
   1998a Entwurf einer Theorie des Tourismus (Draft of a Theory of Tourism). *In* Auf dem Weg zu einer Theorie des Tourismus (Toward a Theory of Tourism), H-P. Burmeister, ed., pp. 54–70. Loccum: s.n.
   1999 Reiselust. Touristen, Tourismus und Urlaubskultur (Wanderlust: Tourists, Tourism and Tourism Culture) (2nd ed). Frankfurt: Suhrkamp.
   2002 Tourism: Enacted Modern Myths. *In* The Tourist as a Metaphor of the Social World, G. Dann, ed., pp. 169–188. Wallingford, CT: CAB International.
Hennig, C. ed.
   1998b Editorial. Voyage. 2:7–9.
Hertogen, J., and D. Naeyaert
   1981 Sociaal Toerisme: Een Schot Naast de Roos? (Social Tourism: A Shot Next to the Target?). De Gids op Maatschappelijk Gebied (Guide on Society) 72(5):403–418.
Hessels, A.
   1973 Vakantiebesteding sinds de Eeuwwisseling: Een Sociologische Verkenning ten Behoeve van de Sociale en Ruimtelijke Planning in Nederland (Holiday Making from the Beginning of the Century: A Sociological Exploration on Behalf of Social and Spatial Planning). Assen: s.n.
Hinske, N. and M. Müller, eds.
   1979 Reisen und Tourismus (Travel and Tourism). Trier: University of Trier.
Hirsch, F.
   1977 Social Limits to Growth. London: Routledge and Kegan Paul.
Hlavin-Schulze, K.
   1998 Man reist ja nicht um anzukommen. Reisen als kulturelle Praxis (After all, Nobody Travels in Order to Arrive. Traveling as Cultural Practice). Frankfurt: Campus.
Hobsbawm, E.
   1962 The Age of Revolution. Europe 1789-1848. London: Abacus.
   2004 Il Secolo Breve (The Short Century) 1914-1991. Milano: BUR.
Hobsbawm, E. and T. Ranger, eds.
   1984 The Invention of Tradition. Cambridge: Cambridge University Press.
Hollinshead, K.
   1993 The Truth about Texas: A Naturalistic Study of the Construction of Heritage. Unpublished PhD thesis, Texas A & M University, USA.
Hömberg, E.
   1977 Tourismus. Funktionen, Strukturen, Kommunikationskanäle (Tourism: Functions, Structures, Communication Channels). München: Tuduv.
   1978 Reisen—zwischen Kritik und Analyse. Zum Stand der Tourismusforschung (Travel. Between Critique and Analysis. The State of Tourism Research). Zeitschrift für Kulturaustausch (Journal of Cultural Exchange) 28(3):36–41.

Hopfinger, H.
2004 Theorien im Tourismus (Theories in Tourism). *In* Von Erholungsräumen zu Tourismusdestinationen (From Spaces of Relaxation to Tourism Destinations), A. Brittner-Widmann, ed., pp. 29–48. Trier: Geographische Gesellschaft.
2007 Versuch einer Standortbestimmung (Attempt at Positioning Tourism Geography). *In* Geographie der Freizeit und des Tourismus. Bilanz und Ausblick (Geography of Leisure and Tourism. Result and Outlook), C. Becker, et al (pp. 1–24. 3rd ed). München: Oldenbourg.

Huck, G.
1980 Freizeit als Forschungsproblem (Leisure as a Research Problem). *In* Sozialgeschichte der Freizeit. Untersuchungen zum Wandel der Alltagskultur in Deutschland (Social History of Leisure. An Examination of Everyday Culture in Germany), G. Huck, ed., pp. 7–17. Wuppertal: Hammer.

Hugo, V.
1842 (1968) Le Rhin (The Rhine). Lettres à un Ami (Letters to a Friend) Paris: Charpentier/Éditions Rencontre.

Huizinga, I.
1949 Homo Ludens: A Study of the Play Element in Culture. London: Routledge and Kegan Paul.

Humanističke vrijednosti turizma (Humanistic Values of Tourism)
1977 Proceedings of a Conference. Zadar: Pedagoška akademija.

Hunziker, W.
1943 System und Hauptprobleme einer wissenschaftlichen Fremdenverkehrslehre (System and Main Problems of Scientific Research on Tourism). St. Gallen: Fehr.
1951 Le Tourisme Social, Caractères et Problèmes (Social Tourism, Characteristics and Problems). Berne: Imprimerie Fédérative, Paris: Alliance Internationale de Tourisme.
1954 Gegenwartsaufgaben der Fremdenverkehrswissenschaft (Current Challenges of Tourism Science). Jahrbuch für Fremdenverkehr (Tourism Yearbook) 2:16–28.
1973 Le Système de la Doctrine Touristique (The System of Tourism Doctrine; Das System der Fremdenverkehrslehre). Bern: Gurtenverlag.

Hunziker, W., and K. Krapf
1941 Beiträge zur Fremdenverkehrslehre und Fremdenverkehrsgeschichte (Contributions to the Teaching and History of Tourism). Bern: s.n.
1942 Grundriß der Allgemeinen Fremdenverkehrslehre (Outline of the General Teaching of Tourism). Zürich: Polygraphischer Verlag.

Huss, R.
1951 Semestern som förebyggande Hälsovård (The Vacation as Prophylactical Health Care). *In* Protokoll, Reso Conference "Samhället och Folksemestern" ("The Society and Popular Vacationing"), pp. 19–30. Ronneby: Brunn.

Høivik, T., and T. Heiberg
  1977 Tourism, Self-Reliance and Structural Violence. Publication S-14-77. Oslo: International Peace Research Institute.
  1980 Centre-Periphery Tourism and Self-Reliance. International Social Science Journal 32(1):69–98.
Iakovidou, O.
  1991 Απασχόληση στον Τουρισμό: Διέξοδος για τον Αγροτικό Πληθυσμό της Χαλκιδικής (Employment in Tourism: A Solution for the Rural Population of Chalkidiki). Επιθεώρηση Κοινωνικίν Επιστημών (Greek Social Science Review) 83:32–47.
  1992 Ο Ρόλος των Γυναικείων Αγροτοτουριστικών Συνεταιρισμών στην Προώθηση του Αγροτοτουρισμού στην Ελλάδα» (The Role of Women's Rural Cooperatives in the Promotion of Agro-Tourism in Greece) Συνεταιριστική Πορεία (Cooperative Course) 27 (July–September), pp. 137–145.
  2007 Mediterranean Tourism beyond the Coastline: New Trends in Tourism and the Social Organisation of Space. Thessaloniki: Ziti.
International Academy for the Study of Tourism
  2008 International Academy for the Study of Tourism (http://www.tourismscholars.org).
International Bank for Reconstruction and Development (IBRD)
  1963 The Economic Development of Spain. Baltimore, MD: Johns Hopkins Press.
Internationales Zentral-Büro Freude und Arbeit, ed.
  1937 Bericht über den Weltkongreß für Freizeit und Erholung vom 23. bis 30. Juli 1936 (Report on the World Congress for Leisure Time and Recreation, 23–30 July 1936). Hamburg: Hanseatische Verlagsanstalt (also English and French editions).
Iovanović, B.
  2008 Tra Urbano e Rurale: Lo Sviluppo del Turismo Sostenibile nella Regione Adriatica Meridionale e Ionica (Between Urban and Rural: Sustainable Tourism Development in the South Adriatic and Ionian Region). *In* Immaginare l'Adriatico. Contributi alla Riscoperta Sociale di uno Spazio di Frontiera (Imagining the Adriatic. Contributions to the Social Rediscovery of a Frontier Space), E. Cocco and E. Minardi, eds., pp. 203–218. Milano: FrancoAngeli.
Jackowski, A.
  1991 Pilgrimage and Tourism. Kraków: Uniwersytet Jagielloński.
Jacobsen, J.
  1983 Moderne Turisme (Modern Tourism). Magister Artium dissertation, Institute of Sociology, University of Oslo, Norway.
  1984 Turistrollen og Turismens Institusjonalisering (The Tourist Role and the Institutionalization of Tourism). *In* Turisme og Reiseliv (Tourism and Travel),

L.-H. Jacobsen and J. Jacobsen, eds., pp. 7–38. Aalborg: The Nordic Summer University.

1985 Hverdag, Fritid og Frihet: Om Turisme som Rekreasjon og som Flukt (Everyday, Leisure, and Freedom: Tourism as Recreation and Escape). *In* Planleggingens Muligheter 3: Reiseliv og Rekreasjon (The Scope of Planning, vol. 3, Tourism and Recreation), N. Veggeland, ed., pp. 11–37. Oslo: Scandinavian University Press.

1993 Motiv-segmentering av feriemarkedet i Lofoten og Vesterålen (Motive Segmentation of Tourism in Lofoten and Vesterålen). *In* Reiselivs- forskning i Norge (Tourism Research in Norway), V. Jean-Hansen and J. Haukeland, eds., pp. 99–131, Research Report 194. Oslo: Institute of Transport Economics.

1997 Transience and Place. Nordlit (Papers on Literature and Culture, University of Tromsø) vol. 1, pp. 23–45.

2000 Anti-Tourist Attitudes: Mediterranean Charter Tourism. Annals of Tourism Research 27(2):284–300.

2001 Nomadic Tourism and Fleeting Place Encounters. Scandinavian Journal of Hospitality and Tourism 1:99–112.

2002 Turisme og Motivasjon (Tourism and Motivation). *In* Turisme: Turister og Samfunn (Tourism: Tourists and Society), J. Jacobsen and K. Eide, eds., pp. 56–99. Oslo: Gyldendal Akademisk.

2003 Theorising Tourism in a Context of Modernities, Working Paper TR 1179/2003. Oslo: Institute of Transport Economics, Norwegian Centre for Transport Research.

2004 Roaming Romantics: Solitude-Seeking and Self-Centredness in Scenic Sightseeing. Scandinavian Journal of Hospitality and Tourism 4:5–23.

2005 Exploring Tourism: Aspects of International European Holiday Travel. Unpublished thesis for Doctor Rerum Politicarum, University of Oslo, Norway.

2007 Monitoring Motoring: A Study of Tourists' Viewpoints of Environmental Performance and Protection Practices. Scandinavian Journal of Hospitality and Tourism 7:104–119.

Jacobsen, J. ed.

1988 Friheten i det Fjerne (The Freedom Afar Off). Aalborg: The Nordic Summer University.

Jacobsen, J., and G. Dann

2003 Images of the Lofoten Islands. Scandinavian Journal of Hospitality and Tourism 3:24–47.

Jacobsen, J., B. Heimtun, and S. Dale Nordbakke

1998 Det Nordlige Norges Image: Innholdsanalyse av Utenlandske Reisehånd- bøker (The Image of Northern Norway: Content Analysis of Foreign Guidebooks). Report 398. Oslo: Institute of Transport Economics, Norwegian Centre for Transport Research.

Jacquemyns, G.
  1998 (1932/1934) Enquête sur les Conditions de Vie Chômeurs Assurés (Inquiry into the Living Conditions of the Unemployed). vol. 5, Liège: s.n.
Jadrešić, V.
  1993 (2001) Nautički turizam (Nautical Tourism). Zadar: Pedagoška akademija.
  2001 Turizam u interdisciplinarnoj teoriji i primjeni (Interdisciplinary Theory and Practice of Tourism). Zagreb: Školska knjiga.
Jafari, J.
  1987 Tourism Models: The Socio-Cultural Aspects. Tourism Management 8: 151–159.
  1990 The Basis of Tourism Education. Journal of Tourism Studies 1:33–41.
  2007 Entry into a New Field of Study: Leaving a Footprint. *In* The Study of Tourism: Anthropological and Sociological Beginnings, D. Nash, ed., pp. 108–121. Oxford: Elsevier.
Jansen-Verbeke, M.
  1988 Leisure, Recreation and Tourism in Inner Cities: Explorative Case Studies. PhD dissertation in geography, Katholieke Universiteit, Nijmegen, Netherlands.
  1990 Toerisme in de Binnenstad van Brugge: Een Planologische Visie (Tourism in the Inner City of Bruges: A Planning Perspective). Nijmeegse Planologische Cahiers (Nijmegen Planning Papers) vol. 35. Nijmegen: Katholieke Universiteit.
Janson, C.-G.
  2000 Scandinavian Sociology. *In* Encyclopedia of Sociology, E. Borgatta and R. Montgomery, eds., vol. 4, pp. 2449–2455. New York: Macmillan Reference.
Jansson, A.
  2007 A Sense of Tourism: New Media and the Dialectic of Encapsulation/ Decapsulation. Tourist Studies 7:5–24.
Jardel, J.-P. ed.
  1994 Le Tourisme International entre Tradition et Modernité (International Tourism between Tradition and Modernity). Actes du Colloque International (Proceedings of the International Colloquium). Nice: Laboratoire d'Ethnologie de l'Université de Nice.
Jensen, Ø., and T. Korneliussen
  2002 Discriminating Perceptions of a Peripheral "Nordic Destination" among European Tourists. Tourism and Hospitality Research 3(4):319–330.
Job, H.
  2003 Reisestile: Modell des raumzeitlichen Verhaltens der Reisenden (Travel Styles: A Model of the Spatio-Temporal Behavior of Travelers). Tourismus Journal 7:355–376.
Jokić, B.
  1994 Turizam u sociokulturnološkoj perspektivi (Tourism in a Social and Cultural Perspective). Zagreb: Mikrorad.

Jokinen, E.
1988 Den Unga Jane: Flickorna, Turismen och Gränserna (The Young Jane: Girls, Tourism and Boundaries). *In* Friheten i det Fjerne (The Freedom Afar Off), J. Jacobsen, ed., pp. 65–72. Aalborg: The Nordic Summer University.

Jokinen, E., and S. Veijola
1988 Ett Försök til Grisfestens Teori (Towards a Theory of the Pork Feast). *In* Friheten i det Fjerne (The Freedom Afar Off), J. Jacobsen, ed., pp. 101–117. Aalborg: The Nordic Summer University.

Jolles, H.M.
1957 Sociologische Notities bij de Openlucht-recreatie (Sociological Notes on Outdoor Recreation). Tijdschrift voor Sociale Geneeskunde (Journal of Social Medicine) 35(8):188–200.

Jorissen, F., J. Kramer, and J. Lengkeek
1990 Het Water op. 400 Jaar Pleziervaart in Nederland (On the Water. 400 Years of Watersports in the Netherlands). Baarn: Uitgeverij Hollandia.

Josiam, B., J. Hobson, U. Dietrich, and G. Smeaton
1998 An Analysis of the Sexual, Alcohol and Drug Related Behavioural Patterns of Students on Spring Break. Tourism Management 19:501–513.

Jovičić, Ž.
1964 Turistička kretanja (Tourism Developments). Beograd: Naučna knjiga.
1966 Turistička kretanja (Tourist Movements). Beograd: Turistička štampa.
1972 Turizmologija (Tourismology), Collected Papers. Beograd: Faculty of Geography, University of Belgrade.
1980 Osnovi turizmologje (Essentials of Tourismology). Beograd: Naučna knjiga.

Jurczek, P.
2007 Disziplingeschichte und Perspektiven (Disciplinary History and Perspectives). *In* Geographie der Freizeit und des Tourismus. Bilanz und Ausblick (Geography of Leisure and Tourism. Result and Outlook), C. Becker, et al (pp. 25–34. 3rd ed). München: Oldenbourg.

Jurdao Arrones, F.
1979 España en Venta: Compra de Suelos por Extranjeros y Colonización de Campesinos en la Costa del Sol (Spain for Sale: Buying Land for Foreigners and the Colonization of the Countryside in the Costa del Sol). Madrid: Ayuso.
1990 España en Venta: Compra de Suelos por Extranjeros y Colonización de Campesinos en la Costa del Sol (New ed). Madrid: Endymión.
1992 Los Mitos del Turismo (Myths of Tourism). *In* Los Mitos del Turismo (Myths of Tourism), F. Jurdao Arrones, ed. Madrid: Endimión.

Jurdao Arrones, F., and M. Sánchez
1990 España, Asilo de Europa (Spain: Asylum of Europe). Madrid: Planeta.

Jurić, B.
1975 Socioekonomske karakteristike turizma (Social and Economic Characteristics of Tourism). Privreda Dalmacije (The Business of Dalmatia) vol. 3/4.

1998a Sociologija turizma (Sociology of Tourism). Zadar: Self-Published.
1998b Ekonomika turizma (Economics of Tourism). Zadar: Self-Published.
Kabiljo, J.
1980 Ekonomika turizma (Economics of Tourism). Beograd: Prevredno finansijski vodič.
Kagelmann, H.
2007 Erlebnisse, Erlebnisgesellschaften, Erlebniswelten (Experiences, Societies of Experience, Worlds of Experience). *In* Tourismusforschung in Bayern. Aktuelle sozialwissenschaftliche Beiträge (Tourism Research in Bavaria: Current Contributions of the Social Sciences), A. Günther, et al, pp. 133–148. München: Profil.
Kagelmann, H. ed.
1993 Tourismuswissenschaft. Soziologische, sozialpsychologische und sozialan-thropologische Untersuchungen (Tourism Science: Sociological, Socio-Psychological and Social-Anthropological Studies). München: Quintessenz.
Kagelmann, H., R. Bachleitner, and M. Rieder, eds.
2004 Erlebniswelten. Zum Erlebnisboom in der Postmoderne (Worlds of Experience. On the Postmodern Boom of Experience (2nd ed). München: Profil.
Kahn, H.
1976 The Next 200 Years—A Scenario for America and the World. New York: Morrow.
Kalfiotis, S.
1976 Τουριστική Οικονομική (μακροοικονομικη επισκοπηση του τουρισμου) (Tourism Economics) (A Macroeconomic View of Tourism). Athens: Τυροβολάς, Interbooks.
Kamphorst, T.
1982 Ten Geleide (Introduction). Vrijetijd en Samenleving (Leisure and Society) 1(1):5–6.
Kamphorst, T., and J. Withagen
1977 Register van Vrijetijdsonderzoek (Register of Leisure Research) Deel 1 (Part 1), SWIDOC. Amsterdam: Noord- Hollandse Uitgeversmaatschappij.
Kantsa, V.
2002 Certain Places Have Different Energy. Spatial Transformations in Eresos, Lesvos. GLQ. A Journal of Lesbian and Gay Studies 8(1):35–57.
Kaplan, M.
1975 Leisure: Theory and Policy. New York: Wiley.
Karagiannis, E.
2004 Αγροτουρισμός: Το μέσο για την ανάπτυξη της υπαίθρου (Agro-Tourism: The Vehicle for the Development of the Countryside). Thessaloniki: Center of Technological Research of Crete.
Kaspar, C.
1975 (1996) Die Fremdenverkehrslehre (Tourismuslehre) im Grundriß (Outline of the Teaching of Tourism) (5th ed.). Bern: Haupt.

Kassimati, K., M. Thanopoulou, and P. Tsartas
(1995) η Γυναικεία απασχόληση στον Τουριστικό Τομέα: Διερεύνηση της Αγοράς Εργασίας και Επισήμανση Προοπτικών (Female Employment in the Tourism Sector: An Investigation of the Labor Market and Future Prospects) Athens: Κέντρο Κοινωνικής Μορφολογιαίς και Κοινωνικής Πολιτικοήος (Center of Social Morphology and Social Policy) (ΚΕΚΜΟΚΟΠ).

Kečkemet, D.
1977 Uloga turizma u humanizaciji i dehumanizaciji ljudskog prostora (The Role of Tourism in the Humanization and Dehumanization of the Human Environment). *In* Zbornik—radova humanističke vrijednosti turizma (Proceedings—Humanistic Values of Tourism), pp. 137–144. Zadar: Pedagoška akademija.

Keitz, C.
1997 Reisen als Leitbild. Die Entstehung des modernen Massentourismus in Deutschland (Travel as a Model. The Origin of Modern Mass Tourism in Germany). München: Deutscher Taschenbuch Verlag.

Keller, P.
1973 (1983) Soziologische Probleme im modernen Tourismus (Sociological Problems in Modern Tourism). Bern: Lang.

Kelly, J.
1987 Freedom to Be: A New Sociology of Leisure. Englewood Cliffs, NJ: Prentice Hall.
1990 Leisure. Englewood Cliffs, NJ: Prentice Hall.

Kenna, M.
1993 Return Migrants and Tourism Development: An Example from the Cyclades. Journal of Modern Greek Studies 11:75–95.

Kentler, H., T. Leithäuser, and H. Lessing
1965 Forschungsbericht Jugend im Urlaub II (Research Report: Youth on Holiday). München: StfT.

Kerstens, A.
1972 Platteland en Recreatie (Countryside and Recreation). Wageningen: Landbouwhogeschool.

Kikkert, J.
1985 Op Stap in Nederland: Toerisme Vroeger en Nu (On the Way: Tourism in the Past and Now). Weesp: Fibula-Van Dishoeck.

Kim, S.
1998 Content Analysis: Annals of Tourism Research and Journal of Travel Research. Unpublished MSc thesis, University of Wisconsin-Stout, USA.

Kitterød, R.
1988 Hvem Reiser Ikke på Ferie? En Analyse av Ikke-reisende i Norge, Sverige, Danmark og Finland (Who Spends their Holiday at Home? An Analysis of Non-Travelers in Norway, Sweden, Denmark and Finland). Oslo: Statistics Norway.

Klemm, K.
1998 Die akademische Tourismus Aus- und Weiterbildung in der BRD (Academic Higher Education in Tourism in the FRG). *In* Tourismus-Management, G. Haedrich, et al (pp. 925–936. 3rd ed). Berlin: de Gruyter.

Klemm, K., and A. Menke
1988 Sanfter Tourismus zwischen Theorie und Praxis (Soft Tourism between Theory and Practice). *In* Fremdenverkehr und Regionalpolitik (Tourism and Regional Politics), Akademie für Raumforschung und Landesplanung, ed., pp. 155–179. Hannover: Jänecke.

Kliment, A.
2000 Elektroničko poslovanje u turizmu (E-Business in Tourism). Zagreb: Mikrorad and Ekonomski fakultet Zagreb.

Kłoskowska, A.
1969 Z historii i socjologii kultury (From the History and Sociology of Culture). Warszawa: Państwowe Wydawnictwo Naukowe.
1981 Socjologia kultury (The Sociology of Culture). Warszawa: Państwowe Wydawnictwo Naukowe.
1996 Kultury narodowe u korzeni (translated into English 2001 as National Cultures at the Grass-Root Level). Budapest: Central European University Press.

Knebel, H.
1960 Soziologische Strukturwandlungen im modernen Tourismus (Sociological Changes in the Structures of Modern Tourism). Stuttgart: Enke.

Knežević-Grubišić, M.
1988 Posredničke organizacije u turizmu (Intermediary Organizations in Tourism). Zagreb: Informator.

Kobašić, A.
1975 Marketing u turizmu (Marketing in Tourism), (Course Material). Dubrovnik: Fakultet za vanjsku trgovinu i turizam.
1987 Turizam u Jugoslaviji (Tourism in Yugoslavia). Zagreb: Informator.

Köck, C. ed.
2001 Reisebilder. Produktion und Reproduktion touristischer Wahrnehmung (Travel Pictures: Production and Reproduction of Tourist Perception). Münster: Waxmann.

Kopper, C.
2004 Neuerscheinungen zur Geschichte des Reisens und des Tourismus (New Publications on the History of Travel and Tourism). Archiv für Sozialgeschichte (Archive of Social History) 44:665–677.

Koster, M.J.
1985 Focus op Toerisme. Inleiding op het Toeristisch Gebeuren (Focus on Tourism. Introduction to the Tourism Issue). Den Haag: VUGA.

Köstlin, K.
1995 Wir sind alle Touristen—Gegenwelten als Alltag (We are all Tourists—Counterworlds as Everyday Life). *In* Arbeit, Freizeit, Reisen. Die feinen

Unterschiede im Alltag (Work, Leisure, Travel: Social Distinctions in Everyday Life), C. Cantauw, ed., pp. 1–12. Münster: Waxmann.

Kousis, M.
1985 Proletarianization under Tourism: A Micro Level Analysis. Working Paper 325. Ann Arbor, MI: Center for Research on Social Organization, University of Michigan.
1989 Tourism and the Family in a Rural Cretan Community. Annals of Tourism Research 16:318–332.
2000 Τουρισμός και Περιβάλλον: η Τοπική Κοινωνική Διαμαρτυρία στην Κρήτη (Tourism and the Environment: Local Social Protest on Crete). *In* Τουριστική Ανάπτυξη: Πολυπολιτισμικές Προσεγγίσεις (Tourism Development: Multidisciplinary Approaches), P. Tsartas, ed., pp.99–122. Athens: Exandas.
2001 Tourism and the Environment in Corsica, Sardinia, Sicily and Crete. *In* Mediterranean Islands and Sustainable Tourism Development: Practices, Management and Policies, D. Ioannides, Y. Apostolopoulos, and S. Sonmez, eds., pp. 214–233. London: Continuum.

Kramer, D.
1982 Aspekte der Kulturgeschichte des Tourismus (Aspects of the Cultural History of Tourism). Zeitschrift für Volkskunde (Journal of Ethnology) 78:1–13.

Kramer, D. and R. Lutz, eds.
1992 Reisen und Alltag. Beiträge zur kulturwissenschaftlichen Tourismusforschung (Traveling and Everyday Life: Contributions to Tourism Cultural Studies). Frankfurt: s.n.

Krapf, K.
1947 Der touristische Konsum (Tourist Consumption). Bern: Habilschrift, Bern: s.n. (printed 1953; French ed. 1964; Spanish ed. 2004).
1953 (1964) La Consommation Touristique: Une Contribution à une Théorie de la Consommation (Touristic Consumption: A Contribution to a Theory of Consumption). Études et Memoires (Studies and Memories, vol. 2).

Krippendorf, J.
1984 Die Ferienmenschen. Für ein neues Verständnis von Freizeit und Reisen (The Holiday Makers: Plea for a New Understanding of Leisure and Travel). Zürich: Orell-Füssli.
1987 The Holiday Makers: Understanding the Impact of Leisure and Travel. Oxford: Butterworth-Heinemann.
1997 Erst wenn der Leidensdruck noch weiter steigt (Only When the Pressure of the Pain Increases Even More). Interview with H. Spode, Voyage—Jahrbuch für Reise- & Tourismusforschung (Yearbook of Travel and Tourism Research) vol. 1, pp. 61–63.

Krippendorf, J., P. Zimmer, and H. Glauber
1985 Für einen anderen Tourismus. Probleme—Perspektiven—Ratschläge (Plea for a Different Tourism: Problems, Perspectives, Advice). Frankfurt: Fischer.

Krzywicki, L.
1950 Sociological Studies. Warszawa: Polski Instytut Wydawniczy.
Księgarnia Zycia Warszawy Webpage
2008 (http://ksiegarnia.zw.com.pl, accessed 23 June).
Kuhn, T.
1962 The Structure of Scientific Revolutions. Chicago, IL: University of Chicago Press, (German ed., 1967).
Kuin, P., and A. Oldendorff
1960 Arbeidstijdverkorting (Reduction in Working Hours). Haarlem: Nederlandsche Maatschappij voor Nijverheid en Handel.
Kušen, E.
2002 Turistička atrakcijska osnoiva (Tourist Attraction Basis). Zagreb: Institut za turizam.
Lacan, J.
1975 La Topique de l'Imaginaire (The Subject of the Imaginary). In Le Séminaire, vol. 1 Les Écrits Techniques de Freud 1953-4 (The Seminar, vol. 1, The Technical Writings of Freud 1953-4), pp. 87–103. Paris: Seuil.
Lafargue, P.
1965 Le Droit à la Paresse (The Right to Idleness). Paris: Maspéro.
La Fontaine, J.
1950 Le Petit Poisson et le Pêcheur (The Little Fish and the Fisherman). In Fables, pp. 167–168. Tours: Maison Mame.
Lamartine, A.
1835 Un Voyage en Orient 1832-1833. Notes d'un Voyageur: Souvenirs, Impressions, Pensées et Paysages (Voyage to the Orient, 1832-1833. Notes of a Traveler. Souvenirs, Impressions, Thoughts, and Landscapes). Paris: Librairie de Charles Gosselin.
Lambiri-Dimaki, E.
1972 Κοινωνιολογική Ανάλυσις (Sociological Analysis). In Mykonos-Dilos-Rinia, Land-Planning Study (in Greek), A. Kalliga and A. Papageorgiou, eds. Athens: Governmental Policy Ministry.
Lambiri-Dimaki, J. ed.
1997 Ν Κοινωνιολογία στην Ελλάδα Σήμερα (Sociology in Greece Today). Athens: Papazisi.
Landes, D.
1969 The Unbound Prometheus. Cambridge: Cambridge University Press.
Lanfant, M.-F.
1972 Les Théories du Loisir: Sociologie du Loisir et Idéologies (Theories of Leisure: Sociology of Leisure and Ideologies). Paris: Presses Universitaires de France, (Dutch Translation: Sociologie van de Vrijetijd. Uitgeverif Het Spectrum. Italian translation: Teorie del Tempo Libero. Sansoni Saggi. Spanish Translation: Sociologia del Ocio. De Bolsillo/URESTI).

1980 Le Tourisme dans le Processus d'Internationalisation (Tourism in the Process of Internationalization). Revue Internationale des Sciences Sociales (International Review of the Social Sciences), numero spécial: L'Anatomie du Tourisme (special issue on the Anatomy of Tourism) vol. XXXII (l), pp. 1–15 (also in English and Spanish).

1987a Presentation. Problems of Tourism 10(2):3–20.

1987b L'Impact Social et Culturel du Tourisme International en Question (Questioning the Social and Cultural Impact of International Tourism). Problems of Tourism 10(2):21–34.

1990 Tourisme International: Phénomène Social Total (International Tourism: Total Social Phenomenon). Paper Presented to the Working Group on International Tourism of the International Sociological Association, Madrid 9–13 July.

1993 Methodological and Conceptual Issues Raised by the Study of International Tourism: A Test for Sociology. *In* Tourism Research: Critiques and Challenges, D. Pearce and R. Butler, eds., pp. 70–87. London: Routledge.

1994 Exposé Introductif: Le Tourisme International entre Tradition et Modernité: Pourquoi ce Thème? (Introductory Presentation: International Tourism between Tradition and Modernity. Why This Theme?). *In* Le Tourisme International entre Tradition et Modernité. Actes du Colloque International (International Tourism between Tradition and Modernity. Proceedings of the International Colloquium), J. Jardel, ed., pp. 11–25. Nice: Laboratoire d'Ethnologie, Université de Nice.

1995 International Tourism, Internationalization and the Challenge to Identity. *In* International Tourism: Identity and Change, M-F. Lanfant, J. Allcock, and E. Bruner, eds., pp. 24–43. London: Sage.

1999 La Sociologie du Tourisme International: "Cadrage Général" (The Sociology of International Tourism: "General Framework"). *In* La Recherche Touristique: Approches Croisées (Tourism Research: Overlapping Approaches). Cahiers du Groupement de Recherche (Papers of the Research Group), no. 2, G. Cazes, ed., pp. 41–50. Paris: Centre National de la Recherche Scientifique.

2002 Gastronomie, Kulturerbe und Welttourismus (Gastronomy, Cultural Heritage, and World Tourism). Voyage 5:30–48.

2004 L'Appel à l'Éthique et la Référence Universaliste dans la Doctrine Officielle du Tourisme (The Appeal to Ethics and the Reference to Universalism in the Official Doctrine of Tourism). International Revue Tiers Monde (International Third World Review) 45(178):125–146.

2005 Tourisme International. Incursions dans les Théories du Tourisme et du Loisir: Moindre Jouissance et/ou Plus-de-Jouir (International Tourism. Entries into the Theories of Tourism and Leisure: Less Pleasure and/or Surplus

Pleasure). Paper Presented to the International Academy for the Study of Tourism, Beijing Hotel, Beijing, July (pages not numbered).

2007 Constructing a Research Project: From Past Definite to Future Perfect. *In* The Study of Tourism: Anthropological and Sociological Beginnings, D. Nash. ed., pp. 122–136. Oxford: Elsevier.

Lanfant, M.-F., J. Allcock, and E. Bruner, eds.
1995 International Tourism: Identity and Change. London: Sage.

Lanfant, M.-F., M. Mollin, D. Rozenberg, M. Picard, and J. de Weerdt
1978 Sociologie du Tourisme: Positions et Perspectives dans la Recherche Internationale (Sociology of Tourism: Positions and Perspectives in International Research). Paris: DGRST-DAFU, CNRS.

Larsen, J., and M. Jacobsen
2008 Zygmunt Bauman vs. John Urry. Sosiologi i dag (Sociology Today) 38(3): 7–36.

Larsen, J., J. Urry, and K. Axhausen
2007 Networks and Tourism: Mobile Social Life. Annals of Tourism Research 34:244–262.

Larsen, S.
2007 Aspects of a Psychology of the Tourist Experience. Scandinavian Journal of Hospitality and Tourism 7:7–18.

Larsen, S., and I. Folgerø
2008 Ansatte, Gjester og Turister: Gjestepsykologi og Servicearbeid (Employees, Guests and Tourists: Working under the Tourist Gaze). *In* Turisme: Fenomen og Næring (Tourism: Phenomenon and Industry), J. Jacobsen and A. Viken, eds., pp. 85–99. Oslo: Gyldendal Akademisk.

Lash, S., and J. Urry
1994 Economies of Signs and Space. London: Sage.

Lavarini, R.
2005 Viaggiatori. Lo Spirito e il Cammino (Travelers. The Spirit and the Way). Milano: Hoepli.
2008 Viaggiare Lento (Slow Travel). Milano: Hoepli.

Lazaridies, G., and E. Wickens
1999 "Us and the Others": Ethnic Minorities in Greece. Annals of Tourism Research 26(3):632–655.

Lazarsfeld, P., B. Berelson, and H. Gaudet
1944 The People's Choice. New York: Duell, Sloan and Pearce.

Lefebvre, H.
1945 Tome I. Introduction à la Première Édition (vol. 1, Introduction to the First Edition).Tome 2. Fondements d'une Sociologie de la Quotidienneté (vol. 2, Foundations of a Sociology of Everyday Life). Paris: L'Arche.
1947 Le Matérialisme Dialectique (Dialectical Materialism). Paris: PUF.
1967 Sur une Interprétation du Marxisme (On an Interpretation of Marxism). L'Homme et la Société (Man and Society) 4:3–22.
1991 The Production of Space. Oxford: Blackwell.

Leiper, N.
2000 An Emerging Discipline. Annals of Tourism Research 27:805–809.
Lekkas, N.
1925 (1996) Ο Περιηγητισμός εν Ελλάδι, (Touring in Greece) Εθνικό Τυπογραφείο 1925 (National Printing House, 1925), Υπουργείο Εθνικής Οικονομίας (Ministry of National Economy), Πανεπιστημιακές Εκδόσεις Αιγαίου (University of the Aegean Publications), Ξενοδοχειακό Επιμελητήριο Ελλάδος (Hellenic Chamber of Hotels), 1996, G.A. Zacharatos, ed., Athens.
Lelli, M.
1983 Dallo Sviluppo all'Equilibrio. Una Nuova Ipotesi sulla Crisi Sarda (From Development to Equilibrium. A New Hypothesis on the Sardinian "Crisis"). *In* Lo Sviluppo che si Doveva Fermare. Saggi e Ricerche sulla Sardegna Post-Agricola e Post-Industriale (The Development which had to be Stopped. Essays and Studies of Post-Agricultural and Post-Industrial Sardinia), M. Lelli, ed., pp. 19–52. Pisa: ETS—Iniziative Culturali.
1989 Tempo e Turismo nella Sardegna Postindustriale (Time and Tourism in Post-Industrial Sardinia). Sociologia Urbana e Rurale (Urban and Rural Sociology) 28:89–101.
Lengkeek, J.
1996 On the Multiple Realities of Leisure: A Phenomenological Approach to the Otherness of Leisure. Loisir et Société (Leisure and Society) 19(1):23–40.
2002 A Love Affair with Elsewhere: Love as a Metaphor and Paradigm for Tourist Longing. *In* The Tourist as a Metaphor of the Social World, G. Dann, ed., pp. 189–208. Wallingford, CT: CAB International.
2006 The Authenticity Discourse of Heritage. Paper Presented to the Research Committee on Leisure of the International Sociological Association, Durban, 23–29 July.
Lengkeek, J., and B. Elands
2006 The Tourist Experience of Out-there-ness: Theory and Practice. Paper Presented to the Research Committee on International Tourism of the International Sociological Association, Durban, 23–29 July.
Lengkeek, J. and M. Swain-Byrne, eds.
2006 Proceedings of the Symposium on Theoretical Innovations in Tourism Studies, Wageningen 9–10 June 2005. Research Committee on International Tourism, International Sociological Association CD-rom. Wageningen: Wageningen University.
Leotta, N.
2005 Approcci Visuali di Turismo Urbano. Il Tempo del Viaggio, il Tempo dello Sguardo (Visual Approaches to Urban Tourism. Time of Travel, Time of the Gaze). Milano: Hoepli.
Leszczycki, S.
1937 Współczesne zagadnienia turyzmu (Contemporary Aspects of Tourism). Kraków: Komunikaty Studium Turyzmu Uniwersytetu Jagiellońskiego no. 3.
Lett, J.
1983 Ludic and Liminoid Aspects of Charter Yacht Tourism in the Caribbean. Annals of Tourism Research 10:35–56.

Leugger, J.

1956 Einige soziologische Aspekte des Fremdenverkehrs (Some Sociological Aspects of Tourism). Revue de Tourisme (Tourist Review) 11(4):145–151.

1958 Weitere soziologische Aspekte des Fremdenverkehrs (Further Sociological Aspects of Tourism). Revue de Tourisme (Tourist Review) 13(1):9–16.

1959 Fremdenverkehr in der modernen Arbeitsgesellschaft (Tourism in the Modern Labor Society). *In* Fremdenverkehr in Theorie und Praxis. Festschrift für W. Hunziker (Tourism in Theory and Practice. Record in Honor of W. Hunziker), pp. 97–108. Bern: s.n.

1966 Verkehrs- und Fremdenverkehrssoziologie (Sociology of Traffic and Tourism). *In* Soziologische Arbeiten (Sociological Works), P. Atteslander and R. Girod, eds., pp. 157–185. Bern: Huber.

Liebman Parrinello, G.

1987 Turismo e Scienze Sociali di Base: Per un Approccio al Turismo Post-Industriale (Tourism and Basic Social Sciences: An Approach to Post-Industrial Tourism). Rassegna di Studi Turistici (Review of Tourist Studies) 3/4:195–218.

1993 Motivation and Anticipation in Post-Industrial Tourism. Annals of Tourism Research 20:233–249.

2006 Rileggendo una Teoria del Turismo di Hans-Magnus Enzensberger (Re-Reading Enzensberger's Theory of Tourism). Quaderno del Dipartimento di Letterature Comparate, Università degli Studi Roma Tre (Occasional Papers of the Department of Comparative Literatures, University of Studies Rome Three) 2:261–275.

2007 Tourismus vs. Fremdenverkehr (Tourism vs. Fremdenverkehr). Quaderno del Dipartimento di Letterature Comparate, Università degli Studi Roma Tre (Occasional Papers of the Department of Comparative Literatures, University of Studies Rome Three) 3:147–155.

2008 Address to the Research Committee on International Tourism of the International Sociological Association, Jaipur, 24–26 November.

Linton, R.

1936 The Study of Man. New York: Appleton-Century.

Lisiecki, S.

1981 Ruch turystyczny z RFN do Polski: zagadnienia społeczne i polityczne (Inbound Tourism from West Germany to Poland: Social and Political Issues). Studium Niemcoznawcze (Studies of German-ness). Poznań: Wydawnictwo Instytutu Zachodniego.

Littré, É.

1872 Dictionnaire de la Langue Française (French Dictionary) (2nd ed). Paris: Published by Émile Littré.

Löfgren, O.

1979 Människan i Naturen (Human in Nature). *In* Den Kultiverade Människan (The Cultivated Human), J. Frykman and O. Löfgren, eds., pp. 45–73. Lund: Liber.

1984 Turism som Kultur– och Klassmöte (Tourism as a Meeting of Culture and Class). *In* Turisme og Reiseliv (Tourism and Travel), L.-H. Schmidt and J. Jacobsen, eds., pp. 98–125. Aalborg: The Nordic Summer University.

1985 Wish you Were Here! Holiday Images and Picture Postcards. Ethnologia Scandinavica (Scandinavian Ethnology) 15:90–107.

1994 Learning to be a Tourist. Ethnologia Scandinavica (Scandinavian Ethnology) 24:103–125.

1999 On Holiday: A History of Vacation. Berkeley, CA: University of California Press.

2001 Know Your Country: A Comparative Perspective on Tourism and Nation Building in Sweden. *In* Being Elsewhere, Consumer Culture, and Identity in Modern Europe and North America, S. Baranowski and E. Furlough, eds., pp. 137–154. Ann Arbor, MI: University of Michigan Press.

2008 The Secret Lives of Tourists: Delays, Disappointments and Daydreams. Scandinavian Journal of Hospitality and Tourism 8:85–101.

Luhmann, N.

1983 Strutture della Società e Semantica (Social Structure and Semantics). Milano: FrancoAngeli.

Luković, T.

2002 Nautički turizam europskog dijela Mediterana (Nautical Tourism of the European Part of the Mediterranean). Split: Hrvatska pan-europska unija.

Lutz, R.

1992 Der subjektive Faktor. Ansätze einer Anthropologie des Reisens (The Subjective Factor: Approaches of an Anthropology of Travel). *In* Reisen und Alltag. Beiträge zur kulturwissenschaftlichen Tourismusforschung (Traveling and Everyday Life: Contributions to Tourism Cultural Studies), D. Kramer and R. Lutz, eds., pp. 229–273. Frankfurt: s.n.

Lytras, P.

1998 Κοινωνιολογία του Τουρισμού (The Sociology of Tourism). Athens: Interbooks.

Łukaszewski, X.

1847 Słownik podręczny wyrazów obcych i rzadkich w języku polskim używanych (Handbook of Foreign Terms and Words Rarely Used in the Polish Language). Królewiec: s.n.

Macbeth, J.

2005 Towards an Ethics Platform for Tourism. Annals of Tourism Research 32:962–984.

MacCannell, D.

1973 Staged Authenticity: Arrangements of Social Space in Tourist Settings. American Journal of Sociology 79(3):589–603.

1976 (1989) The Tourist: A New Theory of the Leisure Class (2nd ed.). New York: Schocken Books.

1992 Empty Meeting Grounds: The Tourist Papers. New York: Routledge.

2005 Il Turista. Una Nuova Teoria della Classe Agiata (The Tourist. A New Theory of the Affluent Class). Torino: UTET-De Agostini.

Mäder, U.

1982 Fluchthelfer Tourismus (Tourism: The Escape Agent). Zürich: Rotpunktverlag.

Magaš, D.

1995 Turistička putovanja kao ekonomska dobra—turistički menadžment (Tourist Travels as Economic Goods—Tourism Management). Opatija: Hotelijerski fakultet.

1997 Turistička destinacija (Tourist Destination). Opatija: Hotelijerski fakultet.

2003 Management turističke organizacije i destinacije (Management of a Tourist Organization and Destination). Rijeka: Adamić.

Maitland, R., L. Minnaert, and G. Miller

2008 Call for Papers on Social Tourism. Current Issues in Tourism.

Malinowski, B.

1922 (1987 reprint) Argonauts of the Western Pacific: An Account of Native Enterprise and Adventure in the Archipelagos of Melanesian New Guinea. London: Routledge.

1935 Coral Gardens and their Magic: A Study of the Methods of Tilling the Soil and of Agricultural Rites in the Trobriand Islands. New York: American Books.

1958 Sketches from the Theory of Culture. Warszawa: Ksiazka i Wiedza.

Malinowski, B., and H. Ellis

1929 (2005 reprint) The Sexual Life of Savages in North-Western Melanesia: An Ethnographic Account of Courtship, Marriage, and Family Life among the Natives of the Trobriand Islands, British New Guinea. Whitefish, MT: Kessinger Publishing.

Manella, G.

2008 Fascia Costiera e Aree Interne nelle Politiche Locali (Coast and Inland Areas in Local Policies). In Spazio Turistico e Società Globale (Tourist Space and Global Society), A. Savelli, ed., pp. 233–253. Milano: FrancoAngeli.

Manera, C.

2001 Renta de Situación y Desarrollo Mercantil: El Crecimiento Económico de Baleares (Renting Locations and Commercial Development: Economic Growth of the Balearics). In Historia Económica Regional de España en los Siglos XIX y XX (Regional Economic History of Spain in the 19th and 20th Centuries), L. Germán, ed., pp. 441–475. Barcelona: Crítica.

Mannheim, K.

1940 Man and Society in an Age of Reconstruction: Studies in Modern Social Structure. London: Routledge and Kegan Paul.

Manologlou, E.

1993 Agro-Tourism Manual (Curriculum of the ALTUR Educational Program). Athens: Greek Tourism Organization.

Manologlou, E., P. Tsartas, A. Markou, and V. Papliakou
1999 Ο Τουρισμός ως παράγοντας κοινωνικής αλλαγής (Tourism as a Factor of Social Change). Athens: EKKE (NCSR) Exantas.
Mariotti, A.
1928 Lezioni di Economia Turistica (Lessons in Tourism Economics). Roma: Tiber.
1952 L'Equilibrio Turistico. Conferenza detta in Pieve di Cadore (The Tourism Balance Conference held in Pieve di Cadore, Belluno). Pubblicazione a cura dell'Ente Provinciale per il Turismo di Belluno (Publication edited by the Tourism Board of the Province of Belluno), Belluno.
1974 Raccolta di Studi sul Turismo (Collection of Studies on Tourism), F. Demarinis, ed. Roma: Arti Grafiche Scalia.
Marković, S., and Z. Marković
1967 Osnove turizma (Essentials of Tourism). Zagreb: Školska knjiga.
1970 Osnove turizma (Essentials of Tourism) (2nd ed). Zagreb: Školska knjiga.
Marković, M., M. Relac, and K. Štuka
1977 Aktivan odmor u turizmu u funkcijihumaniziranja života i rada (Spending the Vacation Actively as a Function of Humanisation of Life and Work). *In* Proceedings Humanističke vrijednosti turizma (Humanistic Values of Tourism), pp. 253–256. Zadar: Pedagoška akademija u Zadru.
Maroudas, L., and A. Kyriakaki
2001 The Perspectives of Ecotourism Development in Small Islands: Some Lessons from Greece. Anatolia: The International Journal of Tourism and Hospitality Research 12(1):59–71.
Maroudas, L., and P. Tsartas
1997 Εναλλακτικές Μορφές Τουρισμού στα Μικρά και Απομονωμένα Νησιά του Αιγαίου: Από την Απομόνωση στην Αειφορική Ανάπτυξη (Alternative Forms of Tourism in the Aegean's Small and Isolated Islands. From Isolation to Sustainable Development). *In* Ν Επιχείρηση στη Αυγή του 21^{ου} Αιίνα (The Enterprise at the Dawn of the 21st Century). Chios: Department of Business Administration, University of the Aegean.
Martinelli, F.
1976 Sviluppo dell'Urbanesimo e Aumento del Tempo Libero dalla Villeggiatura di Élite al Turismo di Massa (Urbanism Development and Increase of Free Time from Elite Vacation to Mass Tourism). *In* Sviluppo del Territorio e Ruolo del Turismo (Territorial Development and the Role of Tourism), C. Stroppa, ed. Bologna: Clue.
Martinengo, M., L. Melocchi, M. Nuciari, and L. Savoja
2001 I Torinesi e il Futuro Turistico della Città (The People of Turin and the Touristic Future of their City). Torino: Leprotto e Bella.
Martinengo, M., and L. Savoja
1998 Sociologia dei Fenomeni Turistici (Sociology of Tourist Phenomena). Milano: Guerini.

2003 Memoria e Fiction nel Turismo Urbano (Memory and Fiction in Urban Tourism). Milano: Guerini.

Martinotti, G.

1993 Metropoli. La Nuova Morfologia Sociale delle Città (Metropolis. The New Social Morphology of Cities). Bologna: Il Mulino.

2004 Urbs Hospitalis (Visitors in the City). *In* Città, Turismo e Comunicazione Culturale (Town, Tourism, and Cultural Communication), A. Savelli, ed., pp. 75–83. Milano: FrancoAngeli.

Marušić, M., and D. Prebežec

2004 Istraživanje turističkog tržišta (Research of a Tourist Market). Zagreb: Adeco.

Marx, K., and F. Engels

1848 (1959) The Communist Manifesto. *In* Basic Writings, L. Feuer, ed. London: Collins.

Mathisen, V.

1978 Tourism and Development: A Sociological Study of Tourism in Morocco, with Emphasis on its Social and Cultural Effects, publication S-6-79. Oslo: International Peace Research Institute.

1980 Turisme: Internasjonal Forståelse eller Kulturpåvirkning? (Tourism: International Understanding or Cultural Influence?), Magister Artium dissertation, Department of Social Science, University of Tromsø, Norway. Published as publication S-4-80. Oslo: International Peace Research Institute.

Mauss, M.

1969 Les Civilisations: Éléments et Formes (Civilizations: Elements and Forms). *In* Essais de Sociologie (Sociological Essays). Paris: Minuit.

1980 (1923–1924) Essai sur le Don: Formes et Raisons de l'Échange dans les Sociétés Archaïques (Essay on the Gift: Types and Reasons of the Exchange in Early Societies). *In* Sociologie et Anthropologie (Sociology and Anthropology). Paris: Presses Universitaires de France (Originally in L'Année Sociologique 1, pp. 30–186).

Mayntz, R.

1961 Urlaub in Almuñecar. Beobachtungen einer Soziologin während einer Urlaubsreise durch Spanien (Holidays in Almuñecar: Observations by a Sociologist during a Holiday Trip to Spain). München: StfT.

Mazi, M.

1965 Inostrani trizam i njegova uloga u privrednom razvoju Jugoslavije (Foreign Tourism and its Role in the Economic Development of Yugoslavia). Doctoral dissertation, University of Belgrade, Beograd, Serbia.

1972 Ekonomika turizma (Economics of Tourism). Beograd: Savremena administracija.

Mazi, M., S. Esminger, M. Stojanovic, Z. Bosnjak, M. Panic, B. Protic, Z. Nikolic, and D. Popov

1967 Osnovi turizma (Tourism Basics). Beograd: Turistička štampa.

Mazzette, A. ed.

2002 Modelli di Turismo in Sardegna. Tra Sviluppo Locale e Processi di Globalizzazione (Tourism Patterns in Sardinia. Between Local Development and the Processes of Globalization). Milano: FrancoAngeli.

Mazzette, A., and C. Tidore

2008 Il Turismo in Sardegna e il Consumo del Territorio. Problemi di Government e di Governance (Tourism in Sardinia and the Consumption of Territory. Problems of Government and Governance). *In* Spazio Turistico e Società Globale (Tourist Space and Global Society), A. Savelli, ed., pp. 128–141. Milano: FrancoAngeli.

Maczka, J.

1974 Definicje i określenia występujace w polskiej literaturze fachowej dotyczacej rekreacji, turystyki i krajoznawstwa (Definitions and Descriptors/Phrases for Leisure, Tourism and Rural Recreation in the Polish Trade Literature). Biuletyn Informacyjny Instytutu Turystyki (Information Bulletin of the Institute of Tourism) 3/12:4–14.

McIntosh, R., and C. Goeldner

1995 Tourism Principles, Practices and Philosophies. New York: Wiley.

Mechelen, F.van.

1964 Vrijetijdsbesteding in Vlaanderen. Een Sociologisch Onderzoek bij de Aktieve Nederlandstalige Bevolking van België (Leisure in Flanders: A Sociological Investigation of the Active Dutch Speaking Population of Belgium). Katolieke Universiteit Leuven, Instituut voor Economisch, Politiek en Sociaal Onderzoek, Centrum voor Sociologisch Onderzoek. Antwerpen: Uitgeverij s.m. Ontwikkeling.

Mehmetoglu, M., G. Dann, and S. Larsen

2001 Solitary Travellers in the Norwegian Lofoten Islands: Why do People Travel on their Own? Scandinavian Journal of Hospitality and Tourism 1:19–37.

Meinke, H.

1968 Tourismus und wirtschaftliche Entwicklung (Tourism and Economic Development). Göttingen: Vandenhoek und Ruprecht.

Melén, O.

1962 Personlig Påverkan och Turism: Rapport från en Undersökning i Malmö om den Personliga Påverkans Roll vid Val av Turistresor m.m. (Personal Influence and Tourism: Report from a Survey in Malmö on Personal Influence on Vacation Travel Decisions). Stockholm: Beredskapsnämnden för Psykologiskt Försvar.

Melotti, M.

2007 Mediterraneo tra Miti e Turismo. Per una Sociologia del Turismo Archeologico (The Mediterranean Sea between Myth and Tourism. For a Sociology of Archaeological Tourism). Milano: Cuem.

2008 Turismo Archeologico. Dalle Piramidi alle Veneri di Plastica (Archaeological Tourism. From Pyramids to Plastic Venuses). Milano: Bruno Mondadori.

Merton, R.
1977 Członkowie grupy i out-siderzy (Group Members and Outsiders). *In* Czy kryzys socjologii? (The Crisis of Sociology?), J. Szacki, ed., pp. 396–465. Warszawa: Czytelnik.

Meyer-Cronemeyer, H.
1960 Verschiedenes (Varieties). Kölner Zeitschrift für Soziologie und Sozialpsychologie. Cologne Journal of Sociology and Social Psychology 12:741–745.

Meyer, W., and G. Meyer
2007 Die Pionierarbeit von Heinz Hahn und des Studienkreises für Tourismus für eine qualitative Tourismusforschung (The Spadework by Heinz Hahn and the Study Circle for Tourism for Qualitative Research). *In* Tourismusforschung in Bayern. Aktuelle sozialwissenschaftliche Beiträge (Tourism Research in Bavaria: Current Contributions of the Social Sciences), A. Günther, et al, pp. 39–50. München: Profil.

Mihalič, T.
1995 Ekonomija okolja v turizmu (Environmental Economics for Tourism). Ljubljana: Ekonomska fakulteta Univerze v Ljubljani.
1997 Turistična podjetja—poslovanje in ekonomika turističkih agencij in gostinskih podjetij (Tourist Firms—The Activities and Economics of Tourist Agencies and Catering Firms). Ljubljana: Univerza v Ljubljani.

Mihalič, T., and J. Planina
2002 Ekonomika turizma (Economics of Tourism). Ljubljana: Univerza v Ljubljani.

Milewski, S.
2006 Podróze blizsze i dalsze czyli urok komunikacyjnych staroci (Travels Near and Far—The Charm of old Travelogs). Warszawa: Iskry.

Mill, J. S.
2008 (1844) Essays on Some Unsettled Questions of Political Economy (http://www.gutenberg.org/files/12004, accessed 9 September 2008).

Miller, D.
1997 Capitalism: An Ethnographic Approach. Oxford: Berg.

Minca, C.
1996 Spazi Effimeri (Ephemeral Spaces). Padova: Cedam.

Minnaert, L., R. Maitland, and G. Miller
2006 Social Tourism and its Ethical Foundations. Tourism, Culture and Communication 7(12):7–17.

Mirić, D., and D. Vlahović
1998 Zdravlje i turizam (Health and Tourism). Split: Turistička zajednica županije splitsko-dalmatinske.

Mitscherlich, A.
1965 Aspekte der Fremdenindustrie (Aspects of the Tourist Industry). Neue Rundschau (New Review) 76(3):530–533.

Mjøset, L.
1991 Kontroverser i Norsk Sosiologi (Controversies in Norwegian Sociology). Oslo: Universitetsforlaget.

Moira-Mylonopoulou, P., K. Tsoumanis, and K. Hatzilekas
2003 Κοινωνιολογία και Ψυχολογία του Τουρισμού (The Sociology and Psychology of Tourism). T.E.E. O.E.D.B.

Mokyr, J.
1996 Il Cambiamento Tecnologico, 1750–1945 (Technological Change, 1750–1945). *In* Storia d'Europa, vol. V, L'Età Contemporanea. Secoli 19–20 (History of Europe, vol. 5, The Contemporary Era. 19th and 20th Centuries), P. Bairoch and E. Hobsbawm, eds., pp. 272–370. Torino: Einaudi.

Montani, A. R.
2005 Turismo, Impatti e Sostenibilità (Tourism, Impacts, and Sustainability). *In* Messer Milione ... Internet. Territorio, Turismo, Comunicazione (Messer Milione ... Internet. Territory, Tourism, Communication), A. Montani, ed., pp. 179–194. Napoli: Liguori.

Moore, R.
1995 Gender and Alcohol Use in a Greek Tourist Town. Annals of Tourism Research 22(2):300–313.

Mordal, T.
1979 Nordmenns Feriereiser (Holiday Trips by Norwegians). Samfunnsøkonomiske Studier (Socio-Economic Studies) No. 41. Oslo: Central Bureau of Statistics of Norway.

Morgenroth, W.
1927 Fremdenverkehr (Tourism). *In* Handwörterbuch der Staatswissenschaften (Concise Dictionary of Political Science) (4th ed.) pp. 394–409. Jena: Fischer.

Morin, E.
1962 (1983) L'Esprit du Temps: Essai sur la Culture de Masse (The Spirit of the Age: Essay on Mass Culture). Paris: Grasset.
1965 Vivent les Vacances (Long Live Holidays). *In* Pour une Politique de l'Homme (For a Politics of Mankind). Paris: Seuil.
1970 Journal de Californie (Californian Diary). Paris: Seuil.

Morra, G.
1988 Homo Turisticus. *In* Il Turismo in una Società che Cambia (Tourism in a Changing Society), P. Guidicini and A. Savelli, eds., pp. 17–21. Milano: FrancoAngeli.

Moß, C.
2000 Briefe der Düsseldorfer Familie Glücksmann (Letters of the Glücksmann Family from Düsseldorf). Düsseldorf: Ev. Kirche im Rheinland.

Moutafi, V.
1990 Tourism on Samos: Implications for Marriage, Dowry and Women's Status. Unpublished PhD dissertation, Graduate School of the City University of New York, New York, NY.

Müller, D.
  2002 German Second Homeowners in Sweden: Some Remarks on the Tourism-Migration Nexus. Revue Européenne des Migrations Internationales (European Review of International Migrations) 18(1):67–86.
  2007 Second Homes in the Nordic Countries: Between Common Heritage and Exclusive Commodity. Scandinavian Journal of Hospitality and Tourism 7:193–201.
Müller, H.
  2002 (2005) Freizeit und Tourismus. Eine Einführung in Theorie und Politik (Leisure and Tourism. An Introduction to Theory and Policy) (10th ed.). Bern: Forschungsinstitut für Freizeit und Tourismus der Universität Bern.
Mundt, J.
  2001 Einführung in den Tourismus (Introduction to Tourism) (2nd ed). München: Oldenbourg.
Nahrstedt, W.
  1972 Die Entstehung der Freizeit, dargestellt am Beispiel Hamburgs (The Formation of Leisure from the Example of Hamburg). Göttingen: Diss.
Nash, D.
  1970 A Community in Limbo: An Anthropological Study of an American Community Abroad. Bloomington, IN: Indiana University Press.
  1981 Tourism as an Anthropological Subject. Current Anthropology 22(5):461–481.
  1989 España en Venta (Spain for Sale) by F. Jurdao Arrones (Book Review). Annals of Tourism Research 16:137–139.
  1993 A Little Anthropology (rev. ed.). Englewood Cliffs, NJ: Prentice-Hall.
  1996 Anthropology of Tourism. Oxford: Pergamon.
Nash, D. ed.
  2007 The Study of Tourism: Anthropological and Sociological Beginnings. Oxford: Elsevier.
National Virtual Translation Center
  2008 National Virtual Translation Center (http://www.nvtc.gov, accessed 30 June 2008).
Naville, P.
  1967 Le Nouveau Léviathan: De l'Aliénation à la Jouissance. Génèse de la Sociologie du Travail chez Marx et Engels (The New Leviathan: From Alienation to Pleasure. Origin of the Sociology of Work in Marx and Engels). Paris: Éditions Anthropos.
Nazou, D.
  2003 Πολλαπλές Ταυτότητες και οι Αναπαραστάσεις τους σ' ένα Τουριστικό Νησί των Κυκλάδων: "Επιχειρηματικότητα" και "Τοπική Ταυτότητα στη Μύκονο" (Multiple Identities and their Representations in a Tourist Island of the Cyclades: "Entrepreneurship" and "Local Identity in Mykonos"). Unpublished doctoral dissertation, Department of Social Anthropology and History, University of the Aegean, Mytilene, Greece.

2005 Συναντώντας τον άλλο στον τουρισμό: Οι γυναίκες επιχειρηματίες, οι τουρίστες και οι διαπολιτισμικές τους ανταλλαγές στη Μύκονο (Meeting the Other in Tourism: Women Entrepreneurs, Tourists and their Intercultural Exchanges in Mykonos). *In* Η Προσέγγιση του Άλλου: Ιδεολογία, Μεθοδολογία και Ερευνητική Πρακτική (Approaching the Other: Ideology, Methodology and Research Practice), Y. Kyriakakis and M. Mihailidou, eds., pp. 197–235. Athens: Metaihmio.

Nedelmann, B., and P. Stztompka, eds.
1993 Sociology in Europe. In Search of Identity. Berlin: de Gruyter.

Nejkov, D.
1980 Koncepcije i metodološka osnovica razvojne politike turizma u Jugoslaviji (Concepts and Methodological Foundations of the Development Policy of Tourism in Yugoslavia). Savjetovanje "Turizam: značajan factor društveno-ekonomskog razvoja Jugoslavije" (Conference: "Tourism as an Important Factor for the Social and Economic Development of Yugoslavia"), p. 12. Split.

Nettekoven, L.
1972 Massentourismus in Tunesien. Soziologische Untersuchungen an Touristen aus hochindustrialisierten Gesellschaften (Mass Tourism in Tunisia: Socio-logical Investigations of Tourists from Highly Developed Societies). Starnberg: Studienkreis für Tourismus.

Nocifora, E.
1993 La Costruzione Sociale dell'Area Mediterranea. Il Ruolo del Turismo (The Social Construction of the Mediterranean Area. The Role of Tourism). *In* Il Turismo Mediterraneo come Risorsa e come Rischio: Strategie di Comunica-zione (Mediterranean Tourism as a Resource and Risk: Communication Strategies), E. Nocifora, ed. Roma: Seam.
1997 Mercato Globale e Società Turistica (Global Market and Tourist Society). *In* Turismatica. Turismo, Cultura, Nuove Imprenditorialità e Globalizza-zione dei Mercati (Tourismatics. Tourism, Culture, New Entrepreneurship, and Market Globalization), E. Nocifora, ed., pp. 17–49. Milano: FrancoAngeli.
2001 Itineraria. Dal Grand Tour al Turismo Postmoderno. Lezioni di Sociologia del Turismo (Itineraries. From Grand Tour to Post-Modern Tourism. Sociology of Tourism Lectures). Milano: Le Vespe.
2004 Turismo Culturale e Promozione della Sostenibilità Ambientale (Cultural Tourism and the Promotion of Environmental Sustainability). Santarcangelo di Romagna: Maggioli.
2008a Oltre il Turismo di Massa. Innovazione di Consumo e Turismo Sociale contro l'Esasperata Standardizzazione del Mercato Turistico Globalizzato (Beyond Mass Tourism. Consumption Innovation and Social Tourism against the Extreme Standardization of the Global Tourist Market). *In* Tracce di Turismo Sostenibile (Traces of Sustainable Tourism), F. Beato, et al, pp. 31–72. Rende: Centro Editoriale e Librario dell'Università della Calabria.

2008b La Società Turistica (The Tourist Society). Napoli: Scriptaweb.

Nordbakke, S.
2000 Reiser Mellom Tid og Sted: En Studie av Ferie og Turisme blant Utenlandske Bilreisende i det Nordlige Norge (Journeys between Time and Place: A Study of Foreign Motor Tourists in Northern Norway). Canadian Political dissertation. Oslo, Norway: University of Oslo.

Norén, C.
1970 Restaurangvanor (Human Behavior in the Restaurant), Special Series in Alcohol Research. vol. 1, Uppsala: Department of Sociology, University of Uppsala.
1971 Restaurangvanor (Human Behavior in the Restaurant), Special Series in Alcohol Research. vol. 2, Uppsala: Department of Sociology, University of Uppsala.

Norval, A.
1936 The Tourist Industry: A National and International Survey. London: Pitman.

Norwood, G.
2006 Buyers Abroad Mind their Language. Sunday Telegraph, Home Living, 19 November, H3.

Nowakowska, A.
1982 Ekonomiczne aspekty turystyki. Zagadnienia wybrane (Economic Aspects of Tourism. Selected Topics). Kraków: Akademia Ekonomiczna.
2003 Ekonomika Turystyki (Economics of Tourism). *In* Nauki o turystyce, czesc I (Studies of Tourism, Part One) (2nd ed.). R. Winiarski, ed., pp. 33–42. Studia i Monografie (Studies and Monographs) no. 7. Kraków: Akademia Wychowania Fizycznego im. Bronisława Czecha w Krakowie.

Nuvolati, G.
2006 Lo Sguardo Vagabondo. Il Flâneur e la Città da Baudelaire ai Postmoderni (The Wandering Gaze. The Flâneur and the City from Baudelaire to Postmodernism). Bologna: Il Mulino.

Nyberg, L.
1955 Zur Grundlagenforschung im Fremdenverkehr (Basic Research on Tourism). Jahrbuch für Fremdenverkehr (Tourism Yearbook) vol. 3, pp. 23–27. Obitelj i turizam (Family and Tourism). Proceedings of Conference.

Odyniec, A.
1876 Listy z podróży (Letters from Travels). Kronika Rodzinna (Family Chronicle) 22:339.

Øllgaard, J.
1984 Turismen som Billede: Billedet som Turisme (Tourism as Picture: The Picture as Tourism). *In* Turisme og Reiseliv (Tourism and Travel), L.-H. Schmidt and J. Jacobsen, eds., pp. 43–67. Aalborg: The Nordic Summer University.

Olsen, K.

2002 Authenticity as a Concept in Tourism Research: The Social Organization of the Experience of Authenticity. Tourist Studies 2:159–182.

2006 Making Differences in a Changing World: The Norwegian Sámi in the Tourist Industry. Scandinavian Journal of Hospitality and Tourism 6:37–53.

Opaschowski, H.

1977 Urlaub—der Alltag reist mit (Holiday—The Everyday Travels Alongside). Psychologie Heute (Psychology Today) 4(6):18–24.

1989 Tourismusforschung (Tourism Research). Opladen: Leske und Budrich.

2002 Tourismus. Eine systematische Einführung (Tourism: A Systematic Introduction). Opladen: Lester und Budrich.

2006 Einführung in die Freizeitwissenschaft (Introduction to Leisure Time Science) (4th ed). Wiesbaden: VS-Verlag.

Oppenheimer, F.

1932 Zur Soziologie des Fremdenverkehrs (On the Sociology of Tourism). Archiv für den Fremdenverkehr (Archive of Tourism) 3:33–36.

Ossowski, S.

1939 Więź społeczna i dziedzictwo krwi (Translated to English in 1966, Social Ties and Blood Heritage). Dzieła (Complete Works). vol. 2, Warszawa: PWN.

1957 (Translated to English in 1963, Class Structure in the Social Consciousness). Trans. S. Patterson. London: Routledge and Kegan Paul.

1962 O osobliwościach nauk społecznych (On the Peculiarities of the Social Sciences). Warszawa: Polish Scientific Publishers.

Ostrowski, P.

1988 Understanding Tourism. Problems of Tourism XI(3):3–20.

Pagenstecher, C.

1998a Enzensbergers Tourismusessay von 1958—ein Forschungsprogramm für 1998? (Enzensberger's Essay on Tourism from 1958—A Research Program for 1998?). Tourismus Journal 2:533–552.

1998b Neue Ansätze für die Tourismusgeschichte (New Approaches to Tourism History). Archiv für Sozialgeschichte (Archive of Social History) 38:591–619.

1999 Immer noch brandet die Ferne. Tourismustheorie nach Enzensberger (Still the Backwash of Tourism. Tourism Theory after Enzensberger). iz3w. Blätter des Informationszentrums 3. Welt, Sonderheft: Fernweh—Wenn Einer Eine Reise tut (241) (Papers of the Third World Information Center, Special Issue, Wanderlust—When One Makes a Journey), 9–11 November.

2003a Der bundesdeutsche Tourismus. Ansätze zu einer Visual History, 1950–1990 (West-German Tourism: Approaches to a Visual History). Hamburg: Kovac.

2003b The Construction of the Tourist Gaze. How Industrial was Post-war German Tourism? *In* Construction d'une Industrie Touristique (Development of a Tourist Industry), L. Tissot, ed., pp. 373–390. Neuchâtel: Éditions Alphil.

Palumbo, M.
1988 Turismo Ligure: La Sfida Viene dall'Entroterra (Ligurian Tourism: The Challenge from Inland). Sociologia Urbana e Rurale (Urban and Rural Sociology) 26:221–244.
1992 Turismo Ligure: Verso una Nuova Immagine (Ligurian Tourism: Towards a New Image). Sociologia Urbana e Rurale (Urban and Rural Sociology) 38:347–363.

Palusci, O. and S. Francesconi, eds.
2006 Translating Tourism: Linguistic/Cultural Representations. Trento: Editrice Università degli Studi di Trento.

Panian, Ž.
2000 Elektoničko trgovanje (Electronic Business). Zagreb: Sinergija.

Paolinelli, P.
1983 Il Turismo come Eccesso: La Costa Smeralda (Tourism as Excess: The Emerald Coast). *In* Lo Sviluppo che si Doveva Fermare. Saggi e Ricerche sulla Sardegna Post-agricola e Post-industriale (The Development which had to be Stopped. Essays and Studies on Post-Agricultural and Post-Industrial Sardinia), M. Lelli, ed., pp. 163–195. Pisa: ETS-Iniziative Culturali.

Papadaki-Tzedaki, S.
1999 Ενδογενής Τουριστική Ανάπτυξη: Διαρθρωμένη και Αποδιαρθρωμένη Τοπική Ανάπτυξη; Η Περίπτωση του Ρεθύμνου, Κρήτης (Endogenous Tourism Development: Structured or Unstructured Local Development: The Case of Rethymnon, Crete). Athens: Papazisi.

Papagaroufali, E.
1986 Ελληνίδα Αγρότισσα και Γυναικείοι Αγροτουριστικοί Συνεταιρισμοί (The Greek Woman Farmer and Women's Cooperatives). Athens: Κέντρο Έρευνας για τις Γυναίκες της Μεσογείου (Research Center for Women of the Mediterranean).
1994 Women's Cooperatives in Rural Greece: An Alternative Form of Work against Unemployment. *In* Participation, Organizational Effectiveness and Quality of Work Life in the Year 2000, L. Nicolaou-Smokoviti and G. Szell, eds., pp. 193–199. Frankfurt: Peter Lang GmBH.

Papageorgiou, F.
1998 The Development of Agro-Tourism in Greece. Sociologia Urbana e Rurale (Urban and Rural Sociology) 26:207–219.

Papakonstantinidis, A.
2002 Αγροτουρισμός: Σταθμός στο Δρόμο για την Τοπική Ανάπτυξη (Agro-Tourism: A Watershed for Local Development). Athens: Agricultural Bank of Greece.

Pappas, N.
2006 Διερεύνηση των οικονομικών, κοινωνικών και χωρικών διαστάσεων του τουρισμού στη Ρόδο, μέσω των αντιλήψεων των πληροφορητών (Investigating the Economic, Social and Spatial Dimensions of Tourism on the Island of

Rhodes through the Perspectives of Key Informants). Unpublished doctoral dissertation, Department of Business Administration, University of the Aegean, Chios, Greece.

Pardi, F.
1992 Il Turismo e il suo Codice (Tourism and its Code). Sociologia Urbana e Rurale (Urban and Rural Sociology) 38:125–129.

Pattie, D.C.
1992 España, Asilo de Europa (Spain: Asylum of Europe) by F. Jurdao Arrones (Book Review). Annals of Tourism Research 19:380–382.

Pauko, F.
1971 Organizacija in poslovanje potovalnih agencij (Organization and Operation of Travel Agencies). Maribor: University of Maribor.

Pearce, D.
1992 España en Venta (Spain for Sale) (2nd ed.) by F. Jurdao Arrones (Book Review). Annals of Tourism Research 19:607–608.

Pearce, P.
1982 The Social Psychology of Tourist Behaviour. Oxford: Pergamon.
1985 A Systematic Comparison of Travel-Related Roles. Human Relations 38(1):1001–1011.

Pearce, P., and G. Moscardo
1986 The Concept of Authenticity in Tourist Experiences. Australian and New Zealand Journal of Sociology 22(1):121–132.

Pennartz, P.
1979 Mensen en Ruimte: Een Studie van de Sociale Betekenis van de Gebouwde Omgeving (People and Spatial Environment: A Study of the Social Meaning of the Built Environment). Wageningen: Landbouwhoge-school.

Perrotta, R.
1985 Aspetti Sociologici del Turismo (Sociological Aspects of Tourism). Promozione del Turismo e Formazione Manageriale (Tourism Promotion and Managerial Training). vol. 8, pp. 119–144. Palermo: Isida.

Persyn, J.
1909 Kiezen, Smaken, Schrijven. Lenzigen op de Leuvense Vakantieleergangen (Choosing, Tasting, Writing. Lectures on Louvain Holiday Courses). Hoogstraten: Jos Haseldonckx.

Petrinjak, S., and J. Sudar
1972 Propaganda turizma (Advertising of Tourism). Zagreb: Vjesnik—agencija za marketing.

Piazzi, G.
1988 Differenziazione Sociale e Turismo (Social Differentiation and Tourism). *In* Il Turismo in una Società che Cambia (Tourism in a Changing Society), P. Guidicini and A. Savelli, eds., pp. 23–37. Milano: FrancoAngeli.

Picard, M.
   1992 Bali: Tourisme Culturel et Culture Touristique (Bali: Cultural Tourism and Touristic Culture). Paris: L'Harmattan.
Pieroni, O.
   2008 Paesaggi, Ecomostri ed Intervento Politico-amministrativo. Una Indagine sul Degrado e l'Abusivismo Lungo le Coste Calabresi (Landscapes, Eco-Monsters, and Political-Administrative Action. A Survey on Decay and Illegal Housing along the Calabrian Coast). *In* Tracce di Turismo Sostenibile (Traces of Sustainable Tourism), F. Beato, et al, pp. 73–101. Rende: Centro Editoriale e Librario dell'Università della Calabria.
Pieroni, O. and T. Romita, eds.
   2003 Viaggiare, Conoscere e Rispettare l'Ambiente. Verso il Turismo Sostenibile (To Travel, to Know, and to Respect the Environment. Towards Sustainable Tourism). Soveria Mannelli, Catanzaro: Rubbettino.
Pikulik, L.
   1979 Romantik als Ungenügen an der Normalität (Romanticism as Displeasure with Normality). Frankfurt: Suhrkamp.
Pine, B., and J. Gilmore
   1999 The Experience Economy. Harvard: Harvard Business School Press.
Pirjevec, B.
   1988 Ekonomski aspekti jugoslavenskog turizma (Economic Aspects of Yugoslav Tourism). Zagreb: Školska knjiga.
   1998 Ekonomska obilježja turizma (Economic Characteristics of Tourism). Zagreb: Golden Marketing.
Pirjevec, B., and O. Kesar
   2002 Počela turizma (Principles of Tourism). Zagreb: Mikrorad and Ekonomski fakultet.
Planina, J.
   1964 Ekonomika turizma (Economics of Tourism). Univerza v.
Podemski, K.
   1981 Turystyka zagraniczna jako przedmiot badań socjologii. Przeglad koncepcji. Propozycje (Foreign Tourism as a Theme for Sociological Research: Review of Concepts and Propositions). Ruch Prawniczy, Ekonomiczny i Socjologiczny (Legal, Economic and Sociological Ideas) 3:249–273.
   2005 Socjologia podrózy (Sociology of Travel). Poznań: Wydawnictwo UAM.
Podilchak, W.
   1991 Distinctions of Fun, Enjoyment and Leisure. Leisure Studies 10:133–148.
Pompl, W.
   1994 Tourismuswissenschaft zwischen Paradigmensuche und Kompilation (Tourism Science between Compilation and the Search for a Paradigm). *In* La Recherche Touristique. Succès, Echecs et Problèmes non Resolus (Tourism Research: Success, Stumbling Blocks and Unresolved Problems), AIEST, ed., pp. 233–248. St. Gallen: Édition AIEST.

Popesku, J.
2002 Marketing u turizmu (Marketing in Tourism). Beograd: Čigaja štampa i CENFORT.
Popov, D.
1979 Putničke agencije (Travel Agencies). Beograd: Turistička štampa.
Pöschl, A.
1962 Fremdenverkehr und Fremdenverkehrspolitik (Tourism and Tourism Politics). Berlin: Duncker und Humblot.
1971 Fremdenverkehr. Volkswirtschaftslehre (Tourism and Economics).Salzburg: Pustet.
Poser, H.
1939 Geographische Studien über den Fremdenverkehr im Riesengebirge (Geographical Studies of Tourism in the Riesengebirge). Göttingen: Vandenhoek und Ruprecht.
Poulain, J.-P., and M. Teychenné
2001 La Recherche en Tourisme (Research in Tourism). Cachan: LT Éditions.
Prahl, H.-W.
2002 Soziologie der Freizeit (Sociology of Leisure). Paderborn: Schöningh.
Prahl, H-W., and A. Steinecke
1979 Der Millionen-Urlaub. Von der Bildungsreise zur totalen Freizeit (Vacation for the Millions—Millions for Vacations: From Educational Journey to Total Leisure). Darmstadt: Luchterhand.
Prahl, H.-W., and A. Steinecke
1981 Tourismus (Tourism). Stuttgart: Reclam.
Prebežec, D.
1998 Poslovna strategija zrakoplovnih kompanija (The Business Strategy of Airline Companies). Zagreb: Golden Marketing.
Przecławski, K.
1973 Turystyka a wychowanie (Tourism and Education). Warszawa: Nasza Ksiegarnia.
1979 Socjologiczne problemy turystyki (Sociological Problems of Tourism). Warszawa: Instytut Wydawniczy CRZZ.
1986 Humanistyczne podstawy turystyki (Humanistic Foundations of Tourism). Warszawa: Instytut Turystyki.
1993 Tourism as the Subject of Interdisciplinary Research. *In* Tourism Research: Critiques and Challenges, D. Pearce and R. Butler, eds., pp. 9–19. London: Routledge.
1994 Tourism and the Contemporary World. Warszawa: Institute of Social Prevention and Adaptation, Center for Social Problems of Education, University of Warsaw.
1996 Człowiek a turystyka. Zarys socjologii turystyki (Man and Tourism. An Outline of the Sociology of Tourism) (2nd ed., 2004). Kraków: Albis.

1997 Etyczne podstawy turystyki (Ethical Foundations of Tourism). Kraków: Albis.

2005 Zycie to podróz: wprowadzenie do filozofii turstyki (Life is a Journey: Introduction to the Philosophy of Tourism). Warszawa: Wydawnictwo Akademickie Zak.

Przecławski, K. ed.

1984 Turystyka, człowiek i społeczeństwo (Tourism, Man, and Society). Warszawa: Instytut Wydawniczy Zwiazków Zawodowych.

Radišić, F.

1981 Turizam i turistička politika (Tourism and Tourist Policy). Pula: Istarska naklada.

Ragone, G.

1992 Su alcuni Fattori che Limitano od Ostacolano la Crescita della Domanda Turistica (On Factors which Limit or Obstruct the Growth of Tourist Demand). Sociologia Urbana e Rurale (Urban and Rural Sociology) 38:85–90.

1998 Turismo (Tourism). *In* Enciclopedia delle Scienze Sociali (Encyclopaedia of the Social Sciences) vol. VIII, pp. 675–683. Roma: Istituto della Enciclopedia Italiana Treccani.

Ramaker, J.

1951 La Sociologie du Tourisme (The Sociology of Tourism). Zeitschrift für Fremdenverkehr (Journal of Tourism) 6(2):73–76.

Ravkin, R.

1983 Sociokulturni aspekti turizma (Social and Cultural Aspects of Tourism). Pula: Istarska naklada.

Raymond, H.

1960 Recherches sur un Village de Vacances: l'Utopie Concrète (Research on a Holiday Village: Concrete Utopia). Revue Française de Sociologie (French Review of Sociology) vol. 3.

RC 50

2008 Research Committee on International Tourism of the International Sociological Association (www.rc50.info, accessed 30 June 2008).

Rebevšek, L.

1966 Raziskava tržišča in ekonomska propaganda v turizmu (Market Research and Advertising in Tourism). Celje: Zveza naravnih zdravilišč in zdraviliškh krajev Slovenije.

Reeh, T.

2005 Der Wunsch nach Urlaubsreisen in Abhängigkeit von Lebenszufriedenheit und Sensation Seeking (The Demand for Holiday Trips in Relation to Life Satisfaction and Sensation Seeking). Göttingen: Diss (also online).

Rekdal, P.

1972 Generering av Materiell Form: Moderne Skupturproduksjon i Livingstone, Zambia (Generating Material Form: Modern Sculpture Production in

Livingstone, Zambia). Magister Artium dissertation, Department of Ethnography, University of Oslo, Oslo, Norway.

1982 Kommersialisering av Kulturelle Ytringer (Commercialization of Cultural Manifestations). *In* Innpassing av Reiseliv i Lokale Samfunn (Adapting Tourism to Local Communities), S. Svalastog, ed., pp. 92–100. Lillehammer: Oppland University College.

1988 Turismens Gjenstander: Et Eksempel fra Zambia (Tourism Objects: An Example from Zambia). *In* Friheten i det Fjerne (The Freedom Afar Off), J. Jacobsen, ed., pp. 145–155. Aalborg: The Nordic Summer University.

Relac, M., and M. Bartoluci
1987 Turizam i sportska rekreacija (Tourism and Sport Recreation). Zagreb: Informator.

Rešetar, M.
1981 Turističke agencije (Tourist Agencies). Zagreb: Informator.

Richards, G.
1996 Cultural Tourism in Europe. Wallingford, CT: CAB International.

Riesman, D.
1950 The Lonely Crowd: Thorstein Veblen Reconsidered. New Haven, CT: Yale University Press.

Ritter, J.
1974 Subjektivität (Subjectivity). Frankfurt: Suhrkamp.

Robinson, M.
1999 Cultural Conflicts in Tourism: Inevitability and Inequality. *In* Tourism and Cultural Conflicts, M. Robinson and P. Boniface, eds., pp. 1–32. Wallingford, CT: CAB International.

Robinson, M., and A. Phipp
2003 Editorial. Tourism and Cultural Change 1:1–10.

Rodríguez, J. C.
2007. El Plan de Estabilización de 1959 (The Stabilization Plan of 1959) (http://www.juandemariana.org/comentario/1105/).

Rogoziński, K.
1975 Wprowadzenie do teorii badań turystyki (Introduction to the Methodology of Tourism Research/Theory of Tourism Research). Nauka Polska (Polish Studies) 9:10.

Rojek, C.
1997 Indexing, Dragging and the Social Construction of Tourist Sights. *In* Touring Cultures: Transformations of Travel and Theory, C. Rojek and J. Urry, eds., pp. 52–74. London: Routledge.

Romita, T.
1999 Il Turismo che non Appare. Verso un Modello Consapevole di Sviluppo Turistico della Calabria (Tourism which does not Appear. Towards a Model of Tourist Development in Calabria). Soveria Mannelli, Catanzaro: Rubbettino.

2008 Stigturismo. Autorganizzazione ed Interazione Sociale attraverso l'Uso dall'Ambiente (Stigtourism. Self-Organization and Social Interaction through the Use of the Environment). *In* Tracce di Turismo Sostenibile (Traces of Sustainable Tourism), F. Beato, et al, pp. 103–132. Rende: Centro Editoriale e Librario dell'Università della Calabria.

Rozwadowski, W.
2007. Konfraternia Turystyczna (Tourism Confraternity) (http://www.biblioteka.wshgit.waw.pl/konfraternia.html, accessed 23 April 2008).

Ruzza, C.
2008 Governance Multilivello, Sostenibilità ed Europa nelle Politiche per il Turismo (Multi-Level Governance, Sustainability, and Europe in Tourist Policies). *In* Tracce di Turismo Sostenibile (Traces of Sustainable Tourism), F. Beato, et al, pp. 133–158. Rende: Centro Editoriale e Librario dell'Università della Calabria.

Saar, E., Z. Skórzyński, M. Strzeszewski, and M. Zürn
1972 Weekendy mieszkańców Krakowa: z badań socjologicznych nad kultura czasu wolnego: raport (Weekends of Kraków Residents: A Report on Sociological Research into the Culture of Leisure). Warszawa: Instytut Naukowy Kultury Fizycznej.

Said, E.
1978 (1991) Orientalism: Western Conceptions of the Orient. Harmondsworth: Penguin.

Salmon, K.
1991 The Modern Spanish Economy: Transformation and Integration into Europe. London: Pinter.

Sand, H.
2008 The Tradition of Norwegian Sociology Textbooks. Current Sociology 56:253–265.

Sargent, S.
1950 Social Psychology. New York: Ronald Press.

Savelli, A.
1989 Sociologia del Turismo (Sociology of Tourism). Milano: FrancoAngeli.
1997a Dai Recinti alle Reti: Uomo e Tecnologia nelle Relazioni Turistiche (From Enclosures to Networks: Man and Technology in Touristic Relationships). *In* Valori, Territorio, Ambiente (Values, Territory, Environment), P. Guidicini and E. Sgroi, eds. Milano: FrancoAngeli.
2001 La Complessità come Attrazione Turistica: Una Ricerca sulla Riviera Adriatica dell'Emilia-Romagna (Complexity as a Tourist Attraction: A Survey on the Adriatic Riviera of Emilia-Romagna). Sociologia Urbana e Rurale (Urban and Rural Sociology) 66:103–126.
2008a Alla Ricerca di Nuovi Spazi per il Turismo (In Search of New Spaces for Tourism). *In* Spazio Turistico e Società Globale (Tourist Space and Global Society), A. Savelli, ed., pp. 9–23. Milano: FrancoAngeli.

2008b Costa, Retroterra e Spazio Marittimo nelle Strategie degli Imprenditori Turistici (Coast, Inland and Maritime Space in the Strategies of Tourist Entrepreneurs). *In* Spazio Turistico e Società Globale (Tourist Space and Global Society), A. Savelli, ed., pp. 211–232. Milano: FrancoAngeli.

2008c Complessità e Differenziazione, Parole Chiave per un Turismo Dinamico e Sostenibile (Complexity and Differentiation, Key Words for a Dynamic and Sustainable Tourism). *In* Tracce di Turismo Sostenibile (Traces of Sustainable Tourism), F. Beato, et al, pp. 159–174. Rende: Centro Editoriale e Librario dell'Università della Calabria.

2008d Mutamenti di Significato del Turismo e Nuovi Rapporti tra Impresa e Territorio (Meaning Changes in Tourism and New Connections between Territory and Enterprise). Sociologia del Lavoro (Sociology of Work) 11:151–166.

Savelli, A. ed.

1997b Turismo e Ambiente. Atti del Terzo Convegno Mediterraneo di Sociologia del Turismo (Tourism and the Environment. Proceedings of the Third Mediterranean Conference on the Sociology of Tourism). Sociologia Urbana e Rurale (Urban and Rural Sociology) vol. 52/53, special issue.

2004a Città Turismo e Comunicazione Globale (City, Tourism and Global Communication). Milano: FrancoAngeli.

2004b Turismo, Territorio, Identità. Ricerche ed Esperienze nell'Area Mediterranea (Tourism, Territory, Identity. Research and Experiences in the Mediterranean Area). Milano: FrancoAngeli.

2008e Spazio Turistico e Società Globale (Tourist Space and Global Society). Milano: FrancoAngeli.

Savoja, L.

2005 La Costruzione Sociale del Turismo (The Social Construction of Tourism). Torino: Giappichelli.

Scheuch, E.

1969 Soziologie der Freizeit (Sociology of Leisure). *In* Handbuch der empirischen Sozialforschung (Handbook of Empirical Social Research), R. König, ed., vol. 11, pp. 1–192. Stuttgart: Enke.

1972 Ferien und Tourismus als neue Formen der Freizeit (Holiday and Tourism as New Forms of Leisure). *In* Soziologie der Freizeit (Sociology of Leisure), E. Scheuch and R. Meyersohn, eds., pp. 304–317. Cologne: Kiepenheuer und Witsch.

1977 Soziologie der Freizeit (Sociology of Leisure). *In* Handbuch der empirischen Sozialforschung, vol. 11, Freizeit—Konsum (Handbook of Empirical Social Research: Leisure—Consumption), R. König, ed., pp. 1–192. Stuttgart: Ferdinand Enke Verlag.

1981 Tourismus (Tourism). *In* Die Psychologie des 20. Jahrhunderts (20th Century Psychology), H. Balmer, ed., vol. 13, pp. 1089–1114. Zürich: Kindler.

Scheuch, E. and R. Meyersohn, eds.

1972 Soziologie der Freizeit (Sociology of Leisure). Köln: Kiepenheuer und Witsch.

Schimany, P.
1999 Tourismussoziologie zwischen Begrenzung und Entgrenzung (Tourism Sociology between Limitation and Limitlessness). *In* Grenzenlose Gesellschaft—grenzenloser Tourismus? (Boundless Society—Boundless Tourism?), R. Bachleitner and P. Schimany, eds., pp. 7–24. München: Profil.

Schivelbusch, W.
1977 Geschichte der Eisenbahnreise: zur Industrialisierung von Raum und Zeit im 19. Jahrhundert (History of Rail Travel: On the Industrialization of Space and Time in the 19th Century). Munich: Hanser (English ed. 1986).
1980 Das Paradies, der Geschmack und die Vernunft: Eine Geschichte der Genußmittel (Paradise, Taste and Reason: A History of Stimulants). Munich: Hanser.

Schmidhauser, H.
1975 Travel Propensity and Travel Frequency. *In* The Management of Tourism: A Selection of Readings, A. Burkart and S. Medlik, eds., pp. 53–60. London: Heinemann.

Schmidt, L.-H.
1984 Rejsen som Konsumtionsform (The Journey as a Form of Consumption). *In* Turisme og Reiseliv (Tourism and Travel), L.-H. Schmidt and J. Jacobsen, eds., pp. 68–77. Aalborg: The Nordic Summer University.

Schmidt, L.-H. and J. Jacobsen, eds.
1984 Turisme og Reiseliv (Tourism and Travel). Aalborg: The Nordic Summer University.

Schmitt, C.
1932 (1993) Land und Meer. Eine weltgeschichtliche Betrachtung (Land and Sea: A World Historical Consideration). Stuttgart: Klett-Cotta.

Schmitz-Scherzer, R. ed.
1973 Freizeit (Leisure). Frankfurt: Akademische Verlagsgesellschaft.
1975 Reisen und Tourismus (Travel and Tourism). Darmstadt: Steinkopff.

Schrand, A.
1998 Transdisziplinäre Tourismuswissenschaft (Transdisciplinary Tourism Science). *In* Der durchschaute Tourist. Arbeiten zur Tourismusforschung (The X-Rayed Tourist: Studies in Tourism Research), R. Bachleitner, et al, pp. 74–82. München: Profil.
2007 Der Studienkreis für Tourismus in Starnberg: Die Institutionalisierung der sozialwissenschaftlichen Tourismusforschung in Deutschland (The Study Circle for Tourism in Starnberg: The Institutionalization of Tourism Social Science Research in Germany). *In* Tourismusforschung in Bayern. Aktuelle sozialwissenschaftlichen Beiträge (Tourism Research in Bavaria: Current Contributions of the Social Sciences), A. Günther, et al, pp. 29–38. München: Profil.

Schullern zu Schrattenhofen, H.v.
1911 Fremdenverkehr und Volkswirtschaft (Tourism and the National Economy). Jahrbücher für Nationalökonomie und Statistik (Yearbooks of the National Economy and Statistics) 3.F 42:433–491.

Schumacher, B.
2002 Ferien. Interpretationen und Popularisierung eines Bedürfnisses. Schweiz 1890-1950 (Vacations. Interpretations and Popularization of a Need: The Case of Switzerland). Wien: Böhlau.

Schumacher, B., D. Gloor, and G. Fierz
1993 Freizeit, Mobilität, Tourismus aus soziologischer Sicht (Leisure, Mobility and Tourism from a Sociological Point of View). Bern: Schweizerischer Wissenschaftsrat.

Schutz, A.
1964 Collected Papers. Studies in Social Theory. vol. II. The Hague: Martinus Nijhoff.

Seitz, E., and W. Meyer
2005 Tourismusmarktforschung (Research on Tourism Marketing) (2nd ed). München: Vahlen.

Selänniemi, T.
1994a A Charter Trip to Sacred Places—Individual Mass-Tourism. *In* Le Tourisme International entre Tradition et Modernité. Actes du Colloque International de Nice (International Tourism between Tradition and Modernity. Proceedings of the International Symposium of Nice), J.-P. Jardel, ed., pp. 335–340. Nice: Laboratoire d'Ethnologie, Université de Nice.

1994b Touristic Reflections on a Marine Venus: An Anthropological Interpretation of Finnish Tourism to Rhodes. Ethnologica Fennica (Finnish Ethnology) 22:35–42.

1997 The Mind in the Museum, the Body on the Beach—Place and Authenticity in Mass Tourism. *In* Tourism and Heritage Management, W. Nuryanti, ed., pp. 293–303. Yogyakarta: Gadjah Mada University Press.

1999 Sakrale Steder og Profane Turister (Sacred Places and Profane Tourists). *In* Turisme: Stedet i en Bevegelig Verden (Tourism: Place in a Moving World), J. Jacobsen and A. Viken, eds., pp. 88–95. Oslo: Scandinavian University Press.

2001 Pale Skin on Playa del Anywhere: Finnish Tourists in the Liminoid South. *In* Hosts and Guests Revisited: Tourism Issues of the 21st Century, V. Smith and M. Brent, eds., pp. 80–92. New York: Cognizant.

2002 Couples on Holiday: (En)gendered or Endangered Experiences? *In* Gender/Tourism/Fun?, M. Swain and J. Momsen, eds., pp. 15–23. New York: Cognizant.

Selstad, L.
2007 The Social Anthropology of the Tourist Experience: Exploring the "Middle Role". Scandinavian Journal of Hospitality and Tourism 7:19–33.
Selwyn, T.
1996 Introduction. *In* The Tourist Image: Myths and Myth Making in Tourism, T. Selwyn, ed., pp. 1–32. Chichester: Wiley.
Senečić, J.
1988 Promocija u turizmu (Promotion in Tourism). Zagreb: Mikrorad and Ekonomski fakultet.
1997 Istraživanje turističkog tržišta (Research on the Tourism Market). Zagreb: Mikrorad and Ekonomski fakultet.
Senečić, J., and A. Kobašić
1989 Marketing u turizmu (Marketing in Tourism). Zagreb: Školska knjiga.
Senečić, J., and B. Vukonić
1993 Marketing u turizmu (Marketing in Tourism). Zagreb: Školska knjiga.
1997 Marketing u turizmu (Marketing in Tourism). Zagreb: Mikrorad and Ekonomski fakultet.
Sessa, A.
1974–1992 Elementi di Sociologia e Psicologia del Turismo (Elements of the Sociology and Psychology of Tourism) (7th ed). Roma: Collana Libri Istruzione Tecnica Turistica.
1979 Turismo e Società (Tourism and Society). Roma: Agnesotti.
Seyfarth, R.
2007 Sehen und Nicht-Sehen am Beispiel des Tourismus (Seeing and Non-Seeing, Exemplified in Tourism). Leipzig: Magisterarbeit.
Sgroi, E.
1988 Culture del Territorio e Modelli di Imprenditorialità Turistica: Due Casi a Confronto (Local Cultures and Patterns of Tourist Entrepreneurship: Two Cases in Comparison). Sociologia Urbana e Rurale (Urban and Rural Sociology) 26:121–141.
2001 Sicilia è Turismo. Dallo Slogan Facile al Progetto (Meno Facile) (Sicily is Tourism. From the Easy Slogan to the (not so Easy) Project). Nuove Effemeridi (New Ephemera) 55:4–10.
Sharpley, R.
1994 Tourism, Tourists and Society. Huntingdon: Elm Publications.
Sheldon, P.
1991 An Authorship Analysis of Tourism Research. Annals of Tourism Research 18:473–484.
Shields, R.
1998 Raumkonstruktion und Tourismus (Spatialization and Tourism). Voyage 2:53–71.

Simmel, G.
1908 Exkurs über den Fremden (Excursus on the Stranger). *In* Soziologie (Sociology), Gesamtausgabe (complete ed.), O. Rammstedt, ed., vol. 11, pp. 764–771. Frankfurt: Suhrkamp.
1923 Exkurs über den Fremden (Excursus on the Stranger). *In* Soziologie (Sociology) (3rd ed.) pp. 509–512. Berlin: Duncker und Humblot (English ed. 1950).
1968[1908] Soziologie: Untersuchungen über die Formen der Vergesellschaftung (Sociology: Investigations of Social Forms). Berlin: Duncker und Humblot.
1969 Socjologia (Sociology). Warszawa: Polskie Wydawnictwo Naukowe.
1992 Alpenreisen (Alpine Travel). *In* Gesamtausgabe (Complete Edition, vol. 5) pp. 91–95. Frankfurt: Suhrkamp.
Simonicca, A.
1997 Antropologia del Turismo. Strategie di Ricerca e Contesti Etnografici (Anthropology of Tourism. Research Strategies and Ethnographic Contexts). Roma: La Nuova Italia Scientifica.
Singh, T. ed.
2004 New Horizons in Tourism: Strange Experiences and Stranger Practices. Wallingford, CT: CAB International.
Skórzyński, Z. and A. Ziemilski, eds.
1971 Wzory społeczne wakacji w Polsce (Social Patterns of Vacation in Poland). Warszawa: Ossolineum.
Sloterdijk, P.
2006 Tractatus Philosophico-Touristicus (Philosophical Touristic Treatise). Berlin (unpublished: online).
Smith, S.
1988 Defining Tourism: A Supply-Side View. Annals of Tourism Research 15:179–190.
Smith, V.
1977a Introduction. *In* Hosts and Guests: The Anthropology of Tourism, V. Smith, ed., pp. 1–14. Philadelphia, PA: University of Pennsylvania Press.
1979 Women: The Taste-Makers in Tourism. Annals of Tourism Research 6: 49–60.
Smith, V. ed.
1977b Hosts and Guests: The Anthropology of Tourism. Philadelphia, PA: University of Pennsylvania Press.
Smits, A., and U. Claeys
2008 Sociaal Toerisme (Social Tourism). Master in Toerisme. Paper Academiejaar 2007–2008. Leuven: Katholieke Universiteit.
Solheim, T.
1982 70-åras Feriereiser (Holiday Travel in the 70s). Oslo: Central Bureau of Statistics of Norway.

Sontag, S.
1977 On Photography. New York: Farrar, Straus and Giroux.
Sørensen, A.
2003 Backpacker Ethnography. Annals of Tourism Research 30:847–867.
Spasić, V.
2005 Poslovanje turističkih agencija i organizatora putovanja (Business Activities of Tourist Agencies and Travel Organizers). Beograd: Rading.
Spode, H.
1982 Arbeiterurlaub im dritten Reich (Working Class Holidays in the Third Reich). *In* Angst, Belohnung, Zucht und Ordnung. Herrschafts-mechanismen im Nationalsozialismus (Fear, Reward, Discipline and Order. Mechanisms of Power in National Socialism), T. Mason, C. Sachse, T. Siegel, H. Spode, and W. Spohn, eds., pp. 275–329. Opladen: Westdeutscher Verlag.
1987 Zur Geschichte des Tourismus (A History of Tourism). Starnberg: StfT.
1995 Reif für die Insel. Prolegomena zu einer historischen Anthropologie des Tourismus (Ready for the Island: Prolegomena for an Historical Anthropology of Tourism). *In* Arbeit, Freizeit, Reisen. Die feinen Unterschiede im Alltag (Work, Leisure, Travel: Social Distinctions in Everyday Life), C. Cantauw, ed., pp. 105–123. Münster: Waxmann.
1997 Editorial: Wohin die Reise geht (Where Travel Goes). Voyage 17–12. (also online).
1998a Geschichte der Tourismuswissenschaft (History of Tourism Science). *In* Tourismus Management (Tourism Management), G. Haedrich, et al, pp. 911–924. Berlin: de Gruyter.
1998b Wie vor 50 Jahren keine theoriegeleitete Tourismuswissenschaft entstand (How 50 Years Ago no Theory-Guided Tourism Science was Born). *In* Der durchschaute Tourist. Arbeiten zur Tourismusforschung (The X-Rayed Tourist: Studies in Tourism Research), R. Bachleitner, H. Kagelmann, and A. Keul, eds., pp. 11–19. München: Profil.
1998c Grau, teurer Freund… Was ist und wozu dient Theorie? (What is Theory, and What is it Good for?). *In* Auf dem Weg zu einer Theorie des Tourismus (Toward a Theory of Tourism), H. Burmeister, ed., pp. 21–40. Loccum: s.n.
1999 Was ist Mentalitätsgeschichte? (What is a History of Mentalities?). *In* Kultu-runterschiede (Cultural Differences), H. Hahn, ed., pp. 9–62. Frankfurt: IKO.
2001 Wie der Mensch zur Freizeit kam. Eine Geschichte des Freizeitverhaltens (How we got Leisure Time: An Historical Outline). Kultur und Technik (Culture and Technology) 25(3):30–37.
2003a Tourismusgeschichte als Forschungsgegenstand (Tourism History as an Object of Research). *In* Tourismus und Entwicklung in Alpenraum/Turismo e Sviluppo in Area Alpina (Tourism and Development in the Alpine Region), H. Heiss and A. Leonardi, eds., pp. 83–100. Innsbruck: Studienverlag.

2003b. Wie die Deutschen "Reiseweltmeister" wurden. Eine Einführung in die Tourismusgeschichte (How the Germans Became Number One in World Travel. An Introduction to Tourism History). Erfurt: Landeszentrale für politische Bildung Thüringen (new ed. 2009).

2005 Der Blick des Post-Touristen. Torheiten und Trugschlüsse in der Tourismusforschung (The Post-Tourist's Gaze: Follies and Fallacies in Tourism Research). Voyage 7:135–161.

2007a Die Bedeutung des Fremdenverkehrs für Bayern. Eine wissenschaftshistorische Grille (The Impact of Tourism for Bavaria: A Footnote to the History of Science). *In* Tourismusforschung in Bayern. Aktuelle sozialwissenschaftlichen Beiträge (Tourism Research in Bavaria: Current Contributions of the Social Sciences), A. Günther, et al, pp. 23–26. München: Profil.

2007b Reisen und Tourismus. Stichpunkte zur Terminologie in Forschung und Statistik (Travel and Tourism Feeds on the Terminology of Research and Statistics). Cestováni Vcera a Dnes (Tourism Yesterday and Today) 4(2):35–41.

2009 Wie die Deutschen Reiseweltmeister wurden. Eine Einführung in die Tourismusgeschichte (How the Germans Became Number One in World Travel: An Introduction to Tourism History). Wiesbaden: VS-Verlag.

Spode, H. ed.
1991 Brüder zur Sonne, zur Freiheit! Beiträge zur Tourismusgeschichte (Brothers, Towards Sun, Towards Freedom! Contributions to Tourism History). Berlin: Verlag für Universitäre Kommunikation.

1996 Goldstrand und Teutonengrill. Kultur- und Sozialgeschichte des Tourismus in Deutschland. 1945–1989 (Golden Beach and Teuton's BBQ: Cultural and Social History of Tourism in Germany). Berlin: Verlag für Universitäre Kommunikation.

Stallybrass, P., and A. White
1986 The Politics and Poetics of Transgression. London: Methuen.

Stavrinoudis, T.
2005 To Time Sharing και οι δυνατότητες αποτελεσματικότερης επιχειρησιακής εφαρμογής του στην Ελλάδα/. (Time Sharing and the Possibilities of its More Effective Operational Application in Greece). Unpublished doctoral dissertation, Department of Business Administration, University of the Aegean, Chios, Greece.

Stavrou, S.
1979–1986 Έρευνα Κοινωνικής Αναγνωρισιμότητας του Τουρισμού στα Νησιά Μύκονο, Νάξο, Κάλυμνο, Λέρο, Πάρο, Σαντορίνη και Κύθηρα (A Study of the Social Recognition of Tourism in the Islands of Mykonos, Naxos, Kalymnos, Leros, Paros Santorini and Kythira). Athens: Research and Development Department, Greek Tourism Organization.

Steinecke, A.
2006 Tourismus. Eine geographische Einführung (Tourism: A Geographical Introduction) (2nd ed). Braunschweig: Westermann.

Stendhal (Beyle, M.-H.)

1838 Letter to Le Temps, 9 August (signed E.B.).

1973 Florence et Rome. Chroniques Italiennes. Prefaces et Notes de D. Fernandez. (Florence and Rome. Italian Chronicles. Introductions and Notes by D. Fernandez). Paris: Gallimard.

1992 (1837–1838) Mémoires d'un Touriste (Memories of a Tourist). *In* Voyages en France (Travels in France). Paris: Gallimard (Bibliothèque de la Pléiade).

Sternberger, D.

1938 Panorama oder Ansichten vom 19. Jahrhundert (Panorama, or Views of the 19th Century). Hamburg: Govert.

Sternheim, A.

1939 Het Probleem van den Vrijentijd in den Totalitaire Staat (The Problem of Free Time in the Totalitarian State). Mensch en Maatschappij (Man and Society) 15(1):25–39.

Stichting Recreatie

1983 De Stichting Recreatie Midden in de Toekomst, 1958-2008 (The Recreation Foundation in the Middle of the Future, 1958-2008). Den Haag: Stichting Recreatie.

Storbeck, D. ed.

1988a Moderner Tourismus. Tendenzen und Aussichten (Modern Tourism: Tendencies and Perspectives). Trier: Geographische Gesellschaft.

Storbeck, D.

1988b *In* Moderner Tourismus. Tendenzen und Aussichten (Modern Tourism: Tendencies and Perspectives), D. Storbeck, ed., pp. 239–256. Trier: Geographische Gesellschaft.

Stott, M.

1973 Economic Transition and the Family in Mykonos. Greek Review of Social Research 17:122–133.

1979 Tourism in Mykonos: Some Social and Cultural Responses. Mediterranean Studies 1(2):72–90.

1985 Property, Labor and Household Economy: The Transition to Tourism in Mykonos, Greece. Journal of Modern Greek Studies 3(2):187–206.

Stradner, J.

1890 Die Förderung des Fremdenverkehrs (The Promotion of Tourism). *In* Kulturbilder aus Steiermark (Cultural Impressions from Styria), G. Wilhelm, et al, pp. 257–279. Graz: Leykam.

1905 (1917) Der Fremdenverkehr. Eine volkswirtschaftliche Studie (Tourism: A Politico-Economic Study) (2nd ed.) Graz: Leykam.

Stroppa, C.

1976 Sviluppo del Territorio e Consumo Turistico (Development of the Territory and Tourist Consumption). *In* Sviluppo del Territorio e Ruolo del Turismo (Territorial Development and the Role of Tourism), C. Stroppa, ed., pp. 21–38. Bologna: Clue.

Studienkreis für Tourismus, ed.

1969 Motive—Meinungen—Verhaltensweisen. Einige Ergebnisse der soziologischen Tourismusforschung (Motives, Opinions, Behavioral Patterns: Some Results of Sociological Tourism Research). Starnberg: Stft.

Suprewicz, J.

2005 Socjologia turystyki (The Sociology of Tourism). Lublin: Katolicki Uniwersytet Lubelski.

Sušić, S.

1985 Turističko pravo (Tourist Law). Dubrovnik: Štampa.

Swain, M.

1995 Gender in Tourism. Annals of Tourism Research 22:247–266.

Swain, M., M. Brent, and V. Long

1998 Annals and Tourism Evolving: Indexing 25 Years of Publication. Annals of Tourism Research 25(Special supplement):991–1014.

Swedner, H.

1971 Om Finkultur och Minoriteter (About Highbrow Culture and Minorities). Stockholm: Almqvist and Wiksell.

Szacki, J.

1981 Historia myśli socjologicznej (History of Sociological Thought). Warszawa: PWN.

Szczepański, J.

1972 Basic Notions in Sociology. Warszawa: PWN.

1980 Sprawy ludzkie (Human Issues). Warszawa: Czytelnik.

Sztompka, P.

1993 The Sociology of Social Change. Oxford: Blackwell.

2002 Socjologia: analiza społeczeństwa (Sociology: Analysis of Society). Kraków: Znak.

2005 Socjologia zmian społecznych (The Sociology of Social Change). Kraków: Wydawnictwo Znak.

Šimić, A.

1991 Turističke agencije—uloga u razvoju turizma (Tourist Agencies—Their Role in Tourism Development). Binghampton: Europatravel.

1994 Turističko poslovanje (Doing Business in Tourism). Zagreb: Informator.

Šmit, V.

1977 Putničke agencije i njeni ugovori s putnicima i davaocima usluga (Travel Agencies and their Contracts with Passengers and Service Providers). Beograd: Savremena administracija.

Štetić, S.

2003 Geografija turizma (The Geography of Tourism). Beograd: LI.

2004 Nacionalna turistička geografija (National Tourist Geography). Beograd: LI.

Tamames, R.

1968 Introducción a la Economía Española (Introduction to the Spanish Economy) (2nd ed). Madrid: Alianza Editorial.

Taxacher, G. ed.
1998 Fernweh, Seelenheil, Erlebnislust (Wanderlust, Salvation and Sensation Seeking). Bensberg and Bergisch-Gladbach: s.n.

Teilhard de Chardin, P.
1985 Zarys wszechświata personalistycznego (Outline of a Personalistic Universe). Warszawa: PAX.

Temprano, A.
1981 Cambios Demográficos y Crecimiento Económico en la España Desarrollista (Demographic Change and Economic Growth in a Developing Spain). *In* Crecimiento Económico y Crisis Estructural en España (1959-1980) (Economic Growth and Structural Crisis in Spain (1959–1980)), R. Carballo, A. Temprano, and J. Moral Santín, eds., pp. 293–304. Madrid: Akal.

Tetsch, E. ed.
1978 Tourismus und Kulturwandel (Tourism and Cultural Change). Stuttgart: s.n.

Thanopoulou, M.
2003 Ισότητα αμοιβών ανδρών και γυναικών στον τουριστικό τομέα: Εμπειρική διερεύνηση της υπάρχουσας κατάστασης και επισήμανση προοπτικών (Wage Equality between Men and Women in the Tourism Sector: Empirical Research of the Existing Situation and Perspectives). Athens: KETHI.

Thanopoulou, M., and P. Tsartas
1991 Tourism and Environment in Greece: What Sociology? Problems of Tourism 14(1/2):23–29.

Theodoropoulou, H.
2005 The Influence of Agrotourism on the Human and Social Environment: The Cases of Trikala and Ikaria in Greece. *In* (Pre) Proceedings of the 6th European IFSA Symposium of the International Farming Systems Association "European Farming and Society in Search of a New Social Contract—Learning to Manage Change", pp. 127–139, Vila Real, Portugal.

Theuns, J.
1984 Toerisme als Multidisciplinair Veld van Studie (Tourism as a Multi-disciplinary Field of Study). Vrijetijd en Samenleving (Leisure and Society) 2(1):65–93.

Thiem, M.
1994 Tourismus und kulturelle Identität (Tourism and Cultural Identity). Bern: FIF.

Thiesse, A. 1996 Organizzazione dei Passatempi dei Lavoratori e Tempi Rubati (1880–1930) (Organization of the Free-Time of Workers and Stolen Time). *In* L'Invenzione del Tempo Libero (The Invention of Free Time), A. Corbin, ed., pp. 327–347. Roma-Bari: Laterza; Roma-Bari: Aubier.

Thomas, W., and F. Znaniecki
1926 The Polish Peasant in Europe and America. New York: University of Illinois Press.

Thomson, D.
1960 The Transformation of Social Life. *In* The New Cambridge Social History, D. Thomson, ed., pp. 42–72. Cambridge: Cambridge University Press.

Thrane, C.
2007 Hospitality Employees' Unemployment Risk: Panel Evidence from Norway. Scandinavian Journal of Hospitality and Tourism 7:347–363.

Thue, F.
1997 Empirisme og Demokrati: Norsk Samfunnsforskning som Etterkrigsprosjekt (Empiricism and Democracy: Norwegian Social Research as a Postwar Project). Oslo: Scandinavian University Press.

Thurot, J.
1981 Tourisme et Communication Publicitaire (Tourism and the Communication of Advertising). Doctoral thesis of 3rd Cycle, Center for Higher Tourism Studies, Université de Droit, d'Économie et des Sciences, Aix-en-Provence.

Tidore, C., and M. Solinas
2002 L'Anglona: Il Passato come Prospettiva Turistica (Anglona: The Past as a Chance for Tourism). *In* Modelli di Turismo in Sardegna. Tra Sviluppo Locale e Processi di Globalizzazione (Tourism Patterns in Sardinia. Between Local Development and Globalization Processes), A. Mazzette, ed., pp. 180–223. Milano: FrancoAngeli.

Timm, A.
1968 Verlust der Muße. Zur Geschichte der Freizeitgesellschaft (The Loss of "Otium": On the History of the Leisure Society). Hamburg-Buchholz: Knauel.

Todorović, A.
1982 Sociologija turizma (The Sociology of Tourism). Beograd: Prevredna štampa.
1984 Sociologija slobodnog vremena (The Sociology of Leisure Time). Beograd: Interpregled.
1990 Teorije turizma i kulturno-umetničke vrednosti (Theories of Tourism, Cultural and Social Values). Beograd: Turistička štampa.

Tokarski, W., and R. Schmitz-Scherzer
1985 Freizeit (Leisure Time). Stuttgart: Teubner.

Tomlinson, A. ed.
1981 Leisure and Social Control. Eastbourne: Brighton Polytechnic.
1986 Leisure and Social Relations: Some Theoretical and Methodological Issues. London: Leisure Studies Association.

Toschi, U.
1947 Appunti per la Geografia del Turismo (Notes for the Geography of Tourism). Annali della Facoltà di Economia e Commercio (Annals of the Faculty of Economics and Business) vol. IV. Firenze.
1952 La Determinazione delle Aree Turistiche (The Determination of Tourist Areas). *In* Atti del Convegno sugli Aspetti Territoriali dei Problemi Economici

(Proceedings of the Conference on Social Aspects of Economic Problems), Bologna.

1957 Aspetti Geografici dell'Economia Turistica (Geographic Aspects of the Tourist Economy). *In* Atti del XVIIIth Congresso Geografico Italiano (Proceedings of the XVIII Italian Geographic Congress), Bari.

Touraine, A.

1998 Social Knowlege and the Multiplicity of Languages and Cultures. Report of the Bureau of International Sociology to the XIVth World Congress of Sociology of the International Sociological Association, Montréal.

Trademark Italia

1985 Il Sistema Turistico (ovvero l'Ospitalità Commercializzata) (The Tourist System (that is Commoditized Hospitality)). Rimini: Trademark.

Tresse, P.

1990 L'Image des Civilisations Africaines à travers les Publications des Services Officiels du Tourisme des Pays d'Afrique Francophone (The Image of African Civilizations through the Publications of the Tourism Authorities of French Speaking Africa). Cahiers du Tourisme (Tourism Papers), série C, no. 110.

Tribe, J.

1997 The Indiscipline of Tourism. Annals of Tourism Research 24(3):638–657.

2000 Indisciplined and Unsubstantiated. Annals of Tourism Research 27:809–813.

2003 The RAE-ification of Tourism Research in the UK. International Journal of Tourism Research 5:225–234.

2005 New Tourism Research. Tourism Recreation Research (Special Issue on Tourism and Research) 30(2):5–8.

Tsartas, P.

1989 Κοινωνικές και οικονομικές επιπτώσεις της τουριστικής ανάπτυξης στον Νομό Κυκλάδων – και ιδιαίτερα στα νησιά Ίος και Σέριφος στην περίοδο 1950-1980 (Social and Economic Consequences of Tourism Development in the Prefecture of the Cyclades and Especially the Islands of Ios, Serifos During the Period 1950-1980). Published doctoral dissertation, National Social Science Research Center, Athens, Greece.

1991 Έρευνα για τα κοινωνικά χαρακτηριστικά της Απασχόλησης, Μελέτη III, Τουρισμός και Αγροτική Πολυδραστηριότητα (Research on the Social Characteristics of Employment, Study III, Tourism and Agricultural Pluriactivity). Athens: EKKE (NCSR).

1995 Κοινωνιολογικές προσεγγίσεις στα χαρακτηριστικά και τις αναζητήσεις των σύγχρονων τουριστών (Sociological Approaches to the Characteristics and the Motives of Contemporary Tourists). Σύγχρονα Θέματα (Current Issues) 55:40–47.

1996 Τουρίστες, Ταξίδια, Τόποι: Κοινωνιολογικές Προσεγγίσεις στον Τουρ ισμό (Tourists, Travel, Places: Sociological Approaches to Tourism). Athens: Exadas.

1997 Θεωρία της κοινωνιολογίας τους τουρισμού: Προσεγγίσεις και προβλήματα (Theory of the Sociology of Tourism: Approaches and Problems). *In* Η Κοινωνιολογία στην Ελλάδα Σήμερα (Sociology in Greece Today), H. Lambiri-Dimaki, ed., pp. 467–476. Athens: Papazisi.

1998 La Grèce: Du Tourisme de Masse au Tourisme Alternatif (Greece: From Mass Tourism to Alternative Tourism), Série: Tourisme et Sociétés (Tourism and Societies). Paris: Éditions L' Harmattan.

2003 Tourism Development in Greek Insular and Coastal Areas: Socio-Cultural Changes and Crucial Policy Issues. Journal of Sustainable Tourism 2/3:116–133.

Tsartas, P., and M. Thanopoulou

1993 Αποτίμηση της λειτουργίας των γυναικείων αγροτουριστικών συνεταιρισμών (A Valuation of the Operation of Women's Agro-tourist Cooperatives). Athens: ΚΕΓΜΕ: Πρόγραμμα NOW (KEGME: Now Program).

1995 Μία πρόταση για το ρόλο που διαδραματίζει ο τουρισμός στην κοινωνικοποίηση της νεολαίας: Η περίπτωση της Ίου και της Σερίφου (A Proposal Concerning the Role of Tourism in the Socialization of the Greek Youth: The Case of Ios and Serifos Islands). Επιθεώρηση Κοινωνικών Ερευνών (Review of Social Research) 86:114–128.

Tsartas, P., E. Manologlou, and A. Markou

2001 Domestic Tourism in Greece and Special Interest Destinations: The Role of Alternative Forms of Tourism. Anatolia: The International Journal of Tourism and Hospitality Research 12(1):35–45.

Tsartas, P., K. Theodoropoulos, R. Kalokardou-Krantonelli, and E. Manologlou

1995 Οι Κοινωνικές επιπτώσεις του Τουρισμού στους Νομούς Κέρκυρας και Λασιθίου (The Social Impacts of Tourism in the Prefectures of Corfu and Lasithi). Athens: EKKE (NCSR).

Turistički proizvod (The Tourist Product)

1974 International Symposium, Fakultet za vanjsku trgovinu, Zagreb.

Turizam zbližava narode (Tourism Brings People Closer)

1975 Conference. Kršćanska sadašnjost, Zagreb.

Turkulin, B., and T. Hitrec

1998 Tourism Research Bibliographic Database. Zagreb: Instutut za Turizam.

Turner, L., and J. Ash

1975 Golden Hordes: International Tourism and the Pleasure Periphery. London: Constable.

Turner, V.

1969 The Ritual Process: Structure and Anti-Structure. London: Routledge and Kegan Paul.

1974 Dramas, Fields and Metaphors: Symbolic Action in Human Society. Ithaca, NY: Cornell University Press.

Turner, V., and E. Turner

1978 Image and Pilgrimage in Christian Culture. Oxford: Blackwell.

Tuulentie, S.
2006 The Dialectic of Identities in the Field of Tourism: The Discourses of the Indigenous Sámi in Defining their Own and the Tourists' Identities. Scandinavian Journal of Hospitality and Tourism 6:25–36.
2007 Settled Tourists: Second Homes as a Part of Tourist Life Stories. Scandinavian Journal of Hospitality and Tourism 7:281–300.
Tuulentie, S., and I. Mettiäinen
2007 Local Participation in the Evolution of Ski Resorts: The Case of Ylläs and Levi in Finnish Lapland. Forest, Snow and Landscape Research 81(1/2):207–222.
Ujma, D.
2002 Channel Relationships between Tour Operators and Travel Agents in Britain and Poland. Unpublished PhD thesis, University of Luton, UK.
Unković, S.
1968 Teorijska razmatranja kategorije potrošača u turizmu (Theoretical Debates on Categories of Consumers in Tourism). Turizam (Tourism) 12:14.
1974 Ekonomika turizma (Economics of Tourism). Beograd: ICIS.
Unković, S., and M. Tourki
1973 Istraživanje turističkog tržišta i turistička propaganda (Research of Tourist Markets and Advertising in Tourism). Beograd: Viša ekonomska škola.
Unković, S., and B. Zečević
1977 Uvod savjetovanju "Humanističke vrijednosti turizma" (Introduction to the Conference "Humanistic Values of Tourism"), Zadar.
2004–2005 Ekonomika turizma (Economics of Tourism). Beograd: Ekonomski fakultet. Uvod Savjetovanju.
Urbain, J.-D.
1993 L'Idiot du Voyage. Histoires de Touristes (The Inexperienced Traveler: Tourist Tales). Paris: Éditions Payot et Rivages.
1997 Auf der Suche nach dem Homo Viator (In Search of Homo Viator). Voyage 1:18–32.
Urry, J.
1990 The Tourist Gaze: Leisure and Travel in Contemporary Societies. London: Sage.
1991 Tourism, Travel and the Modern Subject. Vrijetijd en Samenleving (Leisure and Society) 9(3/4):87–98.
2007 Mobilities. Cambridge: Polity.
van den Abbele, G.
1980 Sightseers: The Tourist as Theorist. Diacritics 10:2–14.
van den Berghe, P.
1994 The Quest for the Other: Ethnic Tourism in San Cristóbal, Mexico. Seattle, WA: University of Washington Press.
van der Duim, R.
2005 Tourismscapes. An Actor-Network Perspective on Sustainable Tourism Development. PhD dissertation, University of Wageningen, The Netherlands.

Vanhove, N.
1973 Het Belgische Kusttoerisme—Vandaag en Morgen (Belgian Coastal Tourism—Today and Tomorrow). West-Vlaams Economisch Studiebureau, nr 3715. Brugge: WES.
2005 The Economics of Tourism Destinations. Oxford: Elsevier/Butterworth Heinemann.

Veblen, T.
1899 (1970) Théorie de la Classe de Loisir (Theory of the Leisure Class), avec une préface de Raymond Aron (with an introduction by Raymond Aron). Paris: Gallimard.
1899 (1994) The Theory of the Leisure Class: An Economic Study of Institutions. New York: Macmillan.

Veijola, S.
1988 What did Jane do to Tarzan: Hustruskap och Resande (What did Jane do to Tarzan: Wifehood and Travel). *In* Friheten i det Fjerne (The Freedom Afar Off), J. Jacobsen, ed., pp. 57–64. Aalborg: The Nordic Summer University.

Veijola, S., and E. Jokinen
1994 The Body in Tourism. Theory, Culture and Society 11:125–151.
2008 Towards a Hostessing Society? Mobile Arrangements of Gender and Labour. NORA—Nordic Journal of Feminist and Gender Research 16(3):166–181.

Velarde, F.J.
2001 Evolución de la Economía Española en el Siglo XX (Evolution of the Spanish Economy in the 20th Century). Estudios Económicos de Desarrollo Internacional (Economic Studies of International Development) 1:1–12.

Vester, H.
1988 Zeitalter der Freizeit. Eine soziologische Bestandsaufnahme (The Age of Leisure: A Sociological Inventory). Darmstadt: Wissenschaftliche Buchgesellschaft.
1997 Tourismus im Licht soziologischer Theorie. Ansätze bei Erving Goffman, Pierre Bourdieu und der World-System-Theory (Tourism in the Light of Sociological Theory. Approaches of Erving Goffmann, Pierre Bourdieu and World System Theory). Voyage 1:67–85.
1998a Soziologische Theorien und Tourismus—eine Tour d' Horizon (Sociological Theories and Tourism—A Tour of the Horizon). *In* Der durchschaute Tourist. Arbeiten zur Tourismusforschung (The X-Rayed Tourist: Studies in Tourism Research), R. Bachleitner, et al, pp. 20–28. München: Profil.
1998b Die soziale Organisation des Tourismus. Ein soziologischer Bezugsrahmen für die Tourismuswissenschaft (The Social Organization of Tourism: A Sociological Frame of Reference). Tourismus Journal 2:133–154.
1999 Tourismustheorie. Soziologischer Wegweiser zum Verständnis touristischer Phänomene (Tourism Theory: A Directory to the Understanding of Tourist Phenomena) (2nd ed., 2005). München: Profil.

Vidal Villa, J.
1981 España y el Imperialismo (Spain and Imperialism). *In* Crecimiento
Económico y Crisis Estructural en España (1959–1980) (Economic Growth
and Structural Crisis in Spain (1959–1980)), R. Carballo, A. Temprano, and M.
Santín, eds., pp. 157–169. Madrid: Akal.

Viken, A.
1997 Turismens Visualitet og Estetisering av Sameland (The Visuality of Tourism
and the Aestheticization of Sámiland). Sosiologi i dag (Sociology Today)
27(1):49–71.
2006 Tourism and Sámi Identity: An Analysis of the Tourism-Identity Nexus in a
Sámi Community. Scandinavian Journal of Hospitality and Tourism 6:7–24.

Vittersø, J., R. Chipeniuk, M. Skår, and O. Vistad
2004 Recreational Conflict is Affective: The Case of Cross-Country Skiers and
Snowmobiles. Leisure Sciences 26:227–243.

Vittersø, J., M. Vorkinn, O. Vistad, and J. Vaagland
2000 Tourist Experiences and Attractions. Annals of Tourism Research 27:
432–450.

Vlaamse Raad
2000 Advies Inzake de Oprichting van een Voortgezette Academisch Opleiding
Toerisme in Vlaanderen (Advice Concerning the Establishment of Higher
Academic Education in Tourism in Flanders). Brussel: Vlaamse Raad voor het
Toerisme.

Volpe, A.
2004 Il Ciclo di Vita delle Località Turistiche. Sviluppi e Limiti di un'Economia
Posizionale (The Life Cycle of Tourist Places. Dynamics and Limits of a
Positional Economy). Milano: FrancoAngeli.

Vrinjanin, J.
1952 Turizam (Tourism). Zagreb: Instruktor.
1957 Putničke agencije (Tourist Agencies). Zagreb: Instruktor.

Vrtiprah, V., and I. Pavlić
2005 Menadžerska ekonomija u hotelijerstvu (Management in the Hotel
Industry). Dubrovnik: Sveučilište u Dubrovniku.

Vukičević, M.
1978 Ekonomika turizma I. i II (Economics of Tourism I and II). Novi Sad: Više
wekonomsko-komercijalna škola.
1981 Poljoprivreda i turizam (Agriculture and Tourism). Senta: Društvo
ekonomista.

Vukonić, B.
1972 Turistička propaganda (Advertising in Tourism). Zagreb: Školska knjiga.
1981 Osnove tržišnog poslovanja—marketing—u turizmu (Basics of Marketing in
Tourism). Zagreb: Školska knjiga.
1983 Marketing u turizmu (Tourism Marketing). Zagreb: Vjesnik—Agencija za
Marketing.

1987 Turizam i razvoj (Tourism and Development). Zagreb: Školska knjiga.

1989 Marketing u turizmu (Marketing in Tourism). Zagreb: Vjesnik.

1990 Turizam i religija (Tourism and Religion). Zagreb: Školska knjiga.

1993 (1970) Turističke agencije (Tourist Agencies). Zagreb: Školska knjiga.

1994 Turizam u susret budućnosti (Tourism Meeting the Future). Zagreb: Ekonomski fakultet and Mikrorad.

1996 Tourism and Religion. Oxford: Elsevier.

1997a Tourism in the Whirlwind of War. Zagreb: Golden Marketing.

1997b Turističke agencije (Tourist Agencies). Zagreb: Mikrorad and Ekonomski fakultet.

2003 Turizam u vihoru rata (Tourism in the Whirlwind of War). Zagreb: MATE.

2005 Povijest hrvatskog turizma (History of Croatian Tourism). Zagreb: HAZU i Prometej.

Vukonić, B. and N. Čavlek, eds.

2001 Rječnik turizma (Dictionary of Tourism). Zagreb: Masmedija.

Vukonić, B., and R. Matović

1973 Turističke agencije (Tourist Agencies). Pula: Viša ekonomska škola.

VV, AA.

2001 Sguardi Antropologici sul Turismo (Anthropological Gazes on Tourism). Afriche e Orienti (Africas and Orients) 3/4:9–81.

Wagner, F.

1970 Die Urlaubswelt von Morgen (The Holiday World of Tomorrow). Düsseldorf: Econ.

Wagner, U.

1977 Out of Time and Place: Mass Tourism and Charter Trips. Ethnos 42(1/2): 38–52.

1981 Tourism in the Gambia: Development or Dependency? Ethnos 46(3/4):190–206.

1982 Reiselivet—Kulturutvikling eller Konflikt? (Tourism—Cultural Development or Conflict?). *In* Innpassing av Reiseliv i Lokale Samfunn (Adapting Tourism to Local Communities), S. Svalastog, ed., pp. 194–202. Lillehammer: Oppland University College.

1985 Turisme og Lokalsamfunn: Det Todimensjonale Bildet (Tourism and Local Community: The Two-Dimensional Picture). *In* Planleggingens Muligheter 3: Reiseliv og Rekreasjon (The Scope of Planning, vol. 3, Tourism and Recreation), N. Veggeland, ed., pp. 56–76. Oslo: Scandinavian University Press.

Wahrlich, H.

1984 Tourismus—eine Herausforderung für Ethnologen (Tourism—A Challenge for Ethnologists). Berlin: Reimer.

Wallerstein, I.

1995 The Language of Scholarship. Letter from the President, No. 3, to members of the International Sociological Association. *In* Letters from the President 1994–1998, pp. 27–33.

1998 Report to the Members, Letters from the President to Members of the International Sociological Association 1994-1998, pp. 3–13.

1999 The Heritage of Sociology and the Promise of Social Science. Presidential Address to the XIVth World Congress of Sociology, Montréal, 26 July 1998. Current Sociology 47(1):1–37.

Walton, J. ed.

2005 Histories of Tourism: Representation, Identity and Conflict. Clevedon: Channel View Publications.

Wang, N.

1996 Logos-Modernity, Eros-Modernity, and Leisure. Leisure Studies 15: 121–135.

1999 Rethinking Authenticity in Tourism Experiences. Annals of Tourism Research 26:349–370.

2000 Tourism and Modernity: A Sociological Analysis. Oxford: Pergamon.

2003 Tourismus und Körper (Tourism and the Body). Voyage 6:127–134.

Waris, H.

1951 The Impact of Sociological Developments on Travel. Zeitschrift für Fremdenverkehr (Tourism Review) 6(2):76–77.

Warszyńska, J.

2003 Geografia turyzmu—zarys problematyki (The Geography of Tourism—An Outline of Issues). *In* Nauki o turystyce. Część I (Studies of Tourism, Part One) (2nd ed.). R. Winiarski, ed. Studia i Monografie (Studies and Monographs) no. 7, pp. 9–32. Kraków: Akademia Wychowania Fizycznego im. Bronislawa Czecha w Krakowie.

Warszyńska, J., and A. Jackowski

1978 Podstawy geografii turyzmu (Foundations of the Geography of Tourism). Warszawa: PWN.

Weber, H. ed.

1989 Vom Wandel des neuzeitlichen Naturbegriffs (On the Transformations of the Modern Notion of Nature). Konstanz: Universitätsverlag.

Weber, S., and V. Mikačić

1994 Osnove turizma (Essentials of Tourism). Zagreb: Školska knjiga.

Whorf, B.

1986 Sprache-Denken-Wirklichkeit (Language-Thought-Reality). Reinbek bei Hamburg: Rowohlt.

Wiberg, H.

1976 Konfliktteori och Fredsforskning (Conflict Theory and Peace Research). Stockholm: Esselte.

Wiese, L.v.

1924 Allgemeine Soziologie als Lehre von den Beziehungen und Beziehungsgebilden der Menschen (General Sociology as a Theory of Human Relations and Relationships). München: Duncker und Humblot.

1930 Fremdenverkehr als zwischenmenschliche Beziehungen (Tourism as an Interpersonal Relation). Archiv für den Fremdenverkehr (Archive of Tourism) 1(1):1–3.

Wikipedia

2007 Mario Gaviria (http://es.wikipedia.org/wiki/Mario_Gaviria, accessed March 31).

Winiarski, R. ed.

2003 Nauki o turystyce. Część I (Studies of Tourism. Part One) (2nd ed.). Studia i Monografie (Studies and Monographs) no. 7. Kraków: Akademia Wychowania Fizycznego im. Bronisława Czecha w Krakowie.

2004 Nauki o turystyce. Część II, (Studies of Tourism. Part Two). Studia i Monografie (Studies and Monographs) no. 7. Kraków: Akademia Wychowania Fizycznego im. Bronisława Czecha w Krakowie.

Wippler, R.

1968 Determinanten van het Vrijetijdsgedrag (Determinants of Leisure Behavior). Assen: Van Gorcum.

Withagen, J.

1984 Register van Vrijetijdsonderzoek (Register of Leisure Research), Deel 2 (Part 2). Amsterdam: Noord-Hollandse Uitgevers Maatschappij.

Wöhler, K.

1998a Sozialwissenschaftliche Tourismusforschung im vorparadigmatischen Zustand? (Tourism Social Science in a Pre-Paradigmatic Stage?). *In* Der durchschaute Tourist. Arbeiten zur Tourismusforschung (The X-Rayed Tourist: Studies in Tourism Research), R. Bachleitner, et al, pp. 29–36. München: Profil.

1998b Eine ökonomische Analyse des Tourismus (An Economic Analysis of Tourism). *In* Auf dem Weg zu einer Theorie des Tourismus (Toward a Theory of Tourism), H. Burmeister, ed., pp. 101–135. Loccum: s.n.

1998c Imagekonstruktion fremder Räume (Constructing Images of Foreign Spaces). Voyage 2:97–114.

2003 Virtualisierung von touristischen Räumen (Virtualization of Tourist Spaces). Tourismus Journal 7:237–250.

2005a Entfernung, Entfernen und Verorten (Distance, Removal and Localization). Voyage 7:121–134.

Wöhler, K. ed.

1997 Editorial. Tourismus Journal. 1:3–12.

2005b Erlebniswelten (Worlds of Experience). Münster: Lit.

Wöhler, K., and A. Saretzki

1996 Tourismus ohne Raum (Tourism without Space). *In* Der Tourismusmarkt von Morgen (The Tourism Market of Tomorrow), A. Steinecke, ed., pp. 26–38. Trier: Geographische Gesellschaft.

Wolf, K., and P. Jurczek

1986 Geographie der Freizeit und des Tourismus (The Geography of Leisure and Tourism). Stuttgart: Ulmer.

Wójcik, W. ed.
  2007 Ks. Karol Wojtyła—Jan Paweł II Miłośnik Gór i Przyrody (Rev. Karol Wojtyla—John Paul II a Lover of Mountains and Nature). Studia i Monografie Nr 40 (Studies and Monographs no. 40). Edited Conference Proceedings 13 October 2005. Kraków: Akademia Wychowania Fizycznego im. Bronislawa Czecha w Krakowie and Polskie Towarzystwo Turystyczno-Krajoznawcze PTTK (Polish Tourist and Sightseeing Association).

World Commission on Environment and Development
  1987 Our Common Future, World Commission on Environment and Development (Bruntland Report). Oxford: Oxford University Press.

Wydawnictwo Znak Website
  2008 (http://www.znak.com.pl/, accessed 21 June 2008).

Wyzsza Szkoła Hotelarstwa Gastronomii i Turystyki w Warszawie (WSHGiT) (University of Hospitality, Catering and Tourism in Warsaw)
  2008 (http://www.biblioteka.wshgit.waw.pl/, accessed 21 June 2008).

Xiao, H.
  2009 Message to TRINET (accessed 24th July).

Xiao, H., and S. Smith
  2006 The Making of Tourism Research: Insights from a Social Sciences Journal. Annals of Tourism Research 33:490–507.

Yeo, E. and S. Yeo, eds.
  1981 Popular Culture and Class Conflict 1590–1914: Explorations in the History of Labour and Leisure. Brighton: Harvester.

Zagkotsi, S.
  2007 Κοινωνική και Επαγγελματική Κινητικότητα στον Τουριστικό Τομέα: Εμπειρικές Προσεγγίσεις σε Τουριστικές Περιοχές του Νομού Χαλκιδικής (Social and Professional Mobility in the Tourism Sector: Empirical Approaches in Tourist Regions of the Prefecture of Chalkidiki). Unpublished doctoral dissertation, Department of Business Administration, University of the Aegean, Chios, Greece.

Zarkia, C.
  1996 *Philoxenia*. Receiving Tourists—but not Guests—on a Greek Island. *In* Coping with Tourists: European Reactions to Mass Tourism, J. Boissevain, ed., pp. 143–173. Oxford: Berghahn Books.

Ziemilski, A.
  1958 Uwagi o problemie socjologii turystyki (Remarks on the Sociology of Tourism). Wychowanie Fizyczne i Sport (Physical Education and Sport) 2(3):487–495.
  1973 Zmiany społeczne pod wpływem rozwoju turystyki (Social Changes Influenced by the Development of Tourism). Biuletyn Informacyjny Instytutu Turystyki (Information Bulletin of the Institute of Tourism) 4–5:8–23.
  1976 Człowiek w krajobrazie. Szkice z pogranicza socjologii (Man in Landscape: Essays from the Margins of Sociology). Warszawa: Sport i Turystyka.

Zimmers, B.
1995 Trierer Tourismus-Bibliographien (Trier Tourism Bibliographies, vol. 7), Geschichte und Entwicklung des Tourismus (Bibliography: History and Development of Tourism).Trier: Geographische Gesellschaft.

Zinovieff, S.
1991 Hunters and Hunted: *Kamaki* and the Ambiguities of Sexual Predation in a Greek Town. *In* Contested Identities: Gender and Kinship in Modern Greece, P. Loizos and E. Papataxiarchis, eds., pp. 203–220. Princeton, NJ: Princeton University Press.

Znaniecki, F.
1931 Studia nad antagonizmem do obcych (Studies on Antagonism to Aliens (Strangers)). [1990 Reprint]. *In* Współczesne narody (Contemporary Nations), F. Znaniecki, ed., pp. 265–358. Warszawa: PWN.

Žabica, T.
1967 Turistička geografija (The Geography of Tourism). Dubrovnik: Visoka turistička škola.

APPENDIX

Table A.1. Tourism Specific and Related General Theoreticians in Continental Europe and Anglophone Countries

Period	Countries									
	Germany, Austria, and Switzerland	France	Italy	Poland	Former Yugoslavia	Scandinavia	Spain	Netherlands and Belgium	Greece	Anglophone Countries
Pre-1930	Brougier Fontane Glücksmann Glücksmann et al Grünthal Guyer-Freuler Morgenroth Sputz Stradner		Bodio Mariotti	Łukaszewski Odyniec				Sternheim	Lekkas	
1930s	Bormann Gölden Jäger Oppenheimer Poser von Wiese			Leszczycki				Blonk et al Jacquemyns		

Table A.1 (*Continued*)

Period	Germany, Austria, and Switzerland	France	Italy	Poland	Former Yugoslavia	Scandinavia	Spain	Netherlands and Belgium	Greece	Anglophone Countries
1940s	Hunziker Krapf Hunziker and Krapf	Bachelard	Toschi					Huizinga		
1950s	Bernecker Enzensberger Günther Leugger Nyberg	Barthes		Ziemilski	Apih Grgasević Vrinjanin	Evang Huss Waris		Berting et al Heinemeyer Jolles Ramaker		
1960s	Adorno Geigant Giesecke Gleichmann Grünthal Hahn and Schade Kentler Kentler et al Knebel Mayntz Meinke Mitscherlich Nahrstedt Pöschl Scheuch	Burgelin Dumazedier Gritti Lafargue	Buccino		Blašković Čulić Jovičić Marković and Marković Mazi Mazi et al Mihovilović Planina Rebevšek Unković	Aubert		Groffen Kuin and Oldendorff		Boorstin Forster

Period	Studienkreis für Tourismus / Timm	Morin / Raymond	Catelli / Stroppa	Bystrzanowski / Skórzyński	Zabica / Zor	Aubert and Arner / Melén	Fraga Iribarne	Van Mechelen / Wippler	Graburn / Mitford
1970s	Armanski	Bruckner and Finkielkraut	Barberis	Abramowska	Alfier	Berggren and Zetterström	Febas	Beckers	Burkhart and Medlik
	Arndt	Cazes	Guidicini	Kloskowska	Blažević and Pepeonik	Ekeroth	Febas and Oresanz	Blok-van der Voort	Cheek and Burdge
	Beutel	Dufour	Martinelli	Maczka	Bunc	Høivik and Heiberg	Gaviria	Groffen	Cohen
	Bodenstein	Lanfant	Sessa	Przecławski	Gavranović	Löfgren	Gaviria et al	Have	Elias
	Bucholz	Lanfant et al		Rogoziński	Jurić	Mathisen	Jurdao Arrones	Hessels	Greenwood
	Eichler			Skórzyński and Ziemilski	Kečkemet	Mordal		Kerstens	Bidgianis
	Fink			Saar et al	Kobašić	Noren		Pennartz	MacCannell
	Hammerich			Ziemilski	Marković et al	Rekdal		Vanhove	Kalfiotis
	Hinske and Müller				Nejkov	Wagner, U.			Nash
	Hömberg				Pauko				Lambiri-Dimaki
	Kahn				Petrinjak and Sudar				Smith, V.
	Kaspar				Popov				Stavrou
	Keller				Savić				Turner and Ash
	Nettekoven				Šmit				Stott
	Opaschowski				Unković				
	Pikulik				Unković and Tourki				
	Prahl and Steinecke				Unković and Zečević				
	Scheuch and Meyersohn				Vukičević				
	Schivelbusch				Vukonić				
	Schmitz-Scherzer				Vukonić and Matović				
	Tesch								
	Wagner, F.								

Table A.1 (*Continued*)

Period	Germany, Austria, and Switzerland	France	Italy	Poland	Former Yugoslavia	Scandinavia	Spain	Netherlands and Belgium	Greece	Anglophone Countries
								Countries		
1980s					Andrić					
	Bernecker et al				Antunac					
	Bopp				Avelini Holjevac					
	Boventer				Bakić					
	Brenner		Bandinu		Cicvarić					
	Fischer		Benini and Savelli		Elaković					
					Gorenc					
	Greverus et al		Costa		Knežević Grabišić			Ashworth		
	Griep and Jäger		Dalla Chiesa		Kovač			Boissevain		
	Gyr		Eco		Marošević					
	Hartmann		Fragola		Nejkov			Bijsterveldt		Crick
	Huck		Guidicini and Savelli		Pirjevec	Flotten and Solvang				
	Kramer		Lelli		Radišić	Gustavsson		Dietvorst and Jansen-Verbeke		Culler
	Krippendorf		Liebman Parrinello		Relac and Bartoluci	Hansen		Hekker		Dann
			Lombardini							
	Krippendorf et al				Rešetar	Haukeland		Hertogen and Naeyaert		Gottlieb
	Mäder		Luhmann		Senečić	Haukeland and Eriksen		Jansen-Verbeke		Jafari
	Spode		Morra	Bartoszewicz	Senečić and Kobašić Jacobsen			Kamphorst		Kelly
	Storbeck		Paolinelli	Burkot	Sirše et al	Jokinen		Kamphorst and Withagen		Lett
	Tokarski and Schmitz-Scherzer		Perrotta	Bystrzanowski and Beck	Sušić	Jokinen and Veijola		Kikkert		Pearce, P.

1990s	Vester	Piazzi	Nowakowska	Todorović	Øllgaard	Koster	Kousis	Pearce, P. and Moscardo
								Smith, S.
								Van den Abbele
								Brown, F.
								Brown, G.
								Bruner
							Papagaroufali	
								Burns and Holden
							Tsartas	
								Dann and Cohen
								Greenblatt
								Harrison
						Theuns	Apostolopolous and Sonmez	Hollinshead
						Withagen		
							Castelberg-Koulma	Lash and Urry
							Chtouris	
							Epitropopoulos	McIntosh and Goeldner
							Galani-Moutafi/ Moutafi	
							Giagou and Apostolopoulos	Pearce, D
					Schmidt			
					Schmidt and Jacobsen		Haralambopoulos and Pizam	
							Iakovidou	
				Vasović				
				Vasović and Jovičić			Kassimati et al	
							Kenna	
			Ostrowski					
			Podemski					
				Bilen				
		Savelli						
		Sgroi						
				Cicvarić				
	Währlich							
	Wolf and Jurcze	Thurot						
				Čavlek				
		Amendola						
		Baraldi and Teodorani						
	Bachleitner et al	Bandinu and Teodorani		Čomić				
	Bachleitner and Schimany			Dulčić				
	Bausinger et al							
	Borghardt							
	Burmeister							
	Cantauw							
	Flitner et al							
	Gemünden							
	George							
	Haedrich et al							
	Hahn and Kagelmann							
	Häußler							
	Hennig	Battistelli						
	Hlavin-Schulze							
	Kaspar							
	Keitz	Bernardi						
	Klemm							
	Köstlin	Bonomi						
	Kramer and Lutz Pagens-techer	Ciacci						

Table A.1 (*Continued*)

Period	Germany, Austria, and Switzerland	France	Italy	Poland	Former Yugoslavia	Scandinavia	Spain	Netherlands and Belgium	Greece	Anglophone Countries
	Pompl		Ferrarotti		Ivošević				Lazaridies and Wickens	Robinson
	Schimany		Gori		Jadrešić				Lytras	Rojek
	Schrand		Martinengo and Savoja		Jokić			Abbink	Manologlou	Selwyn
	Schumacher et al		Martinotti		Magaš			Ashworth and de Haan	Maroudas and Tsartas	Sharpley
	Shields		Minca		Mihalič			Ashworth and Tunbridge	Moore	Singh
	Simmel		Nocifora		Mirić and Vlahović			Beckers and Mommaas	Papadaki-Tzedaki	Sheldon
	Taxacher		Palumbo		Prijevec	Cederholm		Boissevain	Papageorgeiou	Swain
	Thiem		Pardi		Prebežec	Glomnes		Dahles	Selänniemi	Swain et al
	Vester	Jardel	Ragone	Alejziak	Senečić and Vukonić	Heimtun		Descan	Thanopoulou and Tsartas	Tribe
	Wöhler	Picard	Romita	Burszta	Šimić	Jacobsen et al		Jorissen et al	Tsartas and Thanopoulou	Urry
	Wöhler and Saretzki	Tresse	Simonicca	Gaworecki	Turkulin and Hitrec	Vejola and Jokinen	Bote and Esteban	Lengkeek	Zarkia	Van den Berghe
	Zimmers	Urbain	Thiesse	Jackowski	Weber and Mikačić	Viken	Jurdao Arrones and Sanchez	Richards	Zinovief	Wang
			Battilani							
			Beato							
			Benini							
			Bonadei							
			Callari Galli and Guerzoni							
2000 +										

Baranowski
Becker et al
Becker and Job
Bormann, R.
Franke and Hammerich
Freyer
Fritzsche
Graf
Gross
Hachtmann
Heiss and Leonardi
Hopfinger
Job
Jurczek
Kagelmann

Calvi
Cannas and Solinas
Catalano et al
Cocco and Minardi
Corvo
Costa and Corvo
Cubula
De Stasio and Palucci
Ercole
Ercole and Gilli
Fadda
Ferrari
Gasparini
Gemini
Gori
Guala
Gubert and Pollini
Iovanović
Lavarini
Leotta
Manella
Martinengo et al
Martinotti

Bartoluci and Čavlek
Bilen and Bučar
Cerović
Dulčić
Geic
Jadrešić

Birkeland
Birkelund
Berenholdt and Granå
Berenholdt et al
Daugstad
Elsrud
Fennefoss and Jacobsen
Gustafson
Gyimóthy and Mykletun
Haug et al
Jacobsen and Dann
Janson
Jansson
Jensen and Korneliussen
Larsen, J and Jacobsen
Larsen, J. et al

Andriotis
Andriotis and Vaughan
Anthopoulou
Anthopoulou et al
Apostolopoulos et al
Deltsou
Gkrimpa
Kantsa

Table A.1 (*Continued*)

Period	Countries									
	Germany, Austria, and Switzerland	France	Italy	Poland	Former Yugoslavia	Scandinavia	Spain	Netherlands and Belgium	Greece	Anglophone Countries
	Köck		Mazette		Kliment	Larsen, S.			Karagiannis	
	Kopper		Mazette and Tidore		Kušen	Larsen, S. and Folgerø			Liarikos	Botterill
	Meyer and Meyer		Melotti		Luković	Mehmetoglu et al			Maroudas and Kyriakaki	Dann and Jacobsen
	Müller, H.		Montani	Alejziak and Winiarski	Marušić and Prebežec	Müller, D.			Moira-Mylono-poluou et al	Dann and Liebman Parrinello
	Mundt		Nocifora	Gołembski	Mihalič and Planina	Nordbakke		Ateljevic et al	Nazou	Franklin and Crang
	Prahl		Nuvolati	Milewski	Panian	Olsen		Faché	Papakonstanidis	Graburn and Barthel-Bouchier
	Reeh		Pieroni	Rozwadowski	Prijevec and Kesar	Sand		Geilen	Pappas	Graburn and Leite
	Schäfer		Pieroni and Romita	Suprewicz	Popesku	Selstad		Kozak and Decrop	Stavrinoudis	Leiper
	Schrand		Romita	Ujma	Spasić	Sørensen		Lengkeek and Elands	Thanopoulou	Maitland et al
	Schumacher		Ruzza	Warszyńska	Suprewicz	Thrane	Aramberri	Lengkeek and Swain-Byrne	Theodorooulou	Minnaert et al
	Seitz and Meyer		Savoja	Warszyńska and Jackowski		Tuulentie	Aramberri and Butler	Meyer	Tsartas et al	Robinson and Phipp
	Sloterdijk		Tidore and Solinas	Winiarski	Vrtiprah and Pavlić	Tuulentie and Mettiäinen	Martin and Barrado	Smits and Claeys	Zagkotsi	Walton
	Steineche	Poulain and Teychenné	Volpe	Wójcik	Vukonić and Čavlek	Vitterso et al	Germán	van der Duim	Zinovieff	Xiao and Smith

Table A.2. Tourism Specific and Related general Theories in Continental Europe and Anglophone Countries

Period	Countries									
	Germany Austria and Switzerland	France	Italy	Poland	Former Yugoslavia	Scandinavia	Spain	Netherlands and Belgium	Greece	Anglophone countries
Pre-1930	Simmel (Industrialized consumption of nature; strangerhood) Glücksmann (Interpersonal relations, motivation, place, effects)			Łukaszewski (Tourism in Polish language 1847 from Stendhal 1838)				Sternheim (Free time in totalitarian societies (Frankfurt school)) Vliebergh (Holiday-making of workers)	Lekkas (Policy proposals)	
1930s	Bormann (Temporary residence, consumption) von Wiese (Types of stranger: conquering, no interest, friendly)			Leszczycki (Tourism as a set of phenomena comprising sociocultural, economic, nature-based, organizational and legal dimensions)	Vrnjanin (Cites 1933 definition of tourism based on natural and cultural significance)			Blonk and Kruijt (Leisure as a sociological problem) Blonk et al (Leisure patterns and definition of free time) Jacquemyns (Working class leisure)		

Table A.2 (*Continued*)

Period	Countries										
	Germany Austria and Switzerland	France	Italy	Poland	Former Yugoslavia	Scandinavia	Spain	Netherlands and Belgium	Greece	Anglophone countries
1940s	Hunziker and Krapf (Relations by outsiders)	Bachelard (Imaginary of movement)								
1950s	Enzensberger (Critical: motives, alienation escape from capitalist society in vain and ends in disappointment) Leugger (Alienation adventure)				Apih (Travel for entertainment rest, health, nature, curiosity, new regions and people, sport. Links to work of Mariotti, Bormann Glücksmann, Krapf, Hunziker, and Keller)					

Groffen (Determinants of leisure behavior)

Kuin and Oldendorff (Reduction in working hours)

Van Mechelen (Sociological research of leisure including tourism)

Evang (Health complainers better to stay at home in familiar environment. (tourist bubbles in Knebel) holiday-makers: change; tourists: novelty)

Grgašević (Tourism terminology)

Jovičić (Tourism as social movement for recreational and social needs)

Marković and Marković (Distinction between tourism for privileged classes and modern tourism)

Mazi et al (Compendium of local scholars)

Aubert (Life-world themes of tourism, sleep and love. Anti-tourist attitudes Tourism as role,

Skórzyński and Ziemilski (Sociology of tourism, education, mountain climbing)

Krapf (Tourism as a product of consumer society)

Barthes (Semiotics of *Blue Guide*)

Burgelin, Gritti (Alienation, social control, freedom)

Dumazedier (Sociology of leisure)

Barberis (Aristocratic & democratic colonization; effect on countryside)

Catelli (Frenzy of building in country as if it were city)

Kentler (Counter-world allowing departure from society)

Morin (Value of vacations is absence of values)

1960s

Table A.2 (*Continued*)

Period	Countries									
	Germany Austria and Switzerland	France	Italy	Poland	Former Yugoslavia	Scandinavia	Spain	Netherlands and Belgium	Greece	Anglophone countries
						marginality (sailor), escape. Types (cf. Max Weber) of tourist: wilderness, sun, connoisseur, anti-tourist, itinerant sightseer. Tourism as consumption (Knebel) and sacred journey)				Boorstin Mitford (Critique of tourism. Authenticity)
	Knebel (Structural changes and travel with no purpose; mobility relations with hosts, conspicuous consumption, comfort and safety; highbrow view of tourism with social prestige as motive)	Raymond (Club Med)	Stroppa (Desire for novelty)		Mihovilović (Social profile of foreign visitors)	Melén (Opinion leaders and travel, e.g., women (cf. V. Smith))		Wippler (Determinants of leisure behavior)		

Table A.2 (*Continued*)

Period	Germany Austria and Switzerland	France	Italy	Poland	Former Yugoslavia	Scandinavia	Spain	Netherlands and Belgium	Greece	Anglophone countries
	Gleichmann (Motive force of tourism between farness and nearness)	Cazes (Imagery)	Guidicini (Group travel)	Abramowska (Travel as a dichotomous experience linked to information flow and cultural values)		Mathisen (Gigolos in Morocco. Tourism as understanding or conflict. Neither because of bubble and thus no authenticity)	Febas (Semiotics)		Kalfiotis (Tourist demand and supply to adjust to society)	Graburn (Tourism as a sacred journey)
	Kaspar (Systems)	Dufour (Myths)	Martinelli (Local communities)	Maczka (Definitions of tourism especially Przecławski and Hunziker, the latter with links to Simmel and Schutz)	Alfier (Social effects of tourist consumption. Need to enjoy rest not just economics of tourist product. Tourism as resocialization and desocialization)	Mordal (Paid vacation (cf. Dumazedier))	Gaviria (Link to Lefebvre Production of space and Neo-colonialism)	Blok-van der Voort (Role theory of holidays)	Lambiri-Dimaki (Rapid urbanization and shift from imitation to modernization)	MacCannell (Tourist markers, sightseeing authenticity)
	Keller (Tourist way of life as state of mind)	Lanfant (Theories of Leisure; semiology)	Sessa (Motives, decision making, behavior, promotion)	Przecławski (Sociological definition of tourism that includes spatial mobility,	Jovičić (Tourismology predated emergence in France 2005.	Rekdal (Zambian sculptors modifying art to tourist taste. Use of Goffman and	Jurdao-Arrones (Imperialism and nostalgia)	Hessels (Holiday-making since the turn of the century)	Stavrou (Effects are positive on the economy & negative on society)	Nash (Tourism as imperialism)

Countries

1980s

Scheuch (Dis-association from environment but not negation as in Enzensberger)

Link with Krapf

voluntary change of place, rhythm of life, interactive content, experience (cf. Znaniecki); life as a journey (see Teilhard de Chardin)

Even a journal of that name

impression management before MacCannell)

Pi-Sunyer (Socio-cultural impact)

Vanhove (Past, present, and future of coastal tourism)

Stott (Effect of tourism on family role)

Smith, V. (Socio-cultural effects)

Links to France and Germany

Skórzyński and Ziemilski (Sociology of scenery, especially typology of mountains)

Marković, Relac, and Štuka (Tourism as humanization of life)

Wagner (Liminality in the Gambia)

Bandinu (Cultural cost of tourism)

Benini and Savelli (Family)

Costa (Time/space cycle)

Dalla Chiesa (Change in employment, demography, and urbanization. Social effects modifying demand. Compensatory and symbolic functions)

Gustavsson (Conflict of summer holiday-making)

Table A.2 (*Continued*)

Period	Countries									
	Germany Austria and Switzerland	France	Italy	Poland	Former Yugoslavia	Scandinavia	Spain	Netherlands and Belgium	Greece	Anglophone countries
			Lelli (Alienation of industrial factory leads to cultural consumption of post-modernity)			Hansen (Photography with links to Armanski, Bourdieu, Fink, Sontag)				
			Liebman Parrinello (Post-industrial prosumers)			Haukeland and Eriksen (Effects of tourism on communities; sustainable development, see Jafari's adaptancy platform)		Ashworth (Tourism in historic cities. Dark tourism)		
			Morra (Modern society has tourism and consumption)			Jacobsen (Modern tourism with links to Bruckner and Finkielkraut, Keller, Knebel, Opachowski, Scheuch Simmel)		Beckers (Free time as a social problem. Actor-centric leisure. Symbolic Inter-actionism and pheno-menology)		

Boissevain (Tourism as anti-structure European reactions to tourist gaze) Corijn (Cultural studies)

Kousis (Mass tourism leads to proletarianization. Effect on family endogamy and sexual freedom; varies between men and women)

Dann (Push and pull motives)

Hekker (Tourism as a subset of recreation)

Hertogen and Naeyaert (Appraisal of social tourism; change to

Tsartas (Stages of tourism development. Greater development is greater scepticism.

Jokinen and Veijola (Pork feast (cf. Bakhtin, Bourdieu, Schivelbusch))

Löfgren (Charter tour colonialism, (Bruckner and Finkelkraut) bourgeois freedom to and proletarian freedom from (Marx on alienation))

Paolinelli (Tourism as ideological universe of class conflict)

Alfier (Tourism as an epiphenomenon associated with positive and negative features accompanying rapid development of technological civilization)

Perrotta (Collation of Anglophone sources)

Bartoszewicz (Exchange theory: hosts accept aliens)

Øllgaard (Photography (see Schivelbusch's journey as panorama and Urry's tourist gaze))

Jurić (Sociology of tourism)

Schmidt (Guidebooks and planning, repeated journey, tourist bubble (cf. Knebel))

Relac and Bartoluci (Sport and tourism)

Ostrowski (Tourist as a collective alien)

Gyr (Tourist behavior break with ordinary; ritualized concepts of symbols leading to prestige (cf. Knebel))

Piazzi (Meaning of holiday and subjectivity. From Luhmann takes difference)

Bystrzanowski and Beck (Tourism as a socio-cultural factor of change)

Hennig (Link with Enzensberger; tourism as extra-ordinary rite of passage)

Savelli (Motivation, post-industrial tourist space. Reliance on Knebel,

Krippendorf (Ideas from Enzensberger on escape; effects of flight on traveled, tourist as devourer of

Table A.2 (*Continued*)

Period	Countries									
	Germany Austria and Switzerland	France	Italy	Poland	Former Yugoslavia	Scandinavia	Spain	Netherlands and Belgium	Greece	Anglophone countries
	landscape and alternative tourism; as alienation quality of life)		Boyer, Enzensberger, Morin, Burgelin)					tourism for all)	Tourism and various social changes)	
	Spode (Tourism as travel without purpose; link to romanticism and nostalgia)	Thurot (Neo-Marxist Promotion)	Sgroi (Local community as cultural icon)	Podemski (Tourism as 5th dimension of participating in culture)	Vukonić (Tourism and development (political instability of wars and terrorism, religious belief and national indebtedness))	Solheim (Motives for holidays: recreation, experience, family, status)	Aramberri (Critic of conventional wisdom of neo-colonialism, tourism statistics and sociocultural impact)	Jansen-Verbeke (Tourism in inner cities; tourism as a system)	Tsartas et al (Social effects of tourism development. Effects on health, teenagers, environment)	Pearce, P. (Intrinsic motives)
1990s									Apostolopoulos and Sonmez (Mass tourism) Castelberg-Koulma (Females in cooperatives safe from sexual harassment) Chtouris (Tourism as a	

phenomeno-
logical
experience)
Epitropopoulos
(Tourism
development
and the
environment)
Galani-Moutafi
(Female
incorpo-
ration of
tourism
employment
into family
lives; self-
construction
of identity,
esp. mother/
daughter
relationship.
Authenticity)
Haralambo-
poulos and
Pizam
(Positive
development
of women in
tourism
plans)

Iakovidou
(Gender
differences in
tourism
employment)

Amendola (New
urban
renaissance:
differen-
tiation,
identity,
indivi-
dualism,
pleasure)

Baraldi and
Teodorani
(Intercultural
communi-
cation
between
visitor and
host
community)
Battistelli
(Family)

Table A.2 (*Continued*)

Period	Countries									
	Germany Austria and Switzerland	France	Italy	Poland	Former Yugoslavia	Scandinavia	Spain	Netherlands and Belgium	Greece	Anglophone countries
			Bernardi (Tourism as communi-cation of local culture) Buccino (Pioneers of local tourism) Ferrarotti (Mass tourism and escape) Gori (Biographies of daily life and social relationships of tourism) Martinotti (New city users; imagery of post-modern city)						Kassimati et al (Low status of women in tourism employment) Kenna (Clash of return migrants and residents in tourism employment) Lambiri-Dimaki (Sociology of tourism from 1959 to 2000) Lazaridies and Wickens (Albanian migrant workers and tourism workers) Lytras (Sociology of tourism handbook)	

Moore (Effect of drinking on local men and women)

Papadaki-Tzedaki (Effect of tourism growth on employment)

Selänniemi (Motives and behavior of holiday-makers, cultural tourists and pilgrims)

Thanopoulou and Tsartas (Tourism development in urban (integrated) and rural (subversive) areas)

Tsartas (Tourists, travels, places: sociological approaches to tourism)

Bruner (Tourist identity, performance)

Dahles (Anthropology of leisure)

Haukeland (Non-travel)

Minca (Post-modernity and implosion of symbols and non-places)

Nocifora (Different meanings and local identification)

Palumbo (Different readings of identity tourism)

Pardi (Tourism and prolongation of experience)

Ragone (Tourism and class from Veblen; snob effect of tourism)

Alejziak (Curse or blessing of tourism development; definitions of tourism, influence of Hunziker)

Picard (Tourist culture)

Table A.2 (*Continued*)

Period	Countries									
	Germany Austria and Switzerland	France	Italy	Poland	Former Yugoslavia	Scandinavia	Spain	Netherlands and Belgium	Greece	Anglophone countries
	Lutz (Unite different conceptual approaches)	Tresse (Tourism imagery)	Romita (Invisible tourism)	Bartoszewicz (Goals, motives, and forms of outbound tourism)	Mirić and Vlahović (Health and tourism)	Veijola and Jokinen (Body in tourism; gender issues)		Richards (Cultural tourism with the lifestyle approach of Bourdieu)	Zarkia (Comparison of pre and post tourism communities; effect on social class)	Selwyn (Chasing myths)
	Vester (Examine grand theories for sociological relevance)	Urbain (Socio-linguistics)	Simonicca (Ethnography of tourism from French school)	Gaworecki (Functions and roles of tourism, positive and negative effects, future of tourism to 2029)	Senečić (Tourist market)	Selänniemi (Multisensory tourism)		Abbink (Anthropologists leave world intact; tourists spoil it)	Zinovief (Hunting gigolos as way of gaining status)	Urry (The tourist gaze)
2000 +			Beato (Social equity) Benini (Transient identity) Bonadei (In transit experience) Cannas and Solinas (Reading of social relations in protected areas)							

Table A.2 (*Continued*)

Period					Countries						
	Germany Austria and Switzerland	France	Italy	Poland	Former Yugoslavia	Scandinavia	Spain	Netherlands and Belgium	Greece	Anglophone countries
			Gemini (Tourism as meaningful experience; vocational consumption) Guala (Regeneration of city culture) Gubert and Pollini (cf. Manella) (Local community and globalization) Lavarini (Improvization vs. technology) Leotta (Visual sociology and metropolis) Martinengo and Savoja (City and authenticity)						Andriotis (Influence of mass tourism on development)	

Mazzette
(Tourism as
display)

Melotti
(Transfor-
mation of
authenti-
city)

Montani
(Unrealistic
imagery and
exploitation
of locals)

Deltsou
(Ecotourism
and
idealization
of rural past.
Construction
of rurality as
a commodity.
National and
European
identity)

Galani-Moutafi
(Discourses
of travelers
re. self and
other
students'
construction
of male and
female other.
Aromatic
resin and
place identity.
Anthro-
pology of
tourism)

Kantsa (Women
as consumers
of tourism;
gendered
scapes;
tolerance of
lesbian
tourists)

Table A.2 (*Continued*)

Period	Countries									
	Germany Austria and Switzerland	France	Italy	Poland	Former Yugoslavia	Scandinavia	Spain	Netherlands and Belgium	Greece	Anglophone countries
			Nuvolati (Flâneurs)						Kinsis (Environmental protests)	
			Pieroni (Unauthorized building)		Alfier (Collection of scientific papers)	Daugstad (Environmental issues)			Moira-Mylonopolou (Sociology and psychology of tourism)	
			Pieroni and Romita (Sustainable tourism)		Antunac (Collection of scientific papers)	Haug et al (Link to migration)			Nazou (Identity and social/cultural exchange. Gendered hotel business identity and self-perception of younger family members)	
			Ruzza (Governance)		Bartoluci and Čavlek (Tourism and sport)	Heimtun (Imagery; travel identity)			Pappas (Mass tourism on social and land use changes)	

Savoja (Social and touristic sustainability)

Tidore and Solinas (Tourism and local culture)

Volpe (Updating city for tourism)

Podemski (Sociology of travel)

Link of Simmel and Schutz to partial stranger

Kliment (E-tourism)

Kušen (Inter-disciplinarity. "Natural tourist offer" to be replaced by "tourist attraction basis")

Panian (e-tourism)

Jacobsen and Dann (Imagery Multisensory tourism)

Mehmetoglu (Solitary Travelers)

Olsen and Viken (Sámi studies)

Thanopolou (Female occupational mobility in tourism employment)

Ateljevic et al (Critical turn)

Theodoropoulou (Younger, more educated go into agro-tourism)

Lengkeek and Swain (Tourism theory in RC 50)

Zagkotsi (Professional mobility)

Subject Index